SOCIAL STATISTICS

Many fundamentally important decisions about social life are a function of how well we understand and analyze *data*. This sounds so obvious but it is so misunderstood. Social statisticians struggle with this problem in their teaching constantly. This book and its approach are the ally and a support for all instructors who want to accomplish this hugely important teaching goal.

This innovative text for undergraduate social statistics courses is (as one satisfied instructor put it), a "breath of fresh air." It departs from convention by not covering some techniques and topics that have been in social statistics textbooks for 30 years but that are no longer used by social scientists today. It also *includes* techniques that conventional wisdom has previously thought to be the province of graduate level courses.

Linneman's text is for those instructors looking for a thoroughly "modern" way to teach quantitative thinking, problem-solving, and statistical analysis to their students . . . an undergraduate social statistics course that recognizes the increasing ubiquity of analytical tools in our data-driven age and therefore the practical benefit of learning how to "do statistics," to "present results" effectively (to employers as well as instructors), and to "interpret" intelligently the quantitative arguments made by others.

Thomas J. Linneman is Associate Professor of Sociology at the College of William and Mary in Williamsburg, Virginia. He teaches courses on statistics, social change, sexualities, and the media. At William and Mary, he has been the recipient of the Thomas Jefferson Teaching Award, the highest teaching honor given annually to a younger member of the faculty. The citation for his award noted that Linneman has developed a reputation among his students as a demanding professor but one who genuinely cares about them. His teaching evaluations for his statistics course are regularly a standard deviation above the mean.

Contemporary Sociological Perspectives

Edited by Doug Hartmann, University of Minnesota, Valerie Jenness, University of California, Irvine and Jodi O'Brien, Seattle University

This innovative series is for all readers interested in books that provide frameworks for making sense of the complexities of contemporary social life. Each of the books in this series uses a sociological lens to provide current critical and analytical perspectives on significant social issues, patterns and trends. The series consists of books that integrate the best ideas in sociological thought with an aim toward public education and engagement. These books are designed for use in the classroom as well as for scholars and socially curious general readers.

Published:

Political Justice and Religious Values by Charles F. Andrain
GIS and Spatial Analysis for the Social Sciences by Robert Nash Parker and Emily K. Asencio
Hoop Dreams on Wheels: Disability and the Competitive Wheelchair Athlete by Ronald J. Berger
The Internet and Social Inequalities by James C. Witte and Susan E. Mannon
Media and Middle Class Mom: Images and Realities of Work and Family by Lara Descartes and Conrad Kottak
Watching T.V. Is Not Required: Thinking about Media and Thinking about Thinking by Bernard McGrane and John Gunderson
Violence Against Women: Vulnerable Populations by Douglas Brownridge
State of Sex: Tourism, Sex and Sin in the New American Heartland by Barbara G. Brents, Crystal A. Jackson & Kate Hausbeck
Sociologists Backstage: Answers to 10 Questions About What They Do by Sarah Fenstermaker and Nikki Jones
Gender Circuits by Eve Shapiro
Surviving the Holocaust: A Life Course Perspective by Ronald Berger
Transforming Scholarship: Why Women's and Gender Studies Students Are Changing Themselves and the World by Michelle Berger and Cheryl Radeloff
Stargazing: Celebrity, Fame, and Social Interaction by Kerry Ferris and Scott Harris
The Senses in Self, Society, and Culture by Phillip Vannini, Dennis Waskul and Simon Gottschalk
Who Lives, Who Dies, Who Decides? by Sheldon Ekland-Olson
Surviving Dictatorship by Jacqueline Adams
The Womanist Idea by Layli Maparyan

Social Theory Re-Wired: New Connections to Classical and Contemporary Perspectives by Wesley Longhofer and Daniel Winchester

Religion in Today's World: Global Issues, Sociological Perspectives, by Melissa Wilcox

Life and Death Decisions: The Quest for Morality and Justice in Human Societies, Sheldon Ekland-Olson

Understanding Deviance: Connecting Classical and Contemporary Perspectives, Tammy L. Anderson

Titles of Related Interest:

The Connected City by Zachary Neal

Regression Analysis for the Social Sciences by Rachel A. Gordon

Applied Statistics for the Social and Health Sciences by Rachel A. Gordon

GIS and Spatial Analysis: A Tool for the Social Sciences by Robert Parker and Emily Asencio

SOCIAL STATISTICS
MANAGING DATA, CONDUCTING ANALYSES, PRESENTING RESULTS

Second Edition

Thomas J. Linneman

Routledge
Taylor & Francis Group

NEW YORK AND LONDON

First published 2014
by Routledge
711 Third Avenue, New York, NY 10017

Simultaneously published in the UK
by Routledge
2 Park Square, Milton Park, Abingdon, Oxon OX14 4RN

Routledge is an imprint of the Taylor & Francis Group, an informa business

© 2014 Taylor & Francis

The right of Thomas J. Linneman to be identified as author of this work has been asserted by him in accordance with sections 77 and 78 of the Copyright, Designs and Patents Act 1988.

Library of Congress Cataloging-in-Publication Data

Linneman, Thomas John.
  Social statistics : managing data, conducting analyses, presenting results /
by Thomas J. Linneman. — Second Edition.
     pages cm. — (Contemporary sociological perspectives)
  Includes bibliographical references and index.
  1. Social sciences—Statistical methods.   2. Statistics.   I. Title.
HA29.L83118   2014
519.5—dc23   2013029016

ISBN: 978-0-415-66146-1 (hbk)
ISBN: 978-0-415-66147-8 (pbk)
ISBN: 978-0-203-07342-1 (ebk)

Typeset in Times New Roman
by Apex CoVantage, LLC

BRIEF CONTENTS

TABLE OF CONTENTS IN DETAIL

PREFACE TO THE SECOND EDITION

Instructors of introductory social statistics face an unenviable quandary. They want to give their students the skills they need to succeed in the real world of social research, but they realize that if they push their students too far, they risk losing them altogether. Some instructors understandably surrender to this latter concern, opting to teach their students the more basic statistical procedures. Unfortunately, such procedures are seldom used in the real world. If instructors do decide to introduce their students to more contemporary techniques, they encounter course materials that were not developed with the introductory student in mind. This was the position in which I found myself a number of years ago, and I ultimately reached a decision to do something to remedy this dilemma. *Social Statistics: Managing Data, Conducting Analyses, Presenting Results* is my solution. It is the first statistics text that ventures to cover both classic and contemporary techniques in an approachable way that will engage the typical introductory student and make her eager rather than anxious to study this wide array of techniques.

If you compare the table of contents with those of other introductory statistics texts, you will see some similarities and some major differences. The first half of the book contains, on the surface, many of the similarities. The early chapters include many of the topics that one might find in other books: tables and graphs, measures of central tendency and variation, probability distributions, chi-square tests, confidence intervals, *t*-tests, ANOVA, and bivariate regression. I cover these topics innovatively and efficiently in order to prepare the students for the rest of the book. In the second half of the book, students gain significant exposure to a variety of multiple regression techniques that they will find in the real worlds of social research: reference groups, nested modeling, standardized effects, interaction effects, logistic regression, path analysis, and nonlinearity. In stark contrast to many books with such coverage, I handle these topics at a level that introductory statistics students will find approachable and engaging. For most beginning statistics students in the social sciences, this is the one and only statistics course they will take. If they use *Social Statistics: Managing Data, Conducting Analyses, Presenting Results*, they will leave the course with a strong and varied set of skills that will serve them well as they try to navigate the social science literature or acquire a job.

Although some of these regression techniques may appear in other introductory books, they often do so only as afterthoughts, covered in the most cursory of ways in the final chapter of the book. Unfortunately, this is exactly the point at which students need more explanation, not less. I cover these techniques with a significant—though not overwhelming—level of depth. I explain each technique using unique graphics, visual analogies, and real-world examples. The clear emphasis is on interpretation: given a regression model, or having created one of his or her own, what steps should a student take to make sense of what the model is telling him or her? Combined with their instructor's assistance, this book gets students to the point where they can translate a wide variety of statistical results, whether they are reading social science literature or making a presentation at their job. It guides students through the entire statistical research process: from working with data to get it ready for analysis, conducting the analyses (both by hand and with SPSS), and moving from raw SPSS output to professional presentation. Each chapter ends with graphical, step-by-step SPSS demonstrations, followed by short "from output to presentation" sections that teach students how to present results in clear and compelling ways.

Some instructors may be rightfully dubious about the possibility of introducing their students to some of these techniques. Yet I maintain that, with the help of this book, this is completely possible. I use several strategies to accomplish this. Each chapter includes several simple examples that convey the key aspects of the technique at hand. Most of these examples use data from the General Social Survey (GSS), primarily from 2012, but occasionally from other years. Many chapters contain "interchapter connections" that show how techniques are related to one another, and illustrate that some of the more advanced techniques can be considered extensions of more basic techniques. These connections also help the student through the challenging task of choosing the appropriate technique given a research situation. Each chapter ends with an example or two from the social science literature, showing how social researchers used the chapter's technique in an interesting way. I guide the students through these examples, showing them how to decipher tables that, at first, seem daunting. I make further use of the literature in a unique appendix that features descriptions of 86 social science journal articles from a variety of academic fields. I have vetted these articles, including only those that have statistical results that won't overwhelm introductory students. For each article, I offer a brief description, talk about the techniques the authors use to make their points (and what pitfalls to watch out for when reading their results), and end with a few questions for the student about the article's use of statistics.

The book emphasizes visual learning in order to make contemporary techniques more approachable. A series of innovative Excel-based live demonstrations and PowerPoint-based animations make many of the techniques come to life. For example, the Excel-based regression demonstration can, in a brief moment, show students the effect of an outlier on a regression line. A PowerPoint animation walks students through one of the book's path models in order to show the power of indirect effects. Instructors are welcome to integrate these demonstrations and animations into their lectures. There are also innovative videos that demonstrate SPSS procedures. These and other helpful instructor support materials (such as detailed answers to all of the end-of-chapter exercises, and a variety of exam questions) can be found on a companion website at URL: **www.routledge.com/cw/Linneman**

For the end-of-chapter exercises, I use more real-world data from five fascinating datasets: the 2012 American National Election Studies, the 2005 World Values Survey, and three datasets form the Pew Internet & American Life Project (on consumption, health, and cyberbullying). Thus, the end-of-chapter exercises are designed for students of varied interests: sociology, political science, marketing, public health, education, criminal justice, and global studies. Here are some examples that illustrate the range of exercise topics:

- With the exercises from the 2012 American National Election Studies, students explore such questions as "Do voters trust the government more than nonvoters?" and "What propels people to be involved in their communities?"
- With exercises from the 2013 PewShop dataset, students explore such questions as "Do smartphones allow people of all ages to engage in technology-enabled shopping experiences?" and "Do income disparities account for technology consumption differences among racial groups?"
- With exercises from the 2012 PewHealth dataset, students explore such questions as "Do men and women use the Internet to seek health information at the same rate?" and "Do people of all ages use Internet information when discussing their healthcare options with their doctors?"
- With exercises from the 2011 PewKids dataset, students explore such questions as "Do children who have been cyberbullied engage in more empathetic behavior toward the cyberbullied than those who have not?" and "What role does parental age play in the level at which parents monitor their children's technology use?"
- With exercises from the 2005 World Values Survey dataset, students explore such questions as "Is the relationship between health and happiness, on a country-by-country level, linear or nonlinear?" and "What role does societal trust play in citizens' desire for authoritarian leadership?"

At every turn, the book gives students opportunities to understand how researchers use social statistics in the real world, and to conduct and present their own analyses, just as they will be expected to do in their own research in academics or employment.

CHAPTERS OF THE BOOK AND WHAT IS NEW TO THIS EDITION

■ Chapter 1 is all about forms of data: what do they look like and how do you work with them? Since many students may have never even seen a dataset, I describe how you construct a basic dataset and how you can get it into the shape you want through recoding, computing, and indexing. For example, there is a step-by-step GSS example about constructing an index of workplace hostility. I talk about several of the most innovative and extensive data collection efforts in the social sciences. I discuss how we live in an age of endless data, which presents us with myriad research opportunities, and offer literature examples of researchers using Internet-based data (Wikipedia and the Internet Movie Database) to conduct interesting research projects.

■ Chapter 2 covers table construction with one, two, or three variables. I also cover basic graphing, with an emphasis on how to create a graph that accurately represents the data. Examples in this chapter include the effect of childrearing goals on parents' propensity to engage in spanking, and the effects of gender and age on chivalrous behavior. The chapter ends with a fascinating article about racial classification that appeared in a recent issue of a top social science journal, yet featured a greatly exaggerated graph.

■ Chapter 3 covers, using a wide variety of unique graphic-based explanations, the basic descriptive statistics: mean, median, mode, variance, and standard deviation. Given that qualitative diversity is of paramount importance, I also provide extensive coverage of the index of qualitative variation, as well as some coverage of the index of dissimilarity and the Gini Coefficient. Examples in this chapter include variation in Internet use by race, and changing attitudes over time toward government spending on health care, the military, and the environment. A literature example highlights the extensive variation in medical costs for a single surgical procedure.

■ Chapter 4 is the first of four chapters in the book that cover inferential techniques. In each of these four chapters, I discuss in depth how each technique is based on a probability distribution, showing how such distributions are actually created and what they really mean. In this chapter, I cover inference with crosstabs—the chi-square test—using a creative discussion of statistical significance. I emphasize, through a unique graphic, the effect that sample size can have on chi-square results. The chapter's examples include the relationship between age and cynicism and the relationships among age, gender, and gun ownership. Both chi-square literature examples involve the body: one covers gender differences in flatulence habits, whereas the other compares how the French and American media treat the obesity epidemic.

■ Chapter 5 is the second inference chapter. By hand, I build a sampling distribution and show graphically what the standard error of the mean really is. With regard to applications, this chapter covers testing a population claim and building confidence intervals. Examples in this chapter include attitudes toward police use of violence and the relationship between job stress and job satisfaction. The literature example regards how a researcher used confidence intervals to study how blacks are portrayed in a random sample of contemporary films.

■ Chapter 6 is the third inference chapter, and in it, I cover *t*-tests and ANOVA. I construct by hand a sampling distribution of sample mean differences, and I go into significant depth regarding how the tests' formulas actually work. I introduce "interchapter connections," which show students how various techniques are similar or different, and help them understand how to choose among techniques. The examples for the chapter involve the relationships among political party, age, and attitudes toward suicide, and the connection between attitudes toward gender equality in the household and actual behavior within the household. The *t*-test literature example is on gender overcompensation. The ANOVA literature example studies activism through the life course.

■ Chapter 7 covers simple bivariate correlation and regression. The graphical examples fully explain the important concept of explained variation. By examining movie grosses over time, I show how regression can be used in forecasting. Other examples include the effects of income on relaxation time, and intergenerational effects on family size. The literature examples cover attitudes toward relinquishing civil liberties in the age of terror, and the correlations among gender, body size, and physical attractiveness.

■ Chapter 8 is the final chapter on inference. By building one last sampling distribution, I graphically illustrate what the standard error of the slope represents and how we use it to gauge a regression slope's statistical significance. I emphasize the relationship between sample size and statistical significance, and teach students to think critically about the distinction between statistical and substantive significance. Examples in this chapter examine how level of sexual activity is affected by educational achievement, income, and hours worked. Both literature examples involve grades: looking first at the effect of studying at the college level, second at the effect of family size at the grade-school level.

■ Chapter 9 involves the use of various types of variables as independent variables in a regression equation. After covering how to interpret slopes for dichotomous variables, I show in a step-by-step fashion how to use multiple dichotomies to create a set of reference-group variables. I also include an interchapter connection linking *t*-tests with dichotomous slopes. The examples investigate demographic effects on STEM (science, technology, engineering, and mathematics) achievement, partnership-status effects on happiness, and the relationship between political party and political knowledge. The literature examples show how researchers used dichotomies and reference groups to study gender differences in housework, and temporal changes in attitudes toward gay rights.

■ Chapter 10 covers, with the great care that the topic warrants, the very important concept of controlling. I start with some analogies, illustrating how the concept of controlling is actually imbued in our everyday lives. I walk students through the typical tabular construction of a series of nested regression models. I offer an interchapter connection, using the same data to create both an elaborated crosstab and a nested regression model. I show how to judge improvement from model to model, and why it is important to keep sample size constant from model to model. Examples in this chapter involve explaining racial differences in attitudes toward state assistance and gender and in religion's effects on attitudes toward same-sex parenting. The literature examples examine the grade gap between whites and blacks and the media effects on attitudes toward crime.

■ Chapter 11 covers the meaning behind standardized coefficients, or betas. Rather than just handing the students the simple formula for calculating betas, I take them through an in-depth explanation so that they can develop a full understanding of what the betas really are and why they are important. I include an interchapter connection the links betas to *z*-scores. Examples involve religiosity and attitudes toward abortion and the male/female differences in what determines life satisfaction. The literature examples cover the topics of school discipline and of country music's effect on suicide rates.

■ Chapter 12 covers one of the most prominent techniques in current social science literature: interaction effects. I first make an interchapter connection that illustrates how interaction has similarities to elaborated crosstabs. Then, I show students how to work through examples to develop a full understanding of the interaction. Examples in this chapter examine the interaction effect between sex and number of children on relaxation time, the interaction effect between race and education on attitudes toward Muslim civil rights, and the interaction effect between race and sex on religiosity. Literature examples involve the interaction of gender and religious participation on black political activity, and the interaction of gender and work hours on level of family guilt.

■ Chapter 13 explains the difference between regular regression and logistic regression. Without becoming bogged down in the math going on behind the scenes, I show students how to run numerous examples with a logistic regression model in order to understand the probabilities they are calculating. Because so many logistic results are presented as odds ratios, I explain how to interpret such results.

Dichotomous dependent variables in the examples include home ownership, support for gun control, interracial friendships, giving to charity, and condom usage. Literature examples are on the topics of presidential disapproval and global warming.

■ Chapter 14 deals with path analysis. Although more esoteric techniques have emerged, I find that path analysis remains a very useful way for students to visualize indirect effects. I describe how to construct and interpret a path model, and in an interchapter connection, I link path analysis and nested models. To this end, I bring back the same-sex parenting example from an earlier chapter and revise it into a path model. There are also examples concerning drinking behavior, political party identification, and intergenerational socioeconomic status effects. The literature examples involve student activism, and emotion work in the service industry.

■ Chapter 15 covers simple non-linear relationships and basic log transformations. I include a detailed and graphical explanation of how these nonlinear slopes work. For the examples, I use age's non-linear effect on income, education's nonlinear effect on income, income's non-linear effect on political party, and income's non-linear effect on financial satisfaction. The literature examples involve gendered occupations, and congressional effectiveness.

■ Chapter 16 ends the book with a brief look forward, telling students what they might want to look out for as they enter the world of social research. I offer examples of two common regression-related problems: outliers and multicollinearity. Then I very briefly introduce several common advanced techniques that they might encounter in the social research literature, techniques used for specific types of variables (ordered logistic, multinomial), types of samples (multilevel modeling), and types of situations (structural equation modeling, hazard modeling).

I began this preface with a longstanding problem: many of our introductory statistics students do not gain exposure to the techniques they need to know. At academic conferences, from individual discussions to packed workshops on how to transform the introductory statistics course, I have witnessed concern about this situation. Many instructors want to make this type of change, but they simply haven't known how to accomplish it. *Social Statistics: Managing Datasets, Conducting Analyses, Presenting Results* provides instructors with a proven way to achieve this change in their courses. The book markedly improved my own course: I was able to help my students achieve a greater level of understanding of these techniques than ever before. From their reduced stress levels over the material to the improved quality of their class presentations, I witnessed positive change in a number of important ways. I also have heard from other instructors who used the book that students have responded very positively to it and that it has improved their courses. If given the right tools, instructors can teach their students these contemporary techniques. I believe such changes in the introductory social statistics course are not only possible but also necessary in our data-filled world. We must give students the foundation they need to succeed in their courses, their research, their jobs, and their lives. It is my sincere belief that this book will help us accomplish these goals.

ACKNOWLEDGMENTS

First, I'd like to thank the many students in my statistics courses, at the University of Washington and at the College of William and Mary, who helped me through the years craft my teaching of statistics. I'd particularly like to thank students in my recent courses. As this book became a reality, and as I began working on the new edition, they were regular audiences for various examples I was trying, and they were refreshingly candid about what worked and what did not. My research assistants were invaluable to this project. For the first edition, Margaret Clendenen was a big help with getting the datasets in order. For the second edition, Sarah Overton took on every task I threw at her and returned high quality results with amazing speed. The article and variable appendices in particular are much better because of her. My colleagues were, as always, willing to help, particularly Salvatore Saporito and Graham Ousey.

Steve Rutter at Routledge has been an amazing editor. For the second edition in particular, he has provided me with endless and savvy input. Although I occasionally dreaded the arrival of our phone meetings, by the end of them I always felt reinvigorated. Editorial assistant Margaret Moore expertly kept track of every detail, and had the patience of a saint. Project Manager Deepti Agarwal was a pleasure to work with during the production process. I'd also like to thank Series Editors Val Jenness and Jodi O'Brien for their continuing support and advice. The numerous reviewers of the previous edition offered advice with impressive attention to detail, and the book is all the better for it: thanks to Nathan Wright, Yingyi Ma, Michael Abel, Amy Stone, Melanie Arthur, Sally Raskoff, Matthew Green, Dawn Baunach, Linda Henderson, David Sikkink, Mark Handcock, and Matt Huffman. Also thanks to the reviewers of this edition:

Michael Henderson   University of Mississippi
Veena Kulkarni   Arkansas State University

Michael Stern	College of Charleston
Claude Rubinson	University of Houston, Downtown
Justin Berg	University of North Dakota
B. Mitchell Peck	University of Oklahoma
David Merolla	Wayne State University
Sachi Ando	Widener University
Joseph Baker	East Tennessee State University
Tetsuya Matsubayashi	University of North Texas
Paul Warwick	Simon Fraser University
Charles Kaylor	Temple University
Matt Huffman	University of California, Irvine

I wrote most of this book at my home in Richmond, Virginia, often surrounded by pups and within earshot of my partner Farhang. The pups—Miss(ed) Sunshine, Mistah Jack, and Stanley—provided important reality checks ("Sure interaction effects are important, but we want to interact with *you*"). Farhang (who brought me a cup of coffee just moments ago!) has provided a trophy-worthy level of support. When the book revision took on a life far larger than either of us had imagined, we buckled down and got through it together.

Chapter 1

LIFE IN A DATA-LADEN AGE: FINDING AND MANAGING DATASETS

This chapter covers . . .

. . . what data look like in their raw form within a dataset

. . . how to work with data to get them ready to analyze

. . . the wide variety of datasets that are readily available for analysis

. . . the newer forms that data take, from Internet databases to media analyses

. . . types of variables used in statistical analysis

. . . a classification of statistical procedures we'll cover in this book

. . . examples of how researchers used Wikipedia and IMDb to conduct studies

INTRODUCTION

Well, here we are. Long pause. Awkward silence. Let's get one thing out in the open right away: "thrilled" might not be a good description of your mood at this very moment. You are not thrilled to be sitting in front of a book on statistics. Other emotions likely are in play: boredom, trepidation, fear. Maybe not all of these, but if you're like many students taking a course in statistics, the probability is high that some of these emotions are involved. Any effort I make here to dispel such emotions likely will elicit another set of reactions: skepticism, disbelief, anger at my patronizing tone. I realize it might take me a while to win you over. But I will do my best. Mark my words: at some point, perhaps not right away, but somewhere down the road, you will, perhaps secretly, start to like statistics.

OK, you may not get to that point. But I do hope to convince you that understanding statistics is completely possible if you have the right combination of guides (your instructor and me). It is not only possible to understand statistics; it is also absolutely *essential* to being an informed and effective citizen, activist, or employee. We live in an age in which information is overwhelmingly everywhere, and a lot of this information is statistical. Legislators measure the success of social policies based on statistics. A philanthropist considering funding a nonprofit organization may ask for evidence of the organization's prior success, and this evidence is often statistical in nature. Start-up companies have made fortunes by developing better statistical models to help people mine the data created daily by people's Internet searches and by consumer behavior. Therefore, if you can't speak statistics, or read them, you could very well be left out of the loop.

Did I just say, "speak statistics"? Yes, I did. In many ways, for many people, learning statistics is very similar to learning a foreign language. If I started speaking, say, Farsi or Swahili right now, I'd probably lose your interest rather quickly (unless, of course, you're a speaker of these languages). But do I lose you any less slowly when I say. "Adding the squared age term raises the explained variation by 0.04 (with an F-test significant at $p < .01$) and causes the interaction term to lose its statistical significance?" I'd bet not. Right now, to figure out what this sentence meant, you'd need to take it to someone who speaks statistics, and you'd be relying on that person's translation. By the end of this book, you'll be able to figure out on your own what such sentences mean, which means that, among your friends, family, and coworkers, *you* will likely become the statistical translator. And those statistical tables you see in academic journals or policy briefings? You know, those tables that you just skip over because you have no idea what they're saying? I'll be giving you the necessary skills to be able to navigate such tables with ease.

This book differs substantially from other introductory statistics books. I think that's a good thing, but, granted, I'm biased. In addition to using a writing style I hope will not bore or confuse you, I get us through the basic statistics relatively quickly. I do this in order to spend much more time than most books do on the statistical techniques that are used most in the real world. In my opinion, many books spend far too many chapters going over statistical techniques that students likely will never see in practice. Then, before they get to the really good stuff, the book ends. This is akin to a movie that has lots of character and plot development, and then, right at the climax, when the school bus filled with orphans is hanging off the cliff, the screen fades to black and the credits roll. This book, in contrast, not only saves those orphans; it finds them all families and buys each child a puppy. In this book, I cover the basics and then get to the good stuff. Although I've done my best to write as clearly as possible, there inevitably will be points where, the first time you read through them, something just doesn't make sense. Don't give up there. Sometimes this material takes a few readings before you really understand it. But, if you are persistent, you will get there.

WHAT DATA LOOK LIKE

Yes, *look*. The word *data* is the plural form of the singular word *datum*. It may sound weird now, but get used to it, because it's grammatically correct. Stratum, medium, datum; strata, media, data. The data *are* correct. The data *are* available on the Internet. The data *do* not lie. Actually, sometimes they do lie, but more on that later in the book. In our trip together, we'll be calculating and interpreting statistics using lots and lots of data, so the first things I want to go over with you are the basic forms that data take, the major sources of data today, and some useful ways to work with data to answer the questions you want to answer. Here's a hypothetical short conversation between me and a computer:

TL: Hello, computer, I'm a male.
Computer: 00010110110001001?
TL: I am a male.
Computer: 00010110110001001?
TL: (sigh) 01100001010001!
Computer: 01100001010001? 010011011!!!
TL: 011011000011001.

Computers, as amazing as they are, don't understand words very well. Of course, we're getting there; voice recognition is no longer just a dream. But, even with such programs, behind the scenes the computer still is using numbers. Data in the social sciences, then, are almost always reduced to numbers. However, when researchers collect data, it is often through interviews or surveys. We start with a survey interviewer collecting data from a survey respondent. Next, that respondent's answers are translated into numerical codes that the researchers then input into a dataset. The researchers then use the dataset and a statistical program to calculate their statistics. Reducing people's complex behaviors and attitudes to numbers is not a perfect process. Interesting details sometimes get lost in translation. I'll be the first to defend those who use more qualitative techniques to study the social world. However, because this *is* a book on statistics, we'll be working with the more quantitative, survey-driven data.

Before we look at some real datasets, let's start hypothetically, on a very small scale. We conduct a survey of a whopping six people, asking them the following five questions:

1. Their sex (male or female)
2. Their age (in years)
3. Their race (white, black, or other)
4. The highest level of education they have completed (some high school, high school diploma, some college, college degree, advanced degree)
5. Their support of capital punishment for someone convicted of murder (strongly support, support, oppose, strongly oppose).

Here are the tiny surveys for each person:

■ **Exhibit 1.1: A Tiny Set of Data**

Respondent 1:	**Respondent 2:**	**Respondent 3:**
1. Male	1. Male	1. Female
2. 42	2. 75	2. 20
3. White	3. Other	3. White
4. High school diploma	4. College degree	4. Some high school
5. Strongly supports	5. Opposes	5. Supports

Respondent 4:	**Respondent 5:**	**Respondent 6:**
1. Male	1. Female	1. Female
2. 56	2. 33	2. 63
3. Black	3. White	3. Black
4. Advanced degree	4. College degree	4. High school diploma
5. Strongly opposes	5. No answer	5. Strongly opposes

We have data! Now what do we do with them? If we're like most people, we'll enter them into a statistical analysis program. In this book, we'll use SPSS, because it is one of the easiest to use and it is one of the most widely used statistical packages. Most chapters in this book end with a series of SPSS demonstrations that cover the statistical techniques I just went over in the chapter. But, for now, we'll stay hypothetical and get to SPSS at the end of the chapter. First, we need to name our variables. The first four are easy to name: SEX, AGE, RACE, DEGREE. We could name the last one CAPITAL PUNISHMENT, but typically variable names are shorter, so we'll go with CAPPUN. With those decisions made, our dataset looks like this:

■ **Exhibit 1.2: An Empty Dataset**

	SEX	AGE	RACE	DEGREE	CAPPUN
1					
2					
3					
4					
5					
6					

Each variable gets its own column, and each respondent gets his or her own row. Now we need to fill in the cells with the data. For the age variable, we can just put in the actual numbers. However, because the computer doesn't like words, we next need to assign numbers, or **codes**, for each category of the other four of our variables. For SEX, with two categories, we'll use

Male: 0, Female: 1

Now, men, don't ascribe too much meaning to this. I don't think you're zeros. Coding is often arbitrary. I just as easily could have coded females as 0 and males as 1. For RACE, with three categories, we'll use

White: 0, Black: 1, Other: 2

For DEGREE, with five categories, we'll use

Some high school: 0, High school diploma: 1, Some college: 2, College degree: 3, Advanced degree: 4

Finally, the capital punishment variable has four categories:

Strongly support: 0, Support: 1, Oppose: 2, Strongly oppose: 3

With the codes in place, we can fill in our cells:

■ **Exhibit 1.3: A Filled-In Dataset**

	SEX	AGE	RACE	DEGREE	CAPPUN
1	0	42	0	1	0
2	0	75	2	3	2
3	1	20	0	0	1
4	0	56	1	4	3
5	1	33	0	3	.
6	1	63	1	1	3

Be sure to observe how the codes match up with the respondents' survey answers. Notice that Respondent 5 did not give an answer to Question 5, so she gets a dot for that variable (you'll see this a lot, or people will designate particular numbers for "no answer" or "don't know"). Our little dataset, with five variables and six respondents, has 30 cells with 30 pieces of information. As you likely can imagine, most datasets have many more respondents and variables than this one. For example, over the years, the General Social Survey (GSS) has interviewed 57,061 respondents and has 5,548 variables, giving us 316,574,428 cells. That's a lot of information.

MAKING THE DATA WORK FOR YOU

Most of the time, the data aren't exactly in the shape that we need them to be. But this is easy enough to fix. What we do is take the original variable and go through a process called **recoding** in order to create a new variable (always leaving the old variable in its original state). If we wanted to compare whites and nonwhites with regard to whether they either support or oppose capital punishment, we'd want to recode each of these variables. First, we take the original RACE variable and recode it from three categories to two categories, giving us a new variable we'll call RACERE:

■ **Exhibit 1.4: Recoding the RACE Variable**

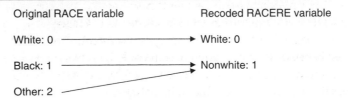

Original RACE variable   Recoded RACERE variable

White: 0 ———————————→ White: 0

Black: 1 ———————————→ Nonwhite: 1

Other: 2 ———————————↗

This gives us a new variable with two categories instead of the original three. Next, we take the CAPPUN variable and from it recode a new variable we'll call CAPPUNRE:

■ **Exhibit 1.5: Recoding the CAPPUN Variable**

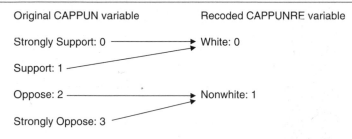

This gives us a new variable with two categories instead of the original four. When we take an original variable and from it create a new variable with fewer categories, we call this process **collapsing**: we are collapsing multiple categories into a smaller number of categories. Here is our dataset with the two new variables and their values:

■ **Exhibit 1.6: Our Tiny Dataset with Two New Variables**

	SEX	AGE	RACE	DEGREE	CAPPUN	RACERE	CAPPUNRE
1	0	42	0	1	0	0	0
2	0	75	2	3	2	1	1
3	1	20	0	0	1	0	0
4	0	56	1	4	3	1	1
5	1	33	0	3	.	0	.
6	1	63	1	1	3	1	1

Notice that when we collapse a variable, we do lose valuable detail. For example, with the new CAPPUNRE variable, we no longer know if someone strongly opposes or simply opposes capital punishment. Therefore, as a general rule, we should collapse categories together only when we have good reason to do so. Don't just collapse willy-nilly just because it's fun. A good reason could be substantive: we really want to compare whites to nonwhites. Or our reason could be statistical: to do what we want to do statistically, we need the variable to be collapsed.

Another way to get new variables is to combine variables in a variety of ways. What if we were studying the household division of labor (a fancy way of saying who does the housework), and we had these two measures:

YOURHWK: number of hours of housework the respondent does per week
PRTNRHWK: number of hours of housework the respondent's partner does per week

We could take these measures and calculate other variables:

TOTALHWK = YOURHWK + PRTNRHWK: this would give us the combined hours of housework.
YOURHWKPCT = YOURHWK/TOTALHWK: this would give us the proportion of housework the respondent does.
PRTNRHWKPCT = PRTNRHWK/TOTALHWK: this would give us the proportion of housework the respondent's partner does.

Another way to combine variables is to find related variables and engage in a process called **indexing**. The simplest (and most common) form of index is an additive index, in which we add variables together. Let's say we had our six respondents from earlier respond not to a single question about capital punishment but to three questions with specific scenarios (e.g., Would you support capital punishment for terrorists responsible for 9/11?), where 0 = NO and 1 YES. We could add respondents' responses together into an index called CAPPUNDX. The dataset might look like this:

■ **Exhibit 1.7: A Dataset with an Additive Index**

	CAPPUN1	CAPPUN2	CAPPUN3	CAPPUNDX
1	0	0	0	0
2	1	1	1	3
3	1	0	0	1
4	0	1	1	2
5	1	1	.	.
6	0	0	0	0

Ornery Respondent 5 is at it again: she was willing to answer the first two questions, but not the third. So, unfortunately, we are unable to compute an index score for her.

Some people use techniques to take care of this, such as "guessing" what the respondent would have said for the question she skipped, based on how she answered other questions, but I'm not a big fan of this.

Indexes (or indices) are a great idea if you're worried that a single variable will not adequately capture what you're trying to get at. Indexing is a real art, and some people get really picky about how you do it, but we won't go into such detail in this book. Just make sure your combinations of variables make sense, not just to you but also to any "reasonable" person. For example, in our original five-variable dataset, if someone said, "Let's add together the age and degree variables," we'd want to meet such a suggestion with great skepticism. Another question we want to ask ourselves when we create an additive index is, "Do our variables give us enough combined cases?" For example, what if our CAPPUN1,2,3 dataset looked like this:

■ **Exhibit 1.8: An Unfortunate Attempt at an Additive Index**

	CAPPUN1	CAPPUN2	CAPPUN3	CAPPUNDX
1	.	0	0	.
2	.	1	1	.
3	.	0	0	.
4	0	1	.	.
5	1	1	.	.
6	0	0	.	.

So very sad. It seems that the survey researchers did not plan things out well. They didn't ask any of the respondents all three CAPPUN questions. So our index ends up with no respondents with valid index scores. If your index involves several variables, sometimes there's just one variable that turns out to be the culprit (later in the book, we'll go over how to figure this out). Removing this variable from the index would likely solve the problem.

OUR DATASETS

In this book, I'm using data from six well-known datasets. For the in-chapter examples, I use the General Social Survey (GSS). For the end-of-chapter exercises, I use the American National Election Studies (ANES), the World Values Survey (WVS), and three surveys from the Pew Internet & American Life Project. Researchers in the social sciences use these datasets quite frequently. Survey researchers have been carrying out the GSS since 1972, doing so every year or—in recent years—every other year. Most of the time, I'll be using data from the 2012 GSS; however, occasionally I'll go back to a different year or look at data over a series of years. The GSS is exactly what it sounds like: researchers design it to be used by a wide variety of people for a wide variety of reasons. It covers a lot of ground topically.

In order to observe trends, it replicates hundreds of questions year to year. But each time they conduct it, the GSS researchers use new questions, often in sets called **modules**. Throughout the years, some of the more interesting modules have been

- 1988: religion,
- 1993: culture,
- 1994: multiculturalism,
- 2000: health,
- 2002: quality of working life,
- 2004: immigration,
- 2006: global warming,
- 2008: scientific knowledge,
- 2010: the environment, and
- 2012: workplace hostility.

In addition to using new questions every year, the GSS uses a new sample of respondents, as opposed to a panel of the same respondents who are reinterviewed year after year, as is done in longitudinal surveys. The researchers take great care in collecting the sample in a highly scientific way. This makes the results highly generalizable to the population from which the sample was drawn: all Americans aged 18 and older not currently institutionalized (in mental institutions or prisons). The size of the sample ranges year to year from around 2,000 respondents to more than 4,500 respondents. The GSS is not the ideal dataset for everyone. For example, if you're interested in people's attitudes toward clowns, I'm afraid you're out of luck. And if you're interested in the attitudes of clowns themselves, again the GSS will let you down.

The ANES is slightly more specialized but still offers the opportunity to study many different topics. Given the name of the survey, you've probably already guessed that the ANES researchers ask a lot of questions about elections, candidates, and political knowledge and attitudes. The researchers carry out the ANES every two years; however, the survey during a presidential election year is quite a bit larger than are those conducted during congressional election years. The ANES I use for the end-of-chapter exercises is from 2012. The 2012 ANES had 5,916 respondents. The researchers interviewed most of these respondents twice: before the election and after the election. In 2012, for the first time, the ANES conducted the survey using two modes: the typical face-to-face interview mode and a new Internet mode. Both sets of data were collected very carefully.

The WVS is a great dataset for studying attitudes and behaviors on a global scale. It is the brainchild of Ronald Inglehart from the University of Michigan, who has written some wonderful books with the data from the WVS. Under Inglehart's careful direction, the 2005 WVS team has carried out surveys in 48 countries, from Argentina to Zambia. In each country, a carefully selected sample of respondents was asked a wide variety of questions about social issues, national pride, immigration, and life satisfaction. The original 2005 WVS dataset had a whopping 67,268 respondents across these 48 countries. To make this dataset more manageable for the end-of-chapter exercises, I converted this dataset to a country-by-country dataset, where each case was a country rather than a person (I describe the process in Appendix A).

The Pew Internet & American Life Project is part of the Pew Research Center, funded by the Pew Charitable Trusts. This project began in 2000 and has been conducting fascinating surveys about the increasing role of the Internet (and other new technologies) in Americans' lives ever since. After they have finished reporting on the findings from a new study, they post the original data on their website. I use data from three of their surveys, each of which used carefully selected random samples. The first I call PewKids: in 2011, it surveyed 799 American parent–child combinations. They asked parents' about their concerns about the Internet and about what they do to protect their children, and they asked children (ages 12–17) about their use of social networking sites and their experiences with cyberbullying. The second Pew survey I call PewHealth: in 2012, it surveyed 3,014 Americans about their health and the extent to which they use the Internet to find health information. The third Pew survey I call PewShop: in 2013, it surveyed 1,003 Americans about what technological devices they had in their home, whether they used a smartphone, and whether they use their cell phones when they're out shopping (in order to call up reviews of products or price comparisons).

OTHER GREAT DATASETS

There are many other great datasets out there, most of which are designed with a specific goal in mind. Here I describe just a few of the most widely used datasets, many of which provide data for the literature examples within the chapters and the articles that appear in Appendix B of the book. Creating such datasets are enormous endeavors involving many researchers and staff.

The Panel Study of Income Dynamics (PSID) runs out of the Institute for Social Research at the University of Michigan. In 1968, the PSID researchers chose a nationally representative sample of more than 18,000 people living in 5,000 families. They have interviewed these same families year after year about changes in their employment, income, family structure, health, and many other topics. The fact that they interview the same people repeatedly is what makes the PSID a panel study. Among the greatest aspects of the PSID is that it allows us to study intergenerational processes. Let's say married couple Mike and Carol were in the original PSID sample in 1968. The PSID gathered data not only on the two of them, but also on their children. As these children went on to create their own families, the PSID continued to track them and *their* children. Now, the PSID is likely collecting data on how Mike and Carol are adjusting to retirement, how their children are faring financially as they enter middle age, and how Mike and Carol's grandchildren are doing in school. This allows researchers unprecedented abilities to study how the financial well-being of one generation affects the well-being of future generations. On its website, the PSID keeps track of what researchers are doing with these data. As I write this, the current counts are 68 books, 469 book chapters, 634 dissertations, and 2,321 journal articles. Another project that is useful for studying family dynamics is the National Survey of Families and Households, which is a longitudinal survey that comes out of the University of Wisconsin. Its researchers conducted interviews with 13,000 people in 1988, 1994, and 2003. Researchers use it to analyze the effects that family structure on children, how parents make child-rearing choices, and how housework is distributed within households.

The National Longitudinal Study of Adolescent Health is another longitudinal survey. Researchers at the University of North Carolina at Chapel Hill oversee the study. Given that the title of the survey is a mouthful, its nickname is Add Health (don't ask me where that extra *d* came from; that's always bugged me). This survey started in 1994 when researchers interviewed tens of thousands of adolescents, their school administrators, parents, siblings, and friends. It has conducted additional interviews with these same people in 1996, 2002, and 2008, allowing researchers to track these people as they become young adults. One of the strengths of this study is its network capabilities. It studied all of students in many schools, asking them to name their friends and romantic relationships. This allows researchers to analyze the effects of social networks among adolescents on such topics as school violence, sexually transmitted diseases, and depression. As I write this, the Add Health website claims that more than 4,600 publications, presentations, dissertations, and unpublished manuscripts have used these data. Other datasets that are useful for studying youth and school issues are the National Longitudinal Survey of Youth (which has been surveying the same people since 1979) and the National Educational Longitudinal Survey (which studied a large sample of youth, as well as their parents and teachers, at five points in time, starting in 1988).

Most of these datasets are available for public use, and finding them on the Internet, downloading them, and running statistics on them isn't difficult. Although it is easy enough to download data, it critical to spend some time understanding how the researchers assembled the dataset and its variables. Most of these datasets provide extensive users' guides and codebooks that are immensely helpful in getting the data up and running. Once you have the data ready to go, you can start creating variables of your own from the original variables. Let's go through an example of this using the most recent GSS data.

GSS EXAMPLE: AN INDEX OF WORK HOSTILITY

In the 2012 GSS is a module of questions regarding the respondent's experiences in his or her workplace. We're going to take three of these questions and combine them into an additive index of workplace hostility. Here are the survey questions:

Please respond to the following statements based on your experience during the past 12 months unless otherwise specified, with reference to your current place of employment only.

LACKINFO: People at work fail to give me information that is necessary for me to do my job.

OTHCREDT: Other people take credit for my work ideas.

PUTDOWN: People at work treat me in a manner that puts me down or address me in unprofessional terms, either publicly or privately.

All of the variables have the same original coding:

■ **Exhibit 1.9: Original Coding of the Workplace Variables**

0	IAP
1	OFTEN
2	SOMETIMES
3	RARELY
4	NEVER
8	DON'T KNOW
9	NO ANSWER

Notice that three of the codes—0, 8, and 9—are for people who don't have valid responses on the question. People who were asked the question but replied "don't know" were coded as an 8 for this question; those who were asked the question but did not give an answer were coded as a 9 for this question. IAP stands for "InAP-plicable," meaning that these respondents weren't asked the question. The GSS does not ask every respondent every question. But each question is answered by a sizable number of respondents. For example, the GSS asked more than half the respondents these work questions, giving us plenty of data with which to work.

Because these variables are all similar in their original coding, this index will be easy to create. We want someone who doesn't experience any hostility to receive a score of 0 on the index. This would be someone who responded "never" to all three questions. This tells us how to recode the variables. Here is the plan:

▨ **Exhibit 1.10: Recode Plan for the Workplace Variables**

Old Value	Value Label	New Value
0	IAP	MISSING
1	Often	3
2	Sometimes	2
3	Rarely	1
4	Never	0
8	Don't Know	MISSING
9	No Answer	MISSING

Each variable will now range from 0 to 3, with the *higher* number meaning *more* hostility. When we combine the three new variables together, someone who experiences no hostility at work will answer "never," "never," and "never" and will have a $0 + 0 + 0 = 0$ for his or her index score. Someone who experiences all kinds of hostility at work will answer "often," "often," "often" and will have a $3 + 3 + 3 = 9$ on the index. Someone who answers "often" on one question, "never" on another, and "sometimes" on the third question will have a $3 + 0 + 2 = 5$ for his or her index score. Here are the results for the LACKINFO variable and the LACKINFORE variable:

■ **Exhibit 1.11: Original Variable Results and Recoded Variable Results**

PPL AT WORK FAIL TO GIVE R NECESSARY INFO

		Frequency	Percent	Valid Percent	Cumulative Percent
Valid	OFTEN	102	5.2	9.0	9.0
	SOMETIMES	362	18.3	31.9	40.9
	RARELY	305	15.5	26.9	67.8
	NEVER	366	18.5	32.2	100.0
	Total	1135	57.5	100.0	
Missing	IAP	795	40.3		
	DONT KNOW	12	0.6		
	NA	32	1.6		
	Total	839	42.5		
Total		1974	100.0		

recoded lackinfo

		Frequency	Percent	Valid Percent	Cumulative Percent
Valid	0.00	366	18.5	32.2	32.2
	1.00	305	15.5	26.9	59.1
	2.00	362	18.3	31.9	91.0
	3.00	102	5.2	9.0	100.0
	Total	1135	57.5	100.0	
Missing	System	839	42.5		
Total		1974	100.0		

Looking at these numbers, things seem to be in order. The 102 who responded "often" on the original variable now get a "3" on the recoded variable. Notice that the three categories that are missing have now been grouped together. One thing that is lacking is value labels on the new variable. You always want to label everything so that if you return to a project in the future, you know what all of your values mean (think of labeling as a nice way to remind your future self what you did in the past). Here are all three original variables alongside their recoded variables (now with value labels):

■ Exhibit 1.12: All Three Original and Recoded Variables

PPL AT WORK FAIL TO GIVE R NECESSARY INFO

		Frequency	Percent	Valid Percent	Cumulative Percent
Valid	OFTEN	102	5.2	9.0	9.0
	SOMETIMES	362	18.3	31.9	40.9
	RARELY	305	15.5	26.9	67.8
	NEVER	366	18.5	32.2	100.0
	Total	1135	57.5	100.0	
Missing	IAP	795	40.3		
	DONT KNOW	12	0.6		
	NA	32	1.6		
	Total	839	42.5		
Total		1974	100.0		

recoded lackinfo

		Frequency	Percent	Valid Percent	Cumulative Percent
Valid	NEVER	366	18.5	32.2	32.2
	RARELY	305	15.5	26.9	59.1
	SOMETIMES	362	18.3	31.9	91.0
	OFTEN	102	5.2	9.0	100.0
	Total	1135	57.5	100.0	
Missing	System	839	42.5		
Total		1974	100.0		

OTHER PEPLE TAKE CREDIT FOR RS WORK OR IDEAS

		Frequency	Percent	Valid Percent	Cumulative Percent
Valid	OFTEN	98	5.0	8.7	8.7
	SOMETIMES	279	14.1	24.7	33.4
	RARELY	324	16.4	28.7	62.0
	NEVER	429	21.7	38.0	100.0
	Total	1130	57.2	100.0	
Missing	IAP	795	40.3		
	DONT KNOW	15	0.8		
	NA	34	1.7		
	Total	844	42.8		
Total		1974	100.0		

recoded othcredt

		Frequency	Percent	Valid Percent	Cumulative Percent
Valid	NEVER	429	21.7	38.0	38.0
	RARELY	324	16.4	28.7	66.6
	SOMETIMES	279	14.1	24.7	91.3
	OFTEN	98	5.0	8.7	100.0
	Total	1130	57.2	100.0	
Missing	System	844	42.8		
Total		1974	100.0		

PPL AT WORK TREAT R IN A MANNER PUTTING R DOWN

		Frequency	Percent	Valid Percent	Cumulative Percent
Valid	OFTEN	38	1.9	3.4	3.4
	SOMETIMES	134	6.8	11.8	15.2
	RARELY	315	16.0	27.8	43.0
	NEVER	645	32.7	57.0	100.0
	Total	1132	57.3	100.0	
Missing	IAP	795	40.3		
	DONT KNOW	14	0.7		
	NA	33	1.7		
	Total	842	42.7		
Total		1974	100.0		

recoded putdown

		Frequency	Percent	Valid Percent	Cumulative Percent
Valid	NEVER	645	32.7	57.0	57.0
	RARELY	315	16.0	27.8	84.8
	SOMETIMES	134	6.8	11.8	96.6
	OFTEN	38	1.9	3.4	100.0
	Total	1132	57.3	100.0	
Missing	System	842	42.7		
Total		1974	100.0		

Once we're sure all the new variables are correct, we can combine them into an index:

HOSTWKINDEX = LACKINFORE + OTHCREDTRE + PUTDOWNRE

Here is a table that summarizes how the respondents fall on the index:

■ **Exhibit 1.13: Index of Work Hostility**

Index of Workplace Hostility

		Frequency	Percent	Valid Percent	Cumulative Percent
Valid	NO HOSTILITY	220	11.1	19.5	19.5
	1	128	6.5	11.4	30.9
	2	172	8.7	15.3	46.2
	3	190	9.6	16.9	63.1
	4	162	8.2	14.4	77.4
	5	120	6.1	10.7	88.1
	6	74	3.7	6.6	94.7
	7	36	1.8	3.2	97.9
	8	14	0.7	1.2	99.1
	VERY HOSTILE	10	0.5	0.9	100.0
	Total	1126	57.0	100.0	
Missing	System	848	43.0		
Total		1974	100.0		

Of the respondents, 220 (or 19.5%) experienced no hostility whereas only 10 (or 0.9%) of the respondents experienced the highest level of hostility. Although GSS respondents are rather bunched up near the "lack of hostility" end, we still have respondents all over the place on the index range, and 1,126 of the 1,974 total respondents have index scores, which is a lot of people with whom to run interesting statistical analyses.

NEW FORMS OF DATA

Although most quantitative social research involves datasets such as the ones I described earlier, there are many other sources of data. As I mentioned at the very beginning of the chapter, we live in an interesting time in which we ourselves have become rapid producers of data. Not to make you paranoid, but nearly every step you make on the Internet also becomes data. I recently clicked on a news story about a band. The following day, I received an e-mail informing me of the band's concert schedule. Today, this sort of thing happens all the time. Everything we do on the Internet—posting a status update, tweeting, "liking" a photo, getting directions to a restaurant—becomes data. When the members of the marketing department were sending e-mails to inform statistics instructors about the first edition of this book, they were very proud that they could tell me who received the e-mail, who opened the e-mail, who clicked on the link within the e-mail, and how much time they spent on the book's website once they clicked on the link. It all becomes data.

With a little programming knowledge (don't worry, we won't be going into that here), you can have your computer pull (or "scrape") information off thousands of web pages and throw it into a dataset ready for analysis. In this age of supposed accountability and transparency, government websites have improved the accessibility of their data. For example, you could pull information from a school district's website, combine it with information from the local police website, and conduct original statistical analyses. As you can imagine, with so much data available on the Internet, you could easily become overwhelmed regarding what to do with the data once you have it. This book should provide you with some guidance in this regard.

Another new development is the pervasive presence and availability of media. A generation ago, if one wanted to study a television show or a news program over time, one had to have the forethought to tape the show, have the ability to travel to a repository at a university or television studio, or have the good fortune of running into a hoarder who happens to be collecting the media you want. Now with Netflix or Hulu, hundreds of seasons of shows are available. Using a social research method called **content analysis**, you can develop a coding mechanism and "ask" each episode of a show a set of questions: Does it feature a particular theme? Does it contain a particular type of interaction among the characters on the show? This age of constant availability has opened up endless research possibilities, but you have to have the knowledge of statistics necessary to make full use of all of these new sources of data.

LEVELS OF MEASUREMENT

Throughout the book, we will be using many variables, but we can't use all of the variables for all of the statistical procedures I'm going to discuss. This is because what you're allowed to do with each variable statistically depends on its **level of measurement**. For example, although we can calculate the average age of the GSS respondents, we can't calculate an average race. "Average race" doesn't even make sense. Nor does "average religious denomination."

Variables such as race and religion have categories that simply represent names used to describe people: that person is black, that person is Jewish, and that person is a black Jew. They allow us to describe, or name people, but that is all. We refer to their level of measurement as **nominal-level** measurement (the French word for name is *nom*, if that helps). Nominal-level variables are simply categories in which we can put the respondents. The categories for a nominal-level variable have no logical order. The GSS race variable's categories are

WHITE = 1
BLACK = 2
OTHER = 3

Yes, we match each category up with a number, but there is no order here. You can't order races; you can't order religions; you can't order marital statuses. Because we can't even order the categories, we can't do much with them mathematically. We simply can say equals or not equals: this person's race equals white; this person's marital status does not equal widowed. Because nominal-level variables are limited mathematically, they are also limited statistically. We can do some procedures, but not others.

If we can order the categories of a variable but can't do anything else with them (I'll explain this in a moment), then we likely have an **ordinal-level** variable. Both the GSS and the ANES have a class variable, a self-reported estimate of the respondent's social class:

GSS Categories:
1 = lower class, 2 = working class, 3 = middle class, 4 = upper class

ANES Categories:
0 = lower class, 1 = average working class, 2 = working class, 3 = upper working class,
   4 = average middle class, 5 = middle class, 6 = upper middle class, 7 = upper class

These variables each provide an ordered set of categories: we know that working class is higher than lower class and that middle class is higher than working class. And we have numbers attached to each category. But these numbers don't really mean anything. For example, the distance between the categories is meaningless. Using the GSS variable, we could try to subtract categories from each other:

3 (middle class) − 1 (lower class) = 2
4 (upper class) − 2 (working class) = 2

Given that both of these equal two, this would imply that

3 (middle class) − 1 (lower class) = 4 (upper class) − 2 (working class),

and this simply doesn't make any sense, because the distances between the categories are meaningless. We have order, but nothing else. Other GSS variables that are ordinal include the following:

PREMARSX: There's been much discussion about the way morals and attitudes about sex are changing in this country. If a man and a woman have sex relations before marriage, do you think it is always wrong, almost always wrong, wrong only sometimes, or not wrong at all?

FAMVSWK: How often do the demands of your family interfere with your work on the job: often, sometimes, rarely, or never?

FECHLD: Now I'm going to read several more statements. As I read each one, please tell me whether you strongly agree, agree, disagree, or strongly disagree with it. a. A working mother can establish just as warm and secure a relationship with her children as a mother who does not work.

With all of these variables, we can order the respondents: Respondent A disagrees more with premarital sex than does Respondent B; Respondent C's family life interferes with her work life more than does Respondent D's family life. But that's all we can do. We can't say, for example, that Respondent A is against premarital sex twice as much as Respondent B is. We can't say that Respondent C's family life is twice as disruptive as Respondent D's family life. Occasionally, this can get tricky. For example, look at the categories for the GSS variable PARTYID (respondent's political party identification):

0   STRONG DEMOCRAT
1   NOT STRONG DEMOCRAT
2   INDEPENDENT, NEAR DEMOCRAT
3   INDEPENDENT
4   INDEPENDENT, NEAR REPUBLICAN
5   NOT STRONG REPUBLICAN
6   STRONG REPUBLICAN
7   OTHER PARTY

It looks pretty darned ordinal: as the number rises, people are moving farther and farther away from Democrat and more and more toward Republican. Until the last category: other party. People who answer this are not more Republican than those who are strong Republicans. Therefore, we'd either have to consider this variable nominal-level or remove those "other party" people (only 2.7% of the respondents in the 2012 GSS chose this category).

Now think about age. We can do lots of math with people's ages. We can add and subtract them:

> Joe is 40, Moe is 30, and Flo is 20. So Joe is $40 - 30 = 10$ years older than Moe, Moe is $30 - 20 = 10$ years older than Flo, and these 10-year differences are the same. That is, the distance of ten years is meaningful.

We can multiply and divide them:

> Pacey is 60, Tracy is 30, and Lacey is 15, so Pacey is $60/30 = 2$ times older than Tracy, and $60/15 = 4$ times older than Lacey. Lacey is half as old as Tracy and a quarter as old as Pacey.

What allows us to do this is the presence of a *meaningful zero*. With age, zero means a lack of something: a lack of age. Income has a meaningful zero, and haven't we all felt that at some point: zero income means a lack of income. The GSS variable CHILDS (number of children the respondent has had) has a meaningful zero: zero means a lack of children. Variables measured in this way are called **ratio-level** variables, because ratios have meaning (as in 60/30 the preceding example). Ratio-level variables give us the full range of mathematical possibilities, and thus statistical capabilities, as we'll see later on in the book.

Last, with regard to levels of measurement, I'd like to talk about two special ratio-level cases. The first is the **dichotomy**: a variable that takes on only two values. For example, earlier we had the variable SEX, coded 0 = Male, 1 = Female. We can claim that there is a meaningful zero, because zero here means (this may sound weird) a "lack of femaleness." In addition, we don't need to worry about the distances between the categories being meaningful, because we have only a single distance: the distance between 0 and 1. The second special case is the index, such as those I mentioned earlier. Many people (me included) consider indexes to be measured at the ratio level. This may seem odd because, as in the GSS example earlier, many indexes are simply the addition of several ordinal-level variables. But we do create them to have a meaningful zero. For example, in the "Index of Work Hostility" GSS example earlier in the chapter, we had zero mean a complete lack of work hostility. Therefore, one can make an argument that an index such as this one can be considered a ratio-level variable. This allows us to use the index in a wide variety of statistical procedures.

It's important to stay mindful of levels of measurement and make sure that your statistical plans will not be ruined by a lack of variables measured at the right levels. I've had to be the bearer of such bad news when people (who shall remain nameless) have come to me with their nominal-level data and asked me, "What can we do with these data?" My response is "Ummm, some things, but not much." Don't let this happen to you. By the end of the book, you'll have a very good idea of what your data should look like if you want to run particular statistical procedures. In addition, a consistent goal throughout the book is to help you understand when to use particular statistical procedures, depending on what your variables look like.

MAJOR TYPES OF STATISTICAL PROCEDURES

The body of statistics I cover in this book can be divided into three categories: descriptive, inferential, and explanatory. Early on in the book, we'll be concentrating on **descriptive statistics**, which are exactly what they sound like: they simply describe the data in clear summary form (in fact, some people call them summary statistics). Sometimes, that's all people want to hear: What's the average income in a neighborhood? What percentage of students at a college resides on campus? How many Americans support gay marriage? To describe a set of data, we use tables, graphs, and simple statistical procedures.

Then there are **inferential statistics**. These procedures are a bit more complicated, but oh so important: these statistics allow us to speak beyond a small sample of people. I'll talk about this much more when we get to it, but we can use inferential statistics to say some pretty specific things about very large populations, even though we haven't surveyed everyone in these populations. Looking at the three questions in the preceding paragraph, it might be possible to survey everyone in a neighborhood about incomes, and it is quite possible to know exactly what percentage of students lives on campus, but for that last question, we would have to ask every single American his or her attitude about gay marriage, and that's just not going to happen. So we sample instead. Although inferential procedures can get complicated, I've developed step-by-step approaches, and I'll show you how all of the inferential techniques are related to one another.

The last set of statistics is **explanatory**. Often, descriptive statistics raise interesting causal questions: some people in this neighborhood make higher incomes than other people in the neighborhood do. Why? Does where you live (on campus or off campus) affect your academic performance? Among which demographic groups has there been increasing support of gay marriage? All of these imply causality:

something causes higher incomes; something causes higher grades; something causes attitudes to change. With this set of statistical procedures, we don't just have variables, we have independent and dependent variables. The **dependent variable** is what we're trying to explain. Why do some students get higher grades than others? Does their residential status have an effect on their grades? That is, do grades depend on residential status? That is why, in this situation, we'd call grades the dependent variable. In this situation, we're saying that residential status is not dependent on anything; therefore we call it the independent variable. The **independent variable** is the variable we're using to explain why the dependent variable varies: we think that grades vary by residential status. The dependent or independent nature of a variable relies on the situation we're investigating. Grades are the dependent variable in the previous example, but in a completely different example, we could use grades as the independent variable to explain why some students pursue certain types of careers.

Of course, all three sets of statistical procedures are related, and any given statistical project likely will involve all three. One of my major goals is that, by the end of the book, you will have a clear picture of how all of these procedures fit together, and you will know how to decide which procedure is appropriate for a given situation. Toward that goal, most chapters end with an example or two from the social science literature illustrating how researchers used the chapter's statistical techniques. Although we didn't cover many techniques in this chapter, following this section are two examples of researchers using new sources of data from popular websites.

LITERATURE EXAMPLE: WIKIPEDIA AS A DATA SOURCE

We've all used Wikipedia. It is a fascinating endeavor that challenges our previous perceptions of expertise: who is an expert? Whose expertise should we trust? The "anyone can contribute" philosophy of everything wiki raises interesting opportunities and challenges. In his article "Governance, Organization, and Democracy on the Internet: The Iron Law and the Evolution of Wikipedia," which appeared in the social research journal *Sociological Forum* in 2009, Piotr Konieczny studied how this endeavor has dealt with a famous phenomenon: the Iron Law of Oligarchy. Robert Michel, the originator of this concept, argued that even if organizations attempt to run completely democratically, there is a natural tendency toward oligarchy (literally: rule by the few). Leaders inevitably rise and gain power, and others start following the leaders. In short, pure democracy where everyone has an equal say is impossible. But Konieczny argues that a wiki organization, because of how it is set up, can avoid some of these tendencies.

To study this phenomenon, Konieczny conducted a content analysis of one small part of Wikipedia: the "Wikipedia: Verifiability Policy." This policy governs what are considered reliable and reputable sources, and it has been edited by more than 500 editors since its creation in 2003. Taking advantage of the fact that every move on Wikipedia is cataloged, he kept track of which editors attempted to make edits to this policy, how often they did so, whether their edits were disputed by other editors, and whether they won the dispute. Starting out with over a thousand edits, he winnowed out edits that were "vandalism," and then minor edits, leaving him with 251 editing events to analyze.

Using these data, Konieczny argues that this wiki culture has, for the most part, staved off oligarchy. Wikipedia administrators' edits were nearly as likely to face disputes, and lose those disputes, as were the edits of non-administrators. Through this finding and others, he disputes the myth that there is a small group of people running Wikipedia. By its very nature, Wikipedia is able to resist this iron law of oligarchy. This is a great example of how a social researcher used publicly available data on the internet in order to advance our understanding of organizational processes.

LITERATURE EXAMPLE: IMDB AS A DATA SOURCE

IMDb—The Internet Movie Database—is another example of a treasure trove of data that was simply unimaginable to previous generations of researchers. The site catalogs nearly every movie ever made (yes, even *Sharknado*), along with the directors, producers, and actors. Social researchers have begun to put this newfound data to fascinating use. In their article "I'd Like to Thank the Academy, Team Spillovers, and Network Centrality," which appeared in the *American Sociological Review* in 2010, Gabriel Rossman, Nicole Esparza, and Phillip Bonacich combined this amazing database with data from the Academy of Motion Picture Arts and Sciences. They constructed a huge dataset of the top 10 credited actors in films eligible for Academy Awards: 147,908 performances by 37,183 actors in 16,392 films from 1936 to 2005.

For their dependent variable, the authors used a dichotomous variable: whether or not an actor's performance was nominated for an Oscar. Then, using all of these data to their full potential, they develop 12 independent variables that they use to explain the Oscar nomination or lack thereof. Two of their independent variables measured human capital (the skill an actor had amassed by that point): number of films the actor had appeared in up to that point, and number of previous Oscar nominations at that point. One of their most interesting (and complicated) variables measured status: how central the actor was within the network of actors in the film. To construct this variable, they looked at where an actor's performance fell in a film's list of credits (because the most important actors are listed first) as well as where his costars' performances within the past five years fell. For example, if an actor's performance for a film was listed higher in the credits than a very famous actor, this raises the former actor's centrality. To corroborate that this measure worked, they turned to another data source: the covers of *Entertainment Weekly* magazine. Their most central actors were far more likely to appear on the covers of the magazine than were other actors.

Although at first it appeared that the human capital of an actor (as measured by number of films in recent years) played an important role, the authors show that it is really how central they are in their network that explains whether they are nominated. Being in a film with others who have been nominated in the past does matter, but being in the film of a previously nominated director or writer matters even more. Rossman and his coauthors used readily available data to build an amazing dataset that advances our understanding of the importance of status and networks. Rossman has conducted similarly cutting-edge research on the diffusion of cultural tastes by studying corporate radio airplay, examining what determines whether a song will climb the charts (Rossman, 2012).

CONCLUSION

Reminiscent of the Chinese saying "May you live in interesting times," we certainly can view living in data-filled times as both a blessing and a curse. We are blessed because at no other point in history has so much data been so readily available at the touch of a button (well, perhaps a few buttons, but not that many). However, if you don't know what to do when you're awash in data, you might feel cursed. By now you should have a good sense of what data are, where they originate, and what you can do with them once you have them. You may not exactly feel blessed at this point, as we do have quite a long way to go, but hopefully you're feeling that being versed in statistics is not only possible, but important as well.

SPSS DEMONSTRATIONS

Please visit the book's website (www.routledge.com/cw/linneman) to view videos of these demonstrations.

Getting to Know SPSS

SPSS has been around since 1968—the same year that I was born. We've both aged reasonably well. When introduced, SPSS stood for "Statistical Package for the Social

Sciences." However, since then, it has made inroads into the business world. If you look at the company's website (www.spss.com), you can tell the program is marketed to businesses to help them use statistics to make accurate forecasts. Although many social scientists still use it, it just goes by the name SPSS now. SPSS can do a *lot* of statistics, only some of which we are going to use. In fact, I would equate our use of SPSS with driving a very expensive sports car to the grocery store down the block: we're going to be using only a small part of SPSS's immense power. SPSS can vary a bit depending on the version you're using, but the procedures we'll be doing should all work fine regardless of version. I highly recommend that you use these SPSS demonstrations while at a computer with SPSS running, because that way you can follow along. When we're working with SPSS, we'll be in two main windows.

The first is the Data Window: this is where we can look at the data, and we can look at it in two ways. The first way is the Data View, called this because we use it to look directly at the data. The other way is the Variable View, called this because we use it to look at aspects of variables. The second main window is the Output Window, and this will pop up once we run some output, such as a table or a statistical test. But let's start with the Data Window, because that's what comes up when you open SPSS. The first thing SPSS asks us is "What would you like to do?" See how nice SPSS is? Within this dialog box, or room (I like to call the boxes that pop-up "rooms," and you'll see why in a bit), we can open up a dataset or another type of file (such as an existing output file that we want to add to). Notice behind this box is an empty data window.

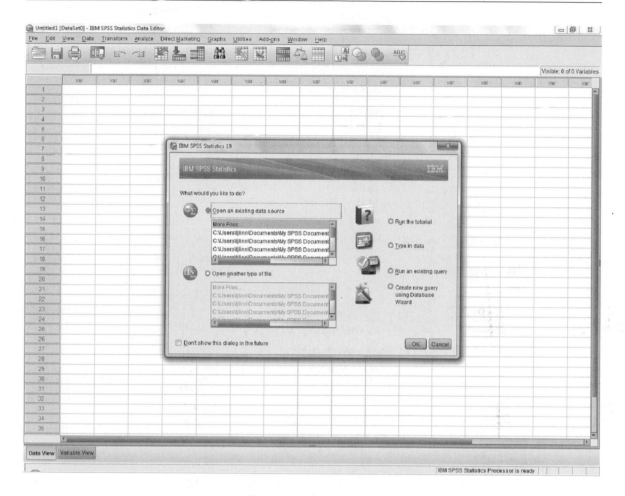

So sadly empty. We fill it by opening up a dataset. I'm going to open up the ANES dataset (the dataset that we will use for these SPSS demonstrations). I can either click on the name of the dataset in the list in the dialog box or click

File ➔ Open ➔ Data . . .

and then find the file just like I would find any other file on the computer or network. Once you open the dataset, it's easy to figure out how SPSS arranges it in the window:

Notice that each column contains a variable, whereas each row contains a case (i.e., a respondent, a person). Each respondent's entire set of answers to all of the survey questions is contained in his or her row. If you scroll to the right, you can see several variables. If you scroll down, you'll see that this dataset has 5,916 cases. Back up at the top, looking at Respondent 1, you can tell that this person is from the state of Alabama (AL), that she is a female, and that she replied "Some of the time" to the "interest_attention" variable. But what does she do some of the time? That is, what was this variable about? There are several ways to figure this out. You could look in a codebook, which, appropriately enough given its name, tells you how each variable was coded. You could also click

Utilities ➜ Variables . . .

and find the interest_attention variable on the left and click on it, and then, in the box on the right, that variable's information will pop up:

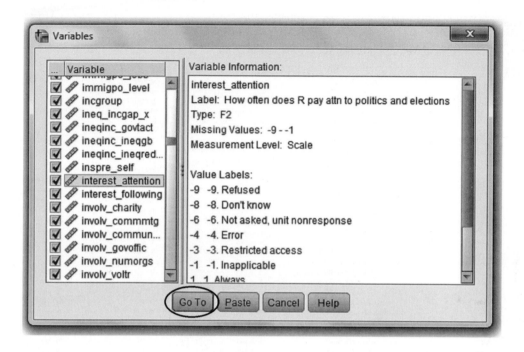

In this box, you can see the Variable Label ("How often does R pay attn to politics and elections"), and the Value Labels (–9 = Refused . . . 1 = Always . . . 5 = Never). Another handy tip about this box is if you click on the "Go To" button (I've circled it in the preceding figure), SPSS will take you right to that variable. This is handy if you have a huge dataset with hundreds of variables.

If you look at the bottom of the Data Window, you will see two tabs: the first says "Data View"; the second says "Variable View." Click on the Variable View tab (I've circled this tab in the next figure). You will now see the second version of the Data Window:

	Name	Type	Width	Decimals	Label	Values	Missing	Columns	Align	Measure	Role
1	caseid	Numeric	4	0	Case ID	None	None	8	Right	Scale	Input
2	weight_ftf	Numeric	7	4	Weight for face-to-face cases	None	None	12	Right	Scale	Input
3	weight_web	Numeric	7	4	Weight for web cases	None	None	12	Right	Scale	Input
4	weight_full	Numeric	7	4	Weight for full sample	None	None	13	Right	Scale	Input
5	mode	Numeric	1	0	Mode of data collection	{1, 1. FTF (f...	None	6	Right	Nominal	Input
6	sample_state	String	2	0	State of respondent's location	None	None	14	Left	Nominal	Input
7	gender_respondent	Numeric	1	0	Gender of respondent	{-1, -1. Inap...	-1	19	Right	Nominal	Input
8	interest_attention	Numeric	2	0	How often does R pay attn to politics and elections	{-9, -9. Refu...	-9 - -1	20	Right	Scale	Input
9	interest_following	Numeric	2	0	Interested in following campaigns standard	{-9, -9. Refu...	-9 - -1	20	Right	Scale	Input
10	voted2008	Numeric	2	0	Did R vote for president in 2008	{-9, -9. Refu...	-9 - -1	20	Right	Scale	Input
11	whovote2008	Numeric	2	0	Presidential vote choice in 2008	{-9, -9. Refu...	-9 - -1, 5	22	Right	Scale	Input
12	media_wkinews	Numeric	2	0	Days in typical week review news on internet	{-9, -9. Refu...	-9 - -1	12	Right	Scale	Input
13	media_wktvnws	Numeric	2	0	Days in typical week watch news on TV	{-9, -9. Refu...	-9 - -1	12	Right	Scale	Input
14	media_wkpaprnws	Numeric	2	0	Days in typical week read news in print newsppr	{-9, -9. Refu...	-9 - -1	12	Right	Scale	Input
15	media_wkrdnws	Numeric	2	0	Days in typical week listen news on radio	{-9, -9. Refu...	-9 - -1	12	Right	Scale	Input
16	congapp_job_x	Numeric	2	0	Approval of Congress handling of job	{-9, -9. Refu...	-9 - -1	15	Right	Scale	Input
17	presapp_track	Numeric	2	0	Are things in the country on right track	{-9, -9. Refu...	-9 - -1	15	Right	Scale	Input
18	presapp_job_x	Numeric	2	0	Approval of President handling of job	{-9, -9. Refu...	-9 - -1	15	Right	Scale	Input
19	presapp_econ_x	Numeric	2	0	Approval of President handling economy	{-9, -9. Refu...	-9 - -1	16	Right	Scale	Input
20	presapp_foreign_x	Numeric	2	0	Approval of President handling foreign relations	{-9, -9. Refu...	-9 - -1	19	Right	Scale	Input
21	presapp_health_x	Numeric	2	0	Approval of President handling health care	{-9, -9. Refu...	-9 - -1	18	Right	Scale	Input
22	ft_hclinton	Numeric	3	0	Feeling Thermometer: Hillary Clinton	{-9, -9. Refu...	-9 - -1	13	Right	Scale	Input
23	ft_gwb	Numeric	3	0	Feeling Thermometer: GW Bush	{-9, -9. Refu...	-9 - -1	8	Right	Scale	Input
24	ft_dem	Numeric	3	0	Feeling Thermometer: Democratic Party	{-9, -9. Refu...	-9 - -1	8	Right	Scale	Input
25	ft_rep	Numeric	3	0	Feeling Thermometer: Republican Party	{-9, -9. Refu...	-9 - -1	8	Right	Scale	Input
26	finance_finpast_x	Numeric	2	0	Better or worse off than 1 year ago	{-9, -9. Refu...	-9 - -1	19	Right	Scale	Input
27	finance_finnext_x	Numeric	2	0	Better or worse off 1 year from now	{-9, -9. Refu...	-9 - -1	19	Right	Scale	Input
28	health_insured	Numeric	2	0	Does R have health insurance	{-9, -9. Refu...	-9 - -1	16	Right	Scale	Input
29	health_2010hcr_x	Numeric	2	0	Support 2010 health care law	{-9, -9. Refu...	-9 - -1	18	Right	Scale	Input
30	health_self	Numeric	2	0	Health of R	{-9, -9. Refu...	-9 - -1	13	Right	Scale	Input
31	health_smoke	Numeric	2	0	Smoked cigarettes	{-9, -9. Refu...	-9 - -1	14	Right	Scale	Input
32	health_smokeamt	Numeric	2	0	If smoked, how many now	{-9, -9. Refu...	-9 - -1	17	Right	Scale	Input
33	libcon_self	Numeric	2	0	Liberal/conservative self-placement	{-9, -9. Refu...	-9 - -1	14	Right	Scale	Input
34	campfin_limcorp	Numeric	2	0	Should gov be able to limit corporate contributions	{-9, -9. Refu...	-9 - -1	17	Right	Scale	Input
35	campfin_banads	Numeric	2	0	Ban corporate/union ads for candidates	{-9, -9. Refu...	-9 - -1	16	Right	Scale	Input
36	ineq_incgap_x	Numeric	2	0	Income gap size compared to 20 years ago	{-9, -9. Refu...	-9 - -1	15	Right	Scale	Input
37	effic_complic	Numeric	2	0	Politics/govt too complicated to understand	{-9, -9. Refu...	-9 - -1	18	Right	Scale	Input

Data View Variable View

Whereas in the Data View the *cases* were in the rows, now each *variable* gets a row. The columns now contain various information about each variable. The most important columns, I believe, are the Label column and the Values column. Here is where we tell SPSS how to label a new variable we create and what each of the variable's values mean. Let's say we needed to add another category to the gender variable because some of our respondents identify as Intersexed (neither male nor female). We could click on the Label cell for the gender_respondent variable, click on the button that pops up, and then tell SPSS that the value 3 will have the label of "Intersexed." Notice that the "Add" button lights up. Once we click this, it adds the new information to the list, and then we can click OK to leave this room.

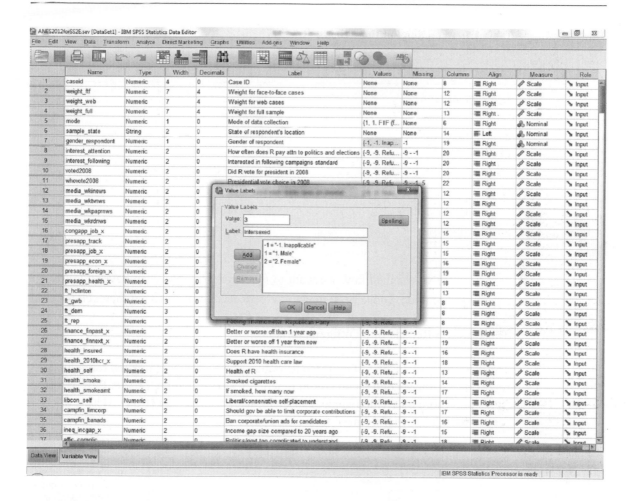

Recoding Variables

As I discussed about earlier in the chapter, often we will want to take an original variable and recode it into a new variable. Let's go through this process doing a very simple recode. What we're going to do is take the original variable for political views (called libcon_self) and recode it into a dichotomy called XYlibcon3cat, which will collapse the original seven categories to three categories (liberal, moderate, and conservative):

Table 1.1: Recoding Political Views

Original Variable: libcon_self	New Variable: XYlibcon3cat
Extremely liberal: 1	Liberal: 0
Liberal: 2	Liberal: 0
Slightly liberal: 3	Liberal: 0
Moderate: 4	Moderate: 1
Slightly conservative: 5	Conservative: 2
Conservative: 6	Conservative: 2
Extremely conservative: 7	Conservative: 2
All other responses	System Missing

Now that we've planned how we want to recode the variable, we have to tell SPSS what we want to do, so we need to go into the Recode room. To get there, click

Transform ➔ Recode Into Different Variables. . .

This takes us into the first of two recode rooms. This is where I think my room imagery really works: the second recode room is actually a *room within a room*. Plus, it makes SPSS into more of a video game, and that makes it more fun (I try). Here's the first recode room and what we need to do:

1.) Move the original libcon_self off of this "variable shelf" by clicking on it and then clicking on this arrow.

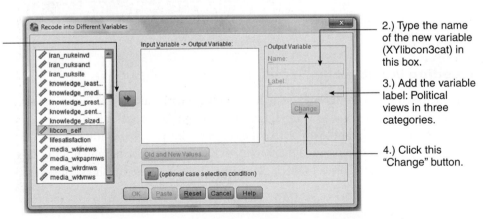

2.) Type the name of the new variable (XYlibcon3cat) in this box.

3.) Add the variable label: Political views in three categories.

4.) Click this "Change" button.

Once you do this, the first room should look like this. Notice that the "Old and New Values . . ." button has become active now. This means we're ready to go into the room within a room.

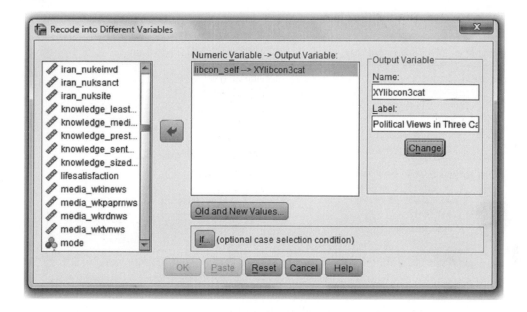

Click on this button (or think of it as a door if you want to). Here is what the next room looks like and what you want to do in it:

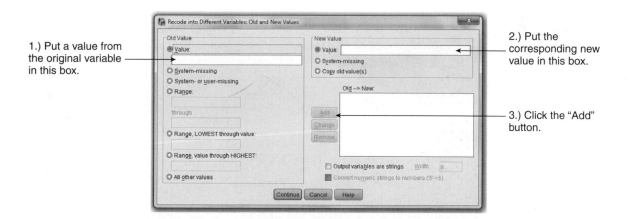

1.) Put a value from the original variable in this box.

2.) Put the corresponding new value in this box.

3.) Click the "Add" button.

Our goal in this room is to take every value of the original variable and make sure that it has a value on the new variable. If you forget a value, your entire recoding of the variable can get messed up. Following are two ways you could fill in this box for the variable we're recoding. In the first box, I put in each old value one by one:

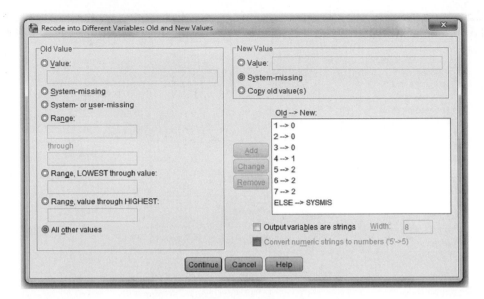

Note that, once I put in all of the valid values (1 through 7), I am telling SPSS to take all the other values and code them as "system-missing" (meaning that if a respondent did not have a valid response on the original variable, he or she will be coded as missing on the new variable). Note at the bottom of the list, SPSS translates this request into the phrase "ELSE → SYSMIS."

An alternative to this is to use the range boxes on the left-hand side, because 1 through 3 take on the same value of 0, and 5 through 7 take on the same value of 2:

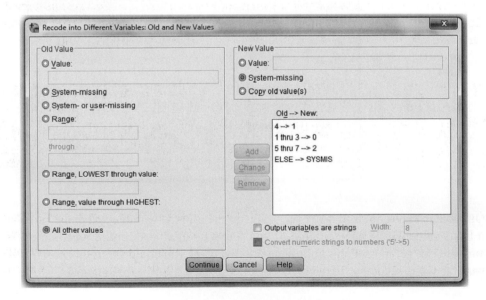

Once you have all of your recode commands entered, click Continue at the bottom of the box and SPSS will create your new variable and place it in the far right of the dataset:

XYlibcon3cat	
	.00
	.00
	-
	-
	.00
	-
	-
	-
	1.00
	2.00
	1.00
	2.00
	.00

Notice that at this point, SPSS does not put labels in, because we haven't told SPSS what the labels are for the new variable. SPSS is smart, but it's not that smart. It can't read our minds and figure out how we want our new variable's categories to be named. So we need to tell it, and here is how we do that. We go to the Variable View of the Data Window and scroll down to the bottom, where our new variable is located:

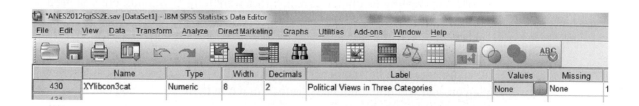

Our new variable already has what is called a Variable Label, because we gave it that when we created the variable. But it does not yet have what are called Value Labels: names for each category. You can see that in the box in the Values column it currently says "None." If you click in that box (as I have done), a button pops up (or, to continue the room analogy, a secret door). Click on this button, and it takes you into the Value Labels room, where we'll tell SPSS what label corresponds to each value, pressing the "Add" button after entering each set. In the next figure, I'm just about the hit Add for the last Value Label:

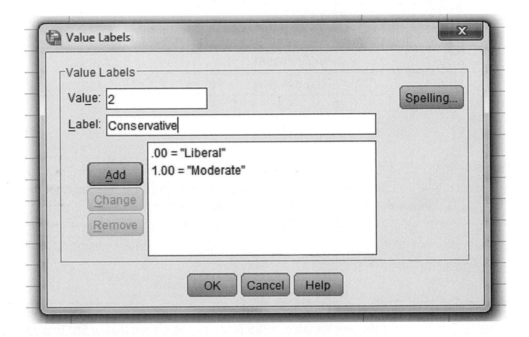

After we click OK to get out of this room, SPSS will add the labels to the values. And every time we use this variable, for example in a table or graph, SPSS will use these value labels in creating its output. It really does want to help you out, but you need to help *it* help *you*.

Bear with me for a second while I make an impassioned plea. Once you get going in SPSS, and you're recoding and creating new variables, the temptation will be to keep plowing on, and you might not take the time to put in these labels. You can remember how you recoded a variable, right? *Wrong*. And I speak from some years of experience with this. You'll create a variable, not give it labels, and after few weeks pass by and you'll return to your dataset, you'll look at this variable you created and have no idea what it means. Trust me on this: it will happen. And, when it happens, your future self will be *so* mad at your past self. I've been there myself, and it's not a pleasant feeling. Labels, labels, labels!!!

Finally, let's look at our old variable and new variable in two ways. First, let's look at the dataset itself:

	libcon_self
205	-2. Haven't thought ...
206	1. Extremely liberal
207	4. Moderate; middle ...
208	3. Slightly liberal
209	5. Slightly conservat...
210	3. Slightly liberal

XYlibcon3cat
.
Liberal
Moderate
Liberal
Conservative
Liberal

You can see that SPSS recoded each respondent's political views correctly. The first person did not give a valid response, so she gets a dot, meaning missing data. Another way to check if SPSS did what you think you asked it to do is to look at a frequency distribution for the old and new variable (we'll talk more about frequency distributions in the next chapter):

Liberal/conservative self-placement

		Frequency	Percent	Valid Percent	Cumulative Percent
Valid	1. Extremely liberal	195	3.3	3.7	3.7
	2. Liberal	638	10.8	12.0	15.7
	3. Slightly liberal	641	10.8	12.1	27.8
	4. Moderate; middle of the road	1830	30.9	34.5	62.3
	5. Slightly conservative	789	13.3	14.9	77.2
	6. Conservative	1001	16.9	18.9	96.1
	7. Extremely conservative	208	3.5	3.9	100.0
	Total	5302	89.6	100.0	
Missing	-9. Refused	32	0.5		
	-8. Don't know	26	0.4		
	-2. Haven't thought much about this	556	94		
	Total	614	10.4		
Total		5916	100.0		

Political Views in Three Categories

		Frequency	Percent	Valid Percent	Cumulative Percent
Valid	Liberal	1474	24.9	27.8	27.8
	Moderate	1830	30.9	34.5	62.3
	Conservative	1998	33.8	37.7	100.0
	Total	5302	89.6	100.0	
Missing	System	614	10.4		
Total		5916	100.0		

Do the extremely liberals, liberals, and slightly liberals become just "Liberal"? Yes: 195 + 638 + 641 = 1,474. Do the 1,830 moderates remain "Moderate"? Yes. Do the slightly conservatives, conservatives, and extremely conservatives become just "Conservative"? Yes: 789 + 1,001 + 208 = 1,998. Do all the missing values add up? Yes: 32 + 26 + 556 = 614. Our task is complete. This recoding process may seem onerous right now, but after you go through it a few times, you will become a pro. Just never forget to label your variables and check your work.

Computing a New Variable

Another common way of creating new variables is through computing: adding, subtracting, multiplying, or dividing variables. To do this, we go to

Transform ➔ Compute Variable . . .

Our goal here is to put an equation in the Numeric Expression box. Let's do a simple one here: we want a new variable called media_index that is an additive index of the number of times per week an ANES respondent connects with the news: through reading a physical newspaper, watching the national news on TV, listening to the news on the radio, and reading the news online. A respondent could do each of these zero times a week, thus getting a $0 + 0 + 0 + 0 = 0$. A respondent could do each of these every day, or seven times a week, thus getting a $7 + 7 + 7 + 7 = 28$. But many respondents will be somewhere in between. Here is what we do in the Compute Variable room:

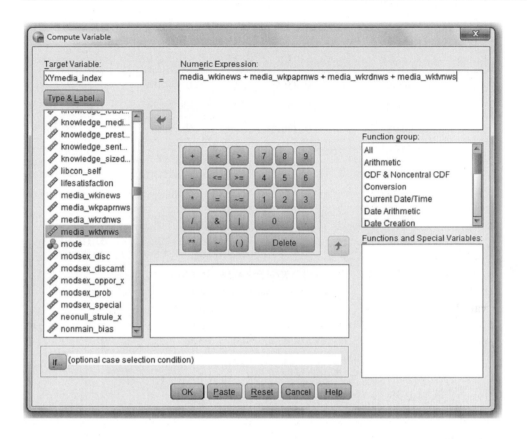

We simply take those three variables and move them into the Numeric Expression box one at a time, with plus signs in between. We then click the "OK" button, and SPSS computes our new variable and puts it at the right-hand side of the dataset. Notice that there's a button in the Compute Variable room called "Type and Label," which we could use to label our new variable, or we could add the label in the Variable View window. Also with regard to labels, it's important to give the endpoint values of the index labels. So, in this situation, we'd give 0 a label of "Never engaged with the news" and 28 a label of "Always engaged with the news."

Here are our old variables, and below them our new variable:

media_wkinews	media_wktvnws	media_wkpaprnws	media_wkrdnws
0. None	0. None	0. None	0. None
2. Two days	7. Seven days	6. Six days	6. Six days
5. Five days	0. None	0. None	0. None
4. Four days	5. Five days	2. Two days	1. One day
-1. Inapplicable	3. Three days	0. None	0. None
0. None	5. Five days	0. None	2. Two days
7. Seven days	7. Seven days	5. Five days	0. None
0. None	7. Seven days	7. Seven days	3. Three days

XYmedia_index
Never engaged with the news
21.00
5.00
12.00
.
7.00
19.00
17.00

Notice a couple of things: first, because I went in and gave the endpoints labels, the person who answered "None" to all four variables gets the "Never engaged with the news" label. Second, notice that last person has a missing value on the first variable but valid values for the other three. This person gets a missing value on the index because we need valid values on all four variables to compute the index score.

FROM OUTPUT TO PRESENTATION

After each chapter's SPSS demonstration(s), I will then go over how to take raw SPSS output and translate it into a format suitable for presentation. Remember, one of your future roles may be translating statistical results for an audience that may or not be versed in statistics. Clearly presenting statistical results is paramount. Slapping some raw SPSS output onto a screen is not the best way to go. These "From Output to Presentation" sections will help you better convey your results. Now, in this chapter we haven't really had much in the way of output. However, we *have* talked about data, and at the start of any presentation (whether it be in oral or written form), it's important to let your audience know about the data from which you will be presenting statistical results. Here are a couple of key questions that you should address:

1. What is the source of the data: who collected it, how, and for what purpose?
2. What are the characteristics of the sample (we'll talk more about sampling in a later chapter): the size of the sample, how was the sample drawn, what was the response rate? To what larger population can the statistical results be generalized?

For example, if you were presenting results from the ANES, here are some things you'd want to say:

1. The ANES is conducted by Stanford University and the University of Michigan.
2. The 2012 study involved nearly 6,000 respondents, carefully selected to complete either a face-to-face interview or a carefully guided Internet-based interview.
3. The ANES population is Americans aged 17 and older.

Basically, you want to assure your audience that the results you will be presenting are based on good data, and that they should listen to what you (and the data) have to say.

EXERCISES

Note: In each chapter's exercises, I have provided my answers to four of the exercises. You can find these answers in the back of the book in Appendix D. I have notated these exercises with (Answer Available in Appendix D).

Exercise 1

The following are variables from the ANES dataset. Describe at which level of measurement each of them should be considered to be, and explain why you think this is the case. You will want to refer to the ANES codebook in Appendix A.

a. dem_hrsnow

b. dem_marital

c. incgroup

d. media_wktvnews

e. smartphone

f. ft_bigbus

g. health_smokeamt

h. owngun

Exercise 2

The ANES dataset has two variables for age: dem_agegrp (the respondent's age in 13 categories) and XYdem_age4cat (age in four categories). This latter variable is a variable that I created using the original age variable. Recode the original age variable to create a new variable that will be identical to this four-category age variable.

Exercise 3 (Answer Available in Appendix D)

For the exercises in this book, I have created numerous indexes using the ANES dataset (see Appendix A). One of them I call the Wiretapping Index, and it is made up of two variables. Take the two original wiretapping variables, recode them into new variables, and then create an additive index exactly like the one I created (where the higher number means more in favor of wiretapping). You know the answer; now all you need to do is figure out how to get there. Here's a hint: keep an eye on the direction of the variables' categories.

Exercise 4

Using the ANES dataset, create a variable called presapp_index, which will combine these four variables: presapp_econ_x, presapp_foreign_x, presapp_health_x, and presapp_job_x. Examine the variables in the Data Window to make sure that SPSS did what you asked it to do.

Exercise 5 (Answer Available in Appendix D)

Following is a list of variables used in the ANES. For each variable, think of a relationship where that variable could be the independent variable; then think of a different relationship where that variable could be the dependent variable. For the other variable in each relationship, you don't need to restrict yourself to variables in the ANES.

a. Level of education

b. Days per week watch TV news

c. Times per month one attends religious services

d. Number of children a person has

e. Feeling thermometer toward big business

f. Political views

g. Having a smartphone

h. Hours one works in a week

i. Whether or not one has a dog

j. Support of environmental movement

Exercise 6

Here's a bad plan for combining two questions into an index. The bad index planner wants to measure concern about China, and he decides to use these two ANES variables:

china_econ: effect of China's economic expansion on U.S.

1. Good

2. Bad

3. No effect

china_mil: China military threat

1. Major threat

2. Minor threat

3. Not a threat

He decides simply to add these two questions together as they are. Clearly explain why this is a bad plan.

Exercise 7

Examine the PewShop dataset and figure out how I took the original variable called "purchase" and recoded it into a new variable called "XYpurchase." Hint: in the Data View, look at cases 15, 19, 23, and 400. In the Variable View, examine the new variable.

Exercise 8

Examine the original PewShop education variable. Take this eight-category variable and plan a recode for a five-category variable, where the educational categories are

Less than high school diploma

High school diploma

Some college

Bachelor's degree

Beyond bachelor's

In your plan, explicitly lay out what new value each old value will be recoded into. Don't carry it out; just plan it.

Exercise 9 (Answer Available in Appendix D)

Here are the results from two variables from the PewHealth dataset:

sample: How was survey conducted?

By landline   1,808 respondents

By cell phone   1,206 respondents

cellphone: Does respondent have a cell phone?

Yes	1,375 respondents
No	432 respondents
Don't know	1 respondent
System Missing	1,206 respondents

Let's say you want to create an overall variable for whether or not the respondent has a cell phone. Talk about how you would do this, considering how these two variables are connected to one another.

Exercise 10

Using the original PewHealth variables "quallife" and "health," plan an index where 0 is lack of good health and quality of life and the highest number is the opposite: excellent health and excellent quality of life. Describe how you would recode the original variables, and describe what your resulting index would look like.

Exercise 11

By examining the PewKids dataset, explain the recodes that went into creating the Child's Own Cyberbullying Enabling Index.

Exercise 12

One concern of survey researchers is social desirability bias: the respondent replies in a way that makes him or her look good. Look through the PewKids dataset and choose five variables that might be particularly subject to this bias and explain why.

Exercise 13

The WVS dataset uses the country as the unit of analysis instead of the individual respondent. Many of the variables in this dataset concern the percentage of a country that feels a particular way. At what level of measurement are such variables? Explain.

Exercise 14 (Answer Available in Appendix D)

The WVS dataset contains these three variables about political participation: SIGNPET (percentage of the country's population that has signed a petition), BOYCOTT (percentage of country's population that has participated in a boycott), and PAXDEM (percentage of country's population that has participated in a peaceful demonstration). Could you combine these variables into a variable that represents the percentage of country's population that has participated in all three behaviors? Explain why or why not.

## Chapter 2

THE ART OF VISUAL STORYTELLING: CREATING ACCURATE TABLES AND GRAPHS

This chapter covers . . .

. . . how to build a frequency distribution to summarize a variable
. . . how to build a crosstabulation to summarize the relationship between two variables
. . . troubleshooting a crosstabulation, and how to fix the trouble you find
. . . elaboration, in which we use crosstabulations across multiple groups
. . . how to choose appropriate graphs for one, two, and three variables
. . . the ways graphs can lie, and how to spot such lies
. . . a graph in a top social science journal that lies

INTRODUCTION

In the next chapter, we'll use statistics to describe a set of data. But, before we do that, I want to go over another major way to describe data: using visuals, such as tables and graphs. In these days of overwhelming amounts of information, tables and graphs are a very common way for people to tell their stories. Or, as we'll find, tell their *lies*! Oh, yes, if you haven't learned this life lesson yet, allow me to break the news: people lie. This chapter will give you a way to catch them in their lies. Creating a good table or graph is not as easy as it might seem at first. There's a real art to visual presentation. Although we won't go into as much detail as one might in a school of graphic design, we'll cover some of the tricks of the trade.

TABLES WITH ONE VARIABLE: FREQUENCY DISTRIBUTIONS

The goal of any table is to let the viewer of the table easily and quickly see the story that the data are trying to tell. A table that is set up incorrectly or unclearly in some way will be distracting, taking away from the power of the story. Often, we simply want to show how the data for a variable are distributed through the various categories of the variable. To do this, we create a **frequency distribution**. It says what it does; it does what it says: it shows how the frequencies are distributed. Hypothetically, we ask a group of 20 people how many children they have. Their answers are

1, 4, 0, 2, 2, 3, 1, 6, 3, 4, 3, 1, 0, 1, 2, 3, 5, 1, 2, 0.

First, we create a column for the categories and a column for the frequencies:

■ **Exhibit 2.1: Creating a Frequency Distribution**

No. of Kids	Frequency
0	3
1	5
2	4
3	4
4	2
5	1
6	1
	$n = 20$

Source: Hypothetical data.

This is a start, but I want to add two more columns to this table. First, I will add a Percentage column that shows what percentage each category contributes to the overall 100%. For example, 3 of the 20 people say they have zero children, so the percentage of people who have zero children is 3/20 = 15%. Next, I will create a Cumulative Percentage column. Each entry in this column tells us the percentage of cases accounted for in this row and above. For example, that 60% in the Cumulative Percentage column tells us that 60% of the people in the table have two kids or fewer. There are 12 people with two kids or fewer: 3 with zero kids, 5 with one kid, and 4 with two kids; thus, 12/20 = 0.60, or 60%. Finally, no table is complete without a title at the top and the source of data at the bottom.

▦ **Exhibit 2.2: A Completed Frequency Distribution**

Frequency Distribution of Number of Children

No. of Kids	Frequency	Percentage	Cumulative Percentage
0	3	15%	15%
1	5	25%	40%
2	4	20%	60%
3	4	20%	80%
4	2	10%	90%
5	1	5%	95%
6	1	5%	100%
	$n = 20$		

Source: Hypothetical data.

With all this information, the viewer can answer a lot of questions really quickly. How many respondents have exactly 3 children? What percentage of the respondents has 3 children? What percentage has 4 children or fewer?

GSS EXAMPLE: NUMBER OF CHILDREN

The GSS variable for the number of children is called CHILDS, and the question reads, "How many children have you ever had? Please count all that were born alive at any time (including any you had from a previous marriage)." When I asked SPSS to give me a frequency distribution for this variable (we'll go over how to do this at the end of the chapter), here is what it gave me:

■ **Exhibit 2.3: A Frequency Distribution from SPSS**

NUMBER OF CHILDREN

		Frequency	Percent	Valid Percent	Cumulative Percent
Valid	0	536	27.2	27.2	27.2
	1	274	13.9	13.9	41.1
	2	569	28.8	28.9	70.0
	3	301	15.2	15.3	85.2
	4	167	8.5	8.5	93.7
	5	56	2.8	2.8	96.5
	6	33	1.7	1.7	98.2
	7	12	0.6	0.6	98.8
	EIGHT OR MORE	23	1.2	1.2	100.0
	Total	1971	99.8	100.0	
Missing	DKNA	3	0.2		
Total		1974	100.0		

Source: GSS 2012 data.

There are several things to point out here. First, notice that the variable has a catchall category at 8 children, so we don't know if those 23 people have 8, 9, 10, 14, whatever children. But it's only 23 cases, so that's not much to worry about. Next, notice that there were 3 cases that are missing data for this variable: 3 people answered "don't know" or "no answer" when asked how many children they had. I sincerely hope it's the latter, because it'd be pretty sad if they didn't know the answer to this question. Notice that, related to this, there is a column called "Percent" and a column called "Valid Percent." The Percent column includes these missing cases in all of its calculations, whereas the Valid Percent column does not include these missing cases in its calculations. That is, the Valid Percent column includes only those cases that have valid values on the variable. Typically, when reporting results, people use the Valid Percent column.

GROUPED FREQUENCY DISTRIBUTIONS

Occasionally, the categories for a variable in a frequency distribution will not be a single number, such as three children, but a range of numbers, such as three to five children. Let's say we jump back in time to when people had many more children and asked 20 people way back then how many children they have. We might end up with data like these:

■ **Exhibit 2.4: A Grouped Frequency Distribution**

Frequency Distribution of Number of Children

No. of Kids	Frequency	Percentage	Cumulative Percentage
0–2	1	5%	5%
3–5	6	30%	35%
6–8	5	25%	60%
9–11	3	15%	75%
12–14	3	15%	90%
15–17	1	5%	95%
18–21	1	5%	100%
	$n = 20$		

Source: Hypothetical data.

The benefit of using a grouped frequency distribution is that it limits the number of categories. Had we given each number its own category, we would have had 22 categories and a very large table. The downside of using a grouped frequency distribution is that we don't know exactly how many children each respondent has. For example, the three people who are in the "12–14" category all could have 12 children; they all could have 14 children; one could've had 12, one 13, one 14. We just don't know. But sometimes this is how the data are presented, so we'll have ways to deal with this in future chapters when we're calculating statistics based on such tables.

TABLES WITH TWO VARIABLES: CROSSTABULATIONS

A major goal of statistics is showing relationships between two variables (or among three or more variables). For example, what is the relationship between gender and attitude toward abortion: Are men more likely to be opposed to abortion than women? What is the relationship between race and attitude toward spanking children: Are blacks more likely to approve of spanking than whites? What is the relationship between age and attitude toward marijuana legalization: are younger people more in favor of legalization than older people? Although we can address these questions with statistics, we may want to start by simply looking at how the data line up, and the most common way to arrange data in order to address these questions is through a **crosstabulation**, or crosstab for short. A crosstab does what it says and says what it does: it crosses two variables over one another so that we can see if there might be a relationship between them.

I will start very simply with a hypothetical example of 12 cases: 5 men and 7 women. I am interested in whether men are more likely to own a dog than women are. So I ask these 12 people whether they own a dog, and here is what they tell me:

■ **Exhibit 2.5: 12 Reponses to the Question, "Do You Own a Dog?"**

Man:	Yes, I own a dog.	*Woman:*	Yes, I own a dog.
Man:	Yes, I own a dog.	*Woman:*	Yes, I own a dog.
Man:	Yes, I own a dog.	*Woman:*	Yes, I own a dog.
Man:	No, I do not own a dog.	*Woman:*	No, I do not own a dog.
Man:	No, I do not own a dog.	*Woman:*	No, I do not own a dog.
		Woman:	No, I do not own a dog.
		Woman:	No, I do not own a dog.

As a first step toward creating a crosstab, I'm going to add lines to the above lists to divide the men from the women and the dog owners from the non-owners:

■ **Exhibit 2.6: Dividing the 12 Responses into Groups**

Man:	Yes, I own a dog.	*Woman:*	Yes, I own a dog.
Man:	Yes, I own a dog.	*Woman:*	Yes, I own a dog.
Man:	Yes, I own a dog	*Woman:*	Yes, I own a dog.
Man:	No, I do not own a dog.	*Woman:*	No, I do not own a dog.
Man:	No, I do not own a dog.	*Woman:*	No, I do not own a dog.
		Woman:	No, I do not own a dog.
		Woman:	No, I do not own a dog.

Next, I'll replace the words with numbers and add up how many of each group I have overall:

■ **Exhibit 2.7: Adding Up the Various Groups**

3 men own dogs	3 women own dogs	6 overall own dogs
2 men don't own dogs	4 women don't own dogs	6 overall don't own dogs
5 men overall	7 women overall	

Next, I'll remove some of the words and move some other words around:

■ **Exhibit 2.8: Putting Categories above the Columns and by the Rows**

	MEN	WOMEN	
OWN DOG	3	3	6
DON'T OWN DOG	2	4	6
	5	7	12

Next, in order to compare men and women, I need percentages. Right now, if I used the frequencies, I might mistakenly say, "Oh, the same number of men and women own dogs, so they are equally likely to own a dog." However, there are more women than men in this sample, so this would be an inappropriate comparison. Of five men, three, or 3/5, or 60%, own dogs; 40% of the men don't. Of the seven women, three, or 3/7, or 43%, own dogs; 57% of the women don't. Adding in these percentages—as well as percentages for the overall frequencies: 6/12 (50%) of the people are dog owners, 6/12 (50%) are not dog owners, 5/5 (100%) of the men are men, 7/7 (100%) of the women are women—to the crosstab, as well as a title and a data source, I now have the following:

■ **Exhibit 2.9: The Completed Crosstab**

Crosstabulation of Dog Ownership by Sex

	MEN	WOMEN	
OWN DOG	3 60%	3 43%	6 50%
DON'T OWN DOG	2 40%	4 57%	6 50%
	5 100%	7 100%	12 100%

Source: Hypothetical data.

There. Done. How do I know I'm done? Well, besides carrying out all the steps I think are necessary to create a crosstab, I can answer yes to this question: does the table tell the story? Yes, it does: a higher proportion of men than women have dogs. I have a couple of simple terms to introduce: the frequencies within the table are called the **cells** and the frequencies outside the boxes are called, appropriately enough, the

marginals. Also, there are a few rules I want to point out in relation to the above crosstab. The dependent variable in this situation is dog ownership: we are trying to see if dog ownership is dependent on sex. That makes sex the independent variable. This leads to the *placement rule* of crosstabs: the independent variable goes on top and the dependent variable goes on the side. This is a rule I follow, and I think it's a good one. On a rare occasion (such as when you have many categories in your independent variable), you may see a crosstab with the independent variable on the side. The next rule is the *percentage rule*: with your independent variable in the columns of the crosstab, you determine the percentage within the columns. This allows you to do what you want to do: compare percentages among columns or among categories of the independent variable. The final rule regarding independent and dependent variables is the *title rule*: the title is always dependent variable by independent variable: dog ownership by sex.

GSS EXAMPLE: SPANKING AND CHILD-REARING GOALS

The GSS regularly asks a question it simply calls SPANKING: "Do you strongly agree, agree, disagree, or strongly disagree that it is sometimes necessary to discipline a child with a good, hard spanking?" Also with regard to children, the respondents are asked to rank various child-rearing goals, such as learning to work hard, learning to help others, or learning to obey. I wanted to see if these child-rearing goals affect attitudes toward spanking. I created three crosstabs, using the spanking variable as my dependent variable, and these child-rearing variables as independent variables. Here are the resulting crosstabs as created by SPSS:

■ **Exhibit 2.10: Crosstabs of Spanking by Childrearing Goals**

FAVOR SPANKING TO DISCIPLINE CHILD* IMPORTANCE OF OBEYING Crosstabulation

		IMPORTANCE OF OBEYING			
		VERY IMPORTANT	SOMEWHAT IMPORTANT	NOT IMPORTANT	Total
FAVOR SPANKING TO DISCIPLINE CHILD	STRONGLY AGREE	30	45	61	136
		31.6%	22.2%	17.3%	20.9%
	AGREE	47	103	161	311
		49.5%	50.7%	45.7%	47.8%
	DISAGREE	14	40	99	153
		14.7%	19.7%	28.1%	23.5%
	STRONGLY DISAGREE	4	15	31	50
		4.2%	7.4%	8.8%	7.7%
Total		95	203	352	650
		100.0%	100.0%	100.0%	100.0%

FAVOR SPANKING TO DISCIPLINE CHILD* IMPORTANCE OF HELPING OTHERS Crosstabulation

		IMPORTANCE OF HELPING OTHERS			
		VERY IMPORTANT	SOMEWHAT IMPORTANT	NOT IMPORTANT	Total
FAVOR SPANKING TO DISCIPLINE CHILD	STRONGLY AGREE	22	90	24	136
		23.4%	20.3%	21.4%	20.9%
	AGREE	39	210	62	311
		41.5%	47.3%	55.4%	47.8%
	DISAGREE	26	106	21	153
		27.7%	23.9%	18.8%	23.5%
	STRONGLY DISAGREE	7	38	5	50
		7.4%	8.6.%	4.5%	7.7%
Total		94	444	112	650
		100 0%	100.0%	100.0%	100.0%

FAVOR SPANKING TO DISCIPLINE CHILD* IMPORTANCE OF HARD WORK Crosstabulation

		IMPORTANCE OF HARD WORK			
		VERY IMPORTANT	SOMEWHAT IMPORTANT	NOT IMPORTANT	Total
FAVOR SPANKING TO DISCIPLINE CHILD	STRONGLY AGREE	40	77	19	136
		22.7%	19.7%	22.9%	20.9%
	AGREE	86	188	37	311
		48.9%	48.1%	44.6%	47.8%
	DISAGREE	35	99	19	153
		19.9%	25.3%	22.9%	23.5%
	STRONGLY DISAGREE	15	27	8	50
		8.5%	6.9%	9.6%	7.7%
Total		176	391	83	650
		100.0%	100.0%	100.0%	100.0%

First, I want to point out one aspect about these crosstabs. Instead of using the word *by*, as in "attitude toward spanking by child-rearing goal," SPSS uses an asterisk (*) in its crosstab title. Now let's examine the results. Only one of these crosstabs shows a relationship between the independent and dependent variable. Look at the first crosstab, the one where obeying is the independent variable. Examining the percentages, we see that as obeying becomes *less* important, respondents are *less* likely to agree with spanking. Among those who think obeying is very important, 31.6% strongly agree with spanking, and an additional 49.5% agree with it, making for a total of 81.1%. Among those who think obeying is not important, only 17.3% strongly agree with spanking, with an additional 45.7% agreeing with it, making for a total of 63%. You can do the same thing with the two disagree categories: those who consider obeying to be unimportant are nearly twice as likely to either disagree or strongly disagree with spanking: $((28.1 + 8.8)/(14.7 + 4.2) = 1.95)$.

In looking at the other two crosstabs, we see that spanking is not related to these child-rearing goals. Look across each row. Notice how the percentages within each column are quite similar to one another. For example, in the crosstab where helping others is the independent variable, the percentages in the strongly agree row are 23.4%, 20.3%, and 21.4%. In the crosstab where hard work is the independent variable, the percentages in the strongly disagree row are 8.5%, 6.9%, and 9.6%. There are no clear trends as there were in the obey crosstab. We are on our way to understanding that there is some kind of relationship between the desire for teaching children to obey and the acceptability of spanking, but spanking seems unrelated to these other child-rearing goals.

GSS EXAMPLE: EDUCATION AND INTERNET ACCESS

Increasingly, the General Social Survey is interested in respondents' use of technology, specifically the Internet. For example, in the 2012 survey, they asked, "Do you have access to the Internet in your home?" What if we wanted to investigate the effect of education on this type of Internet access? Here is a crosstab that tries to get at this, but it does so in a very bad way. A quick note: the GSS tends to use lots of abbreviations: "R'S" is short for "Respondent's."

■ **Exhibit 2.11: A Very Bad Crosstab**

HIGHEST YEAR OF SCHOOL COMPLETED* INTERNET ACCESS IN R'S HOME
Crosstabulation

	Count	INTERNET ACCESS IN R'S HOME		Total
		Yes	No	
HIGHEST YEAR OF SCHOOL COMPLETED	0	1	0	1
	1	0	2	2
	3	2	2	4
	4	3	5	8
	5	1	2	3
	6	3	13	16
	7	0	5	5
	8	10	20	30
	9	8	19	27
	10	13	18	31
	11	22	18	40
	12	195	75	270
	13	53	23	76
	14	121	16	137
	15	40	5	45
	16	161	9	170
	17	33	1	34
	18	40	1	41
	19	19	3	22
	20	31	0	31
Total		756	237	993

Source: GSS 2012 data.

This crosstab has several things wrong with it:

1. The variables are in the wrong places: the dependent variable's categories are across the columns, and the independent variable's categories are across the rows. It should be the other way around.
2. There are no percentages.
3. The "education in years" variable has far too many categories for a crosstab. It is not a good idea to have a crosstab with cells that have such small frequencies.

Here is a much better crosstab. Rather than use education by year, this new crosstab uses a GSS variable called DEGREE, which divides the respondents by their highest degree attainment. "LT" is another abbreviation, meaning "Less Than," meaning that the person did not complete high school.

■ **Exhibit 2.12: An Improved Crosstab**

INTERNET ACCESS IN R'S HOME * RS HIGHEST DEGREE Crosstabulation

		RS HIGHEST DEGREE					
		LT HIGH SCHOOL	HIGH SCHOOL	JUNIOR COLLEGE	BACHELOR	GRADUATE	Total
INTERNET ACCESS IN R'S HOME	YES	56	359	71	174	96	756
		36.1%	75.3%	92.2%	94.1%	97.0.%	76.1%
	NO	99	118	6	11	3	237
		63.9%	24.7%	7.8%	5.9%	3.0%	23.9 %
Total		155	477	77	185	99	993
		100.0%	100.0%	100.0%	100.0%	100.0%	100.0%

Source: GSS 2012 data.

Now we're talking. With the variables in the correct places, and with percentages, we can see the relationship between the two variables very clearly: as educational level rises, the likelihood of having the Internet at home rises very quickly (from 36% to 75% to 92% to 94% to 97%).

TABLES WITH THREE VARIABLES: ELABORATION IN CROSSTABS

Occasionally the relationship we are examining may not be consistent across time, place, or group. That is, the story we're trying to tell with our crosstab is more complicated than we originally thought. Extending the earlier hypothetical example, what if everyone I surveyed earlier had been from urban areas, and then I surveyed 12 more people from rural areas about whether they own a dog? Here is what I might find (again, completely hypothetical data):

The story is now this: among urban residents, men are more likely than women to own dogs. Among rural residents, likelihood of dog ownership is equal between men and women: nearly everyone owns a dog in rural areas: 80% of men, 80% of women, 80% overall. I have engaged in **elaboration**, telling where the relationship exists (urban

▦ **Exhibit 2.13: An Elaborated Crosstab**

Crosstabulation of Dog Ownership by Sex, by Different Residences

| | URBAN RESIDENTS | | | RURAL RESIDENTS | | |
	MEN	WOMEN		MEN	WOMEN	
OWN DOG	3	3	6	4	8	12
	60%	43%	50%	80%	80%	80%
NO DOG	2	4	6	1	2	3
	40%	57%	50%	20%	20%	20%
	5	7	12	5	10	15
	100%	100%	100%	100%	100%	100%

Source: Hypothetical data.

area) and where it doesn't (rural area). Notice that adding another dichotomous variable doubles the number of cells from four to eight. I could add another layer of elaboration (say, owning a home or renting), and that would again double the number of cells from 8 to 16. At this point, it can become difficult to see what is going on, and the frequencies within the cells start to become too small, so typically one level of elaboration is all you'll see. If we want to involve more variables than this, we will use a more advanced statistical technique that we will get to later in the book. Let's look at a series of examples and you'll see why elaboration is an important part of data analysis.

GSS EXAMPLE: CHIVALRY, AGE, AND GENDER

The 2012 GSS asked about two-thirds of the respondents a set of questions regarding altruistic behavior, such as allowing someone to cut in line, or returning change at a store when incorrectly given too much. One such question was, "During the past 12 months, how often have you offered your seat on a bus or in a public place to a stranger?" The possible responses were more than once a week, once a week, once a month, at least two or three times in the past year, once in the past year, or not at all in the past year. I took these responses and collapsed them into a new dichotomous variable: Have you offered your seat, or have you not? I then used this variable as my dependent variable in a crosstab, using a four-category age variable as my independent variable. The resulting crosstab is below. The relationship we would expect definitely shows up in the crosstab. The older you get, the less likely you are to have offered your seat (hopefully because as you get older, people start offering you *their* seat). Notice, however, that this decline doesn't start until the third age group: the first two age groups are nearly identical in their seat-offering behavior. Now we are going to elaborate the crosstab to see if this

■ **Exhibit 2.14: Crosstab of Seat Offering by Age**

OFFERED SEAT TO STRANGER * AGE IN FOUR CATEGORIES Crosstabulation

		AGE IN FOUR CATEGORIES				
		18-33	34-47	48-61	62+	Total
OFFERED BEAT TO STRANGER	NO	139	134	179	231	683
		42.8%	41.7%	53.9%	74.8%	53.1%
	YES	186	187	153	78	604
		57.2%	58.3%	46.1%	25.2%	46.9%
Total		325	321	332	309	1287
		100.0%	100.0%	100.0%	100.0%	100.0%

Source: GSS 2012 data.

relationship between chivalry and age looks different for men and women. It makes sense that it might differ, because chivalry has historically been directed from men to women, and perhaps older women are the least likely to engage in chivalrous behaviors (because they are the most likely to receive it). Here are the elaborated crosstabs:

■ **Exhibit 2.15: Crosstab of Seat Offering by Age, Controlling for Sex**

OFFERED SEAT TO STRANGER * AGE IN FOUR CATEGORIES * RESPONDENT'S SEK Crosstabulation

			AGE IN FOUR CATEGORIES				
			18-33	34-47	48-61	62+	Total
MALE	OFFERED SEAT TO STRANGER	NO	68	52	83	83	286
			44.7%	37.1%	54.6%	63.8%	49.8%
		YES	84	88	69	47	288
			55.3%	62.9%	45.4%	36.2%	50.2%
	Total		152	140	152	130	574
			100.0%	100.0%	100.0%	100.0%	100.0%
FEMALE	OFFERED SEAT TO STRANGER	NO	71	82	96	148	397
			41.0%	45.3%	53.3%	82.7%	55.7%
		YES	102	99	84	31	316
			59.0%	54.7%	46.7%	17.3%	44.3%
	Total		173	181	180	179	713
			100.0%	100.0%	100.0%	100.0%	100.0%

Source: GSS 2012 data.

The men's relationship between age and offering their seat takes an interesting path. First, the chances rise: the men in the second age category (34–47) are *more* likely to have offered their seats than are the men in the first age category. Then, the chances start to fall. But even within the last age category, a third of the old men have offered their seat. Among women, there is a steady decline in seat offering as age rises: from 59% to 55% to 47% and then a whopping drop to 17%. Thus, although the overall relationship does exist among both men and women, this relationship looks rather different for these two groups.

GSS EXAMPLE: RACIAL DIFFERENCES OVER TIME

Another way we can use elaboration is to observe relationships as they exist at different points in time. That's one of the great things about the GSS: because it repeats many of the same questions from year to year, we can observe temporal trends. Take, for example, a question that the GSS repeats yearly:

On the average, blacks have worse jobs, income, and housing than white people. Do you think these differences are because most blacks just don't have the motivation or willpower to pull themselves up out of poverty: yes or no?

That is quite a question to pose to the respondents. Yet respond they do. Here are the responses for whites and blacks at two points in time: 1985 (the earliest available year for which we have data from both whites and blacks) and 2012:

■ **Exhibit 2.16: Crosstab of Lack of Will by Race for Two Years**

DIFFERENCES DUE TO LACK OF WILL * RACE OF RESPONDENT * GSS YEAR FOR THIS RESPONDENT Crosstabulation

GSS YEAR FOR THIS RESPONDENT			RACE OF RESPONDENT		Total
			WHITE	BLACK	
1985	DIFFERENCES DUE TO LACK OF WILL	YES	769	48	817
			60.3%	34.8%	57.8%
		NO	506	go	596
			39.7%	65.2%	42.2%
	Total		1275	138	1413
			100.0%	100.0%	100.0%
2012	DIFFERENCES DUE TO LACK OF WILL	YES	450	98	548
			48.5%	50.0%	48.8%
		NO	478	98	576
			51.5%	50.0%	51.2%
	Total		928	1 96	1124
			100.0%	100.0%	100.0%

Source: GSS 2012 data.

There have been interesting changes over time. In 1985, whites and blacks responded to this question very differently. Nearly two-thirds of whites said yes to this question, whereas only one-third of blacks said yes. Twenty-seven years later, we see a convergence of opinion: a smaller proportion of whites say yes to this question, whereas a larger proportion of blacks now say yes. In fact, if we had looked only at the 2012 data, we would say that whites and blacks don't differ in their responses to this question. However, adding some temporal context shows us that this agreement is really something new, that whites and blacks historically have differed significantly on this issue.

GSS EXAMPLE: GENDER, UNEMPLOYMENT, AND HAPPINESS

Americans just went through one of the most serious recessions in U.S. history. Millions of people lost their jobs, and many remain unable to find work. The loss of a job means not only the loss of income, but often the loss of a significant part of one's identity as well. Given both these reasons, are those who are unemployed more likely to be unhappy? The GSS asks about work status and asks a question called HAPPY: "Taken all together, how would you say things are these days— would you say that you are very happy, pretty happy, or not too happy?" Here's a crosstab using GSS 2012 data that allows us to see the relationship between these two variables:

■ **Exhibit 2.17: Crosstab of Happiness by Employment Status**

GENERAL HAPPINESS * LABOR FORCE STATUS Crosstabulation

		LABOR FORCE STATUS		
		WORKING FULL TIME	UNEMPL. LAID OFF	Total
GENERAL HAPPINESS	VERY HAPPY	293	14	307
		32.2%	13.5%	30.3%
	PRETTY HAPPY	537	60	597
		59.1%	57.7%	58.9%
	NOT TOO HAPPY	79	30	109
		8.7%	28.8%	10.8%
Total		909	104	1013
		100.0%	100.0%	100.0%

Source: GSS 2012 data.

Unemployed people are more than 3 times more likely to say that they are not too happy ($28.8/8.7 = 3.31$). But then I began to wonder: Is holding a job a bigger part of a man's identity than a woman's identity? Might men, who often construct their masculinity around their economic productivity, be more affected by job loss? I elaborated on the crosstab by using the sex variable, and here is what I found:

■ **Exhibit 2.18: Crosstab of Happiness by Employment Status Controlling for Sex**

GENERAL HAPPINESS * LABOR FORCE STATUS * RESPONDENTS SEX Crosstabulation

RESPONDENTS SEX			LABOR FORCE STATUS		Total
			WORKING FULL TIME	UNEMPL. LAID OFF	
MALE	GENERAL HAPPINESS	VERY HAPPY	153	7	160
			31.0%	13.5%	29.3%
		PRETTY HAPPY	297	31	328
			60.1%	59.6%	60.1%
		NOT TOO HAPPY	44	14	58
			8.9%	26.9%	10.6%
	Total		494	52	546
			100.0%	100.0%	100.0%
FEMALE	GENERAL HAPPINESS	VERY HAPPY	140	7	147
			33.7%	13.5%	31.5%
		PRETTY HAPPY	240	29	269
			57.8%	55.8%	57.6%
		NOT TOO HAPPY	35	16	51
			8.4%	30.8%	10.9%
	Total		415	52	467
			100.0%	100.0%	100.0%

Source: GSS 2012 data.

According to this elaborated crosstab, men and women are similarly affected by job loss. Although there are minor variations in the percentages, they are roughly the same: unemployed men are three times as likely as employed men to be unhappy, whereas unemployed women are around three and a half times as likely as employed women to be unhappy. Therefore, the data do not support my idea. Does this mean that this elaboration was a waste of time? Hardly: it's very good to know that men and women are equally affected by being unemployed.

GRAPHS WITH ONE VARIABLE

In addition to tables, graphs are a common way to convey information. In this section, the goal is to figure out what type of graph is best for various types of variables. We'll first deal with three basic types of graphs: bar, line, and pie. What we'll do is look at each of these three types of graphs for the same two variables: an ordinal-level variable with four categories and a ratio-level variable with 17 categories.

The ordinal-level variable is the GSS spanking variable that I used earlier in the chapter. Here are the three types of graphs:

■ **Exhibit 2.19: Three Graphs of Spanking Attitudes**

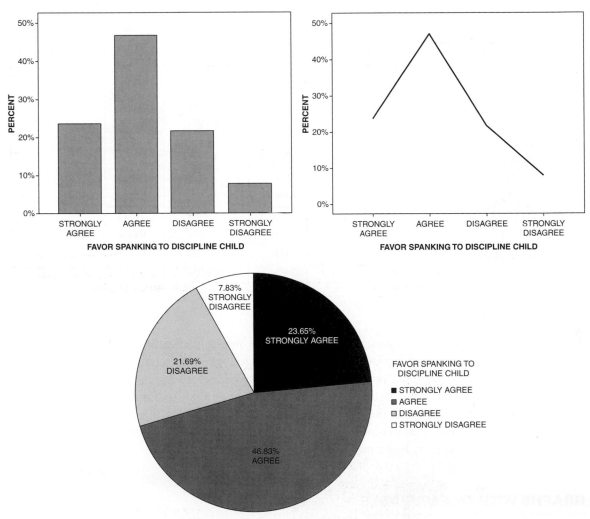

Source: GSS 2012 data.

Clearly, the line graph is out. With a variable with so few categories, a line graph is just not a good way to illustrate these data. So it comes down to the bar graph and the pie graph, and it's a close call. The bar graph captures the flow of the responses and the shape of how the answers are distributed. The pie graph allows the viewer's eye to quickly combine sets of responses. For example, we can see that just under a third of the respondents disagree (either strongly or not) with spanking.

The ratio-level variable is the GSS variable TVHOURS: "On the average day, about how many hours do you personally watch television?" Here are the graphs:

■ **Exhibit 2.20: Three Graphs of Television Watching**

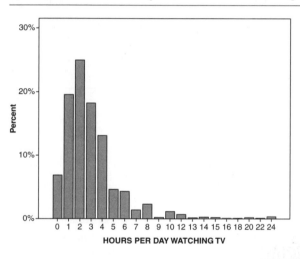

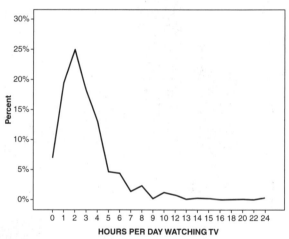

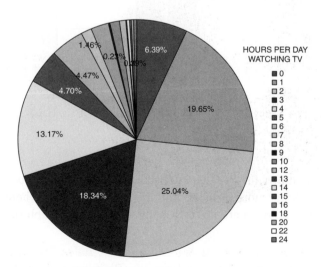

Source: GSS 2012 data.

Now it is the pie graph that is clearly out. Too many categories means too many small slices. The bar graph and the line graph are fairly similar in their ability to get across the shape of how the data are distributed.

GRAPHS WITH TWO VARIABLES

If you want to use a graph to illustrate the relationship between two variables, there are a number of choices. First, there are various types of bar graphs. Let's say we wanted to create a graph to represent the relationship between work status and happiness. We looked at this example in a crosstab earlier in the chapter. Here is a clustered bar graph that represents the information from the crosstab:

■ **Exhibit 2.21: A Clustered Bar Graph**

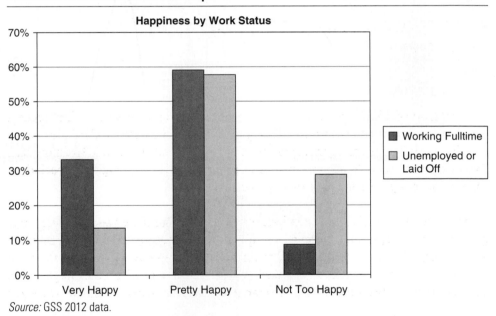

Source: GSS 2012 data.

This graph allows the eye to quickly take in the differences between the working and the nonworking: more of those working are very happy, whereas a larger proportion of those unemployed are not too happy. Another bar graph option is the stacked bar graph:

■ **Exhibit 2.22: A Stacked Bar Graph**

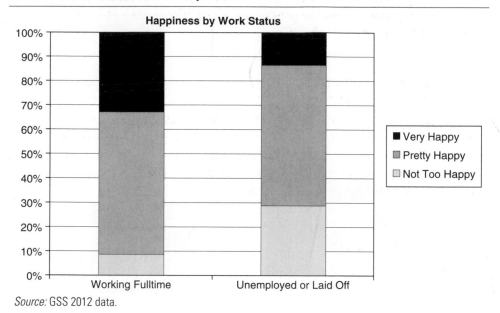

Source: GSS 2012 data.

This bar graph perfectly mimics the crosstab, giving each category of the independent variable (work status) its own bar. This graph works well because the independent variable has only three categories. However, if the independent variable had more than five categories, it would become more difficult to see what is going on, especially if some of the categories had very small percentages.

What if one of our variables is a ratio-level variable? What if we wanted a graph that gave us some insight into the relationship between educational level and the ratio-level variable TV hours per day? One thing we could do graphically is have the computer create a graph that shows, for each level of education, what percentage within each category say they watch TV more than three hours per week. This is what we get:

■ **Exhibit 2.23: A Graph of TV Watching by Education**

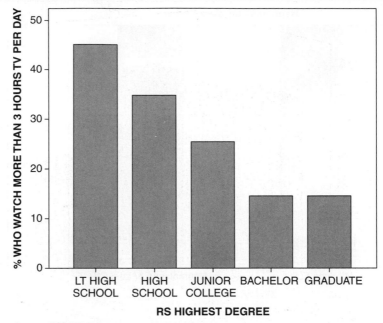

Source: GSS 2012 data.

As we add statistical procedures to our repertoire, I'll mention other types of graphs worth trying.

GRAPHS WITH THREE VARIABLES

If we wanted to use a graph to show the relationships among gender, age, and chivalry (as we did earlier with elaborated crosstabs), we can do this with a graph, but we need to add a third dimension since we have three variables. Both a bar graph and a pie graph allow us to do this, though in different ways. First, let's look at the 3-D bar graph:

■ **Exhibit 2.24: A 3-D Bar Graph**

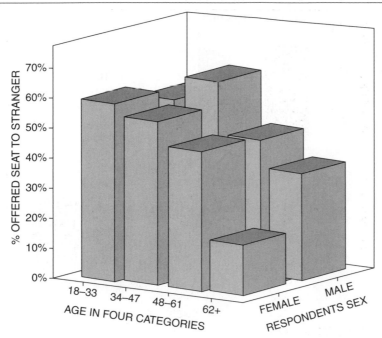

Source: GSS 2012 data.

The independent variable and the control variable make up the "floor" of the graph, and the dependent variable makes up the "wall." This graph immediately allows the viewer to see what we want them to see: that the shape of the relationship for men and women differs: the women's bars start high and go consistently down, whereas the men's goes up and then down. Now, let's look at the pie graph, technically referred to as a plotted pie graph:

▨ **Exhibit 2.25: A Plotted Pie Graph**

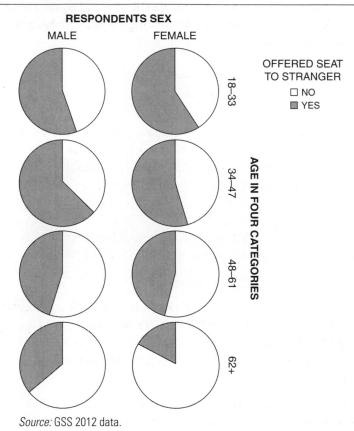

Source: GSS 2012 data.

The pie graph achieves two dimensions in space and one dimension in color. The pie graph may take a little more time for the viewer's eye to figure out, but once it does, it become quite easy to make comparisons by age or by sex.

TUFTE'S LIE FACTOR

Look at the bookshelves of anyone interested in graphic design and you are likely to find Edward Tufte's gorgeous volumes, such as *The Visual Display of Quantitative Information* and *Envisioning Information*. He is very influential in the world of graphic design, particularly those who design tables and graphs. In an early book, Tufte gives us a way to tell whether a graphic is lying to us (Tufte, 2001). Appropriately enough, he calls it the **Lie Factor**. The idea behind the Lie Factor is very simple:

a graphic should accurately reflect what is going on in the data. For example, if the data show a 30% increase over time, then the graphic should also show a 30% increase over time. We calculate the Lie Factor by calculating the ratio of change shown by the graphic divided by change shown by the data:

$$Lie\ Factor = \frac{Change\ Shown\ by\ Graphic}{Change\ Shown\ by\ Data}$$

If the data show a 30% increase, and the graphic shows a 30% increase, then we would have 30%/30% = 1. Therefore, the ideal Lie Factor is 1. If the data show a 30% increase, but the graphic shows a 60% increase, then the Lie Factor would be 60%/30% = 2, meaning that the graphic overrepresents the change in the data by a factor of 2. If the data show a 30% increase, but the graphic shows a 15% increase, then the Lie Factor would be 15%/30% = 0.5, meaning that the graphic under-represents the change in the data. If the Lie Factor is 1.03 or 0.95, that's not a huge deal. However, many graphs have Lie Factors far from 1, and that's a problem.

Before we look at an example, let's talk about how to calculate percentage change. We'll use the example of rising student debt. Let's start hypothetically; say that students used to graduate $10,000 in debt, and now graduate with $20,000. Intuitively, you know that this is an increase of 100%. But how, mathematically, do we do this? We use this tiny formula:

$$Percentage\ Change = \frac{New\ Value - Old\ Value}{Old\ Value}$$

So, in this situation, we would have (20 – 10)/10 = 10/10, or 1, or 100%. Here are some other examples:

■ **Exhibit 2.26: Illustrating Percentage Change**

Old Value	New Value	Percentage Change
40	60	(60 – 40)/40 = + 50%
20	60	(60 – 20)/20 = + 200%
70	35	(35 – 70)170 = – 50%
100	20	(20 – 100)1100 = – 80%
117	372	(372 –117)/117 = + 218%
74	39	(39 – 74)174 = – 47%

To calculate the change in the graphic, we do the same thing, except with a measure of length or space. Now let's do a full example, using this student debt example with real data. According to the College Board, in 2000, among those who borrowed money to earn a bachelor's degree from a public four-year college, the average debt was $20,100, and by 2011, this had risen to $23,800 (The College Board 2013). This is a rise of 18.4%:

(23,800 – 20,100)/20,100 = 0.184, or 18.4%.

Let's say I wanted to alarm people about the rising level of debt, so I wanted to make this rise seem really large. I created the following graph in Microsoft Excel. Actually, when I gave Excel the above dollar amounts and asked for a graph, this is exactly the graph it gave me:

■ **Exhibit 2.27: A Graph that Lies**

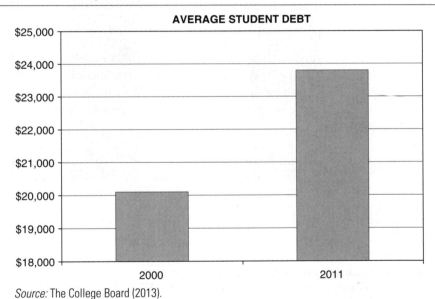

Source: The College Board (2013).

We need to measure the height of the bars. I just held my ruler up to my screen.
Height of bar for the year 2000: 2.5 centimeters
Height of bar for the year 2011: 7.2 centimeters
Now, we can calculate the change in the graphic: (7.2 – 2.5)/2.5 = 1.88, or a 188% increase.

And, finally, we calculate the Lie Factor:

$$Lie\ Factor = \frac{188\%\ increase\ shown\ in\ graphic}{18.4\%\ increase\ shown\ in\ data}$$

This gives us a Lie Factor of 10.21. This graphic drastically overrepresents the change shown in the data. The source of the problem is Excel's default choices for the y-axis. It looked at the low amount of $20,100 and the high amount of $23,800 and decided to have the y-axis go from $18,000 to $25,000. Therefore, to make the graph better, we'll have the y-axis start at 0. Here is the corrected graph:

■ **Exhibit 2.28: A Graph that Doesn't Lie**

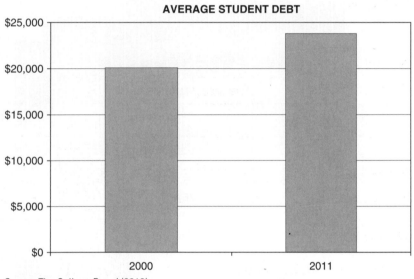

AVERAGE STUDENT DEBT

Source: The College Board (2013).

New height of the bar for the year 2000: 7.0 centimeters
New height of the bar for the year 2011: 8.3 centimeters
Now we recalculate the change in the graphic: $(8.3 - 7.0)/7.0 = 0.186$, or 18.6%.
The Lie Factor is now 18.6 / 18.4 = 1.01.

Now the graph accurately reflects the change in the data.

GSS EXAMPLE: SUPPORT FOR MARIJUANA LEGALIZATION

Attitudes toward marijuana legalization have changed dramatically in the past few decades. Look at these two graphs I made using GSS data. The GSS asks respondents a dichotomous question: Should marijuana be legalized or not? In the first graph, the bars represent the percentage of respondents who believe marijuana should remain illegal. In the second graph, the bars represent the percentage of respondents who believe marijuana should be legalized.

■ **Exhibit 2.29: Two Graphs, Same Data**

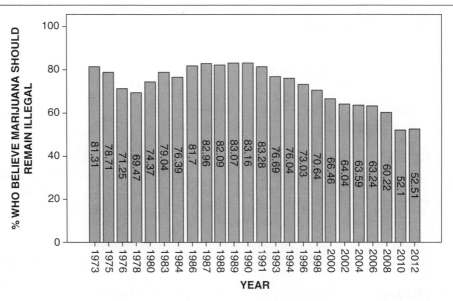

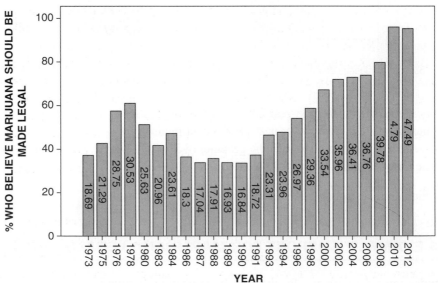

Source: GSS 1973–2012 data.

Clearly, one of these graphs is lying, right? The first graph shows a gradual decline, whereas the second graph shows a rapid growth. Let's calculate the Lie Factor for each graph:

First graph:
Change in graphic: $(6.2 - 9.5)/9.5 - 35\%$ decrease
Change in data: $(52.51 - 81.31)/81.31 = 35\%$ decrease
Lie Factor: $35\%/35\% = 1.00$

Second graph:
Change in graphic: $(11.0 - 4.3)/4.3 = 156\%$ increase
Change in data: $(47.49 - 18.69)/18.69 = 154\%$ increase
Lie Factor: $156\%/154\% = 1.01$

Both graphs offer accurate representations of their respective data. So neither graph is lying, but the eye naturally sees the change in the second graph as being more drastic. A 156% increase, numerically or graphically, just seems bigger than a 35% decrease, even if both of those are just two sides of the same coin.

LITERATURE EXAMPLE: CHANGING RACIAL CLASSIFICATION

We often think of racial classification as constant. For most people, it is. If they self-identify as white one year, they're going to self-identify as white the following year. If they self-identify as black one year, they're going to self-identify as black the following year. Although this is true for most, it's not true for everyone. For some people, race is more fluid. This is particularly true with regard to racial classification: the assigning of a racial category by someone else. In order to study this phenomenon, Aliya Saperstein and Andrew Penner (2012) made brilliant use of data from the National Longitudinal Survey of Youth (NLSY). This survey interviewed 12,686 young men and women in 1979 and every year thereafter until 1994, when they began to interview them every other year. As part of the interview, each year the professionally trained interviewers classified the respondents' race to the best of their ability. Occasionally, the respondent himself was asked to classify his own race.

In their article "Racial Fluidity and Inequality in the United States," which appeared in the *American Journal of Sociology* in 2012, Saperstein and Penner show that for some of the NLSY respondents, racial classification was not constant over the years that the respondents had been interviewed. Here are a few examples, using W for white, B for black, and O for other:

This person was classified consistently as white:	WWWWWWWWWWWWWWW
This person was classified inconsistently:	WWOWOWBOBWWOWBBO
This person's classification changed:	BBBBBWWBWWWWWWWW

Among the 12,686 respondents, 2,588 had "classification discrepancies": 33% of these 2,588 had one discrepancy, 14% had two, 11% had three, 11% had four, and 30% had five or more. But what makes Saperstein and Penner's work very interesting is that these changes are not random: they show that they are linked to changes in social status. Here are two examples that show how a period of extended unemployment affected how two respondents were classified:

Respondent 9266: WOWW – period of unemployment – BOBOWOBBBOBO
Respondent 8857: WOOWWWW – period of unemployment – WOOOOOOWOO

By using a somewhat advanced statistical technique, Saperstein and Penner (2012) figured out the effects of each negative life change. They found that negative life changes make not only the interviewer less likely to classify the respondent as white, but also the *respondent him- or herself* becomes less likely to self-identify as white.

I bring up this piece of research not only because I find it fascinating. I also want to show you one of their graphs. The leftmost bar shows a "baseline" respondent: a 29-year-old married father with a high school education who was classified as white in the previous year. This person has around a 96% chance of being classified as white again. But then, they give this hypothetical person a series of negative life events: he becomes incarcerated, then he loses his job, then he gets divorced, and then he falls into poverty. Here is what happens to his racial classification as these things happen:

■ **Exhibit 2.30: The Effects of Negative Life Events on Racial Classifications**

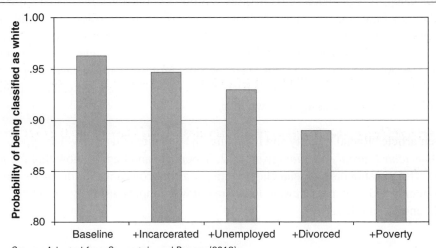

Source: Adapted from Saperstein and Penner (2012).

As these negative things happen, the probability of this person being classified as white goes down. From the looks of the graphic, the probability goes down precipitously. But look at the y-axis: it goes from 0.80 to 1.00. As much as I love this article, I have to call the authors out on this graph: it lies! Let's calculate the Lie Factor for the graph, using the first and last bars:

Change in graphic: (2 cm – 7 cm)/7 cm = –0.71, or a 71% decrease
Change in data: (0.847 – 0.963)/0.963 = –0.12, or a 12% decrease
Lie Factor: 71%/12% = 5.92

The graph overrepresents the change in the data by a factor of nearly six! Granted, any reasonable reader would carefully examine the numbers on the axis and figure out what is going on. But anyone taking a quick look through the article might come away from it thinking that the effect is bigger than it really is. This is not to say that there is no effect. There is, and it is fascinating. But the graph should accurately reflect the effect.

CONCLUSION

Even before we get to actual statistics, we can tell a lot of our stories with simple tables and graphs. However, as we've seen, simplicity can be deceiving, as the simplest of graphs can be deceptive. This chapter has given you tools to spot such deception and to avoid it as you create tables and graphs of your own.

SPSS DEMONSTRATIONS

Please visit the book's website (www.routledge.com/cw/linneman) to view videos of these demonstrations.

Tables

Creating a frequency distribution is one of the simplest things you can do in SPSS. We click

Analyze ➔ Descriptive Statistics ➔ Frequencies . . . This takes us to the Frequencies room:

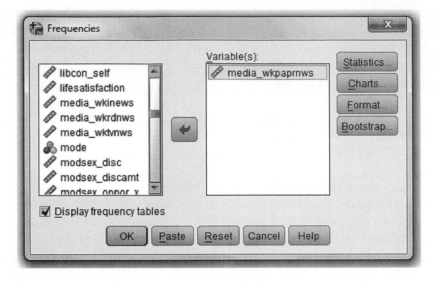

All you do is move the variable (or variables) off the shelf and into the box on the right and press "OK". Yes, some things are really easy. In this example, I'm using the ANES variable for number of times the respondent reads the newspaper. SPSS gives us two boxes of output, only the second of which is necessary:

Days in typical week read news in print newsppr

		Frequency	Percent	Valid Percent	Cumulative Percent
Valid	0. None	2434	41.1	41.2	41.2
	1. One day	911	15.4	15.4	56.6
	2. Two days	549	9.3	9.3	65.9
	3. Three days	402	6.8	6.8	72.7
	4. Four days	211	3.6	3.6	76.3
	5. Five days	303	5.1	5.1	81.4
	6. Six days	188	3.2	3.2	84.6
	7. Seven days	910	15.4	15.4	100.0
	Total	5908	99.9	100.0	
Missing	-9. Refused	3	0.1		
	-8. Don't know	1	0.0		
	-4. Error	4	0.1		
	Total	8	0.1		
Total		5916	100.0		

Notice that the Percent column and the Valid Percent column are almost exactly the same, with one exception: for the category "None," the Percent is 41.1 and for the Valid Percent it is 41.2. The Percent is calculated using all the cases, valid or missing: 2,438/5,916 = 41.1. The Valid Percent is calculated using only the valid cases: 2,438/5,908 = 41.2. You should always use information from the Valid Percent column.

Creating a crosstab in SPSS involves a few more steps, but it's still fairly easy. We'll use ANES data to examine the relationship between gender and capital punishment. That is, we are going to see if gender affects attitudes toward capital punishment. Gender is our independent variable, and capital punishment is our dependent variable. To get to the crosstabs room, we click:

Analyze → Descriptive Statistics → Crosstabs . . .

In this room, we first need to put the variables in the correct boxes. Remember the rule: put the independent variable in the Columns box and the dependent variable in the Rows box. So, for this example, we do this:

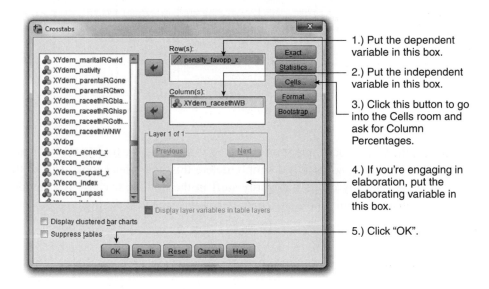

This gives us these two boxes of output:

Case Processing Summary

	Cases					
	Valid		Missing		Total	
	N	Percent	N	Percent	N	Percent
Favor death penalty * recoded raceeth (W=0, 8=1)	4394	74.3%	1522	25.7%	5916	100.0%

Favor death penalty * recoded raceeth (W=0, B=1) Crosstabulation

			recoded raceeth (W=0, B=1)		
			WHITE	BLACK	Total
Favor death penalty	1. Approve strongly	Count	1960	376	2336
		% within recoded raceeth (W=0, B=1)	57.1%	39.1%	53.2%
	2. Approve not strongly	Count	678	147	825
		% within recoded raceeth (W=0, B=1)	19.7%	15.3%	18.8%
	4. Disapprove not strongly	Count	368	164	532
		% within recoded raceeth (W=0, B=1)	10.7%	17.1%	12.1%
	5. Disapprove strongly	Count	427	274	701
		% within recoded raceeth (W=0, B=1)	12.4%	28.5%	16.0%
Total		Count	3433	961	4394
		% within recoded raceeth (W=0, B=1)	100.0%	100.0%	100.0%

The first box, the Case Processing Summary, is useful only to see how many valid and missing cases you have, so usually I simply delete this box after I look at it. In the crosstab itself, I typically delete the wordy stuff in the middle, because it's obvious what the percentages mean. And also I sometimes revise the title. So my crosstab ends up looking like this:

Death Penalty Attitude by Race

		recoded raceeth (W=0 B=1)		
		White	Black	Total
Favor death penalty	1. Approve strongly	1960	376	2336
		57.1%	39.1%	53.2%
	2. Approve not strongly	678	147	825
		19.7%	15.3%	18.8%
	4. Disapprove not strongly	368	164	532
		10.7%	17.1%	12.1%
	5. Disapprove strongly	427	274	701
		12.4%	28.5%	16.0%
Total		3433	961	4394
		100.0%	100.0%	100.0%

Graphs

First we'll create a simple bar graph, using the ANES variable for Internet news reading. We click:

Graphs ➜ Legacy Dialogs ➜ Bar . . .

This takes us to a very small room. Consider it the foyer or entryway to the graph room. Here we need to choose which type of bar graph we want, and we choose Simple, and then Data in Chart Are Summaries for groups of cases:

1. Choose Simple.

2. Click the first button.

3. Click the "Define" button.

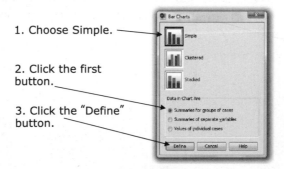

This takes us into the graph room, where we tell SPSS what we want our graph to look like:

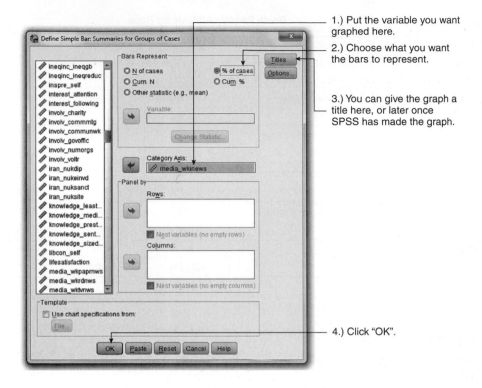

1.) Put the variable you want graphed here.

2.) Choose what you want the bars to represent.

3.) You can give the graph a title here, or later once SPSS has made the graph.

4.) Click "OK".

This gives us this graph:

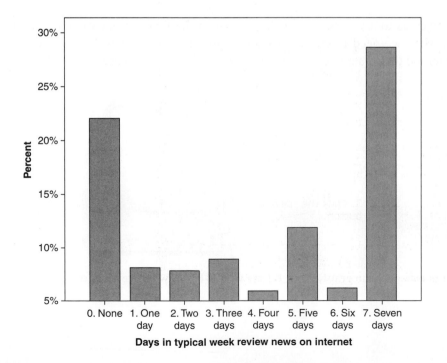

Not the prettiest thing in the world, but that's easy enough to change. To make changes to a graph, double-click on it. This opens up the graph in a Chart Editor. Notice that, when you do this, SPSS puts a "net" over the graph in the regular output window, meaning that you can't work on it here, because it's opened in another window. Once you are in the Chart Editor, you can change the color of the bars by clicking on them, or add a title or subtitle, pretty much anything you'd want to do.

Now let's create a clustered bar graph of capital punishment by race (white/black). We again click

Graphs ➔ Legacy Dialogs ➔ Bar . . .

But this time in this foyer room, instead of Simple, we will choose Clustered. Now, when we go into the big graphing room, it looks a little different:

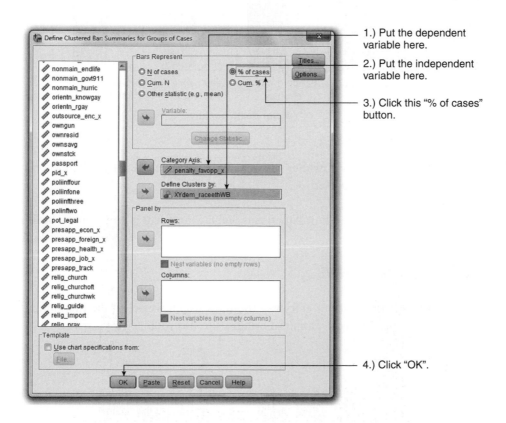

This gives us a graph that nicely illustrates the differences between blacks and whites:

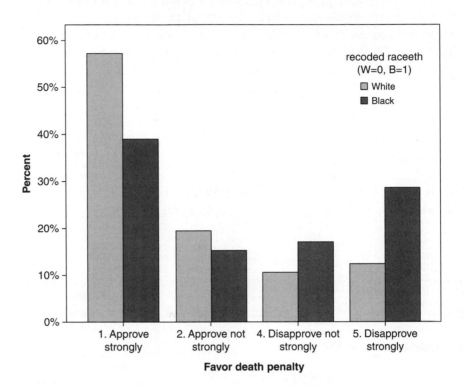

We can see that almost 60% of whites strongly favor the death penalty, whereas only 40% of blacks strongly support it.

Last, let's create a pie graph of how Americans feel the president is doing on the health care issue. We click

Graphs ➔ Legacy Dialogs ➔ Pie . . .

This takes us to another foyer or entryway room, in which we select the first option: Summaries for groups of cases. Doing so brings us to this room:

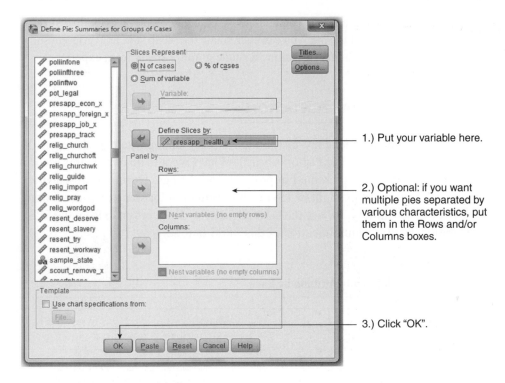

1.) Put your variable here.

2.) Optional: if you want multiple pies separated by various characteristics, put them in the Rows and/or Columns boxes.

3.) Click "OK".

Here is the resulting graph:

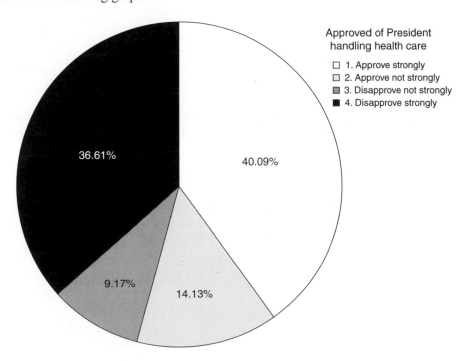

If we double-click on the graph, we can add labels, change colors, or explode a slice of the pie away from the rest of the pie. You can even rotate the pie to start at a different slice. Believe me, you can spend hours formatting a single graph. I speak from experience.

FROM OUTPUT TO PRESENTATION

Creating a professional frequency distribution is easy enough, and with regard to graphs, just make sure their Lie Factor is near 1. What I want to go over in this section is how crosstabs are often presented in professional settings. During a presentation, putting up a whole crosstab might be too much information for some of your viewers, so here is a way to simplify. I'll use the Death Penalty by Race crosstab from the SPSS demonstration. Here is a simplification of this SPSS output:

■ **Exhibit 2.31: Death Penalty Attitude by Race**

Favor death penalty for persons convicted of murder?	Whites	Blacks
	(n = 3,433)	(n = 961)
Approve strongly	57.1%	39.1%
Approve not strongly	19.7%	15.3%
Disapprove not strongly	10.7%	17.1%
Disapprove strongly	12.4%	28.5%

Source: ANES 2012 data.

This allows the viewer to quickly see the differences in percentages without having the frequencies in the way. If someone wanted to change these percentages into frequencies, having the sample size for each group allows her to do so (i.e., 57.1% of 3,433 is 1,960).

EXERCISES

Exercise 1

Here are the wiretapping index scores for the ANES unique group of white women smokers who claim to be in excellent health:

0, 1, 2, 3, 2, 1, 3, 0, 1, 4, 0, 0, 1, 0

Build a complete frequency distribution using these data.

Exercise 2 (Answer Available in Appendix D)

Here are data from the ANES unique group of sad men on two variables: whether a respondent owns a gun and whether he thinks there should be more gun control:

Sad Man 1	no gun, against gun control
Sad Man 2	yes gun, against gun control
Sad Man 3	no gun, for gun control
Sad Man 4	no gun, for gun control
Sad Man 5	no gun, against gun control
Sad Man 6	no gun, against gun control
Sad Man 7	no gun, for gun control
Sad Man 8	yes gun, against gun control
Sad Man 9	no gun, for gun control
Sad Man 10	yes gun, for gun control
Sad Man 11	yes gun, against gun control
Sad Man 12	yes gun, against gun control
Sad Man 13	yes gun, for gun control
Sad Man 14	no gun, against gun control
Sad Man 15	no gun, for gun control
Sad Man 16	yes gun, against gun control
Sad Man 17	no gun, for gun control
Sad Man 18	no gun, for gun control

Sad Man 19   yes gun, against gun control

Sad Man 20   no gun, for gun control

Use this information to create a complete crosstab.

Exercise 3

Create two crosstabs using the ANES dataset to address these two questions:

a.   Does age (in four categories) affect likelihood of having a cell phone?

b.   Does age (in four categories) affect likelihood of having a smartphone?

After you create the crosstabs, address the questions.

Exercise 4

Using ANES data, create a crosstab to address this question:

Does age (in four categories) affect attitude toward marijuana legalization?

After you create the crosstab, address the question.

Exercise 5

Hispanic ANES respondents were asked if they speak Spanish or English in the home. Does where their parents were born affect this? Run a crosstab to find out.

After you create the crosstab, address the question.

Exercise 6 (Answer Available in Appendix D)

Run a series of crosstabs to address these questions:

a.   Do blacks perceive a higher level of discrimination toward blacks than whites or Hispanics perceive toward blacks?

b.   Do Hispanics perceive a higher level of discrimination toward Hispanics than whites or blacks perceive toward Hispanics?

c.   Do blacks personally experience a higher level of discrimination than whites or Hispanics experience?

Exercise 7

Create a frequency distribution and graph for the ANES variable regarding removing a member of the Supreme Court. How could you use these results to argue that Americans *are* in favor of removing a member of the Supreme Court? How could you use these results to argue that Americans *are not* in favor of removing a member of the Supreme Court?

Exercise 8

Are people who have iPods (or a similar MP3 device) more likely to have a smartphone? Using the PewShop data, run a crosstab to find out. Describe your results.

Exercise 9

Using the PewShop dataset, examine the effect of being a parent on work status for both men and women. Use the recoded work status variable that is a dichotomy, and the recoded parent and sex variables. Once you have your crosstabs, explain your results.

Exercise 10

Using the PewShop dataset, create a bar graph that shows how iPod ownership varies by race. Which groups are most likely to have iPods? Which groups are least likely?

Exercise 11 (Answer Available in Appendix D)

Using the PewShop dataset, create a plotted pie graph that shows how smartphone ownership differs by race (white/black) and sex. Among which racial group is there a gender difference?

Exercise 12

Caring for a disabled or sick child can be taxing to say the least. Using the PewHealth dataset, create a crosstab that addresses this question: Does caring for a sick child affect one's family's quality of life, and is this relationship the same for men and women?

Exercise 13

Often you hear about contaminated food problems, such as salmonella or *E. coli*, and such problems often hit children the hardest. Using the PewHealth dataset, create a crosstab that addresses this question: does being a parent make one more likely to search the Internet for information about food safety?

Exercise 14

Going to your doctor well informed and willing to bring up such information with your doctor is a sign of an engaged patient. Using the PewHealth dataset, create a crosstab that addresses this question: Does age (in four categories) affect one's likelihood of raising Internet-located information with your doctor?

Exercise 15

Using the PewKids dataset, run a crosstab that will address this question: What percentage of kids whose parents say the child does *not* use a social networking website actually *do* use a social networking website?

Exercise 16 (Answer Available in Appendix D)

Using the PewKids dataset, run a crosstab that will address this question: Are kids who have been bullied online more likely to have been bullied in person? Then, address this question two more times, once for boys and once for girls.

Exercise 17

Using the WVS dataset, create a grouped frequency distribution of the variable "% OF COUNTRY THAT SAYS THEY USED INTERNET OR EMAIL AS AN INFORMATION SOURCE IN PAST WEEK." Use the following categories: 0–9, 10–19, 20–29, 30–39, 40–49, 50–59, 60–69, 70–79. Use only the countries for which you have valid data.

Exercise 18

I took the WVS variable called PCUSE and created a new dichotomous variable called PCUSE2CAT, where one category of the percentage of a country that uses a PC occasionally or frequently is between 0% and 50%, and the other category is between 51% and 100%. Create a crosstab using this new variable as your dependent variable and the "Country by Category" (COUNTRY5CAT) variable as the independent variable. Include the raw SPSS output as well as a table you've made from this output. Put the country categories in order: from the countries that use a PC the least to the most.

Exercise 19

Here is a graph using WVS data contrasting the importance of religion in the United States and Canada. Calculate the Lie Factor for the graph. Hint: Use the United States as the "old" and Canada as the "new." The actual percentages are 47% for the United States and 34% for Canada.

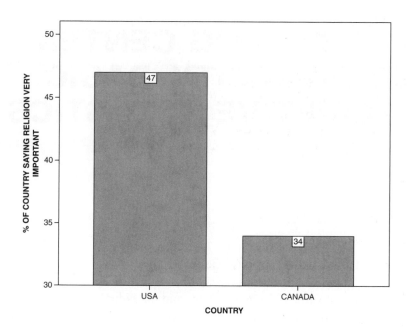

Chapter 3

SUMMARIZING CENTER AND DIVERSITY: BASIC DESCRIPTIVE STATISTICS

This chapter covers . . .

. . . ways to find the center for various types of variables

. . . measures of variation for various types of variables

. . . how to talk about variation, among groups and individuals

. . . an example of extreme variation in medical costs

INTRODUCTION

In addition to representing data in tabular and graphical forms, a key way to describe data is to use, fittingly enough, *descriptive statistics*. By examining just a few descriptive statistics for a variable's scores, we can get a very good idea about where the center of those scores lies, how far the scores are from this center, and what shape the distribution of the scores takes. In this chapter, we'll cover several descriptive statistics that are used for various types of variables: ratio, ordinal, and nominal. We'll start with the ratio level.

THREE WAYS OF THINKING ABOUT THE CENTER

Here is a hypothetical block in a hypothetical neighborhood. There are 11 houses on the block. The number in each box is the value of the house in dollars:

■ **Exhibit 3.1: A Hypothetical Block of 11 Houses**

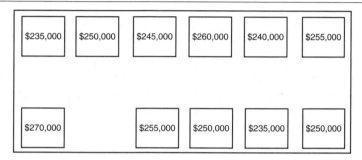

A real estate agent correctly claims that the average house price is $250,000. But then someone buys the house in the lower-left corner. This house was already the highest-valued house on the block. But the new owner is some combination of gaudy, rich, crazy, extravagant, and foolish. He pours money into his new house, adding wall-to-wall carpet made out of the finest cashmere, a hot tub that seats 16 people and their dogs, granite countertops galore, stainless steel—nay, gold—appliances, a 3,000-square-foot master bedroom, and a ballroom for all of his lavish parties. All of this increases the value of his house to a whopping $1,000,000, making him an **outlier** in this set of data. So now the block looks like this:

■ **Exhibit 3.2: The Hypothetical Block after One Heck of a Remodel**

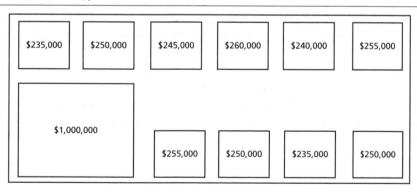

The real estate agent once again claims that the average house price on the block is $250,000. Although this at first may seem outrageously incorrect, we need to keep in mind that there are multiple ways to define where the center of the data falls. Real estate agents often use the **median** home price to describe neighborhoods. Just as a median in a road divides the road into two parts, the median divides an ordered list of data into two parts. Let's order the house prices on the block (as they were before the gaudy guy moved in). Notice that, to keep things simple, I'm switching from dollars to thousands of dollars. So, for example, the $235,000 house is now represented by 235:

235, 235, 240, 245, 250, 250, 250, 255, 255, 260, 270

We can count by hand to figure out which case has an equal number of cases on either side of it. It's that 250 right in the middle: it has five cases to the left of it and five cases to the right of it. So the median house price is 250. Now what about *after* the gaudy guy? Here's the revised ordered list of prices:

235, 235, 240, 245, 250, 250, 250, 255, 255, 260, 1,000

We've replaced the 270 with the 1,000, but notice that this does nothing to the fact that the middle case still has a value of 250. So the real-estate agent is completely correct saying that the median house price remains 250.

There's another way to claim that 250 is the center: 250 is also the *modal* house price. The **mode** is the score that appears most frequently. The highest frequency is three: three houses on the block have prices of 250; therefore, 250 is the mode.

But clearly the rampant renovation of that house must have had *some* effect on the average. There is a third version of the center that we've yet to mention, and that is the version most people think of when we're thinking about the average: the **mean**. To calculate the mean, we take the sum of all the scores and divide this sum by the number of scores. In the original situation (before gaudy guy), if someone wanted to buy the entire block of houses, how much would he or she have had to pay? That is, what was the total value of all of the houses together? We add up all 11 house values and get 2,750 (again, in thousands). To calculate the mean, we divide this 2,750 by the number of houses: 2,750/11 = 250. To calculate the revised mean (after gaudy guy), we calculate the new total value of the houses and divide it by the number of houses: 3,480/11 = 316.363 (or, in dollars, $316,363). The formula for what we're doing intuitively is

$$mean = \frac{sum\,of\,all\,the\,scores}{number\,of\,scores}$$

Or, using the symbols that are most often used for this formula:

$$\bar{x} = \frac{\sum x}{n}$$

The Σ is called "sigma," and it is the formula notation for "sum" or "add up all the ..."
In this case, the sigma notation is telling us to add up all the $\bar{x}$s, or scores. The $\bar{x}$
symbolizes the mean.

Now we have three ways of describing the center, and they alliteratively all start with
m: the mean, the median, and the mode. How should we decide which statistic to
present? My rule of thumb is don't decide; present all three. As we have seen, each
measure of the center tells us something a bit different. If each says the center is
in a different place, then that tells us something very important about our data. For
example, above we saw that, once the rampant renovation was completed, the mean
rose considerably while the median stayed the same. We can generalize this to a rule:

*If the mean is higher than the median, then there is likely a score or small set of
scores at the upper end of the distribution that are considerably higher than the other
scores.*

Now we'll replace that 1,000 with the original 270 and look at a different scenario.
What if one of the people who owned one of the $235,000 houses had done some
horrible renovations of his or her own, ruining the house and lowering its value from
$235,000 (or 235) down to $1,000 (or 1)? Let's recalculate the mean:

Instead of 2,750/11 = 250, we'd have 2,516/11 = 228.73

But the median would stay the same at 250:

1, 235, 240, 245, 250, 250, 250, 255, 255, 260, 270

This leads us to a second rule:

*If the mean is lower than the median, then there is likely a score or small set of scores
at the lower end of the distribution that are considerably lower than the other scores.*

If neither of these rules applies, and the mean and the median are roughly the same,
then there are likely no outliers on either end of the distribution (or there are equal
numbers of outliers at each end).

GSS EXAMPLE: TV WATCHING

The GSS always asks a good number of its respondents how many hours of television they watch per day. Here are some statistics for the black women in the 2012 sample:

Mean: 4.41
Median: 3.00
Mode: 3.00

Based on this, we can make a good guess that a few black women who say they watch a *lot* of television per day. Here is the frequency distribution:

■ **Exhibit 3.3: Frequency Distribution of Black Female Television Watching**

Hours of TV	Frequency
0	7
1	11
2	20
3	27
4	25
5	7
6	6
7	7
8	5
9	2
10	2
12	4
14	2
16	1
18	1
24	1
TOTAL	128

Source: GSS 2012 data.

Sure enough, although most black women say they watch 1, 2, 3, or 4 hours of television, there are a few who say they watch 10 or 12, there's one who claims to watch 18, and there's one who claims to watch 24 hours a day. I'm not sure what it means to say that you watch television 24 hours a day, but to each her own. These outliers at the upper end of the distribution pull the mean up and away from the median. The point of this example is that the descriptive statistics give you a good idea of what the results for a variable look like, even before seeing the actual frequency distribution for the data. Later on in the chapter, after I've introduced a few more descriptive statistics, we'll look at a few distributions visually.

PROCEDURES FOR FINDING THE MEDIAN

Above we had 11 cases, and the middle case was the sixth case, because that put five cases before it and five cases after it. But what if we had a large number of cases, or what if we had an even number of cases? Or even worse, what if we had a large *and* even number of cases? Let's first come up with a procedure that gets us from those 11 cases to picking the sixth case. What can we do to 11 to get us to 6? How about this: we can add 1 to it and divide by 2: $11 + 1 = 12$, $12/2 = 6$. This procedure will work for any odd number of cases. If we had 473 cases, to find the median case we would add one to get 474 and divide by 2 to get 237. Note that this in no way means that the median *is* 237. Rather, the median is whatever value is attached to the 237th *case*. To summarize this procedure,

if you have an odd number of cases, take the total number of cases, add 1 to it, divide it by 2, and that number represents the case you need to find, for the value of that case is the median.

What if the block had 12 houses instead of 11? We can pretty much use the same procedure, but with a twist. Let's add another house to our original block at the upper end of the values:

235, 235, 240, 245, 250, 250, 250, 255, 255, 260, 270, 275

With an even number of cases like this, there is no middle case. If we chose the sixth case, as we did earlier, we would have five cases to the left of it and six cases to the right of it. If we chose the seventh case, we would have six cases to the left of it and five cases to the right of it. So, to find the median when we have an even number of cases like this, we find the two cases that are closest to it (in this situation, the sixth and seventh cases) and we calculate the average of these two cases. This gives us an "imaginary case" in the middle that accomplishes what we want: it has half of the cases on the left of it and half of the cases on the right of it. So in this situation we have

235, 235, 240, 245, 250, 250, 250, 255, 255, 260, 270, 275

The average of 250 and 250 is, of course, 250, so the imaginary median case takes on the value of 250. If the value of the seventh house had been 254, then the value of the imaginary median case would have been: (250 + 254)/2 = 252. To summarize this procedure,

if you have an even number of cases, divide that number by 2 and find the value of that case. Then find the value of the next case. Then find the average of these two values and that is your imaginary median case.

FINDING THE CENTERS WITH A FREQUENCE DISTRIBUTION

Often the data will be presented as a frequency distribution rather than as a list of individual cases. Rather than rewriting the frequency distribution as an ordered list of cases (a chore, even with few cases), if you understand what's going on inside a frequency distribution then it's easy to figure out how to find the mode, the median, and the mean. We'll use the black women's television viewing data from earlier:

▨ **Exhibit 3.4: Frequency Distribution of Black Female Television Watching**

Hours of TV	Frequency	Cumulative Frequency
0	7	7
1	11	18
2	20	38
3	27	65
4	25	90
5	7	97
6	6	103
7	7	110
8	5	115
9	2	117
10	2	119
12	4	123
14	2	125
16	1	126
18	1	127
24	1	128
TOTAL	128	

Source: GSS 2012 data.

The mode is simple, perhaps too simple. The category with the highest frequency is 3 hours, with 27 black women. But notice that the category "4 hours" has a frequency of 25. Had there been just two more women who watched 4 hours, then we would have had two modes. The mode is quite a rough approximation of the center.

Notice that I included a cumulative frequencies column in the preceding figure. This is useful for finding the median. With an even number of cases, we need to find the two nearest cases and average them to get our imaginary case. Because 128/2 is 64, we need the 64th and 65th cases. The cumulative frequency column tells us that the "0 hours" category holds the 1st through 7th cases, so the 64th case is not there. The "1 hour" category holds the 8th through 18th cases, so the 64th case is not there. The "2 hours" category holds the 19th through 38th cases, so the 64th case is not there. The "3 hours" category holds the 39th through 65th cases, so the 64th and 65th cases are in there, and they each have the value of "3 hours." Therefore, the median is $(3 + 3)/2 = 3$. Notice that we're right at the end of this category, so the median was nearly 4.

To find the mean, we need to find the total number of hours of television watched and divide this by the total number of women. We can use the frequency distribution to find the total number of hours:

■ **Exhibit 3.5: Frequency Distribution of Black Female Television Watching**

Hours	f	Contributed Hours of TV Viewing
0	7	These 7 women together contribute 0 hours.
1	11	These 11 women together contribute 11 hours.
2	20	These 20 women together contribute 40 hours.
3	27	These 27 women together contribute 81 hours.
4	25	These 25 women together contribute 100 hours.
5	7	These 7 women together contribute 35 hours.
6	6	These 6 women together contribute 36 hours.
7	7	These 7 women together contribute 49 hours.
8	5	These 5 women together contribute 40 hours.
9	2	These 2 women together contribute 18 hours.
10	2	These 2 women together contribute 20 hours.
12	4	These 4 women together contribute 48 hours.
14	2	These 2 women together contribute 28 hours.
16	1	This 1 woman contributes 16 hours.
18	1	This 1 woman contributes 18 hours.
24	1	This 1 woman contributes 24 hours.
		These 128 women together contribute 564 hours.

Source: GSS 2012 data.

In total, then, these 128 women contribute 564 hours of television viewing; 564/128 = 4.41, and that is our mean. If you understand what we did here, you will understand the slight modification we make in the mean formula when we have a frequency distribution:

$$\bar{x} = \frac{\sum fx}{n}$$

The $\sum fx$ tells us to multiply each value by its respective frequency. Once you have these numbers, then you add them up and then divide by the total number of cases (the sum of all the frequencies). I hope you agree that these formulas aren't so bad if we do it intuitively first.

MEASURES OF THE CENTER AND LEVELS OF MEASUREMENT

Although I think that ideally one should present the mean, the median, and the mode together for comparison's sake, sometimes we are limited by the levels at which the variables are measured. Remember that variables can be measured at the nominal, ordinal, or ratio levels. Here are the measures of center that we can use with each level of measurement:

■ **Exhibit 3.6: Levels of Measurement and Measures of the Center**

	Nominal	Ordinal	Ratio
Mode	Yes	Yes	Yes
Median	No	Yes	Yes
Mean	No	No	Yes

If the variable is measured at the nominal level, the only center we can find is the mode. For example, if we were examining the types of schools students attend (public, private secular, private religious), the type of school with the highest frequency of children would be the mode. If the variable is measured at the ordinal level, there is a mode, but we can also find the median. This is because the median requires ordered data, and we can order the categories of an ordinal-level variable. For example, if we are using an ordinal-level measure of education (less than high school, high school, some college, college degree, graduate degree), we would be able to say, hypothetically, that the modal respondent graduated from high school and the median respondent had some college. If we had a ratio-level variable, then we could find all three measures of the center: the mode, the median, and the mean. For example, if we were measuring education in years, we might find that the mode was 12 years, the median was 13 years, and the mean was 13.27 years of education. If you want to make sure that you have the ability to measure a variable at all three centers, then you have to make sure that you measure that variable at the ratio level.

CLOSE RELATIVES OF THE MEDIAN: QUARTILES AND PERCENTILES

The median, with half the cases above and half below, can be considered by another name: the *50th* **percentile**: 50% of the cases are above and 50% are below. Often in the real world, you will hear other percentiles. A common use of percentiles in today's world is those unsavory standardized tests. If you received your grades, and found out that you were at the 50th percentile, this would mean that 50% of the people who took the test scored lower than your score, and 50% of the people who took the test scored higher than your score. If you found out you were at the 93rd percentile, this would mean that 93% of the people who took the test scored lower than your score, and 7% of the people who took the test scored higher than your score. Although the 50th percentile is the most often used of the percentiles, people sometimes use the 25th percentile and 75th percentile. With these three percentiles, people sometimes organize their results into **quartiles**:

First quartile: from the lowest case to the 25th percentile
Second quartile: from the 26th percentile to the 50th percentile
Third quartile: from the 51st percentile to the 75th percentile
Fourth quartile: from the 76th percentile to the highest case

This provides a nice way to convert a large set of values to a mere four categories.

GSS EXAMPLE: TV WATCHING RERUN

Let's use the frequency distribution from the GSS black women TV watching example from above. Here it is again, with the Cumulative Percent column added:

▪ **Exhibit 3.7: Frequency Distribution of Black Female Television Watching**

Hours of TV	Frequency	Cumulative Percent
0	7	$7/128 \times 100 = 5.47\%$
1	11	$18/128 \times 100 = 14.06\%$
2	20	$38/128 \times 100 = 29.69\%$
3	27	$65/128 \times 100 = 50.78\%$
4	25	$90/128 \times 100 = 70.31\%$
5	7	$97/128 \times 100 = 75.78\%$
6	6	$103/128 \times 100 = 80.47\%$
7	7	$110/128 \times 100 = 85.94\%$
8	5	$115/128 \times 100 = 89.84\%$
9	2	$117/128 \times 100 = 91.41\%$
10	2	$119/128 \times 100 = 92.97\%$
12	4	$123/128 \times 100 = 96.09\%$
14	2	$125/128 \times 100 = 97.66\%$
16	1	$126/128 \times 100 = 98.44\%$
18	1	$127/128 \times 100 = 99.22\%$
24	1	$128/128 \times 100 = 100.00\%$
TOTAL	128	

Source: GSS 2012 data.

From looking at the Cumulative Percent column, we can see that the 25th percentile must take on a value of 2: values of 1 get us only to 14.06%, and values of 2 go through 29.69%. The 75th percentile must take on a value of 5, because that category goes through 75.78%.

ENVISIONING VARIATION

In addition to the center, we want to describe how the data vary around that center. We see variation everywhere we go, throughout the entire day. In the morning, there is variation in the length of showers people take: some take 5-minute showers; others take 25-minute showers. Getting to work, some people have 90-second commutes; others have 90-minute commutes. Some people work at small businesses with 3 employees; others work at large corporations with 10,000 employees. Some people eat a 25-cent noodle cup for lunch; others drop 50 dollars on a three-martini lunch. Some people have no children; others have several children to drive around to various after-school activities. Some people return home to their 1-room apartments; others have 50-room mansions. Some people don't even own a television; some watch five hours of TV per night. Some people get by on four hours of sleep; others need eight or nine. Variation is all around us, and it makes the world an exciting place, for how boring would it be if everyone were exactly the same? In the social sciences, one of our primary goals is to describe this variation and then to try to explain why it exists.

In all of our statistical procedures, we use variables. Say that word aloud five times very slowly: variable, variable, variable, variable, variable. Hopefully this is helping you see that the word *vary* is part of the word *variable*. Or at least I embarrassed you wherever you're reading this. Variables, by their very nature, vary. Vary-able: they are *able* to *vary*. If they weren't able to vary, then they wouldn't be variables; they would be *constants*. If everyone in a room were the same sex, for example, then sex would be, in that situation, a constant: there is no variation in sex in the room. If there were men and women in the room, then we would have variation in sex. If everyone made the same amount of money at his or her jobs, then we would say that income is constant. But, in reality, people make wildly different amounts of money at their respective jobs, so there is lots and lots of variation in income.

ASSESSING VARIATION AMONG GROUPS

At some hypothetical college, you need to take a course, and there are two sections of the course, one taught by Professor L and one taught by Professor H. You are interested in how tough a grader each professor is, so you look up the means for each course. Each course had ten students, and the means for the courses were the same: 3.0 (at this hypothetical college, they use the GPA system, with 0 = F, 1 = D, 2 = C, 3 = B, and 4 = A). With just this information, it seems that there is little difference between the grades in the two courses. However, you want to know more, so you ask to see the list of the grades for the two classes. Here they are:

■ **Exhibit 3.8: Grade Distributions for Two Hypothetical Courses**

Professor L's Grades	Professor H's Grades
3.0	4.0
2.7	3.3
3.4	3.2
3.1	1.6
3.0	3.8
2.8	2.0
2.7	3.9
3.2	1.8
2.9	2.8
3.2	3.6

Source: Hypothetical data.

The courses are not looking so similar any more, are they? Professor L's grades do vary, but they don't vary very much. They are all within a fairly tight range. In contrast, Professor H's grades vary widely. They are all over the place. A first, quick measure of variation is called the **range**: the difference between the highest and lowest values. So, in this situation, we have:

Range of GPAs in Professor L's course: 3.4 – 2.7 = 0.7
Range of GPAs in Professor H's course: 4.0 – 1.6 = 2.4

If you were a very good student, accustomed to getting As, which course would you want to be in? If you were in Professor L's course, even if you worked hard, the highest grade he gave was a 3.4 (or a B+). So you'd want to be in Professor H's course, where very high grades are a possibility. If you were a mediocre student, which course would you want to be in? If you were in Professor H's course, there's a chance she might give you a very low grade. So you'd want to be in Professor L's course, where even if you don't do very well you aren't going to get a very bad grade. It is easy enough to see differing levels of variation among groups when the groups have a small number of cases, but what if we had thousands of cases? Here, the range might mask interesting aspects of the variation. In addition, one very strange score at either end could make the range very wide indeed. Sometimes, people take care of this by using the **interquartile range**: the difference between the 75th percentile and the 25th percentile. But there is a better measure of variation that will allow us easily to contrast variation among groups, and that measure is called the *variance*.

Calculating the variance is straightforward. We'll use the grades from Professor H's course to go through this. The first step is to find how much each person varies from the mean. On a number line, the grades would look like this (sort of drawn to scale, but not exactly):

■ **Exhibit 3.9: Representing Variation Visually on a Number Line**

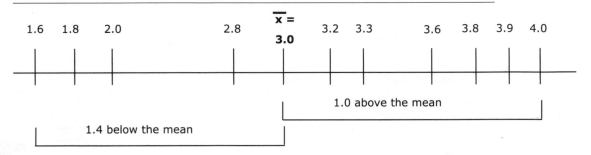

This allows you to visualize this variation. The mean age of these ten students' grades is 3.0, but no one is at the mean. So all the students vary away from the mean. But the amount they vary from the mean differs considerably. The student with the highest grade varies above the mean by 1.0. The student with the lowest grade varies below the mean by –1.4.

Here is the list again, with variations away from the mean:

■ **Exhibit 3.10: Calculating Difference from the Mean**

Student	Grade	Distance of Grade from Mean
Student 1	*Grade of 1.6*	*–1.4*
Student 2	*Grade of 1.8*	*–1.2*
Student 3	*Grade of 2.0*	*–1.0*
Student 4	*Grade of 2.8*	*–0.2*
Student 5	*Grade of 3.2*	*+0.2*
Student 6	*Grade of 3.3*	*+0.3*
Student 7	*Grade of 3.6*	*+0.6*
Student 8	*Grade of 3.8*	*+0.8*
Student 9	*Grade of 3.9*	*+0.9*
Student 10	*Grade of 4.0*	*+1.0*

Add up that last column:

$$-1.4 + -1.2 + -1.0 + -0.2 + 0.2 + 0.3 + 0.6 + 0.8 + 0.9 + 1.0 = 0$$

Zero! Surprised? It's no coincidence. That's the way the mean works: it balances differences on either side of it, so when you add up all the differences, you will always get zero. Notice that the value of the differences matters: there are four negative distances, but six positive distances because some of the negative distances are quite large. In order to deal with this zero-sum problem, what we'll do is square these differences:

■ **Exhibit 3.11: Squaring the Distances**

Student	Grade	Distance	Distance Squared
Student 1	Grade of 1.6	−1.4	1.96
Student 2	Grade of 1.8	−1.2	1.44
Student 3	Grade of 2.0	−1.0	1.00
Student 4	Grade of 2.8	−0.2	0.04
Student 5	Grade of 3.2	+0.2	0.04
Student 6	Grade of 3.3	+0.3	0.09
Student 7	Grade of 3.6	+0.6	0.36
Student 8	Grade of 3.8	+0.8	0.64
Student 9	Grade of 3.9	+0.9	0.81
Student 10	Grade of 4.0	+1.0	1.00

Now add up that last column:

$$1.96 + 1.44 + 1.00 + 0.04 + 0.04 + 0.09 + 0.36 + 0.64 + 0.81 + 1.00 = 7.38$$

But what *is* this 7.38? It's the total amount of *squared variation*. If we take this number and divide it by 9 (the number of cases minus 1), we get 0.82, which is the average squared deviation away from the mean, and this is the **variance**. If it's the average, why don't we simply divide it by the number of cases? Why $n-1$? This is an excellent question, and the answer has to do with the fact that most of our results are based on samples, and it's been shown that samples tend to underestimate variation. To make up for this minor deficiency, we take 1 away from the denominator, thus boosting the overall value a bit. If we had divided by 10 instead of 9, the variance would have been 0.74. Don't get too hung up on this. Just trust me that it's better to overestimate the variance than underestimate it.

How about the students' grades in Professor L's class?

■ **Exhibit 3.12: Professor L's Distances and Distances Squared**

Student	Grade	Distance	Distance Squared
Student 1	Grade of 3.0	0.0	0
Student 2	Grade of 2.7	−0.3	0.09
Student 3	Grade of 3.4	+0.4	0.16
Student 4	Grade of 3.1	+0.1	0.01
Student 5	Grade of 3.0	+0.0	0
Student 6	Grade of 2.8	−0.2	0.04
Student 7	Grade of 2.7	−0.3	0.09
Student 8	Grade of 3.2	+0.2	0.04
Student 9	Grade of 2.9	−0.1	0.01
Student 10	Grade of 3.2	+0.2	0.04

The sum of the third column of numbers is, as expected, zero. The sum of the last column of numbers is 0.48. Divide this 0.48 by 9 and we get 0.05, which is much smaller than variance of 0.82 for students in Professor H's class. How much smaller is it? To figure this out we divide the smaller variance into the larger variance:

$0.82/0.05 = 16.40$

Students in Professor H's course had more than *16 times* the variation of those in Professor L's course.

We've yet to take what we've been doing and create a formula for it. In words, what we've done is take each score, subtract it from the mean and square it. Then we took the sum of these squares and divided it by the sample size minus 1. In formula form,

$$variance = \frac{\sum (score - mean)^2}{sample\, size - 1}$$

Or, using s^2 to stand for the variance (this is the typical symbol for it), x to stand for a score, $\bar{x}$ to stand for the mean, and n for sample size,

$$s^2 = \frac{\sum (x - \bar{x})^2}{n - 1}$$

If you've been following what we've done up to this point, this formula shouldn't upset you, because all it is saying is exactly what we've already done.

GSS EXAMPLE: EDUCATIONAL ATTAINMENT

The GSS always asks respondents how many years of education they have achieved. Here are some statistics using the female respondents who are older than 30 years old:

▨ **Exhibit 3.13: Educational Attainment among Three Racial Groups**

HIGHEST YEAR OF SCHOOL COMPLETED

RACE OF RESPONDENT	N	Median	Mean	Variance
WHITE	662	14.00	13.71	10.166
BLACK	154	13.00	13.47	7.022
OTHER	70	13.00	12.23	20.730

Source: GSS 2012 data, only women over the age of 30.

From these few descriptive statistics, we can say a lot about these distributions. First, regarding where the means and medians fall for each group, for white women, the mean is slightly below the median, so there might be a few low scores among some white women. For black women, the mean is above the median, implying that there are some black women with very high levels of education pulling up on the mean. For women who are neither black nor white, the mean is far below the median, so there are some very low scores among these women pulling down on the mean. The variances add to our understanding. The group with the most variation by far is the women in the "other race" category. Here are a couple of calculations:

Other variance/white variance = 20.73/10.17 = 2.04
Other variance/black variance = 20.73/7.02 = 2.95

Women in the "other race" category have more than twice the variation white women do and nearly three times as much variation black women do when it comes to educational attainment. Let's look at these differences in the following graph, which shows how these other (i.e., neither white nor black) women and black women are distributed on the educational attainment variable:

■ **Exhibit 3.14: Educational Attainment among Black and Other Women**

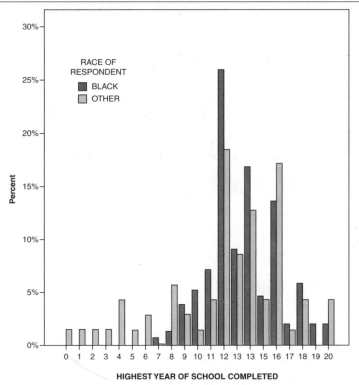

Source: GSS 2012 data for women older than 30 years of age only.

This graph shows what the statistics already implied: in the black women's distribution, the respondents hug the mean, while in the other women's distribution, the cases are spread out much more, and there are some very low scores.

VISUAL VARIATION: THE SHAPES OF DISTRIBUTIONS

Let's bring together some of the ideas we've been covering but looking at four hypothetical distributions. Each have 25 students' grades, but in each, the descriptive statistics, and the shape of the grade distribution, differ in an important way.

■ **Exhibit 3.15: Four Distributions**

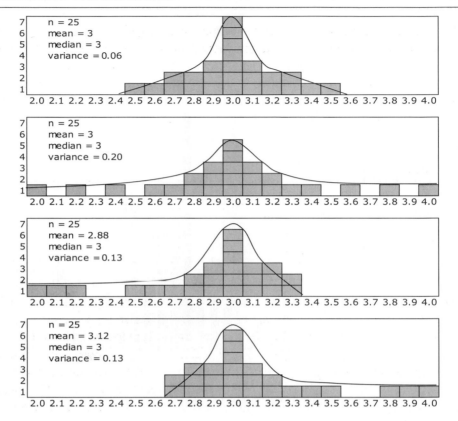

Carefully examine the descriptive statistics of each distribution. In the first distribution, the mean and median are the same, and the distribution has a symmetrical shape. In the second distribution, the mean and median are again equal, but there is more variation than in the first distribution. This is illustrated not only by the higher variance but also by the shape of the distribution, which, although symmetrical, is flatter and has wider tails. The third and fourth distributions have equal amounts of variation, but their shape is different. The third distribution has a mean that is lower than the median. Notice that, visually, this gives the distribution a left **skew** (the distribution's predominant tail is on the left). The fourth distribution has a mean that is higher than the median. Visually, this gives the distribution a right skew (the distribution's predominant tail is on the right). It can be helpful, when comparing distributions' descriptive statistics, to sketch out how the shapes of their distributions likely differ.

ASSESSING THE VARIATION OF INDIVIDUAL CASES

While it is useful to be able to contrast the variation among groups using the variance, we also want to be able to talk about how individual cases vary away from the mean. To do this, we use a close cousin of the variance: the **standard deviation**. To get the standard deviation, we simply take the square root of the variance. Because variance is symbolized by s^2, the standard deviation is symbolized by s. For example, returning to Professor L and Professor H, we see the following:

■ **Exhibit 3.16:**

	Variance	Standard Deviation
Professor H's course	*0.82*	*0.91*
Professor L's course	*0.05*	*0.23*

These numbers are easier to make sense of than the variances. The standard deviation of 0.91 means that, on average, the students' grades in Professor H's course varied away from the mean by 0.91. Some vary away from the mean by a little (for example, the students with the grades of 2.8 and 3.2), and some vary away from the mean by a lot (for example, the students with the grades of 1.6 and 4.0), but on average, they vary away from the mean by 0.91. The standard deviation of 0.23 means that, on average, the students' grades in Professor L's course varied away from the mean by 0.23.

Now we can start looking at the variation of individual cases. We can use the standard deviation to gauge how "unique" certain cases are. One rule we can use is the following, which was developed by my favorite Russian mathematician, Pafnuty Chebyshev:

If our data are distributed in a relatively normal way (with a few cases at each end and most of the cases in the middle, or in other words the classic "bell curve"), then we know that

- *approximately 68% of the cases will fall within one standard deviation of the mean;*
- *approximately 95% of the cases will fall within two standard deviations of the mean;*
- *almost all of the cases will fall within three standard deviations of the mean.*

What if we were looking at a hypothetical group of people and how much money they make? Let's say the mean is 40 (thousand) and the standard deviation is 10 (thousand). According to the preceding rule, the cases would fall as follows. Each tiny triangle represents a person.

■ **Exhibit 3.17: Illustrating Chebyshev's Theorem**

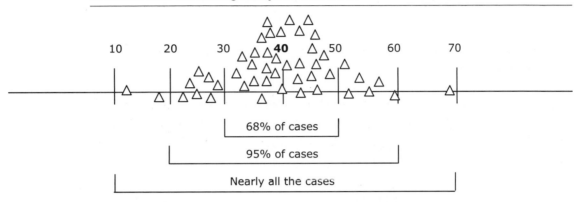

Someone who makes $40,000 doesn't deviate from the mean at all and doesn't stick out at all in terms of his or her income. Someone who makes $50,000 is one standard deviation above the mean and is still within a very normal realm of income. Someone who makes $60,000 is two standard deviations above the mean, and he or she is starting to stick out a bit. Someone who makes $70,000 is three standard deviations above the mean and is quite unique in this income distribution, given that very few cases are this many standard deviations above (or below) the mean. You can see how many standard deviations away various incomes are very easily because of the preceding graphic and because the numbers are very simple. But let's develop a formula for figuring this out. Someone who makes 70 (thousand) is how far above the mean of 40 (thousand)? That's easy, you simply take 70 and subtract 40 to get 30. How many standard deviations is this difference of 30? That's easy, you simply take the 30 and divide it by the value of the standard deviation, which is 10, so 30/10 = 3. Totally simple. So the little formula we'll use to figure out how far a particular case is away from the mean is

$$z = \frac{value - mean}{standard\ deviation}$$

Notice that we're using the symbol z to represent the number of standard deviations away from the mean a particular case is. In fact, these numbers are often called **z-scores**. Using the previous example, what we just did is

$$z = \frac{70 - 40}{10} = 3 \, SDs \, above \, mean$$

One more simple example: an income of 20:

$$z = \frac{20 - 40}{10} = 2 \, SDs \, below \, mean$$

This means that someone who has an income of 20 (thousand) is two standard deviations below the mean.

Back to our two professors. What if a student received a 3.6 from Professor L? What if a student received a 3.6 from Professor H? How many standard deviations would each person be away from the mean? First, Professor L, where the standard deviation is 0.23,

$$\frac{3.6 - 3.0}{0.23}$$

$z = 0.6/0.23 = 2.61$. This person would be almost three standard deviations above the mean, making this a unique grade in Professor L's course. Now Professor H, where the standard deviation was 0.91:

$$\frac{3.6 - 3.0}{0.91}$$

$z = 0.6/0.91 = 0.66$. This person would be within one standard deviation of the mean, so this grade is not so special in Professor H's course. This is usually how we use the standard deviation: to show where various cases lie within a distribution. We will also use it for other procedures later on in the book.

GSS EXAMPLE: INTERNET USAGE AMONG RACIAL GROUPS

Since the advent of the Internet, the GSS has regularly asked respondents how many hours per week they use the Internet. Among male respondents in the 2012 GSS, here are some descriptive statistics:

▨ **Exhibit 3.18: Internet and Email Usage among Men**

WWW HOURS PER WEEK

RACE OF RESPONDENT	N	Median	Std. Deviation
WHITE	373	10.72	14.505
BLACK	50	16.70	21.651
OTHER	50	10.92	12.509

Source: GSS 2012 data, only men.

We can use these descriptive statistics to ascertain how unique various types of people are. What if a man used the Internet 40 hours per week? This may seem like a very long time, but we'll see how unique such a person is for each racial group.

First, a white man:

$$\frac{40 - 10.72}{14.51} = 2.02$$

A white man who uses the Internet 40 hours per week is 2.02 standard deviations above the white mean, which makes him rather unique, but not completely so.

Now, for blacks:

$$\frac{40 - 16.70}{21.65} = 1.08$$

A black man who uses the Internet 40 hours per week is only 1.08 standard deviations above the black mean. This implies that such a person is not really that unique within this distribution; that it is within the range of normality for black men to use the Internet this much.

Finally, for others (i.e., neither white nor black):

$$\frac{40 - 10.92}{12.51} = 2.32$$

A man from the "other" racial group who uses the Internet 40 hours per week is 2.32 standard deviations above the "other" mean, which means that such a man is on his way to being very unique. In other words, such a man would stick out among his racial group for the long time he uses the Internet per week.

FINDING S AND S^2 WITH A FREQUENCY DISTRIBUTION

I want to go over a variation on the formulas we used earlier. Because we often work with frequency distributions, it's useful to see how the formula changes when we have the data in this form. Here are the data for 18- to 30-year-olds in the 2012 GSS for the variable CHLDIDEL: What do you think is the ideal number of children for a family to have? Notice that, for each category, we have multiple respondents:

■ **Exhibit 3.19: Ideal Number of Children Frequency Distribution**

Ideal #	Frequency
0	2
1	7
2	92
3	83
4	22
5	2
TOTAL	208

Source: GSS 2012 data for respondents aged 18 through 29 only.

The mean for this distribution is 2.59, so let's calculate (and square) each variation from the mean:

■ **Exhibit 3.20: Distances and Squared Distances**

Ideal #	ideal# – mean	(ideal# – mean)²	Frequency
0	–2.59	6.71	2
1	–1.59	2.53	7
2	–0.59	0.35	92
3	0.41	0.17	83
4	1.41	1.99	22
5	2.41	5.81	2

But we need to take into account that we don't just have one respondent who said zero kids; we have two respondents who each said zero kids. We don't have one respondent who said one kid; we have seven respondents who each said one kid. So what we do is take the squared deviation and multiply it by the frequency:

■ **Exhibit 3.21: Squared Distances Multiplied by Frequencies**

Ideal #	(ideal# – mean)^2	Frequency	f (ideal# – mean)^2
0	6.71	2	13.42
1	2.53	7	17.71
2	0.35	92	32.20
3	0.17	83	14.11
4	1.99	22	43.78
5	5.81	2	11.62

Adding up this last column gives us the sum of squared deviations: 132.84. We divide this by the sample size minus 1 to get the variance:

$$132.84/207 = 0.64$$

Let's return to our original formula for the variance:

$$s^2 = \frac{\sum (x - \bar{x})^2}{n-1}$$

To revise the formula to take into account multiple frequencies within each category, we need to do what we did earlier: multiply each $(x - \bar{x})^2$ by its corresponding f:

$$s^2 = \frac{\sum f(x - \bar{x})^2}{n-1}$$

This formula does exactly what we did above: it multiplies each squared distance by the frequency of scores located at that distance.

VARIATION WHEN THERE IS NO MEAN

These days, everywhere you turn there is talk of diversity: within the social sciences, within public policy, in the news. We talk of diversity in gender, race, sexual orientation, and religion. All of these variables have something in common: none of them has a mean. There is no mean race. There is no mean religion. If we cannot calculate the mean, then we cannot calculate the variance, because it is based on the variation from the mean. But, because these types of diversity are important, it would be nice to be able to gauge such diversity, especially if it changes over time. Numerous statistical procedures allow us to do this. I'll cover one in depth and briefly describe a couple of others. In depth I will cover the **index of qualitative variation** (IQV). It ranges from 0 to 1. At 0, we have no diversity: all of the cases are exactly the same on our variable of interest. If your classroom had all female students, the IQV for sex would be 0. At 1, we have maximum diversity. This is the situation where the cases are as diverse as possible. If a classroom had equal numbers of freshmen, sophomores, juniors, and seniors, then the IQV for school year would be 1.

We'll start with a simple example. What if we lived in a town with four religious groups: there is a Protestant church, a Catholic church, a Jewish temple, and a Muslim mosque. In order to increase interfaith understanding, we form an eight-person committee with people from all four faiths. However, owing to various scheduling problems, the committee that forms is made up of four Protestants, two Catholics, one Jew, and one Muslim. We'll call them P_1, P_2, P_3, P_4, C_1, C_2, J_1, and M_1. You can tell intuitively that this does not represent the situation of maximum diversity, what with one religion making up half the committee, but we'll return to that very soon.

In order to foster interfaith understanding among committee members, each person of a certain faith is asked to have a one-on-one meeting with each person of a different faith. How many one-on-one pairings could we have with this set of people?

Using the first Protestant, we could make the following one-on-one pairings to match this person up with everyone from a different denomination than himself:

P_1 with C_1, P_1 with C_2, P_1 with J_1, P_1 with M_1, so there's 4 pairs.

Of course, we can match each of the other three Protestants with the same people:

P_2 with C_1, P_2 with C_2, P_2 with J_1, P_2 with M_1, so we're up to 8 pairs.
P_3 with C_1, P_3 with C_2, P_3 with J_1, P_3 with M_1, so we're up to 12 pairs.
P_4 with C_1, P_4 with C_2, P_4 with J_1, P_4 with M_1, so we're up to 16 pairs.

The Catholics can each be matched up with the Jew and the Muslim:

C_1 with J_1, C_1 with M_1, C_2 with J_1, C_2 with M_1, so we're up to 20 pairs.

And finally we can match up the Jew with the Muslim:

J_1 with M_1

So our total number of different-religion pairings is 21. To reiterate, here are the pairs in table form:

▪ **Exhibit 3.22: Locating Different-Religion Pairs**

P_1C_1	P_2C_1	P_3C_1	P_4C_1	C_1J_1	C_2J_1	J_1M_1	
P_1C_2	P_2C_2	P_3C_2	P_4C_2	C_1M_1	C_2M_1		
P_1J_1	P_2J_1	P_3J_1	P_4J_1				
P_1M_1	P_2M_1	P_3M_1	P_4M_1				
4 prs +	4 prs +	4 prs +	4 prs +	2 prs +	2 prs +	1 pr =	21 pairs

But, as we realized earlier, such an eight-person committee does not maximize diversity. To have the maximum possible diversity on our eight-person committee, we would need two people from each of the four faiths, so we would have:

$P_1, P_2, C_1, C_2, J_1, J_2, M_1, M_2$

and with this committee we could form 24 pairings:

▪ **Exhibit 3.23: Locating Different-Religion Pairs with Maximum Diversity**

P_1C_1	P_2C_1	C_1J_1	C_2J_1	J_1M_1	J_2M_1	
P_1C_2	P_2C_2	C_1J_2	C_2J_2	J_1M_2	J_2M_2	
P_1J_1	P_2J_1	C_1M_1	C_2M_1			
P_1J_2	P_2J_2	C_1M_2	C_2M_2			
P_1M_1	P_2M_1					
P_1M_2	P_2M_2					
6 prs +	6 prs +	4 prs +	4 prs +	2 prs +	2 prs =	24 pairs

Exhibit 3.24 offers an alternative illustration of the different possible pairings for the two situations we've been discussing. The gray bars represent pairings of the same person (P_1 with P_1) or a pairing that already is accounted for (when we match P_1 with C_1, we don't want to match C_1 with P_1 again):

■ **Exhibit 3.24: Finding Different-Religion Pairs: Two Scenarios**

Less Than Maximum Diversity: 21 Different-Religion Pairs

	P_1	P_2	P_3	P_4	C_1	C_2	J_1	M_1
P_1		SAME	SAME	SAME	DIFFERENT	DIFFERENT	DIFFERENT	DIFFERENT
P_2			SAME	SAME	DIFFERENT	DIFFERENT	DIFFERENT	DIFFERENT
P_3				SAME	DIFFERENT	DIFFERENT	DIFFERENT	DIFFERENT
P_4					DIFFERENT	DIFFERENT	DIFFERENT	DIFFERENT
C_1						SAME	DIFFERENT	DIFFERENT
C_2							DIFFERENT	DIFFERENT
J_1								DIFFERENT
M_1								

Maximum Diversity: 24 Different-Religion Pairs

	P_1	P_2	C_1	C_2	J_1	J_2	M_1	M_2
P_1		SAME	DIFFERENT	DIFFERENT	DIFFERENT	DIFFERENT	DIFFERENT	DIFFERENT
P_2			DIFFERENT	DIFFERENT	DIFFERENT	DIFFERENT	DIFFERENT	DIFFERENT
C_1				SAME	DIFFERENT	DIFFERENT	DIFFERENT	DIFFERENT
C_2					DIFFERENT	DIFFERENT	DIFFERENT	DIFFERENT
J_1						SAME	DIFFERENT	DIFFERENT
J_2							DIFFERENT	DIFFERENT
M_1								SAME
M_2								

To calculate the IQV, we simply divide the observed pairings with the possible pairings. Our observed committee without ideal diversity had 21 pairings, and the possible committee with ideal diversity had 24 pairings:

$21/24 = 0.875$

For another example using the same scenario, let's make the diversity even worse. What if we had this eight-person committee with the following composition:

$P_1, P_2, P_3, P_4, P_5, C_1, J_1, M_1$

Our pairings would be

$18/24 = 0.75$

■ **Exhibit 3.25: Even Worse Religious Diversity**

P_1C_1	P_2C_1	P_3C_1	P_4C_1	P_5C_1	C_1J_1	J_1M_1
P_1J_1	P_2J_1	P_3J_1	P_4J_1	P_5J_1	C_1M_1	
P_1M_1	P_2M_1	P_3M_1	P_4M_1	P_5M_1		
3 prs +	3 prs +	3 prs +	3 prs +	3 prs +	2 prs +	1 pr = 18 pairs

If we had four religions but the eight-person committee was made up of eight Catholics, the different-religion pairs would be C_1 . . . well, wait a second: we can't match up any Catholics with anyone else, because there are no people from other religions on the eight-person committee, so the IQV would be equal to a big fat zero. Less variation elicits a lower IQV, and the lowest IQV is when there is no variation.

Although pairing people by hand makes it easy to understand what's going on, this gets old fast, so let's develop some formulae. We'll start with our observed pairings, using the original committee:

4 Protestants, 2 Catholics, 1 Jew, 1 Muslim

We need to pair up people with people unlike themselves. To do this, we multiply each group's frequency with the frequencies of all the unlike groups:

The Protestants with the Catholics: 4×2
The Protestants with the Jew: 4×1
The Protestants with the Muslim: 4×1
The Catholics with the Jew: 2×1
The Catholics with the Muslim: 2×1
The Jew with the Muslim: 1×1

And that gives us 21 pairings, exactly what we had earlier. Formula-wise, this represents what we just did:

Observed Differences $= \sum f_i f_j$

It simply says take each frequency and multiply it by each other frequency. Now on to the possible pairings. Instead of

$(4 \times 2) + (4 \times 1) + (4 \times 1) + (2 \times 1) + (2 \times 1) + (1 \times 1) = 21$

we want

$$(2 \times 2) + (2 \times 2) + (2 \times 2) + (2 \times 2) + (2 \times 2) + (2 \times 2) = 24$$

because we know that two of each group gets us maximum diversity. How did we know that two was the magic number? We have eight people on the committee, and we have four religions, so we have $8/4 = 2$. When we pair them, we need 2×2, or 2^2. Next, how many 2^2s do we need? We saw earlier that it's six. But how do we get from four categories to this six? Well, there are many ways, but here's the right way: (4 categories $\times$ (4 – 1) categories)/2 = 6.

Here's a variation on the situation: what if we had 15 people on the committee and five religions? Let's find the possible pairings with maximum diversity:

We'd have $15/5 = 3$, meaning three of each group, so we need 3×3, or 3^2. How many 3^2s do we need?

(5 categories $\times$ (5 – 1) categories)/2 = 10

So we need

$$3^2 + 3^2 + 3^2 + 3^2 + 3^2 + 3^2 + 3^2 + 3^2 + 3^2 + 3^2 = 90 \text{ possible pairings}$$

One more! What if we had 21 people on the committee and 3 religions? We'd have

$$21/3 = 7$$

so we need 7×7, or 7^2. How many 7^2s do we need?

(3 categories $\times$ (3 – 1) categories)/2 = 3

So we have

$$7^2 + 7^2 + 7^2 = 147 \text{ possible pairings.}$$

Formula-wise, here's what we've been doing to find the possible differences (n means total number of cases, c is the number of categories):

Possible Differences $= (n/c)^2 \times ((c \times (c - 1))/2)$

Using the preceding example, we'd have

$$\textit{Possible Differences} = (21/3)^2 \times ((3 \times (3-1))/2) = 147$$

Pulling the entire formula together, we have

$$IQV = \frac{\textit{Observed Differences}}{\textit{Possible Differences}} = \frac{\sum f_i f_j}{(n/c)^2 \times ((c \times (c-1))/2)}$$

I'll be the first to admit that this is a fairly formidable formula, but, as with most formulas, it's just a quicker way to do something intuitive. Let's use this formula one more time with a completely different hypothetical situation. Although ordinal-level variables have medians, they lack means. What if we had an ordinal-level variable that measured diversity in political views among 50 people:

■ **Exhibit 3.26: Hypothetical Political Views of Fifty People**

Political View	Frequency
Very Conservative	3
Conservative	7
Moderate	30
Liberal	8
Very Liberal	2

Source: Hypothetical data.

The total number of observed differences is

■ **Exhibit 3.27:**

3 × 7 = 21	7 × 30 = 210	30 x 8 = 240	8 × 2 = 16
3 × 30 = 90	7 × 8 = 56	30 x 2 = 60	
3 × 8 = 24	7 × 2 = 14		
3 × 2 = 6			

$21 + 90 + 24 + 6 + 210 + 56 + 14 + 240 + 60 + 16 = 737$

There are 737 observed pairings of people with different political views. Now for the possible pairings with maximum variation:

Possible Differences = $(50/5)^2 \times ((5 \times (5 - 1))/2) = 1,000$

This gives us an IQV of $737/1,000 = 0.73$.

Therefore, this set of frequencies is nowhere near maximum diversity.

GSS EXAMPLE: ATTITUDES TOWARD GOVERNMENT SPENDING

The GSS regularly asks respondents about government spending. For example, it asks, "We are faced with many problems in this country, none of which can be solved easily or inexpensively. I'm going to name some of these problems, and for each one I'd like you to tell me whether you think we're spending too much money on it, too little money, or about the right amount. Improving and protecting the nation's health." Here is how the respondents replied in the 2008 GSS:

■ **Exhibit 3.28: Attitudes toward Spending on Health Care**

Too Little	*749*
About Right	*177*
Too Much	*47*
TOTAL	*973*

Source: GSS 2008 data.

We want to pair up people into unlike pairs, so in a sense, what we're doing is pairing people up in "disagreements":

The 749 people who said "too little" matched up with the 177 who said "about right":
   $749 \times 177 = 132,573$ disagreements
The 749 people who said "too little" matched up with the 47 who said "too much":
   $749 \times 47 = 35,203$ disagreements
The 177 people who said "about right" matched up with the 47 who said "too much":
   $177 \times 47 = 8,319$ disagreements

This gives us 176,095 observed disagreements. Now what if there was the maximum amount of controversy over this issue? That is, what if people were all over the map attitudinally? We'd have equal numbers of people in each category:

■ **Exhibit 3.29: Hypothetical Maximum Variation in Attitudes**

Too Little	324.33
About Right	324.33
Too Much	324.33
TOTAL	973

It may seem odd to have 1/3 of a person, but 973/3 = 324.33. Now we need to pair up all the disagreements:

$$324.33^2 + 324.33^2 + 324.33^2 = 315,576$$

This gives us an IQV of 176,095/315,576 = 0.56. Using the formula we developed above, we would get the same result:

$$\frac{\sum f_i f_j}{(n/c)^2 \times ((c \times (c-1))/2)} = \frac{(749 \times 177) + (749 \times 47) + (177 \times 47)}{(973/3)^2 \times ((3 \times (3-1))/2)}$$

Therefore, in the 2008 GSS, respondents veered more toward consensus rather than controversy: a strong 77% of them agreed that we were spending too little. Fast forward to the next GSS, in 2010. Recall that by this point, President Obama had introduced his healthcare plan, and this issue was in the news every day, with a lot of the news regarding how divided Americans were on the issue. When the GSS asked respondents this same survey question in 2010, here were the responses:

■ **Exhibit 3.30: Attitudes toward Health Spending, 2010**

Spending on Health is …	Frequency
… too little	597
… about right	234
… too much	157

Source: GSS 2010 data.

This gives us an IQV of: 270,165 / 325,381.30 = 0.83. There was much less consensus among the respondents this time around. I took the GSS data from 1973 to 2012, from this health care question and two additional spending questions: "the military, armaments, and defense, and "improving and protecting the environment." Observing changes in the IQV over time allows us to track the ebb and flow between consensus and controversy.

■ **Exhibit 3.31: Index of Qualitative Variation over Time for Three Government-Spending Issues**

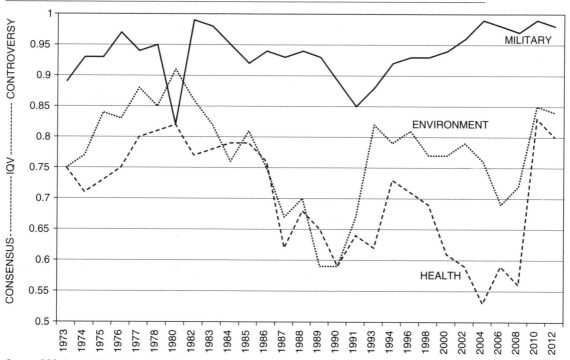

Source: GSS data 1973–2012.

The attitudes toward military spending are relatively laden with conflict: the IQV for this variable is often in the 90–1.00 range, meaning that the frequencies are pretty much evenly divided among the three categories. There are two very temporary dips away from this conflict: in 1980 and in 1991. In these two years, the military was on the minds of Americans. In 1980, the Soviet Union had just invaded Afghanistan, which heated up the Cold War. The percentage of respondents who said we were spending too little on the military went from 29% in the 1978 GSS to 60% in the 1980

GSS. In 1991, the Gulf War had just begun. The percentage of respondents who said we were spending the right amount on the military went from 45% in the 1990 GSS to 58% in the 1991 GSS. We would expect there to be a similar dip, then, after 9/11, but there is not: the IQV remains high, and even rises a bit. This reflects how controversial the U.S. wars in Afghanistan and Iraq were.

The IQV for spending on the environment is lowest in the years 1989 and 1990, and a historical event explains this as well. In these two years, a whopping 75% of the GSS respondents said that the United States was spending too little on protecting the environment. In March of 1989, the *Exxon Valdez*, an oil tanker, crashed off the coast of Alaska, dumping hundreds of thousands of barrels of oil into Prince William Sound. It remains one of the worst environmental disasters in history. Since that time, there has been a move toward controversy, except for a brief dip in 2006 (perhaps resulting from Hurricane Katrina).

From a high of 0.82 in 1980, the health care IQV moved in fits and starts toward consensus: more and more people thought we were spending too little on healthcare. By 2004, when the IQV was at an all-time low of 0.53, 78% of respondents believed this. But all this changed in 2010, when the IQV moved toward conflict: the percentage of Americans who feel we are spending too little on health care began to decrease, and the percentages of Americans who feel we are spending the right amount or spending too much started to rise.

Please notice that, if consensus is increasing, the IQV does not tell us in what direction this consensus is going. We need to look at the actual data to judge this. But the IQV does allow us a quick assessment of the changing diversity in attitudes over time.

OTHER MEASURES OF DIVERSITY

There are two other common measures of inequality-related diversity that I want to mention briefly (but I'll spare you the calculation of these). The first is called the **index of dissimilarity**, and it is used to measure the racial segregation of two groups in geographic areas. Whereas the IQV ranged from 0 (no diversity) to 1 (maximum diversity), the index of dissimilarity ranges from 0 to 100. Imagine two towns: Segville and Desegville. In Segville, all of the whites live on one side of town and all of the blacks live on the other side of town. This is maximum segregation, and the index of dissimilarity would be 100 (the two sides of town are maximally dissimilar). Another way to think about this is that 100% of one of the racial groups would have to move in order to completely desegregate the town. In Desegville, where blacks and whites live equally together on both sides of town, no one (0%) would have to move to achieve desegregation, so the index of dissimilarity is 0 for Descgville. This index is used to contrast the level of segregation in various areas, and to show how segregation levels have changed in a single geographic area over time.

The other common measure is the **Gini coefficient**. Whereas the IQV measures inequality among categories (i.e., Category 1 has 40% of the cases, whereas Categories 2 and 3 each have 20% of the cases), and the index of dissimilarity measures inequality across space, the Gini coefficient measures the level of income or wealth inequality within a society (Wheelan, 2013). Its range is, similar to the IQV, 0 to 1. Zero means total income equality: everyone in a given society has the same exact wealth. One means total income inequality: one person has all the wealth and no one else has any. Obviously, these two extremes are impossible, so typically you'll see Gini coefficients between 0.20 and 0.70. As with the IQV, the Gini coefficient is most useful to track changes across time. For example, there's a lot of concern about growing income inequality in the United States: the Gini coefficient rose from 0.41 in 1997 to 0.45 in 2007. In contrast, Sweden's Gini coefficient went from 0.25 in 1992 to 0.23 in 2005: they have actually experienced a decline in income inequality.

LITERATURE EXAMPLE: COST OF MEDICAL CARE

As we just saw, many Americans think we need to spend more on improving the nation's health. Sometimes it is difficult to find out exactly how much such improvements will cost. Jaime Rosenthal (under the supervision of her advisor, given that she was an undergraduate student at the time) carried out a very simple, but very intriguing research project: she called hospitals to get price quotes for hip replacement surgery. In their article "Availability of Consumer Prices from US Hospitals for a Common Surgical Procedure," which appeared in the *Journal of the American Medical Association Internal Medicine* in 2013, Rosenthal and her coauthors show that although measures of the center are important, sometimes the real story is in the amount of variation.

They studied the 20 top orthopedic hospitals, as well as a random sample of 102 other hospitals that provided this surgery. Then, using a set script, Rosenthal called each hospital to see if she could get a price quote for the surgery for her grandmother who did not have health insurance but could pay for the surgery herself. Here are just a few of their findings:

■ **Exhibit 3.32: Cost of Hip Replacement Surgery**

	Top-Ranked Hospitals	Other Hospitals
Complete Price		
n	12	64
Mean	$53,140	$41,666 .
Range	$12,500–$105,000	$11,100–$125,798
Hospital Price Only		
n	2	21
Mean	$74800	$35,417
Range	$64,600–$85,000	$9,000–$71,200
Physician Price Only		
n	3	1
Mean	$11,117	$9,203
Range	$6,450–$17,500	N/A

Source: Adapted from Rosenthal, Lu, and Cram (2013).

Although she tried numerous times, Rosenthal was unable to get price information from a large proportion of the hospitals. Among those who did provide estimates, the cost of the surgery varied enormously from hospital to hospital. This is definitely a situation where reporting just the mean would not suffice. Diversity of price is the real story here.

CONCLUSION

Well, that was a good chunk of the basics: several measures of the center and several measures of variation. You should have a feel for how to find each of them and how to interpret each of them. You should also understand how to interpret the results when you find that they differ, either among each other (for example, the mean is higher than the median) or among different groups (for example, the IQV for this year is higher than the IQV for that year). Hopefully you're realizing that calculation is but a small part of studying statistics. Interpretation is as important as calculation, if not more so.

SPSS DEMONSTRATION

Please visit the book's website (www.routledge.com/cw/linneman) to view a video of this demonstration.

There are many ways to get descriptive statistics in SPSS, and I'll show you a few of my favorites. First, go into the Frequencies room:

Analyze ➔ Descriptive Statistics ➔ Frequencies

Move whatever variables you want off the shelf and into the Variable(s) box on the right side (we'll use just the ANES internet news variable). Next, click the "Statistics . . ." button:

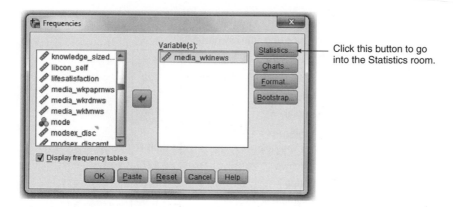

Click this button to go into the Statistics room.

Within this room, you will recognize a lot of what we did in this chapter, and I checked all those boxes in the following figure:

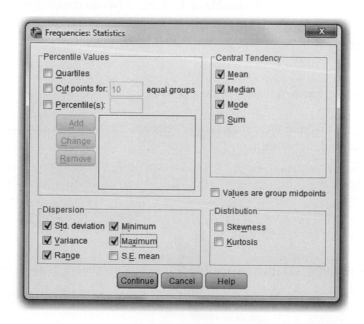

You simply click what you want, then click Continue to exit this room, and then, once you are back in the Frequencies room, click OK. SPSS will run the requested frequency distributions and give you whatever descriptive statistics you requested. Remember that SPSS will do anything you ask it to do, so if, for example, you request it to give you a mean on the race variable, it will do so. However, you should know by now that race is a nominal-level variable, so you shouldn't calculate a mean for it. For the sake of example, I had SPSS give me various descriptive statistics on the ANES dem_raceth variable, and here they are:

statistics

R race and ethnicity group

N	Valid	5887
	Missing	29
Mean		1.70
Median		1.00
Mode		1
Std. Deviation		0.963
Variance		0.927
Range		3
Minimum		1
Maximum		4

SPSS gave me a mean for this variable of 1.70, but it has no meaning whatsoever.

A second way to get some descriptive statistics is the next choice under Descriptive Statistics:

Analyze ➔ Descriptive Statistics ➔ Descriptives

If you click on this and then click on the "Options" button, you can see what your descriptive statistics choices are:

Notice that not all of the descriptive statistics are available in this box. However, in many journal articles, you'll see a table of descriptive statistics, and these are the pieces of information this table usually has: the mean, the standard deviation, the minimum value, and the maximum value.

A third option allows you to start looking at differences between groups:

Analyze ➔ Reports ➔ Case Summaries, which takes you to this room:

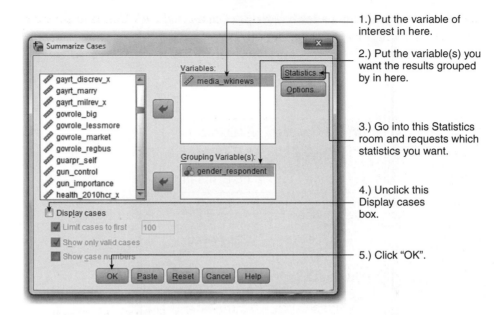

1.) Put the variable of interest in here.

2.) Put the variable(s) you want the results grouped by in here.

3.) Go into this Statistics room and requests which statistics you want.

4.) Unclick this Display cases box.

5.) Click "OK".

One thing you'll want to do in this room is unclick the box under the variable list that says "Display cases." If you don't unclick this box, SPSS will list *all* the cases individually when it runs the output, and you probably don't want that, do you? If you click on the "Statistics" button to go into the Statistics room, you will see that this box is set up much like a variable list, where you move the statistics you want off the shelf.

Here is the resulting output from my request:

Case Summaries

Days in Typical Week Review News on Internet

Gender of respondent	N	Mean	Median	Std. Deviation	Variance
1. Male	2709	4.07	5.00	2.721	7.406
2. Female	2907	3.41	3.00	2.729	7.450
Total	5616	3.73	4.00	2.746	7.539

Finally, you might want to create a graph using a descriptive statistic. For example, you might want a visual representation to show that medians on this Internet news variable for men and women are different. Click

Graphs ➔ Legacy Dialogs ➔ Bar

and then choose Simple, Summaries for groups of cases, and click Define to enter the second graphing room. Rather than asking SPSS to show you the frequencies on the variable, you want to ask it to display the variances for the two sexes. Here's how to ask SPSS for this:

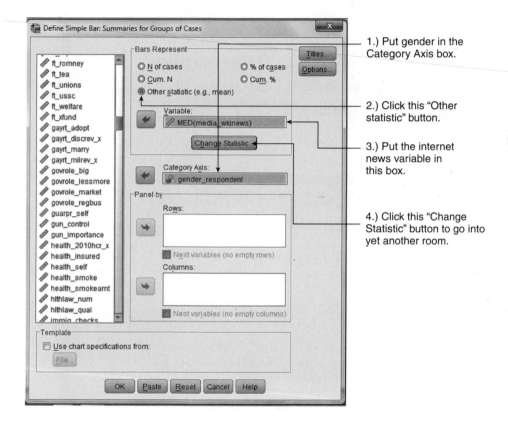

1.) Put gender in the Category Axis box.

2.) Click this "Other statistic" button.

3.) Put the internet news variable in this box.

4.) Click this "Change Statistic" button to go into yet another room.

Yes, now you're within a room within a room within a room! And this room looks like this:

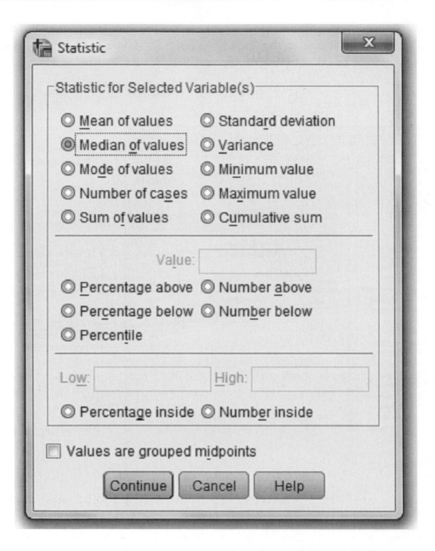

In this room, you want to choose which statistic you want the bars to represent. In this case, I chose Median. But notice you could also have the bars represent the mean (this is the default option), or the mode, or the variance. The options below this can be useful as well. For example, if you wanted the bars to represent the percentage of each group who read internet news more than three times per week, you could do "Percentage above the value of 3." Or, if you wanted the bars to represent the percentage of each group who watch the news one or two times per week, you could do "Percentages inside a Low of 1 and a High of 2." Just play around with these and you'll soon be a pro. But let's see what our median graph looks like. We click Continue to get out of the Statistic room, and then OK to run the graph.

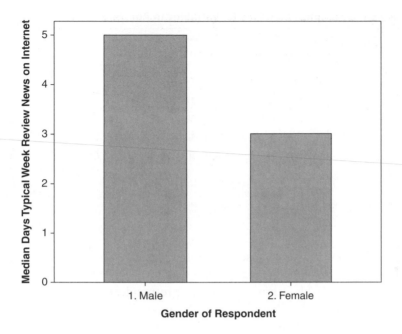

This graph clearly illustrates that the median for the two groups are different. In summary, there are numerous ways in SPSS to get descriptive statistics. You just need to decide on your favorites.

FROM OUTPUT TO PRESENTATION

As I mentioned earlier, it is very common to present a table of descriptive statistics at the beginning of a presentation or report, even if these statistics are not the primary focus of the findings. It is a good way to summarize the variables you will be using in your subsequent analyses. Let's say your report concerned gender and news engagement (similar to one of the earlier SPSS examples but involving all four types of news engagement), your table of descriptive statistics might look like this:

■ Exhibit 3.33: Descriptive Statistics for Variables in Analysis

Variable	Description of variable	x	SD	n
Dependent Variables:				
Internet news	Days/wk check news on Internet	3.73	2.75	5,616
Newspaper	Days/wk read newspaper	2.21	2.61	5,908
Radio	Days/wk listen to news on radio	2.54	2.57	5,906
TV news	Days/wk watch news on TV	4.04	2.59	5,910
Independent Variable:				
Gender	Male = 0, Female = 1	0.52	0.50	5,916

This allows the viewer to quickly see vital information, and notice differences among the variables. For example, looking at the n column, we see that the sample size for the Internet news variable is around 300 fewer respondents than the other variables. This is because if the respondent said he or she doesn't use the Internet, he or she was not asked this question. Note also that it is typical to present the mean and standard deviation for dichotomies. The 0.52 can be interpreted as 52% of the respondents were female. The standard deviation of 0.50 does not have much use.

EXERCISES

EXERCISES

Exercise 1

Use the ANES data and have SPSS calculate the mean and the median for the four feeling thermometers that concern religious groups: atheists, Mormons, Muslims, and Christian Fundamentalists. Discuss each group in terms of the skew. What does this tell you about how Americans likely feel about these groups?

Exercise 2

Use the ANES data to see how the male respondents and then the female respondents score on the feminist feeling thermometer. Have SPSS calculate the mean and the median for each group. Discuss each group in terms of the skew. What does this tell you about how men and women feel about feminists?

Exercise 3 (Answer Available in Appendix D)

Use ANES to get the mean and standard deviation for the recoded income variable for the various marital status groups (use the recoded marital status variable).

Which is more unique: a divorced respondent whose income is $120,000 or a separated respondent whose income is $120,000? Describe specifically and statistically how unique each person is.

Exercise 4

Here are the sample sizes and means for the four racial/ethnic groups on the Political Efficacy Index (only the 17- to 20-year-olds):

Whites: $n = 32$, mean = 6.97

Blacks: $n = 21$, mean = 8.14

Hispanics: $n = 32$, mean = 6.84

Others: $n = 5$, mean = 4.40

Find the overall mean for all 90 respondents.

Exercise 5

Among whom is there more agreement regarding gay marriage: young Hispanics or middle-aged Hispanics? Here are ANES data for this variable:

	Young Hispanics	Mid-Aged Hispanics
Legal marriage	202	81
Civil unions	87	77
No legal recognition	64	72
TOTAL:	353	230

Calculate the IQV for each group and interpret the results, answering the question.

Exercise 6

Here is a list of scores on the Traditionalism Index for the ANES unique group of respondents who simultaneously rated Christian Fundamentalists and Atheists at 100 on the Feeling Thermometer:

7, 10, 5, 6, 5, 8, 5, 12, 4, 11, 11, 9, 10, 13, 8, 8, 7

Use these raw data to the find the mean, median, mode, variance, and standard deviation.

Exercise 7

Here is a frequency distribution for the TV news watching habits of the ANES unique group white women who smoke every day but claim to be in excellent health:

Times/wk TV news	Frequency
0	6
1	2
5	2
6	1
7	6
TOTAL:	17

Use these raw data to the find the mean, median, mode, variance, and standard deviation.

Exercise 8

Using the PewShop dataset, discuss the differences in the variances in income among the three community categories (rural, suburban, and urban).

Exercise 9

Using the PewShop dataset, get the means and the medians for the education variable for the various races (use the recoded income variable and the recoded race variable). Contrast the skew among whites, blacks, and Hispanics.

Exercise 10

Here are the raw data from the PewShop dataset for American Indians on the Technology Index:

1, 1, 1, 2, 2, 3, 3, 5, 4, 1, 3.

By hand, find the mean, median, mode, variance, and standard deviation.

Exercise 11

Here is a frequency distribution for the recoded education variable from the PewShop dataset for the Asian respondents:

Years of Education	Frequency
12	1
13	5
14	3
16	10
19	13
TOTAL:	32

Use these raw data to the find the mean, median, mode, variance, and standard deviation.

Exercise 12 (Answer Available in Appendix D)

Among whom is there more variation in overall health: those in the lowest income bracket of the PewHealth dataset or those in the highest income bracket? Here are data for this variable:

	Lowest Bracket	Highest Bracket
Health excellent	61	87
Health good	115	84
Health only fair	83	9
Health poor	32	3
TOTAL:	291	183

Exercise 13

Use the PewHealth dataset to get the means and the medians on the Cellphone Use Index for the various educational groupings (use the original education variable, not the recoded one). As educational level rises, what is the trend in the skew for this index? What does this imply?

Exercise 14

Using the PewHealth dataset, run the necessary statistics to address these questions:

a. Imagine someone who has four of the six health conditions in the Health Condition Index, yet they say they have excellent quality of life. Among those with excellent quality of life, how unique is it to have four health conditions?

b. Imagine someone who has four of the six health conditions in the Health Condition Index, and they say they have poor quality of life. Among those with poor quality of life, how unique is it to have four health conditions?

Exercise 15 (Answer Available in Appendix D)

Use the PewKids dataset to contrast white kids and American Indian kids on the variable "number of texts sent per day." Contrast the means, the medians, and the variances.

Exercise 16

Use the PewKids dataset to contrast black kids and Hispanic kids on the Child Technology Use Index. Contrast the means, the medians, and the variances.

Exercise 17

WVS respondents were asked to rate how acceptable they believe euthanasia and suicide to be on a scale from 1 (never justifiable) to 10 (always justifiable). Treating these variables as ratio-level, I calculated means for each country to create the country-level variables EUTHAN and SUICIDE. Get the mean, the median, and the variance for these variables and describe what differences you find.

Exercise 18 (Answer Available in Appendix D)

Do Western Europeans and Eastern Europeans differ on how they feel about labor unions? By hand and by using SPSS, calculate the mean and variance for these two groups of countries on the WVS variable CONUNION. Describe the difference between the variances.

Exercise 19

Get the mean and median on the WVS variables JOBMEN and NATJOB. Describe the skewness and predict for each variable where the outlier, or outliers, is (or are). Then look at the raw data in the dataset to find the countries that are outliers for each variable.

## Chapter 4

USING SAMPLE CROSSTABS TO TALK ABOUT POPULATIONS: THE CHI-SQUARE TEST

This chapter covers . . .

. . . why sampling and inference are important to social researchers

. . . what expected frequencies are, and how to calculate them

. . . how to calculate a chi-square value, and what to do with it once you have it

. . . the very important concept of statistical significance

. . . the importance of sample size in a chi-square test

. . . how the chi-square test is based on a chi-square probability distribution

. . . how researchers used chi-square to study how people think about their bodies

INTRODUCTION

I dream of the day when all Americans will have microchips implanted in their brains that will allow social scientists like me to poll all of their minds at any time whenever we want. On second thought, perhaps that dream would turn into a nightmare. Such information could be used for nefarious purposes by anyone, from marketing companies to politicians. But strictly from a social science standpoint, wouldn't that be great? We could know at any time exactly what everyone in the population is thinking. The entire population! All 300,000,000-plus Americans! Until that day comes, however, we must rely on sampling. Instead of asking everyone in the population how he or she behaves or how he or she feels about issues, we ask a tiny sliver of them our questions. Then, using a variety of statistical techniques that are covered in this chapter and subsequent chapters, we can take what we *know* about our sample and make *educated claims*, or **inferences**, about the population from which the sample was drawn.

For example, each year that the good people at the General Social Survey (GSS) carry out their survey, they very carefully select a sample of 2,000 to 4,500 Americans from the GSS population of interest: all non-institutionalized Americans aged 18 and older. With this population, we're talking about roughly 200,000,000 people (given that around 70,000,000 Americans are younger 18 years of age, and millions more are in various institutions, such as prisons, psychiatric wards, etc.). So how can a sample of 2,000 adequately represent 200,000,000? 2,000 divided by 200,000,000 is 0.00001, 0.001%. Can a measly 0.001% of the population of Americans really speak on behalf of all Americans? According to the laws of sampling, as long as the sample is carefully drawn, the answer is *yes*.

Although this is not the place to get into all of these laws (entire courses are taught on sampling theory and techniques), one is very worthy of mention: all members of the population must have some chance of getting into the sample. You intuitively know that it would be wrong to stand in front of the school library, take a sample of students, and expect it to represent the entire student body. You know that such a technique would eliminate the possibility of some students getting into the sample. Some students never even get near the library (and may even take great pride in that fact). A better technique would be find a complete **sampling frame**. Similar to a good picture frame containing the entire picture, a good sampling frame contains all the cases from which you want to sample. You could go to the registrar's office and get an official list of all students. With that list, you could use some sort of random procedure to choose your sample, knowing that everyone on this list had a chance of getting into the sample.

The large national surveys use highly scientific and detailed techniques to choose their samples. For example, the document that describes how the General Social Survey draws its samples is 20 pages long (General Social Survey, 2013)! One technique used by such surveys is called **multistage cluster sampling**. At the first stage, the researchers randomly choose large geographic clusters. At the next stage, within those clusters they randomly choose smaller geographic areas. They carry out more stages, with ever smaller and smaller areas, until they reach the level of the individual. Sometimes these large surveys, for various reasons, will **oversample** particular groups in the population in order to gain adequate numbers of these groups for study. For example, if a researcher were interested in American Indians, a regular random sample would be unlikely to garner enough of them, so he or she might oversample from this specific population. But researchers always keep track of how much they've oversampled so that they can account for this when they start to run their statistical procedures.

This chapter is the first of several that concentrate on statistical inference: making a claim about a population based on information from a sample. Each inferential technique involves numerous steps, so the first time through, it will seem onerous. But keep in mind that the goal for all of these procedures is the same: to see if the relationship we found in our sample data allows us to say that there is a relationship in the population from which the sample was drawn. Inference is important, for it is the major way of connecting samples and populations. Given that most of the data with which you will work will be based on samples rather than populations, inference is key to the claims you'll be making.

A SERIES OF HYPOTHETICAL CROSSTABULATIONS

Imagine two men: Nick and Sam. Nick and Sam are of very different opinions with regard to inference: Nick always claims, regardless of the sample results, regardless of the independent and dependent variables being used, that there is *not* a relationship between our variables in the larger population. In contrast, Sam always claims, regardless of the sample results, that there *is* a relationship between our variables in the larger population. For example, let's say we're interested in examining the relationship between sex and gun ownership. From the population of men and women, we draw a sample of 300 people and get the following results:

■ **Exhibit 4.1: A Hypothetical Crosstab of Gun Ownership by Sex**

	MEN	WOMEN	
OWN GUN	100 *100%*	0 *0%*	100 *33%*
NO GUN	0 *0%*	200 *100%*	200 *66%*
	100	200	300

Nick and Sam both examine these results. Nick says, "Based on these sample results, there's no way that there's a relationship between sex and guns in the population!" Sam says, "Based on these sample results, there's definitely a relationship between sex and guns in the population!" What does your gut say? It sides with Sam, right? The differences in the crosstab based on sample results are so very clear that you feel completely confident saying that in the population there is a relationship between sex and guns. How could there not be? If there weren't a relationship in the population, then how on earth could we take a sample and get these results? Sorry, Nick, but you're wrong.

What if we had taken a sample of 300 people and instead these were the results:

■ **Exhibit 4.2: A Second Hypothetical Crosstab of Gun Ownership by Sex**

	MEN	WOMEN	
OWN GUN	25 25%	50 25%	75 25%
NO GUN	75 75%	150 75%	225 75%
	100	200	300

Nick and Sam both examine these results. Nick says, "Based on these sample results, there's no way that there's a relationship between sex and guns in the population!" Sam says, "Based on these sample results, there's definitely a relationship between sex and guns in the population!" What does your gut say? It sides with Nick, right? The crosstab tells us that in our sample men and women were equally likely to own a gun: overall, 25% (75/300) of the respondents owned a gun. Among men, 25% (25/100) owned a gun. Among women, 25% (50/200) owned a gun. In the sample, men and women were *equally likely* to own a gun. So to claim that, in the population, there is a relationship between sex and guns, that men and women in the population somehow differ in gun ownership, would be positively ludicrous. Sorry, Sam, but you're wrong.

Now imagine that these were our results:

■ Exhibit 4.3: A Third Hypothetical Crosstab of Gun Ownership by Sex

	MEN	WOMEN	
OWN GUN	56 *56%*	91 *44.5%*	147 *49%*
NO GUN	44 *44%*	109 *55.5%*	153 *51%*
	100	200	300

Nick and Sam both examine these results. Nick says, "Based on these sample results, there's no way that there's a relationship between sex and guns in the population!" Sam says, "Based on these sample results, there's definitely a relationship between sex and guns in the population!" Now what does your gut say? Ah, it's torn between siding with Nick and siding with Sam, isn't it? The percentage of men who have guns is indeed higher than the percentage of women who have guns—11.5% higher. But here is the key question: Is this difference we observe in the sample *large enough* so that we can say that there is a relationship in the population? Some might look at these results and side with Nick and say, "No, it's best to be cautious. We should say that these sample results are not clear enough to be able to say with certainty that there is a relationship in the population. We should not claim that, within the population, men are more likely to own guns than women are." Some might look at these results and side with Sam and say, "Yes, there is enough of a relationship in the crosstab. Men and women differ enough in the sample that these results could not have happened simply by chance. There must be a relationship in the population." But, if people have different gut reactions to these results, how can we come to any agreement? Whose gut is right? Whose gut should we trust?

What we're going to do in this chapter is use a standardized gut reaction that we all can agree on. In other words, the results will have to meet a certain standard in order to say that, yes, we are confident that there is a relationship in the population. The way we do this is to compare what we *have observed* in our sample with what we *would expect* if we had taken the sample and there had been absolutely no relationship between the variables. If these differ by enough to meet our standard, then we will say yes, there is a relationship in the population. If what we observed in the sample and what we would expect do not differ by much, then we will say no, there is no relationship in the population.

CALCULATING EXPECTED FREQUENCIES

Before we get to that comparison, we need to figure out how to calculate these **expected frequencies**. Let's look once again at that second crosstab we had:

▨ **Exhibit 4.4: A Crosstab with No Relationship between the Variables**

	MEN	WOMEN	
OWN GUN	25 / 25%	50 / 25%	75 / 25%
NO GUN	75 / 75%	150 / 75%	225 / 75%
	100	200	300

This crosstab represents the situation in which, given the overall number of men and women, and the overall number of gun owners and nonowners, there is no relationship between the variables. What if we just had the marginals?

▨ **Exhibit 4.5: A Crosstab with Only the Marginals**

	MEN	WOMEN	
OWN GUN			75 / 25%
NO GUN			225 / 75%
	100	200	300

How would we go about filling in these cells to elicit no relationship between the variables? Here are the calculations:

25% of the overall people have guns, so we want 25% of the 100 men to have guns:

$0.25 \times 100 = 25$

75% of the overall people don't have guns, so we want 75% of the 100 men to not have guns:

$0.75 \times 100 = 75$

25% of the overall people have guns, so we want 25% of the 200 women to have guns:

$0.25 \times 200 = 50$

75% of the overall people don't have guns, so we want 75% of the 200 women to not have guns:

$0.75 \times 200 = 150$

This gives us what we want:

■ **Exhibit 4.6: A Crosstab Filled with Expected Frequencies**

	MEN	WOMEN	
OWN GUN	25 *25%*	50 *25%*	75 *25%*
NO GUN	75 *75%*	150 *75%*	225 *75%*
	100	200	300

Let's do a couple more of these to make sure you see how to do this. Here's a table with just the marginals:

■ **Exhibit 4.7: A Second Crosstab with Only the Marginals**

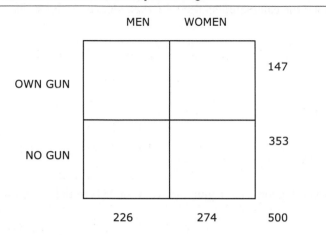

	MEN	WOMEN	
OWN GUN			147
NO GUN			353
	226	274	500

First, we need to figure out the overall percentages for gun ownership:

147/500 = 29.4% of people own guns
353/500 = 70.6% of people don't own guns

So to make sure that there's no difference between men and women, we want

29.4% of the 226 men do have guns: 0.294 × 226 = 66.44
70.6% of the 226 men do not have guns: 0.706 × 226 = 159.56
29.4% of the 274 women do have guns: 0.294 × 274 = 80.56
70.6% of the 274 women do not have guns: 0.706 × 274 = 193.44

■ **Exhibit 4.8: Calculating Expected Frequencies**

	MEN	WOMEN	
OWN GUN	0.294 × 226 66.44	0.294 × 274 80.56	147
NO GUN	0.706 × 226 159.56	0.706 × 274 193.44	353
	226	274	500

It may seem odd to have 0.44 of a person, but we typically keep two numbers after the decimal point. Our completed crosstab of expected values looks like this:

■ **Exhibit 4.9: A Second Crosstab Filled with Expected Frequencies**

	MEN	WOMEN	
OWN GUN	66.44 *29.4%*	80.56 *29.4%*	147 *29.4%*
NO GUN	159.56 *70.6%*	193.44 *70.6%*	353 *70.6%*
	226	274	500

Anyone looking at these sample results would say, "Oh, my, look how similar the men and women in the sample are! Why, it would be positively ludicrous to claim that in the population men and women differ!"

One more, just to make sure you get this. Let's expand the crosstab from a 2 × 2 to a 3 × 2. Instead of sex, we'll use where the person lives as the independent variable:

■ **Exhibit 4.10: A Third Crosstab with Only the Marginals**

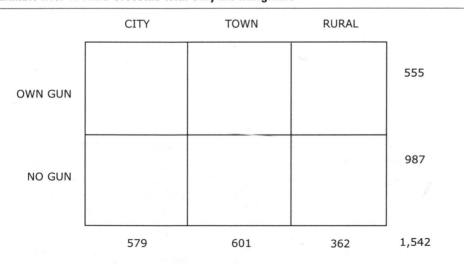

	CITY	TOWN	RURAL	
OWN GUN				555
NO GUN				987
	579	601	362	1,542

First, we calculate the overall percentage of gun owners and nonowners:

555/1,542 = 36% are gun owners
987/1,542 = 64% are not gun owners

Then, we calculate these percentages for each category within the crosstab:

City gun owners: 36% of 579: 0.36 × 579 = 208.44
City gun nonowners: 64% of 579: 0.64 × 579 = 370.56
Town gun owners: 36% of 601: 0.36 × 601 = 216.36
Town gun nonowners: 64% of 601: 0.64 × 601 = 384.64
Rural gun owners: 36% of 362: 0.36 × 362 = 130.32
Rural gun nonowners: 64% of 362: 0.64 × 362 = 231.68

The finished crosstab of expected frequencies looks like the following:

▨ **Exhibit 4.11: A Third Crosstab Filled with Expected Frequencies**

	CITY	TOWN	RURAL	
OWN GUN	208.44 *36%*	216.36 *36%*	130.32 *36%*	555 *36%*
NO GUN	370.56 *64%*	384.64 *64%*	231.68 *64%*	987 *64%*
	579	601	362	1,542

According to this crosstab, do city dwellers have a higher chance than town dwellers of owning a gun? No. Do town dwellers have a higher chance than rural dwellers of owning a gun? No. Do rural dwellers have a higher chance than city dwellers of owning a gun? No. In this table of expected frequencies, geographic area does not affect gun ownership: every group has the same chance of owning a gun as every other group.

INTRODUCING CHI-SQUARE

If you have a crosstab based on sample results, and you want to see if, based on the relationship you observe in your crosstab, you confidently can claim that there is a relationship in the population from which your sample was drawn, the **chi-square test** is the form of inference you likely will use. Chi-square, chi-squared, I've seen both, and I'm not picky. I *am* picky about pronunciation: say *chiropractor* and then take off the *ropractor*. Although I like to drink chai, that's not what we're doing here. Although I appreciate tai chi, that's not what we're doing here. In the world of statistical tests, the chi-square test is a relatively easy one to use. It contrasts the frequencies you observed in the crosstab with the frequencies you would expect if there were no relationship among the variables in your crosstab. It makes this contrast with each cell in the crosstab. We'll use the third sex/gun crosstab from earlier, the one where your gut wasn't completely sure if there was a generalizable relationship. Here it is, with its frequencies expected crosstab next to it:

■ **Exhibit 4.12: Frequencies Observed and Frequencies Expected**

	*F*REQUENCIES *O*BSERVED			*F*REQUENCIES *E*XPECTED	
	MEN	WOMEN		MEN	WOMEN
OWN GUN	56	91	OWN GUN	49	98
NO GUN	44	109	NO GUN	51	102

So let's first find the difference between the frequencies observed (hereafter referred to as f_o) and the frequencies we would expect (hereafter referred to as f_e):

■ **Exhibit 4.13: Differences between Observed and Expected Frequencies**

Cell	f_o	f_e	$f_o - f_e$
Top left	56	49	7
Top right	91	98	−7
Bottom left	44	51	−7
Bottom right	109	102	7

Then we're going to square each of these and divide it by its corresponding f_e:

■ **Exhibit 4.14: Calculating the Chi-Square Value**

Cell	f_o	f_e	$f_o - f_e$	$(f_o - f_e)^2$	$(f_o - f_e)^2/f_e$
Top left	56	49	7	49	1.00
Top right	91	98	−7	49	0.50
Bottom left	44	51	−7	49	0.96
Bottom right	109	102	7	49	0.48

The sum of the last column of numbers is our value for chi-square:

$1.00 + 0.50 + 0.96 + 0.48 = 2.94$

Here is the formula for what we just did:

$$\chi^2 = \sum \frac{(f_o - f_e)^2}{f_e}$$

Notice that the symbol for chi-square is χ^2. It looks like an x with some attitude. Our chi-square value of 2.94 is not an end in itself but rather a means to an end. For now we are going to go shopping, or at least an activity that I consider similar to shopping. When you go shopping (let's say shirt shopping, because everyone loves shirts), you go into a store with one thing (money) and you come out of the store with something else (a shirt). We exchange the money (which really has no use of its own) for something of use (shirts are very useful). What we're going to do now with our chi-square value is quite similar:

Take money ➔ Go into store ➔ Exchange money for shirt
Take χ^2 value ➔ Go into χ^2 table ➔ Exchange χ^2 value for p-value

So we have our chi-square value of 2.94. We take that value into the chi-square table, which is in Appendix C, or you can type "Chi-Square Table" into your Internet browser and one will pop up. We'll look at more of the whole table in a while, but for now here is the first line of it:

■ **Exhibit 4.15: An Excerpt from the Chi-Square Table**

p-value	.20	.10	.05	.02	.01	.001
chi-square value	1.64	2.71	3.84	5.41	6.64	10.83

Within the chi-square table, we're going to play a game called "Let's see how far to the right we can get." With our value of 2.94, we start at the left. Our value of 2.94 is greater than 1.64. So we can move to the right. Our value of 2.94 is greater than 2.71. So we can move to the right. Our value of 2.94 is less than 3.84. Awwww! Because we cannot reach this level, the farthest to the right we can get is that second set of numbers. Our conclusion, then, is that $p < .10$. But we cannot say that $p < .05$, and this point, where $p < .05$, is important, because it is our cutoff for *statistical significance*.

STATISTICAL SIGNIFICANCE

Statistical significance is a very important concept in inference. As a first explanation of this concept, I want to return to our friends from earlier in the chapter, Nick and Sam. They'll help us understand a set of related concepts: type I error and type II error. Remember that Sam erred on the side of saying that, regardless of the sample results, there *was* a relationship in the population. Clearly, he's going to be wrong quite a bit when he says this. For example, based on the second crosstab from earlier, it's ludicrous to say that there is a relationship in the population. By saying that there *is* a relationship in the population when there *is not* a relationship in the population, Sam is making what we call a **type I error**.

Nick, in contrast, erred on the side of saying that, regardless of the sample results, there was *not* a relationship in the population. Clearly, he's going to be wrong sometimes. For example, based on the first crosstab from earlier, it was ludicrous of Nick to say that there is not a relationship in the population when our sample results so clearly suggested otherwise. By saying that there *is not* a relationship in the population when there *is* a relationship in the population, Nick is making what we call a **type II error**.

We're going to try our best to avoid the type of error Sam makes: we do not want to say that there *is* a relationship in the population when in fact there *is not* one. This is where the *p*-value comes in. The *p* stands for *probability*, and it is the probability of making a type I error: it is the probability of claiming that there is a relationship in the population when in fact there is not one. In the social sciences, the typical standard we use is $p < .05$. That is, we want the chance of a type I error to be below 5%. If the chance of making such an error is 5% or above, we conclude that there is not a relationship in the population. We might be making a type II error, but in most cases, we'd rather make a type II error than a type I error. The following summarizes the connections:

■ **Exhibit 4.16: From Differences to Chi-Square Value to *p*-Value**

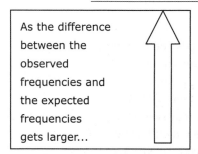 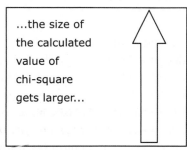 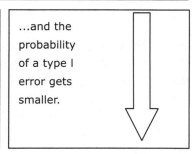

| As the difference between the observed frequencies and the expected frequencies gets larger... | ...the size of the calculated value of chi-square gets larger... | ...and the probability of a type I error gets smaller. |

With our chi-square value of 2.94, the lowest *p*-value we could achieve was $p < .10$. Our chi-square value was not high enough to allow us to get to the *p*-value of $p < .05$. Therefore, with these results, we conclude that there is not a relationship between sex and gun ownership in the population.

What if just two more men did own a gun and two more women did not own a gun? That is, what if our results looked like this:

■ **Exhibit 4.17: Revised Frequencies Observed**

FREQUENCIES **O**BSERVED

	MEN	WOMEN
OWN GUN	58	89
NO GUN	42	111

FREQUENCIES **E**XPECTED

	MEN	WOMEN
OWN GUN	49	98
NO GUN	51	102

Noticed what happened here: the observed frequencies became *more different* from the expected frequencies. For example, in the original results, the difference between the top-left cells was $56 - 49 = 7$. Now the difference between the top-left cells is $58 - 49 = 9$. It's the same for the other cells. Is this increased difference between the f_os and f_es big enough to allow us to claim that there is a relationship in the population? Let's recalculate our chi-square value:

■ **Exhibit 4.18: Recalculating the Chi-Square Value**

Cell	f_o	f_e	$f_o - f_e$	$(f_o - f_e)^2$	$(f_o - f_e)^2/f_e$
Top left	58	49	9	81	1.65
Top right	89	98	−9	81	0.83
Bottom left	42	51	−9	81	1.59
Bottom right	111	102	9	81	0.79

Now our chi-square value is $1.65 + 0.83 + 1.59 + 0.79 = 4.86$.

Next, we take this 4.86 and go to the chi-square table and exchange it for a *p*-value:

■ **Exhibit 4.19: An Excerpt from the Chi-Square Table, Again**

p-value	.20	.10	.05	.02	.01	.001
chi-square value	1.64	2.71	3.84	5.41	6.64	10.83

Can we get past 1.64? Yes!
Can we get past 2.71? Yes!
Can we get past 3.84? Yes!
Can we get past 5.41? No.

Therefore, because we can't get up to that 5.41, we stop at the previous value and our *p*-conclusion is $p < .05$. With our *p*-value below .05, we confidently can conclude that, based on these sample results, there is a relationship in the population between sex and gun ownership. Reflect on what happened here: the differences between our observed frequencies moved farther away from our expected frequencies, far enough away that we are able to achieve **statistical significance**. There is less than a 5% chance of making a type I error, and we can live with that chance. Had our chi-square value been higher than 6.63, then our p-conclusion would have been $p < .01$, meaning that there would have been less than a 1% chance of making a type I error, which would have been even better. But we're satisfied with $p < .05$.

THE EFFECT OF SAMPLE SIZE

Chi-square depends heavily on sample size. To get this point across, I created 44 crosstabs. In the first crosstab, where the total sample size is 40, there is no difference between the two groups: the percentages in the first two cells are 50% and 50%. In the next crosstab (one to the right), I moved one person from the lower-left cell up to the upper-left cell, and this gives me a 5% difference: the percentages in the first two cells are 55% and 50%. In each subsequent crosstab to the right, I adjusted the frequencies to add an additional 5% difference. In the 11th crosstab, all the way to the right, there is a 50% difference: the percentages in the first two cells are 100% and 50%. Then, in the next three rows of crosstabs, I increased the sample size: from 40, to 80, to 120, to 160. Notice that each column has the same percentages: 11/20 and 22/40 are both 55%. With 11 crosstabs across and four different sample sizes, this gives me 44 crosstabs. Then I calculated the chi-square value for each crosstab and traded the chi-square value for the p-conclusion. The p-conclusions are signified in the 44 crosstabs by shading:

No shading: not significant (chi-square value didn't reach $p < .05$ level)
Light shading: $p < .05$
Medium shading: $p < .01$
Dark shading: $p < .001$

▪ **Exhibit 4.20: Illustrating the Effect of Sample Size on Chi-Square**

0% diff.	5% diff.	10% diff.	15% diff.	20% diff.	25% diff.	30% diff.	35% diff.	40% diff.	45% diff.	50% diff.
10 | 10 10 | 10 $\chi^2 = 0$	11 | 10 9 | 10 $\chi^2 = 0.1$	12 | 10 8 | 10 $\chi^2 = 0.4$	13 | 10 7 | 10 $\chi^2 = 0.9$	14 | 10 6 | 10 $\chi^2 = 1.7$	15 | 10 5 | 10 $\chi^2 = 2.7$	16 | 10 4 | 10 $\chi^2 = 4$	17 | 10 3 | 10 $\chi^2 = 5.6$	18 | 10 2 | 10 $\chi^2 = 7.6$	19 | 10 1 | 10 $\chi^2 = 10$	20 | 10 0 | 10 $\chi^2 = 13$
20 | 20 20 | 20 $\chi^2 = 0$	22 | 20 18 | 20 $\chi^2 = 0.2$	24 | 20 16 | 20 $\chi^2 = 0.8$	26 | 20 14 | 20 $\chi^2 = 1.8$	28 | 20 12 | 20 $\chi^2 = 3.3$	30 | 20 10 | 20 $\chi^2 = 5.3$	32 | 20 8 | 20 $\chi^2 = 7.9$	34 | 20 6 | 20 $\chi^2 = 11$	36 | 20 4 | 20 $\chi^2 = 15$	38 | 20 2 | 20 $\chi^2 = 20$	40 | 20 0 | 20 $\chi^2 = 27$
30 | 30 30 | 30 $\chi^2 = 0$	33 | 30 27 | 30 $\chi^2 = 0.3$	36 | 30 24 | 30 $\chi^2 = 1.2$	39 | 30 21 | 30 $\chi^2 = 2.8$	42 | 30 18 | 30 $\chi^2 = 5$	45 | 30 15 | 30 $\chi^2 = 8$	48 | 30 12 | 30 $\chi^2 = 12$	51 | 30 9 | 30 $\chi^2 = 17$	54 | 30 6 | 30 $\chi^2 = 23$	57 | 30 3 | 30 $\chi^2 = 30$	60 | 30 0 | 30 $\chi^2 = 40$
40 | 40 40 | 40 $\chi^2 = 0$	44 | 40 36 | 40 $\chi^2 = 0.4$	48 | 40 32 | 40 $\chi^2 = 1.6$	52 | 40 28 | 40 $\chi^2 = 3.7$	56 | 40 24 | 40 $\chi^2 = 6.7$	60 | 40 20 | 40 $\chi^2 = 11$	64 | 40 16 | 40 $\chi^2 = 16$	68 | 40 12 | 40 $\chi^2 = 22$	72 | 40 8 | 40 $\chi^2 = 30$	76 | 40 4 | 40 $\chi^2 = 41$	80 | 40 0 | 40 $\chi^2 = 53$

With a sample size of only 40, the first crosstab that achieves statistical significance at the $p < .05$ level is the one with a 30% difference. The first crosstab that achieves statistical significance at the $p < .01$ level is the one with a 40% difference. With a small sample, it takes a large difference between the groups in order to achieve statistical significance. If we double the sample size, we achieve statistical significance with less of a difference. With a sample size of 80, the first crosstab that achieves statistical significance at the $p < .05$ level is the one with the 25% difference, and statistical significance at the $p < .01$ level is achieved with a 30% difference. With a sample size of 120, we achieve statistical significance even sooner: significance at the $p < .05$ level with a 20% difference, and significance at the $p < .01$ level with a 25% difference. Whereas with a 25% difference with a sample size of 40 we did not even achieve statistical significance, with a 25% difference with a sample size of 160, we achieve statistical significance at the $p < .001$ level. Sample size really matters.

In fact, it raises an issue that will come up again throughout the book: you need to keep a wary eye on statistical significance when large samples are involved. For example, if we took the second crosstab in Exhibit 4.20, the one with a 5% difference between the groups, the one with a chi-square value of 0.1, and we multiplied the frequencies by 50 (i.e., the cells were 550, 500, 450, and 500), this would elicit a chi-square value of 5.00, significant at the $p < .05$ level. Although the difference between the groups is only 5%, obtaining this difference with such a large sample elicits statistical significance. Never look only at statistical significance; always examine the substantive difference as well. This is particularly important in this age of massive datasets with millions of cases.

CHI-SQUARE WITH LARGER CROSSTABS

So far, we've used chi-square with 2×2 crosstabs, but chi-square works for larger crosstabs, too: 2×3, 3×4, 5×5, just to name a few. However, when we have a larger crosstab, the values we use from the chi-square table are different. The bigger the crosstab, the bigger the values you need to achieve statistical significance. Because of the way the chi-square table is set up, you need to know how many **degrees of freedom** your crosstab has. This is a simple concept to understand, and a simple number to find. A 2×2 crosstab has 1 degree of freedom, and here's why. Let's say we have a crosstab with the marginals filled in, plus one of the cells:

■ **Exhibit 4.21: A 2 × 2 Crosstab with the Marginals and One Cell Filled In**

25		30
		20
40	10	

Based on this information, using subtraction, we can fill in some of the cells:

■ **Exhibit 4.22: Filling in Two More Cells with Subtraction**

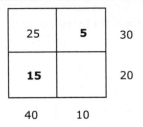

But, if we know those two, then we also can figure out that last cell, either by subtracting 5 from 10 or by subtracting 15 from 20. Therefore, we are free to fill in only one cell before the other cells are spoken for, thus the term 1 degree of freedom. What if we had a 3 × 2 crosstab with one cell filled in?

■ **Exhibit 4.23: A 3 × 2 Crosstab with the Marginals and One Cell Filled In**

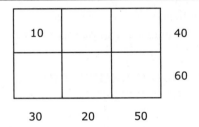

With this information, what else is spoken for? Only one other cell:

■ **Exhibit 4.24: Filling in One Cell with Subtraction**

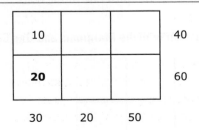

But that's it. We can't fill in the other cells yet; we simply don't have enough information. However, if we fill in just one more cell with a number (16), the rest of the cells become spoken for:

■ **Exhibit 4.25: Filling in the Rest of the Crosstab**

10	**16**	14	40
20	4	36	60
30	20	50	

The 14 is simply $40 - 10 - 16$. The 4 is simply $20 - 16$. And, with these two cells filled in, we know that the last empty cell has to have a 36 in it, because $60 - 20 - 4 = 36$, or $50 - 14 = 36$. Therefore, this 3×2 crosstab has 2 degrees of freedom: we were able to fill in two cells before all the other cells are spoken for. We could play around this way with larger crosstabs, and you're welcome to do so yourself, but here's a quick formula that works just fine:

$df = (\text{# of rows} - 1) \times (\text{# of columns} - 1)$

So, for the 3×2, $df = (3 - 1) \times (2 - 1) = 2 \times 1 = 2$
For a 3×4 crosstab, $df = (3 - 1)(4 - 1) = 2 \times 3 = 6$

Here is a larger excerpt from the chi-square table:

■ **Exhibit 4.26: A Larger Excerpt from the Chi-Square Table**

p-value	.20	.10	.05	.02	.01	.001
$df = 1$	1.64	2.71	3.84	5.41	6.64	10.83
$df = 2$	3.22	4.61	5.99	7.82	9.21	13.82
$df = 3$	4.64	6.25	7.82	9.84	11.34	16.27
$df = 4$	5.99	7.78	9.49	11.67	13.28	18.47

For example, if you have a 3×3 table (where $df = 4$), you'd need to achieve a chi-square value greater than 9.49 in order to claim statistical significance at the $p < .05$ level. Why do larger crosstabs require larger chi-square values to achieve significance? I'll explain this later. But first, a couple of GSS examples.

GSS EXAMPLE: GUN OWNERSHIP AND SEX

Let's run through the whole procedure from start to finish, this time using real GSS 2012 data. Here is the gun and sex crosstab using GSS respondents who are younger 50 years of age:

■ **Exhibit 4.27: Gun Ownership by Sex Crosstab Using GSS Data**

	MEN	WOMEN	
OWN GUN	103 *33.1%*	107 *27.4%*	210 *30.0%*
NO GUN	208 *66.9%*	283 *72.6%*	491 *70.0%*
	311	390	701

Source: GSS 2012; only respondents under 50 years old.

It's definitely one of those crosstabs that makes our guts go "Hmmm." There is a difference between the two groups in the crosstab, but is the difference large enough to say that there is a difference in the population? The next step is to find the expected frequencies. We could, as we did earlier, calculate the overall percentages and then find these same percentages of the men and women. But here is a slightly different way of accomplishing this. To find the expected frequency for a particular cell, multiply the cell's corresponding column total by the cell's corresponding row total and then divide by the total sample size for the crosstab. Here are these calculations for the four cells:

Expected frequency for upper left cell: $311 \times 210/701 = 93.17$
Expected frequency for upper right cell: $390 \times 210/701 = 116.83$
Expected frequency for lower left cell: $311 \times 491/701 = 217.83$
Expected frequency for lower right cell: $390 \times 491/701 = 273.17$

This accomplishes the exact same thing as the other procedure. The only difference is that we're multiplying and dividing in a different order.

Now we have our two tables:

■ Exhibit 4.28: Observed GSS Frequencies and Expected Frequencies

	FREQUENCIES OBSERVED			FREQUENCIES EXPECTED	
	MEN	WOMEN		MEN	WOMEN
OWN GUN	103	107	OWN GUN	93.17	116.83
NO GUN	208	283	NO GUN	217.83	273.17

And now the calculations to get the chi-square value:

■ Exhibit 4.29: Calculating Chi-Square

Cell	f_o	f_e	$f_o - f_e$	$(f_o - f_e)^2$	$(f_o - f_e)^2 / f_e$
Top left	103	93.17	9.83	96.63	1.04
Top right	107	116.83	−9.83	96.63	0.83
Bottom left	208	217.83	−9.83	96.63	0.44
Bottom right	283	273.17	9.83	96.63	0.35

Summing up the last column, we get our chi-square value: 2.66.

We go to the chi-square table and, because we have a 2 × 2 table, we have 1 degree of freedom:

■ Exhibit 4.30: An Excerpt from the Chi-Square Table, Again

p-value	.20	.10	.05	.02	.01	.001
chi-square value	1.64	2.71	3.84	5.41	6.64	10.83

Is 2.66 > 1.64? Yes!
Is 2.66 > 2.71? No.

Therefore, we do not achieve the significance level of $p < .05$. We cannot claim, based on the crosstab, that there is a difference in the populations of men and women who are younger than 50 years old.

But what about those 50 years or older? Here's another crosstab:

■ Exhibit 4.31: Gun Ownership by Sex Crosstab Using GSS Data

	MEN	WOMEN	
OWN GUN	129 *50.2%*	101 *31.8%*	230 *40.0%*
NO GUN	128 *49.8%*	217 *68.2%*	345 *60.0%*
	257	318	575

Source: GSS 2012; only respondents 50 years old and older.

Among these older GSS respondents, there is a large difference between men and women: more than half of the men own guns, whereas fewer than a third of the women do. If your gut thinks the chi-square test on this crosstab elicits statistical significance, your gut is correct. The resulting chi-square value is 20.12, which allows us to go all the way to the right on the chi-square table to the p-conclusion of $p < .001$. Among older people, we can comfortably conclude that a difference exists between the population of men and the population of women.

GSS EXAMPLE: AGE AND CYNICISM

The purpose of this example is to bring to your attention something that sometimes happens in crosstabs larger than 2×2. Following is a 4×2 crosstab using 2012 GSS data. The GSS asked the respondents, "Generally speaking, would you say that most people can be trusted or that you can't be too careful in life?" With the idea that younger people are more optimistic, I decided to use this as my dependent variable, with respondent's age as the independent variable. Here is what I found:

■ **Exhibit 4.32: Crosstab of Cynicism by Age with Four Age Categories**

OFFERED SEAT TO STRANGER * AGE IN FOUR CATEGORIES Crosstabulation

		AGE IN FOUR CATEGORIES				
		18–33	34–47	48–61	62+	Total
CAN PEOPLE BE TRUSTED	CAN TRUST	66	103	110	143	431
		20.8%	32.9%	37.4%	43.7%	33.8%
	CANNOT TRUST	251	210	199	184	844
		79.2%	67.1%	62.6%	56.3%	66.2%
Total		317	313	318	327	1275
		100.0%	100.0%	100.0%	100.0%	100.0%

Source: GSS 2012 data.

I was wrong about younger people, as the opposite is true: the trend is that the younger you are, the *more* cynical you are. A chi-square test on this crosstab gives us a chi-square value of 40.25. With a 4 × 2 crosstab, we have 3 degrees of freedom, so according to the chi-square table, we needed to get above 7.81 to achieve statistical significance. We do so with ease, so we can conclude that in the population from which the GSS sample was drawn, there is a relationship between age and cynicism. In fact, our *p*-conclusion is all the way to the right: $p < .001$. However, look carefully at the cells of the crosstab. Although there is a clear trend along all of the age groups, it's the youngest group that really differs from the other groups. What would happen if we removed this group from the crosstab, as I did in the following.

■ **Exhibit 4.33: Crosstab of Cynicism by Age with Three Age Categories**

CAN PEOPLE BE TRUSTED * AGE IN THREE CATEGORIES Crosstabulation

		AGE IN THREE CATEGORIES			
		34–47	48–61	62+	Total
CAN PEOPLE BE TRUSTED	CAN TRUST	103	119	143	365
		32.9%	37.4%	43.7%	38.1%
	CANNOT TRUST	210	199	184	593
		67.1%	62.6%	56.3%	61.9%
Total		313	318	327	958
		100.0%	100.0%	100.0%	100.0%

Source: GSS 2012 data.

Taking out the youngest group has quite an effect. The chi-square value for this revised crosstab is 8.04, which is a big reduction from the previous chi-square value of 40.25. With a 3×2 crosstab, we have 2 degrees of freedom, so we need a chi-square value greater than 5.99 to claim statistical significance. We make that cutoff, although barely. The moral of this little story is that you shouldn't just look at your chi-square value and significance level; you need to keep an eye on what's going on inside the crosstab. Is there one group that is disproportionately contributing to the chi-square value, perhaps even to the point that it is the only cause of statistical significance?

Because I found this cynicism trend depressing, I hoped it might be a fluke finding. I located two other GSS questions that seemed related:

"Do you think most people would try to take advantage of you if they got a chance, or would they try to be fair?"
"Would you say that most of the time people try to be helpful, or that they are mostly just looking out for themselves?"

Unfortunately, it's no fluke. For both of these, the trend remains: the younger you are, the more cynical you are. And both crosstabs elicit huge chi-square values with $p < .001$. So much for youthful idealism.

THE LANGUAGE OF HYPOTHESIS TESTING

In many pieces of research, authors use the "$p < .05$" language to express their results. However, some researchers use a different way of talking about results: the language of hypothesis testing. The conclusion in either case is the same, but the wording of the conclusion is different. With hypothesis testing, a researcher first states what is called the **null hypothesis**, or H_0, and the **alternative hypothesis**, or H_{alt}. The following table illustrates these hypotheses for two of the situations we examined earlier:

▨ **Exhibit 4.34: Null and Alternative Hypotheses**

Research Question	Null Hypothesis (H_0)	Alternative Hypothesis (H_{alt})
Do men and women differ in gun ownership?	Men and women do *not* differ in gun ownership.	Men and women *do* differ in gun ownership.
Do people of different ages differ in cynicism?	People of different ages do *not* differ in cynicism.	People of different ages *do* differ in cynicism.

As you see, H_0 and H_{alt} are opposites. With the chi-square test, we are pitting one hypothesis against the other. If the chi-square test proves to be statistically insignificant, with p being at .05 or higher, we fail to reject H_0. In other words, we cannot say that there is a difference in the population; we have to conclude that there is *not* a difference. If the chi-square test proves to be statistically significant, with p being below 0.05, we conclude that we can reject H_0 in favor of H_{alt}. In other words, we *can* say that there is a difference in the population. Let's take a moment to make some connections here: if your observed frequencies don't differ enough from the frequencies you would have expected if there were no difference, you will have a low chi-square value and a p greater than .05, and you will fail to reject H_0, which claims that there is no difference. So, if you hear people using this language, don't let it throw you. It's actually quite similar to p-style conclusions.

THE CHI-SQUARE DISTRIBUTION

Now that we've gone through the chi-square procedure a few times, I want to talk about what's really going on here. Where do these various "significance cutoffs" come from? How can we claim that a difference is large enough to be considered statistically significant? To address these questions, I'm going to reverse what we've been doing. Instead of starting with a sample and then saying something about the population from which it is drawn, I'm going to show you a population and then draw samples from it. Let's say we have a small town whose entire population is 300 people, and we're able to ask all 300 of them whether they own a gun. We get the following crosstab for the population:

■ **Exhibit 4.35: Crosstab of Gun Ownership by Sex for a Hypothetical Population**

	MEN	WOMEN	
OWN GUN	42 *35.0%*	63 *35.0%*	105 *35.0%*
NO GUN	78 *65.0%*	117 *65.0%*	195 *65.0%*
	120	180	300

Source: Hypothetical data.

Notice that in this population crosstab, the two groups do not differ: the population of men and the population of women each have a 35% chance of owning a gun.

From this population, I randomly drew a sample of 100 people and created a crosstab based on my sample information:

▨ **Exhibit 4.36: Crosstab of Gun Ownership by Sex for First Sample**

	MEN	WOMEN	
OWN GUN	13 *37.1%*	23 *35.4%*	36 *36.0%*
NO GUN	22 *62.9%*	42 *64.6%*	64 *64.0%*
	35	65	100

Source: Hypothetical data.

Notice how similar the sample results are to the population. From a population where men and women were similarly gun owning, I drew a sample, and surprise, surprise, the men and women in the sample were similarly gun owning. Using this sample crosstab, I calculated the value for chi-square, and it was a very small 0.03. From this same population, I randomly drew a second sample of 100 people, and this is the crosstab that resulted:

▨ **Exhibit 4.37: Crosstab of Gun by Sex for Second Sample**

	MEN	WOMEN	
OWN GUN	18 *48.6%*	19 *30.2%*	37 *37.0%*
NO GUN	19 *51.4%*	44 *69.8%*	63 *63.0%*
	37	63	100

Source: Hypothetical data.

Interesting. This sample was drawn from the same population as the first sample, but it looks much different. In fact, it suggests that there is a difference between men and women. Using this sample crosstab, I calculated the value for chi-square, and it was 3.42. Using this same population of 300, I did this eight more times: I took a random sample of 100 people, built a crosstab, and calculated a chi-square value based on that crosstab. Here is what happened:

■ **Exhibit 4.38: 10 Chi-Square Values Based on 10 Samples**

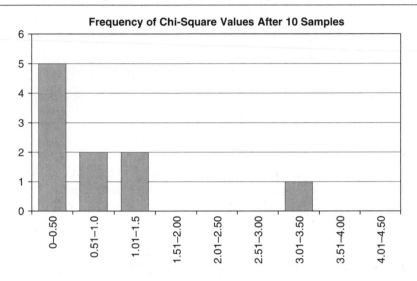

Four of the ten samples were similar to the first, so five of the ten samples resulted in crosstabs that elicited chi-square values between 0 and 0.50. Another two samples had chi-square values between 0.51 and 1.00. Another two samples had chi-square values between 1.01 and 1.50. And then there was that out-of-the-ordinary sample where the chi-square value was 3.42. It's all the way out there to the right. I did all of this again: I drew 10 more samples, created 10 more crosstabs, calculated 10 more chi-square values. Here is a graph with all 20 chi-square values:

▧ **Exhibit 4.39: 20 Chi-Square Values Based on 20 Samples**

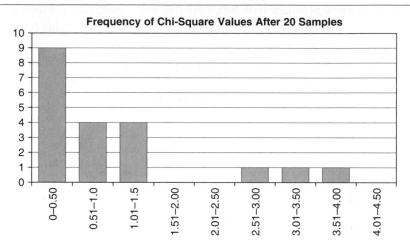

Of the 20 samples, 9 had chi-square values between 0 and 0.50, and 17 had chi-square values of 1.50 or less. As you can see, there was still the occasional odd sample that elicited a higher chi-square value, but this didn't happen very often. Oh, what the heck, let's add 80 more samples into the mix!

▧ **Exhibit 4.40: 100 Chi-Square Values Based on 100 Samples**

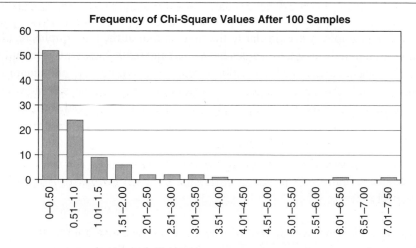

Things are shaping up nicely. More than half of the 100 samples had very low chi-square values of 0.50 or below. Of the samples, 95 had chi-square values of 3.00 or less. But the out of the ordinary occurred again, with one sample each on the sixes and the sevens. One more time, and I promise, that's it. Another 100 samples, another 100 crosstabs, another 100 chi-square values:

■ **Exhibit 4.41: 200 Chi-Square Values Based on 200 Samples**

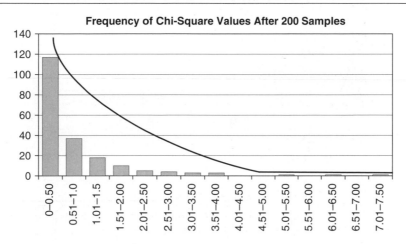

I drew in a line to help illustrate the shape of what we have here: a chi-square distribution that illustrates how the chi-square values are distributed if samples are taken from a population in which the groups don't differ. When we draw samples from a population in which there is no difference between the groups, we are likely to draw samples in which there is little difference between the groups, and when we draw samples in which there is little difference between the groups, we will end up with very low values of chi-square. In the chi-square distribution, most of the chi-square values are very small, and only a very few chi-square values are above 4.00. To reiterate what's going on here:

If there is no difference between groups in a population, then there is a very small probability that there will be large difference between groups in a sample taken from this population.

But remember that the overall goal of inference is to use a sample to say something about a population. So let's take the preceding claim and flip it around:

If there is a large difference between groups in a sample taken from a population, then there is a very small probability that there is no difference between the groups in the population.

Now we can get a better idea of where these critical values of chi-square come from. If we kept taking more and more samples, eventually the distribution would look something like this:

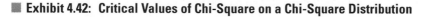

■ **Exhibit 4.42: Critical Values of Chi-Square on a Chi-Square Distribution**

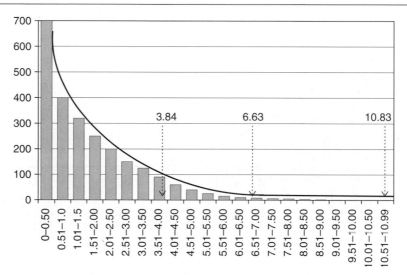

If our 2 × 2 crosstab elicits a chi-square value of just over 3.84, we can see in this distribution that such a chi-square value is unlikely to occur if there is no relationship in the population. Therefore, we can say at the $p < .05$ level of confidence that there is a relationship in the population. If our crosstab had a chi-square value of just more than 6.63, we see that such a chi-square value is very unlikely to occur, so this allows us to say at the $p < .01$ level of confidence that there is a relationship in the population. Finally, if our crosstab had a very large chi-square value, say, 11.00, we see that such a chi-square value is very, very, very unlikely to occur, so this gets us to the $p < .001$ level of confidence.

We can also use a chi-square distribution to understand why larger crosstabs require larger values of chi-square in order to achieve statistical significance. Although I will spare you most of the details, I went through the same 200-sample procedure that I went through earlier, but this time, I used a 3 × 3 crosstab instead of a 2 × 2. Here is the distribution of the 200 values of chi-square using a 3 × 3 crosstab:

■ **Exhibit 4.43: A Chi-Square Distribution Based on a 3 × 3 Crosstab**

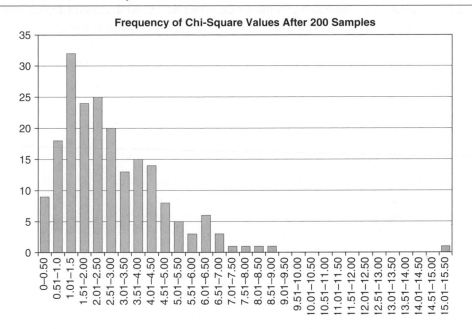

Notice that the chi-square values are, on average, larger in this distribution. For example, in the distribution made from the 2 × 2 crosstab, by the time you get to chi-square values of 3.00, more than 95% of the 200 samples are accounted for. But in the distribution made from the 3 × 3 crosstab, by the time you get to 3.00, only 64% of the 200 samples are accounted for. Why does this happen? Well, nine values contribute to the chi-square value in a 3 × 3 crosstab, rather than four values with a 2 × 2 crosstab. Also, because the frequencies in the nine cells are likely smaller than they would be in four cells, there is more room for random fluctuations. Therefore, with a 3 × 3 crosstab, in order to make a claim with $p < .05$ confidence, we need a chi-square value larger than 9.49, and to get all the way to $p < .001$, we'd need it to be larger than 18.47.

GSS EXAMPLE: CATHOLIC CONFIDENCE IN ORGANIZED RELIGION

The sex scandals in the Catholic Church that occurred in the early 2000s sent shock-waves through American Catholic communities. Were these shockwaves powerful enough to affect Catholics' overall confidence in organized religion? What we are going to do here is use time as our independent variable, and look at confidence in organized religion in the year 2000 (before the sex scandals broke) and the year 2012 (after the sex scandals broke). Our dependent variable will be a GSS variable called CONCLERG, which asked people to assess their confidence in organized religion and gave them three choices: "a great deal," "only some," and "hardly any." To get you more accustomed to that hypothesis-testing language, I'll state my null and alternative hypotheses:

Null hypothesis
There is no difference in Catholic attitudes between 2000 and 2012.

Alternative hypothesis
There *is* a difference in Catholic attitudes between 2000 and 2012.

Here is the output from SPSS. If you want to carry out the math by hand, feel free. Remember that this crosstab includes only Catholics:

■ **Exhibit 4.44: Confidence in Organized Religion by Year**

CONFIDENCE IN ORGANIZED RELIGION * GSS YEAR FOR THIS RESPONDENT
Crosstabulation

| | | GSS YEAR FOR THIS RESPONDENT | | Total |
		2000	2012	
CONFIDENCE IN ORGANIZED RELIGION	A GREAT DEAL	144	77	221
		32.3%	27.1%	30.3%
	ONLY SOME	242	162	404
		54.3%	57.0%	55.3%
	HARDLY ANY	60	45	105
		13.5%	15.8%	14.4%
Total		446	284	730
		100.0%	100.0%	100.0%

Source: GSS 2012 data, only Catholic respondents.

Looking first at the percentages, there does appear to be a loss of confidence between these two years. But they are rather small moves: a 5.2% decrease in those who have a great deal of confidence, a 2.3% increase in those who have hardly any confidence. Are these differences in the sample large enough to claim that there is a trend in the population of Catholics? According to the chi-square test, no. Our chi-square value is 2.47 and, with 2 degrees of freedom, this does not achieve statistical significance (the *p*-value is about .29). Therefore, we accept the null hypothesis and conclude that, in the population of Catholics, there was not a change in attitudes between 2000 and 2012.

Now we are going to engage in that process called *elaboration*: running the same crosstab within different groups of people. My hypothesis is that this trend might look different for men and women. My hunch here is that there might be more of a trend among the female Catholics. Because the church scandals involved the sexual abuse of children, and because women are very protective of their children, Catholic women's confidence in organized religion might have been shaken. I'm not saying that fathers aren't protective of their children, but culturally, mothers are typically depicted as being more protective. We run the same crosstab that we ran earlier, but we run it separately for men and for women. Here are the resulting crosstabs:

■ **Exhibit 4.45: Confidence by Year, Controlling for Sex**

			GSS YEAR FOR THIS RESPONDENT		
			2000	2012	Total
MALE	CONFIDENCE IN ORGANIZED RELIGION	A GREAT DEAL	60	44	104
			29.6%	33.1%	31.0%
		ONLY SOME	118	69	187
			58.1%	51.9%	55.7%
		HARDLY ANY	25	20	45
			12.3%	15.0%	13.4%
	Total		203	133	336
			100.0%	100.0%	100.0%
FEMALE	CONFIDENCE IN ORGANIZED RELIGION	A GREAT DEAL	84	33	117
			34.6%	21.9%	29.7%
		ONLY SOME	124	93	217
			51.0%	61.6%	55.1%
		HARDLY ANY	35	25	60
			14.4%	16.6%	15.2%
	Total		243	151	394
			100.0%	100.0%	100.0%

Source: GSS 2012 data, only Catholic respondents.

Among the male Catholics, there haven't been any clear changes. In fact, the chi-square value is a mere 1.33, giving us a *p*-value nowhere near statistical significance. Therefore, we cannot reject the H_0 that men's attitudes haven't changed over time. We conclude that the attitudes among the population of male Catholics haven't changed over time. The women's crosstab looks quite different from the men's. There has been a precipitous drop in the proportion of Catholic women who have a great deal of confidence in organized religion: from 35% in 2000 to 22% in 2012. There has been a corresponding rise in the percentage of women who have only some confidence—from 51% to 62%—and the percentage who have hardly any confidence has risen a bit as well. The real question, however, is can we say that there has been a shift in opinion among the population of Catholic women. The chi-square value for this crosstab is 7.24, which is larger than the 5.99 we would need to claim $p < .05$ statistical significance, but less than the 9.21 we would need to claim $p < .01$ significance. But this is good enough to claim that, yes, there has been a shift in opinion among the population of Catholic women. We have elaborated where the relationship exists and where it does not exist. It exists among Catholic women, but not among Catholic men. Elaboration is an important process in social research.

GSS EXAMPLE: GUNS, AGE, AND SEX

Please visit the book's website (www.routledge.com/cw/linneman) to view a "From Idea to Presentation" video of this example.

Elaboration is so important, in fact, that let's look at one more example of it, picking up on a set of relationships that was suggested in an example earlier in the chapter. There seemed to be something going on with age, sex, and the likelihood of owning a gun. Let's use elaborated crosstabs to flesh this out. We want to see if the relationship between age and gun ownership differs by sex. Here are the necessary GSS2012 crosstabs:

▪ **Exhibit 4.46: Gun Ownership by Age, Controlling for Sex**

			AGE IN FOUR CATEGORIES				
RESPONDENTS SEX			18-33	34-47	48-61	62+	Total
MALE	HAVE GUN IN HOME	YES	44	49	66	73	232
			29.3%	35.3%	43.7%	57.0%	40.8%
		NO	106	90	85	55	336
			70.7%	64.7%	56.3%	43.0%	59.2%
	Total		150	139	151	128	568
			100.0%	100.0%	100.0%	100.0%	100.0%
FEMALE	HAVE GUN IN HOME	YES	43	53	58	54	208
			24.9%	29.6%	32.6%	30.3%	29.4%
		NO	130	126	120	124	500
			75.1%	70.4%	67.4%	69.7%	70.6%
	Total		173	179	178	178	708
			100.0%	100.0%	100.0%	100.0%	100.0%

Source: GSS 2012 data.

In contrast to the "confidence in religion" example earlier, in this example, the relationship exists among men but not women. As we move up in age categories, women's likelihood of gun ownership goes up a bit, but not by much, and even goes back down in the last age category. In the men's crosstab, we see a clear relationship: the likelihood steadily and sharply increases across the age categories, with the oldest men nearly twice as likely to own a gun as were the youngest men. The chi-square value for the women's crosstab is a small 2.67, and nowhere near statistical significance. The men's chi-square value is a whopping 24.42, giving us a significance level of $p < .001$. We conclude that the relationship between age and gun ownership definitely exists among the male population, but not the female population. Granny, get your gun? Not really. Now to finish the chapter with a couple of examples of how chi-square is used in the social research literature.

LITERATURE EXAMPLE: REAL RESEARCH ABOUT POOP, REALLY

I subscribe to a number of academic journals and, while most of them have interesting stuff in them, very few of them cause me to run down the hallway to show my colleagues an article. This piece of research made me do just that. It's a very interesting article by Weinberg and Williams (2005) about gender differences in farting and pooping. Really. The article appeared in the very well-respected journal *Social Problems*. The title of the article is also classic: "Fecal Matters." Really. Much of the article presents very interesting qualitative data with people expressing their concerns over their own farting and pooping, but it also has some quantitative data. The study involved 172 students from a large Midwestern state university. The researchers recruited the students from sociology courses and e-mail distribution lists. The authors wanted to study not only gender differences but also differences related to sexual orientation. Of these 172 students, there were 69 heterosexual women, 32 nonheterosexual women, 52 heterosexual men, and 19 nonheterosexual men.

Here is an abridged version of their Table 1:

▪ **Exhibit 4.47: Pooping and Farting by Sex/Sexuality**

	Hetero. Women	Non-Hetero. Women	Hetero. Men	Non-Hetero. Men
Hearer of poop feels disgust	50.7%	31.3%	28.8%	47.4%
Hearer of poop thinks it's funny	13.0%	6.3%	26.9%	26.3%
"Not uncomfortable" pooping in public restroom	23.2%	31.3%	50.0%	26.3%
Waits until others leave before pooping	66.7%	37.5%	34.6%	73.7%
Flushes repeatedly while pooping	29.0%	12.5%	0.0%	5.6%
"Often" engages in intentional farting	7.2%	12.5%	23.1%	5.3%

Source: Adapted from Weinberg and Williams (2005).

At the bottom of the table is an important footnote: "Using chi-square analyses, all comparisons between the four groups reach the 0.05 level of significance" (Weinberg and Williams, 2005, p. 325). This is typical in research articles. But let's look carefully at what's going on here. We could translate this table into six crosstabs. Let's do this with the row "Waits until others leave before pooping." First, because chi-square relies on frequencies, not percentages, we'll have to convert the percentages to frequencies:

66.7% of 69 heterosexual women is 46.
37.5% of 32 nonheterosexual women is 12.
34.6% of 52 heterosexual men is 18.
73.7% of 19 nonheterosexual men is 14.

Now we can create the crosstab of observed values:

▪ **Exhibit 4.48: Waiting to Poop by Sex/Sexuality, Observed Frequencies**

	HetW	NHetW	HetM	NHetM	
WAITS	46 *66.7%*	12 *37.5%*	18 *34.6%*	14 *73.7%*	90 *52.3%*
DOESN'T WAIT	23 *33.3%*	20 *62.5%*	34 *65.4%*	5 *26.3%*	82 *47.7%*
	69	32	52	19	172

Based on this crosstab, we can create the expected values:

■ Exhibit 4.49: Pooping and Farting by Sex/Sexuality, Expected Frequencies

	HetW	NHetW	HetM	NHetM	
WAITS	36.09 *52.3%*	16.74 *52.3%*	27.20 *52.3%*	9.94 *52.3%*	90 *52.3%*
DOESN'T WAIT	32.91 *47.7%*	15.26 *47.7%*	24.80 *47.7%*	9.06 *47.7%*	82 *47.7%*
	69	32	52	19	172

And find the chi-square value:

■ Exhibit 4.50: Calculating the Chi-Square Value

f_o	f_e	$f_o - f_e$	$(f_o - f_e)^2$	$(f_o - f_e)^2 / f_e$
46	36.09	9.91	98.21	2.72
12	16.74	4.74	22.47	1.34
18	27.20	9.20	84.64	3.11
14	9.94	4.06	16.48	1.66
23	32.91	9.91	98.21	2.98
20	15.26	4.74	22.47	1.47
34	24.80	9.20	84.64	3.41
5	9.06	4.06	16.48	1.82

This makes our chi-square value 18.51, and with three degrees of freedom this relationship is statistically significant at the $p < .001$ level. However, notice that the crosstab really breaks down into two sides, with heterosexual women and nonheterosexual men on one side (notice how similar their percentages are) and heterosexual men and nonheterosexual women on the other side (notice how similar their percentages are).

If we ran separate crosstabs, comparing each group with each other group, some of the differences would be statistically significant and some would not be. For example, what if we contrasted heterosexual women with nonheterosexual men:

▨ **Exhibit 4.51: Waiting to Poop by Sex/Sexuality, Observed and Expected**

	FREQUENCIES OBSERVED			FREQUENCIES EXPECTED	
	HetW	NHetM		HetW	NHetM
WAITS	46	14	WAITS	47.05	12.95
DOESN'T WAIT	23	5	DOESN'T WAIT	21.95	6.05

You likely can tell by how similar these observed and expected frequencies are to each other that the chi-square value will be low. Indeed, it is 0.32, so there is no statistically significant difference between heterosexual women and nonheterosexual men. Although I love this article, I would have preferred that the authors do these individual contrasts rather than the overall crosstabs that they do show in the table. In fact, the lack of difference between some of these groups is to me a key finding, so I would like to have seen this highlighted a bit more. And, because I'm being critical, I also want to point out that, given their procedures for procuring respondents, their resulting sample is in no way random. If you were a student at this university who was not in one of the recruited classes and was not on the e-mail lists the researchers used, you would have had no way of getting into the sample. To their credit, the authors do talk about this in their article. Given that very few people have studied this topic, I would call this some very good exploratory research. The findings are provocative enough that a larger scale study of pooping and farting is definitely warranted. Care to carry this out? No? Really?

LITERATURE EXAMPLE: OBESITY IN THE UNITED STATES AND FRANCE

Another interesting article appeared in this same journal a few years later, and it made good use of chi-square. Obesity has become a significant public health problem in recent years, but the way the news media frame this problem varies from culture to culture. Abigail Saguy and her coauthors (2010) show how the U.S. and French media have written about this issue by performing a careful content analysis of a sample of 369 news articles and opinion pieces on this topic from 1995 to 2005. They used each country's newspaper of record (the *New York Times* and *Le Monde*) as well as a leading newsmagazine (*Newsweek* and *L'Express*). Using a coding mechanism (which is similar to a survey), they "asked" each article a series of 200 questions. For example, did the article blame an individual for his or her weight gain? Their findings expose interesting differences between the two cultures. The following is an excerpt from their Table 1:

■ **Exhibit 4.52: Proportion of Obesity News Stories Using Specific Frames**

	U.S. ($N = 262$)	France ($N = 108$)	Statistical Significance
Causes			
Individual Choices	0.39	0.46	
Social-structural	0.27	0.47	***
Biological	0.15	0.25	*
Solutions			
Individual	0.56	0.44	*
Any Policy	0.21	0.44	***
Medical	0.24	0.19	

Source: Adapted from Saguy, Gruys, and Gong (2010).

This table is similar to the previous example in that it presents proportions, not frequencies. But because they provide the number of articles for each country, we can transform the proportions to frequencies very easily. For example, using the "cause: individual choice frame" proportions, we can calculate the following:

39% of 262 articles is 102 articles: 102 articles use this frame; 150 of them don't.
46% of 108 articles is 50 articles: 50 articles use this frame; 58 of them don't.

These four frequencies are all we need to carry out this particular chi-square test. First, we build crosstabs with both the observed and expected frequencies:

▨ **Exhibit 4.53: Individual Choice Frame: Observed and Expected Frequencies**

	FREQUENCIES OBSERVED			FREQUENCIES EXPECTED	
	U.S.	France		U.S.	France
USES INDIVIDUAL CHOICE FRAME	102	50	USES FRAME	107.60	44.37
DOES NOT USE INDIVIDUAL CHOICE FRAME	160	58	DOESN'T USE FRAME	154.40	63.63

With these observed and expected frequencies, we calculate that the chi-square value is 1.71, which is not even close to reaching the value we'd need for significance at the $p < .05$ level. Therefore, they cannot claim that French and U.S. media differ in how often they use the "individual choice as cause" frame. This lack of a difference is interesting, because the authors had hypothesized that this frame would be more prominent in the United States because of its culture's emphasis on individualism.

They do find differences in other cross-cultural comparisons. French media were significantly more likely to use the "social-structural cause" frame (the chi-square value for this comparison was 14.01, with $p < .001$). With regard to solutions, U.S. media were significantly more likely than French media to use a "solution is up to the individual" frame ($\chi = 4.17, p < .05$), while French media were significantly more likely than U.S. media to use a "societal policy solution" frame ($\chi^2 = 20.94, p < .001$). American individualism rears its head when people try to create policies that would forbid them from drinking 64 ounces of their favorite soda in one sitting. Give me big gulps or give me death!

CONCLUSION

Chi-square is a *classic*. Mention it to anyone who has taken statistics, even long ago, and they will give you a knowing smile. True, it may be a nervous smile. It is our first example of inference. We took crosstabs based on sample results and made claims about the population from which these samples were drawn. Although many other parts of this book will introduce you to various inferential procedures, keep in mind that they all accomplish the same thing: they allow you to speak beyond the sample and talk about the population.

SPSS DEMONSTRATION

Please visit the book's website (www.routledge.com/cw/linneman) to view a video of this demonstration.

As you can see, the calculations for chi-square are straightforward, but onerous. It's *much* more efficient if we have SPSS do them for us. Having SPSS run a chi-square test is simply a matter of clicking the chi-square button under Statistics in the Cross-tabs dialog box. All we need to do is interpret the output. As is its way, SPSS gives us more output than we need.

Let's try the guns/sex example from earlier in the chapter, but this time using ANES data, and to start, we will use all of the respondents. We go to the Crosstabs room:

Analyze → Descriptive Statistics → Crosstabs . . .

And here is what we do once we get there:

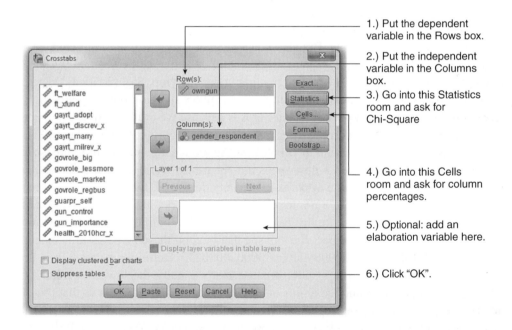

1.) Put the dependent variable in the Rows box.

2.) Put the independent variable in the Columns box.

3.) Go into this Statistics room and ask for Chi-Square

4.) Go into this Cells room and ask for column percentages.

5.) Optional: add an elaboration variable here.

6.) Click "OK".

SPSS gives us three boxes of output: the Case Processing Summary (totally deletable), the crosstab, and the Chi-Square Test. Here is the chi-square output:

Chi-Square Tests

	Value	df	Asymp. Sig. (2-sided)	Exact Sig. (2-sided)	Exact Sig. (1-sided)
Pearson Chi-Square	98.428[a]	1	0.000		
Continuity Correction[b]	97.866	1	0.000		
Likelihood Ratio	98.635	1	0.000		
Fisher's Exact Test				0.000	0.000
Linear-by-Linear Association	98.411	1	0.000		
N of Valid Cases	5728				

a. 0 cells (0.0%) have expected count less than 5. The minimum expected count is 876.32.
b. Computed only for a 2x2 table.

Too much information, I know. But all we need here is that first line of numbers next to Pearson Chi-Square: the chi-square value is 98.43, the degree of freedom is 1, and the significance level is 0.000 (the first number under "Asymp. Sig. (2-sided)." There are a few things here that I want to point out. First, SPSS's value for chi-square might differ just a bit from the one we calculate. This is because we rounded some numbers, whereas SPSS uses all the numbers. Second, and more importantly, notice how SPSS does not give us a "$p < .05$" kind of conclusion. Again, it's a computer program, so it has in its little computer head a ginormous chi-square table and can tell us the *exact* significance level for any value of chi-square at any degree of freedom. We can either report this exact number; or turn it into $p < .05$, $p < .01$, or $p < .001$; or report a lack of significance if that is the case. In this case, SPSS says the significance is 0.000. However, if you click on this number, you can see that beyond these zeros there is indeed a number: 3.37E–23, or 0.0000000000000000000000337. Definitely below 0.001! So our *p*-conclusion would be $p < .001$, because that's usually the lowest *p*-value we report. One more thing to notice in this output: in footnote a, SPSS tells us that 0% of the cells have an expected value of less than 5. It does this because, if these expected values were indeed below 5, chi-square starts to get all wonky. Yes, wonky. It doesn't work very well with very small frequencies. I won't explain why, nor will I go into alternative tests one could use in such an event, as the likelihood of having such small frequencies is pretty small. One thing that might cause this is a crosstab with far too many cells. This might happen if we try to engage in elaboration.

Let's do an elaboration. Let's do this with the ANES data by putting the variable XYdem_age4cat variable into the Layers box in the Crosstab room. Here are the resulting crosstabs and chi-square tests (after I cleaned them up):

Does R own a gun * Gender of respondent * Age in four categories Crosstabulation

Age in four categories			Gender of respondent		Total
			1. Male	2. Female	
17–34	Does R own a gun	1. Yes	161	149	310
			25.8%	20.6%	23.0%
		2. No	462	574	1036
			74.2%	79.4%	77.0%
	Total		623	723	1346
			100.0%	100.0%	100.0%
35–49	Does R own a gun	1. Yes	234	168	402
			35.7%	25.3%	30.5%
		2. No	421	496	917
			64.3%	74.7%	69.5%
	Total		655	664	1319
			100.0%	100.0%	100.0%
50–64	Does R own a gun	1. Yes	382	301	683
			43.2%	31.4%	37.0%
		2. No	503	659	1162
			56.8%	68.6%	63.0%
	Total		885	960	1845
			100.0%	100.0%	100.0%
65+	Does R own a gun	1. Yes	264	148	412
			46.2%	24.6%	35.1%
		2. No	308	454	762
			53.8%	75.4%	64.9%
	Total		572	602	1174
			100.0%	100.0%	100.0%

Chi-Square Tests

Age in four categories		Value	df	Asymp. Sig. (2-sided)
17–34	Pearson Chi-Square	5.172	1	0.023
35–49	Pearson Chi-Square	16.909	1	0.000
50–64	Pearson Chi-Square	27.546	1	0.000
65+	Pearson Chi-Square	59.906	1	0.000

In the crosstab with the youngest respondents, we see that the difference between men and women is small, but according to the chi-square test, we are able to claim statistical significance at the $p < .05$ level. All of the other differences are significant at the $p < .001$ level. Note that as age increases, the differences between men and women grows (as does, of course, the chi-square value).

FROM OUTPUT TO PRESENTATION

Although the SPSS output from a crosstab and chi-square test are fairly straightforward, it is considered gauche in most circles to have such output in a professional presentation. Here is the previous output in professional presentation form:

▨ **Exhibit 4.54: Sex Differences in Gun Ownership, by Age**

Age of Respondent	Number of Men in Age Group	Percentage of Men Owning Guns	Statistical Significance	Percentage of Women Owning Guns	Number of Women in Age Group
17–34	623	26%	$p < .05$	21%	723
35–49	655	36%	$p < .001$	25%	664
50–64	885	43%	$p < .001$	31%	960
65+	572	46%	$p < .001$	25%	602

Source: ANES 2012 data.

This table summarizes a lot of information in a small space, as I felt it important to include both frequencies and percentages. A table with only percentages could be hiding the fact that some of the percentages are based on small frequencies. If one wanted to do so, one could take the information in the table and run the chi-square tests on his or her own, converting the percentages into frequencies as I did earlier in this chapter.

EXERCISES

Exercise 1

Although gay men and lesbians have made great strides in recent years, there are still concerns about health issues. For example, are gays and lesbians more likely to smoke? Use ANES data to create a crosstab that uses the recoded sexual orientation variable (using just gays and lesbians, not bisexuals) as the independent variable, and the recoded smoking variable (not the dichotomous version). Run a chi-square test and explain your results.

Exercise 2 (Answer Available in Appendix D)

Run a crosstab and chi-square test to see if gays and lesbians are more likely to have a dog than heterosexuals are (do not use the sexual orientation variable that includes bisexuals). After you run this crosstab and chi-square test, engage in elaboration by running this crosstab and chi-square test once for men and once for women. Interpret your results.

Exercise 3

Test this hypothesis using ANES data:

Those Americans who don't have passports are more resistant to outsourcing than are those who do have passports.

Exercise 4

Test this hypothesis using ANES data:

Those Americans who are for increased defense spending are against gun control (use the recoded gun control variable).

Exercise 5

You've likely heard of the phenomenon of the bridezilla: women who make their wedding day the most important and stressful day of their lives. This got me to wondering: Do women invest more of their life satisfaction in getting married than men do? First, run a crosstab and chi-square test using the married/partnered variable (the "mvp" variable that includes just those married or partnered) as the independent variable and the dichotomously recoded life satisfaction variable as the dependent variable. Then, elaborate this crosstab (and chi-square test) by running it once for men and once for women. Summarize your results.

Exercise 6

Among the ANES respondents who are 65 years old or older, we find that 51 of the 115 men have dogs, and 50 of the 182 women have dogs. From this information, create a crosstab and run a chi-square test to see if this difference is statistically significant.

Exercise 7

Among the ANES respondents who are aged 17 to 34 and who say that the Bible is the word of God, we find that there might be a relationship between knowing someone gay and support for gay marriage:

Among the 132 people who know someone gay, 53 favor legal marriage, 33 favor civil unions, and 46 say there should be no legal recognition.
Among the 212 people who don't know someone gay, 59 favor legal marriage, 66 favor civil unions, and 87 say there should be no legal recognition.

Use this information to construct a crosstab and run a chi-square test to see if there is a statistically significant difference.

Exercise 8 (Answer Available in Appendix D)

A recent phenomenon is "showrooming": when customers go to a physical store and check out a product, but then go home and order it online, even if they took up the time of the employees in the physical store. Perhaps women are less likely to engage in this behavior because they (sorry for the stereotyping) connect more emotionally with the employees. Using the PewShop data, create a crosstab comparing men and women on the recoded purchase variable. Once you have your crosstab, describe your results.

Exercise 9

Given that smartphones are able to use free Wi-Fi hotspots, which are more likely to be found in urban environments, perhaps there are geographic differences in smartphone ownership. Using the PewShop data, create a crosstab that uses the recoded community variable as your independent variable and the recoded smartphone variable as your dependent variable. Interpret your results.

Exercise 10 (Answer Available in Appendix D)

Among the PewShop respondents younger than 23 years old, 39 of 48 men have gaming consoles, and 24 of 42 women have gaming consoles. From this information, construct a crosstab and carry out a chi-square test. Interpret your results.

Exercise 11

Use the PewHealth dataset to address this question: Are Hispanics born in the United States significantly more likely to have health insurance than Hispanics who were not born in the United States? Use the dichotomously recoded insurance variable and the dichotomously recoded Hispanic born variable in this analysis. Explain your results.

Exercise 12

We often hear in the news that men do not take care of their health as much as women do. Is this supported by the PewHealth dataset? Use both health-tracking variables in your analysis and explain your results.

Exercise 13

Does where you live affect your risk of heart disease, and is this relationship the same for men and for women? Investigate this using the PewHealth dataset by using the recoded community variable and the heart disease variable, and elaborate with the sex variable.

Exercise 14

Use the PewKids dataset to address the following question: is there a significant difference between mothers' and fathers' likelihood of friending their child on a social network?

Exercise 15

Run two crosstabs (with chi-square tests) that investigate the association between parent's worry and parent's action. First, see if the parents' concern over inappropriate content on the Internet affects their likelihood of checking where their child has been on the Internet. Next, see if the parents' concern over how the child treats others on the Internet affects their likelihood of checking where their child has been on the Internet.

Exercise 16 (Answer Available in Appendix D)

If one has been bullied online, does this affect one's willingness to stop cyberbullying of others? Use the bullied online variable as your independent variable. Use the four "what do you do when you see cyberbullying?" variables as your dependent variables. Explain your results.

Exercise 17

Interested in his own campus classmates' experiences with cyberbullying, a student distributes a short survey to his statistics class. He finds, through a crosstab and chi-square test, that there is a statistically significant difference between men and women: men are more likely to have been cyberbullied. Critique.

Exercise 18

I took the WVS DIVORCE variable and from it created a new variable called DIVORCE2CAT:

Lowest value through 4.99: low acceptability of divorce
5.00 through highest value: high acceptability of divorce

Have SPSS create a crosstab using this new variable as the dependent variable and the COUNTRY2CAT (Europe vs. Asia/Africa) variable as the independent variable. Also, run a chi-square test. Fully explain your results.

Exercise 19

I created a variable called PROST2CAT using the PROST variable:

Lowest value through 2.99: low acceptability of prostitution
3.00 through highest value: medium acceptability of prostitution

Have SPSS create a crosstab using DIVORCE2CAT as the independent variable and PROST2CAT as the dependent variable, and run a chi-square test. Explain your results.

Exercise 20

Countries differ in their general level of trust of people. I took the WVS PTRUST variable and created a variable called PTRUST3CAT, where

■ PTRUST values of 0 through 19 get coded as "Low Trust,"
■ PTRUST values of 20 through 39 get coded as "Medium Trust," and
■ PTRUST values of 40 or higher get coded as "High Trust."

Use this PTRUST3CAT variable as your dependent variable, and COUNTRY2CAT as your dependent variable in a crosstab with a chi-square test. Explain your results.

Chapter 5

USING A SAMPLE MEAN OR PROPORTION TO TALK ABOUT A POPULATION: CONFIDENCE INTERVALS

This chapter covers . . .

. . . building a probability distribution of sample means

. . . how to find and interpret the standard error of a sampling distribution

. . . population claims and how to put them to the test

. . . how to build and interpret confidence intervals

. . . how a researcher used confidence intervals to study popular films

INTRODUCTION

In this chapter we continue our exploration of inference, going through some procedures that are strikingly similar to those in the chi-square chapter. Whereas in the chi-square chapter we dealt with variables of the nominal or ordinal variety, here we deal with ratio-level variables. Our attention turns from sample crosstabs and toward sample means (and, at the end of the chapter, proportions). But keep in mind that the inference goal remains the same: we will use sample means in order to make claims about population means. Just as we talked about the chi-square probability distribution, we'll start this chapter with a distribution of sample means.

SAMPLING DISTRIBUTIONS OF SAMPLE MEANS

Imagine a hypothetical class with 100 students in it. These students will serve as our population: it is the entire group of students in which we are interested. They get the following hypothetical grades:

■ **Exhibit 5.1: Grades for a Population of 100 Students: Frequency Distribution**

Grade	# of Students Receiving This Grade
1.0	1
1.1	1
1.2	1
1.3	2
1.4	2
1.5	2
1.6	2
1.7	3
1.8	3
1.9	3
2.0	4
2.1	4
2.2	5
2.3	6
2.4	7
2.5	8
2.6	7
2.7	6
2.8	5
2.9	4
3.0	4
3.1	3
3.2	3
3.3	3
3.4	2
3.5	2
3.6	2
3.7	2
3.8	1
3.9	1
4.0	1

Source: Hypothetical data.

Here is a bar graph of this frequency distribution:

■ **Exhibit 5.2: Grades for a Population of 100 Students: Bar Graph**

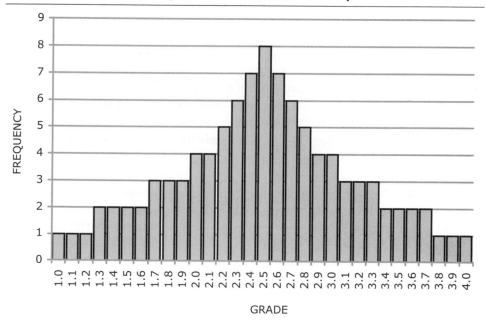

The grades of these 100 students are distributed in roughly the same shape as a bell curve. The population mean, median, and mode for this population are all the same: 2.5. Notice that, in the preceding graph, each little "block" is a person. For example, the block above where it says 1.0 means that one student had a grade of 1.0. The two blocks above where it says 1.3 mean that two students received grades of 1.3. Each block represents the grade of an individual *person*.

Because we're imagining things, let's take full advantage of this. All of a sudden, out of nowhere, a mysterious force appears and prevents me from calculating the population mean. However, the mysterious force *does* allow me to take samples from this population, samples of five students at a time, and the mysterious force says I can take as many samples of five as I want. I took the 100 student scores, and I wrote each score on a small slip of paper, and then I placed these slips into a bowl and mixed them up very well to assure randomness. I then took a sample:

2.5, 2.4, 3.1, 1.8, 2.6

I then calculated a mean for this sample, and it was 2.5 (I'm rounding to the nearest tenth). Wow, the population mean was 2.5 (shhh, don't tell the mysterious force that

I remember this), and the sample mean was also 2.5. I'm such a great sampler! Feeling overly confident, and knowing that the mysterious force will let me draw as many samples as I want, I returned the five students to the bowl, remixed very vigorously, and drew another sample:

4.0 3.0 3.5 3.7 2.4

I calculated the sample mean for this sample, and it was 3.3. Uh oh. Where the first sample mean was a perfect representation of the population mean, this second sample mean is way off: it is 0.8 above the population mean. Did I make a mistake in my sampling when I did it the second time? No, I didn't make an error. However, we do refer to this difference of 0.8 as **sampling error**: simply by chance, the sample that I drew differed from the population mean.

I decided to take full advantage of the mysterious force's strange willingness to let me draw as many samples as I see fit. I replaced the students' scores into the bowl, mixed vigorously, and drew a third sample. I replaced them, mixed vigorously, and drew a fourth, and so on until I had ten samples:

▨ **Exhibit 5.3: Ten Sample Means**

Sample	Scores in Each Sample					Mean of Sample
Sample 1	2.5	2.4	3.1	1.8	2.6	mean = 2.5
Sample 2	4.0	3.0	3.5	3.7	2.4	mean = 3.3
Sample 3	3.3	3.5	3.6	2.8	2.4	mean = 3.1
Sample 4	2.5	1.3	2.3	2.9	4.0	mean = 2.6
Sample 5	2.5	2.3	1.5	2.1	2.4	mean = 2.2
Sample 6	4.0	2.2	2.3	2.5	3.9	mean = 3.0
Sample 7	2.0	2.2	1.7	3.3	1.4	mean = 2.1
Sample 8	3.8	2.3	3.7	1.4	1.6	mean = 2.6
Sample 9	2.4	2.3	3.0	4.0	2.6	mean = 2.9
Sample 10	2.1	2.1	2.2	2.8	3.4	mean = 2.5

Notice that there is a fair amount of variation among these 10 sample means. Some vary above the population mean; some vary below. We have another sample mean that happens to be right on the population mean, and a couple that are just 0.1 above the population mean. To illustrate this, I'll lay these out on a graph deceptively similar to the graph in Exhibit 5.2, but with an important difference:

■ **Exhibit 5.4: A Distribution of 10 Sample Means**

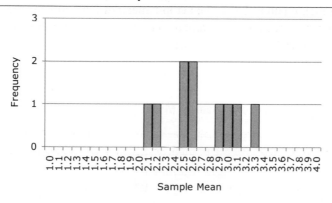

Again, we have a graph with individual "blocks." However, there is a *very* important difference between the blocks in the first graph and the blocks in the second graph. In the first graph, each block was an individual student's grade. In the second graph, that first block above 2.1 represents not an individual student's grade, but rather a *sample mean*. Each of the ten sample means I drew are in the second graph. Be sure you know what is going on in this second graph, because it is absolutely critical for understanding where I'm taking you.

I then took ten more samples and calculated their means. Let's see what the graph looks like now:

■ **Exhibit 5.5: A Distribution of 20 Sample Means**

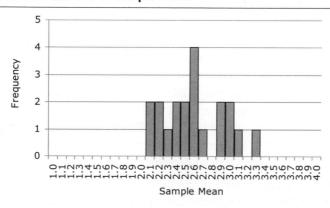

With 20 sample means, there remain some anomalies. Why are there no sample means of 2.8? Why, when there are high sample means of 3.1 and 3.3, are there no corresponding low sample means of 1.7 or 1.9 on the other side? Why, when we know that the population mean is 2.5, is the sample mean of 2.6 happening more frequently than the sample mean of 2.5? This sample taking is fun. No, really, it is. In fact, I love it so much that I'm going to take 30 more samples.

▪ **Exhibit 5.6: A Distribution of 50 Sample Means**

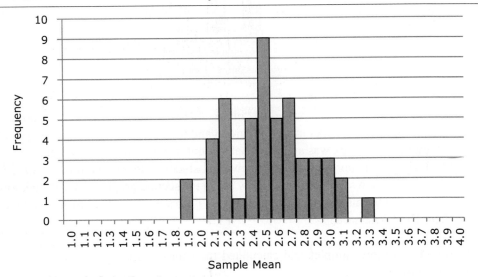

Taking 30 more samples pretty much addresses the three questions from earlier: we now have several sample means of 2.8, we have a couple of lower samples of 1.9 (although still none at 1.7), and the most commonly occurring sample mean is now 2.5, the same as the population mean.

But, I admit, I have become slightly addicted to this little sampling exercise. And I like how these graphs are shaping up. So I took 50 more samples to raise my number of samples to 100 samples. I could have had SPSS randomly draw samples, but I felt drawn to do these by hand. I did a lot of them while I was stuck riding in a plane or a train or a car with nothing better to do (don't worry, I wasn't driving the car at the time). And my partner, my mother, and one of my nephews helped a bit as well. Here is the distribution of sample means after 100 samples:

■ Exhibit 5.7: A Distribution of 100 Sample Means

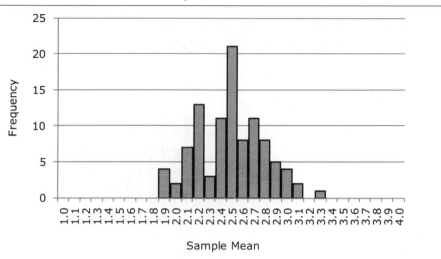

And after 50 more:

■ Exhibit 5.8: A Distribution of 150 Sample Means

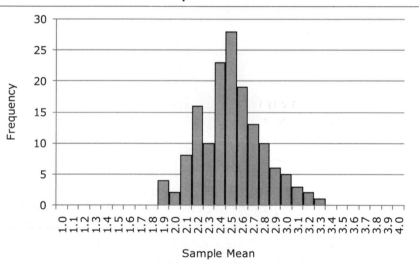

And after 50 more:

■ **Exhibit 5.9: A Distribution of 200 Sample Means**

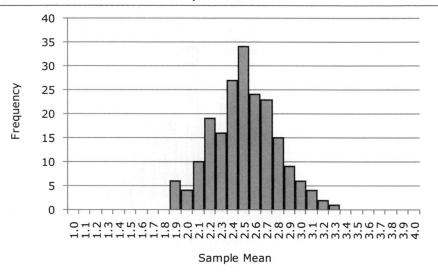

And 50 more:

■ **Exhibit 5.10: A Distribution of 250 Sample Means**

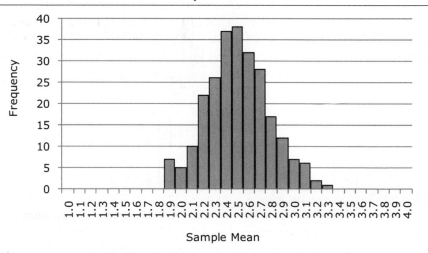

And 50 more:

■ **Exhibit 5.11: A Distribution of 300 Sample Means**

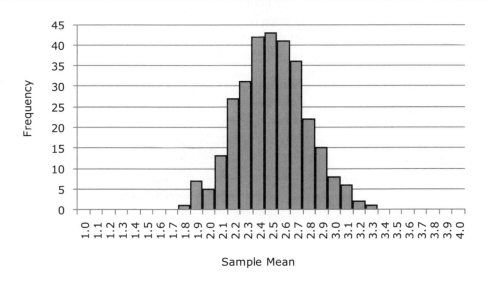

Enough! Three hundred samples will suffice. Some very minor anomalies remain. There are a couple more 1.9s than 2.0s. There's no 1.7 to correspond to the one sample mean of 3.3 on the other side. However, I think I can convince you that, if I were to continue sampling infinitely, the distribution of sample means would get ever closer to being a perfect bell curve, and the laws of randomness would take care of any anomalies. For example, even when I had taken 150 samples, there were strikingly few sample means of 2.3, but, as I took more samples, means of 2.3 finally pulled ahead of means of 2.2.

Let's look closely at this final graph. At the center of the bell, meaning they happened with the highest frequency, are sample means of 2.5, 2.4, and 2.6. From a population of students in which the population mean was 2.5, many of the small samples we drew from the population had sample means very close to the population mean of 2.5. Samples with sample means a bit away from the population mean—2.2, 2.3, 2.7, 2.8—are still common; however, they are less common than the sample means of 2.4, 2.5, and 2.6. The sample means of 1.9 and 3.1 are even less likely to happen, but occasionally they did happen. And once, only once, did I draw a sample where the sample mean was 3.3. Oddly, it was the second sample I drew. The chances of drawing such a sample are very, very slim. Notice that we didn't draw any samples for which the sample mean was as low as 1.2 or 1.3, or as high as 3.7 or 3.8. Think through why such occurrences did not happen. What would have had to fall into place for this to occur? To draw a sample with a mean of 1.2, I would have had to draw, say, a 1.0, 1.1,

1.2, 1.3, and 1.4. To draw a sample with a mean of 3.8, I would have had to draw, say, a 3.6, 3.7, 3.8, 3.9, and 4.0. Given the population of scores, the chances of such things happening are next to nothing. My hope is that all of this is giving you an intuitive feel for how sample means act: most of them will fall near the population mean, some will fall a bit away from the population mean, and a few will, by chance, fall quite far away from the population mean. This is simply how the laws of randomness work. What I have built above is a distribution of sample means, or, as it is more commonly called, a **sampling distribution**. Just as the chi-square distribution was the basis of the chi-square test, sampling distributions form the basis of much of the theory and practice on which mean-based inferential statistical techniques are built.

With this sampling distribution, we can calculate the probability of pulling certain types of samples. To find such a probability, we simply take the total number of attempts (in this situation, 300, because we took 300 samples) and divide that into the number of times a particular event occurred. For example, what is the probability of drawing a sample between 2.3 and 2.7? I took 300 samples, and there were 193 samples with a mean of 2.3, 2.4, 2.5, 2.6, or 2.7:

■ **Exhibit 5.12: Sample Means between 2.3 and 2.7**

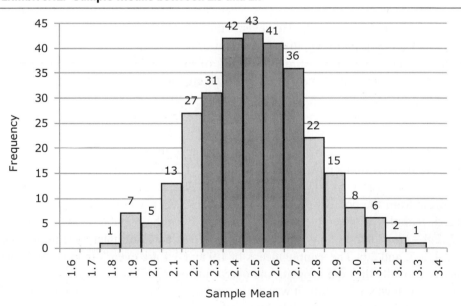

So the probability of such a sample was 193/300 = 0.64. Let's do a few more of these. What was the probability of pulling a sample with a mean of 2.1 or less? I drew 300 samples, and there were 26 samples with a mean of 2.1, 2.0, 1.9, or 1.8:

■ Exhibit 5.13: Sample Means of 2.1 or Lower

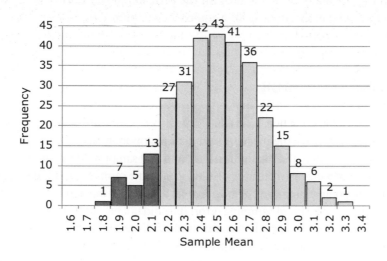

So the probability of such a sample was 26/300 = 0.09. What was the probability of pulling a sample of 3.2 or above? I took 300 samples, and only three had a mean of 3.2 or above:

■ Exhibit 5.14: Sample Means of 3.2 or Higher

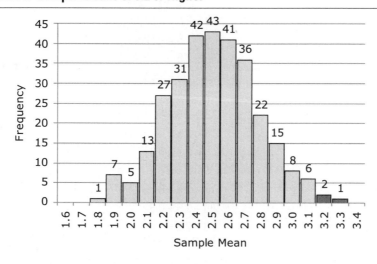

So the probability of such a sample was 3/300 = 0.01. Finally, what was the probability of pulling a sample between 1.8 and 3.3? In other words, when I drew a sample, what was the probability that I drew a sample? That would be 300/300 = 1; 100% of the samples I took are represented in the sampling distribution. This is a key fact: in any sampling distribution, the sum of all the probabilities always adds up to 100%, or, in the form of a proportion, 1.00. Another way to phrase this is "the total area of a sampling distribution is 1."

THE STANDARD ERROR

Remember in Chapter 3 when I introduced you to the standard deviation: the average distance scores were from the mean. A sampling distribution has its own special version of the standard deviation: the standard error. I took 300 samples. Many of them were very close to the population mean (meaning that they had little sampling error: they very nicely represented the population mean). Some were far away from the population mean (meaning that they had quite a bit of sampling error: they did not provide very good estimates of the population mean). We can calculate the average distance that these sample means are from the population mean, the average error, or what we call the **standard error**. We'll do this using exactly the same process we used to calculate the standard deviation. First, we need to calculate the distance each value of the sample mean is from the population mean:

▪ **Exhibit 5.15: Calculating Distances from the Population Mean**

Sample Mean	Sample Mean – Population Mean
1.8	1.8 – 2.5 = –0.7
1.9	1.9 – 2.5 = –0.6
2.0	2.0 – 2.5 = –0.5
2.1	2.1 – 2.5 = –0.4
2.2	2.2 – 2.5 = –0.3
2.3	2.3 – 2.5 = –0.2
2.4	2.4 – 2.5 = –0.1
2.5	2.5 – 2.5 = 0.0
2.6	2.6 – 2.5 = 0.1
2.7	2.7 – 2.5 = 0.2
2.8	2.8 – 2.5 = 0.3
2.9	2.9 – 2.5 = 0.4
3.0	3.0 – 2.5 = 0.5
3.1	3.1 – 2.5 = 0.6
3.2	3.2 – 2.5 = 0.7
3.3	3.3 – 2.5 = 0.8

Next, just as we did when we calculated the standard deviation, we will square these distances. Before we do this, I'm going to switch from words to symbols. For the sample mean, I'll use what I've used before: $\bar{x}$. For the population mean, I'm going to use a Greek symbol (we tend to use Greek symbols when we're talking about populations). That symbol is μ, and it's pronounced /myoo/ (like a French cow).

■ **Exhibit 5.16: Squaring Distances from the Population Mean**

μ	$\mu - \bar{x}$	$(\mu - \bar{x})^2$
1.8	−0.7	0.49
1.9	−0.6	0.36
2.0	−0.5	0.25
2.1	−0.4	0.16
2.2	−0.3	0.09
2.3	−0.2	0.04
2.4	−0.1	0.01
2.5	0.0	0.00
2.6	0.1	0.01
2.7	0.2	0.04
2.8	0.3	0.09
2.9	0.4	0.16
3.0	0.5	0.25
3.1	0.6	0.36
3.2	0.7	0.49
3.3	0.8	0.64

Last, before we add up all the squared variation, we need to take into account that, for most of these sample mean values, we had multiple frequencies. That is, we didn't just have one sample mean of 1.9; we had seven sample means of 1.9 (see Exhibit 5.17).

We add up this final column to get the total squared deviations, and get 22.44, and we divide that by 300 and get 0.075. Just as we did to get from the variance to the standard deviation, we take the square root and get 0.27. This number is the standard error, and it represents the average error in our 300 samples: some of our samples were right at the population mean, some were above, and some were below. On average, they were "off" by 0.27. The symbol that we use for the standard error is another Greek symbol (because the standard error concerns populations). Because we use s for the standard deviation, for the standard error of the mean we use the Greek lowercase sigma, or $\sigma_{\bar{x}}$.

■ **Exhibit 5.17: Accounting for Multiple Frequencies**

$\overline{x}$	$\overline{x} - \mu$	$(\overline{x} - \mu)^2$	f	$f(\overline{x} - \mu)^2$
1.8	−0.7	0.49	1	0.49
1.9	−0.6	0.36	7	2.52
2.0	−0.5	0.25	5	1.25
2.1	−0.4	0.16	13	2.08
2.2	−0.3	0.09	27	2.43
2.3	−0.2	0.04	31	1.24
2.4	−0.1	0.01	42	0.42
2.5	0.0	0.00	43	*0.0*
2.6	0.1	0.01	41	0.41
2.7	0.2	0.04	36	1.44
2.8	0.3	0.09	22	1.98
2.9	0.4	0.16	15	2.40
3.0	0.5	0.25	8	2.00
3.1	0.6	0.36	6	2.16
3.2	0.7	0.49	2	0.98
3.3	0.8	0.64	1	0.64

What you saw earlier, the actual creation of a sampling distribution that we were able to play around with, is highly unusual. Most of the time, people don't sit around pulling hundreds of samples; they have better things to do with their time (as do I, but I really, really wanted to make sure that you understood what a sampling distribution *is*). What we do instead is take a single sample from a population, and then we "imagine" that this sample is part of an imagined sampling distribution. However, if it is imagined, and we haven't actually drawn the samples, how can we calculate the value of the standard error for this imagined sampling distribution? Well, it just so happens that we can estimate the value of the standard error by taking the sample standard deviation and dividing it by the square root of the sample size minus 1:

$$estimate\ of\ \sigma_{\overline{x}} = \frac{s}{\sqrt{n-1}}$$

For example, one of our 300 samples had the following grades:

2.1, 2.2, 2.6, 3.1, 3.3

This sample had a standard deviation of 0.53. Using the preceding formula:

$$estimate\,of\,\sigma_{\bar{x}} = \frac{0.53}{\sqrt{5-1}}$$

and this equals 0.265. Is that cool or *what*? Not all of the sample standard deviations elicit exactly 0.27 for the estimate of the standard error, but many of them are quite close. And, according to the central limit theorem, if the sample had been larger (our samples are tiny at $n = 5$) then its standard deviation would provide a very good estimate of the standard error of the hypothetical sampling distribution. You'll just have to trust me on this one, and also trust me that this little formula is supported by theory, as I'm not going to go into the details behind it.

CLAIMS ABOUT THE POPULATION MEAN

Now let's put all of this to good use. One way we can use the ideas behind a sampling distribution is if someone makes a claim about a population and we want to see how likely it is that this claim could be true. For example, what if we had our original 100-student grade population, and the mysterious force from the beginning of the chapter claimed that the population mean was 3.0? The mysterious force won't allow us to calculate the population mean, but it will allow us to take one sample of 10 student grades from this population. We do so, and these are the scores we get:

1.3, 1.5, 2.0, 2.3, 2.3, 2.3, 2.4, 2.7, 3.5, 3.6

The mean of this sample is 2.4, and the standard deviation for this sample is 0.74. The question we want to ask is, "If the population mean really were 3.0, what is the probability that we could pull this sample or a sample with a lower mean?" First, we calculate the estimate of the standard error:

$$estimate\,of\,\sigma_{\bar{x}} = \frac{0.74}{\sqrt{10-1}}$$

This gives us a standard error of 0.25. Next, we need to figure out how far away a sample mean of 2.4 is from the claimed population mean of 3.0. This sample mean is 0.6 away from the claimed population mean. How many standard errors is this? We divide 0.6 by 0.25 and get 2.4:

■ **Exhibit 5.18: From Distance to Number of Standard Errors**

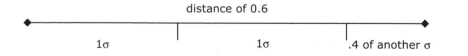

Now that we've "translated" the actual distance of the sample mean from the population mean into a number of standard errors (and it is simply a coincidence that the number of standard errors is the same as the sample mean), we need to perform another "translation": we need to translate this number of standard errors into a probability. We want to figure out what the probability is that this sample (or a sample even lower) could occur. In visual form, here's what's going on:

▨ **Exhibit 5.19: The Situation on a Normal Curve**

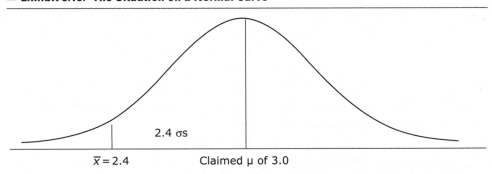

What we do is turn to a table that is set up similarly to the chi-square table we used in Chapter 4. It's called the *t*-table.

Just like the chi-square table, the *t*-table uses degrees of freedom, but it has a slightly different meaning here. Remember that the degrees of freedom (*df*) when using chi-square were the number of cells we were free to fill in before all the cells were "spoken for." But here we don't have cells; we have a sample mean. Let's say we have a three-case sample and the mean of this sample is, say, 2.5:

$$(a + b + c)/3 = 2.5$$

The cases a, b, and c could take on any value: they could all be 2.5; they could be 3, 2.5, and 2; they could be 0, 6, and 1.5; and so on. Let's say the value of the first case, *a*, is 3:

$$(3 + b + c)/3 = 2.5$$

The cases *b* and *c* could still take on any value. They are still free to vary. Let's give the case b a value:

$$(3 + 1 + c)/3 = 2.5$$

Now, all of a sudden, the case c can't vary any more. We can arithmetically solve for c and figure out that the value of c *must* be 3.5. So, with a sample of three, two cases are free to vary; the degrees of freedom when $n = 3$ is 2, or $n - 1$. This works for any sample size: $df = n - 1$. We have a sample size of 10, so our degrees of freedom is 9.

Notice that, once your degrees of freedom reaches 30, the t-table then skips to 40, 50, and so on. If 33, or 47, are your degrees of freedom, what do you do? The easy thing to do is use the degrees of freedom closest to your degrees of freedom, as those values will be pretty darned close to what you need. Some people use a process called interpolation, where they figure out the exact value by doing some math, but we won't go into that. If your degrees of freedom is greater than 100, then the only line you're left with is the ∞ line. This is the line you'll use for any large sample.

With our number of standard errors of 2.4 and our degrees of freedom of 9, we go to the t-table to see how far to the right we can get (see how this is similar to the chi-square procedure?). Going across the row where $df = 9$:

■ **Exhibit 5.20: An Excerpt from the *t*-Table, *df* = 9**

Probability	.100	.050	.025	.010	.005	.001
t-Value	1.38	1.83	2.26	2.82	3.25	4.30

Here's how we can interpret these numbers: Getting a sample mean that is 1.38 standard errors from the claimed population mean is likely to happen less than 10% of the time. Getting a sample mean that is 1.83 standard errors from the population mean is likely to happen less than 5% of the time, and so on. With our 2.4 standard errors, the farthest to the right we can get is 0.025, so we conclude that, if the population mean indeed were 3.0, there is less than a 2.5% chance that we could draw a sample with a mean of 2.4 or below. Therefore, drawing such a sample could happen, but it is unlikely to happen.

Let's go through this one more time. The mysterious force now claims that the population mean is 2.3, and this time allows us to take a sample of $n = 20$. We do so, and get the following grades:

1.3, 1.9, 2.1, 2.3, 2.4, 2.5, 2.5, 2.6, 2.6, 2.7, 2.8, 3.1, 3.2, 3.2, 3.3, 3.4, 3.6, 3.7, 3.7, 3.9

The mean for this sample is 2.8, with a standard deviation of 0.68. The question, of course, is, "If the population mean truly were 2.3, what are the chances of drawing a sample of $n = 20$ whose mean is 2.8?" First, we calculate the estimate of the standard error:

$$estimate\ of\ \sigma_{\bar{x}} = \frac{0.68}{\sqrt{20-1}}$$

This gives us 0.16 for the estimate of the standard error. Our distance is 2.8 – 2.3 = 0.5, and this translates into 0.5/0.16 = 3.13 standard errors. Our degrees of freedom are 20 –1 = 19, so we go to that row in the *t*-table:

■ **Exhibit 5.21: An Excerpt from the *t*-Table, *df* = 19**

Probability	.100	.050	.025	.010	.005	.001
t-Value	1.33	1.73	2.09	2.54	2.86	3.58

Our 3.13 gets us almost all the way to the end (3.13 is larger than 2.86, but less than 3.58), so we can conclude that, if the population mean were indeed 2.3, there would be less than a 0.5% chance of pulling a sample of this size (*n* = 20) with a mean of 2.8 or higher. Here's the visual for what we've been doing:

■ **Exhibit 5.22: The Situation on a Normal Curve**

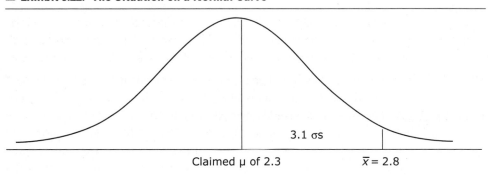

Claimed μ of 2.3 $\bar{x}$ = 2.8

3.1 σs

Recall that the whole goal of inference is to take what we know about the sample and make claims about the population. However, in the two preceding examples, we end up with statements about the likelihood of samples. So what we do is "flip" these statements. Instead of saying, "*If the population mean indeed were 3.0, there is less than a 2.5% chance that we could draw a sample with a mean of 2.4 or below,*" we flip this statement and claim, "*If we draw a sample mean of 2.4 or below, there is less than a 2.5% chance that the population mean is 3.0.*" And instead of saying, "*If the population mean were indeed 2.3, there would be less than a 0.5% chance of pulling a sample with a mean of 2.8 or higher,*" we flip this statement and claim, "*If we draw a sample mean of 2.8 or higher, there is less than a 0.5% chance that the population mean is*

2.3." This gets us to the goal of inference: based on a sample, we make a claim about the population from which that sample was drawn.

GSS EXAMPLE: TV WATCHING AMONG YOUNG WOMEN

Someone, a not very nice person, claims that "women who are ages 20 to 30 who say they're keeping house instead of working at a job, all they're *really* doing is watching television all day. I bet they watch TV seven hours a day." Could this be true? Could this population's mean be 7 hours? We restrict the GSS 2012 sample accordingly (sex = woman, wrkstat = keeping house, age > 19, age < 31) and get the descriptive statistics on the tvhours variable. Here they are:

sample size = 21, mean = 4.52, standard deviation = 3.20

So the sample mean is 4.52. Could the population mean be 7? First, we calculate the estimate of the standard error:

$$estimate\,of\,\sigma_{\bar{x}} = \frac{3.20}{\sqrt{21-1}}$$

This gives us a standard error estimate of 0.72. The difference between the sample mean and the claimed population mean is $7.0 - 4.52 = 2.48$, so the number of standard errors is $2.48/0.72 = 3.44$. Going to the *t*-table, and having *df* = 20, the row we use looks like this:

■ **Exhibit 5.23: An Excerpt from the *t*-Table, *df* = 20**

Probability	.100	.050	.025	.010	.005	.001
t-value	1.33	1.73	2.09	2.53	2.85	3.85

We can get past 1.33, 1.73, 2.09, 2.53, and 2.85. Therefore, we conclude that there is only a 0.5% chance that the population mean is 7.0. Therefore, it is highly unlikely that the population claim is true.

CONFIDENCE INTERVALS

We also can use the logic behind sampling distributions to develop **confidence intervals**. You've probably heard confidence intervals called by a different name: margins of error. Margins of error are typically reported any time you hear poll results: "People favor Candidate W to Candidate L 56% to 44%, with a margin of error of 3 percentage points." In the field of statistics, however, we tend to call them confidence intervals. If confidence is involved, about what exactly are we saying we are confident? When we have a sample mean and want to make an inference and to talk about the population mean, we can develop an interval within which we are confident that the population mean falls. We don't know exactly what the population mean is (if we did know this, then why would we need to sample in the first place?), but we have strong reason to believe it's not greater than this, and not less than that. For example, what if I were interested in building a confidence interval using the TV viewing results from earlier? With the sample mean of 4.52, within what range can I confidently claim that the population mean falls:

4.47 to 4.57?
4.42 to 4.62?
3.77 to 5.27?
3.02 to 6.02?
2.02 to 7.02?
1.52 to 7.52?

There's tension here. On one hand, we want to be as specific as possible: saying that the population mean is between 1.52 and 7.52 isn't very specific and doesn't really help us use the sample results to describe what is going on in the population. On the other hand, we also do not want to be incorrect: saying that the population mean is between 4.47 and 4.57 is very specific, but claiming this doesn't do us much good if the chances are high that the population mean is outside of this range. In other words, we would likely being making a type I error. So we want a happy medium, and the procedure for building confidence intervals is how we find that happy medium.

Speaking of happiness, the level of confidence with which most people are happy is 95%. Recall that, when we performed chi-square tests, we wanted p to be below 0.05. We allowed ourselves a 5% chance of making a type I error. Here we'll use a similar idea: we'll allow a 5% chance that we could be wrong, but we want to be correct 95% of the time, thus the term "95% confidence interval." Some people want to be more sure and want to allow only a 1% chance of error, so we will also cover, you guessed it, a 99% confidence interval. But we'll start with 95%.

So we can be wrong 5% of the time. In other words, we're going to allow a 5% chance that the population mean falls outside of our confidence interval. We're going to take that 5% and cut it into two parts: 2.5% and 2.5%. We're going to use 2.5% for each of the following two scenarios:

1. The population mean is higher than our sample mean.
2. The population mean is lower than our sample mean.

We'll start with the first scenario: there's a possibility that, although the GSS sample mean was 4.52, the population mean is higher than this. Visually, we have this:

■ **Exhibit 5.24: A Sample Mean Lower than the Population Mean**

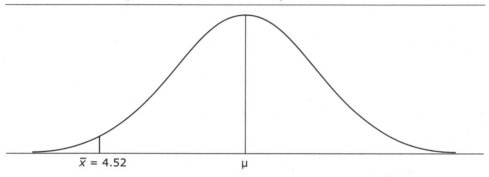

We want to figure out a value for the population mean that is a certain number of standard errors away such that a sample mean of 4.52 or less is likely to happen only 2.5% of the time. Basically, we're going to reverse what we did when we had a claimed population mean:

procedure with claimed population mean:
actual distance ➜ number of standard errors ➜ percentage probability

procedure with confidence intervals:
percentage probability ➜ number of standard errors ➜ actual distance

We already have our percentage probability, 2.5%, and we use the *t*-table to move from this to a number of standard errors. Under the column for 0.025, we go down to the row *df* = 20 (because we have 21 cases in our sample) and see that the number of standard errors is 2.09. The next step is to translate the number of standard errors into a meaningful distance. Earlier, we calculated the value of the standard error, and it was 0.72. We want 2.09 standard errors at a value of 0.72 each: 2.09 × 0.72 = 1.50. We add this distance to the sample mean of 4.52 and get 6.02. Now we have:

■ **Exhibit 5.25: Finding the Upper Limit for a Confidence Interval**

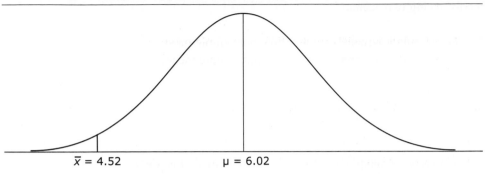

$\bar{x} = 4.52$ $\mu = 6.02$

If the highest claim we make is that the population mean is 6.02, then there is a 2.5% chance that we could draw a sample mean of 4.52 or less. Flipping this, as we have done before, we get the following:

If we draw a sample mean of 4.52, there is a 2.5% chance that the population mean is 6.02 or more.

Employing the second scenario (the population mean is lower than our sample mean), we do the same exact thing on the other side of the sampling distribution:

■ **Exhibit 5.26: Finding the Lower Limit for a Confidence Interval**

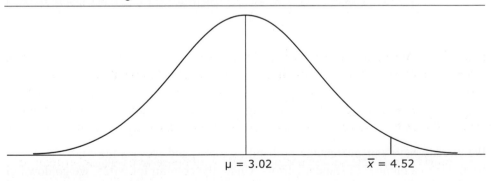

$\mu = 3.02$ $\bar{x} = 4.52$

If the lowest claim we make is that the population mean is 3.02, then there is a 2.5% chance that we could draw a sample mean of 4.52 or higher. Flipping this, we get the following:

If we draw a sample mean of 4.52, there is a 2.5% chance that the population mean is 3.02 or less.

Putting all of this together, we getting the confidence interval:

$3.02 \leq \mu \leq 6.02$

With 95% confidence, we can say that the population mean is somewhere between 3.02 and 6.02. It could be 3.5; it could be 4; it could be 5; it could be 5.5; it could be 4.4; it could be 3.3. We don't know exactly, but with 95% confidence we can say that it's somewhere within that range.

What if we had 41 women instead of 21, but everything else remained the same? What does your gut say will happen to the confidence interval? Here are the old and new results:

■ **Exhibit 5.27: Results with Samples of 21 and 41**

	$n = 21$	$n = 41$
Sample mean	4.52	4.52
Sample standard deviation	3.20	3.20
Estimate of the standard error	0.72	0.51
Number of standard errors	2.09	2.02
Meaningful distance	1.50	1.03
95% confidence interval	$3.02 \leq \mu \leq 6.02$	$3.49 \leq \mu \leq 5.55$

Is this what you expected? Mathematically, a larger sample elicits a smaller standard error and a smaller number of standard errors, so overall the width of the confidence interval is smaller. But, intuitively, does this make sense? One way to look at it is that a larger sample has a better chance of looking more like the population from which it was drawn, so therefore, we are able to make a more precise statement about the population.

I mentioned earlier that some people use 99% confidence intervals rather than 95% confidence intervals. Can you think through intuitively how this will affect the width of the confidence interval?

Here is the comparison (both use samples of 21):

▨ **Exhibit 5.28: 95% and 99% Confidence Intervals**

	95% CI	99% CI
Sample mean	4.52	4.52
Estimate of the standard error	0.72	0.72
Total percentage error allowed	5%	1%
Percentage error for each scenario	2.5%	0.5%
Number of standard errors	2.09	2.85
Meaningful distance	1.50	2.05
Confidence interval	$3.02 \leq \mu \leq 6.02$	$2.47 \leq \mu \leq 6.57$

Is this what you expected? If you want to be more certain that we are not making a mistake, we need to give ourselves more wiggle room.

GSS EXAMPLE: POLICE VIOLENCE

The police often have a problematic relationship with the public. They must simultaneously protect the public and earn the trust of the public. If they use violence to achieve the former, they may not be able to achieve the latter. The GSS asks respondents about the acceptability of the police using violence in various situations:

Are there any situations you can imagine in which you would approve of a policeman striking an adult male citizen?
Would you approve of a policeman striking a citizen who had said vulgar or obscene things to the policeman?
Would you approve of a policeman striking a citizen who was being questioned as a suspect in a murder case?
Would you approve of a policeman striking a citizen who was attempting to escape from custody?
Would you approve of a policeman striking a citizen who was attacking the policeman with his fists?

All of these were asked as yes/no questions. I recoded them so that No = 0 and Yes = 1, and then combined the recoded responses into an index that ranged from 0 (police striking a citizen is never acceptable) to 5 (police striking a citizen is acceptable in all of these situations). Here is a bar graph of the resulting index:

■ Exhibit 5.29: Bar Graph of Police Violence Index

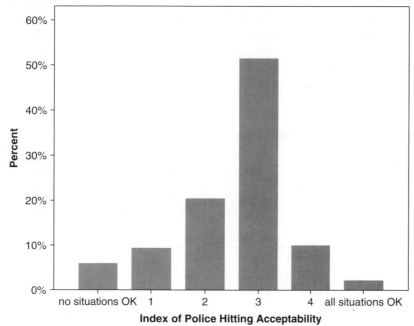

Source: GSS 2012 data.

Most respondents support police violence in several of these situations. However, there is some variation. Historically, race has played a role in community–police relations. Here are descriptive statistics and confidence intervals for five racial groups:

■ Exhibit 5.30: Descriptive Statistics and Confidence Intervals

Racial Group	n	Mean	SD	95% Confidence Interval
Whites	887	2.70	0.99	$2.63 \leq \mu \leq 2.76$
Blacks	171	2.23	1.17	$2.06 \leq \mu \leq 2.41$
Hispanics	52	1.87	1.14	$1.55 \leq \mu \leq 2.18$
Asians	40	2.58	1.24	$2.18 \leq \mu \leq 2.97$
American Indians	16	2.19	1.28	$1.51 \leq \mu \leq 2.87$

Source: GSS 2012 data.

These results illustrate the strong effect that sample size has on the width of the confidence interval. Notice how tight the white confidence interval is. When you have 887 cases, the size of the standard error estimate is going to be very small (remember that the sample size appears in the denominator). In contrast, the American Indian confidence interval, based on a mere 16 cases, is quite wide. Here is a visual representation of the confidence intervals:

▨ **Exhibit 5.31: Confidence Intervals for Various Racial Identities**

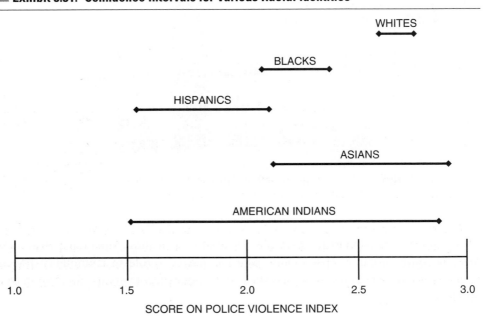

Notice that the confidence interval for blacks does not overlap with the confidence interval for whites. Thus, we can say that we are confident that these two populations differ, since their population means would each have to be outside their confidence intervals in order to be equal. In contrast, even though the American Indian sample mean is quite similar to the black sample mean, we cannot make this same type of assertion of difference with whites. Notice that, because the American Indian confidence interval is so wide, it overlaps with the white confidence interval. Thus, it is possible that that white population mean and the American Indian population mean are the same. In the following chapter, you will learn other ways to test whether we can be confident that population means differ.

GSS EXAMPLE: JOB STRESS AND SATISFACTION

I was concerned about the relationship between job stress and job satisfaction among older men (older than the age of 50). The GSS asks a seven-point job satisfaction question (0 = completely dissatisfied to 6 = completely satisfied). I had SPSS calculate the mean job satisfaction for the eight older men who said they "always found work stressful" (it was 3.63), and the mean job satisfaction for the six older men who said they "never found work stressful" (it was 5.50).

Given the small sample sizes, I knew the confidence intervals might be fairly wide. Here are the intervals SPSS gave me:

95% confidence interval for the eight stressed men: $2.45 \leq \mu \leq 4.80$
95% confidence interval for the six unstressed men: $4.93 \leq \mu \leq 6.07$

Although the width of the confidence interval for the stressed men is 2.35, the width of the interval for unstressed men is only 1.14. Odd, given that there are two fewer unstressed men. The cause? The standard deviations differ greatly:

Standard deviation for the eight stressed men: 1.41
Standard deviation for the six unstressed men: 0.55

The unstressed men are not only more satisfied, but they are also similarly satisfied (3 replied "6," completely satisfied, and 3 replied "5"). Among the stressed men, there were three 2s, two 4s, and three 5s, making for much more variation and eliciting a much wider confidence interval. Some men like stress; some don't. But all men like *not* being stressed.

CONFIDENCE INTERVALS WITH PROPORTIONS

When I began talking about confidence intervals, the example used proportions:

56% of people preferred Candidate W. The proportion equivalent of a percentage of 56% is 0.56.

But notice that, with this kind of result, there is no mean. Proportions have no means. However, we can still use the same confidence interval logic. All we need is a way to calculate the estimate of the standard error for a proportion (P), and we can do so with the following formula:

$$estimate\,of\,\sigma_p = \sqrt{\frac{P(1-P)}{n}}$$

It rather resembles the formula for the standard error of the mean. The sample size is on the bottom. We don't have the standard deviation on the top, but we can consider this a measure of variation if you think about it (and, of course, I'm going to make you think about it). The P is the proportion, and the $1 - P$ is its complement. If you're looking at the probability of something happening, the complement is simply the probability of it *not* happening. For example, if we used that 56% from earlier, P would be 0.56, meaning there's a 56% chance that someone supported Candidate W. The complement, then, would be $1 - P$: $1 - 0.56 = 0.44$. There's a 44% chance that someone did not support Candidate W. The following graph illustrates why their product represents variation:

▨ **Exhibit 5.32: Illustrating the Value of $P(1 - P)$**

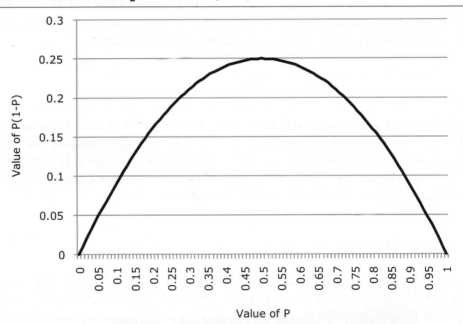

When P and $1 - P$ are equal at 0.50 each, the value of $P(1 - P)$ is at its highest: 0.25. This is the situation of maximum variation: half the respondents feel one way; the other half feel the other way. As P either gets smaller (moves toward 0) or larger (moves toward 1), the value of $P(1 - P)$ gets smaller. For example, when $P = 0.25$, and $1 - P = 0.75$, the value of $P(1 - P)$ is 0.1875. When there is almost no variation in opinion, say, when 95% of the people feel the same way, $P(1 - P)$ would be $0.95(0.05) = 0.0475$.

Instead of using the police violence index from the previous example, what if we wanted to use just one of the survey questions: "Are there any situations you can imagine in which you would approve of a policeman striking an adult male citizen, yes or no?" And let's say we are interested in a particular group who, at least in the media, experiences a disproportionate amount of violence from police: young, black men. In the 2012 GSS, among the 23 black men aged 18 to 35, 70% of them answered yes to this question. Let's build a 95% confidence interval around this sample result.

First, we calculate the estimate of the standard error:

$$estimate\,of\,\sigma_p = \sqrt{\frac{(0.70)(0.30)}{23}}$$

This gives us 0.10. With 23 cases, we go to the *t*-table. Because we don't have a mean, the degrees of freedom is simply the number of cases, so we go to that row and find the number of standard errors is 2.07. The meaningful distance is $0.10 \times 2.07 = 0.21$. We add and subtract this from our 0.70 to get the confidence interval:

$0.49 \leq \Pi \leq 0.91$

With 95% confidence, we can say that the percentage of the population of young black men who is approve of police violence is between 49% and 91%. This is quite a wide interval. What if we used *all* black men in the 2012 GSS who responded to this question? Of the 68 black men, 63% approved. The revised standard error is 0.06. From the *t*-table, the closest degree of freedom is 60, so for a 95% confidence interval we use 2.00 standard errors. This gives us a meaningful distance of $0.06 \times 2.00 = 0.12$, resulting in this confidence interval:

$0.51 \leq \Pi \leq 0.75$

Not as wide, but still pretty wide. Notice that the symbol we use for the population proportion is, not surprisingly, a Greek letter that starts with a *P*: pi. Don't confuse this with the 3.14-type pi—not the same things at all. Also, be careful not to get confused by the fact that you have lots of percentages going on here: you have the percentages that make up the confidence interval, and you have the percentage chance of a type I error—not the same things at all. Finally, if you wanted to report this 95% confidence interval as a "margin of error" that you typically see in news reports, you would say: 63% of black men approve of police violence, with a margin of error of ± 12%.

GSS EXAMPLE: SUPPORT FOR MARIJUANA LEGALIZATION

Imagine that a politician for whom you are working is about to give a speech to a group that is made up of two constituencies: young people (aged 18–29) and old people (aged 65 and older). The topic of the speech is marijuana legalization. She asks you what is the best stance to take, given these specific constituencies. We go to the 2012 GSS and see that there is a variable called GRASS: Should marijuana be made legal, yes or no? We decide to use the data from this question and these age groups to build 99% confidence intervals and then make a recommendation to the politician. Here are the statistics:

■ **Exhibit 5.33: Marijuana Legalization Attitudes for Two Ages Groups**

	Age 18–29	Age 65 and older
Proportion supporting legalization	0.55	0.33
Sample size	200	254
Estimate of the standard error	0.04	0.03
Number of standard errors	2.58	2.58
Meaningful distance	0.10	0.08
Confidence interval	$0.45 \leq \prod \leq 0.65$	$0.25 \leq \prod \leq 0.41$

If the politician wants to take *one* stance on marijuana legalization, based on these results, if should be against legalization. Let's examine the confidence intervals. Among the old population, we are very confident that the majority opinion is against legalization. The interval goes from 25% to 41%, so a majority in favor of legalization (i.e., 51%) is far outside this range. Among the young population, there is a possibility that less than 50% favor legalization: the interval goes from 45% to 65%. Therefore, the safest stance is to be against legalization, as there is at least a chance that both populations feel this way. There is essentially no chance that both of these populations favor legalization. Of course, you might want to ask your politician boss how she personally feels about the issue . . . nah! Political stances based on statistics are *much* more fun.

LITERATURE EXAMPLE: BLACK CHARACTERS IN FILM

Researcher Matthew Hughey noticed a trend among mainstream movies: more and more were featuring what he calls "magical negros": "lower-class, uneducated, magical black characters who transform disheveled, uncultured, or broken white characters into competent people" (Hughey 2009, p. 543). From dramas (*The Green Mile*) to science fiction (*The Matrix*) to comedies (*Bruce Almighty*), this type of character is appearing quite frequently. He analyzed this trend in his article "Cinethetic Racism: White Redemption and Black Stereotypes in 'Magical Negro' Films," which appeared in the journal *Social Problems*. As you can glean from the title, he argues that these films, although giving these black characters some power, ultimately reinforce longstanding racial stereotypes.

Hughey and his research assistant drew a random sample of 26 films featuring such characters and conducted a careful content analysis of the films in 30-second segments. They coded the frequency with which various themes appeared, themes regarding stereotypes of blacks or whites. For example, one stereotype was the magical negro who quickly appears or disappears. He often appears out of nowhere to help the white character, and once his job of transforming the white character is complete, the black character quickly rides off into the sunset or disappears into thin air. Hughey argues that this represents the impermanence of the black–white relationship. Another stereotype involved socioeconomic mobility: the white characters showed the ability to move between social classes by pulling themselves up by their bootstraps. In Table 3 of his article, Hughey presents descriptive statistics for the themes, as well as confidence intervals. Here are the statistics for these two themes:

■ **Exhibit 5.34: Two Themes from "Magical Negro" Films**

	(Dis)appearing Acts	Socioeconomic Mobility
Mean frequency per film	6.08	9.88
Standard deviation	3.09	13.07
Number of films	26	26
Confidence interval	$4.89 \leq \mu \leq 7.27$	$4.86 \leq \mu \leq 14.90$

Source: Adapted from Hughey (2009).

The (dis)appearing acts theme appeared more consistently in the 26 films than the mobility theme. Only one film (*Down to Earth*) didn't feature the (dis)appearing acts theme, and the highest frequency was only 13 times (*Dogma*). This results in a small standard deviation and a relatively tight confidence interval. In contrast, the mobility theme didn't appear at all in 15 of the films, but quite frequently in others (36 times in *The Legend of Bagger Vance* and 37 times in *Bruce Almighty*). This results in a larger standard deviation and a much wider confidence interval. That is, with regard to the mobility theme, Hughey cannot be as precise in his claims about the population of films from which he drew the sample, given that the occurrence of the theme was inconsistent.

Although I really enjoy this article, and think it offers a great example of confidence intervals, I do want to criticize Hughey briefly. It took me a while to do the math and figure out how exactly he calculated his confidence intervals. As far as I can tell, he made two minor deviations from the procedures we've covered in this chapter. First, in calculating the standard error estimates, he divided by the square root of 26 (n), and not 25 ($n - 1$). Second, rather than using 2.06, which is the t-value for building a 95% confidence interval with 25 degrees of freedom, he used 1.96, which is the t-value for large samples. Both of these modifications make the confidence intervals just a bit narrower than they should be. For example, when I calculated his confidence interval for the (dis)appearing acts theme, my confidence interval was $4.80 \leq \mu \leq 7.36$. This is only slightly different from his interval. Little did Hughey know I would be poring over his results with such a fine-toothed comb!

CONCLUSION

This chapter certainly has covered a lot of ground. After some introductory sampling, sampling, and more sampling, we went over two ways that we can apply these inferential ideas in order to make connections between sample means and population means:

1. using a sample mean to judge the legitimacy of claims about a population; and
2. using a sample mean to build a confidence interval within which we can confidently predict that the population mean falls.

These procedures are based on the same underlying ideas. If you understand the sampling distributions and how they contribute to these procedures, then you're in good shape.

SPSS DEMONSTRATIONS

Please visit the book's website (www.routledge.com/cw/linneman) to view videos of these demonstrations.

Selecting Cases

Since this chapter has involved a lot of sampling, I think it's a good time to go over how you can have SPSS take samples from a dataset. This might be useful if you want to conduct a sampling exercise of your own. But keep in mind that, if you take a sample from a GSS or ANES dataset, you really are taking a sample of a sample (however, for learning purposes, you could *pretend* that the entire dataset sample is a population). The way to get to this procedure is

Data → Select Cases

When you click on this, SPSS takes you into this room:

We'll be using the top three options:

- ■ "All cases": the button to click when you want SPSS to return to using all the cases in the dataset.
- ■ "If condition is satisfied": the button to click when you want SPSS to select cases on a certain condition.
- ■ "Random sample of cases": the button to click when you want SPSS to draw a random sample of a certain number of cases.

Let's start with that second option: selecting cases on a condition. Sometimes, when running statistics, you'll want to limit your analyses to a subset of your dataset. For example, you might want to analyze only the female respondents, or only the black respondents, or only those younger than 25 years of age. All you have to do is tell SPSS what your condition is. When you click on the "If condition is satisfied" button, the "If . . ." button below it activates, and when you click on this "If . . ." button, it takes you into the following room within a room:

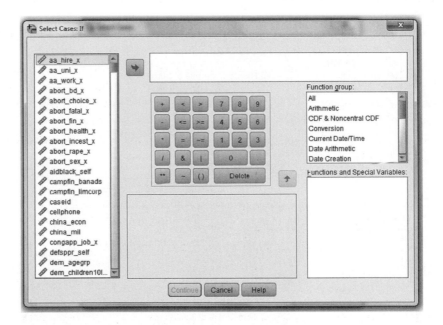

In this room, you tell SPSS your condition or set of conditions. Here are a few examples using the ANES dataset. If you wanted to look at only those younger than 25 years of age, you would move the XYdem_age variable over into the top box and then after it type < 25, so that you end up with:

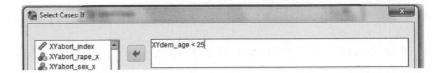

If you wanted to look at only the females in the sample, you'd look up how the variable XYgender_respondent was coded, see that the codes were Male = 0, Female = 1, so your condition would be XYgender_respondent = 1. If you wanted to look at only those respondents who are married or partnered, you could do any of the following:

XYdem_marital = 0 or XYdem_marital = 1 or XYdem_marital = 2
XYdem_marital < 3
XYdem_marital < = 2

One thing you *wouldn't* want to do in order to find those who are married and those who are partnered and those who are married but whose spouse is absent is:

XYdem_marital = 0 & XYdem_marital = 1 & XYdem_marital = 2

This might seem right at first: you want to find the married people *and* the partnered people *and* the people who are married but whose spouse is absent, so using the "&" might make sense. But think about what you're asking SPSS to do if you ask this: find all the respondents that have a 0 on the variable and a 1 on the variable and a 2 on the variable. Given that, for this variable, no respondents have more than one value, you would end up with no cases selected. So let's go with the second one: XYdem_marital < 3. I put this in the top box and clicked the "Continue" button to get out of this room and back to the first room, which now looks like this:

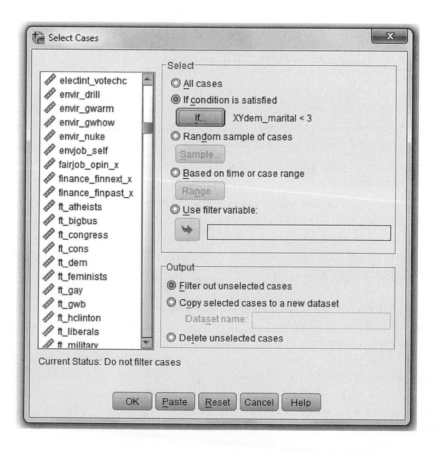

Notice that next to the "If . . ." button is our condition. We now want to click OK, but before we do, I want to caution you regarding something you *shouldn't* do. The default procedure is for SPSS to filter out the unselected cases: that button is automatically selected. But below this is an option "Delete unselected cases," and I really don't think you'd ever want to do this, because you *always* want to keep your original data. So don't do this. Once we click OK, when we look back at the dataset, notice what SPSS has done:

	XYdem_marital
31	Divorced
32	Partnered
33	Married
34	Married, spouse absent
35	Married, spouse absent
36	Never married
37	Married, spouse absent
38	Never married
39	Partnered
40	Never married

For all the cases that do not satisfy our condition, SPSS has put a line through, meaning that that case is temporarily unselected. What SPSS actually does to accomplish this is to create a new variable called "filter_$" (which it places at the far-right end of the dataset), assign each case a value of "Selected" or "Not Selected," and select the cases based on these values.

You can also give SPSS a set of conditions. For example, if you wanted to analyze only the divorced women, your condition would be "XYdem_marital = 4 & XYgender_respondent = 1." If you wanted to select only people with dogs who are Strong Republicans (the people, not the dogs), your condition would be "XYdog = 1 and Xpid_x = 6."

Now what if, instead of giving SPSS conditions to select on, we wanted to have SPSS select a random sample of cases from the dataset. We click Data → Select Cases to get back into the Select Cases room, and then we click the "Random sample of cases" button. The "Sample . . ." button below it becomes active, and we click on this to go into the following room:

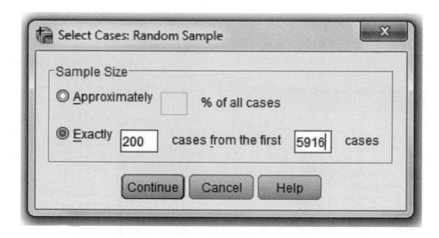

This is how I would draw a random sample of 200 cases from the 5,916 cases in the ANES dataset. Then you click the "Continue" button to exit this room, and then the "OK" button to run the sample. SPSS uses a random-number generator to select a random sample of cases and then it crosses off all of the other cases.

One thing to remember that even I sometimes forget: once you are finished doing analyses using only a subset of your data, *always* remember to go back into the Select Cases room and tell SPSS to select all cases. This will remove all of the little lines on the side and put all of the cases back into play. SPSS tries to keep you apprised of when you have cases selected, but it's subtle: at the bottom right of the data window, right next to where it usually says "IBM SPSS Statistics Processor is ready," there will be a tiny "Filter On" notice. Once you go back in and select all cases, this notice will go away. I can't tell you how many times I've been cruising along in my analyses, only to realize after amassing a good amount of output that I mistakenly left the filter on the whole time, and so I have to go back and redo all of those analyses. Don't let this happen to you.

Running Confidence Intervals

The other SPSS procedure pertinent to this chapter is confidence intervals. The room you need to go into is:

Analyze → Descriptive Statistics → Explore

Here is the room and what you want to do in it. In this example, we will get confidence intervals for each racial group on the Egalitarian Concern Index:

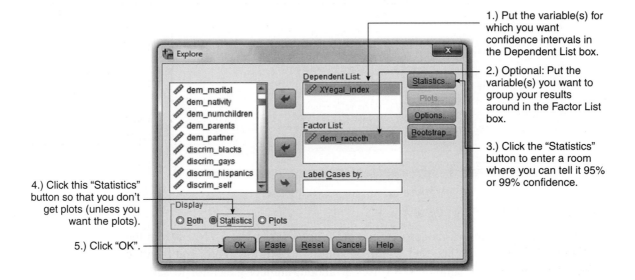

1.) Put the variable(s) for which you want confidence intervals in the Dependent List box.

2.) Optional: Put the variable(s) you want to group your results around in the Factor List box.

3.) Click the "Statistics" button to enter a room where you can tell it 95% or 99% confidence.

4.) Click this "Statistics" button so that you don't get plots (unless you want the plots).

5.) Click "OK".

This is the output that SPSS gives you. Because I'm really only interested here in the means and confidence intervals, I've deleted information impertinent to this:

Case Processing Summary

		Cases					
		Valid		Missing		Total	
	R race and ethnicity group	N	Percent	N	Percent	N	Percent
Egalitarianism Concern Index	1. White non-Hispanic	3234	92.5%	261	7.5%	3495	100.0%
	2. Black non-Hispanic	946	93.1%	70	6.9%	1016	100.0%
	3. Hispanic	908	90.2%	99	9.8%	1007	100.0%
	4. Other non-Hispanic	347	94.0%	22	6.0%	369	100.0%

Descriptives

R race and ethnicity group				Statistic	Std. Error
Egalitarianism Concern Index	1. White non-Hispanic	Mean		13.44	0.088
		95% Confidence Interval for Mean	Lower Bound	13.27	
			Upper Bound	13.61	
		Std. Deviation		5.002	
	2. Black non-Hispanic	Mean		17.93	0.135
		95% Confidence Interval for Mean	Lower Bound	17.66	
			Upper Bound	18.20	
		Std. Deviation		4.162	
	3. Hispanic	Mean		15.09	0.147
		95% Confidence Interval for Mean	Lower Bound	14.80	
			Upper Bound	15.38	
		Std. Deviation		4.432	
	4. Other non-Hispanic	Mean		14.67	0.284
		95% Confidence Interval for Mean	Lower Bound	14.12	
			Upper Bound	15.23	
		Std. Deviation		5.293	

FROM OUTPUT TO PRESENTATION

Presenting confidence intervals is sometimes done in conjunction with presenting descriptive statistics. Here are the previous results in a typical tabular format:

Scores on the Egalitarian Index by Race of Respondent

▧ **Exhibit 5.35: Scores on Egalitarian Index by Race of Respondent**

Group	Mean (95% c.i.)	sd	*n*
Whites	13.44 (13.27, 13.61)	5.00	3,234
Blacks	17.93 (17.66, 18.20)	4.16	946
Hispanics	15.09 (14.80, 15.38)	4.43	908
Others	14.67 (14.12, 15.23)	5.29	347

EXERCISES

Exercise 1

I drew a bunch of samples to get my points across in this chapter, and I hope it was worth it. Now it's your turn. Develop a sampling exercise to test one of the following claims:

1. The sampling exercise at the beginning of the chapter was based on a bell-shaped distribution of population data, and the resulting sampling distribution was bell-shaped (eventually). However, if the population data distribution were not bell-shaped (i.e., highly skewed to the left or to the right), drawing samples from this population would still eventually produce a bell-shaped sampling distribution.
2. The sampling exercise at the beginning of the chapter used sample sizes of 5. Drawing larger samples would result in a sampling distribution with a smaller standard error.
3. Larger samples produce better estimates of the standard error than smaller samples do.

Exercise 2

When someone rates a group at 10 on the ANES feeling thermometer, that's a pretty serious sign of dislike. I make the claim that the population of African American, female strong Democrats aged 17 to 34 on average rate Republicans at a chilly 10 degrees. Is this possible? Test this claim.

Exercise 3

Run confidence intervals by state using the ANES Muslims feeling thermometer and report the 95% confidence intervals for the first five states: Alaska (AK), Alabama (AL), Arkansas (AR), Arizona (AZ), and California (CA). Explain why the confidence intervals differ in width for these states.

Exercise 4

According to the ANES, 22 of the 32 blacks aged 17 to 20 have smartphones. Build a 95% confidence interval with this information.

Exercise 5 (Answer available in Appendix D)

Among those aged 17 to 34, does having a smartphone instead of a regular cell phone make one more likely to review news on the Internet? Select cases to look at this age group, and then run an Explore to get 95% confidence intervals on the Internet news variable for those who have smartphones and those who don't have smartphones. Do the confidence intervals for the two groups overlap? What does this tell you?

Exercise 6

Here are the raw data for the ANES unique group of widows with three or more kids at home:

Number of days read newspaper per week: 3, 2, 1, 7, 1, 0, 0, 0, 0, 2, 2

Use these raw data to construct a 95% confidence interval.

Exercise 7

Here are the raw data for the ANES unique group of people in educationally unequal households:

Economic Peril Index Score: 17, 13, 10, 12, 11, 21, 16, 16

Use these raw data to test the following claim: the population mean for people in educationally unequal households on the Economic Peril Index is 20.

Exercise 8

Use the PewShop dataset to build 99% confidence intervals for the Technology Index variable for the various racial groups. Which intervals are widest, and why?

Exercise 9

According to the PewShop dataset, 49 of 253 respondents aged 65 and older own tablet computers. Build a 99% confidence interval with this information.

Exercise 10 (Answer available in Appendix D)

In survey after survey, people from the state of Colorado are named the healthiest people in the United States. Use the PewHealth dataset to run 95% confidence intervals on the Health Condition Index for the various races. Warning: you're going to get some odds results. Be sure to explain why these results happened.

Exercise 11

Using the PewHealth dataset, find out what proportion of Hispanics in the sample don't have health insurance (use the recoded race variable and the dichotomously recoded insurance variable), and by hand, build a 99% confidence interval with this information.

Exercise 12

Using the PewKids dataset, build confidence intervals by parents' race. Use the Child's Negative Social Networking Consequences Index as your variable of interest. Describe two reasons why the resulting American Indian confidence interval is comically wide in contrast to some of the other confidence intervals.

Exercise 13 (Answer available in Appendix D)

We suspect that kids who sext (send nude photos by text) text more than kids who don't sext. Get 95% confidence intervals that will help you address this suspicion. Based on the confidence intervals, could the population means be the same? What is problematic about the results? Why did this happen?

Exercise 14

Use the WVS variables concerning how people feel about citizenship: CITANC, CITBORN, CITADOPT, and CITLAWAB. Run 95% confidence intervals for these variables, and then answer this question: Could the population mean for each of these variables be similar to that of the other three variables?

Exercise 15 (Answer available in Appendix D)

In the WVS countries as cases dataset, we see that 27% of American respondents had a great deal or quite a lot of trust in major companies. Can we build a confidence interval around this percentage, using information we have in the WVS dataset? Why or why not?

## Chapter 6

USING MULTIPLE SAMPLE MEANS TO TALK ABOUT POPULATIONS: *T*-TESTS AND ANOVA

This chapter covers . . .

. . . building another probability distribution, this time of mean differences

. . . conducting and interpreting a *t*-test

. . . how a *t*-test really works

. . . conducting and interpreting an ANOVA

. . . how ANOVA really works

. . . the similarities and differences between ANOVA and chi-square test

. . . how researchers used *t*-tests to study gender overcompensation

. . . how researchers used ANOVA to study student activism

INTRODUCTION

In the previous chapter, we used inferential techniques with a single mean or proportion. We dealt with claims about a population mean, seeing how likely the claim was to be true given what we had found in our sample. We also covered confidence intervals, developing an interval within which we could confidently claim that the population mean is likely to fall. Notice that, in both of these procedures, we are dealing with only a single sample mean (or a single proportion). This chapter applies our inferential ideas to situations where we have more than one sample mean and are seeking to make claims about more than one population mean. For example, rather than stating where a single population mean falls, we want to be able to say whether or not two population means differ significantly. Or we want to be able to say whether three or more population means differ significantly. To answer these questions, respectively, we use two additional inferential techniques: the difference-of-means test (or the *t*-test for short) and the analysis of variance (or ANOVA for short). Because we'll be talking about differences among groups, you will see some similarities to the chi-square test. And just as the last two chapters were based on probability distributions (the chi-square distribution and the sampling distribution of sample means), in this chapter, we start with another sampling distribution.

A DIFFERENT KIND OF SAMPLING DISTRIBUTION

This new sampling distribution is the one that allows us to compare two means. Fittingly, it is called the sampling distribution of sample mean differences. Let's go back to our original population of 100 students I used in the last chapter. What if this population had 50 women and 50 men in it, and the population mean for men and the population mean for women were identical? I took my 100 slips of paper and divided them accordingly, by placing them a bowl for women and a bowl for men and making sure that they had similar grades in their bowls and the means for both the men's population and the women's population were exactly 2.5. That is, the population means are equal. I then took a sample of five from the men's bowl and a sample of five from the women's bowl, calculated the sample means for each sample, and then calculated the difference between those sample means. I then put the numbers back in their respective bowls, mixed vigorously, and took a second set of samples. I did this a total of 100 times. Yes, really. Here is one of the sets of samples:

Men's sample: 1.8, 2.1, 2.2, 3.0, 3.5   Mean = 2.52
Women's sample: 2.1, 2.5, 2.6, 2.7, 2.7   Mean = 2.52

Male mean − female mean = 0

This is what we would expect, right? If the population means are equal, and we draw samples, ideally the sample means should be equal as well, so that, if we subtract one sample mean from the other sample mean, we should get zero. However, here is another set of samples I took:

Men's sample: 2.3, 2.4, 2.5, 2.6, 3.5   Mean = 2.66
Women's sample: 1.3, 1.9, 2.5, 2.6, 3.1   Mean = 2.28

Male mean − female mean = 0.38

With this set of samples, the male sample mean was above its population mean, whereas the female sample mean was below its population mean. When we subtract the female mean from the male mean, we get 0.38. Owing to sampling error, if we looked at just these samples, it would seem that men's grades were higher than women's grades, when in the population they are the same. Here is a third set of samples:

Men's sample: 1.0, 2.3, 2.3, 2.6, 2.7   Mean = 2.30
Women's sample: 2.3, 2.6, 2.9, 2.9, 4.0   Mean = 2.94

Male mean − female mean = −0.64

With this set of samples, the female sample mean was high, whereas the male sample mean was low. When we subtract the female mean from the male mean, we get −0.64. Owing to sampling error, if we just looked at these samples it would seem that women's grades were higher than men's grades when in the population they are the same.

I took these 3 sample mean differences, as well as the 97 other sample mean differences, and placed them on a bar graph:

■ **Exhibit 6.1: A Sampling Distribution of Sample Mean Differences**

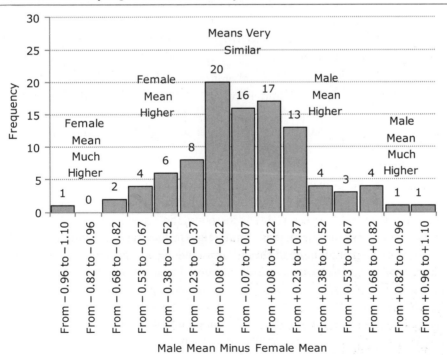

The resulting distribution resembles a normal curve. Take a moment to process what these bars represent. In a frequency distribution, each block represents an individual score. In a sampling distribution of sample means, each block represents a sample mean. Now, in the **sampling distribution of sample mean differences**, each block represents not an individual's score, nor a sample mean, but rather the difference between two sample means. For example, that first tiny block on the left represents the situation in which I took a male sample and a female sample and the female sample mean was much higher than the male sample mean. That tiny block all the way to the right represents the situation in which I took a male sample and a female sample and the male sample mean was much higher than the female sample mean. Be sure you understand this distribution before you read on.

As was the case in the previous chapter, there are some anomalies, but if I continued taking pairs of samples, these anomalies eventually would go away. At the center of this distribution is zero, where the male sample mean and female sample mean did not differ at all. Notice that many of the sample pairs were quite similar: more than half the male mean/female mean pairs ($20 + 16 + 17 = 53$) were within 0.22 of each other. As we move away from the center on either side, as the sample mean differences become larger, the probability that such differences occur goes down quickly. Only in one instance did the sample means differ by 1.0 or more (1.08, to be exact). This phenomenon leads us to three claims:

1. If we have Population A and Population B, and the population means are equal $\mu_A = \mu_B$, then the probability is high that, if we take a sample from each population, the two sample means will be equal or approximately equal $\bar{x}_A = \bar{x}_B$
2. If we have Population A and Population B, and the population means are equal $\mu_A = \mu_B$, then the probability is lower that, if we take a sample from each population, the two sample means will be somewhat unequal (either $\bar{x}_A > \bar{x}_B$ or $\bar{x}_A < \bar{x}_B$).
3. If we have Population A and Population B, and the population means are equal $\mu_A = \mu_B$, then the probability is very low that, if we take a sample from each population, the two sample means will be very unequal (either $\bar{x}_A > \bar{x}_B$ or $\bar{x}_A < \bar{x}_B$).

Make sure you understand how these three relate to the graph in Exhibit 6.1, because now I'm going to take all three of these claims and apply that flipping logic I've used before in order to get us to some useful inferential rules (remember the goal of inference: to take information from samples and talk about populations):

1. If we take two samples from two different populations, and the two sample means are equal or approximately equal $\bar{x}_A = \bar{x}_B$, then the probability is high that the two population means are equal $\mu_A = \mu_B$.

2. If we take two samples from two different populations, and the two sample means are somewhat unequal (either $\bar{x}_A > \bar{x}_B$ or $\bar{x}_A < \bar{x}_B$), then the probability is lower that the two population means are equal $\mu_A = \mu_B$.
3. If we take two samples from two different populations, and the two sample means are very unequal (either $\bar{x}_A > \bar{x}_B$ or $\bar{x}_A < \bar{x}_B$), then the probability is very low that the two population means are equal $\mu_A = \mu_B$.

TESTING DIFFERENCES BETWEEN TWO MEANS: THE *T*-TEST

These statements are at the heart of what is called the difference-of-means test, which is also called the **t-test**. In a *t*-test, we take information from two samples and calculate a *t*-value. This *t*-value represents the number of standard errors away from the center of the sampling distribution of sample mean differences. If our sample means differ by enough, and the number of standard errors is high enough, then we can conclude with confidence that the population means cannot be equal. In the language of hypothesis testing, we state the null hypothesis that the population means are equal:

$$H_0: \mu_1 = \mu_2$$

Then, typically, the alternative hypothesis is

$$H_{alt}: \mu_1 \neq \mu_2$$

Here is the formula we use to calculate the *t* value:

$$t = \frac{\overline{X}_1 - \overline{X}_2}{\sqrt{\frac{S_1^2}{n_1} + \frac{S_2^2}{n_2}}}$$

What this formula essentially does is take the difference between the sample means and "standardize" it into a number of standard errors.

Once we do this a few times, it will make sense, so on to examples!

GSS EXAMPLE: BACK TO TV WATCHING

We'll start with the 21 women from the example in the previous chapter: the ones who were keeping house and were aged 20 to 30. Their descriptive statistics on the TVHOURS variable were

Sample mean = 4.52   Standard deviation = 3.20 $n = 21$

We'll contrast them to women ages 20 to 30 but working part-time, whose descriptive statistics are

Sample mean = 2.48   Standard deviation = 2.45 $n = 25$

So the big question is, although the sample means clearly differ, by more than two hours, do they differ *enough* to enable us to say that the population means are not the same?

Our null and alternative hypotheses are

H_0: Young women working part-time *do not* differ in television watching from young women keeping house.

H_{alt}: Young women working part-time *do* differ in television watching from young women keeping house.

We calculate the *t*-value:

$$t = \frac{4.52 - 2.48}{\sqrt{\frac{10.24}{21} + \frac{6.00}{25}}} = 2.40$$

We take this 2.40 to the *t*-table. But which line do we use? Because we have two means, the degrees of freedom is determined by $n_1 - 1 + n_2 - 1$, or $n_1 + n_2 - 2$, so here we have $df = 44$, which is closest in the *t*-table to $df = 40$, where the values are

▪ **Exhibit 6.2: An Excerpt from the *T*-Table, *df* = 40**

Probability	.200	.100	.05	.02	.01	.001
t-value	1.30	1.68	2.02	2.42	2.70	3.55

We work our way as far to the right as we can, and we are stopped by that 2.42, so we conclude that $p < .05$. But what does this p stand for? The probability of what? Let's return to the idea of type I error, which in general is the error of making a claim about a population and being wrong. With a *t*-test, the type I error would be to claim that two population means differ when in reality they do not differ. So our $p < .05$ means that, if we claim that there is a difference between the populations we are contrasting (in this situation, young women who are keeping house and young women who are working part-time), there is less than a 5% chance that we are incorrect. Therefore, we can feel safe, but just barely, in making the claim that the population means are different. In terms of hypothesis testing, we can confidently reject the null hypothesis of no difference in favor of the alternative hypothesis that there is a difference.

LOOKING MORE CLOSELY AT THE FORMULA

I'm going to take our statistics from the previous example and hypothetically change them several times so we can look more closely at how the t-test works. Remember that our original results just barely achieved significance. I'll first decrease the mean difference:

Original results
Group 1: $\bar{x} = 4.52$, $s = 3.20$, $n = 21$
Group 2: $\bar{x} = 2.48$, $s = 2.45$, $n = 25$
$t = 2.40$, $p < .05$

Revised results
Group 1: $\bar{x} = 4.52$, $s = 3.20$, $n = 21$
Group 2: $\bar{x} = $ **3.00**, $s = 2.45$, $n = 25$
$t = 1.79$, $p < .10$, or not statistically significant

With the revised results, the difference between the sample means is no longer large enough to allow us to be confident enough to claim that there is a difference between the population means. We would accept the null hypothesis in this situation, since the probability of making a type I error has increased above the 0.05 cutoff for the p-value.

Now what if we take the original results and increase the sample sizes?

Original results
Group 1: $\bar{x} = 4.52$, $s = 3.20$, $n = 21$
Group 2: $\bar{x} = 2.48$, $s = 2.45$, $n = 25$
$t = 2.40$, $p < .05$

Revised results
Group 1: $\bar{x} = 4.52$, $s = 3.20$, $n = $ **30**
Group 2: $\bar{x} = 2.48$, $s = 2.45$, $n = $ **35**
$t = 2.83$, $p < .01$

If everything else remains the same, having larger samples increases our certainty in our claim that there is a difference in the population means. Mathematically, it lowers the value of the denominator, giving us a larger t-value. Conceptually, if we achieved the same mean difference with larger samples, we can be more certain that the difference didn't simply occur by chance and that there is a difference in the populations. Last, I'll take the original results and increase the standard deviations:

Group 1: $\bar{x} = 4.52$, $s = 3.20$, $n = 21$
Group 2: $\bar{x} = 2.48$, $s = 2.45$, $n = 25$
$t = 2.40$, $p < .05$

Revised results
Group 1: $x = 4.52$, $s = \mathbf{4.00}$, $n = 21$
Group 2: $x = 2.48$, $s = \mathbf{3.00}$, $n = 25$
$t = 1.92$, $p < .10$, or not statistically significant

We're back to lacking statistical significance. Mathematically, increasing the standard deviations increases the size of the denominator, making the overall t value smaller. Conceptually, this one is the trickiest. Why does increasing the variation in the samples decrease our chances of claiming a population difference? If our samples have more variation, their means may not be as good at representing their respective population means, so the formula takes this into account.

GSS EXAMPLE: SUICIDE, AGE, AND POLITICAL PARTY

The 2012 GSS asks this set of four yes/no questions regarding the acceptability of suicide:

Do you think a person has the right to end his or her own life if this person:

a. Has an incurable disease?
b. Has gone bankrupt?
c. Has dishonored his or her family?
d. Is tired of living and ready to die?

I took these four questions and combined them into an index where 0 meant the respondent didn't support the right to suicide in any of these situations and 4 meant the respondent supported the right to suicide in all four situations. Here is the resulting index in the form of a bar graph:

■ **Exhibit 6.3: Index of Suicide Support**

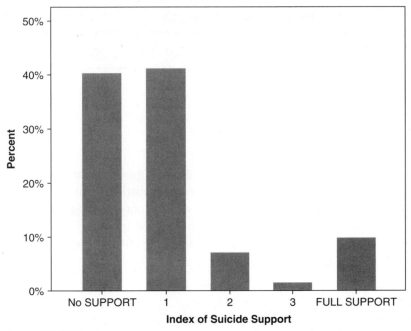

Source: GSS 2012 data.

I decided to examine the support for suicide based on two factors: age and political party. I divided the GSS respondents into three age groups (putting roughly a third of the respondents in each group: young (18–37), middle (38–55), and old (56 and older). For political party, I restricted my analysis to strong Democrats and strong Republicans. Here are the results for the six groups I examined:

■ **Exhibit 6.4: Suicide Support among Six Groups**

Group	*n*	Mean on Index	Standard Deviation
Young Democrats	55	1.04	1.11
Young Republicans	22	0.82	1.37
Middle Democrats	69	1.01	1.11
Middle Republicans	43	0.51	0.91
Old Democrats	89	0.93	1.19
Old Republicans	51	0.59	0.90

Source: GSS 2012 data.

I then ran three t-tests, one for each age group. Here are my results:

■ **Exhibit 6.5: 3 *T*-Tests Using Suicide Support Index**

Comparison	Mean Difference	t-value	p-conclusion
Young Dem. vs. Young Rep.	0.22	0.67	Not Sig.
Middle Dem. vs. Middle Rep.	0.50	2.63	$p < .01$
Old Dem. vs. Old Rep.	0.34	1.89	$p < .10$

Source: GSS 2012 data.

The size of the difference varies from age group to age group. Among the young group, the difference is small and does not even approach statistical significance. Among the old group, the difference is a bit larger. However, it is not quite large enough to garner statistical significance at the $p < .05$ level. The middle age group has the largest difference, and achieves statistical significance at the $p < .01$ level (though it just barely achieved this level, according to my calculations).

TESTING THE DIFFERENCES AMONG MORE THAN TWO MEANS: ANOVA

Often, we want to compare two groups: whites to blacks, Republicans to Democrats, Catholics to Protestants. Occasionally, however, we want to compare more than two groups: whites to blacks to Hispanics, Republicans to Democrats to Independents, Catholics to Protestants to Jews to Muslims. We could run t-tests comparing all the groups, but if we have many groups, this process becomes tedious and can complicate matters with regard to sampling error. When researchers have more than two groups they want to compare, they will likely use a procedure called analysis of variance, or **ANOVA** for short. Psychologists and market researchers, who tend to use several smaller groups, are more likely to use ANOVA than other social scientists. It's a procedure that's fairly simple to carry out, but there's a lot of math involved, so eventually we'll have SPSS do it all. But, first, let's do it step by step, by hand, in order to see how it works.

The reason ANOVA is called ANalysis Of VAriance is that it does just that: It analyzes the variance, both within our groups and between our groups, in order to accomplish its inferential task: to see if it is safe to claim that the population means differ. Notice the similarity here to the t-test:

With a *t*-test, the null hypothesis we're seeking to refute is $\mu_A = \mu_B$
With ANOVA, the null hypothesis we're seeking to refute is $\mu_A = \mu_B = \mu_C \ldots$

For our first example, we'll extend the original TV-watching *t*-test example from earlier to include a third group of young women: those currently in school. Here are the individual TV hours for the women in the three groups:

Young women who are working part-time ($n = 25$):

1, 2, 1, 0, 1, 8, 7, 7, 4, 1, 1, 2, 1, 3, 2, 3, 1, 1, 0, 2, 8, 0, 1, 2, 3

Young women who are in school ($n = 14$):

3, 3, 2, 1, 3, 0, 1, 3, 1, 3, 1, 1, 3, 4

Young women who are keeping house ($n = 21$):

4, 12, 3, 5, 0, 4, 3, 4, 2, 1, 6, 3, 0, 6, 4, 1, 6, 6, 5, 10, 10

Notice that we have roughly the same number of cases in each group, which is a good thing to have with ANOVA. You don't want one group to have 5 cases and another group to have 500. First, we need to calculate the means for each group:

Mean for young women who are working part-time: 2.48
Mean for young women who are in school: 2.07
Mean for young women who are keeping house: 4.52

And we will need the overall mean for all 60 women. We could calculate the overall mean in two ways:

1. Add up the values of all the individual cases and divide by 60:

    $1 + 2 + 1 + 0 + 1 + 8 + 7 + 7 + 4 + 1 + 1 + 2 + 1 + 3 + 2 + 3 + 1 + 1 + 0 +$
    $2 + 8 + 0 + 1 + 2 + 3 + 3 + 3 + 2 + 1 + 3 + 0 + 1 + 3 + 1 + 3 + 1 + 1 + 3 + 4 + 4 +$
    $12 + 3 + 5 + 0 + 4 + 3 + 4 + 2 + 1 + 6 + 3 + 0 + 6 + 4 + 1 + 6 + 6 + 5 + 10 + 10 = 186;$
    $186/60 = 3.10$

2. By rearranging our formula for the mean, use the fact that

    $$\bar{x} = \frac{\Sigma x}{n} \quad \text{is the same as} \quad (\bar{x})(n) = \Sigma x$$

in order to calculate the grouped mean:

$$((2.48 \times 25) + (2.07 \times 14) + (4.52 \times 21))/60 = 186/60 = 3.10$$

The way ANOVA works is that it imagines a situation where all the cases for each group are at their group's sample mean. So, instead of these 14 scores for the young women in school,

3, 3, 2, 1, 3, 0, 1, 3, 1, 3, 1, 1, 3, 4,

we would imagine that the individual 14 scores are

2.07, 2.07, 2.07, 2.07, 2.07, 2.07, 2.07, 2.07, 2.07, 2.07, 2.07, 2.07, 2.07, 2.07.

We want to find how far each of these scores is from the overall mean:

$$2.07 - 3.10 = -1.03$$

But, because we're talking about the variance, we square this distance:

$$-1.03^2 = 1.0609.$$

So we'd have 14 squared distances of 1.0609, or $14 \times 1.0609 = 14.8526$.

We do this for the other two groups:

The 25 young women working part-time:
Distance of this group mean from overall mean: $2.48 - 3.10 = -0.62$
$25 \times -0.62^2 = 9.61$

The 21 young women keeping house:
Distance of this group mean from overall mean: $4.52 - 3.10 = 1.42$
$21 \times 1.42^2 = 42.3444$

Adding all these up gives us $14.8526 + 9.61 + 42.3444 = 66.807$.

So these are the squared deviations *if* all the cases were on their group's mean. Because this is a measure of the deviation between groups, we call this the between-group sum of squares, or BGSS.

But the cases are *not* all the same: they vary away from their respective sample means. The next step is to calculate the total amount of variation that exists *within* the groups. To do this, we calculate the sum of squares within each group, or within-groups sum of squares (WGSS). What we do here is very similar to the procedure in Chapter 3 for calculating the variance. For example, we take the 14 cases for the women in school, calculate their distance from their sample mean (which was 2.07), square these distances, and add up those squared distances:

■ **Exhibit 6.6: Squaring Distances for the In-School Group**

Woman	Hours TV	Distance from Mean	Squared Distance
1	3	0.93	0.8649
2	3	0.93	0.8649
3	2	−0.07	0.0049
4	1	−1.07	1.1449
5	3	0.93	0.8649
6	0	−2.07	4.2849
7	1	−1.07	1.1449
8	3	0.93	0.8649
9	1	−1.07	1.1449
10	3	0.93	0.8649
11	1	−1.07	1.1449
12	1	−1.07	1.1449
13	3	0.93	0.8649
14	4	1.93	3.7249
Total Squared Distances:			18.9286

Source: GSS 2012 data.

I did this for the other two groups:

Women working part-time: 144.24
Women keeping house: 205.2384

So our total within-groups sum of squares is

18.9286 + 144.24 + 205.2384 = 368.41

So far, we have

BGSS = 66.807

WGSS = 368.407

We are ready to calculate the big statistic for the ANOVA test. Just as the chi-square test had a chi-square value and the *t*-test had a *t*-value, for ANOVA we have what is called the *F*-value. It is calculated as follows:

$$F = \frac{BGSS / (\#\, of\ groups - 1)}{WGSS / (\#\, of\ cases - \#\, of\ groups)}$$

So we have

$$F = \frac{66.807 / (3 - 1)}{368.407 / (60 - 3)} = 5.17$$

Just as with a chi-square test or a *t*-test, we go to a statistical table to see how our *F*-value of 5.17 measures up and to see if we can confidently state that the population means differ from one another. There are two *F*-tables, one for the 0.05 level of confidence and another for the 0.01 level of confidence. Notice that this differs from both the chi-square table and the *t*-table, where we move our way as far to the right as we can. With ANOVA, we first see if our *F*-value exceeds the value for the 0.05 table. Notice that this table is set up with degrees of freedom on each side: df_1 and df_2. For df_1, we use number of groups minus 1. For df_2, we use number of cases minus number of groups. So our *F*-value has to be greater than 3.15 (I used $df_1 = 2$ and $df_2 = 60$, the closest value to my true df_2 of 57). Because $5.17 > 3.15$, I can at least conclude $p < .05$. Looking at the 0.01 *F*-table, our *F*-value has to be greater than 4.98. Because $5.17 > 4.98$, we can also conclude that $p < .01$. But what probability is this? We can say, with 99% confidence, that the three population means are not equal. In terms of hypothesis testing, we can confidently reject the null hypothesis that the sample means are equal, and we reject this in favor of the alternative hypothesis that the sample means are not equal. Notice how this is phrased: the three means are not equal. We cannot claim with ANOVA that particular population means differ from each other. We are studying the means as a group.

Just as we did with the *t*-test, let's take the original results and slightly modify them in order to get a better feel for how ANOVA works. What I'm going to do is remove the three women from the keeping house group who watch an extreme amount of television: the two women who watch 10 hours and the one woman who watches 12 hours. These women raised the overall mean, raised the overall amount of variation, raised their group's mean, and raised their group's variation. Here are the original and revised results:

■ Exhibit 6.7: Original and Revised ANOVA Results

	Original Results	Revised Results
Mean for part-time group	2.48	2.48
Mean for school group	2.07	2.07
Mean for keeping house group	4.52	3.50
BGSS	66.807	18.261
WGSS	368.407	233.669
F-value	5.17	2.11
p-conclusion	$p < .01$	$p > .05$

Source: GSS 2012 data, with several cases removed.

Removing these three cases lowers both the BGSS and WGSS, but it lowers the BGSS by 73% $((18.261 - 66.807)/66.807 = 0.73)$ and the WGSS by 37% $((233.669 - 368.407)/368.407 = 0.37)$. Therefore, when we recalculate the *F*-value, it goes down from 5.17 to 2.11. When we go to the *F*-table, we see that this lower *F*-value doesn't allow us to achieve statistical significance at the $p < .05$ level. We made the mean for one of the groups (women keeping house) more similar to the means of the other groups, and this change was enough to change the outcome of the overall ANOVA result. Whereas originally we could claim with confidence that the means as a group differed, with the revised results, we cannot claim this.

A COMPARATIVE GRAPHICAL APPROACH TO UNDERSTANDING ANOVA

Now I'm going to take the preceding example, hypothetically simplify the numbers, and show you three different ANOVAs using bar graphs. I conducted an ANOVA using Groups A, B, and C; a second ANOVA using Groups D, E, and F; and a third ANOVA using Groups G, H, and I. Notice the following things: (1) each group has 14 people in it; (2) each set of three groups has the same means: a mean of 3 in the first group, a mean of 4 in the second group, and a mean of 5 in the third group; (3) there is the least variation in the first set of groups (A, B, C): almost all of the cases are at their group's mean; the next set of groups (D, E, F) has more variation, and the last set of groups (G, H, I) has the most variation. Notice that, in terms of overlap, there is more overlap in the second set of groups than in the first set, and there is the most overlap in the third set of groups.

■ **Exhibit 6.8: 3 ANOVAs with Different Levels of Variation**

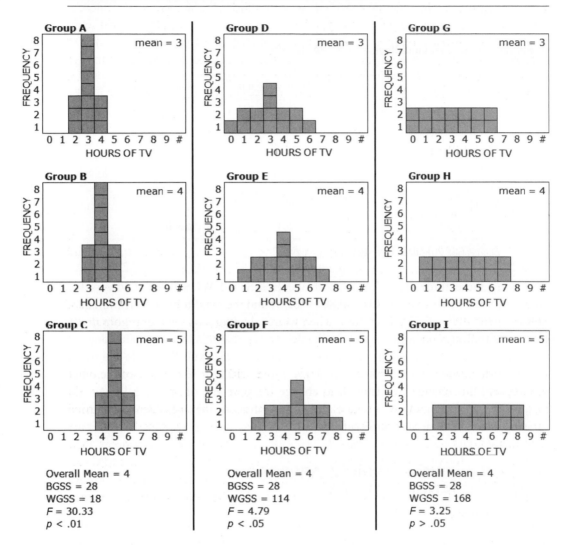

Overall Mean = 4
BGSS = 28
WGSS = 18
$F = 30.33$
$p < .01$

Overall Mean = 4
BGSS = 28
WGSS = 114
$F = 4.79$
$p < .05$

Overall Mean = 4
BGSS = 28
WGSS = 168
$F = 3.25$
$p > .05$

The BGSS for each set of groups is the same: 28. Do you see why this is? Because the overall mean is the same for each set of groups, and because each set has groups with means of 3, 4, and 5, these similarities give us the same BGSS. Where the sets start to differ is the WGSS. More variation makes the WGSS get larger: notice how it grows from 18 to 114 to 168. This growth in the WGSS makes the F-value go down: from

30.33 to 4.79 to 3.25. And, when the *F*-value goes down, the *p*-value goes up. In the first set of groups, where there is little variation and little overlap, we are confident at the $p < .01$ level in rejecting the null hypothesis that $\mu_A = \mu_B = \mu_C$. In the second set of groups, where there is more variation and more overlap, we are confident at the $p < .05$ level in rejecting the null hypothesis that $\mu_D = \mu_E = \mu_F$. In the third set of groups, we cannot reach the $p < .05$ level, and therefore, we must accept the null hypothesis that $\mu_G = \mu_H = \mu_I$. Even though, in the third set of groups, the three means differed by the same amount as in the other two sets of groups, it is the *variance* within the groups in the third set that diminishes our ability to claim there are population mean differences among the groups.

GSS EXAMPLE: ATTITUDES VERSUS BEHAVIOR ABOUT HOUSEWORK

The 2012 GSS asks numerous questions regarding housework, some attitudinal and some behavioral. On the attitude side, here is one of the questions:

It is much better for everyone involved if the man is the achiever outside the home and the woman takes care of the home and family: strongly agree, agree, disagree, or strongly disagree.

Among married people, 9% of men strongly agree with this statement, and another 32% agree. Among married women, 5% strongly agree and another 27% agree. Of married men, 10% strongly disagree with this statement, whereas 24% of married women strongly disagree. On the behavioral side, respondents are asked to estimate how many hours of housework they do per week, as well as how many hours their spouse does. I took these two variables and calculated a new variable called PCTH-HWK: the percentage of the total amount of housework in a household that the respondent does. Overall, men say they do just over a third of the housework, whereas women say they do about two-thirds.

The question is, do people who respond differently on the attitudinal question actually behave differently? That is, do men who answer the attitudinal question by espousing traditional gender roles actually do *less* housework, and do men who espouse progressive gender roles actually do *more* housework? Do women who espouse traditional gender roles actually do *more* housework, and do women who espouse progressive gender roles actually do *less* housework? Given that this attitudinal question has four responses, this gives us four groups to compare, so we will use ANOVA. First, here are the results for the men:

■ **Exhibit 6.9: Housework ANOVA Results for Men**

	n	Mean % Housework	Standard Deviation
Strongly Agree	27	32.98	20.20
Agree	96	29.62	23.12
Disagree	154	40.73	22.15
Strongly Disagree	37	42.60	28.33
Total	314	36.89	

$(32.98 - 36.89)^2 \times 27 =$	412.78
$(29.62 - 36.89)^2 \times 96 =$	5,073.88
$(40.73 - 36.89)^2 \times 154 =$	2,270.82
$(42.60 - 36.89)^2 \times 37 =$	1,206.35
BGSS	8,963.83
$20.20^2 \times 27 =$	11,017.08
$23.12^2 \times 96 =$	51,315.30
$22.15^2 \times 154 =$	75,555.87
$28.33^2 \times 37 =$	29,695.79
WGSS	167,584.04

$$F = (8{,}963.83/3) / (167{,}584.04/310) = 5.53$$

With an F-value of 5.53, we go to the first F-table and see that this value exceeds 2.60 (the value at the bottom of the table under the $df_1 = 3$ column). Looking at the second F-table, we see that this value exceeds 3.78 (the value at the bottom of the table under the $df_1 = 3$ column). Therefore, our p-conclusion is $p < .01$. We can conclude that the population means are not equal. Examining the means, we see that men who answered progressively (say they) do around 40% of the housework, whereas men who answered traditionally do around 30% of the housework. Now let's look at the women's results:

■ **Exhibit 6.10: Housework ANOVA Results for Women**

	n	Mean % Housework	Standard Deviation
Strongly Agree	19	75.73	17.50
Agree	91	68.29	26.75
Disagree	173	66.91	26.02
Strongly Disagree	94	64.38	26.65
Total	377	67.05	

$(75.73 - 67.05)^2 \times 19 =$	1,431.51
$(68.28 - 67.05)^2 \times 91 =$	137.67
$(66.91 - 67.05)^2 \times 173 =$	3.39
$(64.38 - 67.05)^2 \times 94 =$	670.12
BGSS:	2,242.69
$17.50^2 \times 19 =$	5,818.75
$26.75^2 \times 91 =$	65,116.19
$26.02^2 \times 173 =$	117,127.99
$26.65^2 \times 94 =$	66,760.92
WGSS:	254,823.85

$$F = (2242.69/3)/(254823.85/373) = 1.09$$

Our *F*-value of 1.09 is less than the 2.60 (the value at the bottom of the table under the $df_1 = 3$ column). Therefore, we cannot reach the *p*-conclusion of $p < .05$. We cannot claim that the population means are not equal. Examining the means, we see that the women's differences between the four groups are smaller than the differences among the men, and the amount of variation within the women's groups is a bit larger. This results in a smaller *F*-value. In summary, it seems as though men's attitudes affect their behavior, whereas women's attitudes do not affect their behavior. As you've likely noticed from my parenthetical phrases earlier, one reason to be skeptical of these findings is the fact that the housework behavior questions ask the respondents to self-report how many hours of housework they do. This is not only difficult to estimate accurately on the spot, but people may not be truthful about this behavior.

INTERCHAPTER CONNECTION: ANOVA AND CHI-SQUARE

Before we get to another example, I want to talk briefly about how ANOVA and the chi-square test are doing something similar. They both set up hypothetical situations to which we then compare our real data. Recall that, in the chi-square test, we created a hypothetical situation where the two variables were completely independent of one another. That is, we created a table of expected frequencies, where we expected the frequencies we would achieve if the variables were completely unrelated. We then compared our observed values to the expected values. If there was enough of a relationship between the variables within the samples, then our observed values were different enough from the expected values. This elicited a chi-square value that was large enough and a p-value that was small enough to claim that in the population there is a relationship between the two variables.

With ANOVA, we also set up a hypothetical situation. However, here the situation is that all the scores are at their respective sample means (this is what BGSS is). Then we use our actual data to calculate the WGSS. We then, just as with the chi-square test, compare the actual to the hypothetical. But, in order to claim confidently that the population means differ, in ANOVA we want WGSS to be *similar* to BGSS, not *different*, as was the case with chi-square. If WGSS is quite a bit larger than BGSS (meaning that the scores within the samples vary dramatically, making it more difficult to claim that there are differences in the populations based on these widely varying samples), then when we calculate the F-value it will be smaller (recall that WGSS is in the denominator), and a smaller F-value elicits a larger p-value. If the WGSS is similar to the BGSS (meaning that the scores within the samples are similar), the F-value will be more likely to be large enough to claim that the population means differ.

GSS EXAMPLE: INTERNET USE, RACE, AND GENDER

The 2012 GSS asked respondents how many hours per week they spend using the Internet. Here are the means for six groups:

Mean for white men: 10.72   Mean for white women: 9.87

Mean for black men: 16.70   Mean for black women: 9.21

Mean for other men: 10.92   Mean for other women: 8.83

I conducted an F-test comparing the three groups of men, and with an F-value of 3.42, the significance level was $p < .05$. Therefore, we can conclude that the men's population means differ. I then conducted an F-test comparing the three groups of women. The *F*-value was a mere 0.17, making the significance level far above 0.05, meaning that we cannot conclude that the women's population means differ. However, what I want you to notice here is that the real cause of the higher *F*-value in the men's *F*-test is that the black men differ from the other two groups. This allows us to conclude that the population means differ, because the black men differ from the white men and the black men differ from the other men. But look how close the white and other men are: they differ by only 0.20 hours. In fact, they differ by less than white women and black women differ (0.66), or black women and other women differ (0.38). An ANOVA that gives you a statistically significant result does not imply that all of the means differ from one another. It can simply mean that one of the means differs from the other means. So don't just rely on the significance level; examine the means carefully.

LITERATURE EXAMPLE: OVERDOING GENDER

Within the gender literature, there is what is known as the "masculine overcompensation thesis: if a man's masculinity is threatened (that is, he is accused of being "less than a real man"), he will overcompensate, engaging in overly masculine behaviors. Although this might be considered common knowledge, few have put it to an empirical test. Robb Willer, Christabel Rogalin, Bridget Conlin, and Michael Wojnowicz developed a set of innovative ways to examine this thesis, and published their findings in the *American Journal of Sociology* in 2013, in an article called "Overdoing Gender: A Test of the Masculine Overcompensation Thesis."

They first conducted a laboratory experiment on 60 female college students and 50 male college students (all from Cornell University). The students were given a "gender identity survey" to fill out, and then they were given their score on the survey, ranging from 0 (*very masculine*) to 50 (*very feminine*). What the students didn't know was that they were assigned their scores at random: half the men received scores of 11 (on the masculine side); half received scores of 32 (on the feminine side). Half the women received score of 39 (on the feminine side); half received scores of 18 (on the masculine side). Thus, the "gender threat" was receiving a feminine score if you were a male and receiving a masculine score if you were a female. Willer then had the students fill out a survey of political attitudes, and from these responses built a 7-point index of support for the Iraq War (with a higher number meaning more support) and a 7-point index of hostility toward homosexuality (with a higher number meaning more hostile). Finally, the students were asked to fill out a "Car Purchasing Survey," in which they read about four types of vehicles (an SUV, a minivan, a sedan, and a coupe), and then rated each vehicle (higher numbers being more positive) and how much they would be willing to pay for each vehicle. Here are their results:

■ **Exhibit 6.11: The Effects of Gender Threat on Men and Women**

	Gender Threat	No Gender Threat	*t*
Means for Men (*n* = 50)	*n* = 25	*n* = 25	
Support for Iraq War	3.64 (1.85)	2.65 (1.52)	2.06
View of Homosexuality	4.03 (1.68)	2.77 (1.60)	2.70
SUV Desirability	6.56 (2.63)	4.84 (3.16)	2.09
SUV Pay ($1,000s)	28.00 (13.76)	20.68 (10.63)	2.10
Means for Women (*n* = 60)	*n* = 30	*n* = 30	
Support for Iraq War	2.52 (1.59)	2.40 (1.39)	0.30
View of Homosexuality	2.54 (1.81)	2.20 (1.52)	0.80
SUV Desirability	5.20 (3.03)	5.17 (2.74)	0.05
SUV Pay ($1,000s)	22.52 (14.60)	25.38 (19.52)	0.63

Note: Standard deviations are in parentheses.
Source: Adapted from Willer et al. (2013).

Willer uses *t*-tests to see if there is a difference between the threat and no-threat groups. The rightmost column has the *t* values (if you want more practice calculating the *t* values by hand, you have all the statistics you need to do so: sample sizes, means, and standard deviations). All of the men's *t*-values are statistically significant at the $p <$ .05 level (except for the 2.70, which is significant at the $p < .01$ level). None of the women's *t*-values was statistically significant. These results are predictable, but nonetheless fascinating. The men whose gender was threatened were significantly more likely to support the Iraq War, express hostility toward homosexuality, positively rate the SUV, and pay more for the SUV than were the men whose gender was not threatened. Among the women, gender threat had no effect: all of the differences are small and fail to achieve statistical significance. These findings were in line with what Willer predicted based on the gender literature: men react much more strongly to gender threat than women do.

However, because Willer uses *t*-tests, and *t*-tests are a type of inference, let's be critical for a moment. One of the rules of inference is that the sample must be drawn randomly and everyone in the population must have some chance of getting into the sample. Given that the experiment participants were all from Cornell University, and they were not drawn randomly from a registrar's list (they received payment and the option of extra credit in a sociology class), this rule is broken. However, we can also defend Willer in numerous ways. First, inference is commonly used in experiments such as this. Second, even though he does not select the study participants at random, he does use a random mechanism to distribute them into the two groups (threat and no threat). Third, in the article, he then goes on and conducts more studies, using survey research based on random samples to show that the gender threat effect exists in these other research sites. Personally, I will never look at a guy driving an SUV in the same way again.

LITERATURE EXAMPLE: ACTIVISM THROUGH THE LIFE COURSE

Once an activist, always an activist? This is the question that concerned James Max Fendrich and Kenneth Lovoy in their article "Back to the Future: Adult Political Behavior of Former Student Activists," which appeared in the journal *American Sociological Review* in 1988. They wanted to see if those who were activists in college were politically active a generation later. But they didn't simply want to compare activists to non-activists, which would have called for *t*-tests. They wanted to examine three groups: students who were not active, students who were "institutional activists" (i.e., in college government), and students who were "radical activists" (i.e., those in engaging in on-the-street protest activities). Thus, having three groups to compare, they used ANOVA in their analyses.

They conducted a survey with 85 former students from the Florida State University, which during the civil rights movement in the 1960s was a hotbed of civil rights activity. During this period, there were students who did not get involved, students who worked within the university's institutions and with university administration to seek change, and students who engaged in confrontational protest activities. Fenrich and Lovoy built a sample of each group (*n*s: 32 noninvolved, 30 institutional activists, 23 radical activists) and asked them a series of questions about their level of political activity in 1986. They asked them about their current engagement in institutional politics (i.e., campaign participation and voting) and noninstitutional politics (i.e., protest and community activism), and then ran several ANOVAs to see if there were differences among the three groups. Here are some of their results:

■ **Exhibit 6.12: Political Activity among Three Groups**

	Mean	Std.Dev.	*F*-value	*p*-conclusion
Protest			13.03	$p < .001$
Radical activists	5.61	1.99		
Institutional activists	3.80	1.85		
Noninvolved	3.47	0.92		
Community activism			4.67	$p < .05$
Radical activists	13.04	4.43		
Institutional activists	12.20	4.89		
Noninvolved	9.78	3.18		
Party and campaign work			3.12	$p < .05$
Radical activists	8.00	2.95		
Institutional activists	7.87	3.08		
Noninvolved	6.28	2.80		
Voting and patriotism			17.71	$p < .001$
Radical activists	8.87	2.32		
Institutional activists	11.33	1.12		
Noninvolved	10.91	1.22		

Source: Adapted from Fendrich and Lovoy (1988).

Twenty years after college, these respondents for the most part continued their activism (or lack thereof). All of the ANOVAs resulted in statistically significant differences, meaning that we can claim that the population means differ. However, this begs these questions: What is the population? All college students? All students at state colleges? All students at large state colleges? Again, we see that inference is used in a less than ideal situation. Site-specific studies are quite common and many use inferential statistics, although the sample is less than ideally random.

Note that the general trend in ANOVA we discussed previously holds for these results. The first ANOVA had differences between the means and a low amount of variation within the groups, resulting in a high *F*-value and a quite significant *p*-conclusion. The second ANOVA, compared to the first, had similar differences between the means. However, notice that the amount of variation is higher for each group. This results in a lower *F*-value and a *p*-conclusion of only $p < .05$.

CONCLUSION . . . WITH INTERCHAPTER CONNECTIONS

Your inference arsenal is getting fuller all the time. With chi-square, confidence intervals, *t*-tests, and ANOVA, you have the ability to take many types of sample information and say a lot about the populations from which they were drawn. One of your major goals now should be to understand *when* you use *which* of these procedures. This is a critical skill to develop with statistics: looking at your variables and making these decisions. For example, in deciding whether to use a chi-square test or a *t*-test or ANOVA, the following are some possible scenarios.

You have an independent variable and a dependent variable, and both of those variables are measured at the nominal, the ordinal level, or are dichotomies: you would want to create a crosstab and run a chi-square test. For example, if you wanted to compare blacks and whites on a single "Is suicide acceptable, yes or no?" question, you would have two dichotomies, so you would want to create a crosstab and run a chi-square test. If you wanted to compare blacks with whites with people from other races on this same suicide question, you would still use a crosstab and chi-square.

Now say you have an independent variable that is a dichotomy, but now your dependent variable is measured at the ratio level. If this is the variable combination you have, you'd want to use a *t*-test. For example, if you wanted to compare blacks and whites on a ratio-level suicide acceptability index, you would want to run a *t*-test comparing blacks and whites.

Last, say you have an independent variable that is nominal or ordinal but not a dichotomy, and you still have a ratio-level dependent variable. In this scenario, you would want to use ANOVA. For example, if you wanted to compare blacks, whites, and others on the ratio-level suicide index, you would want to run an ANOVA comparing these three groups.

In summary, before you run a statistical test, carefully consider what your variables are.

SPSS DEMONSTRATIONS

Please visit the book's website (www.routledge.com/cw/linneman) to view videos of these demonstrations.

Running a *T*-Test

As with most procedures in SPSS, running a *t*-test is simple, but interpreting the output is where things get a bit complicated. We'll go through the procedure with a simple question: If you were born outside the United States, do you have a higher score on the Immigration Index? To run a *t*-test, we click

Analyze → Compare Means → Independent-Samples T-Test . . .

This brings us to this room:

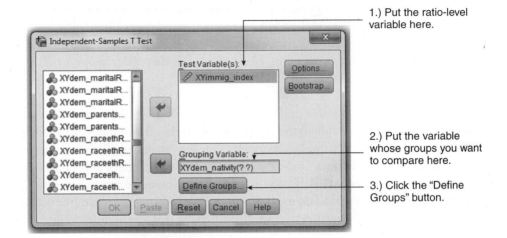

1.) Put the ratio-level variable here.

2.) Put the variable whose groups you want to compare here.

3.) Click the "Define Groups" button.

Notice that, when you place a variable in the Grouping Variable box, SPSS gives you two question marks. This is its way of asking you which two groups you want to compare. When you click on the "Define Groups" button, SPSS will take you to a "room within a room" where you tell it what your two groups are. Even if there are only two valid groups within the variable, as we have in this case, it is still necessary to do this. After putting in our two valid groups (0 for "Born in U.S." and 1 for "Not born in U.S."), the original room now looks like this:

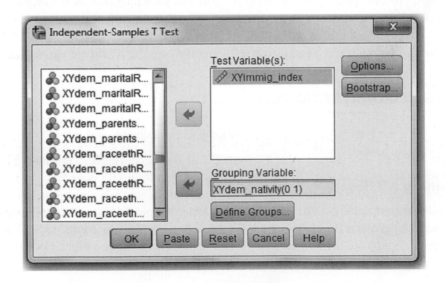

Notice that, once we tell SPSS what groups to compare, the "OK" button becomes active. Once we click it, here is the output we get

Group statistics

	recoded dem_nativity (1=foreign)	N	Mean	Std. Deviation	Std. Error Mean
Immigration Index	Born in U.S.	4720	1.9639	0.99523	0.01449
	Not born in U.S.	586	2.4804	0.96371	0.03981

Independent Samples Test

		Levene's Test for Equality of Variances		t-test for Equality of Means						95% Confidence Interval of the Difference	
		F	Sig.	t	df	Sig. (2-tailed)	Mean Difference	Std. Error Difference		Lower	Upper
Immigration Index	Equal variances assumed	1.416	0.234	-11.890	5304	0.000	-0.516	0.043		-0.602	-0.431
	Equal variances not assumed			-12.192	748.544	0.000	-0.516	0.042		-0.600	-0.433

As we have done before, we can cut this output significantly:

Group Statistics

	recoded dem_nati...	N	Mean	Std. Deviation
Immigration Index	Born in U.S.	4720	1.96	0.995
	Not born in U.S.	586	2.48	0.964

Independent Samples Test

		t-test for Equality of Means			
		t	df	Sig. (2-tailed)	Mean Difference
Immigration Index	Equal variances not assumed	-12.192	748.544	0.000	-0.516

Perhaps you're wondering why I deleted the first row of the second box, Equal variances assumed. And what is that "Levene's Test for Equality of Variances"? This is one of those points where I could spend pages and pages going over this issue, but I have decided against it because, in the thousands of *t*-tests I have run over the years, this difference between equal and unequal variances simply does not matter 99.9% of the time. So I opt to use the more statistically conservative line (equal variances not assumed) and just go with that.

We find that the sample means do differ enough to claim that the population means differ: those born outside the United States score about half a point higher on average on the Immigration Index. The *p*-value is 0.000, or *p* < .001. We reject the null hypothesis that there is no difference between the two populations.

Running an ANOVA

We'll use the same dependent variable—the Immigration Index—as we did with the *t*-test. But we'll use an independent variable that has more than two groups. We'll use the original ANES variable called dem_parents, which has three groups:

1. Both parents born in the U.S.
2. One parent born in the U.S.
3. Both parents born outside the U.S.

We will also run this only using Hispanics who are under the age of 25 (your Select Cases command is: dem_raceeth = 3 & XYdem_age < 25)

We click

Analyze → Compare Means → One-Way ANOVA . . .

This takes us to this room:

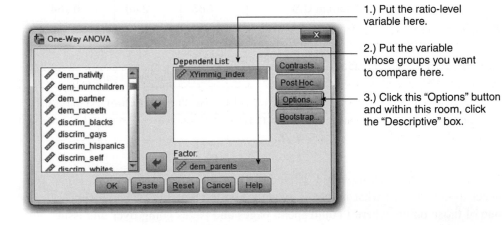

1.) Put the ratio-level variable here.

2.) Put the variable whose groups you want to compare here.

3.) Click this "Options" button and within this room, click the "Descriptive" box.

This gives us this output:

Descriptives

Immigration Index

	N	Mean	Std. Deviation	Std. Error	95% Confidence Interval for Mean		Minimum	Maximum
					Lower Bound	Upper Bound		
1. Both parents born in the U.S.	38	2.42	0.905	0.147	2.13	2.72	0	4
2. One parent born in the U.S.	22	2.61	1.054	0.225	2.14	3.08	1	4
3. Neither parent born in the U.S.	55	2.90	0.566	0.076	2.74	3.05	2	4
Total	115	2.69	0.817	0.076	2.54	2.84	0	4

ANOVA

Immigration Index

	Sum of Squares	df	Mean Square	F	Sig.
Between Groups	5.167	2	2.583	4.081	0.019
Within Groups	70.910	112	0.633		
Total	76.077	114			

We see that the sample means differ, and according to the ANOVA these differences are large enough to be able to claim confidently that the population means differ: the significance level is at 0.019, which is just under our $p < .05$ cutoff.

FROM OUTPUT TO PRESENTATION

In a typical results presentation, you will likely have multiple *t*-tests you want to present, so the key is to do so as clearly and efficiently as possible. Here is an example that combines ideas from the *t*-test SPSS demonstration and the ANOVA SPSS demonstration. It looks at the effects of nativity on Immigration Index score among the four age groups of Hispanics.

▨ **Exhibit 6.13: Effects of Nativity on Immigration Attitudes for Four Hispanic Age Groups**

Age Group	Born in U.S. $\bar{x}$	sd	n	Born Outside of U.S. $\bar{x}$	sd	n	Statistical Significance
17–34	2.65	0.84	251	2.79	0.74	59	n.s.
35–49	2.31	0.98	126	2.90	0.71	97	$p < .001$
50–64	2.37	0.88	105	2.55	0.93	103	n.s.
65+	2.28	0.94	56	2.60	0.75	68	$p < .05$

Note: sd = standard deviation; n.s. = not significant.

Although this table presents a lot of information, it's clearly presented. You could take the statistics and reconstruct each *t*-test yourself.

EXERCISES

Exercise 1

Do those who vote differ from those who don't vote with regard to how much they trust the government? Using ANES data, run a *t*-test comparing those who voted in the 2012 election with those who didn't vote. Compare them on the Trust in Government Index. Interpret your results.

Exercise 2 (Answer Available in Appendix D)

Although poor people are the predominant recipients of welfare, they are not one and the same, especially with regard to how people feel about each group. Using ANES data, run *t*-tests comparing people who claim they are extremely liberal with those who claim they are extremely conservative. Compare them on two of the feeling thermometers: for the poor, and for people on welfare. Interpret your results.

Exercise 3

Most smartphones are made in China. If you have a smartphone, and you have it with you all the time, and you think it makes your life wonderful, are you perhaps less concerned about China's progress? Run a *t*-test using ANES data comparing those who have smartphones with those who don't have smartphones, using the China Concern Index. Interpret your results.

Exercise 4

Among the ANES unique group of people who simultaneously rate Christian Fundamentalists and atheists at 100 on the feeling thermometer, is there a difference between men and women with regard to how they score on the Traditionalism Index? Here are the raw data:

Men's scores: 7, 10, 12, 11, 9, 10, 13, 8, 7
Women's scores: 5, 6, 5, 8, 5, 4, 11, 8

Carry out a *t*-test by hand and explain your results.

Exercise 5 (Answer Available in Appendix D)

Among the ANES unique group of widows who have three or more children at home, is there a difference between those with a high school education or less and those who have some college or more with regard to household income? Here are the raw data:

High school or less: 21.25, 2.5, 72.5, 2.5, 11.25
Some college or more: 32.5, 32.5, 47.5, 2.5, 72.5, 37.5

Carry out a *t*-test by hand and explain your results.

Exercise 6

Using ANES data, carry out an ANOVA using the Muslims Feeling Thermometer. Compare the groups on the original religion variable regarding the Bible (whether or not it is the word of God). Explain your results.

Exercise 7

Using ANES data, carry out an ANOVA that will allow you to see if you can claim that the four age categories differ (use the recoded age variable that has four age categories) on the Election Integrity Index. Explain your results.

Exercise 8

Using the ANES unique group of sad men, here are the raw data for the recoded religious attendance variable for three groups on the Word of God variable:

Literal Word of God: 0, 1.5, 3, 1.5, 8, 0
Word of God, not Literal: 4, 4, 0, 0, 8, 8
Not Word of God: 0, 0, 0, 0, 0, 0, 0

By hand, conduct an ANOVA to see if you can claim that the population means are not equal.

Exercise 9

Use the PewShop dataset to address this question: is there a significance difference between men and women on the Technology-Enabled Shopping Index?

Exercise 10

Use the PewShop dataset to address this question: Do people who are parents have significantly more technology overall?

Exercise 11

Use the PewShop dataset to address this question: do people in various types of communities (rural, suburban, urban) have significantly different behavior with regard to technology-enabled shopping (i.e., the shopindex)?

Exercise 12

Use the PewShop dataset to address this question: Among the Asian respondents, do people of different work statuses have different levels of education (measured with the recoded education variable of education in years)?

Exercise 13 (Answer Available in Appendix D)

Use the PewHealth dataset to address this question: Is there a difference between men and women with regard to their willingness to seek out health information on the Internet (as measured by the Internet Health Use Index)?

Exercise 14

Use the PewHealth dataset to address this question: Is there a difference between parents and nonparents with regard to the number of things they use their cell phones for (as measured by the Cellphone Use Index)?

Exercise 15

When I lived in Texas, I recall leaving my city, Houston, and going out into the suburbs and rural areas and noticing very different levels of health. Is this reflected in the PewHealth data? Select cases to look only at Texans; then run an ANOVA to see if there are community differences with regard to the Health Conditions Index.

Exercise 16

Just as in Exercise 15, let's stay in Texas, and only look at the whites, blacks, and Hispanics. With regard to the Health Conditions Index, is there a difference among these groups?

Exercise 17

Using the PewKids dataset, compare kids in married and divorced/separated families: Do they significantly differ on the Experiences with Being Bullied Index?

Exercise 18

Does experience with social networking make kids more savvy about what they post? Compare kids who say they have refrained from posting something online to kids who say they haven't refrained from posting something online. Compare them on the Child's Social Networking Uses Index.

Exercise 19 (Answer Available in Appendix D)

Does geography influence texting? Perhaps kids who live in communities with more face-to-face interaction text less than people from other types of communities. Run an ANOVA using the three types of communities and compare them on the number of texts per day variable. Explain your results. Why do you think the results turned out the way they did?

Exercise 20

Under communism, religion was frowned on in the countries of Eastern Europe. Do these countries still differ from the countries of Western Europe? Use the variable RELPER in a *t*-test to find out, and explain your results.

Exercise 21

Does a higher percentage of people from Asian countries live with their parents compared to people from South American countries? Run a *t*-test by hand, and then check your work by running the *t*-test in SPSS.

Exercise 22

Do groups of countries differ on their concern over global warming? Run an ANOVA using the COUNTRY5CAT and GLWARM variables. Run it twice: with all the sets of countries, and then with all the sets except the Asian countries.

## Chapter 7

GIVE ME ONE GOOD REASON WHY: BIVARIATE CORRELATION AND REGRESSION

This chapter covers . . .

. . . a review of linear equations
. . . how to calculate and interpret a regression equation
. . . how to calculate and interpret a correlation coefficient
. . . what explained variation really means
. . . how to use regression in forecasting
. . . how researchers used correlations to study support for the war on terror
. . . how a researcher used correlations to study physical attractiveness

INTRODUCTION

I am five feet six inches tall. And proud! The average height of the American male is five feet nine inches, so I am a bit on the shorter side, but not dramatically so. Occasionally, I experience what I consider to be discrimination, but these are minor occurrences, such as when clothing store sizes start at "M" instead of "S." So imagine my absolute horror when I heard that studies had found a very serious form of discrimination: shorter men actually make less money than do taller men. I thought that this would be a good example to start our exploration of **simple regression**, as the variables involved are so very visual: you can see when someone's short or tall, and you can see when someone's poor or rich. These are also good variables because both of them are measured at the ratio level. Regression in its simple form is bivariate, involving two ratio-level variables that are related to one another in a linear fashion. One of these variables serves as the independent variable, and the other serves as the dependent variable.

LINEAR EQUATIONS

What ordinary regression does is create a linear equation, so, before we get to how it does that, it might be a good idea to review the simple algebra behind it. You might remember the basic format of a linear equation as $y = m(x) + b$, where m is the slope and b is the constant. I'm going to revise that a bit in order to ease you into regression-ese. The typical format of a regression equation is $Y = a + b(X)$, where Y is the value of the dependent variable, X is the value of the independent variable, b is the value of the slope, and a, also called the y-intercept, is the constant. Let's do a few examples and this should all come back to you. Say the slope is 2 and the constant is 1. Our equation would be $Y = 1 + 2(X)$. In terms of a visual graph, it would look like the thick line in Exhibit 7.1:

■ **Exhibit 7.1: Three Positive Linear Equations**

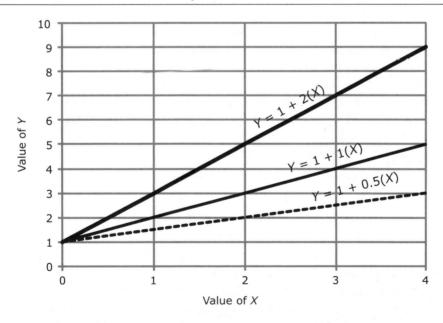

We have the values of X going from left to right across the bottom on what we call the horizontal axis. We have the values of Y going from bottom to top along what we call the vertical axis. When $X = 0$, we have $Y = 1 + 2(0)$, or 1. So a, the constant, is what Y equals when X is equal to 0. The slope, or b, is 2, which means that every time X goes to the right by 1, Y goes up by 2. For example, when X changes from 0 to 1, Y changes from 1 to 3. When X changes from 1 to 2, Y changes from 3 to 5. If we decrease the value of the slope (going from 2 to 1 to 0.5), notice that the line becomes less steep, as illustrated by the other lines on the graph.

Just a couple more of these to be sure you remember how this works. This time, we'll do a negative relationship: $Y = 9 - 2(X)$. The line crosses the Y-axis at 9 this time (for that is what Y equals when X is 0). Then, every time X goes to the right by 1, Y will go down by 2, as the thick solid line on in Exhibit 7.2 shows.

■ **Exhibit 7.2: Two More Linear Equations**

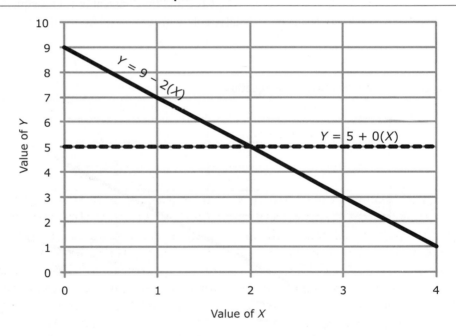

What if our slope were zero? That would mean that whatever X was simply doesn't matter, because any value multiplied by zero is going to be zero. Y will simply take on the value of whatever the constant is, regardless of the value of X, and we will have a horizontal line coming straight out from the y-intercept. This is illustrated in Exhibit 7.2 by the dotted line representing the equation $Y = 5 + 0(X)$. This will prove useful a bit later on in this chapter.

CALCULATING THE REGRESSION EQUATION

Let's get back to our example. Our dependent variable—the variable that is dependent on the other variable—is salary. We are saying that what your salary is *depends* on your height. Height is the independent variable, because it does not depend on anything, at least in this scenario. We are going to use a small hypothetical dataset to investigate this relationship. We locate six men who are equivalent in many ways, except for their heights, and we ask them for their salaries. Here are the data:

Exhibit 7.3: Six Men's Heights and Salaries

Man	Height	Salary (in $10,000s)
Floyd	4	2
Ernie	5	3
Dave	6	4
Charlie	6	7
Buck	7	9
Andre	8	5

Source: Hypothetical data.

First look at Floyd, Ernie, and Dave. If we were looking at just these three guys, it would seem that there is a perfect relationship between height and salary: every time height goes up by 1 foot, salary goes up by the same amount of salary (in this case, $10,000). It seems that height explains all of the increase in salary. But then we add Charlie into the mix. Charlie is the same height as Dave, but makes $30,000 more than he does. So this throws off our perfect relationship, as does the next jump from Charlie to Buck, where the 1-foot increase in height delivers a $20,000 increase in salary, rather than the $10,000 increase we observed at first. And then we get to Andre, who is an uncomfortable 8 feet tall. His salary is actually *less* than Buck's by quite a bit. So it is not a perfect relationship by far. Here's what the points look like on a **scatterplot**:

■ **Exhibit 7.4: A Scatterplot of Six Hypothetical Men's Heights and Salaries**

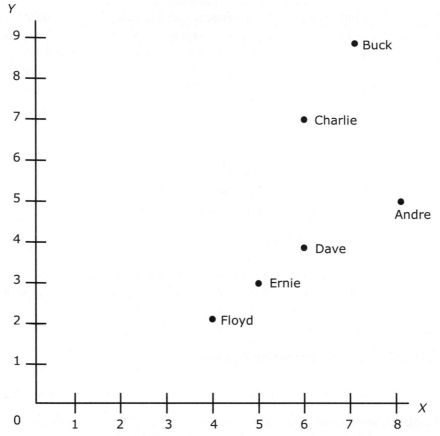

There is clearly a relationship, but it's nowhere near perfect. In a perfect relationship (as we would have if it were just Floyd, Ernie, and Dave), all of the points would be *on* the line. There is no way to draw a single straight line that would touch all of the points.

However, there is *one best* line. Mathematically, one line gets closer, on average, to all of the points than any other line. That line is the regression line that we get by using our data to calculate the regression equation, a linear equation with a slope and a constant. Without further ado, let's calculate it.

Because the regression formulas rely a lot on the means of the variables, we'll need the means right away. The mean height is 6. The mean salary is 5. That's one of the things I love about hypothetical data: the numbers always work out so nicely. Now we need to calculate the distance each man is away from each mean

■ Exhibit 7.5: Calculating Distances from the Mean

Man	Height	Height – Mean	Salary	Salary – Mean
Floyd	4	4 – 6 = –2	2	2 – 5 = –3
Ernie	5	5 – 6 = –1	3	3 – 5 = –2
Dave	6	6 – 6 = 0	4	4 – 5 = –1
Charlie	6	6 – 6 = 0	7	7 – 5 = 2
Buck	7	7 – 6 = 1	9	9 – 5 = 4
Andre	8	8 – 6 = 2	5	5 – 5 = 0

Notice that, if we added up these differences for each variable, we'd get zero:

$$-2 + -1 + 0 + 0 + 1 + 2 = 0$$
$$-3 + -2 + -1 + 2 + 4 + 0 = 0$$

Such is the nature of the mean. So we're going to square each number first to get rid of those negative signs, just as we did when we calculated the variance earlier in the book.

■ Exhibit 7.6: Squaring Distances from the Mean

Man	Height – Mean	(Height – Mean)^2	Salary – Mean	(Salary – Mean)^2
Floyd	4 – 6 = –2	4	2 – 5 = –3	9
Ernie	5 – 6 = –1	1	3 – 5 = –2	4
Dave	6 – 6 = 0	0	4 – 5 = –1	1
Charlie	6 – 6 = 0	0	7 – 5 = 2	4
Buck	7 – 6 = 1	1	9 – 5 = 4	16
Andre	8 – 6 = 2	4	5 – 5 = 0	0

Now we have the total squared distances from each mean:

$$4 + 1 + 0 + 0 + 1 + 4 = 10$$
$$9 + 4 + 1 + 4 + 16 + 0 = 34$$

The last component we need in order to calculate our regression equation is called the **covariance**, which is a measure of how the two variables vary together. When a point is above the mean on one variable, is it above the mean on the other variable? Alternately, if we're looking at a negative relationship, when a point is above the mean on one variable, is it below the mean on the other variable? In our situation, the tendency is toward the former, giving us a positive relationship:

▪ **Exhibit 7.7: The Scatterplot with Means Added**

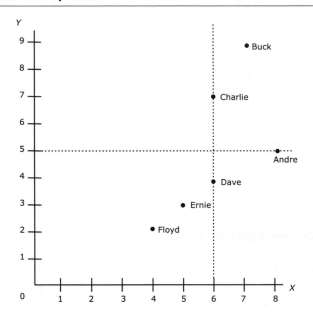

In Exhibit 7.7, I drew the means in as dotted lines. Notice that Floyd and Ernie are below both means, and Buck is above both means. To calculate the covariance, we multiply—OK, this is going to be a mouthful, but you'll see in a second what it means—we multiply the distance each point is from one mean by the distance that same point is from the other mean:

■ **Exhibit 7.8: Calculating the Covariance**

Man	Height – Mean	Salary – Mean	Product
Floyd	4 – 6 = –2	2 – 5 = –3	–2 × –3 = 6
Ernie	5 – 6 = –1	3 – 5 = –2	–1 × –2 = 2
Dave	6 – 6 = 0	4 – 5 = –1	0 × –1 = 0
Charlie	6 – 6 = 0	7 – 5 = 2	0 × 2 = 0
Buck	7 – 6 = 1	9 – 5 = 4	1 × 4 = 4
Andre	8 – 6 = 2	5 – 5 = 0	2 × 0 = 0

Adding this column up, we get 6 + 2 + 0 + 0 + 4 + 0 = 12, and that is the covariance. Finally, we can start calculating parts of the regression equation. First, the slope. To calculate the slope, we divide the covariance by the total squared distances from the independent variable (height).

If you've been keeping up with me so far, the following formula shouldn't freak you out:

$$b = \frac{\sum(X - \bar{X})(Y - \bar{Y})}{\sum(X - \bar{X})^2}$$

Therefore, given what we calculated above, $b = 12/10 = 1.2$.

This slope of 1.2 means that, on average, every 1-foot increase in height produces a 1.2 (or $12,000) increase in salary. So far, our regression equation looks like this:

$Y = a + 1.2(X)$

Or, replacing the X and the Y with their respective variable names:

SALARY = a + 1.2(HEIGHT)

To figure out what the value of the constant is, we use a fun fact: the regression line *always* passes through the intersection of the means of the two variables (illustrated earlier by the intersection of the two dotted lines). Knowing that the regression line passes through the point where $X = 6$ and $Y = 5$, we can simply plug in these numbers in order to solve for a:

$5 = a + 1.2(6)$
$5 = a + 7.2$
$-2.2 = a$

An interpretation of this constant is initially confusing: how can one have a *negative* salary? Remember that the constant is the value the dependent variable takes on when the independent variable is zero. And being zero feet tall is just as ridiculous. But, if a man were unfortunate enough to be zero feet tall, he would have the additional burden of his salary being –$22,000. Ouch! Our finished regression equation is

$$Y = -2.2 + 1.2(X)$$

or, using the variable names: SALARY = –2.2 + 1.2(HEIGHT).

Graphically, here is what things look like:

■ **Exhibit 7.9: The Scatterplot with Regression Line Added**

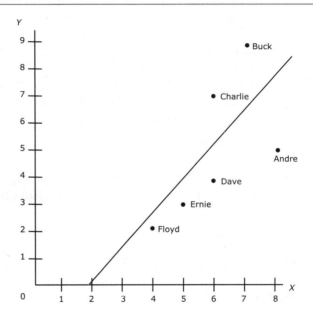

The regression line in this situation does not touch any of the points. Yet it is the *best-fitting* line for these points. The squared distances it is from the points are, cumulatively, less than for *any* other line. In fact, we call basic regression ordinary least squares regression, or OLS regression: it gives us an ordinary straight line whose squared distances from the points (measuring distance straight up and down) are the least of any line.

CALCULATING THE CORRELATION COEFFICIENT

But exactly how well does this line do? This is answered in the next step, where we calculate what is called the **correlation coefficient**. Symbolized by the letter r, it is calculated by taking the covariance (which we already used earlier) and dividing it by—here's another doozy, so bear with me—the square root of the product of the summed squared distances of each variable. Confused? Here it is in formula notation:

$$r = \frac{\Sigma(X - \bar{X})(Y - \bar{Y})}{\sqrt{\left[\Sigma(Y - \bar{Y})^2\right]\left[\Sigma(X - \bar{X})^2\right]}}$$

The correlation coefficient is a sort of index. It ranges from 0 to 1 if we have a positive relationship (the slope is positive: as the independent variable goes up, the dependent variable also tends to go up). It ranges from 0 to –1 if we have a negative relationship (the slope is negative: as the independent variable goes up, the dependent variable tends to go down). It gives us a measure of the strength of the relationship. At one end, 0 means *no* relationship. Whatever the value of X is doesn't matter, as it doesn't have any effect on Y. For example, look at the following scatterplot of points. I asked Excel to give me 30 random numbers between 0 and 10 and made 15 of them Xs and 15 of them Ys, and based on numbers, I plotted points.

■ **Exhibit 7.10: The Scatterplot with No Relationship**

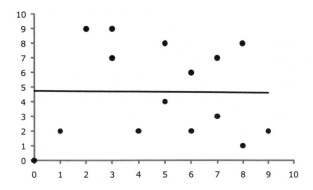

Because of the random nature of the points, there is no relationship between the variables. The value of r is zero because the value of the covariance is zero. I took Exhibit 7.10 and added a line for the mean of X and a line for the mean of Y. Then I placed on top of the points a "+" if the point contributed a positive value to the covariance or a "–" if the point contributed a negative value to the covariance:

■ **Exhibit 7.11: Illustrating a Covariance of Zero**

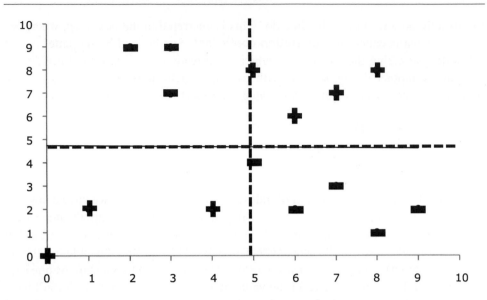

The points in the upper right part of the graph contribute positive values to the covariance because they all are above the mean of X and above the mean of Y. The points in the lower-left part of the graph also contribute positive values to the covariance because they all are below both means (and any negative multiplied by another negative gives you a positive). Points in the other two areas all contribute negative values, because each of them is above one mean while being below the other mean. Notice that the pluses and minuses cancel each other out, so when they are added up you'd get zero, or no relationship.

A correlation coefficient of 1 means a perfect relationship: all of the points are *on* the regression line:

■ **Exhibit 7.12: A Perfect Relationship**

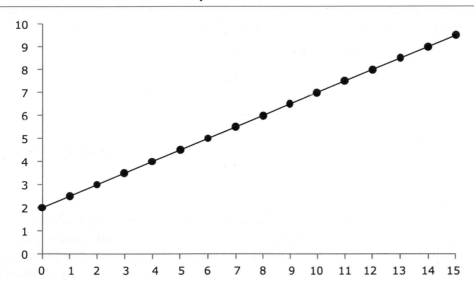

Everyone agrees on these. For points between, people use various descriptors. Here are the ones I use:

■ **Exhibit 7.13: The Meaning of the Correlation Coefficient**

0	No relationship
±0.1	Very weak
±0.2	Weak
±0.3	Weak to moderate
±0.4	Moderate
±0.5	Moderate
±0.6	Moderate to strong
±0.7	Strong
±0.8	Strong
±0.9	Very strong
±1	Perfect

Sometimes these vary depending on the specific field of study. If certain social scientists get a 0.3, they get all excited and may call this moderate rather than weak. But the above guidelines are pretty safe.

Now we'll calculate the correlation coefficient for the situation with our six men. We already calculated the summed squared distances earlier; they were 10 for the independent variable and 34 for the dependent variable. And so we calculate:

$$r = \frac{12}{\sqrt{[10][34]}}$$

This gives us an *r*-value of 0.65. The relationship described by these six points is moderately strong.

THE EFFECTS OF AN OUTLIER

With such a small number of cases, one oddball case could throw the whole thing off. We call such a case an outlier, as it lies out far from where the other points are. In our situation, Andre is sort of an outlier. But let's make him even more so. Perhaps he destroys the top of one too many doorways, gets demoted, and his salary is reduced from $50,000 to $20,000. What effect does this have on the regression equation and correlation coefficient? Its first effect will be that it will change the mean salary from 5 to 4.5. The necessary summations are

Sum of squared distances for independent variable:	10
Sum of squared distances for dependent variable:	41.50
Covariance:	6

This gives us the following changes to our equation:

Slope = 6/10 = 0.6
Constant = 4.5 − 0.6(6) = 0.9
Regression equation: $Y = 0.9 + 0.6(X)$

And the correlation coefficient changes to the following:

$$r = \frac{6}{\sqrt{[10][41.50]}} = 0.29$$

Huge changes! The slope decreased by a factor of two. The constant switched from negative to positive. The correlation coefficient decreased to weak. Why? Let's look at the graph:

■ **Exhibit 7.14: Revised Regression Line after Andre's Misfortune**

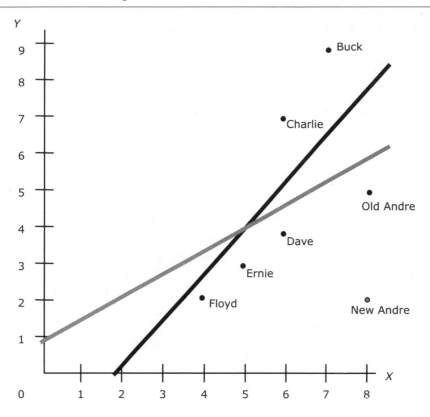

I've symbolized the new Andre point and the new regression line by using gray. Notice how the gray line, in an attempt to get closer to the new Andre point, gets farther away from many of the other points. In trying to please everyone, it pleases no one, giving us a low correlation coefficient. Mathematically, the new Andre point contributes a substantially *negative* value to the otherwise positive covariance, with the covariance contributions for each of the six points being 5, 1.5, 0, 0, 4.5, and (for Andre) –5. Usually, outliers do not have this big an effect, but because we have such a small number of points, the effect of an outlier is likely to be large. I'll talk more about the effect of outliers late in the book.

EXPLAINED VARIATION

If we take the value of the correlation coefficient and square it, we get what is called the **coefficient of determination**. Because this is a mouthful, and a relatively meaningless name at that, most people just call it **r-squared** (r^2). And now, here is another one of those lines that will not make sense right away, but before long, if I explain it as well as I think I can, you will understand it. The value for r^2 represents the proportion of the variation in the dependent variable that can be explained by its relationship with the independent variable. In our original situation, (we'll give poor Andre his $30,000 back), our value for r was 0.65, which makes the value of r^2 0.42; this means that 42% of the variation in salary can be explained by the men's height, and 58% is left unexplained, possibly relating to other factors:

■ **Exhibit 7.15: Explained and Unexplained Variation**

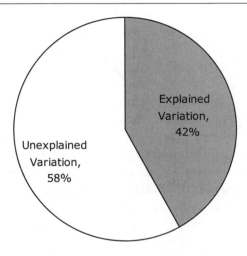

But what does this idea of explained variation really mean? Over the next few pages, I will guide you through an explanation of explained variation. Let's first imagine a situation where the two variables were not at all related. That is, there is variation in salary, but it is not explained at all by height. In this case, r^2 would be zero, as would r. Well, if r is zero, then b has to be zero as well, because they both have the same value of the covariance in common. Because $r = 0$, the covariance must be zero, because we can't have zero in the denominator. So $b = 0$. Notice that, in the scatterplot in Exhibit 7.10, where there was no relationship, the regression line was totally horizontal, meaning that the slope was zero. If the mean salary is 5 and $b = 0$, let's calculate the constant of the regression equation:

$Y = a + b(X)$
Plugging in the slope: $Y = a + 0(X)$
Plugging in the means: $5 = a + 0(6)$

So the constant is $a = 5$, and our regression equation is $Y = 5 + 0(X)$. For any value of height, because height is unrelated to salary, our best bet is to predict the mean salary. In other words, if all I told you was that there was a group of six men with a mean salary of 5, and I asked you to predict each man's salary, your best bet, for each man, would be to say 5. If you did this, you'd be off for most of the men:

■ **Exhibit 7.16: Calculating Error from Using the Mean**

Man	Prediction	Actual Salary	Off By
Floyd	5	2	−3
Ernie	5	3	−2
Dave	5	4	−1
Charlie	5	7	2
Buck	5	9	4
Andre	5	5	0

Because we've squared these distances up to this point, let's do it again: $-3^2 + -2^2 + -1^2 + 2^2 + 4^2 + 0^2 = 34$. Actually, we've seen this number before, as it was part of the calculation for the correlation coefficient. This 34 is the sum of the squared differences between each point and the mean, or the total amount of squared variation in the dependent variable.

But we *do* have an independent variable that we found *was* related to the dependent variable, and we have a regression equation of their relationship: $Y = -2.2 + 1.2(X)$. Let's use this equation to make predicted salaries for each of the men based on his height:

■ **Exhibit 7.17: Making Predictions with the Regression Equation**

Man	Height	Predicted Salary
Floyd	4	$-2.2 + 1.2(4) = 2.6$
Ernie	5	$-2.2 + 1.2(5) = 3.8$
Dave	6	$-2.2 + 1.2(6) = 5.0$
Charlie	6	$-2.2 + 1.2(6) = 5.0$
Buck	7	$-2.2 + 1.2(7) = 6.2$
Andre	8	$-2.2 + 1.2(8) = 7.4$

Now let's take each of these predicted salaries and see how far off from their real salaries they are:

■ **Exhibit 7.18: Estimating Error from Using the Regression Equation**

Man	Predicted Salary	Actual Salary	Difference
Floyd	2.6	2	0.6
Ernie	3.8	3	0.8
Dave	5.0	4	−1.0
Charlie	5.0	7	−2.0
Buck	6.2	9	−2.8
Andre	7.4	5	2.4

Notice that, for most of the men, our prediction using the regression equation is better than our prediction using the mean. For example, using the mean, we predicted a salary for Buck of 5, which was off by 4. Using the regression equation, we predicted a salary for Buck of 7.4, which was off by only 2.4, an improvement of 1.6 (see Exhibit 7.19 for an illustration of this).

■ **Exhibit 7.19: Illustrating Explained and Unexplained Variation**

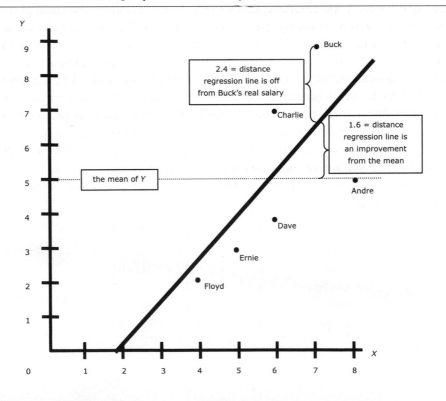

Stay with me, because we're almost to the cool part. Let's take the differences from above and, as always, square them:

$$0.6^2 + 0.8^2 + 1^2 + 2^2 + 2.8^2 + 2.4^2 = 19.6$$

This is the squared distances we are still off, even after taking into account the regression predictions. The total amount off we were without the regression was 34, so we've improved by $34 - 19.6 = 14.4$. The improved part, or the *explained variation*, is 14.4, and the total amount of variation is 34. Therefore, the proportion of the total variation that is explained is $14.4/34 = 0.42$, and the total variation that is left unexplained is $19.6/34 = 0.58$. Get it? *0.42 and 0.58!* The original r^2 we calculated at the beginning of this section was 0.42. Come on, you have to admit that's pretty cool. Hopefully, this gives you a much better idea of what explained variation really is. It is how much our regression predictions improve on the next best thing: making predictions using the mean of the dependent variable. We will be using r-squared throughout the rest of the book, so make sure you have a good understanding of how it represents the variation we can explain.

EXAMPLE: FORECASTING WITH REGRESSION

One of the uses of regression is to create an equation that we can then use to make predictions, or forecasts. This example uses something near and dear to my heart: movies. As you know, movies are big business. Some have noted that, recently, the strategies of moviemakers have changed. The new rule is to pack the theaters to make as much money as you can early on. With companies building new multiplexes everywhere you turn, it is possible for a big new movie to open on thousands of screens. Movie companies try to create buzz that will make their movie a must-see on its opening weekend so that people can talk about it around the water cooler on Monday morning. Looking at the numbers, have things changed? Do movies make more of their money early on? Exhibit 7.20 shows the top movies for the years 1990 through 2012, what they made their first weekend, what their overall American gross was, and what percentage of this gross was made on the first weekend. The data are from the website boxofficemojo.com.

■ **Exhibit 7.20: Movie Grosses over Time**

Year	Movie	Weekend ($ million)	Gross ($ million)	%
1990	Home Alone	17	286	6.0
1991	Terminator 2	32	205	15.5
1992	Aladdin	19	217	8.9
1993	Jurassic Park	47	357	13.2
1994	Forrest Gump	24	330	7.4
1995	Toy Story	29	192	15.2
1996	Independence Day	50	306	16.4
1997	Titanic	29	601	4.8
1998	Saving Private Ryan	31	217	14.1
1999	Star Wars: The Phantom Menace	65	431	15.0
2000	How the Grinch Stole Christmas	55	260	21.2
2001	Harry Potter and the Sorcerer's Stone	90	318	28.4
2002	Spider-Man	115	404	28.4
2003	Lord of the Rings: Return of the King	73	377	19.3
2004	Shrek 2	108	441	24.5
2005	Star Wars: Revenge of the Sith	108	380	28.5
2006	Pirates of the Caribbean 2	136	423	32.2
2007	Spider-Man 3	151	337	44.8
2008	The Dark Night	158	528	29.9
2009	Avatar	77	750	10.3
2010	Toy Story 3	110	415	26.5
2011	Harry Potter Deathly Hallows Pt. 2	169	381	44.4
2012	The Avengers	207	623	33.2

Source: www.boxofficemojo.com.

Looking at the following scatterplot, there does seem to be a trend over time:

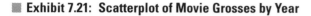

■ Exhibit 7.21: Scatterplot of Movie Grosses by Year

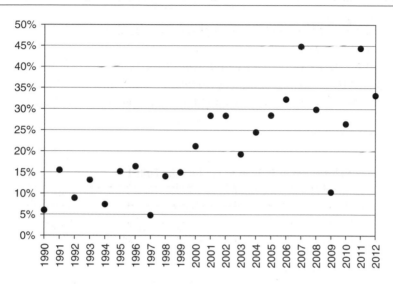

What if we wanted to make a forecast: given this clear trend, in what year is it expected that the first weekend box office receipts will constitute around 50% of the total gross? To answer this, we'll create a regression equation. To start, we'll set the year 1990 equal to "YEAR 0" and proceed from there (1991 will be 1, 1992 will be 2, etc.). YEAR will be my independent variable, and PCTGROSS (meaning the percentage of the total gross that was made in the first weekend) will be my dependent variable. I won't go through all of the math to get to the regression equation (if you want to do that on your own, you can see if you get similar results, although they may differ slightly because of rounding). The regression equation is

PCTGROSS = 7.30 + 1.26(YEAR)

According to the equation, for each additional year that passes, the percentage of total gross made in the first weekend rises 1.26%. How strong is the relationship? The value for the correlation coefficient is 0.76, making this a strong relationship. This makes the r^2 value 0.57, meaning that we can explain 57% of the variation in PCTGROSS through its relationship with time.

Now for the prediction. We want to know when PCTGROSS will be 50%. So we plug in 50 for PCTGROSS and solve for YEAR:

50 = 7.30 + 1.26(YEAR)
42.7 = 1.26(YEAR)
33.89 = YEAR

We'll round this up to 34. Because 1990 was "Year 0," Year 34 will be 2023. If the trend suggested by these data continues, in 2023, the top movie will make about 50% of its gross in its first weekend, as illustrated by the graph in Exhibit 7.22, where I have added the regression line and extended it into the future:

■ **Exhibit 7.22: Scatterplot with Trend Line into the Future**

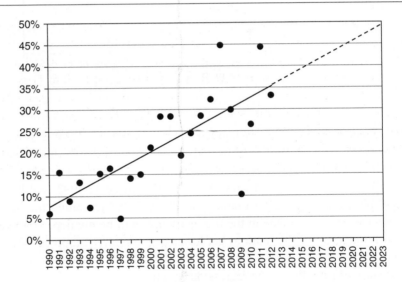

What if, just for the sake of example, we wanted to explore what this relationship would look like if we removed three of the outliers that all have something in common. Notice from the original data that the three movies that were directed by James Cameron—*Terminator 2*, *Titanic*, and *Avatar*—fall far away from the regression line. I removed these three films and recalculated everything:

PCTGROSS = 6.03 + 1.49(YEAR) $r = 0.88, r^2 = 0.78$

By removing these three films, one of which pulled up on the left-hand side of the line (*Terminator 2*), one of which pulled down on the right-hand side of the line (*Avatar*), and one of which had the lowest percentage gross, even though it wasn't the earliest movie (*Titanic*), big changes occur. The slope increases from 1.26 to 1.49. The correlation coefficient goes from strong (0.76) to very strong (0.88), and the explained variation rises from 57% to 78%. If we used this new equation to predict the 50% gross, we end up with a predicted of four years earlier:

$$50 = 6.03 + 1.49(YEAR)$$
$$43.97 = 1.49(YEAR)$$
$$29.51 = YEAR, \text{ or } 2019$$

As with the "height and income" example, a few outliers among a small number of cases can seriously affect the results.

GSS EXAMPLE: EDUCATION AND INCOME

Unfortunately, we can't make our hypothetical height–salary example a reality by using GSS data, as the GSS does not ask the respondents their heights. It *does* ask respondents about their incomes. However, it doesn't ask for income as a dollar amount, because people are somewhat wary about answering such a question. They are more willing to answer an income question if they are given a set of categories in which they can place their income. This is what the GSS does. Unfortunately, this gives us an ordinal-level variable, not a ratio-level variable. I took this original variable and constructed a makeshift ratio variable by using the midpoints of each of the 25 income categories. Here are a number of these categories and their new dollar amounts:

■ **Exhibit 7.23: Recoding Income**

Category	Dollar Amount for New Variable
Under $1,000	$500
$1,000–$2,999	$1,500
$3,000–$4,999	$4,000
. . .	
$30,000–$34,999	$32,500
$35,000–$39, 999	$37,500
. . .	
$75,000–$89,999	$82,750
$90,000–$109,999	$100,000
$110,000–$129,999	$120,000
$130,000–$149,999	$140,000
$150,000+	$160,000

Although this gives us a ratio variable (we now have people's incomes in dollar amounts), notice that I am doing some guessing here. For example, if a woman really made $76,000, she would answer the survey question by choosing the "$75,000–$89,999" category, and I then made her value on the new ratio variable $82,750, which is not exactly her income. But it is close. The last category poses a problem, because it is "$150,000 and over," which doesn't have an upper endpoint. I treated this category as if it were as wide as the previous category: $20,000, making the upper endpoint $170,000. So, for these people (who make up around 3% of the respondents), the possibility is there that I am *way* off: they could make millions and I'm giving them a measly $160,000. And then we have the additional annoyance that another 9% of the respondents refused to answer this question (or said they didn't know the answer), even when given categories. But, with existing data such as these, we do the best we can. The new variable I created isn't perfect, but it will suffice.

Instead of using height as the dependent variable, I will use another variable we all understand: education. The GSS asks this question in two ways: it asks respondents what is the highest degree they have achieved, and it asks them how many years of education they have. Although the degree variable is a good variable, it is not a ratio-level variable. The categories for this variable (less than high school, high school diploma, some college, college degree, advanced degree) are not such that we can say that Category 4 is twice the education of Category 2. For regression purposes, we want to use the years of education, as this is a ratio-level variable. This variable has problems as well, as it does not measure the quality of education in those years. Two people each with 16 years of education could have very different educational experiences, one with a degree from Harvard and one with a high school degree who repeated the fourth grade four times and says, without lying, "I was in school for 16 years."

Although the GSS has a total of around 2,000 respondents in its 2012 survey, when we remove people who are not working (and therefore do not have incomes), those who refused to answer the income question, and those who refused to answer the education question, we have 1,142 respondents for whom we have data for both variables. We could take these 2,284 numbers (that's 1,142 × 2) and go through the math we did earlier, but that would take more time than you and I have. Instead, we'll let SPSS crunch the numbers. We ask SPSS to do this and it thinks for, oh, 0.00000003 seconds and then presents the output (we'll go over how to read the output in Chapter 8). The regression equation it gives us is

INCOME = –29.23 + 4.94(YEARS OF EDUCATION)

Having zero years of education is definitely not a good idea, because the regression equation predicts that you will make –$29,230. This is another one of those nonsensical constants that result when having zero on the independent variable is highly unlikely (although there are indeed three people who answered zero on the education variable). Each additional year of education produces a $4,940 increase in income. Keep in mind that this is an average increase. It is likely that the jump in income one receives going from 14 to 15 years of education is substantially smaller than the jump one receives going from 15 to 16 years of education (the point at which one usually gets a bachelor's degree). There is a special regression technique we could use to test this, a technique that I cover in Chapter 9, but OLS regression simply gives you the linear equation and, in a sense, suggests that each year produces the same increase.

The relationship is a moderate one, with an r-value of 0.42. This makes the r^2 value 0.18. Income varies: some people make a little; some people make a lot. This variation can be explained partially by people's education: 18% of the variation, to be exact. That means 82% of the variation is left unexplained, or remains to be explained, possibly by other independent variables. This 0.18 may seem small in contrast to the values of r^2 we had in our previous examples: 0.42 in the hypothetical height–income example and 0.57 in the first movie grosses example. Actually, for a simple regression equation using a large dataset, this is a very high value for r^2. It is very common, as you will see in later chapters, for regressions to have r^2 values of 0.07, 0.03, or even 0.01. The world is a complex place, especially when we have variables dealing with the behavior of thousands of people, so often we have to settle for explaining only a small part of the picture. So, when you run your own regressions and end up with low r^2 values, don't get discouraged. Findings with a low r^2 are often just as intriguing as findings with a higher r^2. However, if you consistently end up with an r^2 of 0.00, you may want to rethink what you are trying to accomplish.

Another way to get a feel for regression results is to run some examples. Let's do three using this equation, the first for someone with 10 years of education, then someone with 16 years, and finally someone with 19 years:

INCOME = −29.23 + 4.94(10) = 20.17
INCOME = −29.23 + 4.94(16) = 49.81
INCOME = −29.23 + 4.94(19) = 64.63

Another way to think about these results is that these are the means predicted by the regression equation for each year: among those with 10 years of education, the regression equation predicts that such people will have a mean income of $20,170. Among those with 16 years of education, the regression equation predicts that such people will have a mean income of $49,810. Looking at the actual means, the regression equation makes fairly accurate predictions: Among the 16 respondents who have 10 years of education, the actual mean income is \$18,940. Among the 196 respondents who have 16 years of education, the actual mean income is \$57,000.

GSS EXAMPLE: INCOME AND HOURS TO RELAX

Now let's use income as an *in*dependent variable, addressing the question, Does making more money garner one more time to relax? The GSS in 2010 (but, unfortunately, not in 2012) asked this question: "After an average work day, about how many hours do you have to relax or pursue activities that you enjoy?" One might think that people who make lots of money will have the ability to "hire out" many of their chores, leaving them more time to relax. Here are the regression results:

HRSRELAX = $3.87 - 0.005$(INCOME IN 1000S); $n = 971, r = 0.064$

Well, this one didn't work out very well, did it? First, the correlation coefficient is very close to zero, so the relationship between income and relaxation is very weak. Second, the relationship goes in the opposite direction I had hypothesized: the *more* money one makes, the *less* time one has to relax. However, as I've continually emphasized, sometimes when a hypothesis is not supported by statistics, this makes for an even more interesting finding. Perhaps money really *can't* buy everything, including free time.

GSS EXAMPLE: EXPLAINING CYNICISM

Recall earlier in the book we found that age had an interesting effect on level of cynicism: the older you get, the less cynical you are. To look at this, I used crosstabs with age categorized into four age groupings, giving me an ordinal-level variable. Now that we're using regression, we can use the original ratio-level version of age (age in years) as our independent variable. For the dependent variable, I combined three questions that got at cynicism (Can people be trusted? Are people fair? Are people helpful?) into an index that ranges from 0 (*people can't be trusted, aren't fair, and aren't helpful*) to 6 (*people can be trusted, are fair, and are helpful*). Here are my regression results:

CYNICISM = $1.45 + 0.03$(AGE) $n = 1,311, r = 0.22, r^2 = 0.05$

This produces an effect similar to the crosstab, though notice the additional information we have with regression: we see, on average, what happens with each additional year of age (0.03). We see how much variation in cynicism age can explain (5%). We can make predictions: 20-year-olds, on average, score 2.05 on the cynicism index, whereas 80-year-olds, on average, score 3.85.

What other ratio-level variables could we use to explain variation in cynicism? How about years of education? Here are the results:

$$CYNICISM = -0.07 + 0.21(YRSEDUC) \quad n = 1,314, r = 0.30, r^2 = 0.09$$

Education by itself explains more of the variation in cynicism than age does by itself. Looking at the correlation coefficient, we would call this relationship weak to moderate. Where someone with 10 years of education scores, on average, 2.03, someone with 20 years of education scores over two points higher, on average, 4.13. One more independent variable, shall we? Family income in thousands of dollars:

$$CYNICISM = 2.00 + 0.014(INCOME) \quad n = 1,177, r = 0.28, r^2 = 0.08$$

In terms of variation explained, we get a picture similar to the previous example: family income alone can explain 8% of the variation in cynicism. Someone whose family income is a mere $10,000 has a predicted cynicism score of 2.14, whereas someone whose family income is $100,000 scores a 3.40. Each additional $1,000 moves one away from cynical by 0.014 (due to the smallness of the slope, I kept an extra decimal point).

GSS EXAMPLE: INTERGENERATIONAL FAMILY SIZE

Do people who come from large families tend to have large families themselves? The GSS asks respondents how many siblings they have and how many children they have had. Let's regress number of children onto number of siblings to see if those from larger families tend to then have larger families themselves. But we will run three separate equations: one for white respondents, one for black respondents, and one for respondents whose race is "other" (neither white nor black). In addition, we will limit the sample to those 50 years or older, because that lets most people's fertility end (i.e., very few people are still having babies in their 50s). Here are the three equations, using GSS 2012 data:

For white respondents:

$$\#CHILDREN = 1.82 + 0.12(\#SIBLINGS) \quad n = 714, r = 0.19, r^2 = 0.035$$

For black respondents:

#CHILDREN = 2.50 + 0.05(#SIBLINGS) $n = 131$, $r = 0.10$, $r^2 = 0.01$

For "other" respondents:

#CHILDREN = 2.01 + 0.19(#SIBLINGS) $n = 44$, $r = 0.37$, $r^2 = 0.13$

The relationship differs among the three racial groups. Using number of siblings, we are able to explain 13% of the variation in number of children. In contrast, with the white equation, we can explain only 3.5% of the variation and, among blacks, only 1% of the variation. In Chapter 12, we will look at a technique that allows us to examine this type of phenomenon using a single regression equation.

LITERATURE EXAMPLE: SUPPORT FOR THE WAR ON TERROR

Within the field of political science, there is a longstanding concept called authoritarianism. Common aspects of authoritarianism are obedience to authority and aggression toward out-groups, particularly in times of threat. Marc Hetherington and Elizabeth Suhay add to our understanding of this concept in their article "Authoritarianism, Threat, and Americans' Support for the War on Terror." This article appeared in the *American Journal of Political Science* in 2011. They wanted to see how people who subscribe to the tenets of authoritarianism felt about new policies considered or employed during the U.S. war on terrorism. They used data from the Cooperative Congressional Election Study and the American Barometer Survey.

Although they use more complicated forms of regression analysis later in their article, early on in their results, they present simple correlations between authoritarianism and support for war-on-terror policies that affect average citizens. They measure authoritarianism using an index used in the American National Election Studies. To create the index, respondents are asked to choose between traits they believe a child should have (notice that one of each of these points to authoritarianism): respect for elders versus independence, obedience versus self-reliance, good manners versus curiosity, and being well behaved versus being considerate. Among the policies they asked about were media censorship (should the media not report information about secret methods the government is using to fight terrorism) and national ID cards (cards that citizens would be required to carry with them at all times). Here are some simple percentages and correlations illustrating the association between these variables:

■ **Exhibit 7.24: Authoritarianism and Support for the War on Terror Policies**

	Support Media Censorship	Support National ID Cards
Minimum Authoritarianism	27%	23%
Midpoint of Authoritarianism	69%	32%
Maximum Authoritarianism	79%	49%
Correlation	0.40	0.23

Source: Adapted from Hetherington and Suhay (2011).

As expected, those who scored higher on the authoritarian index were more likely to support policies that restricted civil liberties. However, the extent of the correlation varies by policy. Support for national ID cards was only weakly correlated with the authoritarian index. Looking at the percentages, you can get a feel for this: the difference between the low authoritarians and high authoritarians is 26%. Support for media censorship was moderately correlated with the authoritarian index, and this is reflected in the percentages: the difference between the low authoritarians and high authoritarians is 52%. Hetherington and Suhay go on to show that people who do not subscribe to authoritarianism, if faced with enough threat, will be willing to support the restriction of civil liberties.

LITERATURE EXAMPLE: PHYSICAL ATTRACTIVENESS

Beauty is in the eye of the beholder. But when a bunch of beholders are asked to assess beauty at the same time, that's when things get interesting. In his article "'A Thing of Beauty is a Joy Forever'?: Returns to Physical Attractiveness over the Life Course," which appeared in the journal *Social Forces* in 2011, Mads Meier Jæger used the Wisconsin Longitudinal Survey (WLS) to assess the effects of physical attractiveness. Among other things, he found that taller men and more attractive women make more money. But I want to focus here on a set of statistics that he uses early on in his article.

But, first, a little more about this fascinating survey. The WLS is famous for its extreme longitudinality: it first surveyed more than 10,000 Wisconsin high school students in 1957 and then conducted follow-up interviews with the same students (or their parents) in 1964, 1975, 1992/1993, and 2004. Thus, the 18-year-olds in 1957 were 65 years old in 2004, allowing for a lot of interesting research. In addition to asking about attitudes, behavior, and life achievements, the WLS also kept track of respondents' height and BMI (body mass index, a commonly used, although simplistic measure of fatness based on the person's height and weight: a BMI of 18.5 is underweight, 23 is normal weight, 28 is overweight, and 30 or greater is obese; whereas a 170-pound 6-foot-tall man has a BMI of 23, a 170-pound 5-foot tall man has a BMI of 33). Most interestingly, the WLS includes a measure of "facial attractiveness": in 2004, they had 12 raters (6 men, 6 women, aged 63–91) rate the attractiveness of the WLS respondents' senior high school yearbook photos, resulting in average ratings ranging from –3 (unattractive) to +3 (attractive).

Exhibit 7.25 is called a **correlation matrix**: it summarizes the correlations between a set of variables.

▪ Exhibit 7.25: Attractiveness Correlation Matrix

	Attr 18	BMI 18	BMI 54	BMI 65	Hgt 54	Hgt 65
Attr 18	–	0.038	0.091	0.059	–0.014	0.027
BMI 18	–0.239	–	0.328	0.256	–0.034	–0.047
BMI 54	–0.145	0.293	–	0.817	–0.002	0.028
BMI 65	–0.142	0.237	0.843	–	0.003	–0.030
Hgt 54	–0.019	0.025	–0.094	–0.040	–	0.929
Hgt 65	0.020	0.019	–0.082	–0.085	0.906	–

Note: Attr 18 = attractiveness at age 18; BMI 18 = body mass index at age 18; Hgt 18 = height at age 18. Correlations for men are above the diagonal, and correlations for women are below the diagonal.
Source: Adapted from Jæger (2011).

The correlation between a man's BMI at age 18 and his physical attractiveness at age 18 is 0.038, meaning that there is essentially no correlation between how fat a boy was and how attractive he was. In contrast, the correlation between a woman's BMI at age 18 and her physical attractiveness at age 18 is –0.239, meaning that there is a correlation (albeit a weak-ish one), and it is a negative correlation: the fatter a woman was, the lower the attractiveness rating this woman received. Another interesting contrast is between height at age 54 and BMI at age 54. The women's correlation between these two variables is –0.094: the taller the woman, the lower the BMI. However, among the men, the correlation between these two variables is –0.002, meaning there is no relationship between these two variables. Whereas the women's correlation is weak, it's something compared to the men's lack of correlation. In summary, Jæger finds more correlation among the women's body measures than among the men's.

CONCLUSION

Our trip through the wonderful, sometimes scary, sometimes geeky, always exciting world of regression has left the station. Face it: you're intrigued by this technique and can envision the possibilities it offers. You may even be starting to see the world as a series of regression equations. What independent variables will raise your score on the next exam you take? What independent variables will lower the anger your significant other has because of the stupid thing you just did? OK, perhaps not. But hopefully you see how this technique has many possible uses. In the following chapters, you will see regression used to explain a wide variety of phenomena, most of which (I think) will be interesting you.

SPSS DEMONSTRATION: CREATING A SCATTERPLOT

Please visit the book's website (www.routledge.com/cw/linneman) to view a video of this demonstration.

At the end of the next chapter, I'll go over how to run regressions in SPSS. But, for now, let's go over how to have SPSS run a scatterplot. We'll do a scatterplot using one of the ANES unique groups I created: gay men who own guns. Among this group is there a correlation between how often they review news on the Internet and how often they read a newspaper? Although it's somewhat arbitrary in this situation, I'm going to say that Internet news reading is the independent variable: how often you read the news on the Internet affects how often you'll read an old-school newspaper. My hypothesis is that there is a negative effect: the more you read Internet news, the less you'll read a newspaper. We click

Graphs ➔ Legacy Dialogs ➔ Scatter/Dot . . .

Then we choose "Simple Scatter," and this brings us to the following room, where we do the following:

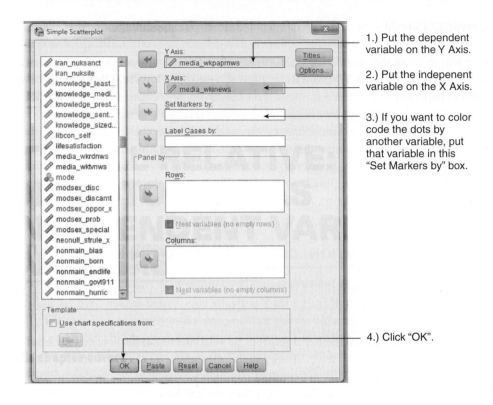

1.) Put the dependent variable on the Y Axis.

2.) Put the indepenent variable on the X Axis.

3.) If you want to color code the dots by another variable, put that variable in this "Set Markers by" box.

4.) Click "OK".

This gives us the following scatterplot:

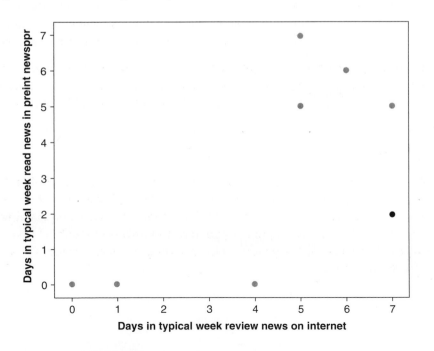

There is a clear relationship, but it is a positive relationship, not a negative one like I had hypothesized. One tiny detail in the scatterplot to point out. Look at the person at $X = 7$, $Y = 2$: this dot is a bit darker than the others. This is SPSS's way of telling us that there is really more than one person at this point. There are other settings for this, such as dot size.

EXERCISES

EXERCISES

Exercise 1

Using the ANES unique group of antimilitary dog owners, determine whether there is a relationship between score on the Resentment Index and score on the Affirmative Action Index. Here are the raw data:

Case	Resentment Index	Affirmative Action Index
A	1	12
B	8	7
C	4	18
D	10	16
E	8	13
F	12	2
G	8	6

Use these data to calculate a regression equation with resentment index score as the independent variable and affirmative action index score as the dependent variable. Also calculate the value of r and r^2. Then provide a full interpretation of all of your results.

Exercise 2

Using the ANES unique group of respondents who have less than a high school diploma but who have spouses with a graduate degree, investigate the relationship between scores on the Government Role Index and scores on the Environmental Index, with the thinking that if you think the government should do more, you will think it is OK for the government to carry out environmental legislation. Here are the raw data:

Case	Government Role	Environmentalism
A	14	18
B	6	30
C	10	16
D	16	16
E	2	0
F	1	6
G	1	18

Use these data to calculate a regression equation. Also calculate the value of r and r^2. Then provide a full interpretation of all of your results.

Exercise 3

Among the ANES unique group of conspiracy theorists, is there a relationship between age and score on the Ownership Index?

Case	Age of Respondent	Ownership Score
A	42	2
B	62	3
C	62	1
D	67	1
E	37	0
F	47	0

Using these data, create a regression equation, calculate values for r and r^2, and offer an interpretation. Then, using the regression equation, calculate predicted scores on the ownership index for a 25-year-old and an 80-year-old.

Exercise 4 (Answer Available in Appendix D)

Among the ANES antimilitary dog owners, is there a relationship between age and how one scores on the Traditionalism Index?

Age	Traditionalism Score
52	13
47	7
42	7
57	13
67	7
42	8
37	8
22.5	3

Using these data, calculate the regression equation, correlation coefficient, and r^2. Calculate predicted traditionalism scores for a 30-year-old and a 70-year-old.

Exercise 5

Among the ANES gay gun owners, is there a relationship between income and how one rates Republicans on the feeling thermometer?

Income	Republican FT
95	60
57.5	30
85	40
95	14
37.5	20
77.5	0
42.5	0
16.25	0
2.5	15
52.5	15

Using these data, create a regression equation, correlation coefficient, and r^2. Calculate predicted feeling thermometer scores for someone who has an income of $10,000 and someone who has an income of $200,000.

Exercise 6

Among the ANES respondents who claim to be strong Republicans but have voted for Obama twice, assess the relationship between days respondent reads a physical newspaper and their score on the Knowledge Index. Calculate the regression equation, r, and r^2 and interpret your results. What is the predicted difference between someone who never reads the newspaper and someone who reads the newspaper every day of the week? Here are the raw data:

Days rd. news	Knowledge Score
7	7
5	6
0	4
0	6
7	4
4	9
1	3
7	8
7	5
0	5
0	4

Exercise 7

Using data from the PewShop dataset, investigate the relationship between education and income using only the American Indian respondents. Calculate the regression equation, r, and r^2 and interpret your results. Here are the raw data:

Yrs Education	Income in 1,000s
12	25
19	25
13	5
12	15
13	45
19	35
16	125
10	15
12	25
13	5
13	5

Exercise 8 (Answer Available in Appendix D)

Using data from the PewShop dataset, investigate the relationship between income and score on the Technology Index using only the American Indian respondents. Calculate the regression equation, r, and r^2 and interpret your results. Here are the raw data:

Income in 1,000s	Tech. Index Score
25	1
25	1
5	1
15	2
45	2
35	3
125	3
15	5
25	4
5	1
5	3

Exercise 9

Typically, education has a positive effect on health. Here are data from the American Indian men in the PewHealth survey:

Education	Health Condition Index
16	0
16	3
13	0
12	1
16	0
13	1
13	0
16	3
12	1
12	0

Using these data, calculate a regression equation, correlation coefficient, and r^2. What is the punch line of this equation?

Exercise 10 (Answer Available in Appendix D)

One of the unhealthiest states in the United States is Mississippi. Run a scatterplot using black women from Mississippi that shows the relationship between years of education and score on the Health Conditions Index. From this scatterplot, what would you say is the relationship between these two variables?

Exercise 11

Do higher family incomes lead to more technology use among children? Among the American Indian children in the PewKids dataset, is there a relationship between family income and the child's score on the Child Technology Use Index? Use the below data to calculate a regression equation, correlation coefficient, and r^2. Explain your results.

Family Income	Child's Tech. Score
125	2
125	1
63	2
35	3
5	3
88	4

Exercise 12

Is there a relationship between what parents do and what their children *think* they do? Here are data comparing the Parent's Checking and Blocking Index to the Child's Perception of Parent's Checking and Blocking Index (using parents who identified as "Other Race"). Use the following data to calculate a regression equation, correlation coefficient, and r^2. Explain your results.

Parent Index	Child Index
2	0
4	1
1	2
3	3
0	0
4	4

Exercise 13

As I suggested at the end of the chapter, regression possibilities are all around you. Think about your everyday life, and think of a simple regression equation you could run if you hypothetically collected data from your life. Don't actually collect the data; just propose a little study. What would the dependent variable be and how would you measure it? What would the independent variable be and how would you measure it?

Exercise 14

Using the WVS dataset, create a scatterplot that shows the relationship between the percentage of a country that doesn't want people with AIDS as their neighbors (put this on the *x*-axis) and the percentage of a country that doesn't want homosexuals as their neighbors (put this on the *y*-axis). In addition, put the COUNTRY5CAT variable in the "Set Markers by" box in the Scatterplot room. Which countries seem to be outliers? Why do you think this is?

Exercise 15 (Answer Available in Appendix D)

If the people of a country are healthy, are they happy? Using only the WVS countries from Western Europe and Eastern Europe, create a scatterplot that allows you to look at this relationship. Then, by looking at the scatterplot, answer this question: Does health have more of an effect at the lower end of the health spectrum or on the upper end of the health spectrum?

Chapter 8

USING SAMPLE SLOPES TO TALK ABOUT POPULATIONS: INFERENCE AND REGRESSION

This chapter covers . . .

. . . one last probability distribution, this time using sample slopes

. . . what the standard error of the slope really means

. . . how to test a slope for statistical significance

. . . the role of sample size in testing a slope for significance

. . . how a researcher used regression to study how studying and grades are related

. . . how a researcher used regression to study how family size and grades are related

INTRODUCTION

The goal of this chapter is to take the inferential techniques we're already covered and apply them to the regression slopes you learned about in the previous chapter. Given that you are a seasoned pro at inference by this point, you will undoubtedly experience some déjà vu (or because you're reading this, déjà lu). Inferential techniques have a lot in common with one another, so once you learn the overall goal of inference, it's really just a variation on a theme. The goal of inference with slopes is to be able to claim that, in the population, the independent variable has an effect on the dependent variable.

ONE MORE SAMPLING DISTRIBUTION

Chapter 4 included a distribution of hundreds of chi-square values. Chapter 5 had a distribution of hundreds of sample means. Chapter 6 involved a sampling distribution of sample mean differences. Here, I do roughly the same thing, but instead of chi-square values, or sample means, or differences between sample means, my building blocks will be sample slopes. I went back to my original hypothetical dataset of 100 grades I used in previous chapters. To each student's grade, I added another piece of information: the percentage of classes that student attended during the semester. For example, here are ten of the 100 cases:

▩ **Exhibit 8.1: Percentage of Classes Attended and Grades: 10 Cases**

Percentage of Classes Attended	Grade
10	1.0
40	1.6
60	2.0
50	2.2
71	2.5
90	2.7
76	3.0
85	3.2
97	3.6
100	3.9

Source: Hypothetical data.

I did this for all 100 cases in the population. Then, using the entire population, I calculated a regression equation:

GRADE = 1.274 + 0.018(ATTENDANCE)

Therefore, 0.018 is the *population slope*: in the population, for every additional percentage of classes a student attended, his or her grade went up by 0.018. However, just as I did in Chapter 5, I'm going to draw small samples again and again, this time with a sample size of 10. I did this 150 times: I had SPSS draw a random sample of ten cases from this population of 100, and then I had it calculate the regression equation using only these 10 cases. If you're seeing the similarities to what happened in Chapter 5, you already know what's going to happen next. Because of sampling error (especially with these small samples), the resulting regression equations differed widely. Here are 3 of the 150 equations:

GRADE = 1.317 + 0.018(ATTENDANCE)
GRADE = 0.544 + 0.027(ATTENDANCE)
GRADE = 1.931 + 0.006(ATTENDANCE)

In the first equation, the sample slope is exactly the same as the population slope. The second sample slope is higher than the population slope. The third slope is lower than the population slope. The lowest of the 150 sample slopes was 0.000. The highest of the 150 sample slopes was 0.041. Here is a graph of all 150 sample slopes:

■ **Exhibit 8.2: Sampling Distribution of 150 Sample Slopes**

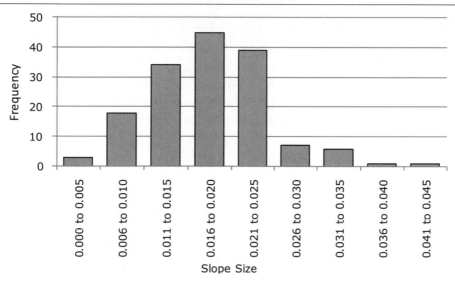

The distribution of these slopes is fairly normally shaped, and would become even more normal if I had taken more and more samples and calculated more and more slopes. Most of the slopes are actually quite close to the population slope of 0.018. Notice that at the center of this distribution is the bar containing this population slope. Some slopes, however, have quite a bit of error, either underestimating or overestimating the slope.

What is the average—or *standard*—error of these slopes? To find this, I used the same procedure we used to find the standard error of the sampling distribution of sample means:

1. I calculated how far each sample slope was from the population slope of 0.018.
2. I squared these distances.

3. I added up these squared distances to get 0.007208.
4. I divided the 0.007208 by 150 to get 0.000048053.
5. I took the square root of this 0.000048053 to get 0.007.

So the standard error—the average error of these slopes—is 0.007.

Recall that, when we were working with sample means, we had a way to estimate the standard error using information from just a single sample: we took the sample standard deviation and divided it by the square root of the sample size. There also is a way to estimate the **standard error of the slope** using information from a single sample-based set of regression results. We will use this formula to estimate the standard error of the slope:

$$estimate\ standard\ error\ of\ the\ slope = \frac{s_y}{s_x}\sqrt{\frac{1-r^2}{n-2}}$$

How good an estimate does this provide? Well, as we found in Chapter 5, this depends on several things, most importantly the size of the sample. But even with samples of ten, the estimate is pretty good. For example, one of the samples had the following results:

$r^2 = 0.46$, $n = 10$, $s_y = 0.48$, $s_x = 21.25$

$$estimate\ standard\ error\ of\ the\ slope = \frac{0.48}{21.25}\sqrt{\frac{1-0.46}{10-2}} = 0.006$$

And this is pretty darned close to 0.007. As in Chapter 5, this is powerful, because it is through the standard error that we can use inferential techniques.

FROM STANDARD ERROR TO A *T*-VALUE TO A *P*-CONCLUSION

At the center of the sampling distribution of sample means, we had the population mean. At the center of the sampling distribution of sample mean differences, we had the claim that two population means were equal, for that was our null hypothesis. If we were able to move far enough away from the center of this distribution, we were able to reject the null hypothesis and conclude that our population means did differ. What we're going to have at the center of the sampling distribution of sample slopes is the null hypothesis that the population slope is zero. If our sample slope is far enough away from this claim, then we will be able to reject the null hypothesis and conclude that the population slope is not zero. To calculate this distance, we turn our sample slope into a number of standard errors. That is, we want to know how far away our sample slope is from this center claim.

It's time for an example to make all of this clear. The example we will use is similar to that in Chapter 6, using height as the independent variable and salary as the dependent variable. Here are the data for 10 men, hypothetically randomly drawn from a population of men:

■ **Exhibit 8.3: Height and Salary from a Sample of Ten Men**

Height in Feet	Salary in $10,000s
4.0	1.2
5.0	2.0
5.5	3.0
5.5	3.5
5.8	3.5
5.9	4.5
6.0	5.2
6.1	6.0
6.2	9.0
6.5	7.0

The regression equation derived from these data is:

SALARY $= -11.17 + 2.77$(HEIGHT)

The value of r^2 for this regression is 0.70, meaning that height explains 70% of the variation in salary. The last two pieces of information we need are the standard deviations for the two variables:

standard deviation for height $= 0.72$
standard deviation for salary $= 2.37$

With this information, we can calculate the estimate of the standard error of the slope:

$$estimate\ standard\ error\ of\ the\ slope = \frac{2.37}{0.72}\sqrt{\frac{1-0.70}{10-2}} = 0.64$$

With this, we can calculate how many standard errors away the slope of 2.77 is from 0:

$2.77/0.64 = 4.39$

Is this far enough to be confident that we can reject the claim that the population slope is zero? We take our number of standard errors and the sample size and, you guessed it, it's off to the t-table. The degrees of freedom are $n - 2$ (we take away 1 degree of freedom for each variable), so we use the row where $df = 8$:

■ **Table 8.1: An Excerpt from the t-Table**

Level of significance	0.10	0.05	0.01	0.001
$df = 8$	1.86	2.31	3.36	5.04

Our t-value is 4.39. So we begin moving to the right:

Our 4.39 is greater than 1.86. We can keep moving rightward.
Our 4.39 is greater than 2.31. On to the right we go.
Our 4.39 is greater than 3.36. Right on(ward).

But 4.39 is less than 5.04. Because our t-value is less than 5.04, we cannot use the p-value of $p < .001$. So, we settle for $p < .01$, which is pretty darned good.

The p again stands for probability: the probability that the population slope is indeed zero. To say that the population slope is not zero (that is, to say that there is a real effect), we need the probability that the population slope *is* zero to be below 5%, or 0.05. In our example, the conclusion is that $p < .01$, meaning that there is less than a 1% chance that the population slope is zero. Let me apply that "flipping logic" I've used before. If the population slope were indeed zero, then the probability of drawing a sample of 10 that then had a slope of 2.77 is very, very small. Now, we flip this statement: because we *did* draw a sample of 10, which then had a slope of 2.77, we can say that the probability that the population slope is zero is very, very small.

For the sake of illustration, let's take the preceding example and change only the size of the slope: we'll halve it, going from 2.77 to 1.39. Now that the slope is smaller (and thus closer to the center of the sampling distribution), can we still reject the null hypothesis that the population slope is zero? The t-value is now

$1.39/0.64 = 2.17$

Looking at the excerpt from the t-table again, we see that our t-value of 2.17 does not get past 2.31, which is what we would need to say that $p < .05$. So in this situation, we cannot reject the null hypothesis that the population slope is zero.

The chart below should help you make some sense of what is going on. I took the preceding example and ran a variety of versions of it, modifying the size of the effect and the size of the sample. I kept everything else the same: the standard deviations and the r^2 (I realize it is somewhat unlikely to change the slope and not have the r^2 be affected, but I wanted to keep this simple). Going from top to bottom on the left, we have the size of the effect, ranging from a small 0.4 to a large 4.0. Going from left to right across the top, we have the sample size, from a very small 5 to a sizable 122. The numbers within the table are t-values calculated by plugging in the corresponding sample size and slope. For example, the first number, 0.38, is calculated by using the slope of 0.4 and the sample size of 5.

■ **Exhibit 8.4: Slope, Size, Sample Size, and Statistical Significance**

					SAMPLE SIZE				
	5	**10**	**15**	**20**	**25**	**32**	**42**	**62**	**122**
0.4	0.38	0.63	0.80	0.94	1.06	1.22	1.40	1.72	2.43
0.6	0.58	0.94	1.20	1.41	1.60	1.82	2.11	2.58	3.65
0.8	0.77	1.26	1.60	1.88	2.13	2.43	2.81	3.44	4.86
1	0.96	1.57	2.00	2.35	2.66	3.04	3.51	4.30	6.08
1.2	1.15	1.88	2.40	2.83	3.19	3.65	4.21	5.16	7.29
1.4	1.35	2.20	2.80	3.30	3.73	4.26	4.91	6.02	8.51
1.6	1.54	2.51	3.20	3.77	4.26	4.86	5.62	6.88	9.73
1.8	1.73	2.83	3.60	4.24	4.79	5.47	6.32	7.74	10.94
2	1.92	3.14	4.00	4.71	5.32	6.08	7.02	8.60	12.16
2.2	2.11	3.45	4.40	5.18	5.86	6.69	7.72	9.46	13.37
2.4	2.31	3.77	4.80	5.65	6.39	7.29	8.42	10.32	14.59
2.6	2.50	4.08	5.20	6.12	6.92	7.90	9.13	11.18	15.81
2.8	2.69	4.39	5.60	6.59	7.45	8.51	9.83	12.04	17.02
3	2.88	4.71	6.00	7.06	7.98	9.12	10.53	12.90	18.24
3.2	3.08	5.02	6.40	7.53	8.52	9.73	11.23	13.76	19.45
3.4	3.27	5.34	6.80	8.00	9.05	10.33	11.93	14.61	20.67
3.6	3.46	5.65	7.20	8.48	9.58	10.94	12.64	15.47	21.88
3.8	3.65	5.96	7.60	8.95	10.11	11.55	13.34	16.33	23.10
4	3.84	6.28	8.00	9.42	10.65	12.16	14.04	17.19	24.32

The left axis is labeled **SLOPE**.

☐	= Slope is not statistically significant.
☐	= Slope is statistically significant at $p < .05$ level.
☐	= Slope is statistically significant at $p < .01$ level.
☐	= Slope is statistically significant at $p < .001$ level.

Let's walk through this chart by sample sizes, starting with the smallest. With a sample size of a mere 5, it takes a very large effect to get to a point where we'd feel comfortable saying that the population slope is not zero. A slope of 3.4 is the first one that breaks through the $p < .05$ barrier. With a slightly larger sample of 10, you don't need as big an effect to make the claim that the population slope is not zero. The first slope that gets to the $p < .05$ level is 1.6. And, with a slope of 3.4, your p-value is $p < .001$, not $p < .05$. With a sample size of 15, the $p < .05$ level comes even earlier, with an effect of 1.2. Why is this? Why is it easier to make the "population slope is not zero" claim with a larger sample than it is with a smaller sample? Think about it: with a very small sample, you may have a single outlier that would have the ability to throw things off, seriously affecting the size of the slope. Because of this, we need to make sure the effect is huge in order to have the certainty to make the claim. With a larger sample, outliers do not have the same power, so if there is a sizable slope we can be that much more certain that it is "real," giving us the confidence to say, at a lower level of effect, that the population slope cannot be zero. Notice that, with the larger samples, the effects can be quite small and still achieve statistical significance. Granted, part of this might be that I have not varied the r^2 from its original 0.7. But the point remains: it is sometimes easy—too easy—to achieve statistically significant results if your samples are quite large, as you will see later when we get to some examples using real data.

The shadings I used earlier to signify the various levels of statistical significance in Exhibit 8.4 are nice and all, but in the real world of regression, rather than shadings, we use something even prettier: stars. Yes, in what I like to think of as a tribute to Dr. Seuss's beloved Sneetches, we use stars to represent statistically significant findings. Typically, here is what the stars mean:

▪ **Exhibit 8.5: The Typical Meaning of Significance Stars**

No stars:	slope is not statistically significant.
* One star:	slope is statistically significant at the $p < .05$ level.
** Two stars:	slope is statistically significant at the $p < .01$ level.
*** Three stars:	slope is statistically significant at the $p < .001$ level.

So, if a slope has a star by it (e.g., 1.23*), it means that the researchers performed the preceding calculations (or, more likely, had their computer do them), and their t-value yielded this p-conclusion. I will use this set of symbols in subsequent chapters. If you're looking at research in journal articles, the specific use of stars should be described at the bottom of each table. While most research uses the set of star meanings shown in Exhibit 8.5, a few researchers may use slightly different combinations. For example, sometimes they use one star to represent $p < .10$, as in some circles this is considered a statistically significant effect (the typical cutoff, as you know, is $p < .05$). So always look at the bottom of any regression table before you make any conclusions.

Also at the bottom of many regression tables you will see, next to the typical "*$p < .05$, **$p < .01$, ***$p < .001$," the following parenthetical phrase: "(two-tailed tests)."

Nearly all inferential regression results involve two-tailed tests, because we seldom can say for certain in which direction any given relationship is going to go, and therefore there are two possibilities (thus we need to look at both tails of the sampling distribution). For example, in the illustrations that follow, I hypothesize that education affects sexual activity. Although I have some idea about the direction of the relationship, it is theoretically possible that the direction of the relationship could go either way: more education leads to more sex; more education leads to less sex—two possibilities, two-tailed tests. Only in rare circumstances when we know that one direction for the relationship is simply not possible (e.g., "Live people have more sex than dead people") would we do a one-tailed test.

GSS EXAMPLE: EDUCATION AND SEXUAL ACTIVITY

It is rumored that people from the working class have different amounts of sex than people than do the those in the middle and upper classes. Let's investigate this possibility by using 2012 General Social Survey data. I'll use years of education as a marker of social class (imperfect though it may be). For the dependent variable, I will use a rendition of the variable SEXFREQ, which is the number of times the respondent says he or she had sex in the past year. Here is a bar graph for this variable:

■ **Exhibit 8.6: Bar Graph of Sexual Frequency**

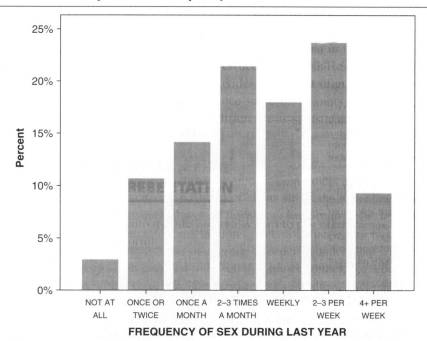

Source: GSS 2012 data.

That's a great deal of variation. I recoded this ordinal-level variable into more of a ratio-level variable called SEXMONTH: the number of times per month that the respondent says she has sex. For example, someone who said once a month would be coded 1 on SEXMONTH, whereas someone who said weekly would be coded 4. I'll run the simple regression for four age groups: 30-somethings, 40-somethings, 50-somethings, and 60-somethings. First, for the people in their 30s, here are the results:

$$SEXMONTH = 11.85 - 0.34(EDUC) \quad r^2 = 0.028, n = 323$$

There is an effect: the more education you get, the less sex someone in his or her 30s has. But this is the effect for the *sample*. Can we generalize and say that an effect exists in the population of 30-somethings? SPSS, rather than giving us a "$p <$" conclusion, gives us the *actual p*-value it derived from its trip to the *t*-value store, and in this case, it is 0.002. Because we can't say that $p < .001$, our *p*-conclusion would be $p < .01$. We can say with much confidence that the population slope is not zero. In other words, we can say that, among the population of 30-somethings, education does affect sexual frequency. Notice that we don't say that this exact sample slope can be generalized to the population. Rather, all we're able to conclude is that we know with a good degree of certainty that there *is* an effect within the population.

Here are the results for the 40-somethings:

$$SEXMONTH = 8.52 - 0.18(EDUC) \quad r^2 = 0.009, n = 268$$

The *p*-value for this slope is 0.114, so we cannot even conclude that $p < .10$. We cannot say that, in the population of 40-somethings, education affects sexual frequency.

The results for the 50-somethings are

$$SEXMONTH = 2.90 + 0.09(EDUC) \quad r^2 = 0.003, n = 198$$

If a slope of 0.18 with a sample size of 268 was not statistically significant, you can already guess that a slope of 0.09 with a sample size of 198 is not going to make it either. The *p*-value is 0.418, so we conclude that, among the population of 50-somethings, there is no statistically significant relationship between education and sexual frequency.

Finally, these are the results for the 60-somethings:

$$SEXMONTH = -0.68 + 0.19(EDUC) \quad r^2 = 0.042, n = 139$$

The *p*-value for this last situation is .016, so here we can conclude that $p < .05$ and that in the population of 60-somethings, there is a relationship between education and sexual frequency.

You may have noticed something counterintuitive: with the 268 people in their 40s, a slope of 0.18 did not achieve statistical significance, but with the 139 people in their 60s, a slope of 0.19 did achieve statistical significance. How can we achieve statistical significance with essentially the same size slope but half the sample size? That just doesn't seem right. Here is what is going on:

■ **Exhibit 8.7: Variation, Standard Error, and Statistical Significance**

	40-somethings	60-somethings
SD for education	3.21	2.62
SD for sexmonth:	5.94	2.49
s_y/s_x	1.85	0.95
standard error of slope	0.113	0.080
slope	0.18	0.19
slope/standard error	1.59	2.38
p-value:	$p > .10$	$p < .05$

It turns out that the 40-somethings have greater variation in sexual frequency than do the 60-somethings. Recall that this figures into the calculation of the standard error of the slope. Because the standard error for 40-somethings is larger, when we divide this into the value of the slope, we get a smaller *t*-value than we do for the 60-somethings. Conceptually, because there's more variation in the sexual behavior of 40-somethings, we can't be as confident in speaking about that population. Sample size plays an important role, but it isn't everything.

You may have noticed something else about the two groups that produce statistically significant relationships: the 30-somethings and the 60-somethings. For the 30-somethings, education has a negative effect on sexual frequency: the more education you have, the less sex you have. But among the 60-somethings, education has a positive effect on sexual frequency: the more education you have, the more sex you have. For these two groups, education and sexual frequency are related, but the relationship is the opposite. We'll return to this example later in the book.

GSS EXAMPLE: INCOME AND SEXUAL ACTIVITY

Now we'll use a different measure of social class: income. The purpose of this example is to distinguish between statistical significance and substantive significance. I ran a regression with 2012 GSS data, using SEXMONTH as my dependent variable and respondent's income in thousands as my independent variable. Here are the results I received:

$$\text{SEXMONTH} = 5.96 - 0.014(\text{INCOME}) \qquad r^2 = 0.007, n = 807$$

The p-value is .015, so we can claim that it is a statistically significant effect and that in the population sexual frequency is related to income. However, let's say you wanted to have sex one more time per month and were willing to give up some of your income to make this happen (no, I'm not talking about paying for sex). We ask, "How many thousands of dollars of income decline would it take to raise sexual frequency by one time?"

$$1/0.014 = 71.43$$

You would need to make more than \$70,000 less in income in order to get sexual frequency to go up by one. That's a lot of money. Granted, this is a rather ridiculous example, but it does drive home the point that you cannot look only at the statistical significance. You have to grapple with the actual size of the effects and determine if they are substantively significant as well. Don't get (significance) starstruck!

GSS EXAMPLE: WORK TIME AND SEXUAL ACTIVITY

Obsessed with what explains variation in sexual activity, we try yet another independent variable: the number of hours you work in a week. The thought is that if someone is working many hours per week, he or she won't have time, or will be too tired, to have sex. Here are the regression results, using 2012 GSS data:

$$\text{SEXMONTH} = 5.96 - 0.00005(\text{HRSWRKD}) \qquad r^2 = 0.000, n = 796$$

This tiny slope has a p-value of .997, meaning that, if we were to claim that hours worked affected sexual activity in the population, we would have a 99.7% chance of being incorrect. However, rather than saying, "No statistical significance, no substantive finding," I say, "How interesting!" And, really, the fact that no relationship exists between hours worked and sexual activity speaks well of American productivity, in multiple ways. Overworked does not necessarily mean undersexed.

LITERATURE EXAMPLE: GRADE POINT AVERAGES

Here is a piece of research that I think will be of interest to you. It's on the older side: an article published in 1985 in the journal *Social Forces*, with data collected all the way back in 1973. But it addresses a question near and dear to many hearts: Does studying affect grade point averages? In this study, Howard Schuman and his students collected data from a random sample of 424 undergraduate students at the University of Michigan. By asking their respondents a series of questions about their study habits, Schuman et al. constructed an index of hours studied per day, which the researchers then used as an independent variable. Their dependent variable was grade point average (GPA). One would think (and hope) that there would be a relationship between the two. Before we get to the regression, here are some summary results:

■ **Exhibit 8.8: Studying and GPA**

Hours Studied	Number of Students	Average GPA
0.0–1.9	46	2.94
2.0–2.9	69	2.91
3.0–3.9	100	2.97
4.0–4.9	89	2.86
5.0–5.9	53	3.25
6.0–6.9	45	3.18

So far, not an impressive relationship. Among the first four categories, in fact, there seems to be no relationship. GPA does shoot up in the fifth category, but in the sixth category, it goes back down. Once Schuman et al. averaged out this effect using regression, did it achieve statistical significance? Just barely. They don't report the slope, but they do report an r^2 of 0.012 and a p-value of .03. Therefore, they could say that the relationship between hours studied and GPA *does* exist within the University of Michigan undergraduate student body, but it's a squeaker. Don't be disheartened. And *definitely* don't stop studying. There are numerous possibilities why they hardly found a relationship. I think one of the biggest potential culprits here is the fact that these data were self-reported by the students. Not that the students were liars, but I imagine that estimating this with any accuracy is difficult. There's time spent studying, and then there's time spent Studying with a capital *S*.

Schuman and his students also had data on what percentage of classes their respondents said they attended. When they carried out a regression with this as the independent variable, and GPA as the dependent variable, the results were considerably more heartening. The r^2 for the regression was 0.076, and the p-conclusion was $p < .001$. There is almost certainly a relationship between class attendance and GPA within the population of University of Michigan undergraduate students. One possible lesson to take away from this is that, if you have to choose between studying an extra hour or going to class for that hour, you might want to opt for going to class.

LITERATURE EXAMPLE: FAMILY SIZE AND GRADES

Let's stick with the dependent variable of grades, but let's look at a different age group and a different independent variable. It is from an article by Douglas Downey on the effects of family size on grades (Downey, 1995). The data come from a highly reputable project called the National Educational Longitudinal Study, which followed a large, scientifically drawn sample of students throughout their educational careers. These data were collected when the students were in the eighth grade. The students were asked to self-report what their grades were since the sixth grade, ranging from 0.5 (mostly below D) to 4 (mostly As). Downey also knew how many siblings the students had. The goal of his study was to explore the effects of family size on grades, the expectation being the larger the family, the lower the grades. He started with simple regression. His sample size was a very large 16,933. Using grades as the dependent variable, the slope for "number of siblings" was −0.059. This slope is significant at the $p < .001$ level. But keep in mind a point I made earlier: it can be easy to attain statistical significance with very large sample sizes. Let's think about the substantive significance for a moment. Let's imagine that a child with no siblings has grades of 3.00. What happens to this child's grades as we, hypothetically, give him or her more and more siblings? Exhibit 8.9 shows the expected grades (assuming a starting point of 3.00) for a variety of family sizes:

◼ **Exhibit 8.9: Number of Siblings and Predicted Grades**

Number of Siblings	Grades
0	3.00
1	2.94
2	2.88
3	2.82
4	2.76
5	2.71

Does number of siblings have an effect on grades? Yes. Is it an effect that allows us to say that in the population of eighth graders from which this sample was drawn that family size affects grades? Yes. Is it a substantively significant effect. Hmmm. Let's look at this more closely. The difference between an only child who has no siblings and a child who has five siblings is fairly small: about the difference between a B and a B–. We would have to give an only child *17* siblings in order to lower his grades by an entire grade point ($0.059 \times 17 = 1.00$). Yes, the −0.059 is a generalizable effect, but in the grand scheme of things, it's a substantively small effect.

CONCLUSION

With this chapter, we complete our tour of inferential techniques. Whether we're using crosstabs, means, proportions, or slopes, the goal is always the same: using what we've learned about a sample to make a statement about the population from which the sample was drawn. In regression analysis, the inferential goal is to say that, in some population, the independent variable has an effect on the dependent variable. If the size of the sample-based slope is large enough, we're able to do this with confidence. If it is not large enough, we can't.

SPSS DEMONSTRATIONS

Please visit the book's website (www.routledge.com/cw/linneman) to view videos of these demonstrations.

Regression

Having SPSS run a regression is quite easy. Making sense of the output is the more difficult part. But even this is not that hard once you know what to look for. That's what this demonstration is all about. We'll use ANES data to investigate the relationship between age and score on the Traditionalism Index. We click

Analyze → Regression → Linear

and once in the regression box, it's simply a matter of putting the variables in the correct boxes and then clicking OK:

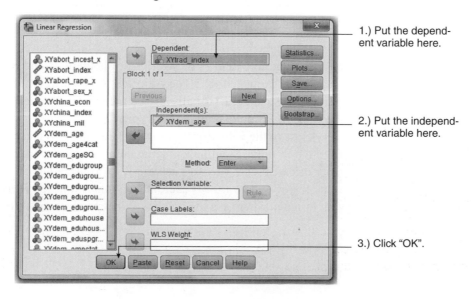

When you ask SPSS to run an ordinary least squares (OLS) regression model, it gives you four boxes of output. It may seem like a lot of output, but I'll show you exactly what to look for in each box. Here are the four boxes and what useful information you can garner from each of them:

Variables Entered/Removed[b]

Model	Variables Entered	Variables Removed	Method
1	Age in Years[a]	.	Enter

a. All requested variables entered.
b. Dependent Variable: Traditional Values Index.

The first box is simply SPSS's way of telling you that it did what you asked it to do. It lists the independent variables within the box and states the dependent variable below the box. If SPSS had a problem running your regression and, say, one of the variables did not work out, here is where SPSS would tell you this. By "not work out," I'm talking about something such as if a variable turned out to be a constant (all the cases have the same value on the variable) or the combinations of variables you're using don't elicit any cases in common.

Model Summary

Model	R	R Square	Adjusted R Square	Std. Error of the Estimate
1	0.235[a]	0.055	0.055	3.529

a. Predictors: (Constant), Age in Years.

The second box gives you your value for r and r^2 or, as SPSS calls them, R and R^2. It also gives you what is called the "Adjusted R^2." The Adjusted R^2 is a way of taking into account the fact that the R-Squared is (usually) based on sample data and is not a perfect estimate of the value of R^2 in the population. Typically, the value for the Adjusted R^2 will be very, very close to the value for R^2, or even the same, as it is here. It will be quite different from the R^2 only if you have a large number of independent variables and a small number of cases. One way to raise the R^2 is to use a bunch of independent variables, so this is a way to ward off such inclinations. Adjusted R^2 is calculated with the following formula, where k is the number of independent variables and n is the sample size:

$$Adjusted\ R^2 = R^2 - \left(\frac{k}{(n-k+1)}\right) \times (1 - R^2)$$

In this case, we have

$$Adjusted\ R^2 = .055 - \frac{1}{5417 - 1 + 1} \times 1 - .055 = .055$$

It's highly unlikely that you'll ever need to use this calculation on your own, because SPSS will do it for you, but it's good to know what's going on behind the scenes sometimes. I'll be using the unadjusted R^2 throughout the book.

ANOVA[b]

Model		Sum of Squares	df	Mean Square	F	Sig.
1	Regression	3938.819	1	3938.819	316.262	0.000[a]
	Residual	67439.954	5415	12.454		
	Total	71378.774	5416			

a. Predictors: (Constant), Age in Years.
b. Dependent Variable: Traditional Values Index.

The third box is titled ANOVA, meaning ANalysis Of VAriance. This is a cousin to the ANOVA procedure we did in Chapter 6. Remember in Chapter 7 when we calculated the total amount of error made with and without the regression equation? That is what we have here. The Sum of Squares Regression is the equivalent of the total amount of explained variation, the Sum of Squares Residual is the equivalent of the total amount of unexplained variation, and the Sum of Squares Total is the total amount of variation. If we take that 3,938.819 and divide it by the 71,378.774, we get 0.055, which is the value of R^2, or the proportion of variation explained. The other important thing we can glean from the third box is the total number of cases in the regression. In the column headed "df" (standing for degrees of freedom), we take the bottom number, add 1 to it, and we have n. There are 5,416 + 1 cases in this regression.

Coefficients[a]

Model		Unstandardized Coefficients		Standardized Coefficients		
		B	Std. Error	Beta	t	Sig.
1	(Constant)	6.446	0.152		42.467	0.000
	Age in Years	0.052	0.003	0.235	17.784	0.000

a. Dependent Variable: Traditional Values Index.

This last box is full of good stuff. In the first column of numbers, going from top to bottom, is the regression equation. The first number is the constant, and then we have the slope. In this example, the regression equation is

TRADINDEX = 6.446 + 0.052(AGE)

To the right of the slope, we have its standard error: 0.003 is the standard error of the slope for the variable education. If we take this standard error and divide it into the slope, we get the *t*-value over to the right: 0.052/0.003 = 17.33. This differs slightly from the SPSS calculation because of rounding. SPSS has a full *t*-table "in its head," so it gives you, based on the *t*-value and sample size, the significance level. Here, the significance is reported as 0.000, meaning that $p < .001$ (because p can never be exactly zero). So we can feel very confident in saying that, in the population from which the ANES sample was drawn, there is a relationship between age and traditionalism. The only other piece of information in this box is the Standardized Coefficient, or Beta. Chapter 11 is all about the betas, so just remember where it is in the output and we'll get back to it.

Creating a Correlation Matrix

Please visit the book's website (www.routledge.com/cw/linneman) to view a video of this demonstration.

If you want to look at correlations among a number of different variables, you might want to create a correlation matrix, and this is very easy to do in SPSS. Click

Analyze → Correlate → Bivariate

This brings us to this room, where we're going to correlate the feeling thermometers for the President, Congress, and the Supreme Court:

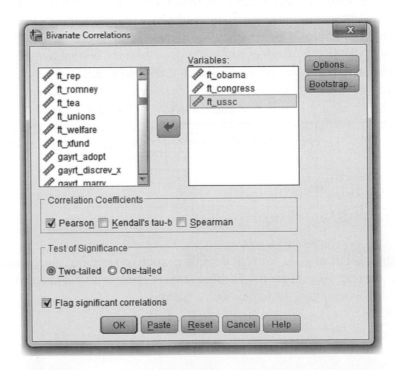

As you can see, it's simply a matter of filling the box with the variables of interest and then pressing the "OK" button. Here is the output from this request:

Correlations

		Feeling thermometer: Democratic Presidential candidate	Feeling thermometer: CONGRESS	Feeling thermometer: THE U.S. SUPREME COURT
Feeling thermometer: Democratic Presidential candidate	Pearson Correlation	1	0.317**	0.301**
	Sig. (2-tailed)		0.000	0.000
	N	5495	5450	5432
Feeling thermometer: CONGRESS	Pearson Correlation	0.317**	1	0.479**
	Sig. (2-tailed)	0.000		0.000
	N	5450	5458	5428
Feeling thermometer: THE U.S. SUPREME COURT	Pearson Correlation	0.301**	0.479**	1
	Sig. (2-tailed)	0.000	0.000	
	N	5432	5428	5439

**Correlation is significant at the 0.01 level (2-tailed).

This at first seems like a lot of information, but it's really not so bad. We have all three variables across the top and then again along the side. Notice this gives us a diagonal full of 1.000s, because correlating a variable with itself should darned well better give us a perfect correlation. Notice also that above and below this diagonal, it's a mirror image: the 0.317 appears twice, because it's the same correlation (Obama with Congress, Congress with Obama). Therefore, often people will delete everything under the diagonal. Or, occasionally, you will see people have, for example, the women's correlations above the diagonal and the men's correlations below the diagonal (e.g., see the "physical attractiveness" literature example in Chapter 7). Notice that SPSS tells us which correlations are statistically significant. We didn't talk about inference and correlations, but it's the same old story: a significant correlation means we can say with confidence that the correlation between these variables in the population is not zero.

FROM OUTPUT TO PRESENTATION

Now we can start to talk about how people typically present regression results. We'll go into this in-depth in Chapter 10, but here is a preview. Here is our regression equation from the preceding SPSS demonstration:

TRADINDEX = 6.446 + 0.052(AGE) $r^2 = 0.055$, $n = 5,417$

What we're going to do is basically turn the equation 90 degrees:

▪ **Exhibit 8.10: Effect of Age on Traditionalism**

Independent Variable	Slope
Age in Years	0.055***
Constant	6.446
R^2	0.055
n	5,417

***$p < .001$.
Source: ANES 2012 data.

This may not seem like much of an improvement, but you'll soon see what it is useful to present results this way. Notice that we're also starting to use stars to symbolize statistical significance, which is very typical in results presentation.

EXERCISES

EXERCISES

Exercise 1

Several of the ANES feeling thermometers concern religion. Run three simple regression equations, all of them using the Christian Fundamentalist feeling thermometer as your independent variable. For the first equation, use the Mormon feeling thermometer. For the second equation, use the Muslim feeling thermometer, and for the last equation, use the Atheist feeling thermometer. Clearly present the three regression equations, the value for r-squared, the sample size, and the statistical significance. Then, write a short paragraph about your results.

Exercise 2

A common lament is that younger people don't follow the news any more. Is this a valid observation? The ANES asks respondents how many times a week they review news on the Internet, read a physical newspaper, listen to the news on the radio, and watch the news on television. Using these four variables as dependent variables, regress age onto each of them (i.e., use age as your independent variable; be sure to use the recoded age variable that uses age in years). Write up your results, describing the effect of age on each of these news-getting behaviors. In your explanation, contrast a 20-year-old to an 80-year-old.

Exercise 3 (Answer Available in Appendix D)

Younger people these days are developing a reputation for not caring about privacy. Therefore, we might expect that the younger you are, the less concerned you might be about the government's wiretapping. Run a simple regression equation using ANES data, using the recoded age variable as your independent variable and the Wiretapping Index as your dependent variable. Interpret your results, distinguishing between statistical significance and substantive significance.

Exercise 4

Which political party has the most dedicated constituencies? Looking at correlations among various ANES feeling thermometers that are stereotypically associated with the major political parties is a good way to look for such connections. Run one correlation matrix using the following feeling thermometers: big business, the military, the tea party, Christian Fundamentalists, and the Republican Party. Then run a second correlation matrix using the following feeling thermometers: feminists, poor people, labor unions, gays and lesbians, and the Democratic Party. Which correlation matrix has stronger correlations? What does this tell you about the cohesiveness of each party?

Exercise 5

Many people claim that with the election of Barack Obama, the racial terrain of the United States has changed. Others claim that resentment still lingers. Run a simple regression equation using the Obama feeling thermometer as the dependent variable and the Resent Blacks Index as the independent variable. Fully interpret your results, addressing the question, Do those who still harbor resentment toward blacks feel more negatively toward Obama?

Exercise 6

I used one of the Unique Groups—those who rated Christian Fundamentalists and atheists at 100 on the feeling thermometer—and ran a simple regression equation using the abortion index as my dependent variable and number of times attend religious services per month as my independent variable. Here are some results:

Standard Deviation of the Dependent Variable: 12.14
Standard Deviation of the Independent Variable: 3.25
Value for r^2: 0.14
Number of cases: 15
Value of the slope: −1.41

Determine if this slope is statistically significant. Explain your results.

Exercise 7 (Answer Available in Appendix D)

I used another one of the Unique Groups—strong Republicans who have twice voted for Obama—and ran a sample regression equation using the economic peril index as my dependent variable and family income as my independent variable. Here are some results:

Standard Deviation of the Dependent Variable: 5.10
Standard Deviation of the Independent Variable: 92.06
Value for r^2: 0.52
Number of cases: 10
Value of slope: −0.04

Determine if this slope is statistically significant (hint: because your standard error will be very small, keep three decimal places). Explain your results.

Exercise 8

Does the presence of technology in people's homes influence how they use technology when they are out shopping? Use the PewShop dataset to investigate this relationship. Use the Tech Index as your independent variable and the Shop Index as your dependent variable. Run this regression once for white respondents and once for Hispanic respondents. Examine the results and discuss the importance of sample size for statistical significance.

Exercise 9

Using the PewShop dataset, investigate the relationship between the Tech Index and the Shop Index, but now run the regression once for men younger than 40 years old and then again for women younger than 40 years old. Examine the results and contrast the statistical significance of the two slopes.

Exercise 10

Often, various health conditions are related. That is, if one has one condition, one is likely to have another condition. Using the PewHealth index, run a correlation matrix using the five recoded health condition variables (leave out the variable for "other conditions"). Which health conditions are highly correlated with one another?

Exercise 11

Select cases in the PewHealth dataset so that you are analyzing only the Asian respondents. Assess the relationship between years of education (use the recoded variable) and the Internet Health Use Index.

Exercise 12 (Answer Available in Appendix D)

Among the elderly, is there a relationship between education and health? Using the PewHealth dataset, select cases so that you are looking only at those aged 80 and older. Assess the relationship between years of education (use the recoded variable) and the Health Conditions Index.

Exercise 13

Do kids engage in more bad cyberbehavior as they get older? Use the Child's Bad Cyberbehavior Index as your dependent variable, and use child's age as your independent variable. Interpret your results.

Exercise 14

Does parents' checking and blocking behavior affect kids' behavior, or is it more the kids' perceptions of what parents do in this respect? Use the Child's Own Cyberbullying Enabling Index as your dependent variable, and then run two regressions: one with the Parental Checking and Blocking Index as your independent variable and one with the Child's Perception of Parental Checking and Blocking Index as your independent variable. Explain your results.

Exercise 15 (Answer Available in Appendix D)

Here is a hypothesis: The larger the percentage of people in a country that experiences environmental problems in their community, the larger the percentage of the people in that country will be willing to pay more to protect the environment. Test this hypothesis by creating and interpreting a correlation matrix with the following WVS variables:

INCENV, TAXENV, WATER, AIRQUAL, and SEWAGE.

Exercise 16

In this exercise, use the WVS dataset to see if a relationship between education and attitudes toward gays and lesbians exists on a country-by-country level. Using SPSS, create a simple regression equation using the EDUC variable as the independent variable and the NEHOMO variable as the dependent variable. Fully interpret the results.

Exercise 17

A long-standing topic in the social sciences is the authoritarian personality: there are certain characteristics that lead people to favor a very strong government. One of these factors is trust. Is trust related to favoring a strong leadership? Using the WVS dataset and SPSS, run a simple regression using PTRUST as your independent variable and STRLEAD as your dependent variable. Fully interpret your results.

## Chapter 9

IT'S ALL RELATIVE: DICHOTOMIES AS INDEPENDENT VARIABLES IN REGRESSION

This chapter covers . . .

. . . how to use dichotomies as independent variables in regression

. . . how to use reference groups in regression

. . . how researchers used reference groups to study gender differences in housework

. . . how a researcher used reference groups to study attitude changes over time

INTRODUCTION

In the previous two chapters, all of the independent variables we have used have been ratio-level variables: height, income, hours, and grade point average, for example. Often we want to use other types of variables in regression that are not naturally measured at the ratio level. For example, we may want to use sex as an independent variable: do men and women significantly differ on some dependent variable of interest? We (usually) consider sex to be a dichotomy: you are either male or female. Or we may want to compare people of various religious backgrounds: Catholic, Protestant, Jewish, Muslim, and so on. As you recall from Chapter 1, religious background is a nominal-level variable: it simply puts people into categories without any means of ranking them (there's no natural way to rank religious backgrounds). This chapter covers simple techniques we can use when we want to include these kinds of variables in a regression as independent variables.

DICHOTOMIES

Let's start with an easy question: Do men become fathers at an age later in life than women become mothers? We all know that the answer to this one is, on average, yes. But let's get a regression equation just to be sure. First, we need to see how the gender variable is coded, and recode the variable if necessary. In the General Social Survey, the variable SEX is coded Male = 1, Female = 2. I recoded it so that Female = 0, Male = 1:

■ **Exhibit 9.1: Recoding the Sex Variable**

	Original Variable Codes	New Variable Codes
Male	1	1
Female	2	0

Then I ran a regression using a variable called AGEKDBRN (respondent's age when first child was born) as the dependent variable and the recoded SEX variable as the independent variable. I used GSS 2012 data. Here are my results:

Age at first marriage = 22.99 + 2.68(SEX)
Number of cases: 1,430
$r^2 = 0.06$, slope significant at $p < .001$ level

To interpret, let's plug in numbers for both a woman and a man:

Age of woman when first child was born = 22.99 + 2.68(0) = 22.99
Age of man when first child was born = 22.99 + 2.68(1) = 25.67

The woman, coded as a 0, *doesn't* get those additional 2.68 years. The man, coded as 1, *does* get those 2.68 years. Imagine, if you will, that I had coded things differently, with the men coded as 0 and the women coded as 1. How would the equation differ? It would instead look like this:

Age at first marriage = 25.67 − 2.68(SEX)

The story is exactly the same. In the first equation, women were denied those extra years that the positive slope gives the men (their being coded as 0 makes this positive slope go away). In the second equation, women get those extra years taken away from them, whereas the men do not get those extra years taken away from them (their being coded as 0 makes this negative slope go away). Just for practice, here are two more equations using the same variables. I used a different age group for each equation.

Age group: 40 or younger
Age when first child born = 22.18 + 1.94(SEX)
Number of cases: 421
$r^2 = 0.04$, slope significant at $p < .001$ level (two-tailed test)

Age group: 65 or older
Age at first marriage = 22.29 + 3.35(SEX)
Number of cases: 350
$r^2 = 0.10$, slope significant at $p < .001$ level (two-tailed test)

The punch line from these additional two equations: the age difference between men's and women's ages at first child has decreased over time. Among the older respondents, men and women differed on average by almost three and a half years. Among the younger respondents, men and women differed on average by just less than two years.

INTERCHAPTER CONNECTION: *T*-TESTS VERSUS REGRESSION

At this point, you may be wondering why we are using regression here. We already learned in Chapter 6 how to tell the difference between two groups: we used a *t*-test. In fact, let's run a *t*-test to get the exact same results as we did just with those 65 and older:

▨ **Exhibit 9.2:** *T*-Test Comparing Men and Women at Age First Child Is Born

	RESPONDENTS SEX	*N*	Mean	*SD*
R'S AGE WHEN 1ST CHILD BORN	MALE	145	25.64	5.526
	FEMALE	205	22.29	4.325

	t-test for Equality of Means			
	t	*df*	Sig. (2-tailed)	Mean Difference
R'S AGE WHEN 1ST CHILD BORN	6.078	262.980	0.000	3.349

Source: GSS 2012 data.

Notice that the difference between men and women is exactly the same, 3.35 years, and the *p*-conclusion is the same, $p < .001$. So why use regression? One reason is that regression tells us how much variation in age at first child can be explained by sex, and the *t*-test doesn't tell us that. A second reason is that, as we will see in the next chapter, regression allows us to control for other variables; this is not as easy to do with a *t*-test. Sometimes, *t*-tests are fine, but regression is more powerful.

CATEGORICAL VARIABLES

Let's say we wanted to see if people of different races differed on this same dependent variable: age when first child was born. If we look at the General Social Survey, the basic RACE variable has three categories: white = 1, black = 2, other = 3. One solution that would allow us to use this variable in a regression would be to dichotomize it, comparing whites with nonwhites, for example. So we could collapse the "black" and "other" categories into one category called "nonwhite." I did this, coding whites as 0 and nonwhites as 1:

■ **Exhibit 9.3: Recoding Race into a Dichotomy**

	Original Variable Codes	New Variable Codes
White	1	0
Black	2	1
Other	3	1

I then ran the regression using 2012 GSS data, and here are the results:

AGEKDBRN = 24.52 − 1.69(RACE)
Number of cases: 1,430
$r^2 = 0.017$, slope significant at $p < .001$ level (two-tailed test)

The equation shows a significant difference of 1.69 years between whites and non-whites, with nonwhites having their first child earlier (notice that nonwhites are coded as 1, so they get the 1.69 years taken away). However, what if we *didn't* want to collapse the categories? What if we wanted to contrast whites with blacks and whites with others? To do this, we use a simple technique called **reference grouping**. There are a couple of steps to this technique, but the results are easy to understand. First, we decide which group is going to be the reference group. In this case, let's use whites. For every other category that is *not* the reference group, we create a dummy variable:

RACEBLACK, where black = 1, whites and others = 0
RACEOTHER, where other = 1, whites and blacks = 0

Then all we do is run a regression that includes these dummy variables in the equation:

AGEKDBRN = 24.52 − 2.10(RACEBLACK) − 0.99(RACEOTHER)
Number of cases: 1,430
$r^2 = 0.020$

Notice that there is no slope for whites. Whites are the reference group, or because they are not represented by a slope in the equation, sometimes people refer to this as the **omitted category**. Both of the slopes are statistically significant, the black slope at the $p < .001$ level, and the other slope at the $p < .05$ level (two-tailed test). So what do we have here? Let's calculate predictions for all three races:

AGEKDBRN = 24.52 – 2.10(RACEBLACK) – 0.99(RACEOTHER)
AGEKDBRN, white: 24.52 – 2.10(0) – 0.99(0) = 24.52
AGEKDBRN, black: 24.52 – 2.10(1) – 0.99(0) = 22.42
AGEKDBRN, other: 24.52 – 2.10(0) – 0.99(1) = 23.53

Let me talk you through what I did here. I gave the white person zeros on both the RACEBLACK and RACEOTHER variables because this white person is indeed not black and is indeed not other. The white person, therefore, doesn't get that 2.10 taken away from him or her, nor does he or she get the 0.99 taken away from him, so this person's age at first child is simply the value of the constant. The black person gets a 1 for the RACEBLACK variable, but gets a 0 for the RACEOTHER variable (because this person is not an "other"). So he or she gets the 2.10 taken away, but he or she doesn't get the 0.99 taken away. For the person who is "other," we give him a 0 on RACEBLACK and a 1 on RACEOTHER. So he or she gets the 0.99 taken away because of being an "other," but he or she doesn't get the 2.10 taken away because the person is not black.

Here is a visual way to think about reference groups using an old-fashioned number line. The slopes we get help us to see where people's ages are *in reference* to the reference group:

■ **Exhibit 9.4: A Number Line Showing Differences in Age at First Child**

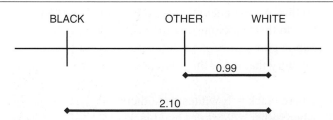

Notice that all of the comparisons we are making are *to* the reference group. Although it may look like blacks' age at first child is younger than people in the "other" category, the regression equation is not set up to state this definitively. We don't know if the 1.11 difference (2.10 – 0.99 = 1.11) between the others and the blacks is statistically significant, because the slope that would allow us to make that comparison was not part of the regression equation.

There is one critical question left unanswered: How do you choose which of the groups to make your reference group? One way is by sample size: let the group that makes up the largest part of the sample be the reference group. However, I think a better way is to make the decision based on substance: In the end, which groups do you want to compare? If all of your comparisons involve blacks, for instance, then you might want to make blacks your reference group. If we really wanted to compare blacks to those in the "other" category, then we should set up the reference-group variables to allow us to see if that was a statistically significant difference.

GSS EXAMPLE: VARIATION IN STEM ACHIEVEMENT

Many people these days are stressing the importance of education in STEM (science, technology, engineering, and math). The 2012 GSS asked some questions that allow us to measure to some extent the respondents' STEM training. We know, for a subset of the GSS respondents, whether they took a biology class, chemistry class, physics class, and advanced math class (trigonometry, precalculus, or calculus) in high school. Now we don't know how *well* they did in these classes, or the quality of these classes, just whether they took them at all. Using these four questions, I created a small index of STEM training. It ranged from 0 (a respondent had taken none of these four courses) to 4 (a respondent had taken all of these courses). Here is a bar graph of how the respondents were distributed on the index:

■ **Exhibit 9.5: Bar Graph of STEM Achievement**

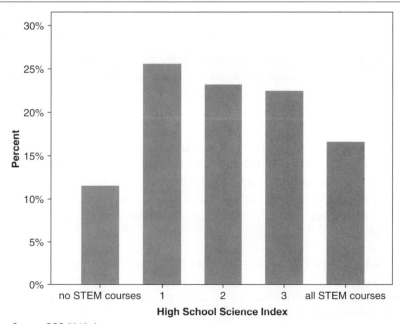

Source: GSS 2012 data.

There is a lot of variation in STEM achievement. Using dichotomies and reference groups, we'll try to explain some of this variation. We start with a dichotomy: sex. Although a higher proportion of women than men now seek higher education, women remain underrepresented among the STEM fields. Does this difference manifest itself in high school STEM achievement? Here is a simple regression equation with sex (coded M = 1, F = 0) as the independent variable:

STEM = 1.95 + 0.26(SEX)
Number of cases: 841
$r^2 = 0.01$

The slope was statistically significant at the $p < .01$ level. But the effect is fairly small: men say they have, on average, taken about a quarter of a STEM class more than women. Notice that we are able to explain only 1% of the variation in STEM achievement.

On to another demographic: race. However, instead of using the race variable I used earlier, I'm going to use a different race variable that allowed the respondents to be more specific in their racial identifications. I will still use whites as my reference group, but now I will use variables to assess the differences between whites and four racial groups: blacks, American Indians, Hispanics, and Asians. Here is my regression equation:

STEM = 2.05 – 0.16(BLACK) – 0.34(AMIND) + 0.27(HISPANIC) + 1.10(ASIAN)
Number of cases: 835
$r^2 = 0.035$

Although there seem to be some differences here, the only slope that achieved statistical significance was the slope for Asians, who had over one additional course than whites. Because the slopes were not significant, we cannot say that, in the population, whites differ from blacks, American Indians, or Hispanics.

There has been a lot of talk lately about how political conservatives may be hostile to science. Does this manifest itself with regard to STEM achievement? I used the GSS variable that measures political views, and created a set of reference-group variables that would allow me to contrast extreme liberals with moderates, and extreme conservatives with moderates. Here are my regression results, using political moderates as my reference group:

STEM = 2.00 + 0.21(EXTLIBERAL) – 0.50(EXTCONSERVATIVE)
Number of cases: 346
$r^2 = 0.013$

Although it does seem that extreme conservatives differ from moderates, with conservatives having fewer STEM courses, the p-value for this slope is . . . $p = .06$! Oh so close to statistical significance. The p-value for the extreme liberals slope was $p = .38$, so this difference of 0.21 courses is not significant. However, I wondered if the 0.71 (0.50 + 0.21 = 0.71) difference between extreme liberals and extreme conservatives might be statistically significant. I can't use this equation to tell this, because I didn't set up my reference groups in this way. So I went back and rearranged my reference group variables so that my reference group was extreme liberals, and now my two independent variables will be moderates and extreme conservatives. Here is the resulting equation:

STEM = 2.00 – 0.21(MODERATES) – 0.71(EXTCONSERVATIVE)
Number of cases: 346
$r^2 = 0.013$

Although the slope for the difference between moderates and the reference group (extreme liberals) was not significant (because it has the same p-value as before: .38), the difference between extreme liberals and extreme conservatives did prove to be statistically significant: the p-value was .037. Therefore, we can say that there is a statistically significant difference between extreme liberals and extreme conservatives, with extreme liberals taking 0.71 more STEM courses in high school than extreme conservatives. In other words, we can conclude with confidence that among the population of extreme liberals and extreme conservatives, there is a difference in STEM achievement.

GSS EXAMPLE: TV WATCHING AND WORK STATUS

Does your work status affect how much television you watch? Although we could investigate this by using a ratio-level variable such as number of hours worked per week, let's use the GSS variable for working status (WRKSTAT) and the reference-group technique. Making "working full-time" my reference group, I created a set of five dummy variables:

Working part-time: Yes = 1, No = 0
Unemployed: Yes = 1, No = 0
Retired: Yes = 1, No = 0
In school: Yes = 1, No = 0
Keeping house: Yes = 1, No = 0

Note that the nature of the question insisted that respondents choose one of these options. Although I can see how someone might be able to simultaneously answer that he or she was working part-time, keeping house, and in school, the question asked the respondents to choose one option. I ran a regression using these five dummy variables as independent variables and the variable TVHOURS as my dependent variable. I used 2012 GSS data. The coefficient for the slope for "in school" had a p-value of only .69, far from significant, so we conclude that people in school do not differ from people working a full-time job and remove this slope from the equation. What remains is

TVHOURS = 2.34 + 0.59(PTIME) + 1.96(RET.) + 1.33(UNEMP.) + 1.70(HOUSE)
Number of cases: 1,231
$r^2 = 0.08$, slopes significant at $p < .001$ level, except for part-time slope, which is significant at the $p < .05$ level (two-tailed test)

Graphically, here are the results:

■ **Exhibit 9.6: A Number Line Showing TV Viewing Differences**

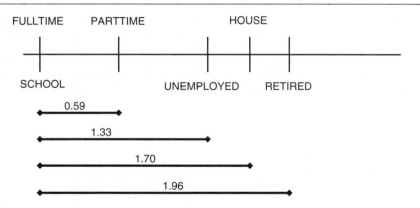

Describing the differences between various working statuses this way is far more illuminating than simply looking at the incremental effect of each additional hour worked.

GSS EXAMPLE: HAPPINESS AND PARTNERSHIP STATUS

Does being married make people happier? I'm not just talking about being with someone. I'm talking about being officially married. The GSS has always asked a regular marital status variable, but given recent social changes, they've also started asking about relationships in other ways. I used one of these newer variables and created a set of reference-group variables:

Reference group: living with married partner
PARTLIV: Have partner, living with partner as if married

PARTNOLIV: Have partner, but not living with partner
NOPART: No steady partner

I then used a 7-point happiness scale variable (0 = *completely unhappy* to 6 = *completely happy*) as my dependent variable. Here is the resulting equation:

HAPPINESS = $4.72 - 0.03$(PARTLIV) $- 0.55$(PARTNOLIV) $- 0.46$ (NOPART)
Number of cases: 647
$r^2 = 0.06$, slopes significant at $p < .001$ level, except for PARTLIV slope, which is not
   significant (two-tailed test)

Among the most interesting findings from this equation is a lack of difference between those who are officially married and those who are not married but living with a partner. In these times when people are fighting for marriage equality for many reasons, it is somewhat heartening to know that, regarding happiness, legal marriage makes no difference. Living with a partner can make one just as happy. But woe to those who have a partner but, for some reason, do not live with him or her. Such people are significantly less happy than those who are married. It even seems that they are even less happy than those who have no partner at all; however, we can't say this for sure. We would have to rearrange the reference group configuration in order to see if this is a statistically significant difference.

GSS EXAMPLE: PARTY IDENTIFICATION AND POLITICAL KNOWLEDGE

Everyone knows someone who is a political junkie. You know, those people who constantly check political websites, people who actually watch C-SPAN for fun. It seems to me that those people are also more partisan than other people are. That is, people who claim to be knowledgeable about politics also seem to identify strongly with a particular political party. Does my observation hold up to statistical scrutiny? I constructed a little index of self-reported political knowledge, using two Likert scale GSS questions:

"I feel that I have a pretty good understanding of the important political issues facing
   our country."
"I think that most people are better informed about politics and government than I am."

After recoding these variables so that they went in the same direction, I ended up with an index ranging from 0 (respondent rates his political knowledge as very low) to 8 (respondent rates his political knowledge as very high). Then, on the independent side of the equation, I used the Party Identification variable to construct a set of reference-group variables:

Reference Group: those who identify as Independent
STRD: those who identify as Strong Democrats
DEM: those who identify as Democrats
REP: those who identify as Republicans
STRR: those who identify as Strong Republicans

POLKNOW = 3.92 + 1.27(STRD) + 0.43(DEM) + 0.66(REP) + 1.37(STRR)
Number of cases: 492
$r^2 = 0.09$, slopes significant at the $p < .001$ level, except for the DEM slope, which is significant at the $p < .05$ level, and the REP slope, which is significant at the $p < .01$ level (two-tailed test)

This set of reference-group variables explains 9% of the variation in self-reported political knowledge, which is a healthy proportion. To illustrate the differences, rather than a number line, I've opted for a bar graph:

■ **Exhibit 9.7: Self-Reported Political Knowledge by Political Party**

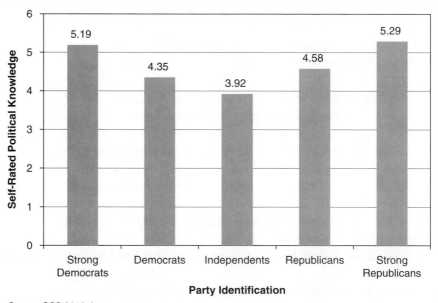

Source: GSS 2012 data.

My observation seems to hold: as people become more partisan, in either direction, their self-reported level of political knowledge goes up, particularly among those who identify as strong in their partisan identification. Now whether these people are *actually* more knowledgeable is subject to debate.

LITERATURE EXAMPLE: GENDER AND HOUSEWORK

A number of researchers have investigated how housework is distributed among the members of a household. In their article "Housework in Marital and Nonmarital Households," which appeared in *American Sociological Review*, Scott South and Glenna Spitze (1994) used regression with reference groups to examine differences among people from different types of households, and they show these differences for both women and men. They used the well-respected National Survey of Families and Households for their data. Because they are interested in differences between men and women, they restricted their analyses to heterosexual households. The article is primarily concerned with how married households differ from other types of households, so for this reason, the authors made "married" the reference group. Here, in list form, are the slopes for women and for men:

■ **Exhibit 9.8: Housework Slopes for Women and Men**

Slopes for Women:	
Never married/living in parental home:	−17.41**
Never married/living independently:	−11.62**
Cohabitating	−5.54**
Married	Reference group
Divorced/separated	−5.30**
Widowed	−9.08**

$R^2 = 0.08$
Number of cases = 6,764
**$p < .01$ (two-tailed test)
Source: South and Spitze (1994).

Slopes for Men:	
Never married/living in parental home:	−2.90**
Never married/living independently:	1.09
Cohabitating	1.34
Married	Reference group
Divorced/separated	3.73**
Widowed	5.66**

$R^2 = 0.02$
Number of cases = 4,252
**$p < .01$ (two-tailed test)
Source: South and Spitze (1994).

Notice first that, with these results, we cannot directly compare the amount of housework men and women do. However, the results still tell an interesting (although maddening) story. Going from living with one's parent(s) to being married has a huge effect on women's housework: a married woman does 17.41 hours more per week than her living-with-their-parents female friends do. A man who makes the same transition increases his housework by only 2.90 hours—not a huge jump; however, it is statistically significant.

One of the things South and Spitze wanted to do in this article was contrast married people with those who cohabitate. Their reasoning is that perhaps cohabiters, given that they're apparently resistant to the norm of marriage, may also resist stereotypical gender norms when it comes to housework. That is, perhaps in homes in which the couple are cohabiting, they more equitably distribute the housework, so that the man would do more and the woman would do less. From what I see in these results, one difference is that cohabiters' houses may be a bit messier. A woman in a cohabiting relationship with a man does significantly less housework than a married woman does (5.54 hours less), but a cohabiting man does *not* do more housework than a married man does (the slope of 1.34 is not statistically significant), so in such households, 5.54 fewer hours of housework get done.

What about the poor women whose husbands leave them, through either divorce or death? Well, although they indeed may be quite sad for a variety of reasons, they can take solace in the fact that having the man out of the house reduces their housework per week by 5.30 hours and 9.08 hours, respectively. Divorced and widowed men, on the other hand, do *more* housework, most likely because they no longer have a wife around to do it for them. Men!

This same article offers a nice contrast between ratio-level variables and dichotomies. South and Spitze were also interested in the effect that various ages of children have on the hours of housework each parent does. For example, one independent variable is "Number of Children Ages 0 to 4." For the women's sample, the slope for this variable is a statistically significant 3.63, meaning that, for each baby, the woman does 3.63 more hours per week. So a woman with twin babies does 3.63 hours more than a woman who has just a single baby and does 7.26 hours more than a woman with no children aged 0 to 4. The slope for the men's sample is, ahem, not significant. Yes, you heard that right: having a baby does *not* increase the hours of housework a man does.

As the children age and, eventually, become adult children living in the home, the sex of the children becomes more significant, so South and Spitze create separate variables for adult children. They include two dummy variables:

1. whether an adult female child is present
2. whether an adult male child is present

For this first variable, the slope turned out to be –2.46 (and statistically significant). But notice that this does not mean "for every additional adult female child," because this is a dichotomy. Instead, we end up with this interpretation: women who have an adult female child in the house do 2.46 fewer hours of housework per week than do women who do not have an adult female child in the house. That is, the adult female child pitches in and relieves the mother of 2.46 hours of housework per week. The slope for the "adult male child" variable is also statistically significant, but it is a *positive* 1.79 hours of housework per week, meaning that an adult male child actually *adds* to the total amount of housework a mother does. Rather than pitching in, he simply pitches his clothes on the floor and his dishes into the sink. Sorry, guys, but these numbers don't lie. Men!

LITERATURE EXAMPLE: TRACKING CHANGES OVER TIME

We saw in an earlier chapter that one set of ratio-level variables we can use is measures of time, from minutes to years. However, normal linear regression averages the effects over time. If every year does have the same effect, then that's fine. But often this is not the case. If this is a concern, what you can do is set one year as the reference group (typically the beginning or ending year of the period you are examining) and then create independent variables for the other years. This is what Jeni Loftus did in her article "America's Liberalization in Attitudes toward Homosexuality," which appeared in the journal *American Sociological Review* in 2001. The article concerned changes over time in willingness to restrict civil liberties for homosexuals. She used GSS data from 1973 to 1998 for her analyses. Her dependent variable is a three-point index that counts the number of civil rights a respondent would deny "a man who admits that he is a homosexual" (a biased way to start the question, if you ask me, but unfortunately the survey writers didn't—granted, I was only five years old when the survey was first administered). Anyway, the questions read as follows:

1. Suppose this admitted homosexual wanted to make a speech in your community. Should he be allowed to speak, or not?
2. Should such a person be allowed to teach in a college or university, or not?
3. If someone in your community suggested that a book he wrote in favor of homosexuality should be taken out of your public library, would you favor removing this book, or not?

Her index went from 0 (unwilling to restrict any of these rights) to 3 (willing to restrict all three of these rights). Before she introduced many, many other independent variables, she looked first at the effect of time. She set 1998 as her reference group and then created dummy variables for the five other years she used in her analyses: 1973, 1980, 1985, 1990, and 1994. Her resulting equation is as follows:

index = 0.67 + 0.68(1973) + 0.51(1980) + 0.48(1985) + 0.24(1990) + 0.09(1994)
$R^2 = 0.03$
Number of cases = 19,413

However, the 1994 slope was not significant, meaning that the average score on the index in 1994 did not differ from the average score in 1998. So the revised equation is

index = 0.67 + 0.68(1973) + 0.51(1980) + 0.48(1985) + 0.24(1990)

Plugging in the right numbers, we get the following averages for each of the years:

$average_{1973}$ = 0.67 + 0.68(1) + 0.51(0) + 0.48(0) + 0.24(0) = 1.35
$average_{1980}$ = 0.67 + 0.68(0) + 0.51(1) + 0.48(0) + 0.24(0) = 1.18
$average_{1985}$ = 0.67 + 0.68(0) + 0.51(0) + 0.48(1) + 0.24(0) = 1.15
$average_{1990}$ = 0.67 + 0.68(0) + 0.51(0) + 0.48(0) + 0.24(1) = 0.91
$average_{1994}$ = 0.67 + 0.68(0) + 0.51(0) + 0.48(0) + 0.24(0) = 0.67
$average_{1998}$ = 0.67 + 0.68(0) + 0.51(0) + 0.48(0) + 0.24(0) = 0.67

Graphically, it looks like this:

■ **Exhibit 9.9: Changes in Attitudes toward Gay Rights over Time**

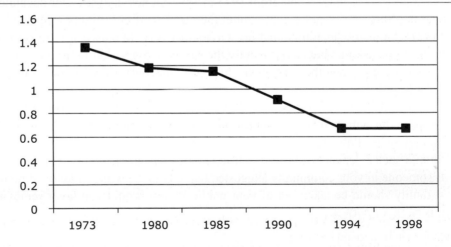

The result is fairly linear, but some jumps from year to year are bigger than others. Had we run a simple linear equation, we would not have known that there was little change from 1980 to 1985, or from 1994 to 1998. Since there was no movement from 1994

to 1998, I wondered if there had been any changes since 1998. Scores in the index remained steady through 2008, but then started to liberalize further in 2010 and 2012.

CONCLUSION

In the end, this entire chapter has been about dichotomous variables and about how to interpret their effects. The reference-group technique calls for us to look at *sets* of dummy variables, but they are each dummies nonetheless. As long as your dummy variables' categories are coded as 0 and 1, their effects should be quite easy to interpret: either a respondent gets the effect (because he or she is coded as a 1) or the respondent doesn't get the effect (because he or she is coded as a 0). It is critical, then, to remember how variables are coded. And, as I said earlier in this book, if you created these variables, it is of paramount importance to give your variables *labels*. If you don't do this, you'll eventually feel like, well, a dummy.

SPSS DEMONSTRATION: REFERENCE GROUPING

Please visit the book's website (www.routledge.com/cw/linneman) to view a video of this demonstration.

In this demonstration, we'll go over how to create a set of reference groups. We'll use the ANES recoded variable XYrelig_guide, which measures the guidance religion provides in the respondent's life, and it is coded as follows:

■ 0: Unimportant (n=1780);
■ 1: Provides some guidance (n=838);
■ 2: Provides quite a bit of guidance (n=1225);
■ 3: Provides a great deal of guidance (n=2035).

We'll make "Unimportant" the reference group, to which we will compare the other three groups. Because we have four categories, we need to create three dummy variables:

XYrel_guideREFsome
XYrel_guideREFquite
XYrel_guideREFgreat

So we will recode the XYrel_guide variable three times. Here are the recode commands for each recoded variable:

XYrel_guideREFsome: recode XYrel_guide: 0→0, 1→1, 2→0, 3→0, ELSE→SYSMIS
XYrel_guideREFquite: recode XYrel_guide: 0→0, 1→0, 2→1, 3→0, ELSE→SYSMIS
XYrel_guideREFgreat: recode XYrel_guide: 0→0, 1→0, 2→0, 3→1, ELSE→SYSMIS

And then, after giving each variable's values labels, we have our three new dummy variables:

Religion provides some guidance = 1

		Frequency	Percent	Valid Percent	Cumulative Percent
Valid	Not some guidance	5040	85.2	85.7	85.7
	Some guidance	838	14.2	14.3	100.0
	Total	5878	99.4	100.0	
Missing	System	38	0.6		
Total		5916	100.0		

Religion provides quite a bit of guidance = 1

		Frequency	Percent	Valid Percent	Cumulative Percent
Valid	Not quite a bit of guidance	4653	78.7	79.2	79.2
	Quite a bit of guidance	1225	20.7	20.8	100.0
	Total	5878	99.4	100.0	
Missing	System	38	0.6		
Total		5916	100.0		

Religion provides great deal of guidance = 1

		Frequency	Percent	Valid Percent	Cumulative Percent
Valid	Not a great deal of guidance	3843	65.0	65.4	65.4
	A great deal of guidance	2035	34.4	34.6	100.0
	Total	5878	99.4	100.0	
Missing	System	38	0.6		
Total		5916	100.0		

You can see that the frequencies for each new variable are what they should be by comparing them to the frequencies of the original variable. For example, in the original variable, 838 respondents answered "Provides some guidance," and this is how many people scored a 1 on the new variable XYrelguideREFsome.

Let's use these new variables to see if the extent to which religion guides your life affects how you feel about people on welfare. We simply put our three reference-group variables into a regression with the welfare feeling thermometer as the dependent variable. Here is the last box of the regression output:

Coefficients[a]

Model		Unstandardized Coefficients		Standardized Coefficients	t	Sig.
		B	Std. Error	Beta		
1	(Constant)	47.785	0.549		87.023	0.000
	Religion provides some guidance = 1	0.945	0.982	0.015	0.962	0.336
	Religion provides quite a bit of guidance = 1	2.237	0.861	0.040	2.597	0.009
	Religion provides great deal of guidance = 1	6.342	0.754	0.134	8.409	0.000

a. Dependent Variable: Feeling thermometer: PEOPLE ON WELFARE.

From the other output boxes, I'll tell you that the sample size was 5,418 and the R^2 was a low 0.014.

We see that those who say religion provides some guidance do not significantly differ from those for whom religion is unimportant (the p-value was .336). Those who say religion provides quite a bit of guidance score 2.24 points higher on the welfare feeling thermometer than do people who say religion is unimportant, and this difference is statistically significant at the $p < .01$ level, so we can say that in the population from which the ANES was drawn, there is a difference between those who say religion is unimportant and those who say religion provides quite a bit of guidance. Those who say religion provides a great deal of guidance score 6.34 points higher than people who say religion is unimportant, and this difference is statistically significant at the $p < .001$ level.

FROM OUTPUT TO PRESENTATION

Now flipping the equation onto its side will really start to pay off. Here are the preceding results in presentation form:

▨ **Exhibit 9.10: The Effect of Religiosity on Attitudes toward Welfare Recipients**

Dependent Variable: Score on Welfare Feeling Thermometer

Independent Variable	Slope
Religion unimportant	reference group
Religion provides some guidance	0.95
Religion provides quite a lot of guidance	2.24**
Religion provides a great deal of guidance	6.34***
Constant	47.79
R^2	0.014
n	5,418

$**p < .01.$ $***p < .001.$
Source: ANES 2012 data.

Another option instead of putting "Religion unimportant" in the body of the table is to have a note at the bottom of the table that says "The reference group for religion is 'Religion unimportant.'" Either one of these ways is fine, and you'll see both of them used widely.

EXERCISES

EXERCISES

Exercise 1

Does greater education bring one a greater sense of political efficacy? Run a regression equation using the politically efficacy index as your dependent variable and the four education-level reference-group variables for respondents as your independent variables (which use those with less than a high school diploma as the reference group). Write out the resulting equation and explain your results.

Exercise 2 (Answer Available in Appendix D)

Does education also affect one's propensity to believe in various conspiracy theories? Use the Non-Mainstream Views Index as your dependent variable and the four education-level reference-group variables for respondents as your independent variables (which use those with less than a high school diploma as the reference group). Write out the resulting equation and explain your results.

Exercise 3

There is variation in people's attitudes toward how big the government's role should be. Does race and ethnicity play a role in explaining this variation? Run a regression equation using the Government Role Index as your dependent variable and the three race reference-group variables as your independent variables (which uses whites as the reference group). Write out the equation and explain your results.

Exercise 4

Use three dichotomous variables to explain some of the variation in how people feel towards gays and lesbians: gender, race (measured as white and black) and Bible belief (measured as Word of God or not Word of God). Write out your resulting equation. Develop two examples: the type of person who would feel most negatively toward gays and lesbians and the type of person who would feel most positively toward gays and lesbians. Use the equation to calculate predicted feeling thermometer scores for these two people.

Exercise 5

Does one's personal employment situation affect how optimistic one is about the state of the economy? Run a regression equation that uses the Economic Optimism Index as the dependent variable and the five employment-status reference-group variables (which use employed as the reference group). Write out the equation (remember to include only those variables that have statistically significant effects). Interpret your results.

Exercise 6 (Answer Available in Appendix D)

Does race play a role in technology-enabled shopping? Use the PewShop dataset's Shop Index as your dependent variable and the race reference group variables as your independent variables. Interpret your results, and predict Shop Index scores for each racial group.

Exercise 7

Use the PewShop dataset to see if people from different types of communities (rural, suburban, urban) have different levels of technology use (as measured by the Technology Index). That is, use the community reference-group variables as your independent variables.

Exercise 8

Use the same reference-group variables as in Exercise 7, but this time, use recoded income (in 1,000s) as your dependent variable. Predict incomes for all three community groups.

Exercise 9

Use the PewHealth dataset to run a regression that contrasts whites with the other racial groups on the Health Conditions Index. How much variation do these variables explain? Which groups significantly differ from whites?

Exercise 10

Use the PewHealth dataset to run a regression that contrasts whites with other racial groups on the Cellphone Use Index. How much variation do these variables explain? Make predictions for each racial group.

Exercise 11 (Answer Available in Appendix D)

Does having a smartphone increase the propensity to review health ratings on the Internet? Run a regression with the Review Index as the dependent variable and the recoded smartphone variable as the independent variable, once using only white respondents, and once using only Asian respondents. Contrast the slope size, sample size, and statistical significance for these two groups.

Exercise 12

Does geography affect parental Internet surveillance behavior? In the PewKids dataset, use the Parental Checking and Blocking Index (what the parents actually *do*, not what the kids think they do) as your dependent variable and then community reference groups as your independent variables. Explain your results.

Exercise 13

Use the PewKids dataset to run two regression models, both using family income as the dependent variable. In the first, use the five race reference-group variables. In the second, use the race (white/ nonwhite) dichotomy. After interpreting your results, address these questions: Which slopes in the first model are closer in value to the slope in the second model? Why do you think this happened?

Exercise 14

Which countries' citizens see themselves more as citizens of the world: European countries or Asian/African countries? Run a simple regression equation using WVS data in SPSS. Use the COUNTRY2CAT variable as your independent variable and the WRLDCIT variable as your dependent variable. Explain your results.

Exercise 15

Address the same question as in Exercise 14, but instead of a single dichotomy as the independent variable, use the set of reference-group variables for country categories: CCAFRICA, CCASIA, CCEASTEUR, and CCSTHAMER (note that the Western European category is the reference group). Interpret your results.

Exercise 16 (Answer Available in Appendix D)

This exercise uses WVS data to examine variation in the level of support for female business executives. As independent variables, use the set of reference-group variables for country categories: CCAFRICA, CCASIA, CCEASTEUR, and CCSTHAMER (note that the Western European category is the reference group). As the dependent variable, use the variable MENEXEC ("Men make better business executives than women do"). Fully interpret your results.

Chapter 10

ABOVE AND BEYOND: THE LOGIC OF CONTROLLING AND THE POWER OF NESTED REGRESSION MODELS

This chapter covers . . .

. . . the logic of controlling

. . . a different way to present regression results when you have multiple models

. . . how to tell different types of nested stories

. . . how to judge improvement from model to model

. . . the importance of constant sample size

. . . how researchers used nested models to examine how race affects grades

. . . how a researcher used nested models to study media and fear of crime

INTRODUCTION

In this chapter, I cover one of the most important concepts in social statistics: **statistical control**. Controlling with regression allows us to tell some very interesting stories. Speaking of stories, I'm going to start this chapter with a few, just to show you that the idea of controlling exists within our daily lives, although we may not think about it as statistical in nature. So forget about statistics for a minute and just listen to a few stories.

Jane lives in a house with four dogs: Alfie, Buster, Casey, and Draco, and she lets all of them have the run of the house while she's out. Jane also has a vast collection of decorative throw pillows, of which she is very proud. You already see where this is headed, don't you? On Monday, Jane comes home from work to find one of her beloved pillows ripped to shreds on the floor. She has no idea which dog did it. So she devises a plan: she'll put one dog in a room away from the pillows when she goes to work the next day. Tuesday, she puts Alfie away and lets the other three dogs run free. She returns home to another pillow destroyed. Wednesday, she lets Alfie back out and puts Buster away. She returns home to another pillow destroyed. Thursday, she puts Casey away and lets the other three dogs run free. She returns home to another pillow destroyed. Friday, she puts Draco away, and when she gets home, no new pillows have been destroyed. Jane deduces that Draco is the culprit.

Ted is baking cookies. He has a number of possible recipes that range from extremely simple (only one ingredient) to more complex (four ingredients). Of course, he starts with the dough, which has little taste on its own. Then he adds an ingredient: chocolate chips. A sensible start. He bakes a batch. He tastes a cookie, and it's filled with the flavor of chocolate chips. However, Ted doesn't stop there. Instead, he follows another recipe that has not only chocolate chips but also another ingredient: rainbow sprinkles (or, depending on where you grew up, "jimmies"). Sprinkles, though beautiful, have little if any taste. He bakes this new batch. He tastes a cookie, and all the flavor of the chocolate chips comes through loud and clear. In fact, he can't even taste the sprinkles. Ted moves on to a third recipe, same as the second except for the addition of another ingredient, one that does have some taste to it: brown sugar. He bakes this batch and tastes a cookie. He can still taste the chocolate chips, but their flavor is slightly less than the previous recipes, owing to the presence of the brown sugar. For his fourth and final recipe, Ted pulls out all the stops and, just for the fun of it, adds a big heaping spoonful of hot sauce. Ted's resulting cookie-eating experience is not a pleasant one. The addition of a single ingredient drastically affects the taste of the other ingredients. Ted can definitely taste the hot sauce, but that's all he can taste. The taste of the chips is gone, as is the taste of the brown sugar and, needless to say, that of the poor sprinkles.

Kathy runs The Lab of Obvious Findings. One day, she runs an experiment involving a group of volunteers. She randomly assigns each volunteer into one of two groups: the control group or the stimulus group. She has each volunteer complete a fifty-piece puzzle and times how long it takes each volunteer to complete the task. Then, she makes each member of the stimulus group wear a blindfold and has each volunteer complete the puzzle again. She discovers that, on average, it takes the members of the stimulus group much longer this time to complete the puzzle, whereas the members of the control group complete it in the same amount of time as before. Because the only thing she has changed about the stimulus group is the blindfolds, she concludes— drum roll, please—that the *blindfolds* caused the increase in time to complete the puzzle.

Jack's car is making a funny noise, and he doesn't know why. He takes it to the local garage, which is named Swindle Brothers. The mechanic takes the car and tells Jack to come back tomorrow. When Jack returns to the shop, the mechanic says, "I changed the spark plugs, the alternator, the muffler, and the brake pads. Your car doesn't make the sound anymore. That'll be $2,000 please." Jack says, "Wait a minute, how do you know what the problem was?" The mechanic replies, "Well, I don't know exactly, because I changed all four things at once, but because the car doesn't make the noise anymore, we know it was one of those four things, right?" Joe asks, "Why didn't you switch out the parts one at a time?" The mechanic replies, "That would have taken longer, and I wanted to save you on labor costs."

The point of these stories is to show that the logic of controlling exists within our everyday lives. People practice this logic all the time; however, they may not consciously realize it. Keep all of this in mind as we now turn to controlling as it exists within the world of regression. We start with two similar GSS examples, both using income as the dependent variable.

GSS EXAMPLE: GENDER AND INCOME

Women have long been behind men with regard to income. Although there has been some progress in recent years, significant differences remain, as shown by the following simple regression equation, which I created using 2012 GSS data:

INCOME = 51.47 – 16.48(SEX)
The slope is significant at the $p < .001$ level (two-tailed test) SEX is coded M = 0, F = 1
$R^2 = 0.05$
$n = 983$

According to this equation, the average man makes $51,470. The coefficient for the sex slope means that the average woman makes $16,480 less than the average man, making her income $34,990—quite a large difference. Some might try to explain away this difference by arguing that women make less than men do because women work fewer hours than men do. First, we'll check to see if women do indeed work fewer hours than men by looking at another simple regression equation, this time with "Hours Worked Per Week" as the dependent variable:

HRSWORKED = 43.52 – 6.49(SEX)
The slope is significant at the $p < .001$ level (two-tailed test) SEX is coded M = 0, F = 1
$R^2 = 0.04$
$n = 1166$

So far, it seems as though this argument is supported: men *do* work longer hours than women do, six-and-a-half hours per week. But does this difference fully account for the income difference? To see, we'll go back to the first regression equation and *add* hours worked as a *second* independent variable in the equation to see if this changes the original effect of sex. Let me rephrase this last sentence using terminology from earlier in the chapter: we'll go back to the original recipe and add the new ingredient "hours worked" to the recipe to see if this changes the original taste of the original ingredient "sex." If the addition of this new ingredient makes the taste of the original ingredient go away, then the income difference is actually due to the fact that women work less than men do. Let's look at the equation:

INCOME = 19.06 − 11.67(SEX) + 0.74 (HRSWORKED)
Both slopes are significant at the $p < .001$ level (two-tailed test)
$R^2 = 0.15$
$n = 983$

So is the argument correct? Partially. Once we introduce the new ingredient (hours worked), the taste of the original ingredient (sex) does diminish, but we can definitely still taste it. The slope has gone from −16.48 to −11.67, or a decrease in the difference of 29% ((11.67 −16.48)/16.48 = 0.29). If the argument were completely correct, then the taste of the original ingredient (sex) would have gone away completely, decreasing to a level of nonsignificance (i.e., the significance level would have risen above 0.05). This is not the case, however: there remains a statistically significant $11,670 difference even after we take hours worked into account.

I want to look at this more closely by calculating incomes for two examples. Let's say we have two men, Joe and Bob, who each work a full-time job of 40 hours per week. The equation would predict that each of them would make $48,660:

Joe's income = 19.06 − 11.67(0) + 0.74(40) = 48.66
Bob's income = 19.06 − 11.67(0) + 0.74(40) = 48.66

Now let's say that Bob decides that he wants to transition to become a woman named Bobette. The only thing that's changed about Bobette is her sex. She still works 40 hours per week. However, according to the equation, her income will change:

Joe's income = 19.06 − 11.67(0) + 0.74(40) = 48.66
Bobette's income = 19.06 − 11.67(1) + 0.74(40) = 36.99

Notice we are holding constant the number of hours worked by each person: each works 40 hours. The only thing being allowed to vary is the sex of the person (this would be a good time to think back to the dog analogy, or the experiment analogy). With this one small change, Bobette's income goes down $11,670. Those who claim that the income difference exists simply because of the difference in hours worked are not correct: even after we take hours worked into account, or, in other words, even after we control for hours worked, a significant difference between the sexes remains.

A DIFFERENT WAY TO PRESENT RESULTS

Now that we are going to be looking at the results of multiple equations at the same time, it is best to move to a different presentation style where the results are side by side. Basically, we're taking the equations and flipping them sideways. We've already covered this somewhat in the "From Output to Presentation" sections in preceding chapters, so this won't be completely new to you. Here are the income equations from earlier:

■ **Exhibit 10.1: Two Models Involving Income and Sex**

Dependent Variable: Respondent's Income in $1,000s		
Independent Variable	Model 1	Model 2
Sex (M = 0, F = 1)	–16.48***	–11.67***
Hours Worked	—	0.74***
Constant	51.47	19.06
R^2	0.05	0.15
n	983	983

***$p < .001$ (two-tailed test).
Source: GSS 2012 data.

I have a number of things to point out, and I'll start from the top. Notice that, instead of the word *equation* (or "recipe"), I've switched to the word *model*. This is generally the term people use rather than *equation*. Why? I think it's to make it sound more scientific, but to tell you the truth, I'm not really sure. A second change is that I'm using the star notation I introduced in Chapter 8, where no stars mean that the slope is not statistically significant, one star means that $p < .05$, two stars mean that $p < .01$, and three stars mean that $p < .001$. This is fairly standard, though infrequently you will see one star meaning $p < .10$. The third thing to point out is the series of three dashes in Model 1 for Hours Worked. This is our way of saying, "This variable is not included in Model 1, but it will be added in future models."

When we have a series of models, each subsequent model with more independent variables than the last model, we call these *nested models*. Here are some imageries to make sense of this. First, think of a bird, any bird—well, any nest-building bird. When building a nest, it adds twigs, one by one; looks at the nest; and then flies off to look for another branch. The idea here is similar, with the variables as twigs. We're starting off with a single independent variable in Model 1, and then we fly off, bring back, and add in a second independent variable in Model 2. Then we see how our nest looks, or cookies taste, or car runs. Another way to understand this "nesting" imagery involves dolls. When I lived in Moscow during a semester in college, as a gift for my mother, I brought back a beautiful set of Matroshka dolls—the wooden dolls that when you open up the biggest doll, you find a smaller doll inside; then you open up this smaller doll and find an even smaller doll inside, and so on, and so on. Instead of nested dolls, we have nested models, and we work from smaller models to larger models, as illustrated by this exhibit:

■ **Exhibit 10.2: Envisioning Nested Models**

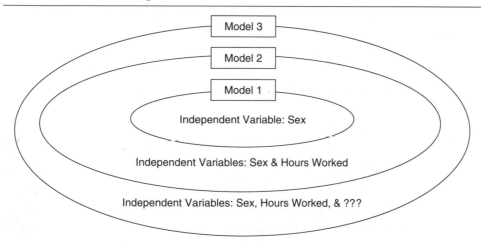

Model 1, the smallest circle, has just one independent variable: Sex. Model 1 is then nested inside Model 2 (the middle-sized circle), where we add the second independent variable: Hours Worked. But because Model 1 is nested inside Model 2, although we have added Hours Worked as a second independent variable, we still include Sex as an independent variable. Model 1 and Model 2 are nested inside Model 3, the largest circle, which contains not only Sex and Hours Worked but also a third independent variable. There are sometimes variations on this theme, as we add variables, take them out, and then add them in again, but the overall idea remains the same: to see how the effect (taste) of our key independent variable (ingredient) changes once we add in other independent variables (ingredients). Let's keep on cooking!

GSS EXAMPLE: AGE AND INCOME

Remember that in the sex-and-income example from earlier, once we controlled for hours worked, the effect of the sex variable decreased somewhat, but stayed substantial, and quite statistically significant. Let's see if the same thing happens when, instead of sex, we use age as the first independent variable. We will use GSS 2012 respondents who are 50 years or older. Here are the regression models in the new side-by-side format:

■ **Exhibit 10.3: Two Models Involving Age and Income**

Dependent Variable: Respondent's Income in $1,000s		
Independent Variable	Model 1	Model 2
Age in Years	–0.69*	–0.26
Hours Worked	—	1.10***
Constant	88.06	18.32
R^2	0.01	0.17
n	328	328

$*p < .05. ***p < .001$ (two-tailed test).
Source: GSS 2012 data for respondents 50 years old or older.

In Model 1, we see that age has a statistically significant effect: for every year you get older, you make around $700 less in annual income. A logical comment on this finding is: shouldn't you consider the fact that as people get older, going from 50 to 60 to 70, they tend to start working less? To deal with this possibility, in Model 2 we add Hours Worked Per Week as an independent variable. In contrast to the sex example earlier in the chapter, adding in the Hours Worked variable takes away the effect of the original independent variable. Once we control for hours worked, the effect of age goes away. The actual coefficient decreases by around two-thirds of its former value, and it loses its statistical significance (its p-value in Model 2 is .39, nowhere near the $p < .05$ we would need). A few examples to make this clear:

a 50-year-old who works 30 hours per week: $18.32 + 1.10(30) = 51.32$
a 70-year-old who works 30 hours per week: $18.32 + 1.10(30) = 51.32$
a 50-year-old who works 50 hours per week: $18.32 + 1.10(50) = 73.32$
a 70-year-old who works 50 hours per week: $18.32 + 1.10(50) = 73.32$

Although I varied age among the examples, having two 50-year-olds and two 70-year-olds, age doesn't matter in the equation: it is *only* how much you work that matters.

To summarize the story: at first it seemed that the older you are, the less money you make. However, once you control for how much you work, taking into account the fact that older people work less, the original effect of age disappears. Late in the book, I cover a technique that allows us to investigate the effect of age on income through the entire life course.

GSS EXAMPLE: PERCEPTIONS OF U.S. RACIAL MAKEUP

In the 2000 General Social Survey (and unfortunately *only* in the 2000 version), the researchers asked the respondents to do something very interesting: they asked them to estimate what percentage of the population of the United States they thought was black. The actual percentage is about 13% (www.census.gov). However, when people are asked out of the blue to estimate this percentage, their answers vary wildly. The mean guess is 31.5%, and the median is 30%. As Exhibit 10.4 and high standard deviation show, people's estimates are all over the place:

■ **Exhibit 10.4: Americans' Estimates of Percentage of U.S. Population that is Black**

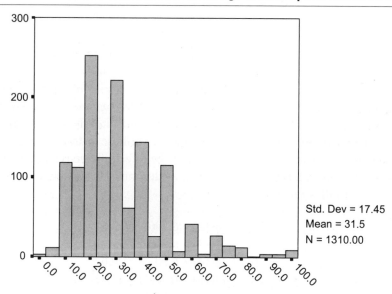

Std. Dev = 17.45
Mean = 31.5
N = 1310.00

WHAT PERCENTAGE OF POPULATION IS BLACK

Source: GSS 2000 data.

Yes, the graph does indeed show that six respondents thought that the United States was 100% black. Intrigued by these six people, I investigated further and found that three of these six were white (and clearly not very good at math). Although these may be peculiar cases, notice that large numbers of respondents answered 40, 50, 60, and 70. In other words, there is a lot of variation. Now let's try to explain some of this variation. We'll start with two independent variables: the respondent's years of education and the respondent's race.

■ **Exhibit 10.5: Racial Differences in Demographic Perceptions**

Dependent Variable: Respondent's Estimate of % Black in U.S.	
Independent Variable	Model 1
Years of Education	–1.48***
Race (W = 0, B = 1)	6.90***
Constant	50.30
	$R^2 = 0.09$
	$n = 1,191$

***$p < .001$ (two-tailed test).
Source: GSS 2000 data.

This first model has two interesting findings. First, the more educated you are, the smaller percentage black you think the United States is: for every additional year of education a person gets, his or her estimate goes down by 1.46%. Let's assume that this is because, with more education, you may have been exposed to the actual statistics (hey, it's happening to you at this very moment, isn't it?). Notice that the correct percentage is low compared to the average guess, so those with more education are estimating closer to the correct number. Second, the effect of race is significant: blacks think that the United States is more black than whites think it is, by about 7%. Here are some examples to illustrate this:

white with H.S. diploma:	$50.30 – 1.48(12) + 6.90(0) = 32.54$
black with H.S. diploma:	$50.30 – 1.48(12) + 6.90(1) = 39.44$
white with college degree:	$50.30 – 1.48(16) + 6.90(0) = 26.62$
black with college degree:	$50.30 – 1.48(16) + 6.90(1) = 33.52$

Here is a possible explanation for what is going on: if you are a member of a minority group, you may want to think that your group is a significant proportion of the population. For that reason, when asked to estimate the size of your group, you might offer a larger estimate. This argument implies that the cause of a respondent's higher estimate is *because* he or she is black.

However, let's add another model with another independent variable that appeared in the 2000 GSS: the respondent's estimate of the makeup of his or her *local* community. The GSS people were smart to ask respondents to estimate the racial makeup of both their nation *and* their local community. Perhaps it is the case that a typical GSS respondent came up with his or her national estimates based on what he or she experiences locally. This makes sense: you're asked a rather odd question, so a natural inclination might be to go with what you know, and people often base their claims on what surrounds them. This is an important consideration, given that racial residential segregation persists in the United States: many blacks live in neighborhoods with mostly blacks, and many whites live in neighborhoods with mostly whites. The average white respondent estimated that his or her local community was about 15% black, whereas the average black respondent estimated that his or her local community was about 51% black. With all this in mind, let's introduce Model 2:

■ **Exhibit 10.6: Racial Differences in Demographic Perceptions**

Dependent Variable: Respondent's Estimate of % Black in U.S.		
Independent Variable	Model 1	Model 2
Years of Education	−1.48***	−1.31***
Race (W = 0, B = 1)	6.90***	−0.12
% Black Local	—	0.21***
Constant	50.30	44.95
	$R^2 = 0.09$	$R^2 = 0.14$
	$n = 1,190$	$n = 1,190$

***$p < .001$ (two-tailed test).
Source: GSS 2000 data.

An intriguing story emerges. A respondent's estimate of his or her local community has the expected effect on the respondent's estimate of the nation: the higher the estimate he or she gives for the local population, the higher the estimate he or she gives for the national population. The effect of education decreases by a bit, but not dramatically so. The key finding is this: on introducing this new independent variable, look at what happens to the effect of being black. Its significance *completely* disappears (notice that not only has the original coefficient decreased dramatically but that it has also lost all of its significance stars). So it's not *what race you are*, it's *where you live*. Blacks tend to live among other blacks, so when asked to provide a national estimate they look around and estimate a high national number. Whites tend to live among other whites, so their national estimates are lower. Here are some examples to help you understand this (all of these respondents have college degrees):

white in a 20% black community: $44.95 - 1.31(16) + 0.21(20) = 28.19$
black in a 20% black community: $44.95 - 1.31(16) + 0.21(20) = 28.19$
white in an 80% black community: $44.95 - 1.31(16) + 0.21(80) = 40.79$
black in an 80% black community: $44.95 - 1.31(16) + 0.21(80) = 40.79$

If a white person and a black person live in a racially similar community, their national perceptions will be exactly the same. The original effect of race has lost its taste.

INTERCHAPTER CONNECTION: CONTROLLING WITH CROSSTABS

In order to give you a better idea of what's going on here, and what controlling really means, I'm going to make some connections between regression and cross-tabs. Remember the crosstab examples where we ran a simple crosstab, but then we elaborated the relationship? We were engaging in controlling when we did so. For example, when we investigated whether the relationship existed separately among men and among women, we were controlling for sex, holding sex constant at female for one crosstab and then holding sex constant at male for the other crosstab. Exhibit 10.7 is a simplified hypothetical 40-case dataset based on the preceding example.

■ **Exhibit 10.7: A Forty-Case Hypothetical Dataset**

Person	Race	Local	Nat'l	Local2	Nat'l2
1	WHITE	8	15	LOW	LOW
2	WHITE	15	25	LOW	LOW
3	WHITE	10	10	LOW	LOW
4	WHITE	5	23	LOW	LOW
5	WHITE	23	60	LOW	HIGH
6	WHITE	19	27	LOW	LOW
7	WHITE	17	30	LOW	LOW
8	WHITE	14	24	LOW	LOW
9	WHITE	22	16	LOW	LOW
10	WHITE	6	21	LOW	LOW
11	WHITE	9	13	LOW	LOW
12	WHITE	15	26	LOW	LOW

Person	Race	Local	Nat'l	Local2	Nat'l2
13	WHITE	14	20	LOW	LOW
14	WHITE	10	23	LOW	LOW
15	WHITE	80	65	HIGH	HIGH
16	WHITE	75	40	HIGH	LOW
17	WHITE	55	55	HIGH	HIGH
18	WHITE	65	75	HIGH	HIGH
19	WHITE	70	60	HIGH	HIGH
20	WHITE	75	80	HIGH	HIGH
21	BLACK	20	15	LOW	LOW
22	BLACK	15	25	LOW	LOW
23	BLACK	10	70	LOW	HIGH
24	BLACK	25	14	LOW	LOW
25	BLACK	12	18	LOW	LOW
26	BLACK	18	10	LOW	LOW
27	BLACK	60	65	HIGH	HIGH
28	BLACK	80	80	HIGH	HIGH
29	BLACK	90	75	HIGH	HIGH
30	BLACK	75	54	HIGH	HIGH
31	BLACK	85	80	HIGH	HIGH
32	BLACK	59	72	HIGH	HIGH
33	BLACK	67	63	HIGH	HIGH
34	BLACK	83	76	HIGH	HIGH
35	BLACK	76	59	HIGH	HIGH
36	BLACK	68	62	HIGH	HIGH
37	BLACK	72	65	HIGH	HIGH
38	BLACK	86	81	HIGH	HIGH
39	BLACK	70	70	HIGH	HIGH
40	BLACK	80	40	HIGH	LOW

Source: Hypothetical data.

The first three columns are the respondent's race, his or her local percentage black perceptions, and his or her national percentage black perceptions. Before you knew about controlling with regression, if I had asked you to control for local perceptions, you might have thought back to controlling with crosstabs and say, "I can do that, but I'll have to turn the variables into dichotomies first." That is what the last two columns are: dichotomies of the two perception variables (0 to 50 in the low category, and 51 to 100 in the high category). Once you had these, you could run a simple crosstab comparing whites and blacks and then an elaborated set of crosstabs: one for people with low local perceptions and one for people with high local perceptions. Here is what these crosstabs look like:

■ Exhibit 10.8: Crosstabs from Hypothetical Forty-Case Dataset

PERCEIVED % U.S. DICHOTOMY * RACE Crosstabulation

		RACE		
		WHITE	BLACK	Total
PERCEIVED% U.S. DICHOTOMY	LOW	14	6	20
		70.0%	30.0%	50.0%
	HIGH	6	14	20
		30.0%	70.0%	50.0%
Total		20	20	40
		100.0%	1 00.0%	1 00.0%

Chi-Square Tests

	Value	df	Asymp. Sig. (2-sided)
Pearson Chi-Square	6.400	1	0.011

PERCEIVED % U.S. DICHOTOMY * RACE * LOCAL % BLACK DICHOTOMY Crosstabulation

			RACE		
			WHITE	BLACK	Total
LOW	PERCEIVED% U.S. DICHOTOMY	LOW	13	5	18
			92.9%	83.3%	90.0%
		HIGH	1	1	2
			7.1%	16.7%	10.0%
	Total		14	6	20
			100.0%	100.0%	100.0%
HIGH	PERCEIVED% U.S. DICHOTOMY	LOW	1	1	2
			16.7%	7.1%	10.0%
		HIGH	5	13	18
			83.3%	92.9%	90.0%
	Total		6	14	20
			100.0%	100.0%	100.0%

Chi-Square Tests

LOCAL% BLACK DICHOTOMY		Value	df	Asymp. Sig. (2-sided)
LOW	Pearson Chi-Square	0.423	1	0.515
HIGH	Pearson Chi-Square	0.423	1	0.515

PERCEIVED % U.S. DICHOTOMY * LOCAL % BLACK DICHOTOMY * RACE Crosstabulation

			LOCAL% BLACK DICHOTOMY		
RACE			LOW	HIGH	Total
WHITE	PERCEIVED% U.S. DICHOTOMY	LOW	13	1	14
			92.9%	16.7%	70.0%
		HIGH	1	5	6
			7.1%	83.3%	30.0%
	Total		14	6	20
			100.0%	100.0%	100.0%
BLACK	PERCEIVED% U.S. DICHOTOMY	LOW	5	1	6
			83.3%	7.1%	30.0%
		HIGH	1	13	14
			16.7%	92.9%	70.0%
	Total		6	14	20
			100.0%	100.0%	100.0%

Chi-Square Tests

RACE		Value	df	Asymp. Sig. (2-sided)
WHITE	Pearson Chi-Square	11.610	1	0.001
BLACK	Pearson Chi-Square	11.610	1	0.001

In the first crosstab, there is a clear relationship: blacks are more likely than are whites to be in the High category of the dependent variable, and according to the chi-square test, the relationship is statistically significant. However, once we elaborate the relationship and control for the perceived local % black variable, the original relationship disappears. In the next set of crosstabs, we see that there is very little difference between whites and blacks, making the statistical significance go away.

What happens if instead we elaborate the other way, and control for the race variable? The last set of crosstabs shows this. Controlling for race, the relationship between perceived local % black and the perceived % U.S. black variables in these crosstabs is very clear, and highly statistically significant. The picture is now clear: it's not race, but rather the local perceptions that are affecting national perceptions.

However, now you *do* know how to control with regression, so you don't need to dichotomize these variables and lose all that detail. Here are the regression models using these hypothetical data:

■ **Exhibit 10.9: Regression Models from Hypothetical 40-Case Dataset**

Dependent Variable: Respondent's Estimate of % Black in U.S.		
Independent Variable	Model 1	Model 2
Race (W = 0, B = 1)	19.30*	1.10
% Black Local	—	0.67***
Constant	35.40	15.10
	$R^2 = 0.15$	$R^2 = 0.70$
	$n = 40$	$n = 40$

$*p < .05.$ $***p < .001$ (two-tailed test).
Source: Hypothetical data.

These regression models tell the same story as the crosstabs: In Model 1, it seems that there is a difference between blacks and whites. In Model 2, once we add the percent local variable, the effect of race goes away, and we see that the real relationship is between the local perception variable and the national perception variable. We are simply going about the controlling in a different way, and use all the detail in our data. And finding out how much variation we are explaining. Crosstabs have their place, but when possible, regression is usually the way to go.

GSS EXAMPLE: ATTITUDES TOWARD STATE ASSISTANCE

Please visit the book's website (www.routledge.com/cw/linneman) to view a "From Idea to Presentation" video of this example.

Whether the topic is welfare or health care, the role of government is constantly a source of heated debate. Some people think that the government should play a minimal role in people's lives. Others think that the government's role needs to be expanded. The 2012 GSS asked several interesting questions regarding this topic. I used some of them to create an index of attitudes toward government assistance. I chose four questions that each got at a different area of life: paying for child care, paying for care for the elderly, providing assistance to the poor, and providing assistance to the sick. I combined these questions into an index that ranges from 0 to 16. Free-Market Frank, who believes that the government should not assist with any of these, would score a 0. Welfare Waldo, who believes that the government should pay for all of these, would score a 16. Here is the resulting index in bar graph form:

■ **Exhibit 10.10: Americans' Attitudes toward Government Assistance**

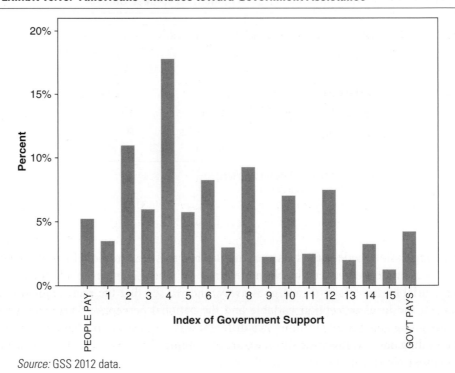

Source: GSS 2012 data.

As you might expect, American attitudes on this topic vary greatly. When I see such variation, my impulse is, of course, to try to explain it. I'm going to focus on the effect of race, using a set of reference-group variables. I'll use whites as my reference group, so the variables in Model 1 are the race variables for blacks and for others (those respondents who are neither white nor black). Then, I will complicate my recipe by throwing in an ingredient that has historically been connected to race *and* to attitudes toward government assistance: political party. Finally, because income has been known to vary by race, and since income may affect one's attitude toward government assistance, I will add a family income variable. This gives me three regression models:

■ **Exhibit 10.11: Explaining Assistance Attitudes: Three Models**

Dependent Variable: Respondent's Score on Assistance Index			
Independent Variable	Model 1	Model 2	Model 3
Race Black	4.17***	2.34***	1.98**
Race Other	1.52*	1.46*	1.51*
Party	—	–0.80***	–0.74***
Total Family Income	—	—	–0.02***
Constant	5.92	8.30	9.54
	$R^2 = 0.12$	$R^2 = 0.23$	$R^2 = 0.28$
	$n = 355$	$n = 355$	$n = 355$

Note: The reference category for race variables is white. Political party is measured from 0 = strong Democrat to 6 = strong Republican.
*$p < .05$. **$p < .01$. ***$p < .001$ (two-tailed test).
Source: GSS 2012 data.

There is a lot going on here. But let's take it step by step, model by model, and develop the overall story that these models are telling as a group. In Model 1, we see that there is a very large and highly statistically significant difference between blacks and whites: more than 4 points on a 16-point scale, with blacks more in favor of government assistance. Whites and others differ as well, but not by as much: 1.5 points, with $p < .05$: statistically significant, but barely so. These differences explain more than 12% of the variation in attitudes, which is a lot for just one set of reference-group variables. Remember that we can't say that blacks and others significantly differ, as that was not how I set up the reference groups, but they differ by more than 2.5 points, which seems like a lot to me.

In Model 2, I added the political party variable. It adds quite a bit to the explanation of these attitudes: the R^2 nearly doubles. Its effect is as you would expect: strong Republicans are nearly five points lower ($6 \times -0.80 = -4.8$) on the index than strong Democrats. The addition of this variable affects one of the race variables, but not the other. The coefficient for blacks decreases by 44% (($2.34 - 4.17)/4.17 = -0.44$), whereas the coefficient for others decreases by a mere 4% (($1.46 - 1.52)/1.52 = -0.04$). This tells us something about the relationship between political party and race: black Republicans still differ from white Republicans, but not as much as black Democrats differ.

In Model 3, I added the family income variable. Once again, the explained variation rises, to 0.28. This income effect is highly statistically significant, but the substantive size of the effect is questionable: it would take an additional $50,000 to move someone one point down on the index ($-0.02 \times 50 = -1.00$). I was thinking that adding the income variable would lower the effect of the party variable (because Republicans tend to have higher incomes than Democrats), but it does so only marginally (lowering it by only 8%). Similar to what happened when I added the party variable, in Model 3 the race variables are differentially affected. The effect of the black variable decreases (by another 15%), whereas the effect of the other variable essentially remains the same as before. Although the black variable's effect remains a bit larger, the "race other" variable's effect is notable for its robust nature: it doesn't budge when other variables are added. In summary, the black–white difference can be partially explained away by political party and income, but the other–white difference cannot be explained away by these variables.

GSS EXAMPLE: SUPPORT FOR SAME-SEX PARENTING

Attitudes toward gay men and lesbians have shifted dramatically in recent decades. The General Social Survey has adjusted accordingly, adding questions in recent years regarding gay marriage, sexual identity, and, in the 2012 GSS, same-sex parenting. Rather than asking whether a gay couple or a lesbian couple should have children, the GSS asked a much more provocative question: Can such couples raise a child *as well as* a male–female couple? They asked separate questions about same-sex male couples and same-sex female couples. The responses signal continued resistance to same-sex families. 41% of the respondents either disagreed or strongly disagreed that a same-sex female couple could do as well as a male-female couple, and 44% either disagreed or strongly disagreed that a same-sex male couple could do as well. Using these two Likert-scale variables, I created an index of support, where 0 signified no support and 8 was full support. Here is the resulting bar graph:

▦ **Exhibit 10.12: Support for Same-Sex Parenting**

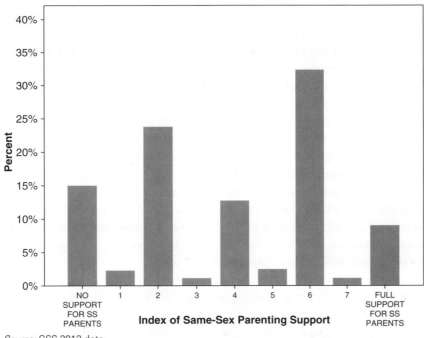

Source: GSS 2012 data.

Before I present the regression results, I want to pause for a moment to review the types of nested stories we've examined thus far and preview what makes this new set of models relatively unique. Until this point, we've seen the three types of nested stories:

Nested Story 1: The independent variable in Model 1 has a statistically significant effect. After introducing a second independent variable in Model 2, the first independent variable's effect does not change, and maintains its statistical significance. This likely means that the effects of the variables are completely separate, as the introduction of the second effect in no way affects the first effect (its recipe ingredient corollary would be the sprinkles). An example of this from above is the government assistance example, where the effect of the "other race" variable hardly changed as I introduced other independent variables.

Nested Story 2: The independent variable in Model 1 has a statistically significant effect. After introducing a second independent variable in Model 2, the first independent variable's effect decreases somewhat, but maintains an effect that is statistically significant. This likely means that the original variable's effect is connected to the effect of the second independent variable's effect, but only partially (its recipe ingredient corollary would be the brown sugar). An example of this is the sex and income example from earlier, where the effect of the sex variable decreased somewhat when I introduced the hours worked variable, but a lot of the effect remained.

Nested Story 3: The independent variable in Model 1 has a statistically significant effect. After introducing a second independent variable in Model 2, the first independent variable's effect decreases dramatically and loses its statistical significance. This likely means that the original dependent variable was simply a "stand in" for the second independent variable, so once we add in the second independent variable in Model 2, the original effect of the first independent variable goes completely away (the recipe ingredient corollary would be the hot sauce). An example of this is the race and racial perception example from earlier, where the racial difference between blacks and whites completely went away once I added the local racial perception variable. Another way to put this is that we have identified an **intervening relationship**. Local racial perception intervenes between race and national racial perception: what race you are affects your local perceptions, and your local perceptions affect your national perceptions.

In this next example, you'll see Nested Story 4, and this one may throw you at first. What's going to happen is that a variable will *not* have a statistically significant effect at first, but then after introducing a new independent variable, the original variable will *gain* a significant effect. This probably sounds odd, but I'll get you through it. The closest recipe ingredient corollary I could think of for this is salt: sometimes when you're cooking, and you add salt, it enhances the other flavors that were already in there, allowing you to taste them whereas you couldn't before.

The first (and key) independent variable here is respondent's sex: Are women more supportive of same-sex parenting than men are? Then, I will add as an independent variable an index of support for "nontraditional" parenting. This index is the combination of three variables that each gets at support for a particular parenting situation: full-time working mother, non-married parents, and single parent. It ranges from 0 (no support for nontraditional parenting) to 12 (full support for nontraditional parenting). With regard to timing, I'll argue that people likely have had longstanding attitudes toward non-traditional parenting ("but that's how I was raised . . ."), but only recently have people formed their attitudes toward same-sex parenting. Finally, I throw religiosity into the mix (measured rather simplistically by number of times respondent goes to religious services in a month). Here are the models:

■ **Exhibit 10.13: Explaining Support for Same-Sex Parenting: Three Models**

Dependent Variable: Respondent's Score on Same-Sex Parenting Index

Independent Variable	Model 1	Model 2	Model 3
Sex (M = 0, F = 1)	0.75***	0.13	0.34**
Support for Nontrad. Par.	—	0.58***	0.51***
# of times attend per month	—	—	–0.26***
Constant	3.53	0.41	1.20
	$R^2 = 0.02$	$R^2 = 0.33$	$R^2 = 0.38$
	$n = 1175$	$n = 1175$	$n = 1175$

**p < .01. ***p < .001 (two-tailed test).
Support for Nontraditional Parenting is measured from 0 = no support to 12 = full support.
Source: GSS 2012 data.

In Model 1, we find that sex has an effect: on the 8-point index, women are 0.75 points more supportive than men are. This is a sizable effect; however, notice that sex explains only 2% of the variation in attitude. In Model 2, we see an example of Nested Story 3. Once we control for attitudes toward nontraditional parenting, the difference between men and women disappears. The coefficient for sex decreases by 83% $((0.13 - 0.75)/0.75 = 0.83)$, and goes from $p < .001$ to statistical nonsignificance. The effect of the nontraditional parenting variable is huge: someone who is not at all supportive of nontraditional parenting is 7 points lower on the 8-point same-sex parenting index than someone who is fully supportive of nontraditional parenting. Plus, it raises the R^2 to 0.33. Women are more supportive of nontraditional parenting than men are (I checked this out in a separate regression). When we control for this, given that support for nontraditional parenting is positively related to support for same-sex parenting, the separate effect of sex goes away. Another way to say this is that if a man and a woman have similar attitudes toward nontraditional parenting, then they will also have similar attitudes toward same-sex parenting.

In Model 3, we have an example of Nested Story 4. I added religiosity in Model 3. It has a statistically significant effect of its own: the more often you attend religious services, the less supportive you are of same-sex parenting. However, adding the religiosity variable causes the sex variable to come back to life (zombie variable! Run!). The effect of sex returns and is now once again statistically significant (at the $p < .01$ level). Women attend religious services more often than men do (I checked this out in a separate regression). When we control for this, given that attendance at religious services is negatively related to support for same-sex parenting, the separate effect of sex comes back. Another way to look at this is that in Model 2, men and women had similar attitudes toward same-sex parenting, but I had yet to control for religiosity.

When I control for religiosity in Model 3, I am essentially "giving" the men more religiosity so that they are equally religious as the women, and when I do this, they become less supportive of same-sex parenting, pushing the women back ahead of the men on this index. I realize that might be a lot to get your head around, so give this some thought. If it's any consolation, this type of nested story is relatively rare. But to me, that makes it all the more interesting.

JUDGING IMPROVEMENT FROM MODEL TO MODEL

One obvious question that arises when dealing with nested models is, How do we know a new model is an improvement over a previous model? For example, if we have Model 1 with one independent variable and then, in Model 2, we add a second independent variable, how can we tell if Model 2 is an improvement over Model 1? An easy way is to look at the values of R^2. If the second model's R^2 is higher than the first model's R^2, that is a sign that this second model is a better model. But this raises a question: How much bigger does the R^2 need to be? Is a jump from 0.05 to 0.12 enough to be called an improvement? Or 0.05 to 0.07? Or 0.05 to 0.06? We can use a version of the **F-test** (we used F when we covered ANOVA in Chapter 6) in order to tell if the improvement is statistically significant. To calculate F, we need the following information:

BMR^2: the R^2 for the bigger model
SMR^2: the R^2 for the smaller model
df_1 = the number of independent variables in the bigger model minus the number of independent variables in the smaller model
df_2 = 1 plus the sample size of the bigger model minus the number of independent variables in the bigger model

Here's the formula:

$$F = \frac{\dfrac{\left(BMR^2 - SMR^2\right)}{df_1}}{\dfrac{1 - BMR^2}{df_2}}$$

Here is an example of this using Models 2 and 3 from the Government Assistance Model from earlier in the chapter:

BMR^2: 0.28, SMR^2: 0.23, $df_1 = 1$, $df_2 = 352$

$$F = \frac{\dfrac{0.28 - 0.23}{1}}{\dfrac{1 - 0.28}{352}}$$

This gives us $F = 25$. This value is much larger than the 3.84 in the F-table that we would need to achieve significance at the $p < 0.05$ level, so Model 3 is a significant improvement over Model 2. What if the Model 3 R^2 were only 0.24, and we had 200 cases instead of 355? Does the addition of the income variable significantly increase the explanatory power of the model with these revised figures?

$$F = \frac{\dfrac{0.24 - 0.23}{1}}{\dfrac{1 - 0.24}{197}}$$

This gives us $F = 2.56$, which is lower than the 3.84 we would need to achieve a p-value of less than .05. Therefore, with these figures, we would conclude that Model 3 is not an improvement over Model 2.

SAMPLE SIZE FROM MODEL TO MODEL

An additional concern when we're dealing with nested models relates to the fact that different models have different combinations of variables. For various reasons, the number of valid cases we have for one variable might differ from the number of valid cases we have for another variable. For example, we might use a variable in Model 1 for which we have information on all of the respondents, but then in Model 2, we add a variable for which we have information for only a third of the respondents. When we run the regression for Model 2, it will involve only those cases for which we have information on *all* of the variables. Therefore, Model 2 will have only a third of the sample size that Model 1 has. As you've learned, sample size can have a big effect on the results, especially where statistical significance is concerned. You may have noticed that in all the preceding examples, all the models in a set of nested models have the same sample size. This is because I used a technique that assures that this will occur: it looks at all the variables I'm using throughout all the models and uses only those cases for which I have information on all of those variables.

As an example of the importance of this, we'll return to explaining the income difference between men and women. Instead of using hours worked as an independent variable, we realize that the GSS asked people how many college-level science courses they had taken. Given the unfortunate gender gap in science, we decide this could be an interesting independent variable. However, respondents were asked this question only if they had replied yes to the question, "Have you taken any college science courses?" Of course, to answer this question, you would have had to attended at least some college. This drastically affects the sample size. Examine these models:

▪ **Exhibit 10.14: The Importance of Sample Size in Nested Models**

Dependent Variable: Respondent's Income in $1,000s

Independent Variable	Model 1	Model 2	Model 3
Sex (M = 0, F = 1)	−15.53***	−24.72***	−22.70***
# of college science courses	—	—	1.76***
Constant	47.77	63.64	50.03
R^2	0.05	0.09	0.25
n	1,142	252	252

***$p < .001$ (two-tailed test).
Source: GSS 2012 data.

Model 1 is a simple regression of the effect of sex on income, with all cases that had information on those two variables. Model 2 is the same simple regression but uses only those cases that have information on these two variables *plus* the science courses variable. Notice the greatly reduced sample size. Model 3 uses the same cases as Model 2. The mistake would be to compare the effect of sex in Model 1 with the effect of sex in Model 3, because the sample sizes are so different. The correct way would be to compare the effect of sex in Model 2 with the effect of sex in Model 3, since both of these models share the same cases. Occasionally, you might see someone's models differ by a few cases. Although this is not completely correct, it happens. However, if the models differ by many cases, that's a problem.

LITERATURE EXAMPLE: OPPOSITIONAL CULTURE IN SCHOOLS

Now for a couple of examples from the research literature. This first one comes from an article that appeared in the top journal *American Sociological Review*: "Assessing the Oppositional Culture Explanation for Racial/Ethnic Differences in School Performance," by James Ainsworth-Darnell and Douglas B. Downey (1998). They started with the fact that, on average, blacks perform worse than whites do in school. One explanation for this is that American blacks, after centuries of oppression by whites, have developed their own culture that is in "opposition" to white culture. For example, the explanation holds that, where whites believe that performing well in school is a good thing, blacks, in opposition to this idea, think that it is a bad thing. Black students who perform well in school are accused of "acting white." You may have heard this term before. Up to this point, however, no one had tested this explanation using large-scale data.

Ainsworth-Darnell and Downey (1998) used the National Educational Longitudinal Study to build a series of regression models. This dataset is highly complex: it surveyed high school sophomores, their teachers, their principals, and their parents over time. Their article presents pages and pages of regression results. Exhibit 10.15 is a simplified version of their Table 5:

■ **Exhibit 10.15: Race's Effect on Grades**

Dependent Variable: Student Grades (ranges from 0 (mostly below Ds) to 7 (mostly As))				
Independent Variable	Model 1	Model 2	Model 3	Model 4
Race Variable				
W = 0, B = 1	−0.17***	−0.09**	+0.02	−0.13***
Social Class Variables				
Family Income	—	+0.02***	+0.01***	+0.01**
Parental Prestige	—	+0.10***	+0.06***	+0.04***
Parental Education	—	+0.18***	+0.08***	+0.07***
Skills and Habits				
Effort (acc. to teachers)	—	—	+0.28***	+0.21***
In trouble	—	—	−0.05***	−0.03***
Homework	—	—	+0.05***	+0.03***
Attitudes				
Treatment by teachers	—	—	—	+0.02**
OK to break rules	—	—	—	+0.01*
OK to cheat	—	—	—	−0.01
R^2	0.04	0.08	0.36	0.44

$*p < .05.$ $**p < .01.$ $***p < .001$ (two-tailed test).
Source: Adapted from Ainsworth-Darnell and Downey (1998).

Let's slowly walk through these nested models and see how the oppositional culture explanation holds up. Model 1 has but one independent variable that contrasts blacks with whites, and the slope shows that blacks' grades do lag behind whites' grades by 0.17 on a 7-point scale—not a huge difference, but it is statistically significant.

Model 2 introduces a number of social class variables. Research has shown that some of the differences we observe between blacks and whites may be due not to race but to social class (Conley 1999). Model 2 supports this: when the researchers control for social class, around half of the race effect goes away (dropping from –0.17 to –0.09, a reduction of 47%). In other words, if we look at a black and a white student from similar class backgrounds (both being middle class, for example), their grades will differ by only 0.09. However, this remains a statistically significant difference. This is an example of Nested Story 2 I talked about earlier in the chapter.

Model 3 adds variables regarding the amount of effort the student puts in. Previously in the article, the researchers showed that blacks, according to the measures used in this survey, tend to put in less effort than whites do. When such variables are taken into account, the difference between whites and blacks completely disappears. For example, if you have a black student and a white student from similar class backgrounds *and* who each put in similar effort, their grades will not differ. This is an example of Nested Story 3 I talked about earlier in the chapter.

It is in Model 4, however, where things get really interesting, albeit daunting at first glance. We have an example of Nested Story 4 I described earlier in this chapter. In Model 4, the researchers add a set of attitude variables. They argue that, if a student feels he or she is treated poorly by teachers, thinks it's OK to break the rules, and thinks it's OK to cheat, then that's a pretty good sign that he or she is opposed to school and the rules that it has in place. Earlier in the article, the researchers show that black students actually have *less* oppositional attitudes than do whites: they're more likely to think the teachers treat them well, that it's not OK to break the rules, and that it's not OK to cheat. Therefore, blacks have advantageous attitudes compared to whites, attitudes that help them do better in school. So, in Model 4, when the researchers control for these attitudes and take away this advantage, the difference between blacks and whites *comes back*: whites once again perform better than blacks. Looking at our two students, here would be the story: The black student has an advantage over the white student in that he has better pro-school attitudes. Well, let's say we give the white student the same pro-school attitudes as the black student. That is, we hold these attitudes constant. When we do this, the white student benefits, and once again pulls ahead of the black student. Based on these regression results, Ainsworth-Darnell and Downey claim that the oppositional culture explanation does not hold up very well under statistical scrutiny. Not only are the anti-school attitudes less prevalent among black students compared to white students, but also it seems to be exactly these attitudes that help black students in school.

LITERATURE EXAMPLE: MEDIA EXPOSURE AND FEAR OF CRIME

I love watching the local television news, particularly because I live in a small city. I sometimes feel sorry for the newscasters, who are trying to do a good job, but often they just don't have enough juicy news to fill up the allotted time. Because they are reporting about a small city, sometimes not much happens on any given day. When something notable does happen, such as a crime, they milk it for all it's worth, and put it at the start of the newscast. A long-standing mantra in news is "If it bleeds, it leads." Also sensational are the "ripped from the headlines" dramatic programs, as well as reality-based TV shows about crime. Imagine someone watches all of this on a steady basis. Will such a person be affected by such media? That is, will he think the chances of crime are greater in his neighborhood, and will he be more fearful of crime (thus staying inside his house and watching even more crime shows)? These are some of the questions Valerie Callanan addresses in her article "Media Consumption, Perceptions of Crime Risk and Fear of Crime: Examining Race/Ethnic Differences," which appeared in the journal *Sociological Perspectives* in 2012. She uses data from a telephone survey of a random sample of Californians: 2,500 whites, 777 Latinos, and 435 blacks. Respondents were asked about their experiences with crime, their attitudes about various crime policies, and their media usage. Her dependent variable was fear of crime, measured on a scale from 0 (no fear) to 10 (very fearful). The independent variable perceived risk of neighborhood crime was measured similarly (0 = no risk to 10 = high risk). Exposure to various types of media were measured on a scale from 1 (no exposure) to 5 (high exposure). Exhibit 10.16 presents an abridged version of her Table 2.

■ **Exhibit 10.16: Fear of Crime: Two Models**

Dependent Variable: Fear of Crime (0 = no fear, 10 = much fear)		
Independent Variable	Model 1	Model 2
Black	0.269*	−0.160
Latino	1.045***	0.903***
Newspapers	0.017	0.024*
Local TV news	0.056***	0.021*
Crime dramas	0.043	−0.006
Crime reality TV	0.115**	−0.069
Crime victim	0.427***	0.170***
Perceived risk of crime	—	0.532***
Constant	4.232	1.195
Adjusted R^2	0.166	0.439
n	3,142	3,114

*$p < .05$. **$p < .01$. ***$p < .001$.
*$p < .05$. **$p < .01$. ***$p < .001$ (two-tailed test).
Source: Adapted from Callanan (2012).

One of her goals was to see how perceived risk of crime acts as an intervening variable: if you watch local TV news, your perceived risk of crime might go up, and then your fear of crime might go up. We'll walk through Model 1 first. Looking at the race variables, we see that both blacks and Latinos are more fearful than whites, but Latinos much more so. Among the media variables, only two of the four—watching local TV news and watching reality TV—significantly raise the respondent's fear of crime. It should come as no surprise that if one has been a victim of crime in the past, one will have a higher fear of crime.

Model 2 adds the perceived risk of neighborhood crime variable. It has quite an effect, and raises the explained variation from 0.17 to 0.44. Notice also that the addition of this variable slightly lowers the number of cases. The change is so small that we'll give the author a pass, but she really should have removed those cases from Model 1. But what effect does introducing this variable have on the effects of the other independent variables? Similar to one of the examples earlier in the chapter, one of the race variables is affected whereas the other one is not. Notice that the effect of the black variable switches signs from positive to negative, although ultimately this doesn't matter because the negative coefficient is not statistically significant. Having a coefficient switch signs from model to model does happen, and I was considering making this Nested Story 5, but it's really rare. Because this effect has lost its significance, we conclude that if a black person and a white person perceive the same risk in crime, then they will have the same fear of crime. In contrast, because the Latino coefficient remains highly significant, we conclude that, even if a Latino person and a white person perceive the same risk of crime, the Latino person will still have a higher fear of crime. Controlling for perceived risk of crime alters the effects of the media variables: the local TV news effect decreases (but remains significant), while the reality TV effect disappears altogether. If watching reality TV does not increase your perceived risk of crime, it won't affect your fear of crime. Finally, the victim variable decreases as well, by 60% ((0.170 − 0.427)/0.427 = 0.60). An interpretation of this change is that being a victim of crime not only directly, but also indirectly, causes increased fear of crime. If you are a victim of crime, you will subsequently perceive a greater risk of crime, and this will raise your fear of crime. I'll talk more about these direct and indirect effects later on in the book.

CONCLUSION

Controlling is at the heart of regression analysis. Hopefully the examples above have shown you how controlling for a second (or third, or fourth . . .) independent variable can be used to tell some very interesting statistical stories. Often, people will look at regression results and say, "Well, the real reason for your findings is . . .," such as in the income/sex example from earlier: "Well, the real reason for your finding that men make more money than women is that men work more hours than women." You've seen that regression allows you to deal with such arguments by controlling for additional variables. Using nested models is one way we can start to explore the interrelated nature of social forces. For, if taking into account an additional variable changes the effects of other variables, that indeed tells us how these variables might be related. It's a complex world out there, so sometimes a set of increasingly complex models is necessary to make sense of it.

SPSS DEMONSTRATION

Please visit the book's website (www.routledge.com/cw/linneman) to view a video of this demonstration.

Now that we are running multiple, related models, it's a good idea to go over how to do this in SPSS. It is possible to run a regression model, look at the results, go back into the regression room, add another independent variable, run that regression model, look at the results, and so on. However, although this may be an OK way to start, once you see what your set of models is going to look like you should have SPSS run them all at once because of the sample-size issue I talked about earlier in this chapter. So back into the regression room we go, where we'll run a set of models similar to the sex and income example from earlier in the chapter. Here are the variables for the first model, where we're using family income as the dependent variable and our only independent variable is the respondent's sex. In order to add a second model, I'm going to do the following things:

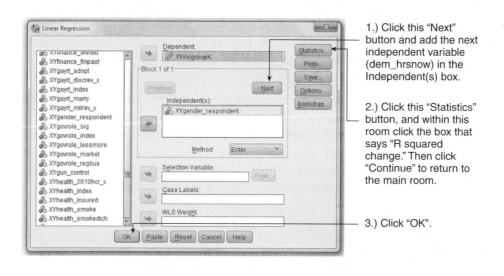

1.) Click this "Next" button and add the next independent variable (dem_hrsnow) in the Independent(s) box.

2.) Click this "Statistics" button, and within this room click the box that says "R squared change." Then click "Continue" to return to the main room.

3.) Click "OK".

If you had a third model, you would click the "Next" button again and add your next independent variable into this third box. Notice that, as you do this, between the Dependent and Independent boxes it says Block 1 of 3, 2 of 3, and so on. Here is the output when you run two models at the same time:

Variables Entered/Removed[b]

Model	Variables Entered	Variables Removed	Method
1	recoded gender (M=0, F=1)	.	Enter
2	How many hours R works	.	Enter

a. All requested variables entered.
b. Dependent Variable: Family Income in 1000s

This first box tells you which new independent variable SPSS added for each model.

Model Summary

Model	R	R Square	Adjusted R Square	Std. Error of the Estimate	Change Statistics R Square Change	F Change	df1	df2	Sig. F Change
1	0.098[a]	0.010	0.009	57.015	0.010	30.107	1	3130	0.000
2	0.176[b]	0.031	0.030	56.401	0.022	69.524	1	3129	0.000

a. Predictors: (Constant), recoded gender (M=0,F=1)
b. Predictors: (Constant), recoded gender (M=0,F=1), How many hours R works

This second box tells you if the addition of the second independent variable significantly improved the model. It carries out the F-test described near the end of the chapter and shows us that, indeed, this second model is an improvement. Look at the last column, Sig. F Change: the second 0.000 tells you that Model 2 is an improvement because that number is below 0.05.

ANOVA[c]

Model		Sum of Squares	df	Mean Square	F	Sig.
1	Regression	97871.190	1	97871.190	30.107	0.000[a]
	Residual	10174777.38	3130	3250.728		
	Total	10272648.57	3131			
2	Regression	319034.345	2	159517.172	50.146	0.000[b]
	Residual	9953614.234	3129	3181.085		
	Total	10272648.57	3131			

a. Predictors: (Constant), recoded gender (M=0,F=1)
b. Predictors: (Constant), recoded gender (M=0,F=1), How many hours R works
c. Dependent Variable: Family Income in 1000s

This third box of output gives us our number of cases: 3,132. Notice that, when you run the models this way, SPSS uses only the cases for which we have valid values for *all* of the models, and this is what we want.

Coefficients[a]

Model		Unstandardized Coefficients		Standardized Coefficients	t	Sig.
		B	Std. Error	Beta		
1	(Constant)	72.895	1.410		51.713	0.000
	recoded gender (M=0, F=1)	-11.191	2.040	-0.098	-5.487	0.000
2	(Constant)	45.012	3.623		12.423	0.000
	recoded gender (M=0, F=1)	-7.330	2.070	-0.064	-3.541	0.000
	How many hours R works	0.663	0.079	0.151	8.338	0.000

a. Dependent Variable: Family Income in 1000s

The fourth box gives us all our coefficients, and we can see how the coefficients change as we add in the additional variables. We will come back to the fifth box of output later in the book.

FROM OUTPUT TO PRESENTATION

If you've been following the "From Output to Presentation" sections for the last couple of chapters, you should be getting accustomed to presenting the results "sideways," and now you should really understand why this is the preferred way to present such results. In Exhibit 10.17, I have taken the output from the above SPSS demonstration and created a professional table.

Exhibit 10.17: The Effects of Sex and Hours Worked on Family Income

Dependent Variable: Family Income in $1,000s		
Independent Variable	Model 1	Model 2
Sex (M = 0, F = 1)	–11.19***	–7.33***
Hours Worked Per Week	—	0.66***
Constan	72.90	45.01
R^2	0.01	0.03
n	3,132	3,132

***$p < 0.001$
Source: ANES 2012 data.

Although the dependent variable here is Family Income rather than Respondent's Income, the ANES results are strikingly similar to the GSS results. The original $11,190 difference between men and women is decreased to $7,330 once we control for hours worked. Taking into account hours worked does lower the effect of sex, but it in no way fully dissipates the effect of sex.

Here are some additional thoughts about presenting regression results. Some may not agree with me, but I find stating the dependent variable to be an acceptable title for this type of table. If you want to provide a title, just make it clear. Two options would be "The Effects of Sex and Hours Worked on Family Income" or "The Regression of Family Income onto Sex and Hours Worked." As long as the audience can see what the dependent variable is and how it was measured, you're good.

Even if you describe elsewhere in your presentation or paper how you measured the independent variables, it is nice to make sure that this information appears in the table as well so that the audience does not have to look elsewhere for this information. For example, you wouldn't want to say simply "Sex" for this independent variable, because this would not tell the audience how you coded this variable, and without this information, they cannot interpret the slopes for this variable. Alternately, instead of "M = 0, F = 1," you might see "Female," which implies that the slopes you see are the effect on females (i.e., the "−11.19" in Model 1 above means that females get $11,190 taken away from them).

Notice that the SPSS output gives you the statistical significance of the constant, but I have not included this in the professional table. We are concerned with whether the slopes are statistically significant, not whether the constant is significant. Given that the constant will go up and down depending on which independent variables are in the model, its statistical significance may come and go, but this doesn't imply anything. In some professional tables, they may include the statistical significance of the constant (i.e., it may have stars by it), but I don't think whether you do or don't do this is a big deal.

EXERCISES

Exercise 1

First, using ANES data, run a simple regression that investigates the relationship between age (use the recoded age variable) and environmental views (use the environmental index). Then, add political views to the regression model. Create a table that contains both models. Tell the story that these models are telling as a group.

Exercise 2

The 2010 health care act was highly controversial, and many people chose sides based on political party. Run a simple regression with ANES data that uses the Health Care Index as your dependent variable and the recoded party identification variable as your independent variable. Then, examine the possibility that part of the effect of political party could be that the different parties have different ideas regarding the role that government should play in people's lives. That is, add the Government Role Index as an independent variable and run the regression again. Create a table that contains both models, and fully interpret your results.

Exercise 3

No surprise here: African Americans, on average, favor affirmative action more than whites do. Do feelings toward egalitarianism play a role in this difference? Run a simple regression with the ANES dataset using the Affirmative Action Index as the dependent variable and the dichotomous race variable (white/black) as the independent variable. Then, run a second model in which you add the Egalitarianism Index as an independent variable. Create a table that contains both models and fully interpret your results.

Exercise 4

Are women more concerned about discrimination against women than men are? Probably. But is this difference due to the fact that women tend to be more liberal than men? Using ANES data, run a simple regression model using the Women Discrimination Index as the dependent variable and gender as the independent variable. Then, run a second model, adding the (recoded) political views variable. Create a table that contains both models and fully interpret your results.

Exercise 5 (Answer Available in Appendix D)

What propels people to be involved in their communities? Income might play a role: households with higher incomes might give people the luxury of time to be involved. Using ANES data, run a simple regression using household income in thousands as your independent variable and the Involvement Index as your dependent variable. Then, examine the possibility that it is really household education that plays a role: educated people have more skills to bring to their involvement, and they have higher incomes. Run a second regression model, adding education of the household as a second independent variable. Create a table that contains both models and fully interpret your results.

Exercise 6

Although immigrants to the United States come from all over the world, when many people think of immigrants, they think of Hispanics. Do Hispanics have different attitudes toward immigration than whites do? Using ANES data, run a regression that uses the Immigration Index as the dependent variable and the three race reference groups as your independent variables. Then, consider the possibility that if one is himself an immigrant, this may affect attitudes toward immigration (that is, add the recoded nativity variable to create a second regression model). Finally, consider that if one's parents were born outside the United States, this could affect attitudes as well (that is, to a third regression model, add the two reference group variables that concern where the respondent's parents were born). Create a table that contains all three models and fully interpret your results.

Exercise 7

In the news, it is often reported that younger people have much more positive attitudes toward gay policy issues than older people have. See if this is true according to ANES data by running a simple regression with age as the independent variable (the recoded version: age in years) and the Gay Rights Index as the dependent variable. Then, consider the possibility that may be more supportive in general of nontraditional lifestyles: create a second regression model by adding the Traditional Values Index as an independent variable. Finally, consider that both of these former effects may be affected by the fact that younger people are more likely to know a gay man or lesbian: create a third regression model by adding the variable for gay acquaintance (use the recoded version of this). Create a table that contains all three models and fully interpret your results.

Exercise 8

Use the PewShop data to investigate the interplay between race, education, and income. First, use the race reference-group variables as your independent variables, with recoded income (in 1,000s) as your dependent variable. Then, in a second model, add the recoded education variable. Create a table that contains both models, and fully interpret any changes that occur between Model 1 and Model 2 with regard to racial effects.

Exercise 9

Do racial differences in technology presence change once we take into account that different races have different average incomes? Use the PewShop dataset to address this question. First, use the race reference variables as your independent variables, with the Technology Index as your dependent variable. Then, in a second model, add the recoded income variable. Create a table that contains both models, and fully interpret any changes that occur between Model 1 and Model 2 regarding racial effects.

Exercise 10

Run a set of nested models with the PewShop dataset that will test an idea from early in this chapter: men typically have higher incomes than do women, but once we control for work status (use the reference-group variables), this difference will go away. Create a table that presents the nested models and explain your findings.

Exercise 11

Run a set of nested models with the PewShop dataset that will test this idea: younger people tend to use technology more to shop (use the shop index), but this is only because (as we've seen) younger people are more likely to have smartphones than are older people. Create a table that presents the nested models and explain your findings by doing four examples:

a.   a 25-year-old who doesn't have a smartphone

b.   a 25-year old who does have a smartphone

c.   an 80-year-old who doesn't have a smartphone

d.   an 80-year old who does have a smartphone

Exercise 12

Those who use their cell phones for a wide variety of activities are more likely to use the Internet to find health information, but perhaps this is only because of age (younger people are more likely to use their cell phones for a wide variety of activities *and* to use the Internet to find health information). Test this idea using the PewHealth dataset. Create a table that presents the nested models and address whether this idea is supported or not by the findings.

Exercise 13 (Answer Available in Appendix D)

Using the PewHealth dataset, run a set of nested models using the Internet Health Use Index as your dependent variable. First, use the Health Conditions Index as your only independent variable. Then, add age as an independent variable. Create a table that presents the nested models and interpret the models as a set.

Chapter 11

SOME SLOPES ARE BIGGER THAN OTHERS: CALCULATING AND INTERPRETING BETA COEFFICIENTS

This chapter covers . . .

 . . . why comparing regular regression slopes is problematic
 . . . how to standardize slopes and interpret them
 . . . how standardization and z-scores are related
 . . . how researchers used betas to study race and school discipline
 . . . how researchers used betas to study country music and suicide

INTRODUCTION

Now that you've learned how to use multiple independent variables in the same regression equation, you may have started to wonder: How do you know which independent variable has the biggest effect on the dependent variable? One might be tempted to use the significance levels, but that's not what significance levels are meant to be used for. Plus, in many situations, all of the independent variables we're using have significant effects, all at very high ($p < .001$) levels. To add to the confusion, variables often are measured in very different units. For example, in a single regression model you could use as independent variables:

■ sex: measured as 0 or 1
■ attendance at religious services: measured in times to church per month, from 0 to 10

■ education: measured in years, from 0 to 20
■ income: measured in dollars, from 0 to 100,000

So, with all of these different units, imagine trying to compare their various slopes in their original forms. Let's say the slope for SEX was 0.73 and the slope for EDUCATION was 0.25. At first glance, it might seem that sex has a larger effect, because it has the larger slope. But think about this for a minute. True, the variable SEX, if it changes from 0 to 1, can change the dependent variable by 0.73. But that is *all* it can do. SEX cannot go onward to 2, 3, or 4. Education, in contrast, can go from 0 to 1 to 2, 3, 4, 5, 6, 7, 8, 9, 10, 11, 12, 13, 14, 15, 16, 17, 18, 19, 20. EDUCATION has a larger range than does SEX, and that gives it a greater chance to affect the dependent variable. In fact, in this situation the change it causes in the dependent variable could be anywhere from 0 (with 0 years of education) to 5.0 (with 20 years of education; $20 \times 0.25 = 5.0$).

What we need is a way to standardize these effects. To get you in the mood, here is a very brief history lesson (I'm sure economic historians would be horrified at this over-simplification, so don't tell them about this). A long time ago, countries subscribed to what was called the gold standard. Each country had its own type of money (for example, dollars, pounds, francs, pesos, deutschmarks, yen). As you likely know, each of these currency units is not the same: 1 dollar traditionally equaled around half a pound, around 5 francs, and more than 100 yen. But, even with their disparate currencies, these countries knew the value of their economies because they had the ability to translate the total value of their currencies into a single unit: the gold standard. Each country's total value was calculated in gold, so that everyone knew what each country was worth. This way, a country couldn't simply print billions of sheets of currency and then go, "We're all rich!" So a standard, in this sense, allows us to compare across disparate units of measurement.

That is what we are looking for: a way to standardize our variables' units so that we can compare and contrast their effects. Hmmm. Standard. Where have we seen that term used before? Perhaps the standard deviation? Definitely.

THE PROCESS OF STANDARDIZING SLOPES

What we are going to do is convert all of the slopes into units measured in standard deviations. So instead of saying, "For each year increase in education, income increases _____ dollars," we are going to end up with something that looks like this: "For each standard deviation increase in education, income increases by _____ standard deviations." This way, all of our variables will be on something akin to a gold standard: everything will be measured in the same units, so then we will be able to compare and contrast their effects. Throughout this chapter, because I'll be using the term *standard deviation* so many times, I'll just use *SD*.

As usual, let's start quite simply. We'll use the number of children a person has as our dependent variable, and only two independent variables: education (expectation: the more educated you are, the fewer children you will have had) and age (expectation: the older you are, the more children you will have had; people from older generations had more children, generally). I restricted the 2012 GSS sample so that I am looking only at people aged 46 and older. If we included everyone in the GSS, including the 20-year-olds, we would have many people in the sample who have not yet had children, so that would be misleading. Using only respondents older than 45 greatly reduces this problem. Also, for this analysis, I'm using only the white respondents. Here are the regression results:

■ **Exhibit 11.1: The Effects of Education and Age on Number of Children**

Dependent Variable: Number of Children Respondent Has Had	
Independent Variable	Slope
Education	–0.11***
Age	0.03***
Constant	1.73
	$R^2 = 0.11$
	$n = 828$

***$p < .001$.
Source: GSS 2012 data for all white respondents age 46 and older.

At first glance, it may seem that, because both of the independent variables are measured in the same units (years), we wouldn't need to standardize them. However, look at the standard deviations—whoops, I mean SDs—for the variables:

SD for number of CHILDREN   1.60
SD for years of EDUCATION   3.19
SD for AGE   11.53

The SD for AGE is much higher than the SD for EDUCATION. This is possible to see just by thinking about the ranges of the variables: education ranges from 0 to 20, age ranges from 46 to 90. But, besides this, here is a rule: in order to compare and contrast the effects of multiple independent variables, you must standardize them.

Our first question is, If EDUCATION increases by one SD, by how many SDs does CHILDREN increase? To answer this, we need to convert the slope into standard deviations. Here is the slope in its original form:

CHILDREN goes down by 0.11 children/EDUCATION goes up by one year. Let's start with the CHILDREN part. How much of one SD is 0.11 children? To figure this out, we divide 0.11 by 1.60:

$0.11/1.60 = 0.06875$

Note that because I'm dividing and multiplying small numbers several times, I'm going to keep five decimal places for this example.

Now we have the following:

CHILDREN goes down by 0.06875 SD/EDUCATION goes up by one year

Let's do the same thing to the EDUCATION part: How much of one SD is one year of education? We divide 1 by 3.19:

$1/3.19 = 0.31348$

Now we have the following:

CHILDREN goes down by 0.06875 SD/EDUCATION goes up by 0.31348 SD

Just as with any slope, we want the bottom to be 1, so we divide the top and the bottom by 0.31348:

$0.06875/0.31348 = 0.22$
$0.31348/0.31348 = 1$

Our end result is that

CHILDREN goes down by 0.22 SD/EDUCATION goes up by 1 SD

Or, we can say that for every standard deviation increase in education, number of children goes down 0.22 SD. This slope is now standardized. It goes by a number of names:

- **standardized slope** (bet you didn't see that one coming)
- standardized regression coefficient
- beta weight
- **beta** (this is the name *I* use, because it reminds me of that cute little fish)

Let's calculate the beta for the AGE slope by going through the same process. The original slope is that

CHILDREN goes up by 0.03 children/AGE goes up by one year

Our first question is, How much of one SD is 0.03 children? The answer:

0.03/1.60 = 0.01875

Next question is, How much of one SD is one year of age? The answer:

1/11.53 = 0.08673

So far, we have the following:

CHILDREN goes up by 0.01875 SD/AGE goes up by 0.08673 SD

To get one on the bottom,

0.01875/0.08673 = 0.22
0.08673/0.08673 = 1

Our end result is that

CHILDREN goes up by 0.22 SD/AGE goes up by 1 SD

Or, we can say that for every one SD increase in age, number of children goes up 0.22 standard deviations. Pulling all of this together, we now have two versions of the slopes: unstandardized and standardized:

■ Exhibit 11.2: Unstandardized and Standardized Slopes

Independent Variable	Unstandardized Slope	Standardized Slope
Education	−0.11***	−0.22
Age	0.03***	0.22

*** $p < .001$.

We conclude that age and education have the same effect on number of children. We're looking at the magnitude of the effect, so we don't consider the negative sign in front of the education beta. Had we mistakenly contrasted the unstandardized slopes, we would have concluded that education has nearly *four times* the effect of age, and this would have been quite wrong.

A SHORTCUT

The preceding procedure for standardizing slopes, although step by step and therefore (hopefully) clear, is a bit lengthy. If you promise that you understand what I showed you earlier, I will show you a shortcut. Promise? OK, here goes: to calculate a standardized slope, use this little formula:

$$Standardized\ Slope = Original\ Slope \times \frac{SD_{IV}}{SD_{DV}}$$

Don't take this personally, but, had I simply shown you this formula first, I highly doubt you would understand what betas really are. If you played around with all of this, you could see that this is really doing the exact same thing that the long way is doing. Here are the slopes we did above:

Beta for EDUCATION: $-0.11 \times 3.19/1.60 = -0.22$
Beta for AGE: $0.03 \times 11.53/1.60 = 0.22$

Remember that if you calculate the betas by hand, they may differ slightly from SPSS output, because SPSS doesn't round. For example, in SPSS output, the beta for age is 0.219 and the beta for education is –0.212.

INTERCHAPTER CONNECTION: STANDARDIZATION AND *Z*-SCORES

In the preceding procedure, we went through a process of standardizing the slopes. As a way of even better understanding betas, I'm going to show you a different procedure: standardizing the actual values and then using those in a regression model. In other words, we'll turn our actual values into *z*-scores. Remember those from Chapter 3? Following are a few hypothetical examples to jog your memory. Respondent A is 50 years old, so his or her *z*-score for age is

(A's age – mean of age)/standard deviation of age = $(50 - 62.71)/11.53 = -1.10$

This means that Respondent A's age is 1.10 standard deviations below the mean.

▨ **Exhibit 11.3: Actual Values and z-Scores**

Respondent	Age	Age z	Educ	Educ z	Child	Child z
A	50	–1.10	10	–1.11	0	–1.37
B	70	0.63	14	0.14	3	0.50
C	90	2.37	18	1.40	6	2.37

I had SPSS calculate all of the z-scores for all the respondents for these three variables, creating three new variables (AGEZ, EDUCZ, and CHILDRENZ). I then reran the original regression model from the previous example, but this time I used these three new variables. Here are both the unstandardized and the standardized slopes that resulted:

▨ **Exhibit 11.4: The Effects of Education and Age on Number of Children, z-Score Version**

Dependent Variable: Z-Score of Number of Children Respondent Has Had		
Independent Variable	Unstandardized Slope	Standardized Slope
z-Score of Education	0.219***	0.219
z-Score of Age	–0.212***	–0.212
Constant	0.00	
	$R^2 = 0.11$	
	$n = 828$	

Note: Dependent variable: z-scorer of number of children respondent has had.
***$p < .001$.
Source: GSS 2012 data for all white respondents age 46 and older.

The cases that I put into the regression model were, for these three variables, already all in terms of standard deviations, because all of the values were z-scores. Therefore, the unstandardized slopes and standardized slopes are exactly the same, because they both tell you the exact same thing: for each standard deviation increase in an independent variable, how much does the dependent variable change, in terms of standard deviations?

GSS EXAMPLE: RELIGION AND ABORTION ATTITUDES

The abortion debate continues, and religion plays a role in people's attitudes toward this contentious topic. But religion is not a single-faceted phenomenon. Which aspects of a person's religious life most influence his or her abortion attitudes? I chose three

GSS variables, each one getting at a different aspect. First, as a measure of connection to a religious community, I used the number of times per month one attends religious services. Next, as a measure of religious identity, I used whether or not the respondent has ever had a "born again" experience. Finally, as a measure of religious belief, I used whether or not the respondent thinks the Bible is the literal word of God. As my dependent variable, I used an index of seven questions that asked the respondent whether or not abortion should be an option in a variety of circumstances. It ranges from 0 (*abortion should not be allowed in any of the circumstances*) to 7 (*abortion should be allowed in all of the circumstances*). Here is the regression model with both the unstandardized slopes (typically called just slopes) and the betas:

■ **Exhibit 11.5: Religion and Attitudes toward Abortion**

Dependent Variable: Abortion Index Score (0 = Pro-Life — 7 = Pro-Choice)		
Independent Variable	Slope	Beta
Times Attend Per Month	−0.33***	−0.30
Reborn? (Y = 1, N = 0)	−0.67***	−0.13
Bible Literal (Y = 1, N = 0)	−1.05***	−0.19
Constant	5.53	
	$R^2 = 0.23$	
	$n = 1,061$	

***$p < .001$.
Source: GSS 2012 data.

The unstandardized slopes give the actual effects: as a person attends religious services one more time per month, he or she goes down on the index (i.e., becomes more pro-life) by a third of a point. Those who take the Bible literally are slightly more than a point lower on the index than those who do not take the Bible literally. Someone who attends religious services 10 times per month, has been reborn, and takes the Bible literally would be predicted to score a 0.51 on the index, whereas someone who never attends, has not been reborn, and who doesn't take the Bible literally who be predicted to score a 5.53 on the index. These variables together explain nearly a quarter of the variation in abortion attitudes. But let's get to the real question of this chapter: which independent variable has the largest effect? According to the betas, it is clearly attendance at religious services, which has the largest beta by a healthy margin. Next is the Bible effect, followed by the reborn effect. This is not to imply that the reborn variable has a small effect, as 0.67 on a 7-point index is nothing to sneeze at. But in contrast to these other two independent variables, it does have the smallest effect.

Just in case you'd care to practice coming up with the betas yourself, here are the standard deviations for these variables:

Abortion Index	2.54
Religious Attendance	2.31
Reborn Experience	0.49
Biblical Belief	0.46

GSS EXAMPLE: FOLLOWING IN YOUR PARENTS' EDUCATIONAL FOOTSTEPS

Is the level of education that men and women achieve affected by the educational levels of their mothers and fathers? If so, does the mother's education or the father's education have a bigger effect? And, if there are differences, do they differ for male and female respondents? Here are two regression models, one for male respondents, one for female respondents. The dependent variable is the years of education the respondent attained. The independent variables are the respondent's mother's education (in years) and the respondent's father's education (in years). I restricted the sample to those respondents older than 25 years old, because those younger than that may still be pursuing their education.

▪ **Exhibit 11.6: The Effects of Parental Education on Child's Education**

Dependent Variable: Respondent's Education in Years		
Independent Variable	Men	Women
Mother's Education	0.16**	0.34***
Father's Education	0.39***	0.21***
R^2	0.27	0.26
n	552	668

**p < .01. ***p < .001 (two-tailed test).
Source: GSS 2012 data for respondents age 25 and older.

We find what you might expect: there is a gendered pattern to the results. For the male respondents, their education is more strongly influenced by their fathers' education: the beta is 0.39 compared to the beta of 0.16 for mothers' education. For the female respondents, their education is more strongly influenced by their mothers' education: the beta is 0.34, compared to the beta of 0.21 for fathers' education. One other thing to point out in these models is that they both explain a healthy chunk of the variation in respondent's education: more than a quarter of the variation can be explained by just these two independent variables. That sort of thing just doesn't happen very often.

GSS EXAMPLE: GENDER AND HAPPINESS

Here is another research question that contrasts men and women: is there a difference in their sources of happiness? I used three independent variables in which people gauged their level of satisfaction with various aspects of their lives:

Family: from 0 (completely dissatisfied) to 6 (completely satisfied)
Job: from 0 (completely dissatisficd) to 6 (completely satisfied)
Health: from 0 (poor health) to 4 (excellent health)

For my dependent variable, I used a measure of happiness that ranged from 0 (completely unhappy) to 6 (completely happy). I then ran two regression models: one for men and one for women. I admit that my expectations were based on stereotypes: I thought that women's happiness would be more reliant on family satisfaction and men's happiness would be more reliant on job satisfaction. Here is what I found:

■ **Exhibit 11.7: Effects on Men's and Women's Happiness**

Dependent Variable: Happiness (0 = very unhappy — 6 = very happy)				
Independent Variable	Men		Women	
	b	Beta	b	Beta
Family	0.45***	0.54	0.29***	0.33
Job	0.19***	0.25	0.13**	0.17
Health	0.13***	0.14	0.14**	0.16
Constant	1.31		2.28	
R^2	0.52		0.25	
n	382		359	

$**p < .01.$ $***p < .001$ (two-tailed test).
Source: GSS 2012 data.

That's the great thing about stereotypes: they can so easily be proved wrong. The first thing that jumped out at me is the vast difference between the values for R^2: these three variables explain more than half of the variation in men's happiness but only a quarter of the variation in women's happiness. The betas soundly dismiss my expectations: family satisfaction has the largest effect in both the women's and men's models, and the beta for men's family satisfaction dwarfs the other two betas in the men's model. Exhibit 11.8 illustrates the relative importance of family for men's happiness. Assuming a very satisfied work life and excellent health, it shows that satisfaction with family has a larger effect on men's happiness than on women's.

■ **Exhibit 11.8: The Differential Effect of Family Satisfaction**

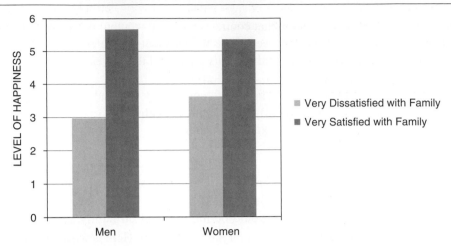

■ Very Dissatisfied with Family
■ Very Satisfied with Family

LITERATURE EXAMPLE: RACIAL THREAT AND SCHOOL DISCIPLINE

The majority of social science research uses the individual as the unit of analysis. For example, with regard to school discipline, we might ask, "Do black students receive harsher punishments than white students do?" However, researchers conduct interesting projects where the unit of analysis is not the individual. In their article "Racial Threat and Punitive School Discipline," which appeared in the journal *Social Problems* in 2010, Kelly Welch and Allison Ann Payne asked a similar research question, but at a different unit of analysis: Do schools with larger percentages of black students use harsher discipline policies? They explained this racial threat hypothesis as follows: "Rooted in the conflict perspective, the racial threat hypothesis suggests that as the proportion of blacks increases in relation to whites, intensified measures of control will proliferate in response to the perceived growing threat derived from closer proximity to minorities" (Welch and Payne 2010, p. 29). To test this hypothesis, Welch and Payne use the National Study of Delinquency Prevention in Schools, which surveyed hundreds of schools in the United States about their characteristics and policies. They used the public, non-alternative middle and high schools for their study. Their primary empirical claim is that, among all of the independent variables they examine, the percentage of blacks in a school has the largest effect on punishment policies. To make such a claim, they use multiple regression models with betas. Exhibit 11.9 is an excerpt that includes only the variables that were statistically significant in their first model. In addition to the percentage black, they include a measure of socioeconomic disadvantage: the percentage of students who receive a free or a reduced-cost lunch at the school. The survey also interviewed principals at the school, and from some of these questions Welch and Payne created a measure called "principal leadership," where a low number meant an uninvolved principal and a high number meant a very involved principal. Here is an excerpt from their Table 2:

■ **Exhibit 11.9: Racial Threat and School Discipline**

Dependent Variable: Punitive Disciplinary Response (1 = low — 3 = high)		
Independent Variable	Slope	Beta
Percent black students	0.007***	0.404
Percent free/reduced lunch	0.002*	0.184
Principal leadership	0.250***	0.263
	$R^2 = 0.21$	

$*p < .05.$ $***p < .001.$
Source: Adapted from Welch and Payne (2010).

If one were to examine only the unstandardized slopes, one might conclude that Principal Leadership has the largest effect, given that the slope's size is so huge compared to the other two slopes. However, this variable ranged from only 2 to 4, in contrast to the other variables, which each range from zero to 100. Welch and Payne also present the betas in their tables, so we can observe which independent variable has the largest effect. By far, it is the percent black students variable. In fact, in four out of five of their primary regression models (which each measure a different aspect of school disciplinc), the percent black students variable has the largest beta in each model. Welch and Payne conclude that the racial threat hypothesis is indeed supported by their findings. They conclude by calling on schools to reevaluate their discipline policies to ensure that they are not racially biased.

LITERATURE EXAMPLE: COUNTRY MUSIC AND SUICIDE

This next example also uses a unit of analysis different from the individual. At the individual level, we often wonder what characteristics propel an individual to commit suicide. But we may also examine this topic at a different level of analysis: What causes certain geographic areas to have higher suicide rates than other areas? Steven Stack and Jim Gundlach (1992) used, to put it mildly, an interesting independent variable to address this question: the proportion of radio airtime in a metropolitan area that is devoted to country music. They argued that country music, with its themes of cheating hearts, empty bank accounts, and lack of luck infuses the country subculture with a predisposition toward feelings that could lead to suicide.

Remember that they weren't looking at this at the individual level. They were not saying that if you listen to country music, you will commit suicide. Rather, they were saying that if country music pervades a geographic area's airwaves, this might affect what is on people's minds and, combined with other factors, could lead to a higher rate of suicide.

Because country music might overlap with other factors that might also be related to suicide, they controlled for these factors. For example, if an area has a high divorce rate, this could be a factor leading to a higher suicide rate. In addition to the divorce rate, other factors they considered were the level of poverty, the availability of guns (as measured by presence of gun stores), and whether the area was in the South. Their regression tables include both unstandardized and standardized slopes:

■ **Exhibit 11.10: Country Music and Suicide**

Dependent Variable: Suicides Per 100,000 People		
Independent Variable	Slope	Beta
Percent airtime country music	0.13*	0.27
Structural poverty	0.28	0.13
Southern region (Y = 1)	2.17*	0.27
Divorce rate	0.74*	0.30
Gun availability	0.20	0.08
Constant	7.73	
	$R^2 = 0.51$	
	$n = 49$	

*$p < .05$.
Source: Adapted from Stack and Gundlach (1992).

Three of the five independent variables have statistical significant effects, and country music is among them. These variables together explain a whopping 51% of the variation in suicide rates. The other two significant variables were the divorce rate and the southern region. All three of these variables have positive effects on the suicide rate. But which had the largest effect? It's pretty much a draw: although the beta for the divorce variable is a tad larger, the other two variables are right there behind it (0.27 compared to 0.30). So we can say that country music has a similarly sized effect as the divorce rate, which is a powerful finding. Interestingly, they ran this model using data for whites and data for blacks, and they found that all of these relationships hold only for the white suicide rate. Therefore, the black suicide rate needs to be explained by other factors.

CONCLUSION

Though betas are hard to interpret directly (visualizing standard deviations is difficult), they are quite useful. My hope for you, having concluded this chapter, is that you have developed a real feeling for how we actually *derive* the standardized coefficients. If all you got out of this chapter is "Line up the variables by their betas," please give it another read so that you develop a deeper understanding of what's going on. Remember to keep an eye out in the research literature for which type of coefficients the authors are using and interpret accordingly.

SPSS DEMONSTRATION

You don't have to do anything special to get betas in SPSS, as the betas are part of the standard issue regression output. Here is an output box from a previous SPSS demonstration:

Coefficients[a]

Model		Unstandardized Coefficients		Standardized Coefficients	t	Sig.
		B	Std. Error	Beta		
1	(Constant)	72.895	1.410		51.713	0.000
	recoded gender (M=0, F=1)	-11.191	2.040	-0.098	-5.487	0.000
2	(Constant)	45.012	3.623		12.423	0.000
	recoded gender (M=0, F=1)	-7.330	2.070	-0.064	-3.541	0.000
	How many hours R works	0.663	0.079	0.151	8.338	0.000

a. Dependent Variable: Family Income in 1000s

Notice the column headed "Standardized Coefficients" and subheaded "Beta." The two betas in Model 2 tell us the relative size of the effects. The beta for hours worked is 0.151, higher than the beta for sex (−0.064), so we can conclude that the variable hours worked has a larger effect than the sex variable.

If you want practice going from unstandardized to standardized slopes, there is a way in the regression room to ask for the descriptive statistics you need to do this. Simply click on the "Statistics" button and then click the Descriptives box. You could ask for these descriptive statistics in other ways, but the nice thing about doing this in the Regression room is that the descriptive statistics you'll get use only the cases that are in the requested regression model.

FROM OUTPUT TO PRESENTATION

In professional tables, you will see a lot of variation with regard to the betas. Sometimes researchers will present the unstandardized coefficients without the betas, sometimes they will present both, and sometimes they will present only the betas. Although it makes for a lot of numbers, I think it's preferable to present both, especially if you want to directly interpret the effects (by using the unstandardized coefficients) and talk about the relative size of the effects (by using the betas). Here is the professional table from last chapter's "From Output to Presentation," only this time with the betas added:

Exhibit 11.11: The Unstandardized and Standardized Effects of Sex and Hours Worked on Family Income

Independent Variable	Model 1		Model 2	
	b	Beta	b	Beta
Sex (M = 0, F = 1)	−11.19***	−0.10	−7.33***	−0.06
Hours Worked Per Week	—	—	0.66***	0.15
Constant	72.90		45.01	
R^2		0.01		0.03
n		3,132		3,132

***$p < .001$.
Source: ANES 2012 data.

I have positioned the R^2 and the sample size in between the unstandardized and standardized slopes in order to emphasize that these models go together.

EXERCISES

Exercise 1

Being engaged with the news is likely to make one more knowledgeable about politics, but are all types of news equally important? Use the ANES Knowledge Index as your dependent variable and the four media variables as your independent variables. Create a table that presents both the unstandardized and standardized coefficients. If someone has no news exposure, what is the predicted knowledge score? If someone has full news exposure (i.e., all types seven days a week), what is the predicted knowledge score? Talk about the relative size of the effects of the variables.

Exercise 2

It is commonly known that religion plays an important role in attitudes toward both abortion and homosexuality. However, do the various aspects of religiosity play the same role? Run two regressions using ANES data: in one, use the abortion index as the dependent variable; in the other, use the gay rights index as the dependent variable. For both regressions, use the following independent variables: attendance at religious services (the recoded Church variable), frequency of prayer (the recoded pray variable), and belief in the Bible (the recoded Word of God variable). Create a table that presents both the unstandardized and standardized coefficients for the two models. Compare the betas for the two models and provide an interpretation.

Exercise 3

Atheists are a much-maligned group in American society. Use the Atheist Feeling Thermometer as your dependent variable and then the three other religion-oriented feeling thermometers (toward Christian Fundamentalists, Mormons, and Muslims) as your independent variables. Create a table that presents both the unstandardized and standardized coefficients for the model and interpret the results.

Exercise 4 (Answer Available in Appendix D)

Hillary Clinton comes to you and asks you which of the following three issues people most connect with her: abortion rights, gay rights, or health care? Use her Feeling Thermometer as your dependent variable and then these three indices as your independent variables. Create a table suitable for Hillary (present both unstandardized and standardized slopes) and explain to her your results.

Exercise 5

We know that there is a relationship between conservatives and big business, but let's explore this relationship further. Use the big business feeling thermometer as your dependent variable and the conservative and liberal feeling thermometers as your independent variables. Run this regression twice: once for respondents with incomes less than or equal to $43,000 and once for respondents with incomes greater than $43,000. Create a table that presents unstandardized and standardized coefficients for both models. Interpret your results.

Exercise 6

Using the PewShop data, determine which of these factors has the largest impact on the use of technology in shopping: sex, age, or race (white/black). Create a table that presents unstandardized and standardized coefficients. Interpret your results.

Exercise 7 (Answer Available in Appendix D)

Using the PewShop data, determine which of these factors has the largest impact on the ownership of technology (i.e., the Technology Index): whether one is a parent, family income, or education (use all the recoded variables for these). Create a table that presents unstandardized and standardized coefficients. Interpret your results.

Exercise 8

Using the PewHealth data, determine which of these factors have the largest impact on the Health Conditions Index: age, recoded education, and recoded income. Create a table that presents unstandardized and standardized coefficients. Interpret your results.

Exercise 9

Using the PewHealth data, determine which of these factors have the largest impact on the Internet Health Use Index: age, recoded education, and recoded sex. Create a table that presents unstandardized and standardized coefficients. Interpret your results.

Exercise 10 (Answer Available in Appendix D)

Using the PewHealth data, run a regression with the Cellphone Use Index as your dependent variable, and then recoded education and recoded family income as your independent variables. In the regression dialog box, click on the "Statistics" button and ask for Descriptive statistics. Once you get your results, use the beta shortcut formula to show, by hand, how you get from the unstandardized coefficients to the betas.

Exercise 11

Use the PewKids dataset to run a single regression model to see which of these variables has the largest effect on family income: parent's age, parent's education, or parent's sex. Create a table that presents unstandardized and standardized coefficients. Interpret your results.

Exercise 12

Use the PewKids dataset to run a single regression model to see which of these variables has the largest effect on the number of devices the child has used the internet on: child's age, child's sex, or family income. Create a table that presents unstandardized and standardized coefficients. Interpret your results.

Exercise 13

Use the Western and Eastern European countries of the WVS dataset to run two models: one with the euthanasia variable as the dependent variable and one with the abortion variable as the dependent variable. In both models, use ATTEND and PRAYMED as the independent variables. Describe the results, paying attention to the betas.

Exercise 14

Using the WVS dataset, run a regression with the "% of country that approves of a woman being a single parent" variable (WSNGLPAR) and three independent variables in a single model: DIVORCE, ABORT, and HOMOSEX. Contrast the betas and the levels of statistical significance among the independent variables.

Exercise 15 (Answer Available in Appendix D)

If a high percentage of a country participates in sports, does this affect the level of the country's health and happiness? Run two simple regression equations, both of which use the "% participation in sports or recreation group" as the independent variable. For one equation, use the HAPPY variable as your dependent variable. For the other equation, use the HEALTH variable as your dependent variable. Contrast the betas to answer the question, Does sport have any larger effect on health or happiness?

## Chapter 12

DIFFERENT SLOPES FOR DIFFERENT FOLKS: INTERACTION EFFECTS

This chapter covers . . .

. . . which research questions lead us to looking at interaction effects

. . . how interaction and elaborated crosstabs are related

. . . interaction effects between a dichotomy and a ratio-level variable

. . . interaction effects between two dichotomies

. . . interaction effects between two ratio-level variables

. . . how researchers used interactions to study religion and political participation

. . . how researchers used interactions to study work-related guilt

INTRODUCTION

Some friends of ours were supposed to visit us in a few weeks with their three young children. Unfortunately, they just informed us that they were canceling their trip. It seems their two-year-old is not quite ready for the road, as her terrible-twos behavior on a recent weekend had proved to them. Let's face it: children change your life. Stereotypically, a childless couple has all the time in the world to hang out, pursue their hobbies, see movies, and do whatever they want to. A child comes along, and pretty much all their free time disappears. First, there are diapers, then play dates, then carpools to numerous activities.

The General Social Survey actually provides us a way to document this, as it occasionally asks this question: "After an average work day, about how many hours do you have to relax or pursue activities that you enjoy?" Following is a regression model that uses hours to relax as the dependent variable, with number of children and hours worked as the independent variables. I restricted the sample to respondents 50 years and younger, as those are the people who are likely to have children still in the home. Unfortunately, the GSS didn't include this question in the 2012 version, so I had to go back to the 2010 version:

■ Exhibit 12.1: The Effects of Children and Hours Worked on Relaxation Time

Dependent Variable: Hours Respondent Has to Relax Per Day	
Independent Variable	Slope
Number of children	−0.26***
Hours worked per week	0.03***
Constant	4.90
	$R^2 = 0.05$
	$n = 773$

***$p < .001$ (two-tailed test).
Source: GSS 2010 data.

The effect of children is in the expected direction: for each additional child you have, your free time decreases by 0.26 hours per day. Now we'll bring gender into the picture. Historically, women who work outside the home come home from their jobs, only to have a "second shift" of work to do: taking care of the kids and doing housework. I added sex into the regression model:

■ Exhibit 12.2: The Effects of Children, Hours Worked, and Sex on Relaxation Time

Dependent Variable: Hours Respondent Has to Relax Per Day	
Independent Variable	Slope
Number of children	−0.25***
Hours worked per week	0.03***
Sex (F = 0, M = 1)	0.51**
Constant	4.80
	$R^2 = 0.06$
	$n = 773$

**$p < .01$, ***$p < .001$ (two-tailed test)
Source: GSS 2010 data.

Another effect that we would expect: given a man and a woman who each work the same hours and have the same number of children, the man will have half an hour more free time per day.

So we know that number of children and sex affect relaxation time, but now we're going to add an additional possibility, which will sound a little confusing at first, but before long you will understand what's going on. Our question now is not "Do children affect relaxation time?" nor is it "Does sex affect relaxation time?" Rather, it is "Does sex affect how number of children affects relaxation time?" Or, to phrase this question another way, "Does number of children affect relaxation time *differently* for men than for women?"

Well, if the "second shift" holds true, we should see different effects for men and for women. Adding a child should produce a greater reduction in relaxation time for women than it does for men. However, our latest regression model doesn't allow us to observe this. It gives us the separate effects of number of children and of sex, but it doesn't tell us how these variables interact. We know our independent variables each have an effect, but do they interact in interesting ways to produce an additional effect? This is the key question of this chapter, and to address it, we're going to explore what are called **interaction effects**. Such effects are among the cooler findings these days in the social sciences. Unfortunately, some think that interaction effects are difficult to interpret. This chapter shows that this is not necessarily the case, especially if you take a graphical approach to describing the interaction effect.

INTERCHAPTER CONNECTION: ELABORATED CROSSTABS

It is possible to examine relationships akin to regression interaction effects by using elaborated crosstabulations. We explored elaboration in earlier chapters, but let me refresh your memory and make some connections. Let's stick with the sex/children/ relaxation example from earlier. We know that number of children affects relaxation time, but now we want to elaborate this relationship to see if, among various subgroups, the relationship is stronger, is weaker, or even remains at all. So we run two crosstabulations of number of children and relaxation time: one for men and one for women. To accomplish this, I collapsed the children and relaxation time variables into three categories each (otherwise, I would have had laughably large crosstabs). I also used only those respondents who were 50 years old or younger and who were working full time.

■ Exhibit 12.3: Sex, Children, and Relaxation Time: Elaboration with Crosstabs

RESPONDENTS SEX			Number of Children			Total
			0 kids	1–2 kids	3+ kids	
MALE	Hours to Relax Per Day	0–1 hrs	13 10%	18 16%	12 16%	43 13%
		2–3 hrs	52 40%	61 53%	24 32%	137 43%
		more than 3 hrs	66 50%	37 32%	38 51%	141 44%
	Total		131 100%	116 100%	74 100%	321 100%
FEMALE	Hours to Relax Per Day	0–1 hrs	12 12%	49 33%	19 36%	80 26%
		2–3 hrs	37 36%	54 36%	21 40%	112 37%
		more than 3 hrs	55 53%	45 30%	13 25%	113 37%
	Total		104 100%	148 100%	53 100%	305 100%

Chi-Square Tests

RESPONDENTS SEX		Value	df	Asymp. Sig. (2-sided)
MALE	Pearson Chi-Square	12.763	4	0.012
FEMALE	Pearson Chi-Square	24.303	4	0.000

Source: GSS 2010 data.

It is easy to see from the crosstabs what is going on. There is a stronger relationship in the women's crosstab than in the men's crosstab. Look across the top row in the men's crosstab: the percentages don't really indicate a trend: as number of children goes up, the percentage of men with little free time goes from 10% to 16% to 16%. In the women's crosstab, the relationship is clearer: 12%, 33%, 36%. Now look across the bottom row of cells, where we would expect that as number of children goes up, the percentages of people with lots of free time should decrease. Among men, this is not really the case: the percentage goes from 50% to 32%, but then back up to 51%.

Among women, the relationship is clear: 53%, 30%, 25%. The chi-square tests reiterate this: although the men's crosstab does achieve statistical significance, it does so just barely: $p < .05$. The women's crosstab is statistically significant at the $p < .001$ level. Although elaboration with crosstabs is quite simple, and gives us some idea where the relationship most exists, it has limitations. First, if you use variables that have several categories, you will end up with unwieldy crosstabs. The preceding crosstabs are 3×3, with nine cells each. But this involved a lot of collapsing, which gets rid of a lot of detail. Another limitation is that it is difficult to control for other variables. For example, I wanted to take hours worked into account, but to do this with a crosstab, I simply restricted the sample to full-time workers. I could have run separate crosstabs for those working full-time, part-time, or not working outside the home, but then the frequencies in my crosstab cells would have started to get really small. Regression with interaction effects is totally doable (once you get the hang of it), and much prettier (oh, the graphs we're going to draw!).

CREATING THE INTERACTION EFFECT

To observe the interaction between two independent variables, we need to take those variables and create what is called an *interaction term*. So, if we want to look at the interaction between sex and number of children, we create an interaction term called INTSEXCHILD, which is simply the *product* of the two independent variables:

SEX:	males coded as 1, females coded as 0
CHILD:	measured in number of children
INTSEXCHILD:	SEX × CHILD

At first, it may sound odd to say that we are going to multiply variables together. You know how to multiply numbers together, but *variables*? Here are four examples using hypothetical cases:

▪ **Exhibit 12.4: Examples of the Interaction Term**

Sample Cases	SEX	# CHILDREN	INTSEXCHILD
Female Case 1	0	1	0 × 1 = 0
Female Case 2	0	5	0 × 5 = 0
Male Case 1	1	2	1 × 2 = 2
Male Case 2	1	4	1 × 4 = 4

Notice that, because the women are coded as 0, their values for the interaction term end up as 0, regardless of their number of children. The value of the men's interaction term in this example is simply their number of children.

To see if the interaction term has a significant effect, we put the interaction variable into a regression with the two original independent variables. I like to call the two variables that go together to create the interaction effect the **parent variables** and their slopes the parent slopes: they are getting together, and out of their union comes a new variable. As in the previous regression models, we will control for the number of hours people work by including this variable in the regression model.

GSS EXAMPLE: SEX, NUMBER OF CHILDREN, AND RELAXATION

Here is the resulting regression model:

■ **Exhibit 12.5: Explaining Hours to Relax with an Interaction Term**

Dependent Variable: Hours Respondent Has to Relax Per Day	
Independent Variable	Slope
Sex (F = 0, M = 1)	0.06
Number of children	−0.43***
Interaction: Sex × # of children	0.35**
Hours worked per week	−0.03***
Constant	5.10
	$R^2 = 0.06$
	$n = 773$

**p < .01. ***p < .001 (two-tailed test).
Source: GSS 2010 data.

The first slope may seem like quite a shock, since it contradicts a result we saw earlier in the chapter: it implies that sex has no effect at all, as the slope does not reach significance at the $p < .05$ level. However, here is an important point regarding the interpretation of slopes when using interaction effects: it is necessary to interpret the interaction slope and its parent slopes *as a group* in order to understand what is going on. They've got a story to tell, but they must tell this story together, not separately. And the way we're going to interpret this interaction story is to draw a set of line graphs. Using these slopes, let's first create an equation:

RelaxTime = 5.10 + 0.06(SEX) − 0.43(#KIDS) + 0.35(SEX)(#KIDS) − 0.03(HRS)

Notice how I've put in the interaction term: it's the product of three things: the slope for the interaction term, the value of sex, and the number of children. Notice also that I've included the slope for sex, even though it was not statistically significant. This is necessary for interpreting the complete interaction effect. So, although it is not statistically significant, we include it in the equation along with the other parent slope and the interaction slope (which, as you notice, is quite statistically significant). Now we plug in some examples. We'll do four: two men and two women. We're going to draw a line for men and a line for women, and to draw a line we need two points. We'll have all four people work full-time jobs of 40 hours per week (that is, we'll hold hours worked constant). We'll need to vary number of children, so we'll put in zero kids for two of the people and six kids for the other two:

$$\text{RelaxTime}_{F, \text{0kids}} = 5.10 + 0.06(0) - 0.43(0) + 0.35(0)(0) - 0.03(40) = 3.90$$
$$\text{RelaxTime}_{F, \text{6kids}} = 5.10 + 0.06(0) - 0.43(6) + 0.35(0)(6) - 0.03(40) = 1.32$$
$$\text{RelaxTime}_{M, \text{0kids}} = 5.10 + 0.06(1) - 0.43(0) + 0.35(1)(0) - 0.03(40) = 3.96$$
$$\text{RelaxTime}_{M, \text{6kids}} = 5.10 + 0.06(1) - 0.43(6) + 0.35(1)(6) - 0.03(40) = 3.48$$

With these four points, we get the following lines:

■ **Exhibit 12.6: Illustrating the Interaction Effect between Sex and Number of Children**

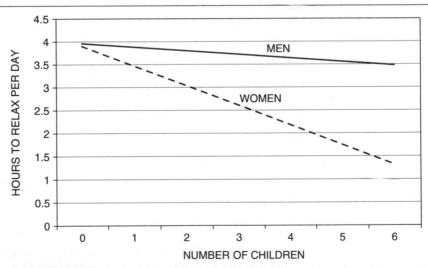

Source: GSS 2010 data.

So here's the story: when they have zero children, men and women essentially have the same amount of time to relax: just less than 4 hours per day. However, as children start to arrive in a household, men and women are differentially affected by this. Although children produce somewhat of a decrease in free time among men, the decrease in free time among women is much more drastic. By the time there are six children involved, the time gap between men and women has grown to more than 2 hours ($3.48 - 1.32 = 2.16$).

Let's examine more closely what is going on here on a child-by-child basis. We'll look at what happens as we move from zero children to one child. Exhibit 12.7 is essentially a magnified version of the left side of the full graph in Exhibit 12.6:

■ **Exhibit 12.7: The Interaction Effect, Year to Year**

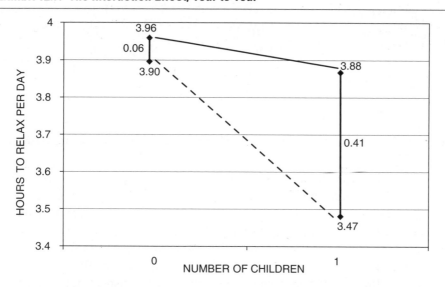

With zero children, women are only 0.06 hours behind men. With one child, women are 0.41 hours behind. So, with an additional child, women fall behind an additional $0.41 - 0.06 = 0.35$. Notice that this is the value of the interaction slope. For every additional child, women fall behind 0.35 hours more.

With the way we coded sex (with F = 0, M = 1), this is how the interaction effect is manifested: for each additional child, the men initially get 0.43 hours taken away from them, but then the interaction effect "gives them back" 0.35 of this, so that the decline per child for men is a mere 0.08. Women, however, get the full 0.43 hours taken away per child.

What if, for the sake of driving the point home, we had coded sex the *opposite* way, with F = 1 and M = 0? I reran the regression equation this way, and here are the models side by side:

■ **Exhibit 12.8: Two Versions of the Interaction Effect Models**

Dependent Variable: Hours Respondent Has to Relax Per Day

Independent Variable	Model 1: Sex (F = 0, M = 1)	Model 2: Sex (M = 0, F = 1)
	Slope	Slope
Sex	0.06	–0.06
Number of children	–0.43***	–0.08
Interaction: Sex × # of children	0.35**	–0.35**
Hours worked per week	–0.03***	–0.03***
Constant	5.10	5.16
	$R^2 = 0.06$	$R^2 = 0.06$
	$n = 773$	$n = 773$

**p < .01, ***p < .001 (two-tailed test)
Source: GSS 2010 data.

Although the slopes are different for the two models, they tell exactly the same story. In Model 2, both men and women get 0.08 taken away from them per child, but because of the interaction effect, women get an additional 0.35 taken away from them on top of the original 0.08, whereas the men do not get this taken away. One more thing to note: notice that in Model 2, the "number of children" parent slope is not statistical significant, whereas in Model 1 it was. Remember that with interaction effects, the statistical significance of the parent slopes isn't important; it's the statistical significance of the interaction slope that matters.

GSS EXAMPLE: WORK HOURS AND JOB SATISFACTION

We'll stick with sex as one of our parent variables, but this time, we'll move "hours worked per week" up to parent variable status. I created an interaction effect between these two variables:

■ **Exhibit 12.9: Examples of the Interaction Term**

Sample Cases	SEX	HOURS WORKED	INTSEXHRSWK
Female Case 1	0	25	$0 \times 25 = 0$
Female Case 2	0	40	$0 \times 40 = 0$
Male Case 1	1	15	$1 \times 15 = 15$
Male Case 2	1	55	$1 \times 55 = 55$

I'm not exactly sure what my expectation was here, but I do know that sometimes men and women think about their jobs differently, and so their job satisfaction might be differently affected by hours worked. Here is the regression model:

■ **Exhibit 12.10: Explaining Job Satisfaction with an Interaction Term**

Dependent Variable: Job Satisfaction (0=very dissatisfied — 6=very satisfied)	
Independent Variable	Slope
Sex (M = 0, F = 1)	0.59*
Hours Worked Per Week	0.015**
Interaction: Sex × hrs worked	–0.012*
Constant	3.71
	$R^2 = 0.02$
	$n = 761$

$*p < .05$, $***p < .001$ (two-tailed test)
Source: GSS 2012 data.

Before we draw some graphs, take a minute to examine the regression model to see if you can figure out what the interaction effect is saying.

▪ **Exhibit 12.11: Illustrating the Interaction between Sex and Hours Worked**

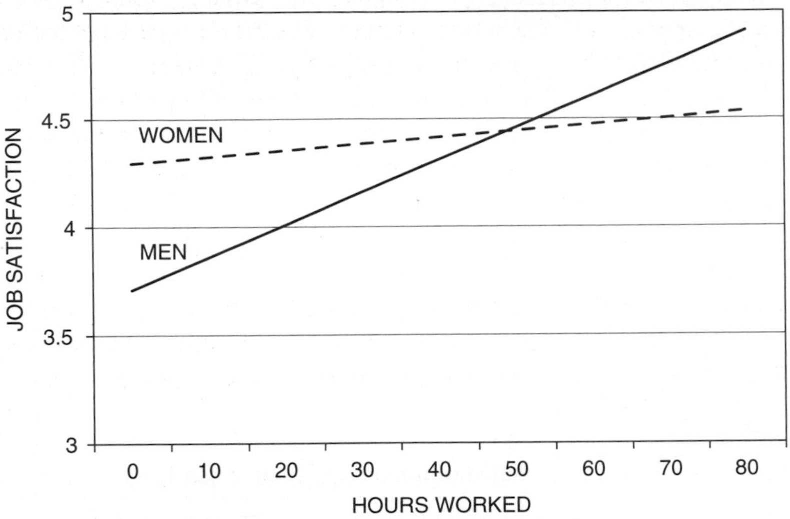

Source: GSS 2012 data.

A confession: I adjusted the satisfaction axis to make the graph lie a bit so that you could observe the interaction effect more clearly. Hours worked does have a different effect for men and women. It certainly doesn't tell the whole story, because a mere 2% of the variation is explained. However, men who work few hours are less satisfied with their jobs than are women who work few hours. As hours are added on, men's job satisfaction goes up more quickly than does women's satisfaction. By the time we're at 50 hours, the men's line surpasses the women's line. Men working long hours are more satisfied with their jobs than are women who work long hours. One potential explanation for this is that, connected to the children example earlier, women appreciate the flexibility of part-time work more than men do, so they don't mind shorter work hours, but they do mind really long work hours.

GSS EXAMPLE: CIVIL RIGHTS AND RACE

Please visit the book's website (www.routledge.com/cw/linneman) to view a "From Idea to Presentation" video of this example.

Every year that it is conducted, the GSS asks what are affectionately referred to (well, at least by me) as the civil rights questions. It asks about various types of people and about whether such people should be able to teach at a college or university. It asks if such a person wrote a book espousing his or her views, should it be removed from the public library. It asks if such a person wanted to make a public speech about his or her views, should the person be allowed to. Some of the groups it asks about are racists, homosexuals, communists, and anti-religionists. For the most part, according to GSS trends, Americans have been moving toward protecting these rights. For example, in 1973, just fewer than half of the GSS respondents would allow a homosexual to teach at a college, but by 2012, this rose to 85%. In 1973, 45% of the respondents wanted to remove the communist's book from the library, and by 2012, this fell to 27%. In 1973, 66% would allow an anti-religionist to speak, and by 2012 this rose to 78%. However, in 2008, the GSS added a new set of these college-library-speech questions, this time about "a Muslim clergyman who preaches hatred of the United States." Wow. As you might imagine, this really stretched people's willingness to extend these rights. In 2012, only 34% said they would allow such a person to teach at a college, 50% said to remove his or her book from the public library, and 56% said such a person should not be allowed to give a public speech.

I took the 2012 data from the "U.S.-hating Muslim clergyman" questions and combined these three questions into a small index that ranged from 0 (no rights support) to 3 (full support). As you can see, this results in an index with a lot of variation:

■ **Exhibit 12.12: Index of Rights Support for Anti-U.S. Muslim**

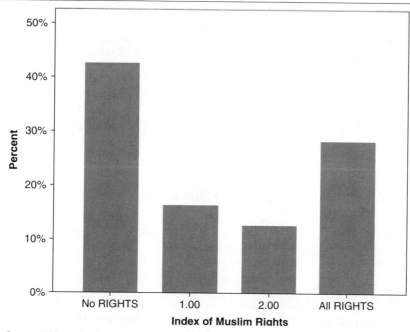

Source: GSS 2012 data.

I wondered what explains such variation. I decided to examine the roles of education, race, and the interaction of the two. I also included attendance at religious services per month. Here is my resulting regression model:

■ **Exhibit 12.13: Explaining Rights Support with an Interaction Term**

Dependent Variable: Support for Anti-U.S. Muslim Rights (0 = none—3 = full)	
Independent Variable	Slope
Education in years	0.14***
Race (W = 0, NW = 1)	0.74*
Interaction: Educ × Race	−0.08**
# times relig. attend/month	−0.07***
Constant	−0.46
	$R^2 = 0.13$
	$n = 1251$

$*p < .05, **p < .01, ***p < .001$ (two-tailed test)
Source: GSS 2012 data.

The interaction term is highly significant. But to get a true feel for what these relationships look like, we need a graph. For the graph, I held religious attendance constant at two times per month:

■ **Exhibit 12.14: Illustrating the Muslim Model Interaction Effect**

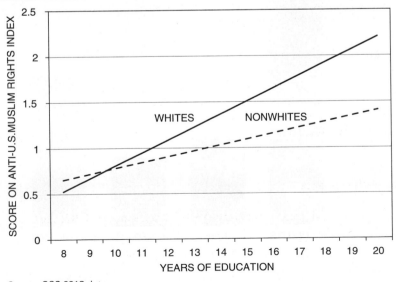

Source: GSS 2012 data.

The effect of education is stronger for whites than for non-whites. At the low end of the education spectrum, whites and nonwhites don't differ much, but as education increases, white support for anti–U.S. Muslim rights increases twice as fast as support among nonwhites does.

GSS EXAMPLE: RACE, SEX, AND RELIGION

All of the interactions we have looked at thus far have involved interactions between a dichotomy and a ratio-level variable. For example, we interacted sex (a dichotomy) with number of children (ratio-level variable); we interacted race (collapsed into a dichotomy) with years of education (ratio-level variable). This is the most common interaction you will see or use. However, there are other combinations. Here is a simple example that interacts two dichotomies: sex and a black/white race variable. I was interested in what determines attendance at religious services. I know that sex plays a role, as does race, but I wondered if, in addition to these effects, they interacted in any way. I also included age in the model. Here are the regression results:

■ **Exhibit 12.15: Explaining Religious Attendance with an Interaction Term**

Dependent Variable: Number of Times Attend Religious Services Per Month	
Independent Variable	Slope
Sex (M = 0, F = 1)	0.41***
Race (W = 0, B = 1)	0.58*
Interaction: Sex × Race	0.74*
Age	0.02***
Constant	0.29
	$R^2 = 0.07$
	$n = 1,767$

*$p < .05$, ***$p < .001$ (two-tailed test)
Source: GSS 2012 data.

This gives us the equation

$$attendance = 0.29 + 0.41(sex) + 0.58(race) + 0.74(sex)(race) + 0.02(age)$$

And now for some examples (I held age constant at 50, which was very close to the mean age):

a 50-year-old white man:

attendance = 0.29 + 0.41(0) + 0.58(0) + 0.74(0)(0) + 0.02(50) = 1.29

a 50-year-old white woman:

attendance = 0.29 + 0.41(1) + 0.58(0) + 0.74(1)(0) + 0.02(50) = 1.70

a 50-year-old black man:

attendance = 0.29 + 0.41(0) + 0.58(1) + 0.74(0)(1) + 0.02(50) = 1.87

a 50-year-old black woman:

attendance = 0.29 + 0.41(1) + 0.58(1) + 0.74(1)(1) + 0.02(50) = 3.02

Black women far surpass the other groups. In the calculation, not only do they get the value for the race slope, and the value for the sex slope, but they also are the only group to get the interaction effect (because they are the only group without a zero in that interaction product). Understanding interaction effects is a straightforward endeavor if you simply run some examples.

GSS EXAMPLE: AGE, EDUCATION, AND SEXUAL ACTIVITY

In Chapter 8, there appeared to be something interesting going on involving sexual activity, age, and education. Among 30-somethings, education had a negative relationship with sexual frequency. Among 60-somethings, education had a positive relationship with sexual frequency. Can we use an interaction effect to analyze these relationships more closely? Uh oh. Both of these independent variables are at the ratio level. One option is to dichotomize age: create a variable with the 30-somethings coded as 0 and the 60-somethings coded as 1, and make everyone else go away. Or we could dichotomize education by using the median to divide people into two groups. Or we could go all in and use the original ratio-level variables and see what happens. You were afraid I was going to say that, weren't you? Yes, we're going to create an interaction effect with two ratio-level variables. Here is the regression model (just as in the previous sexual activity example, I'm using only people aged 30–69):

■ **Exhibit 12.16: Explaining Sexual Activity with an Interaction Effect**

Dependent Variable: Number of Times Have Sex Per Month	
Independent Variable	Slope
Education in years	−1.03***
Age in years	−0.43***
Interaction: Educ. × Age	0.019**
Constant	27.23
R^2	0.12
	$n = 877$

**$p < .01$, ***$p < .001$.
Source: GSS 2012 data, respondents aged 30 to 69.

The interaction effect is certainly statistically significant. But how on earth do you interpret it? Examples, of course! With education going from 0 to 20, and age going from 30 to 69, if we did every possible combination, that would be 840 examples. How about 16 instead—four ages: 34, 45, 55, and 65, and four educational levels: 8, 12, 16, 20. This should give us a good idea of what is going on. I plugged in these 16 combinations, and decided to go with a 3-D bar graph to illustrate the relationships:

■ **Exhibit 12.17: Illustrating the Sexual Activity Interaction Effect**

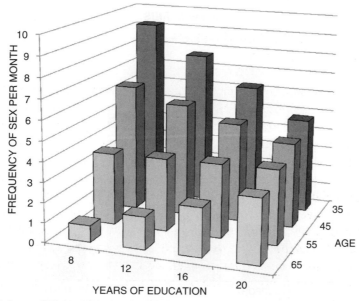

Source: GSS 2012 data for respondents ages 30 to 69.

This allows us to see clearly what is going on: among 30-somethings (and, to a lesser extent, among the 40-somethings), as education goes up, sexual frequency goes down. Among the 50-somethings, education doesn't seem to matter at all. Among 60-somethings, as education goes up, sexual frequency goes up. You could also interpret the graph another way: among those with little education, the effect of age is huge: younger people have lots of sex, while older people have very little sex. As education rises, the differences among the ages decreases. Any way you look at it, it's an interaction story, and that's what we want.

GSS EXAMPLE: KNOWING SOMEONE WITH AIDS

For our last GSS example, we turn to a matter of public policy. And we're turning back the clock. We go all the way back to 1988, when paranoia over AIDS was at its zenith. Because of the importance of AIDS at the time, the GSS asked a number of interesting questions about AIDS-related policies. Here are three of them, all of which were asked as dichotomous yes/no questions:

- Allow insurers to test applicants for AIDS.
- Have the government pay for all AIDS health care.
- Prohibit students with AIDS from attending public schools.

I put these three questions together into a 3-point index:

■ **Exhibit 12.18: Attitudes toward People with AIDS**

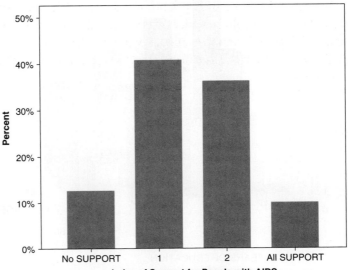

Source: GSS 1988 data.

Notice that there is a good deal of variation. Our goal now is to try to explain at least some of this variation. An important independent variable is personal knowledge: does knowing someone with AIDS affect how one feels about AIDS policies? In addition, I want to see how this variable interacts with another variable: political views (ranging from 0, extremely conservative, to 6, extremely liberal). Are liberals and conservatives differently affected by knowing someone with AIDS? Here are the regression results:

■ **Exhibit 12.19: The Interaction of Political Views and Knowing a Person with AIDS**

Dependent Variable: AIDS Policy Index (0 = no support, 3 = full support)	
Independent Variable	Coefficient
Political Views	0.11***
Know Someone w/ AIDS?	−0.45**
Interaction Effect	0.23***
Constant	1.11
	$R^2 = 0.09$
	$n = 544$

Note: Political Views measured 0 = extremely conservative to 6 = extremely liberal.
***$p < .001$ (two-tailed test)
Source: GSS 1988 data.

As with the other interaction effects, it is not a good idea to try to interpret each slope individually. For example, if we tried to interpret the slope for the variable "Know Someone with AIDS?" we would conclude that people who know someone with AIDS have more anti-AIDS attitudes than do people who don't know someone with AIDS, and this is unlikely to be true. So, as before, we draw a set of line graphs to get a real feel for what is going on:

▨ **Exhibit 12.20: Illustrating the Interaction of Political Views and Knowing a Person with AIDS**

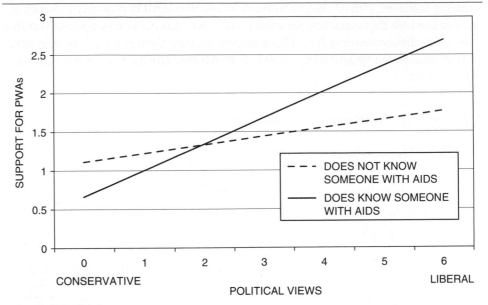

Source: GSS 1988 data.

What the graphs give us is an interesting story. Among those who do not know someone with AIDS, attitudes are relatively uniform: conservatives and liberals do not differ by much (the political extremes differ by only two-thirds of a point on the index). Knowing someone with AIDS, however, amplifies the effect of political views, creating more extreme differences between conservatives and liberals. An extreme conservative who knows someone with AIDS and an extreme liberal who knows someone with AIDS differ by more than 2 points on the 3-point index.

LITERATURE EXAMPLE: RELIGION AND POLITICAL PARTICIPATION

Earlier, we found that African American women, and to some extent African American men, attend religious services more than other groups. Some argue that religious participation can lead to greater political participation: as one becomes involved in religious activities, one can gain valuable skills that can then be used in political activities. But is this effect the same for women as it is for men? Isn't that the quintessential interaction question? Belinda Robnett and James Bany use interaction effects to great, well, effect in their article "Gender, Church Involvement, and African-American Political

Participation," which appeared in the journal *Sociological Perspectives* in 2011. They used the perfectly suited National Black Politics Study to investigate whether African American men are indeed more politically active than African American women are (Robnett and Bany found that they are), and what role does religious participation play in this difference? Exhibit 12.21 is an excerpt from their Table 3. Yes, it involves a set of four nested models and two sets of interaction effects, but don't worry, we'll get through it.

Exhibit 12.21: Explaining African American Political Participation

Dependent Variable: Political Activity (0 = none — *7* = all types)

Independent Variable	Model 1	Model 2	Model 3	Model 4
Gender (F = 1)	–0.483**	–0.643***	–0.250	0.055
Church Active (Y = 1)	—	0.984***	1.440***	1.031***
Interaction: G × C.A.	—	—	–0.802**	–0.549*
Church Political Activity	—	—	—	0.494***
Ineraction: G × C.P.A.	—	—	—	–0.160*
R^2	0.092	0.158	0.168	0.282

Note: n = 1,206. C.P.A. = church political activity; C.A. = church activity. C.P.A. is measured on a scale from 0 (church is not politically active) to 5 (church is very politically active).
***$p < .001$ (two-tailed test).
Source: Adapted from Robnett and Bany (2011).

Each model adds a layer to the story. Model 1 tells us that men are indeed more politically active than women: because women are coded 1, they get this slope of 0.483 taken away from their political activity. In Model 2, the authors add whether or not the respondent is active in their church (besides just going to services). Being active in your church raises your political activity by nearly a point. Elsewhere in the article, they show that women are more active in their church. Therefore, when we control for church activity, in a sense, raising men's church activity up to the level of women's church activity, the gender difference in political activity grows to 0.643. Model 3 introduces the interaction effect between gender and church activity. Although we're not using the full equation, doing some examples helps us figure out what the interaction effect means:

equation: –0.250(gender) + 1.440(active) – 0.802(gender)(active)

woman who is not church active: $-0.250(1) + 1.440(0) - 0.802(1)(0) = -0.250$
man who is not church active: $-0.250(0) + 1.440(0) - 0.802(0)(0) = 0$
woman who is church active: $-0.250(1) + 1.440(1) - 0.802(1)(1) = 0.388$
man who is church active: $-0.250(0) + 1.440(1) - 0.802(0)(1) = 1.440$

We see that being church active raises men's political activity much more than women's. Model 4 introduces both the church political activity variable and its interaction with gender. Although it's getting complicated, we carefully construct the part of the equation we have and plug in some examples:

equation:

$$0.055(\text{gender}) + 1.031(\text{active}) - 0.549(\text{gender})(\text{active}) + 0.494(\text{church}) - 0.160(\text{gender})(\text{church})$$

active woman in a nonpolitical church:

$$0.055(1) + 1.031(1) - 0.549(1)(1) + 0.494(0) - 0.160(1)(0) = 0.537$$

active man in a nonpolitical church:

$$0.055(0) + 1.031(1) - 0.549(0)(1) + 0.494(0) - 0.160(0)(0) = 1.031$$

active woman in a very political church:

$$0.055(1) + 1.031(1) - 0.549(1)(1) + 0.494(5) - 0.160(1)(5) = 2.207$$

active man in a very political church:

$$0.055(0) + 1.031(1) - 0.549(0)(1) + 0.494(5) - 0.160(0)(5) = 3.501$$

The examples show that being in a political church has a smaller effect on women than it does on men. Therefore, although being active in one's church does raise political activity, it also has the unsavory effect of exacerbating the difference in African-American women's and African-American men's political participation.

LITERATURE EXAMPLE: GENDER, WORK, AND GUILT

There is an entire body of literature on the conflict between the demands of home and the demands of work. This topic is becoming all the more important now that many workers have smartphones that tether workers to their jobs outside of the office. Are women more affected by this work–home conflict than men are? Another perfect question for an interaction effect. Paul Glavin, Scott Schieman, and Sarah Reid explored this effect in their article "Boundary-Spanning Work Demands and Their Consequences for Guilt and Psychological Distress," which appeared in the *Journal of Health and Social Behavior* in 2011. They used data from the Work, Stress, and Health Survey, which asked 1,042 Americans about their work and home lives and the conflict between them. One of their dependent variables is guilt, which they measured quite simply as the number of days in the past week that the respondent said she felt guilty. Among the independent variables they use are

Gender: with males coded as 0, and females coded as 1

Work Contact: how often do work demands happen after normal work hours? ranges from 1 = never to 5 = once or more times a day

Work–Family Conflict: an index of how often work negatively affects family life, ranging from 1 = never to 5 = very often

Interaction between gender and work contact.

Here is an excerpt from their Table 2:

■ **Exhibit 12.22: Explaining Days of Guilt**

Dependent Variable: Number of Days in Past Week Felt Guilty

Independent Variable	Model 1	Model 2	Model 3
Gender (F = 1)	0.212	0.176	0.158
Work Contact	0.082	0.061	−0.063
Work–Family Conflict	—	0.305***	−0.302***
Interaction: Gender × Work Contact	—	—	0.215**
R^2	0.063	0.077	0.083

$*p < .05, **p < .01, ***p < .001$ (two-tailed test)
Source: Adapted from Glavin et al. (2011).

At first, just looking at Models 1 and 2, it seems that there is no gender difference in guilt, and work contact doesn't affect guilt. However, we want to concentrate on the interaction effect, which is statistically significant at the $p < .01$ level. To observe what the effect looks like, we'll do four examples (even though we don't have the full equation here). For work–family conflict, I'm plugging in the mean of 2.33 that they provide in the article:

Equation: Guilt = 0.158(gender) – 0.063(contact) + 0.302(conflict) + 0.215(gender) (contact)

Man with no work contact:

$$0.158\,(0) - 0.063(1) + 0.302(2.33) + 0.215(0)(1) = 0.64$$

Man with work contact once or more a day:

$$0.158(0) - 0.063(5) + 0.302(2.33) + 0.215(0)(5) = 0.39$$

Woman with no work contact:

$$0.158(1) - 0.063(1) + 0.302(2.33) + 0.215(1)(1) = 1.01$$

Woman with work contact once or more a day:

$$0.158(1) - 0.063(5) + 0.302(2.33) + 0.215(1)(5) = 1.62$$

From these examples, we see that as work contact goes up, a man's guilt goes down slightly, but a woman's guilt rises, meaning that when work comes home with them, women experience a higher level of guilt about this than men do. Here is a graph of the relationship, adapted from their article. In this graph, all of the other variables that I did not put in the abridged version are controlled for, and it includes the constant, so the numbers are slightly different from the examples earlier, but the story remains the same:

◼ **Exhibit 12.23: Illustrating the Interaction between Sex and Work Contact**

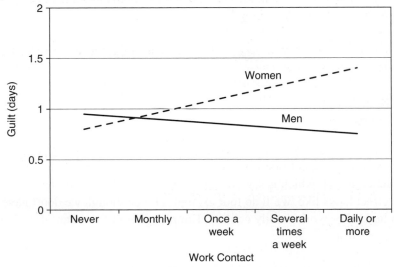

Source: Adapted from Glavin et al. (2011).

We started this chapter with an example that showed that women have less time to relax as their families grow larger, and this effect is much larger for women than for men. This literature example additionally shows that women whose work lives seep into their home lives are also more affected by this than men are.

CONCLUSION

I considered walloping you with more complicated interaction situations, such as those that involve three or more variables, but I decided to spare you this fun. The majority of interaction effects involve the interaction between two variables, so you now should be well equipped to understand many of those encounters. As I have said, interaction effects are among the more interesting things in current social science research, and people are using them more and more. For me, drawing those graphs is the quickest and easiest way to grasp what is going on. However you decide to grapple with them, be sure this is part of your plan.

SPSS DEMONSTRATION

Please visit the book's website (www.routledge.com/cw/linneman) to view a video of this demonstration.

In this demonstration, we'll use ANES data to address the question

Religious attendance affects attitudes toward abortion, but does this effect look the same for blacks as it does for whites?

Therefore, our interaction will be between race and religious attendance. Using the ANES data, our variables will be

XYdem_raceethWB
XYrelig_church

The interaction between these two: XYdem_raceethWB × XYrelig_church

To create the interaction, I go to the Compute room:

Transform ➔ Compute

In this room, I place our interaction variable name on the left and the product of the parent variables on the right:

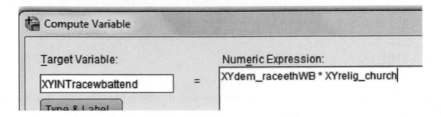

After creating the interaction term and giving it a label, I ran my regression using these three independent variables and the abortion index as my dependent variable. Here is the last box of SPSS output:

Coefficients[a]

Model		Unstandardized Coefficients		Standardized Coefficients		
		B	Std. Error	Beta	t	Sig.
1	(Constant)	41.509	0.329		126.170	0.000
	recoded raceeth (W=0, B=1)	-2.108	0.764	-0.051	-2.761	0.006
	Religious attendance times per month	-3.516	0.114	-0.515	-30.975	0.000
	Interaction: RaceWB and Attendance	1.929	0.219	0.186	8.815	0.000

a. Dependent Variable: Abortion Index

For your information, the R^2 for this regression was 0.20 and the sample size was 4,026. For example purposes, we can rewrite this output as an equation:

ABINDEX = 41.51 – 2.11(RACE) – 3.52(ATTEND) + 1.93(RACE)(ATTEND)

FROM OUTPUT TO PRESENTATION

It would be easy enough to calculate by hand various examples, but graphs are definitely the way to present interaction effects. I prefer Excel for these kinds of graphs, and it's pretty easy. First, let's take the preceding equation and write it out for whites and blacks, filling in the zeros and ones where they belong and doing a little math to make the equation as simple as possible:

WHITES:
ABINDEX = 41.51 − 2.11(0) − 3.52(ATTEND) + 1.93 (0)(ATTEND)
ABINDEX = 41.51 − 3.52(ATTEND)

BLACKS:
ABINDEX = 41.51 − 2.11(1) − 3.52(ATTEND) + 1.93(1)(ATTEND)
ABINDEX = 39.40 − 3.52(ATTEND) + 1.93(1)(ATTEND)
ABINDEX = 39.40 − 1.59(ATTEND)

This gives us two easy equations to plug into an Excel worksheet. I make a column for ATTEND and put the possible values—0 through 8—in it. Then I make a column for WHITE and a column for BLACK. In these columns, I put the equations to generate the predictions:

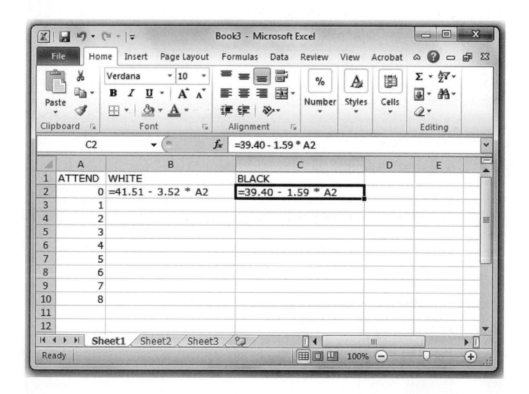

Notice that in cell B2 I placed the equation for whites whose ATTEND value is 0, and in cell C2, I placed the equation for blacks whose ATTEND value is 0. Now I'll copy this into the rest of the cells that follow and I'll get my predicted values:

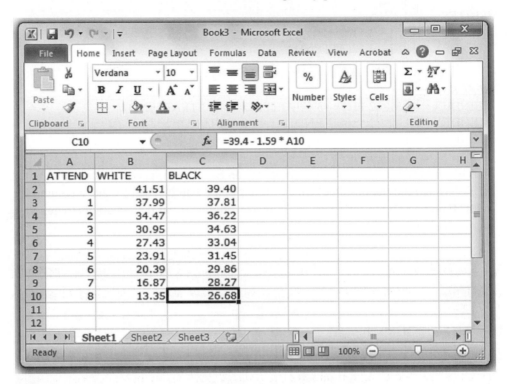

Now for the graph. If you highlight the cells in columns B and C (starting with headings WHITE and BLACK) and then click Insert Line Graph, Excel will create the graph:

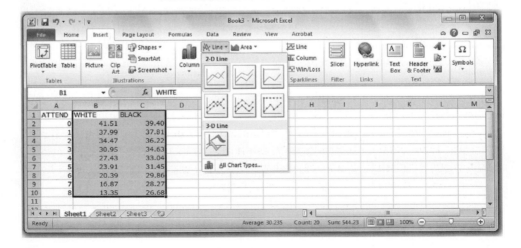

Here is the graph Excel gives you:

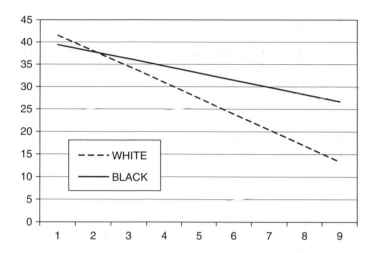

Now all we have left to do is change the numbers on the bottom axis: we don't want them to read 1 through 9; we want them to read 0 through 8 (the values on the ATTEND variable). To accomplish this, we do the following (this gets a bit tedious, so just bear with me):

1. Right-click on those numbers on the *x*-axis (any one of them).
2. Choose Select Data. A box pops up.
3. Click the "Edit" button underneath where it says "Horizontal (Category) Axis Labels." Another box pops up.
4. Click and drag over the cells that have the 0 through 8 (immediately to the left of the whites' and blacks' predicted scores). Excel will add some gibberish in the box under where it says "Axis label range," and it will immediately add these numbers to the graph.
5. Click the "OK" button in that box.
6. Click the "OK" button in the first box.

Of course, you may want to format things to your liking, but I'll leave that up to you. For example, sometimes I'll delete the legend and add words to the prediction lines. Making these graphs takes a bit of time, but once they're done they provide an important visual representation of the interaction effect. For example, we can see clearly from the graph the religious attendance has a much larger effect on abortion attitudes of whites than it does on abortion attitudes of blacks.

EXERCISES

Exercise 1 (Answer Available in Appendix D)

There is a huge wealth gap between whites and blacks. Even blacks who have high incomes have, for a variety of reasons, difficulty building wealth. Investigate this by creating an interaction model with the ANES Ownership Index as the dependent variable. For the independent variables, use race (the recoded version with whites and blacks only), income, and the interaction between these two variables. Create a table of your results; draw a graph that illustrates your results and interpret the graph.

Exercise 2

Whites and blacks typically have different ideas about the importance of working toward equality. People's incomes also affect how they feel about equality: those with higher incomes care a bit less about equality. But does income affect attitudes towards equality the same for whites and blacks? This calls for investigating a possible interaction effect. Create a regression equation using the ANES Egalitarianism Index as your dependent variable and three independent variables: recoded race (white/black), family income (in 1,000s), and the interaction between these two variables. Create a table of your results; then draw a graph that illustrates your results and interpret the graph.

Exercise 3

Does religiosity have the same effect on attitudes toward feminism for women as it does for men? Use the ANES feminist feeling thermometer as the dependent variable. For the independent variable use the recoded sex variable, the recoded religious attendance variable, and the interaction between the two. Create a table of your results; then draw a graph that illustrates your results and interpret the graph.

Exercise 4

There's a good chance that men and women may have different attitudes toward women working. But does how much men and women work affect these attitudes as well, and does this effect differ for men and women? Using the ANES Women Working Index, run a regression using the recoded sex variable, the original hours worked variable, and the interaction between these two. Create a table of your results; then draw a graph that illustrates your results and interpret the graph.

Exercise 5

Do political views and income interact in interesting ways with regard to how people feel about income inequality? Run a regression using the ANES Income Inequality Concern Index as your dependent variable. As your independent variables, use the recoded political views variable, family income in 1,000s, and the interaction between the two. Create a table of your results. Note that these two variables are both ratio-level variables (well, political view is a pseudo-ratio). So for the graph you should make, I suggest you create three lines: one for liberals (political views = 0), one for moderates (political views = 3), and one for conservatives (political views = 6). Explain your graph.

Exercise 6

We've seen using the PewShop data that whites have more technology than do blacks and that the more income you have, the more technology you have. But does race affect how income affects technology? Run a regression model with race (white/black), income in 1,000s, and the interaction between these two. Explain what you see in the output.

Exercise 7 (Answer Available in Appendix D)

We've seen using the PewShop data that people with smartphones use technology when shopping more than people without smartphones and that the older you are, the less likely you are to use technology when shopping, but do age and smartphone interact to create an additional effect? Run a regression model with age, the recoded smartphone variable, and the interaction between these two. Create a table of your results as well as a graph, and explain your graph.

Exercise 8

Does education have the same effect on technology acquisition for men as it does for women? Use the PewShop dataset to run a regression model with sex (recoded), education (recoded, in years), and the interaction between these two. Create a table of your results as well as a graph and explain your graph.

Exercise 9

Using the PewHealth dataset, address this question: As they age, do whites and blacks develop health conditions at the same rate? Use the Health Conditions Index as your dependent variable, and age, race (white/black), and the interaction between the two as your independent variables. Create a table of your results as well as a graph and explain your graph.

Exercise 10

Using the PewHealth dataset, address this question: does education have the same effect on men and women with regard to seeking out health information on the Internet? Use the Internet Health Use Index as your dependent variable, and recoded sex, recoded education, and the interaction between the two as your independent variables. Create a table of your results as well as a graph and explain your graph.

Exercise 11

Using the PewHealth dataset, address this question: does age have the same effect on men and women with regard to cell phone use? Use the Cellphone Use Index as your dependent variable, and recoded sex, age, and the interaction between the two as your independent variables. Create a table of your results as well as a graph and explain your graph.

Exercise 12 (Answer Available in Appendix D)

Perhaps gender—of both the checker and the checkee—plays a role in the extent to which a parent checks and blocks the technology of his or her child. Use the PewKids dataset to run a regression model that uses the Child's Perception of Parental Checking & Blocking Behavior as the dependent variable. For the independent variables, use parent's sex, child's sex, and the interaction between the two. Note: we are assuming here that the parent who responded to the survey is the one who the child thinks is doing the checking/blocking. Create a table of your results and run the following examples:

a. a male parent and a male child

b. a male parent and a female child

c. a female parent and a male child

d. a female parent and a female child

Interpret your results.

Exercise 13

A child's age likely has an effect on the number of ways he or she uses social networking websites, but is this effect the same for boys and girls? Investigate this (use the Child's Social Networking Uses Index). Create a table of your results as well as a graph and explain your graph. Although in the survey, children's ages only went from 12 through 17, just for the fun of it, extrapolate from this information and include in the graph ages 9 through 21.

Exercise 14

We know that health affects happiness: the healthier a country is, the happier it is. Does this relationship vary by country set? Using the WVS dataset, run a regression equation using HAPPY as the dependent variable, and three independent variables: HEALTH, COUNTRY2CAT, and the interaction between HEALTH and COUNTRY2CAT. Describe your results by calculating predicted percentage happiness for four examples:

- a European country with 40% healthy people
- a European country with 80% healthy people
- an Asian/African country with 40% healthy people
- an Asian/African country with 80% healthy people

Exercise 15

Religiosity affects attitude toward suicide: the more religious a country, the less support for suicide. Does this relationship vary by country set? Using the WVS dataset, run a regression equation using SUICIDE as the dependent variable, and three independent variables: RELGIMP, COUNTRY2CAT, and the interaction between RELGIMP and COUNTRY2CAT. Describe your results by calculating the predicted suicide support score for four examples:

- a European country with 10% religious people
- a European country with 90% religious people
- an Asian/African country with 10% religious people
- an Asian/African country with 90% religious people

Exercise 16 (Answer Available in Appendix D)

Does saving money lead to happiness? Does this relationship hold for all countries? Using the WVS dataset, run a regression equation using HAPPY as the dependent variable and three independent variables: FAMSAV, COUNTRY2CAT, and the interaction between FAMSAV and COUNTRY2CAT. Describe your results by calculating predicted percentage happiness for four examples:

- a European country where no one saves
- a European country where 60% of the country saves
- an Asian/African country where no one saves
- an Asian/African country where 60% of the country saves

Exercise 17

Now that we've covered nested models and interaction models, it's important to understand which kinds of scenarios will lead you to which kinds of models.

Below are several scenarios. For each one, describe whether you think it is a nested-model situation or an interaction situation and explain why.

a. A school district implements a new curriculum and then measures for an increase in test scores, but there is some concern that the curriculum might be better designed for schools that were already performing well and that it won't work well in schools that have performance problems.

b. If a sports team spends more money and brings in some big-name talent, is the improvement in the team's performance due to this talent, or is it due to the increased attendance at games that all players on the team respond to by performing better?

c. People in cities tend to be in better shape than do people in the suburbs. Is this because of the shorter commutes that people in cities have?

d. Who experiences more health benefits from having an active social network, men or women?

Chapter 13

EXPLAINING DICHOTOMOUS OUTCOMES: LOGISTIC REGRESSION

This chapter covers . . .

. . . why we need logistic regression

. . . what logistic regression does

. . . what odds ratios are

. . . how a researcher used logistic regression to study presidential approval

. . . how researchers used logistic regression to study attitudes toward global warming

INTRODUCTION

Think about all of the dependent variables we've used throughout this book so far. Income. Number of times people have sex in a month. Hours of television watched. Student grade point averages. They all have something in common: they are all ratio-level variables. They all start at zero and continue on from there: 1 hour, 2 hours, 5 hours, 10 hours, 24 hours of television a day (yes, there were actually five people in the 2012 GSS who claimed to watch television 24 hours a day). Much of the variation we want to explain involves ratio-level variables.

However, in social research we often want to explain phenomena that involve not ratio-level variables but dichotomies. There are things that people either do or don't do, did or didn't do, have or don't have, believe or don't believe. Some variables we may indeed be able to measure at the ratio level, but it makes more sense to think about them as dichotomies. For example, you might be interested in what explains how many times someone has been married: 0, 1, 2, 3, and 9. But for the vast majority of people it makes more sense to ask what explains *whether* they have ever been married. You might want to know what explains why people get involved in car accidents, and measure the dependent variable as 0 accidents, 1 accident, 2 accidents, 3 accidents, and 4 accidents, but thankfully few people would have had more than one serious accident. It would make more sense to ask people, "In the past five years, have you been in a serious car accident?" and to measure this variable as a dichotomy, where 0 = no and 1 = yes. Sometimes the GSS asks only one question about a topic of interest and offers only two possible responses to the question. For example, let's say we are interested in using the GSS to study variation in people's attitudes toward capital punishment. The GSS regularly asks only one question about capital punishment, called CAPPUN, which reads, "Do you favor or oppose the death penalty for persons convicted of murder?" There are just two valid response choices: favor or oppose. That's it. If we really wanted to use the GSS to study capital punishment, we would be limited to using this dichotomous variable as our dependent variable.

When we have a dichotomy as our dependent variable, we do not use regular linear regression. We use a special type of regression called **logistic regression**. But before we get to that, I first want to explain why using linear regression is not appropriate when our dependent variable is dichotomous.

REGULAR REGRESSION WITH A DICHOTOMOUS DEPENDENT VARIABLE: WHAT COULD POSSIBLY GO WRONG?

I won't go into all of the nasty mathematical details regarding why it's inappropriate to use regular regression when you have a dummy dependent variable. To tell the truth, sometimes people do still use it; however, it's frowned upon in most polite circles. When we use regular regression with a ratio-level variable, we then can use the resulting regression equation to make predictions about various types of cases. For example, using a regression equation, we could predict that someone with 16 years of education, on average, will make $50,000. Let's say we're trying to use regular regression with the CAPPUN variable I described earlier, with Oppose = 0 and Favor = 1. SPSS will gladly run the regression with whatever independent variables we want. Then we would use the resulting equation to make predictions about various types of cases and about how they would stand on capital punishment. However, what if the regression equation predicted these values for CAPPUN:

0.28, 0.50, −0.13, 1.15

What do these numbers mean? This is where using regular regression becomes problematic: it becomes difficult to comprehend these resulting predictions. Is the 0.28 a percentage, meaning 28%? Not really. Does the −0.13 mean that that respondent is really, really against the death penalty? And how would we interpret that 1.15, especially because the highest value that CAPPUN can take on is 1.00? Questions, questions, with no great answers available. That's why we need a different kind of regression.

WHAT LOGISTIC REGRESSION DOES

Logistic regression is that different kind of regression. This type of regression uses logarithms (bet you didn't see *that* coming) to elicit dependent variable scores that are limited to values between 0 and 1 (so, no −0.13 or 1.15). The value that we get at the end of a set of logistic regression calculations is actually the *percentage chance* that a particular case gets a "1" on the dependent variable. To use the capital punishment example, we'd be able to say something like "Such-and-such type of person has a 75% chance of supporting capital punishment" or "Such-and-such type of person has a 37% chance of supporting capital punishment." To accomplish this, we're going to use the natural logarithm called "*e*." The "natural" aspect of it is that there are things in nature, such as bacteria, that grow exponentially, and they all do so in similar ways. Remember good old pi? Pi represents something that occurs in the natural world: it's the ratio between any circle's circumference and diameter. Well, e is another one of those: it's the growth experienced by things that grow exponentially. Similar to pi being represented by a specific number (3.14159), *e* is also represented by a specific number: 2.71828. There's a whole lot of math going on behind the scenes here, but basically we're going to multiply *e* to the power of some number: e^z. When SPSS gives us a logistic regression model, we take it and use it to calculate what is called a z-value (not the same thing as a z-score). After this, we have one additional step: we take the z-value and use the following equation to calculate a probability:

$$p = \frac{e^z}{1 + e^z}$$

If $z = 0$, the value of e^z is 1, giving us a probability of 0.50 (1/2). If the value of z is less than 0, the value of e^z is less than 1, making the probability less than 0.5 (any number less than 1 divided by itself plus 1 is going to be less than 0.5). If we have a value of z that is greater than 0, the value of e^z is larger than 1, giving us a probability greater than 0.5 (any number larger than 1 divided by itself plus 1 is going to be greater than 0.5). If you try plugging in very large positive or negative values of z, you will see that the p this elicits is never lower than 0 or greater than 1. This is simply how the logarithm works. This may seem a bit overwhelming right now, but just think of it as regular regression with an extra step at the end (the step to get from a *z*-value to a probability). On to some examples!

GSS EXAMPLE: HOME OWNERSHIP

Here is a great example of a dichotomous dependent variable: what factors determine whether people own a home? Yes, some people "sort of" own their home, with the bank owning it until the mortgage is paid off. So we technically could think of this as a ratio-level variable: What percentage of your mortgage have you paid off? But generally we think of home ownership as a dichotomy: "Do you own or rent?" is a common question. Home ownership is viewed as part of the American dream. Let's look at an equation that tries to explain some of the variation in home ownership. I'm using GSS 2012 data with three independent variables:

▪ Age: My thinking here is that older people will be more likely to own their homes.
▪ Born in U.S.: I want to see if immigrants are less likely to own their homes, or if the American Dream is equally available to them.
▪ Party Identification: Are Republicans more likely to own their home than Democrats are?

▪ **Exhibit 13.1: Explaining Variation in Home Ownership**

Dependent Variable: Home Ownership (No = 0, Yes = 1)	
Independent Variable	Slope
Age in Years	0.03***
Born in U.S. (0 = No, 1 = Yes)	0.66***
Party ID (0 = Dem, 6 = Rep)	0.11**
Constant	−1.91
R^2	0.12
	$n = 1{,}241$

**p < .01. ***p < .001.
Source: GSS 2012 data.

This gives us the equation:

$$Z = -1.91 + 0.03(\text{AGE}) + 0.66(\text{BORNINUS}) + 0.11(\text{PARTYID})$$

Now, to illustrate the effects of each variable, we need to run some examples. Let's first compare a strong Democrat to a strong Republican. For the other variables, I'll put in the mean for age and the mode for the born variable, which is born in U.S.:

$$z_{\text{Democrat}} = -1.91 + 0.03(48) + 0.66(1) + 0.11(0) = 0.19$$

$$z_{\text{Republican}} = -1.91 + 0.03(48) + 0.66(1) + 0.11(6) = 0.85$$

Now we need to carry out the additional step involved in logistic regression: use a calculator or a computer to calculate the natural logarithm:

$$e^{0.19} = 1.21$$

$$e^{0.85} = 2.34$$

We then take these two values and use the formula to calculate the probabilities:

$$p_{\text{Democrat}} = \frac{1.21}{1 + 1.21} = 0.55$$

$$p_{\text{Republican}} = \frac{2.34}{1 + 2.34} = 0.70$$

Strong Republicans are more likely to own their homes than are strong Democrats: 70% versus 55%. Next, let's examine the effect of age. We'll make our hypothetical people political moderates who are U.S. born, and contrast a 25-year-old to a 75-year-old:

$$z_{\text{age}=25} = -1.91 + 0.03(25) + 0.66(1) + 0.11(3) = -0.17 \qquad p = .46$$

$$z_{\text{age}=75} = -1.91 + 0.03(75) + 0.66(1) + 0.11(3) = 1.33 \qquad p = .79$$

We observe what we would expect: a 25-year-old has less than 50% chance of owning a home, whereas a 75-year-old has a 79% chance. Finally, the effect of being an immigrant:

$$z_{\text{immigrant}} = -1.91 + 0.03(48) + 0.66(0) + 0.11(3) = -0.14 \qquad p = .47$$

$$z_{\text{nonimmigrant}} = -1.91 + 0.03(48) + 0.66(1) + 0.11(3) = 0.52 \qquad p = .63$$

This illustrates a large difference: immigrants are quite a bit less likely to own their homes. Finally, let's do the two extremes: a 25-year-old strong Democrat immigrant and a 75-year-old strong Republican nonimmigrant:

$$z = -1.91 + 0.03(25) + 0.66(0) + 0.11(0) = -1.16 \quad p = .24$$

$$z = -1.91 + 0.03(75) + 0.66(1) + 0.11(6) = 1.66 \quad p = .84$$

This shows that these three variables together can have quite an effect on home ownership. However, keep in mind that the R^2 is only 12%, so there remains a lot of variation that is unexplained.

GSS EXAMPLE: SUPPORT OF GUN CONTROL

Few public policy issues are more contentious than gun control. Fortunately, the GSS asks a gun control question every year it is conducted. Unfortunately, it is a single question, and it is a favor/oppose question: "Would you favor or oppose a law which would require a person to obtain a police permit before he or she could buy a gun?" Although this may not be an ideal question, the GSS has asked this question since its inception in 1972, and it needs to keep the question wording consistent to assess any trend in opinion. A strong majority of the GSS respondents who were asked this question supported gun control: 74%. Only 26% opposed such a measure. But there are factors that make people more or less likely to support gun control. The following model uses three: sex, age, and whether one owns a gun:

▪ **Exhibit 13.2: Explaining Variation in Support for Gun Control**

Dependent Variable: Support for Gun Law (No = 0, Yes = 1)	
Independent Variable	Slope
Sex (M = 0, F = 1)	0.58***
Age in years	0.02***
Own gun (N = 0, Y = 1)	–1.10***
Constant	0.34
R^2	0.12
	$n = 1,252$

***$p < .001$.
Source: GSS 2012 data.

It is quick and easy to decipher the direction of the relationships, simply by looking at the directions of the slopes:

women have a higher probability than do men of supporting gun control
older people have a higher probability than do younger people
gun owners have a higher probability than do those who do not own a gun

However, it's always best to run some examples to illustrate the size of the effects. Here is the equation from the model:

$$z = 0.34 + 0.58(SEX) + 0.02(AGE) - 1.10(OWNGUN)$$

From this, we can run various combinations of characteristics to get a full picture of who supports gun control. For example, to illustrate the effect of owning a gun, we'll use the mode for sex and the mean age:

$$z_{no\ gun} = 0.34 + 0.58(1) + 0.02(48) - 1.10(0) = 1.88 \quad p = .87$$

$$z_{gun} = 0.34 + 0.58(1) + 0.02(48) - 1.10(1) = 0.78 \quad p = .69$$

No surprises here: owning a gun significantly lowers the probability that you support gun control (as measured by this simple question). Here is a graph with a set of examples that illustrates the effect of all three independent variables:

■ Exhibit 13.3: Illustrating Variation in Support for Gun Control

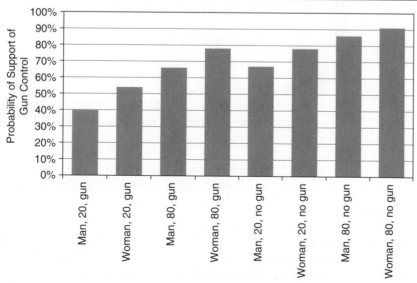

Source: GSS 2012 data.

Although the overall support of gun control is high, this graph illustrates important variation in this attitude. A young male gun owner has less than a 50% chance of supporting gun control, whereas an old woman who does not own a gun has over a 90% probability of supporting it.

GSS EXAMPLE: INTERRACIAL FRIENDSHIPS

The 1998 GSS used a very interesting question: it asked the white respondents how many "good friends who are black" they have, and they asked black respondents how many "good friends who are white" they have. Here is a graph of the results:

▪ **Exhibit 13.4: Interracial Friendships among American Whites and Blacks**

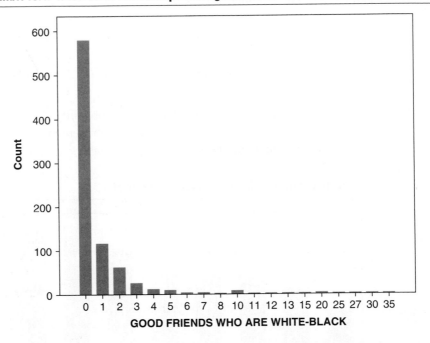

Note that, for the purposes of this variable, we are considering only two races: white and black. As you can see, the majority of people (almost 70% of the respondents!) do not have any interracial friendships. But some do, and it would be nice to be able to explain this variation. We could use regular regression to try to explain the limited variation in this variable, but when things are so lopsided, it makes more sense to turn the variable into a dichotomy, where 0 = no interracial friendships and 1 = one or more interracial friendships. So that is what I did, and I'll use that as my dependent variable. For my logistic regression equation, I decided to use the following independent variables:

- Education: My thinking was that people with more education will have had more opportunities to form interracial friendships, especially given that people with more education tend to have more liberal views on race.
- Live in City: My thinking was that people who live in big cities also have more opportunities to meet people of different races.
- Age: Younger people, having grown up with the benefits of the civil rights movement, will be more likely to have interracial friendships.
- Race: My guess was that blacks will be more likely to have an interracial friendship than whites, simply because there are more whites than blacks (overly simplistic, I know).

Here is the model:

■ **Exhibit 13.5: Explaining Interracial Friendships**

Dependent Variable: Have Interracial Friendship (No = 0, Yes = 1)	
Independent Variable	Slope
Education (in years)	–0.06*
Live in City (0 = No, 1 = Yes)	0.52*
Age	0.00
Race (W = 0, B = 1)	1.08***
Constant	–0.39
R^2	0.07

Note: $n = 787$.
*$p < .05$. ***$p < .001$.
Source: GSS 1998 data.

So how did I do? I'll run through some examples in a minute, but for now, let's just interpret the signs and the significances:

- Education: Although it's a statistically significant effect, my thinking was completely wrong: the more education you get, the *less* likely you are to have interracial friendships. I'm not off to a good start here.
- Live in City: My thinking was right: living in a big city significantly raises the probability that you will have an interracial friendship. I'm one for two now!

- Age: So much for the future. Age has absolutely no effect. This is one of those times that a *lack* of significance elicits an interesting finding.
- Race: My guess was totally on the mark: blacks are much more likely to have an interracial friendship than whites are.

So I end up getting a 2 out of 4. Not bad. And now a list of eight examples that show the range of the effects:

The equation (notice that age is not included):

$$z = -0.39 - 0.06(EDUC) + 0.52(CITY) + 1.08(RACE)$$

A very educated white person, not living in city:

$$z = -0.39 - 0.06(20) + 0.52(0) + 1.08(0) = -1.59 \qquad p = .17$$

A very educated white person, living in city:

$$z = -0.39 - 0.06(20) + 0.52(1) + 1.08(0) = -1.07 \qquad p = .26$$

A noneducated white person, not living in city:

$$z = -0.39 - 0.06(10) + 0.52(0) + 1.08(0) = -0.99 \qquad p = .27$$

A noneducated white person, living in city:

$$z = -0.39 - 0.06(10) + 0.52(1) + 1.08(0) = -0.47 \qquad p = .38$$

A very educated black person, not living in city:

$$z = -0.39 - 0.06(20) + 0.52(0) + 1.08(1) = -0.51 \qquad p = .38$$

A very educated black person, living in city:

$$z = -0.39 - 0.06(20) + 0.52(1) + 1.08(1) = +0.01 \qquad p = .50$$

A noneducated black person, not living in city:

$$z = -0.39 - 0.06(10) + 0.52(0) + 1.08(1) = +0.09 \qquad p = .52$$

A noneducated black person, living in city:

$$z = -0.39 - 0.06(10) + 0.52(1) + 1.08(1) = +0.61 \qquad p = .65$$

These differences are stark, and say a lot about racial interactions in the United States.

Perhaps you've noticed this already, but if not, I want to point it out: when you're calculating the effects of each variable, it sometimes depends at what level you set the other variables. For example, let's say we wanted to show the effect of race and say something like "Blacks are some % more likely than whites." Well, look at this:

Examining racial difference by looking at

A less-educated black person, living in city	0.65
A less-educated white person, living in city	0.38
Difference:	*0.27*
A highly educated black person, not living in city	0.38
A highly educated white person, not living in city	0.17
Difference:	*0.21*

The difference between 0.27 and 0.21 is not huge, but it's worth pointing out that this happens. Therefore, you need to be clear about this when you're describing the effects. Here is generally what I do: for any variable whose effect I am interpreting, I use the average categories for the other variables (whatever makes sense given the variable: the mode, the median, or the mean).

GSS EXAMPLE: CHARITABLE GIVING

My mother, 82 years young, regularly laments about the amount of mail she receives from charities asking for a donation. Perhaps she ends up on their mailing lists because she does regularly give to numerous groups. However, another possibility is that these organizations realize that older people may have a higher probability of giving to charity. The 2012 GSS asked a battery of questions about altruistic behavior, including asking respondents how often they give money to charity. This question elicited an ordinal-level variable (once a week, once a month, etc.). I could have transformed it into a pseudo-ratio-level variable (i.e., the number of times per year the respondent gives to charity), but I instead chose to dichotomize it so that 0 equals "did not give to charity in the past year" and 1 equals "did give to charity in the past year." I then ran a set of nested regression models using GSS respondents aged less than 60. The first model includes only age. In the second model, I considered the fact that older people tend to have higher incomes than younger people, and possibly this could possibly play a role (I limited the age because at some point, people retire and their incomes go down; more on that in a later chapter). Here are the logistic models:

■ **Exhibit 13.6: Explaining Variation in Charitable Giving**

Dependent Variable: Given Money to Charity in Past Year (No = 0, Yes = 1)		
Independent Variable	Model 1	Model 2
Age in years	0.04***	0.03***
Family Income in $1,000s	—	0.016***
Constant	–0.66	–1.19
R^2	0.06	0.17
	$n = 842$	$n = 842$

***$p < .001$.
Source: GSS 2012 data for respondents younger than 60 years old only.

Note I kept another decimal place for the income variable in Model 2 because it is such a small number. Model 1 shows that age has a statistically significant effect: the older you are, the higher the probability is that you give to charity. Does this effect go away when we control for family income? Although it does decrease slightly, it remains highly statistically significant. Now, for some examples to put together the story of what is going on in these models. Here is the equation from Model 2:

$$z = -1.19 + 0.03(\text{age}) + 0.016 \, (\text{income})$$

First, we'll set income at its mean of 60 and let age vary:

$$z = -1.19 + 0.03(20) + 0.016(60) = 0.37 \quad p = .59$$

$$z = -1.19 + 0.03(40) + 0.016(60) = 0.97 \quad p = .73$$

$$z = -1.19 + 0.03(60) + 0.016(60) = 1.57 \quad p = .83$$

$$z = -1.19 + 0.03(80) + 0.016(60) = 2.17 \quad p = .90$$

This makes it fairly clear why my 82-year-old mother gets constant solicitations from charities: the probability of old people giving to charity is very high. Now setting age at its mean of 48, we'll manipulate income:

$$z = -1.19 + 0.03(48) + 0.016(10) = 0.41 \quad p = .60$$

$$z = -1.19 + 0.03(48) + 0.016(50) = 1.05 \quad p = .74$$

$z = -1.19 + 0.03(48) + 0.016(100) = 1.85 \quad p = .86$

$z = -1.19 + 0.03(48) + 0.016(150) = 2.65 \quad p = .93$

Income has a similar effect. Although those with low incomes are likely to give to charity, the probability increases as family income rises. Finally, here are two extremes:

$z = -1.19 + 0.03(20) + 0.016(10) = -0.43 \quad p = .39$
$z = -1.19 + 0.03(80) + 0.016(150) = 3.61 \quad p = .97$

This is perhaps why you don't see too many poor 20-year-olds on high-powered charity boards.

GSS EXAMPLE: CAPITAL PUNISHMENT

Let's return to a variable I mentioned earlier in the chapter: in the 2012 GSS, 69% of the male respondents favored capital punishment for someone convicted of murder, and 31% opposed it (I'm using only men because most of death row is made up of men). Let's try to explain some of this variation. Just as in the last example, in which I combined logistic regression with nested models, here I'm going to throw you another curveball: we're going to combine logistic regression with an interaction effect. Don't worry; we're going to follow the exact same procedures we've done so far. It'll be fine. The model is

■ **Exhibit 13.7: Explaining Support for the Death Penalty**

Dependent Variable: Support for Death Penalty (No = 0, Yes = 1)	
Independent Variable	Slope
Education (in years)	−0.10**
Race (W = 0, B = 1)	−2.92**
Interaction: Race × Educ	0.14*
Constant	2.43
R^2	0.06
	$n = 733$

$*p < .05. \ ***p < .001$ (two-tailed test).
Source: GSS 2012 data, only men only.

First, we rewrite this as an equation:

$$z = 2.43 - 0.10(EDUC) - 2.92(RACE) + 0.14(RACE)(EDUC)$$

Then, we run four examples:

A less-educated white person:

$$z = 2.43 - 0.10(10) - 2.92(0) + 0.14(0)(10) = 1.43 \qquad p = .81$$

A highly educated white person:

$$z = 2.43 - 0.10(20) - 2.92(0) + 0.14(0)(20) = 0.43 \qquad p = .61$$

A less-educated black person:

$$z = 2.43 - 0.10(10) - 2.92(1) + 0.14(1)(10) = -0.09 \qquad p = .48$$

A highly educated black person:

$$z = 2.43 - 0.10(20) - 2.92(1) + 0.14(1)(20) = 0.31 \qquad p = .58$$

Finally we create a graph:

▪ **Exhibit 13.8: Illustrating Support for the Death Penalty**

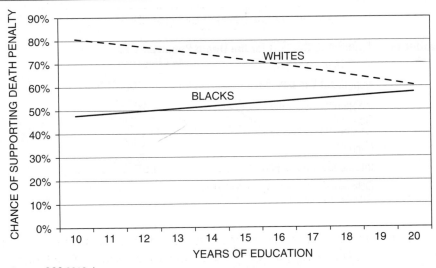

Source: GSS 2012 data.

What emerges is fascinating and relatively rare: the effect of education is opposite for black men and white men. Whites and blacks with little education differ hugely on the issue of capital punishment: whites are nearly twice as likely to support the death penalty as are blacks. As whites and blacks rise in education, this gap shrinks until by the end of the lines the two groups differ by only 3%. There, that wasn't so bad, was it? It's all a matter of running examples and graphing it out.

GSS EXAMPLE: CONDOM USAGE

The 2012 GSS asked respondents about condom usage. How valid the responses are, we'll never know. This is obviously a very personal question, and people may have been prone to the survey problem of social desirability, where they answer the way they thought they should answer. When asked if they used a condom the last time they had sex, 22% of the respondents answered yes and 78% answered no. Let's try to explain this variation with a logistic model that, similar to the last example, uses an interaction effect. We'll use two independent variables related to sexual behavior: the number of times the respondent had sex in the last month and the number of sexual partners the respondent has had in the past five years, as well as an interaction variable combining these two variables:

■ **Exhibit 13.9: Explaining Condom Usage**

Dependent Variable: Used Condom Last Time? (No = 0, Yes = 1)	
Independent Variable	Slope
# of times sex in past month	−0.002
# of partners in past 5 yrs.	0.078***
Interaction: times sex × partners	−0.004**
Constant	−1.52
R^2	0.03
	$n = 1,151$

**p < .01. ***p < .001 (two-tailed test).
Source: GSS 2012 data.

Given that the two parent variables are both ratio-level variables, and given that this is a logistic model, it is best to figure out these effects using a series of examples. First, we write the model out as an equation:

$z = -1.52 - 0.002(\text{times sex}) + 0.078(\text{partners}) - 0.004\,(\text{times sex})(\text{partners})$

To fully assess these effects, I calculated 16 examples and created the following three-dimensional bar graph:

■ **Exhibit 13.10: Illustrating Variation in Condom Usage**

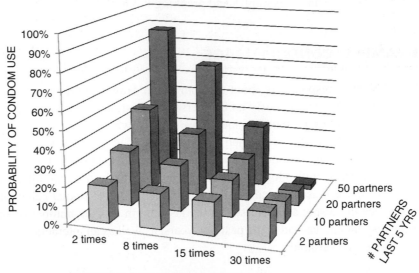

Source: GSS 2012 data.

This graph should give public health officials pause. Among those who have sex infrequently, the more partners one has, the more likely one is to have used a condom. But as sexual frequency increases, the effect of number of partners dissipates. By the time sexual frequency is daily, the effect of number of partners is actually slightly negative. In fact, the person least likely to use a condom is someone who has sex 30 times per month and 50 partners in the past five years. Fortunately for public health, such a person is quite rare.

ANOTHER WAY OF LOOKING AT THINGS: ODDS RATIOS

A significant number of researchers prefer to describe their logistic regression results in a different way. Rather than saying, "Here's the probability for Group A, and here's the probability for Group B," they use what is called an **odds ratio**. Before we get to that, it will help to review what odds are. Let's say the probability of a non-immigrant owning a home was around 0.75. To translate this into odds, we divide the probability of "success" (getting a 1 on the dependent variable, in this case owning a home) by the probability of "failure" (getting a 0 on the dependent variable, in this case not owning a home): 0.75/0.25 = 3.0, or 3 to 1. For nonimmigrants, in other words, we expect for every three people who own a home there will be one person who will not own a home. Among immigrants, if the probability was 0.50, the odds would be 0.50/0.50, or 1 to 1 (we also call these *even odds*): we expect for every one immigrant who owns a home there will be one immigrant who does not own a home. If the probability had been 0.25, then the odds would have been 0.25/0.75, or 1/3, or 1 to 3: we would expect for every one person who owns a home there would be three who did not own a home. Here is a list of various probabilities and their respective odds:

■ **Exhibit 13.11: Examples of Probabilities and Odds**

Probability of	Probability against	Odds
0.10	0.90	0.10/0.90 = 0.11
0.20	0.80	0.20/0.80 = 0.25
0.25	0.75	0.25/0.75 = 0.33
0.33	0.67	0.33/0.67 = 0.50
0.40	0.60	0.40/0.60 = 0.67
0.50	0.50	0.50/0.50 = 1.00
0.60	0.40	0.60/0.40 = 1.50
0.67	0.33	0.67/0.33 = 2.00
0.90	0.10	0.90/0.10 = 9.00

The odds ratio is exactly what it sounds like: the ratio of the odds for the two groups we are comparing at any given time. So, if the odds for nonimmigrants are 3.0, and the odds for immigrants are 1.0, the odds ratio for nonimmigrants versus immigrants is:

Odds for nonimmigrants/Odds for immigrants = 3.0/1.0 = 3

Regarding home ownership, a nonimmigrant's odds are three times the odds of an immigrant. But because I wanted to start this out simply, that ratio is based on hypothetical numbers. Here were the actual probabilities from earlier in the chapter:

Probability that a nonimmigrant owns a home: 63%
Probability that an immigrant owns a home: 47%

Here is how we translate these into odds, and then how we calculate the odds ratio:

Odds for nonimmigrants: 0.63/0.37 = 1.70
Odds for immigrants: 0.47/0.53 = 0.89
1.70/0.89 = 1.91

A nonimmigrant's odds of home ownership are 1.91 times an immigrant's odds of home ownership. Although the meaning of this is not really intuitive, many researchers present their results this way when using logistic regression, so it is important to know about this.

Because logistic regression results are presented as both probabilities and odds, it is important to note that they are *not* the same thing. For example, say Group A has a 60% chance of owning a home, and Group B has a 20% chance of owning a home. We would say that someone from Group A is three times more likely to own a home than is someone from Group B, because 60%/20% = 3. But if we state this as an odds ratio, we would have the following:

Odds for Group A: 0.60/0.40 = 1.50
Odds for Group B: 0.20/0.80 = 0.25
Odds ratio: 1.50/0.25 = 6.00

Although you can say that the odds are six times greater, it would be an incorrect interpretation to say that Group A is six times more likely to own a home than is Group B. In examining the social research literature, I have seen this mistake. So be wary when reading people's interpretations of odds ratios.

Another interesting thing you can do in relation to odds ratios is to combine e with any given slope by taking e and raising it to the power of the slope. For example, if the slope were 2, we'd want e^2; if the slope were –5, we'd want e^{-5}; and if the slope were 0.27, we'd want $e^{0.27}$. Let's use the home ownership example again. The coefficient for party identification was 0.11. If we calculate $e^{0.11}$, we get 1.12. Put that number on the back burner; we'll return to it in a moment. But now let's calculate two hypotheticals using the equation: one person who is very much a Democrat (scoring a 0 on party id) and another person who is the next step up toward being a Republican (scoring a 1 on party id):

$$z_{partyid=0} = -1.91 + 0.03(48) + 0.66(1) + 0.11(0) = 0.19 \qquad p = .5474$$

Odds of home ownership = 0.5474/0.4526 = 1.2095

$z_{partyid=1} = -1.91 + 0.03(48) + 0.66(1) + 0.11(1) = 0.30$ $\qquad$ $p = .5744$

Odds of home ownership = 0.5744/0.4256 = 1.3496

So the odds ratio for these two people is 1.3496/1.2095 = 1.12. Remember that's what we calculated earlier for $e^{0.11}$. Therefore, e to the power of any given slope is the odds ratio between adjoining groups on that slope.

Let's do another one of these using one of the dichotomies from the gun control example from earlier in the chapter: the effect of owning a gun. The slope was −1.10, so $e^{-1.10} = 0.33$, meaning that the odds ratio between those who own a gun and those who don't own a gun is 0.33. Here are the odds for the two groups:

Own a gun: $p = .69$, making the odds 0.69/0.31 = 2.2258
No gun: $p = .87$, making the odds 0.87/0.13 = 6.6923

This gives us an odds ratio of: 2.2258/6.6923 = 0.33. Again, not the most intuitive thing in the world, but you have to admit that's just a little bit cool.

GSS EXAMPLE: CAPITAL PUNISHMENT REVISITED

To bring all this together and make sense of it all, I'll return to race and capital punishment, using a very simple example. We'll start as simple as it gets: a crosstab, using 2012 GSS data:

■ **Exhibit 13.12: A Crosstab: Capital Punishment by Race**

		RACE		
		WHITE	BLACK	Total
SUPPORT CAPITAL PUNISHMENT	NO	415	139	554
		30.4%	51.9%	33.9%
	YES	952	129	1081
		69.6%	48.1%	66.1%
Total		1367	268	1635
		100.0%	100.0%	100.0%

Source: GSS 2012 data.

But we can also run this with logistic regression and get the same results. I ran two models, each with race as the independent variable, but I recoded race two ways:

Model 1: whites coded as 0, blacks coded as 1
Model 2: blacks coded as 0, whites coded as 1

This gave me the following results:

▨ **Exhibit 13.13: Results from Two Very Similar Logistic Models**

	Model 1	Model 2
Whites coded as	0	1
Blacks coded as	1	0
Slope	−0.9050	0.9050
Constant	0.8300	−0.0750
z-value for whites	0.8300	0.8300
Probability for whites	0.6964	0.6964
Odds for whites	2.2938	2.2938
z-value for blacks	−0.0750	−0.0750
Probability for blacks	0.4813	0.4813
Odds for blacks	0.9279	0.9279
Odds ratio	0.4045	2.4720
e^{slope}	0.4045	2.4719

The point of all this is to show that, though the predicted probabilities are of course the same as they were in the crosstab (70% for whites and 48% for blacks), the odds ratios differ because one odds ratio is blacks to whites and the other is whites to blacks. In Model 1, the odds ratio expresses the odds for blacks divided by the odds for whites: $0.9279/2.2938 = 0.4045$. In other words, the odds of a black respondent being in favor of capital punishment are two-fifths of the odds of a white respondent being in favor of capital punishment. Notice that we can find the odds ratio by taking e to the power of the slope ($e^{-0.9050}$). In Model 2, the odds ratio expresses the odds for whites divided by the odds for blacks: $2.2938/0.9279 = 2.4720$. In other words, the odds of a white respondent being in favor of capital punishment are nearly two and a half times the odds of a black respondent being in favor of capital punishment. Thus, though the odds ratios for the two models are different, they tell the same story: 2/5 flipped around is 5/2.

LITERATURE EXAMPLE: WAR AND PRESIDENTIAL DISAPPROVAL

The Gallup Organization regularly asks Americans if they approve or disapprove of the job the president is doing. During the Iraq War, they also asked respondents whether they knew someone serving in the war and whether or not they had a connection to someone who had been killed or wounded in the war (a family member, a close friend, or a coworker). Political scientist Scott Sigmund Gartner used these survey data in his article "Ties to the Dead: Connections to Iraq War and 9/11 Casualties and Disapproval of the President," which appeared in the journal *American Sociological Review* in 2008. His dependent variable was a dichotomy: approve of the job the president is doing (coded as 0) or disapprove (coded as 1). Therefore, he used logistic regression in his analyses. He controlled for a variety of factors: race, political party, education, age and income. I didn't include these in the following simplified model:

■ **Exhibit 13.14: Explaining Disapproval of the President**

Dependent Variable: Attitude toward President (Approve = 0, Approve = 1)	
Independent Variable	Slope
Know someone serving in Iraq	−0.424**
Know Iraq casualty	0.724**
Constant	0.750
R^2	0.41
	$n = 905$

***p < .01* (two-tailed test).
Source: Adapted from Gartner (2008).

Using this simplified model (I've controlled for all of his control variables), we can predict the probability that someone disapproves of the president:

$z = 0.750 - 0.424$(knows someone serving) $+ 0.724$(knows casualty)

A respondent who doesn't know anyone serving:

$z = 0.750 - 0.424(0) + 0.724(0) = 0.750 \quad p = .68$

A respondent who knows someone serving, but not a casualty:

$z = 0.750 - 0.424(1) + 0.724(0) = 0.326 \quad p = .58$

A respondent who knows someone serving, and knows a casualty:

$$z = 0.750 - 0.424(1) + 0.724(1) = 1.050 \quad p = .74$$

Gartner argued that these results show that social networks matter: those who know someone serving are more likely to approve (that is, less likely to disapprove) than were others. But knowing a casualty has the opposite effect: the probability of disapproval is highest among respondents who know someone who has been killed or hurt. Gartner also showed that someone who knew a casualty from 9/11 was more likely to disapprove of the president. Whether the casualty is military or civilian, such connections matter.

LITERATURE EXAMPLE: GLOBAL WARMING

Among the most contested public policy issues is global warming. Although the scientific community is essentially in agreement that the effects of global warming are already happening and that we are the cause of it, among the American public there remains significant variation in opinion on these issues. In their article "The Politicization of Climate Change and Polarization in the American Public's Views of Global Warming, 2001–2010," which appeared in the journal *The Sociological Quarterly* in 2011, Aaron McCright and Riley Dunlap analyzed this variation. They used a series of environmental polls conducted by the Gallup Organization. In these polls, some of the questions about global warming were asked as yes/no questions, so McCright and Dunlap use logistic regression in their analyses. Here we will focus on only one of their dependent variables, which concerned whether the effects of global warming have already begun. Not only does their analysis involve logistic regression, but they also include two interaction effects. This may make this table daunting at first, but let's work through it.

■ **Exhibit 13.15: Explaining Attitudes toward Global Warming**

Dependent Variable: Global warming effects have already begun (N = 0, Y = 1)

Independent Variable	Slope
Political ideology (1 = very conservative, 5 = very liberal)	0.271***
Party identification (1 = Republican, 5 = Democrat)	0.179***
Educational attainment (1 = H.S. or less, 4 = more than college)	0.166***
Self-rep. G.W. understanding (1 = not at all, 4 = very well)	0.363***
Year (1 = 2001, 10 = 2010)	0.007
Environmental movement identity (1 = unsymp., 4 = active)	0.599***
Gender (0 = male, 1 = female)	0.265***
Age (in years)	−0.008***
Race (0 = white, 1 = nonwhite)	−0.358*
Annual income (1 = < 20K, 5 = > 75K)	0.081***
Religiosity (1 = never attend, 5 = attend once a week)	−0.112***
Political ideology × educational attainment	0.091***
Political ideology × self-reported understanding	0.317***
Constant	−3.682
R^2	0.24
	n = 9,113

*$p < .05$. ***$p < .001$ (two-tailed test)
Source: Adapted from McCright and Dunlap (2011).

There's a lot going on here. I'll tell just one of the interesting stories from this article, using three examples. I plugged in these values, and the averages for all of the other variables. I'll spare you all of the math I did, especially because, for the interaction, effects the authors calculated their numbers using what is called "center scoring" (basically the real value minus the mean on that variable). Here are the z-values I calculated, and the resulting probabilities:

a highly educated liberal Democrat who claims to understand global warming very well: z-value = 3.32, predicted probability of saying the effects of global warming have already begun = 97%

a highly educated conservative Republican who claims to understand global warming very well: z-value = −0.62, predicted probability of saying the effects of global warming have already begun = 35%

a noneducated conservative Republican who claims to understand global warming not at all: z-value = 0.00, predicted probability of saying the effects of global warming have already begun = 50%

McCright and Dunlap's findings illustrate the interconnections between political ideology and knowledge. Educated liberals are almost guaranteed to believe that the effects of global warming already have begun. Educated conservatives are much less likely to believe this, even though they claim high levels of understanding about global warming. These educated conservatives are even *less* likely than are noneducated conservatives to believe this. The article then goes on to examine the effects of time. They provide an immense amount of evidence (36 graphs total!) that points to a polarization of American attitudes on this issue: the gap between liberals and conservatives grows wider by the year.

CONCLUSION

If you flip through recent scholarly journals, you will notice that a *lot* of researchers use logistic regression these days. I'm not sure what it says about the social sciences that we are so intrigued by dichotomies, especially because I see the world in so many shades of gray. But as we've realized, many interesting things are dichotomous, and many times surveys ask about issues in dichotomous ways. Hopefully you have seen that logistic regression is really very similar to regular regression, just with an extra step and a few extra taps on the calculator (or computer keyboard).

SPSS DEMONSTRATION: RUNNING A LOGISTIC REGRESSION MODEL

Please visit the book's website (www.routledge.com/cw/linneman) to view a video of this demonstration.

Running logistic regression in SPSS is easy: under the Regression menu, you simply go down a few more to Binary Logistic. And, as you've seen, once you have the equation, interpreting the results is not that bad. The one possibly scary thing about SPSS and logistic regression is the output, because it's a case of Too Much Information. So let me show you what you need from all of this output. Similar to an example from earlier in this chapter, the dependent variable I'll be using is the recoded ANES variable XYinvolv_charity, which relates to answers respondents gave to the question of if they have given money to a church or charity in the past 12 months. To this, 72% of the respondents said yes (which is coded as 1), and 28% of the respondents said no (which is coded is 0). We'll use basic demographics as independent variables: age, family income, and race (white/black). To run a logistic regression, you click

Analyze → Regression → Binary Logistic . . .

and add the variables just as in any regular regression. However, the output we get is quite different, and much longer: *nine* boxes, not four. But most of the boxes we won't use. As I've said, there's a lot of fancy math going on behind the scenes in logistic regression. The very first box has your number of cases:

Case Processing Summary

Unweighted Cases		N	Percent
Selected Cases	Included in Analysis	4070	68.8
	Missing Cases	1846	31.2
	Total	5916	100.0
Unselected Cases		0	0.0
Total		5916	100.0

We see that, of the 5,916 total cases in the ANES sample, 4,070 cases have full data. Scroll down, and you'll see a box called Model Summary:

Model Summary

Step	-2 Log likelihood	Cox & Snell R Square	Nagelkerke R Square
1	4313.093[a]	0.083	0.122

a. Estimation terminated at iteration number 5 because parameter estimates changed by less than .001.

Because it's a special kind of regression, logistic regression has a special kind of R^2. Actually, two special kinds. I prefer the Nagelkerke because it allows for perfect relationships (i.e., an R^2 of 1). Plus, it's fun to say Nagelkerke. Finally, scroll down to the last box and you'll find the information you need to build the regression model:

Variables in the Equation

		B	S.E.	Wald	df	Sig.	Exp(B)
Step 1[a]	XYdem_age	0.028	0.002	148.166	1	0.000	1.028
	XYincgroupK	0.011	0.001	152.686	1	0.000	1.011
	XYdem_raceethWB	0.324	0.091	12.686	1	0.000	1.382
	Constant	-1.012	0.130	60.519	1	0.000	0.363

a. Variable(s) entered on step 1: XYdem_age, XYincgroupK, XYdem_raceethWB.

Just as in regular regression, what you need here is the B column and the Sig. column. But have you noticed what is missing? That's right: the betas. Why are they missing? Because betas rely on standard deviations, and the standard deviations for dichotomies are quite hard to interpret. So, instead, we run examples. Let's just do two extremes, and then I'll show you how to do a graph.

A 20-year-old white person with a family income of $10,000:

$$z = -1.01 + 0.028(20) + 0.011(10) + 0.32(0) = -0.34 \qquad p = .42$$

An 80-year-old black person with a family income of $150,000:

$$z = -1.01 + 0.028(80) + 0.011(150) + 0.32(1) = 3.20 \qquad p = .96$$

We see that these three variables together cause large changes in the probability of charitable giving.

Notice the last column on the right: Exp(B). This stands for e to the power of the slope, which I talked about earlier regarding odds ratios. For example, the Exp(B) for race is 1.382, meaning that the odds ratio between blacks and whites is 1.382. Let's do a couple of examples to show that this works. We'll put in average values for the other variables: 49 for age and 59 for family income:

A white person:

$$z = -1.01 + 0.028(49) + 0.011(59) + 0.32(0) = 1.01 \qquad p = .73$$

giving us odds of $0.73/0.27 = 2.70$

A black person:

$$z = -1.01 + 0.028(49) + 0.011(59) + 0.32(1) = 1.33 \qquad p = .79$$

giving us odds of $0.79/0.21 = 3.76$

This makes the odds ratio: $3.76/2.70 = 1.39$, which is pretty darned close to the 1.382 from above.

FROM OUTPUT TO PRESENTATION

Just as in the previous chapter, using Excel to create a graph that illustrates the regression model is easy. We'll use the example from just above to illustrate the effect of age (similar to an example from earlier in the chapter). To show the effect of age, we'll keep race constant at 0 (white, the modal category) and income constant at 59 (the mean). This allows us to shorten our equation:

$z = -1.01 + 0.028(\text{AGE}) + 0.011(59) + 0.32(0)$
$z = -0.36 + 0.028(\text{AGE})$

I take this equation to Excel and, just like in the last chapter, set up a column for AGE (which we'll have range from 20 to 80, in increments of 10). Then we'll need a column for the z-value and a column for the p-value. The formula to place in the z-value cells is easy: it's simply

$= -0.36 + 0.028 * (\text{whatever your corresponding age cell is})$

For the p column, we need to go over how we can get Excel to calculate the natural logarithm. The command in Excel is EXP. For example, if our z-value is located in cell B2,

$= \text{EXP(B2)/(1 + EXP(B2))}$

This gives us the p-values, which we can use to create a graph, such as the following:

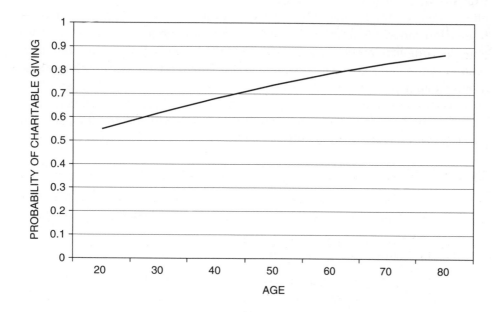

EXERCISES

Exercise 1

The ANES asks people about their smoking behavior. I took these variables and created a dichotomous variable: 0 = don't currently smoke, 1 = currently smoke. Use this as your dependent variable and these as your independent variables: family income in 1000s, gender (recoded version), recoded religious attendance, and the three race reference groups. Create a table of your results and describe them. Finally, predict the probability of currently smoking for

a. a Hispanic woman whose family income is $150,000, and she attends religious services eight times a month.

b. a black man whose family income is $10,000, and he never attends religious services.

Exercise 2 (Answer Available in Appendix D)

Only 42% of the ANES respondents say they have current passports. What explains whether one has a passport? First, we posit that political party has an effect. Then, we think it might be wise to control for income. Run a set of logistic regression models with the recoded passport variable as your dependent variable. In your first model, use only the recoded political party variable. In the second model, add family income in 1,000s. Create a table with both models in it and explain your results. Use Model 1 to predict probability of passport for a strong Democrat and then a strong Republican. Use Model 2 to predict probability of passport for someone whose family income is $10,000 and then someone whose family income is $150,000.

Exercise 3

Gun control is a highly controversial issue in the United States today. The ANES asks a question about gun control, and here is how the respondents weighed in:

Make it more difficult: 49.2%
Make it easier: 5.5%
Keep these rules about the same: 45.3%

I created a dichotomy with 0 = keep the same or easier and 1 = make harder. Use this recoded variable as the dependent variable in a logistic regression model, with the recoded "own gun?" question, the recoded gender variable, and age in years. Create a table of your results. Then run predictions for

a. a 20-year-old male gun with a gun

b. an 80-year-old female without a gun

Exercise 4

The ANES asks the respondent if she is married, and if she is not and there is another adult living in the household, they ask the respondent if she has a partner. Use the recoded marital status partner variable as your dependent variable in a logistic regression model. When you run the model, select cases so that the recoded marital status variable < 2 (this will limit the model to those who are married and those who are partnered). Use two independent variables: age and whether the respondent is gay, lesbian, or bisexual.

Create a table of your results. Then run predictions for

a. a 50-year-old heterosexual

b. a 50-year-old nonheterosexual

Turn these predictions into odds, and then calculate the odds ratio of non-heterosexual versus heterosexual. Does it match up with the corresponding result in the output?

Exercise 5

When people are asked, "Is the country on the right track?" some will think of economic issues, whereas others will think of social issues. Use the recoded "right track/wrong track" variable as your dependent variable, and the Traditionalism Index and the Economic Optimism Index as your independent variables. Create a table of your results. Then, make predictions for

a. Someone who is at the mean of 7 on the Economic Optimism Index and a 0 on the Traditionalism Index

b. Someone who is at the mean of 7 on the Economic Optimism Index and a 16 on the Traditionalism Index

c. Someone who is at the mean of 9 on the Traditional Values Index and a 0 on the Economic Optimism Index

d. Someone who is at the mean of 9 on the Traditional Values Index and a 16 on the Economic Optimism Index

What do these examples tell you regarding which independent variable has the larger effect on the dependent variable?

Exercise 6

Blacks are less likely than whites to have health insurance. But is this because blacks tend to have lower incomes than whites do? Using the ANES data, run a logistic regression model with the recoded health insurance variable as your dependent variable and the recoded race (white/black) variable as your independent variable. Then, run a second model in which you control for family income in 1,000s. Create a table that includes both models. Then, using Model 1, calculate probabilities for a white person and a black person. Finally, using Model 2, calculate probabilities for a white person and a black person who both make $59,000 (the mean income).

Exercise 7

Using the PewShop data, run a logistic regression model that uses whether you have a smartphone (use the recoded variable) as the dependent variable and the following as independent variables: age, education (recoded, in years), income (recoded, in $1,000s), sex (recoded), and the race reference-group variables. Create a table of your results. Describe the type of person who is most likely to have a smartphone.

Exercise 8 (Answer Available in Appendix D)

Many young men play video games. But does the probability of owning a game console change as one ages, and does this change look the same for men and women? Using the PewShop dataset, run a logistic regression model using whether or not you have a gaming console (use the recoded variable) as the dependent variable and the following as independent variables: sex (recoded), age, and the interaction between the two. Because children play such an important role in whether one has a gaming console, select cases so that you are looking only at people who are not parents. Create a table of your results and then a graph, and explain your graph.

Exercise 9

In an exercise in an earlier chapter, we examined the effect of being a parent on work status for men and women. But this analysis didn't control for age, which is an important factor. Run a logistic regression equation using the PewShop dataset that uses the dichotomously recoded work status variable as the dependent variable. For independent variables, use the recoded sex variable, the recoded parent variable, the interaction between these two, and the age variable. Create a table of your results and then a graph (do a clustered bar graph), and explain your graph.

Exercise 10

One of the crises within the healthcare system is the use of emergency rooms, where many people go for primary care instead of going to a typical doctor, particularly if they don't have health insurance. Using the PewHealth dataset, run a logistic regression model that uses the recoded ER-usage variable as your dependent variable. For your independent variables, first use just the recoded income variable; then, add the dichotomously recoded insurance variable. Create a table that includes both models. Tell the story of what is going on in this set of nested models by running four examples:

a. someone whose family income is $10,000 and he or she doesn't have health insurance

b. someone whose family income is $10,000 and he or she does have health insurance

c. someone whose family income is $150,000 and he or she doesn't have health insurance

d. someone whose family income is $150,000 and he or she does have health insurance

Exercise 11

In the U.S. health care system, whether one has insurance is often related to one's work status. Using the PewHealth dataset, run a logistic regression model that uses the dichotomously recoded health insurance variable as your dependent variable. First, use the work status reference-group variables as your independent variables. Then, add the recoded family income variable. Create a table that includes both models. Just by looking at what happens to the effects of the work status variables from model to model, tell the story of these nested models.

Exercise 12

The stereotype is that women are more concerned about their weight than men are concerned about their own weight. Is this true across the education spectrum? Using the PewHealth dataset, run a logistic regression model using the recoded "looked for information about weight on the Internet" variable as your dependent variable, and then for your independent variables, use the recoded sex variable, the recoded education variable, and the interaction between the two. Create a table of your results as well as a graph and explain your graph.

Exercise 13

Use the PewKids data to run a logistic regression equation to see if being bullied online is affected by the other three types of bullying: in person, by phone, and by text message. Create a table of your model, and then address these questions: What is the probability of being bullied online if someone has not been bullied in the other ways? What is the probability of being bullied online if someone has been bullied in all the other ways?

Exercise 14 (Answer Available in Appendix D)

Family income likely affects the probability that a child will have a smartphone: more money, higher probability. But does this probability change in the same way for white and black families? Using the PewKids dataset, run a logistic model with an interaction effect to find out. Create a table, create a graph, and explain your graph.

Exercise 15

First, using the WVS dataset, run a regular regression model using PCUSE as the dependent variable and FAMSAV as the independent variable. Then imagine you didn't have the PCUSE variable and instead had only the PCUSE2CAT dichotomous variable. Run a logistic regression model using PCUSE2CAT as the dependent variable and FAMSAV as the independent variable. Interpret both models by making predictions for a country that doesn't save and a country in which 60% of the country's population saves.

Exercise 16

First, using the WVS dataset, run a regular regression model using DIVORCE as the dependent variable and RELGIMP as the independent variable. Then, imagine you didn't have the DIVORCE variable, and instead had only the DIVORCE2CAT dichotomous variable. Run a logistic regression model using DIVORCE2CAT as the dependent variable and RELGIMP as the independent variable. Interpret both models by making predictions for a country where 10% of the population says religion is very important and then for a country where 90% of the population says religion is very important.

Exercise 17 (Answer Available in Appendix D)

First, using the WVS dataset, run a regular regression model using PROST as the dependent variable and JOBMEN as the independent variable. Then, imagine you didn't have the PROST variable, and instead had only the PROST2CAT dichotomous variable. Run a logistic regression model using PROST2CAT as the dependent variable and JOBMEN as the independent variable. Interpret both models by making predictions for a country where 20% of the population says men should have more right to a job than should women and then for a country where 70% of the population says men should have more right to a job than should women.

Chapter 14

VISUALIZING CAUSAL STORIES: PATH ANALYSIS

This chapter covers . . .

. . . how to build and interpret a path model

. . . how to calculate direct, indirect, and total effects

. . . how path analysis and nested modeling are related

. . . how a researcher used path analysis to study the effects of activism

. . . how a researcher used path analysis to study emotions at work

INTRODUCTION

As I've said in earlier chapters, the world is a complicated place. So far, each of our examples has used a single dependent variable. What affects people's income, for example? Education served as an independent variable, affecting income. But, given that the world is complicated, what about the possibility that other variables affect one's level of education? Education could serve, simultaneously, as an independent *and* a dependent variable. For example, people often achieve levels of education similar to that of their parents, simply because all children want to be like their parents (right?). Also, parents' income may play a role in all of this: if your parents are rich, they will be more likely to pay for your college education, which might raise the probability that you will seek such an education. So now we have your parents' education affecting their income, which affects your education, which affects your income.

The regression techniques we've learned so far can deal with such complex relationships in only the most basic of ways. We've learned that adding another variable to a model can sometimes change the effect that the original independent variables had on the dependent variable, as well as adding its own new effect. This chapter adds another technique to your growing arsenal. It allows you to model these complex interrelationships using a visual map to which we will add standardized regression coefficients. The technique is called **path analysis**.

GSS EXAMPLE: HOUSEWORK

In the 2012 GSS, respondents were asked to estimate how many hours of housework they do (this variable was called RHHWORK), as well as how many hours of housework their spouse does (this variable was called SPHHWORK). Using these variables, I calculated a new variable: THHWORK, which is the sum of these two variables:

THHWORK = RHHWORK + SPHHWORK

If a respondent did 30 hours of housework and his or her spouse did 10 hours of housework, we would have

THHWORK = 30 + 10 = 40

Then, I calculated another variable: the percentage of the total housework that the respondent does:

R%HHWORK = (RHHWORK/THHWORK) × 100

Our respondent's value would be

R%HHWORK = (30/40) × 100 = 75

So this respondent does 75% of the housework in her household.

Here is the distribution of this variable, arranged by sex of respondent:

■ **Exhibit 14.1: Distribution of Housework Variable**

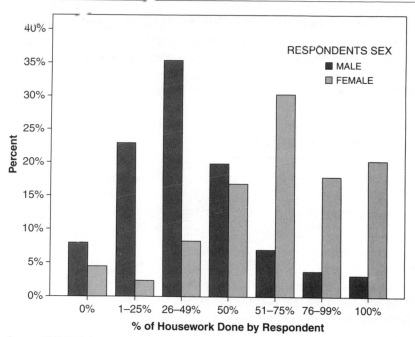

Source: GSS 2012 data.

We clearly see the gender difference in housework. Nearly 20% of the female respondents said they do 100% of the housework, whereas fewer than 5% of the male respondents said this. Most of the women are on the right side of the graph. Most of the men are on the left side of the graph.

I used this R%HHWORK variable as my dependent variable in a regression equation with two independent variables:

HRSWRKD: the number of hours you work at an outside job. My thinking was that if you worked very long hours at an outside job, you might not have the time to do a large share of the housework at home.

%INCOME: the percentage of the household income that the respondent brings home. My thinking was that if you bring home the majority of the household income, you might feel like you shouldn't have to do housework.

Here are my regression results:

▪ **Exhibit 14.2: Explaining Percentage of Housework Respondent Does**

Dependent Variable: % of Housework Completed by Respondent				
Independent Variable	Model 1		Model 2	
	Slope	Beta	Slope	Beta
Hours R Works at Job	−0.50***	−0.314	−0.31**	−0.196
% of Income from R	—	—	−0.29***	−0.328
Constant	70.27		79.46	
	$R^2 = 0.10$		$R^2 = 0.19$	
	$n = 295$		$n = 295$	

Note: R = respondent.
**p < .01. *** p < .001.
Source: GSS 2012 data.

We observe the expected effects: the more you work at an outside job, the lower the percentage of housework that you do. The greater percentage of household income you bring home, the lower the percentage of housework you do. Here are two examples:

Someone who works 10 hours per week at an outside job and brings home 5% of the household income:

$$\%RHHWORK = 79.46 - 0.31(10) - 0.29(5) = 74.91$$

The model predicts that such a person would do around 75% of the housework.

Someone who works 70 hours per week at an outside job and brings home 90% of the household income:

$$\%RHHWORK = 79.46 - 0.31(70) - 0.29(90) = 31.66$$

The model predicts that such a person would do around a third of the housework.

We can visually model these effects in Model 2 by drawing a causal model and adding the betas to the arrows in the model:

■ **Exhibit 14.3: The Start of a Housework Casual Model**

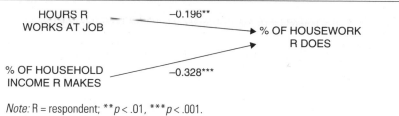

Note: R = respondent; **p < .01, ***p < .001.
Source: GSS 2012 data.

We use the betas for these models because we want to compare and contrast the size of the effects, and for that we use the betas. This model shows that both independent variables—hours worked at job and percentage of household income that the respondent makes—have effects on the percentage of the housework that the respondent does.

Although Percentage of Household Income is an independent variable explaining percentage of housework, we could also treat it as a dependent variable. The number of hours the respondent works at a job likely affects the percentage of household income the respondent contributes. Therefore, Percentage of Household Income can simultaneously be a dependent and independent variable. We can visualize this with a revised causal model:

■ **Exhibit 14.4: Revised Housework Casual Model**

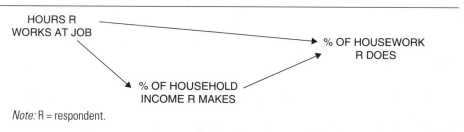

Note: R = respondent.

In this model, notice that percentage of household income has an arrow going to it (meaning that it is a dependent variable whose variation is being explained by hours at job) *and* it has an arrow going away from it (meaning that it is an independent variable explaining variation in percentage housework). To find the beta to attach to the arrow going from hours at job to percentage household income, we need to calculate another regression equation:

▪ **Exhibit 14.5: Explaining the Percentage of Income a Respondent Contributes**

Dependent Variable: % of Income Respondent Contributes		
Independent Variable	Slope	Beta
Hours R Works at Job	0.64***	0.361
Constant	31.42	
	$R^2 = 0.13$	
	$n = 295$	

Note: R = respondent.
*** $p < .001$.
Source: GSS 2012 data.

Now we can add this beta to the revised causal model:

▪ **Exhibit 14.6: Revised Housework Causal Model with Betas**

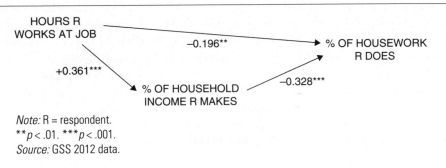

Note: R = respondent.
** $p < .01$. *** $p < .001$.
Source: GSS 2012 data.

We are starting to get a fuller picture of the interrelationships between these variables. What we have here is called a path model, for it allows us to assess the effects of variables by following the various paths from left to right. There are paths that are a straight shot from one variable to another, and these are called **direct effects**. Hours at Job has a direct effect on percentage of housework: as Hours at Job goes up by one standard deviation, Percentage of Housework goes down by 0.196 standard deviations. Hours at Job also has an **indirect effect** on Percentage Housework through Percentage Income Contributed. To calculate the indirect effect, we multiply the paths:

Path from Hours at Job to Percentage of Income Contributed: +0.361
Path from Percentage of Income Contributed to Percentage Housework: × −0.328

Indirect effect: −0.118

We can add the indirect effect of −0.118 to the direct effect of −0.196 in order to calculate what we call the total effect:

−0.118 + −0.196 = −0.314

Last, we can calculate what percent of the total effect is direct and indirect:

% of total effect that is direct = direct effect/total effect = 0.62, or 62%
% of total effect that is indirect = indirect effect/total effect = 0.38, or 38%

Now for a couple of terms. Any variable with an arrow going towards it is called an **endogenous variable**. In this model, we have two endogenous variables: Percentage of Income and Percentage of Housework. Both of these variables are being affected at some point by other variables in the model. Any variable without arrows going toward it is called an **exogenous variable**. Our only exogenous variable in this model is hours at job: we have no variables that are trying to explain how many hours the respondent works. You may have heard these prefixes in other contexts. *Endo–* means "inside" (as in *endoskeleton* and *endogamy*, for example). The endogenous variables are on the inside of the model. *Exo–* means "outside" (as in *exoskeleton* and *exogamy*, for example). The exogenous variables are on the outermost left side of the model. Keep in mind that the exogenous or endogenous nature of a variable isn't inherent, but rather specific to the model in question. We may well try to explain hours at job with other variables in other models and, if we did, hours at job would then be an endogenous variable. But, in this specific path model, hours at job is an exogenous variable. Using these new terms, here is a rule for building path models: you need to run a regression model for each endogenous variable.

INTERCHAPTER CONNECTION: NESTED VERSUS PATH

Before we move on to more examples, I want to make a couple of connections between path analysis and nested modeling, as they are indeed related. Recall that in the original set of nested models in this example, in Model 1, the beta for Hours at Job was −0.314. In Model 2, after I added the "% of Income from R" variable, the beta for Hours at Job decreased to −0.196. Notice that, in the path model, this is the value of the direct effect in the path model.

This beta decreased *to* –0.196, meaning that it decreased *by*

$$-0.314 - -0.196 = -0.118$$

This is the value of the indirect effect in the path model. Therefore, nested modeling does allow us to parse out these separate effects. However, path modeling does this as well, and it does so in a clear and visually pleasing way.

GSS EXAMPLE: SAME-SEX PARENTING REVISITED

In the nested modeling chapter, there was an example that explained support for same-sex parenting. In this example, sex, religious attendance, and support for nontraditional parenting all played roles, but these independent variables all seemed related: adding one variable affected the effects of the others. Let's revisit this example using path analysis. Here is a path model with all of the variables:

■ **Exhibit 14.7: Path Model Explaining Support for Same-Sex Parenting**

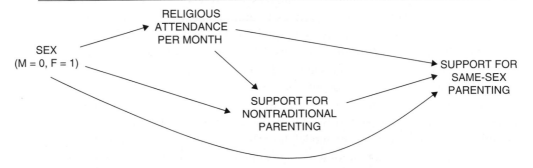

This model has three endogenous variables. Therefore, in order to fill in this model with the necessary betas, we need three regression models:

1. a model with support for same-sex parenting as the dependent variable
2. a model with support for nontraditional parenting as the dependent variable
3. a model with religious attendance as the dependent variable

Here they are:

Exhibit 14.8: Three Models Needed to Complete Parenting Path Model

Dependent Variable: Support for Same-Sex Parenting	
Independent Variable	Beta
Sex (M = 0, F = 1)	0.070**
Religious Attendance Per Month	−0.245***
Support of Nontrad. Parenting	0.498***

Dependent Variable: Support for Nontraditional Parenting	
Independent Variable	Beta
Sex (M = 0, F = 1)	0.247**
Religious Attendance Per Month	−0.287***

Dependent Variable: Religious Attendance Per Month	
Independent Variable	Beta
Sex (M = 0, F = 1)	0.103**

$**p < .01.$ $***$ $p < .001.$
Source: GSS 2012 data.

Now we can place these betas into the path model:

Exhibit 14.9: Parenting Path Model with Betas

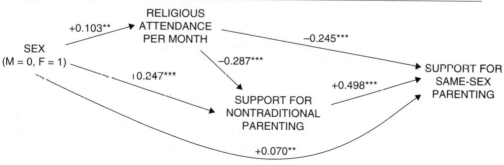

$**p < .01.$ $***p < .001.$
Source: GSS 2012 data.

Let's use this model to practice calculating different types of effects. First, the effect of attendance is as follows:

Direct effect	−0.245
Indirect effect through nontrad. parenting: −0.287 × +0.498 =	−0.143
Total effect	−0.388

We can conclude from these calculations that about two-thirds of the effect of religious attendance on attitudes toward same-sex parenting is a direct effect. One-third of the effect comes from the fact that religious attendance makes one more critical of nontraditional parenting in general, and this leads one to be more critical of same-sex parenting.

Calculating the effect of sex is trickier, because there are three indirect effects:

Direct effect	+0.070
Indirect effect through nontrad. parenting: +0.247 × +0.498 =	+0.123
Indirect effect through attendance: +0.103 × −0.245 =	−0.025
Indirect through att. & n.t.p.: +0.103 × −0.287 × +0.498 =	−0.015
Total effect	+0.153

Notice that by the time we multiply three paths together, the indirect effect gets rather small. Calculating the direct and indirect effects gives us a clear picture of the interrelationships among these variables. It is interesting that the total sex effect is primarily made up of indirect effects. Also notice that the first two effects are positive, while the other effects (although small) are negative. This helps us see in a different way a finding from the nested model when we looked at these relationships before: women are more supportive of same-sex parenting, but a little less so because of their higher religious attendance, than are men.

GSS EXAMPLE: EDUCATION, INCOME, AND POLITICAL PARTY

There is a long-running assumption that education will change your politics: many parents worry that they will send their child away to college a Republican and their child will return a Democrat. National statistics show that the vast majority of college professors vote for Democratic candidates. However, when I ran a simple regression equation with GSS 2012 data, using years of education as my independent variable and political party identification as my dependent variable, there was no relationship: the slope did move in this expected direction, but it was far from statistically significant. Let's look at this among a more specific group, however. Here is a path model:

■ Exhibit 14.10: Causal Model Explaining Party Identification

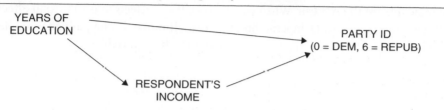

You likely can see where I'm going with this. I'm suggesting that education has a direct effect on party identification: people with more education might be more likely to vote Democrat. But education might also have an indirect effect through income: the more education you get, the more money you make, and there's a common belief that the more money you make, the more likely you are to vote Republican. Therefore, education may have conflicting effects on party identification: the direct effect moves in one direction, whereas the indirect effect moves in the opposite direction. Here is the path model with betas. Note that I ran this using only the respondents who were in their 50s.

■ Exhibit 14.11: Party Identification Model with Betas

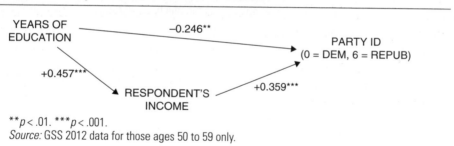

$**p < .01.$ $***p < .001.$
Source: GSS 2012 data for those ages 50 to 59 only.

Looking at the direct and indirect effects produces an interesting story. Here they are:

Direct effect of education on party identification	−0.246
Indirect effect of education on party through income: = +0.457 × +0.359 =	+0.164
Total effect	−0.082

The direct effect of education on political party is what we expected earlier: the more education you get, the more you move down on the scale toward Democrat. However, the indirect effect moves things in the opposite direction: the more education you get, the more money you make, and the more money you make, the more you move up on the scale toward Republican. When we combine these effects to get the total effect, we still get a move toward Democrat, but it is a small move. Using path analysis helped us to understand what was really going on among these variables.

GSS EXAMPLE: EXPLAINING DRINKING BEHAVIOR

Between 1990 and 1994, the General Social Survey asked a set of questions pertaining to the respondent's drinking behavior (this example is a modification of an example from Bohrnstedt & Knoke, 1988). The first question was, "Do you ever have occasion to use any alcoholic beverages such as liquor, wine, or beer, or are you a total abstainer?" Those respondents who said they did drink were asked the second question: "Do you sometimes drink more than you should?" Using these two questions, I created a little index of drinking behavior:

▨ **Exhibit 14.12: An Index of Drinking Behavior**

Score	Meaning	Frequency
0	Do not drink	1,061
1	Drink, but never too much	1,627
2	Drink, sometimes too much	795

Source: GSS 1990–1994 data.

We have variation. Now let's build a path model to try to explain it. We'll use two common variables: Age and Years of Education. We'll also use an uncommon variable: an assessment by the respondent of how often he/she goes to bars, ranging from 0 (I never go to bars) to 6 (I go to bars on an almost daily basis). This gives us the following coefficientless path model:

▨ **Exhibit 14.13: Path Model Explaining Level of Drinking**

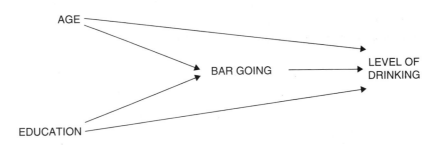

Before we run the regressions, let's go over what we are saying with this model. We are positing that age and education each have direct effects on drinking: how old you are and how educated you are will have a direct influence on how much you drink. We are also positing the existence of indirect effects: how old you are and how educated you are affect how frequently you go to bars, and, wild guess here, how frequently you go to bars affects how much you drink. First, we need a regression model using drinking behavior as the dependent variable. Here it is:

■ **Exhibit 14.14: Explaining Drinking Behavior**

Dependent Variable: Drinking Behavior	
Independent Variable	Beta
Age	−0.09***
Education	+0.10***
Bar Going	+0.46***

***$p < .001$ (two-tailed test)
Source: GSS 1990–1994 data.

Then we need a regression model using bar going as the dependent variable. Here it is:

■ **Exhibit 14.15: Explaining Going to Bars**

Dependent Variable: Going to Bars (0 = never, 6 = almost every day)	
Independent Variable	Beta
Age	−0.32***
Education	+0.10***

***$p < .001$.
Source: GSS 1990–1994 data.

This gives us the necessary betas to fill in the model:

■ **Exhibit 14.16: Completed Path Model for Drinking Behavior**

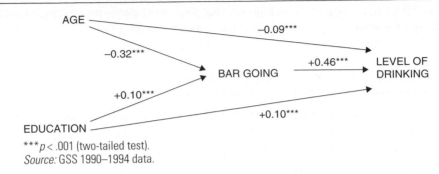

***$p < .001$ (two-tailed test).
Source: GSS 1990–1994 data.

A quick comment on beta placement: it doesn't really matter whether you put it above or below the arrow. The key is that it is crystal clear to which arrow a beta belongs.

Let's calculate the direct, indirect, and total effects:

Effect of age on drinking

Direct effect	-0.09
Indirect effect	$-0.32 \times +0.46 = -0.15$
Total effect	-0.24
Percentage of total effect that is indirect	$-0.15/-0.24 = 63\%$

Effect of education on drinking

Direct effect	$+0.10$
Indirect effect	$+0.10 \times +0.46 = +0.05$
Total effect	$+0.15$
Percentage of total effect that is indirect	$+0.05/+0.15 = 33\%$

Age has the expected effect: the older you get, the less you drink. The interesting finding from the model, however, is that a big part (63%) of this effect stems from the fact that, as you get older, you go to bars less frequently, and that lowers your alcohol consumption. The effect of education is smaller, but goes in (at least from my perhaps classist perspective) a counterintuitive direction: the more education you get, the more you drink. A part (33%) of this effect is indirect: the more educated you are, the more you go to bars, and therefore, the more you drink. But the larger part of education's effect is direct, in contrast to the effect of age. In the end, when we compare the total effects of the two exogenous variables, we find that age has a larger effect on drinking than does education.

GSS EXAMPLE: LIKE FATHER, LIKE SON?

As I suggested at the beginning of the chapter, a very common way to use path diagrams is to show the interconnections between parents and their children with regard to the levels of education the children achieve and the careers they choose. We like to believe that children can achieve anything, but their family backgrounds often have strong effects on how their lives turn out. For example, if your father was a janitor, what are the chances that you will end up as a physician? It can happen, and we love it when we hear a story like this, as it shows that the American dream is still a possibility. But I think you'd agree the possibility that you'd become a physician would be higher if your father had been a physician. But why? Well, the story is a bit complicated. A son could achieve a similar level of career to his father because he wanted to follow in his footsteps (awwwww). However, if a father has a high-level career, he is in a better position to finance his son's education. If the son achieves a high level of education, this will likely affect the level of career he achieves. Do you see how path analysis might help us to figure all this out?

Before we get to the paths, I should explain two things. First, you've likely noticed that in the preceding paragraph I talked only about the careers of fathers and sons, leaving women out of the picture. This is quite typical in this type of analysis. Although many women these days work outside of the home, many of their mothers—even though they worked many hours inside the home—did not have careers outside of the home. This puts a big wrench in this kind of analysis. So researchers typically restrict their analyses to fathers and sons. Second, I need to explain how we're going to measure one of the concepts I used earlier: level of career. In the social sciences, the term for this is *occupational prestige*. Some jobs have more prestige than others. By quantifying this prestige, we can study its causes and effects in our regression models. But how do we quantify it? We leave that up to the good people at the GSS, who, through surveys, have calculated the prestige level of hundreds of occupations and have given each occupation an index score. For example, a physician gets an occupational prestige score of 86, whereas a janitor gets a score of 22. Exhibit 14.17 shows some other occupations and their scores:

■ **Exhibit 14.17: Occupational Prestige Scores for Selected Occupations**

Lawyer	75
Accountant	65
Police officer	60
Mail carrier	47
Child care worker	36
Garbage collector	28
Shoe shiner	9

Now, of course, this quantification system is not perfect. For example, there may be a fair amount of variation in prestige *within* a given occupation. You could be head of surgery at the acclaimed Cedars-Sinai Medical Center in Los Angeles, or you could be one of those "docs in a box" at one of those urgent care enterprises. But, in general, these prestige numbers do provide some semblance of reality.

The GSS has occupational prestige scores for nearly all respondents. It also has data on the respondents' parents: their levels of education and their occupational prestige scores. With all of this in mind, here is the model we're going to work on:

■ **Exhibit 14.18: Prestige Path Model**

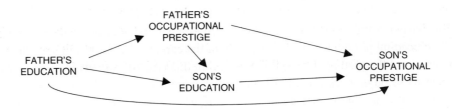

Before you look at the following models with numbers in them, answer this question: What regression models do you need to run to put betas into the model?

Exhibit 14.19 is the path model using 2010 GSS data (for some reason, the 2012 GSS did not contain some of these variables). I limited the samples so that we're looking only at respondents 30 years or older. I did this to allow the men to finish their education and attain their first careers.

■ Exhibit 14.19: Completed Prestige Path Model

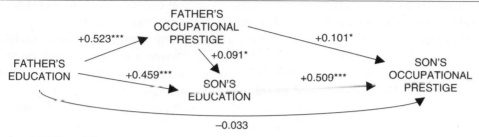

*p < .05. ***p < .001.
Source: GSS 2010 data for male respondents 30 years old or older.

There is no significant direct effect between father's education and son's occupational prestige. But there are plenty of indirect effects:

Indirect effect through son's education: +0.459 × +0.509 =	+0.234
Indirect effect through father's occupational prestige: +0.523 × +0.101 =	+0.053
Indirect effect through f's prestige, then s's educ: +0.523 × +0.091 × +0.519 =	+0.023
Total effect:	+0.310

The largest indirect effect is through son's education. A son sees the level of occupation his father attained and attains a similar level. The second indirect effect shows us that a son sees the prestige of his father's occupation and achieves a higher level of education because of this, which leads him to a prestigious occupation. The third indirect effect is small because it multiplies three paths together, but here is the story: a father gets a lot of education, which allows him to achieve prestige; the son sees this prestige and seeks more education in order to achieve similar prestige.

LITERATURE EXAMPLE: THE EFFECTS OF ACTIVISM

In the summer of 1964, around a thousand upper-middle-class college students from around the country participated in the Mississippi Freedom Summer Project. They traveled south to educate blacks and to register them to vote. The political climate in Mississippi at the time was very hostile towards blacks and those who fought for blacks' civil rights. For many of these students, who until this point had led fairly sheltered lives, this proved to be a very intense activist experience, one that changed their lives forever. Sociologist Doug McAdam wanted to understand how this experience affected the students in the years following their participation in the project (McAdam, 1989). He conducted a lengthy survey with those who participated in the project and with those who applied to participate in the project but, for some reason, did not participate. He used his survey results to construct several ordinary least squares (OLS) and logistic regression models. He also constructed some impressive path models that tell interesting stories. I present here only a tiny excerpt from one of these models from one of his scholarly articles (in 1990, he also wrote a wonderful book on the topic called *Freedom Summer*). But, first, here are descriptions of the variables used in the model. He was interested in how the students' subsequent level of activism during the rest of the 1960s was affected by their participation in Freedom Summer, so he used this as the dependent variable in the model. To measure this, he asked the survey respondents what activism they were involved in during those years and built an index. The only exogenous variable in the model is whether the student participated in Freedom Summer. He also asked the respondents how many Freedom Summer volunteers they were still in contact with in 1966, two years after the Freedom Summer project (he called these "ties"). Finally, he asked them to rate their political stance after Freedom Summer on a scale from 0 (very politically to the left) to 9 (very politically to the right). Although he found in earlier models that participation in Freedom Summer affected subsequent activism, the path model helps to flesh out these relationships. Here it is:

▣ **Exhibit 14.20: Activism Path Model**

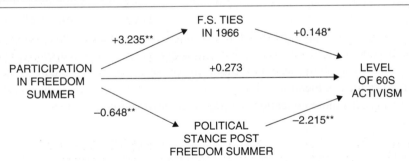

*p < .05. **p < .01 (two-tailed test).
Source: Adapted from McAdam (1989).

The most important finding is smack dab in the middle of the path model: participation in Freedom Summer does *not* have a direct effect on level of 1960s activism. That is, nothing inherent in the project itself propelled people to continue living activist lives. Although there is a beta on the arrow, the beta does not have stars, and therefore, it is not statistically significant. Participating in Freedom Summer did have a large effect, but it was *mediated* through the other two variables. A student who participated in Freedom Summer was much more likely to maintain multiple ties to other Freedom Summer volunteers, compared to those who applied for the project but did not go. The intensity of the experience forged strong bonds that kept these people tied into networks of activism. Those who didn't participate were more likely to be left out of the loop, and if you don't know where the next big protest is, it is difficult to participate (keep in mind that this research was conducted before the advent of the Internet). Those who participated in Freedom Summer were also affected in that they witnessed firsthand extreme injustices, often perpetrated by the government. This affected their political stance, moving them further to the political left than they were prior to Freedom Summer. Those who did not participate may have followed the events in Mississippi via the media, but this did not have the strong effect that seeing it face to face did. Those who had experienced a shift to the left subsequently participated in other activism, which was almost exclusively leftist in its orientation in the 1960s.

Through which of these variables does participation in Freedom Summer have the largest effect? To answer this, we do a little multiplication:

Indirect effect of ties $+3.235 \times +0.148 = +0.48$

Indirect effect of political stance $-0.648 \times -2.215 = +1.44$

Although participating in Freedom Summer has a larger effect on ties than it does on political stance, the effect of ties on activism is smaller than that of political stance on activism, so in the end the path through political stance elicits the larger effect, three times that of ties.

LITERATURE EXAMPLE: EMOTIONS IN SERVICE WORK

Does it really matter whether service employees smile at or make eye contact with their customers? This is one of the questions S. Douglas Pugh sought to address in his article "Service with a Smile: Emotional Contagion in the Service Encounter," which appeared in the *Academy of Management Journal* in 2001. He used path analysis to track the connections among every aspect of the service encounter at a bank. He and a research assistant conducted this study at 39 branches of a regional bank, and the research involved both survey research and observational research. They studied 131 employees and 220 customers. Here are some of their variables:

Transaction busyness: how many people were waiting in line to see the teller

Employee display of emotion: an index involving four behaviors: greeting, smiling, eye contact, and thanking the customer at the end of the transaction; a high number on the index meant that the employee engaged in all of these behaviors, sometimes multiple times

Customer positive affect: a survey measure of the customer's mood after the transaction

Customer service quality perceptions: a survey measure of the customer's satisfaction with the transaction

Here is Pugh's resulting path model:

■ **Exhibit 14.21: Employee Emotion Path Model with Betas**

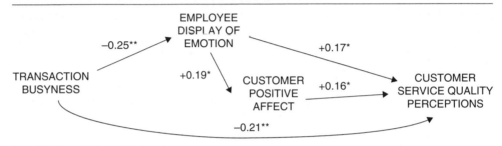

*$p < .05$. **$p < .01$ (two-tailed test).
Source: Adapted from Pugh (2001).

There are some interesting indirect effects going on here. Transaction busyness has a direct effect on customer satisfaction: customers who felt rushed felt less satisfied. But there is also an indirect effect through employee display of emotion: if the transaction was busy, the employee was less likely to use these emotional cues, and the customer was less satisfied because of this. Employee display of emotion has a direct effect on customer satisfaction: if the customer was greeted, smiled at, given eye contact, and thanked, he or she was more satisfied. But there is also an indirect effect through customer positive affect: if the employee engaged in these positive behaviors, signaling a positive mood, there was emotional contagion, and the customer's mood was positive as well, and the customer's positive mood itself led to higher customer satisfaction.

Here are the direct, indirect, and total effects of transaction busyness:

Direct effect	−0.21
Indirect: through employee emotion: −0.25 × +0.17 =	−0.04
Indirect: through emp. em. and cust. pos. affect: −0.25 × +0.19 × +0.16 =	−0.01
Total effect	−0.26

An implication of these findings: transaction busyness affects customer satisfaction, but if the employee maintains positive emotional cues throughout the transaction, he or she can somewhat counteract this effect.

CONCLUSION

Path analysis is a useful way to visualize all of the relationships you're investigating and see the relationships among them all. It is not used terribly often in the social science literature but often enough to warrant attention. In recent years, it has been supplanted by more advanced techniques, such as structural equation modeling (I talk about this technique briefly in Chapter 16). However, I believe that path analysis is an interesting and useful technique that more than holds its own among the stable of regression techniques.

SPSS DEMONSTRATION

Please visit the book's website (www.routledge.com/cw/linneman) to view a video of this demonstration.

Recall in the nested model chapter that I made a big deal about keeping the number of cases constant from model to model. Well, the same issue arises with path models, since the model represents multiple equations. However, unlike nested models, which all had the same dependent variable, our equations in path models have different dependent variables. A variable will be an independent variable in one equation and a dependent variable in another. That's pretty much the whole point of path models. This makes it difficult to keep the number of cases constant, but here's a tricky way to accomplish this.

Our example will involve the following path model:

The education level of household variable combines the educational levels of the respondent and his or her spouse, and it ranges from 0 (both have less than a high school degree) to 8 (both have graduate degrees). To fill in the betas, we need to run two regression models:

Model 1: DV: ownership index   IVs: education and income
Model 2: DV: income   IV: education

Model 1 will use only those cases that have valid values on all three variables. However, Model 2, if we just ran it with income and education, will use cases that don't have a valid value on the ownership index, because this variable is not in Model 2. So here's the trick: When you run Model 2, run it as a set of nested models, with education as the independent variable in the first model of the set, and then the ownership index as the independent variable in the second model of the set. Now, of course, we're not going to use that second model of the nested set (it doesn't even make sense; how can score on the ownership index affect income?). However, this will keep the cases constant across the two models you need for the path model.

Here is the SPSS output needed to put together the model:

Coefficients[a]

Model		Unstandardized Coefficients		Standardized Coefficients	t	Sig.
		B	Std. Error	Beta		
1	(Constant)	0.984	0.035		28.032	0.000
	Combined education of respondent and spouse	0.147	0.008	0.301	17.319	0.000
	Family Income in 1000s	0.005	0.000	0.316	18.225	0.000

a. Dependent Variable: Ownership Index.

Coefficients[a]

Model		Unstandardized Coefficients		Standardized Coefficients	t	Sig.
		B	Std. Error	Beta		
1	(Constant)	20.130	2.110		9.542	0.000
	Combined education of respondent and spouse	13.230	0.458	0.463	28.865	0.000
2	(Constant)	0.285	2.280		0.125	0.900
	Combined education of respondent and spouse	9.263	0.487	0.324	19.033	0.000
	Ownership Index	18.160	0.996	0.311	18.225	0.000

a. Dependent Variable: Family Income in 1000s.

FROM OUTPUT TO PRESENTATION

Pulling the betas from the above output, we can fill in the path model:

■ **Exhibit 14.22: Path Model of the Effects of Education and Income on Ownership**

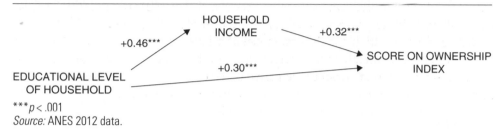

***p < .001
Source: ANES 2012 data.

The model shows us that education has both a direct and indirect effect on ownership index score.

EXERCISES

EXERCISES

Exercise 1

Using the ANES data, run the necessary regression equations to get the betas that go into the following model (use the recoded variable for religious attendance, as well as the recoded age variable). Then calculate the direct, indirect, and total effect of age. Finally, think about and write the story that is implied by your results.

Exercise 2 (Answer Available in Appendix D)

Let's stick with age and religious attendance, but switch our dependent variable to the ANES abortion index. First, run a simple regression with age as the independent variable and the abortion index as your dependent variable. Then, run regressions to add betas to the following model:

By contrasting what you found with the simple regression to what you found in the path model, tell the interesting story that is going on here.

Exercise 3

Political views are linked to attitudes toward the tea party: conservatives align more closely with it than liberals do. Is this a direct relationship, or does attitudes toward the government's role in society play a part?

Run the regression models you need to fill in the path model. Calculate the direct, indirect, and total effects and summarize the overall finding of the model.

Exercise 4

Using ANES data, create a path model that addresses this question: Does household educational level affect life satisfaction directly, indirectly through household income, or a combination of the two? Be sure to use the recoded variables in your analysis. Once you have your path model, explain what is going on.

Exercise 5

Using ANES data, create a path model that addresses this question: Does (recoded) party identification affect one's score on the affirmative action index directly, indirectly through resentment toward black (use the index), or a combination of the two? Once you have your path model, explain what is going on.

Exercise 6

Using the PewShop dataset, run the regressions you need for the following path model. Then, convey the story the path model is telling.

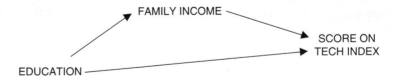

Exercise 7 (Answer Available in Appendix D)

Using the PewShop dataset, first run a simple regression of education on the Shopping Index (just retrieve the beta from this model). Then, run the regressions you need for the following path model. Explain what the path model tells you that the simple regression does not.

Exercise 8

We posit that the effect of education on seeking health information on the Internet has a direct and indirect effect that are in opposition to one another. The more education you have, the more you will use the Internet to look for health information on the Internet. However, the more education you have, the fewer health conditions you will have, and the less you will use the Internet to look for health information on the Internet. Create a path model of the preceding ideas, and then Use the PewHealth dataset to fill in the model with betas. Interpret your results, addressing the ideas earlier.

Exercise 9

We posit that the effect of age on seeking health information on the Internet has a direct and indirect effect that are in opposition to one another. The older you are, the less you will use the Internet to look for health information on the Internet. However, the older you are, the more health conditions you will have, and the more you will use the Internet to look for health information on the Internet. Create a path model of the preceding ideas, and then use the PewHealth dataset to fill In the model with betas. Interpret your results, addressing the ideas earlier.

Exercise 10

We are interested in the relationships among the various measures of technology use among children. Use the PewKids dataset to fill in the betas on the following model, calculate the direct and indirect effects, and explain your results.

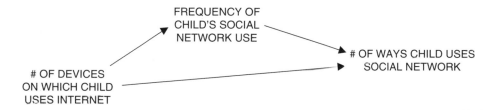

Exercise 11

We found in an exercise in an earlier chapter that parent's age affects how much they do (from the perception of their child) to check/block their child's technology. Complicate this story by filling in the below path model with the necessary betas and explaining what happens in the model.

Exercise 12

Using the WVS dataset, investigate the relationship between trust, happiness, and favoring a strong leadership. Run regression models to fill in the following path model and explain your results:

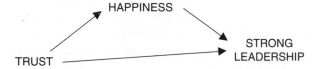

Exercise 13

Run the model in Exercise 12 twice more: once for the European countries and once for the Asian/African countries. Describe the differences you observe in the models.

Exercise 14 (Answer Available in Appendix D)

Using the WVS dataset, address the following question: Does religiosity (as measured by RELGIMP) affect number of children (CHILD) directly, or indirectly, through the importance of family (FAMIMP)?

## Chapter 15

QUESTIONING THE GREATNESS OF STRAIGHTNESS: NONLINEAR RELATIONSHIPS

This chapter covers . . .

. . . why some relationships may be nonlinear rather than linear

. . . how to use a squared term in a regression model

. . . how to tell the shape of the curve

. . . the use of logarithms to straighten out a relationship

. . . how a researcher examined how occupation affects housework

. . . how researchers examined the effectiveness of members of the U.S. Congress

INTRODUCTION

When I first began talking about regression, I said that one of the names for regular regression is linear regression. All the regression models we've examined so far have made a very large assumption: that the relationship between our variables is linear. For example, a relationship we've examined again and again has been that between education and income. Here is a model using education and hours worked as the independent variables and respondent's income as the dependent variable (using 2012 GSS data):

Holding hours worked constant at 40 hours, we get the following graph:

■ **Exhibit 15.4: Illustrating the Nonlinear Effect of Education on Income**

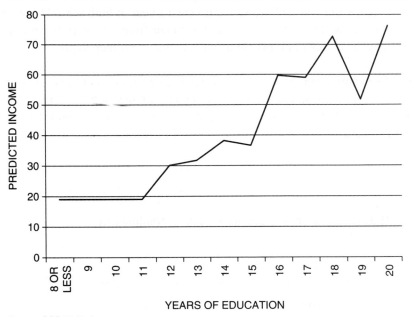

YEARS OF EDUCATION

Source: GSS 2012 data.

According to the regression equation, education doesn't significantly affect income until the move from 11 to 12 years. This makes sense, because this is the point at which people received a high school diploma. Then, in fits and starts, it rises quickly. So is the linear equation wrong? No. It's just doing what we asked it to do: describe the average increase in income as education increases year to year. Is the second equation more right? That is, is the second equation a better reflection of reality? Yes, a bit. Look at the R^2s. The second model has a value of 0.33, compared to 0.29 in the first model, meaning that it does fit the data better. The point I want you to get from this first example is that not all the relationships are linear in nature. Some of them may follow a different, curvier path.

MODELING NONLINEAR RELATIONSHIPS

Consider this example: Does age affect the number of car accidents people have? Think about driving over the life course. When drivers are young, they're still perfecting the art of driving, they have distracting young friends in their cars, and some of them even *text while driving* (oh, don't get me started on that one). All of these factors mean that younger drivers get in more accidents than do older drivers. As people get older, they get wiser, get more driving practice, and drive alone more often, and the number of accidents they have goes down. But, as people move into old age, the number of accidents rises again. Their reaction time gets longer, their eyesight worsens, and if they're anything like my mother, they're shrinking and can't see over the steering wheel any more. Here are completely hypothetical data for 16 completely hypothetical people:

■ **Exhibit 15.5: 16 Hypothetical People's Ages and Number of Car Accidents**

Person	Age	# of Car Accidents in Past Year
Alison	16	8
Brandon	18	7
Caitlin	23	5
Darren	25	4
Emily	29	3
Fernando	33	3
Gina	39	2
Hank	42	1
Isabel	45	1
Jack	54	1
Kay	60	3
Leroy	67	4
Marion	73	5
Nancy	79	7
Otis	83	7
Peggy	90	8

This gives us the equation:

$$\text{ACCIDENTS} = 13.62 - 0.49(\text{AGE}) + 0.005(\text{AGE})^2$$

or

$$\text{ACCIDENTS} = 13.62 - 0.49(\text{AGE}) + 0.005(\text{AGE})(\text{AGE})$$

As the R^2 shows us, this model does extremely well at explaining the variation in accidents. Look at how close its predicted curved line is to all of the points:

■ **Exhibit 15.9: Illustrating the Nonlinear Relationship**

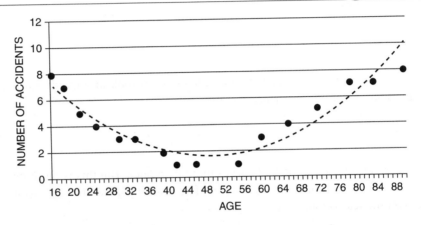

Let's look at these numbers more closely so you can get a real feel for what's going on here:

■ **Exhibit 15.10: Looking at the Predicted Accidents More Closely**

Person	AGE	−0.49 × AGE	+0.005 × AGE × AGE	Sum	Predicted Accidents
A	16	−7.84	1.28	−6.56	7.06
B	18	−8.82	1.62	−7.20	6.42
C	23	−11.27	2.65	−8.62	5.00
D	25	−12.25	3.13	−9.12	4.50
E	29	−14.21	4.21	−10.00	3.62
F	33	−16.17	5.45	−10.72	2.90
G	39	−19.11	7.61	−11.50	2.12
H	42	−20.58	8.82	−11.76	1.86
I	45	−22.05	10.13	−11.92	1.70
J	54	−26.46	14.58	−11.88	1.74
K	60	−29.40	18.00	−11.40	2.22
L	67	−32.83	22.45	−10.38	3.24
M	73	−35.77	26.65	−9.12	4.50
N	79	−38.71	31.21	−7.50	6.12
0	83	−40.67	34.45	−6.22	7.40
P	90	−44.10	40.50	−3.60	10.02

Notice in the graph that the point at which the regression line "bottoms out" and starts going back up is at around age 50. What I have in the table are the calculations for each part of the regression equation. The third column is the part involving AGE. The fourth column is the part involving AGE × AGE. Then, in the fifth column, I have the sum of these two parts. Finally, the last column has the predicted number of accidents. Notice what happens between Isabel and Jack: Isabel, aged 45, is the last person for whom the sum of these parts is increasingly negative (−11.92), making the predicted number of accidents go down. Jack, aged 54, is the first person for whom the sum of these parts becomes less negative (−11.88) and thus, when combined with the constant, is the first step toward making the number of accidents go back up. Why does this happen? Notice that, as age goes up, the column with AGE × AGE starts to go up more quickly. This is the nature of the square of a whole number: it rises more quickly than the number itself. This is why we see the predicted number of accidents bottom out and then start to rise again.

I'd like to say something about the size of squared slopes. Even though the slope for the squared term seems very small at 0.005, we need to keep in mind the range of the squared variable. Whereas the range of the age variable is 16 to 90, the range of the age-squared variable is 256 to 8,100. Because of this, I tend to keep more decimal points for the squared slopes. For example, if I had rounded the 0.005 up to 0.01, because I'd be multiplying this by Peggy's squared age (a whopping 8,100), Peggy's predicted number of accidents would have gone from 10 to 50!

Let's do one more hypothetical example, and we'll even use these same people and their ages again. For this example, let's imagine a statistics-savvy grocery-store check-out person who observes our 16 people and keeps track of how much on average they spend at her grocery store per week:

■ **Exhibit 15.11: 16 People's Ages and Weekly Grocery Bills**

Person	Age	Amount Spent per Week on Groceries
Alison	16	$20
Brandon	18	$25
Caitlin	23	$40
Darren	25	$42
Emily	29	$55
Fernando	33	$60
Gina	39	$100
Hank	42	$150
Isabel	45	$175
Jack	54	$150
Kay	60	$130
Leroy	67	$100
Marion	73	$60
Nancy	79	$40
Otis	83	$30
Peggy	90	$20

Here is a scatterplot of these data:

■ Exhibit 15.12: Scatterplot of Ages and Weekly Grocery Bills

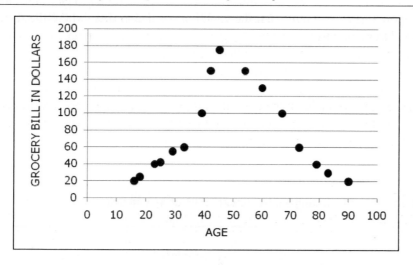

As before, let's see how badly regular linear regression does trying to fit a straight line to these data:

GROCERIES = 70.64 + 0.09(AGE) $R^2 = -0.07$

Significance of slope: 0.882

Wow, that's bad. Let's instead use a curvilinear relationship. We again add the age-squared variable, and here is the resulting this model:

■ Exhibit 15.13: Explaining Grocery Bills with a Squared Term

Dependent Variable: Amount per Week Spent on Groceries	
Independent Variable	Slope
Age	10.24***
Age Squared	−0.10***
Constant	−136.82
R^2	0.76

Note: $n = 16$.
*** $p < .001$ (two-tailed test)

This gives us the equation

GROCERIES = –136.82 + 10.24(AGE) – 0.10(AGE)(AGE)

Notice how this is different from the equation we had earlier, where the dependent variable was accidents:

ACCIDENTS = 13.62 – 0.49(AGE) + 0.005(AGE)(AGE)

With the groceries equation, the first slope is positive, and the slope for the square is negative. With the accidents equation, the first slope is negative, and the slope for the square is positive. Here is the graph of this relationship:

■ **Exhibit 15.14: Illustrating the Nonlinear Effect of Age on Grocery Bills**

With the much more reasonable R^2 of 0.76, we know that this curved line does a much better job than the straight-line model. It's not perfect. For example, it predicts that 90-year-olds will spend a negative amount of money on groceries. But, now that I think about it, I once had an elderly neighbor who was an absolute wizard with coupons, so, who knows, maybe the model isn't that far off.

To drive the point home one more time, let's do the same calculations for this model as we did with the previous model:

■ Exhibit 15.15: Looking at the Predicted Grocery Bills More Closely

Person	AGE	$10.24 \times AGE$	$-0.10 \times$ $AGE \times AGE$	Sum	Predicted Grocery Bill
A	16	163.84	−25.6	138.24	1.42
B	18	184.32	−32.4	151.92	15.10
C	23	235.52	−52.9	182.62	45.80
D	25	256.00	−62.5	193.50	56.68
E	29	296.96	−84.1	212.86	76.04
F	33	337.92	−108.9	229.02	92.20
G	39	399.36	−152.1	247.26	110.44
H	42	430.08	−176.4	253.68	116.86
I	45	460.80	−202.5	258.30	121.48
J	54	552.96	−291.6	261.36	124.54
K	60	614.40	−360.0	256.40	119.58
L	67	686.08	−448.9	237.18	100.36
M	73	747.52	−532.9	214.62	77.80
N	79	808.96	−624.1	184.86	48.04
O	83	849.92	−688.9	161.02	24.20
P	90	921.60	−810.0	111.60	−25.22

Notice that the sum rises until it gets to Jack, and then after that it begins to fall. This creates a line that rises, first quickly and then slowly, to an apex; then it starts to fall, first at a slow rate and then more rapidly as age reaches its highest point. Still not getting how this all works? Let's try a visual approach. Take a look at this graph:

▨ **Exhibit 15.16: Looking at the Predicted Grocery Bills More Closely**

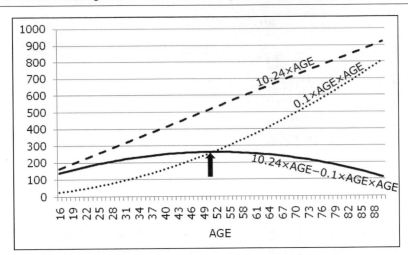

Let's say we're pulling for the thin dotted line, which represents the product of 0.1 × AGE × AGE. It's trying really hard to climb up and catch the thick dotted line (which represents 10.24 × AGE). But, at first, it falls further and further behind the thick dotted line: notice that on the left side of graph, the gap between these two lines is widening. Because this gap is widening, when we subtract 0.1 × AGE × AGE from 10.24 × AGE this difference grows, which makes the solid line rise. But don't give up hope for our thin dotted line, because where the arrow is, the thin dotted line reaches a point where it starts to catch up to the thick dotted line, because the product of AGE × AGE starts to get pretty big. Notice that this is *also* the point where the solid line changes direction. As the thin dotted line really starts to catch up to the thick dotted line, the difference between 10.24 × AGE and 0.1 × AGE × AGE starts to get smaller, thus making the solid line go down.

Before we get to a few examples using real data, I want to reiterate what we've learned about the shape of these curves, as there is a general set of rules about how quadratic equations work:

If you have a quadratic equation with a slope for a variable X and the slope for X^2:

If the slope for X is *negative* and the slope for X^2 is *positive*,
then the curve of the line will have a U shape,
with the line going from high to low to high.

If the slope for X is *positive* and the slope for X^2 is *negative*,
then the curve of the line will have a ∩ shape,
with the line going from low to high to low.

Although these rules give you a good idea of what the relationships look like, I think it is preferable to do enough examples and actually create a graph in order to see its exact shape.

GSS EXAMPLE: AGE AND INCOME

Here we examine a classic nonlinear relationship: age's effect on income. Young people don't make much money. As you get older, your income rises. As you enter old age, your income begins to fall. That's the story. Let's see if the data support it. First, a simple regression with age and income using 2012 GSS data:

■ **Exhibit 15.17: Linear Model of Age's Effect on Income**

Dependent Variable: Respondent's Income in 1000's	
Independent Variable	Model 1
Age	0.50***
Constant	18.13
R^2	0.04
	$n = 1,140$

***$p < .001$ (two-tailed test)
Source: GSS 2012 data.

Age has an effect, but the R^2 value is small. We add a Model 2 that has the square of the Age variable:

■ **Exhibit 15.18: Adding a Nonlinear Model of Age's Effect on Income**

Dependent Variable: Respondent's Income in 1000's		
Independent Variable	Model 1	Model 2
Age	0.50***	4.30***
Age Squared	—	−0.042***
Constant	18.13	−60.02
R^2	0.04	0.11
	$n = 1,140$	$n = 1,140$

***$p < .001$ (two-tailed test)
Source: GSS 2012 data.

One thing I want you to notice is that, just as with interaction terms, you cannot interpret the slopes of a quadratic regression equation individually. For example, the slope for age in Model 2 suggests that each year of age garners you an additional $4,300. That's a big increase, and no 90-year-olds I know make $327,000 a year. We can't interpret the slope this way; when there is a squared term, we have to interpret the non-squared term along with its squared term. Similarly, just as we did for interaction effects, if the slope for the squared term is statistically significant, we keep the slope for the non-squared term in the prediction equation, regardless of whether it is itself statistically significant.

How can we tell if the curvilinear model is the better fit? Two ways: the age-squared variable is highly statistically significant, and the value for R^2 nearly triples. The graph tells us when income reaches its peak and then starts to decline: between the ages of 51 and 52:

■ **Exhibit 15.19: Illustrating the Nonlinear Effect on Income**

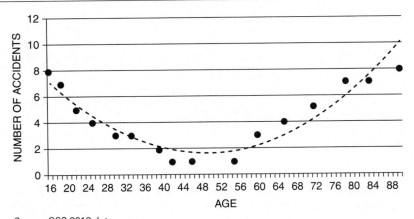

Source: GSS 2012 data.

As you know, I'm a big fan of drawing the graph, as this is the best way to show your non-stats audience what is going on. However, if you are for some reason resistant to graphs (due to a bad childhood experience, or an allergy), here's a quick equation that gives you the point at which the graph turns: take the negative of the linear slope and divide it by two times the nonlinear slope:

$$-(\text{linear slope})/(2 \times \text{nonlinear slope})$$

For example, using the slopes from Model 2 from earlier:

$$-4.30/(2 \times -0.042) = -4.30/-0.084 = 51.19$$

Let's also look at this same nonlinear relationship, but for different groups, something akin to the process of interaction. Here are models for those with a high school degree or less versus those with a bachelor's degree or higher:

■ **Exhibit 15.20: The Nonlinear Relationship among Two Educational Groups**

Dependent Variable: Respondent's Income in 1000's		
Independent Variable	H.S. or Less	Bachelor's or More
Age	2.40***	6.89***
Age Squared	−0.022***	0.068***
Constant	−30.20	−98.32
R^2	0.12	0.12
	$n = 672$	$n = 374$

***$p < .001$ (two-tailed test)
Source: GSS 2012 data.

As you might expect, the curve for those with more education is steeper than the curve for those with less education. But it is steeper on both ends:

■ **Exhibit 15.21: Illustrating the Nonlinear Relationship among Two Groups**

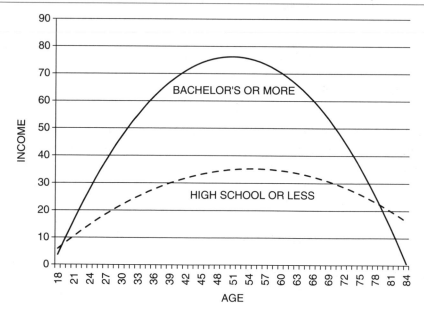

The educated people rise faster above the less educated, and their incomes decline faster as well. This could be because those who have less education may need to work longer hours in their older age to maintain incomes, whereas those with more education were able to put money aside earlier in their lives (when their incomes were very high) and therefore don't need to work as much as they get older. That is, they have wealth, and therefore do not need any income.

GSS EXAMPLE: INCOME AND FINANCIAL SATISFACTION

In this example, we're going to move income to the dependent side of the equation and square it (if only we really could square our incomes!). The GSS asks respondents how satisfied they are with their financial situations, with the response choices being: 0 (not at all satisfied), 1 (more or less satisfied), and 2 (satisfied). Not an ideal variable for regression, but we'll use it for now. Our question is, "As income increases, does financial satisfaction increase in a linear or non-linear fashion?" First, the linear model:

▪ **Exhibit 15.22: The Linear Relationship Between Income and Financial Satisfaction**

Dependent Variable: Respondent's Financial Satisfaction	
Independent Variable	Model 1
Income in 1000s	0.006***
Constant	0.711
R^2	0.086
	$n = 1{,}140$

***$p < .001$ (two-tailed test)
Source: GSS 2012 data.

There is a relationship: for each $1,000 you make, you get more 0.006 more financially satisfied (notice that because I'm dealing with very small values, I'm keeping more decimal places). However, perhaps the phenomenon of diminishing returns comes into play here. At lower income levels, a $10,000 increase in income might make a large difference in financial satisfaction. But a high-income person's response to a $10,000 increase might be "Meh. Who cares?" And so we introduce a squared income term:

■ **Exhibit 15.23: The Nonlinear Relationship between Income and Financial Satisfaction**

Dependent Variable: Respondent's Financial Satisfaction		
Independent Variable	Model 1	Model 2
Income in 1000s	0.006***	0.010***
Income Squared	—	0.00003026***
Constant	0.711	0.635
R^2	0.086	0.092
	$n = 1,141$	$n = 1,141$

$*p < .05, ***p < .001$ (two-tailed test)
Source: GSS 2012 data.

A slight improvement: the R^2 increases from 0.086 to 0.092. I ran one of those F-tests on this improvement, and it was statistically significant. Perhaps it is slightly ridiculous to keep that many decimal places for the slope of the squared term, but I feel this is justified since the dependent variable takes on such small values and the independent variable takes on such large values once squared. Here is the resulting graph:

■ **Exhibit 15.24: Illustrating the Nonlinear Relationship Between Income and Financial Satisfaction**

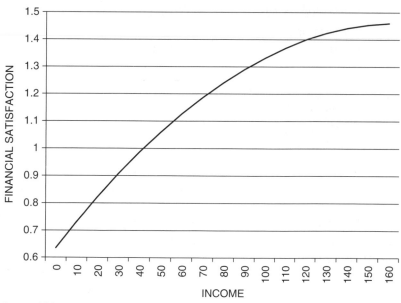

Source: GSS 2012 data.

I must admit, to make the effect look really big, I messed with the vertical axis, making it go only from 0.6 to 1.5. I couldn't resist, as I wanted to clearly illustrate that we do indeed have diminishing returns here. Here are a few examples:

as income goes from $10,000 to $20,000, financial satisfaction increases by 0.09
as income goes from $60,000 to $70,000, financial satisfaction increases by 0.06
as income goes from $110,000 to $120,000, financial satisfaction increases by only 0.03.

Although it is the same income increase each time, the effect it produces gets smaller and smaller. In other words, the returns it produces are diminishing.

What if we felt uneasy about using a dependent variable that had only three categories? One thing we could do would be to turn the variable into a dichotomy, where $0 =$ not at all satisfied or more or less satisfied and $1 =$ satisfied (27% of the respondents said they were satisfied, by the way). You have that sinking feeling, don't you? Yes, I'm going to combine curvilinearity with logistic regression. It's really not that big a deal. We'll take it a step at a time. First, the model:

■ **Exhibit 15.25: A Nonlinear, Logistic Model**

Dependent Variable: Are You Financially Satisfied? (No=0, Yes=1)	
Independent Variable	Model 1
Income in 1000	0.008***
Income Squared	0.00007456*
Constant	−1.987
R^2	0.090
	$n = 1,141$

$*p < .05, ***p < .001$ (two-tailed test)
Source: GSS 2012 data.

This gives us the equation:

$$z = -1.987 - 0.008(\text{INCOME}) + 0.00007456(\text{INCOME})(\text{INCOME})$$

And the graph looks like this:

■ **Exhibit 15.26: Illustrating the Nonlinear, Logistic Model**

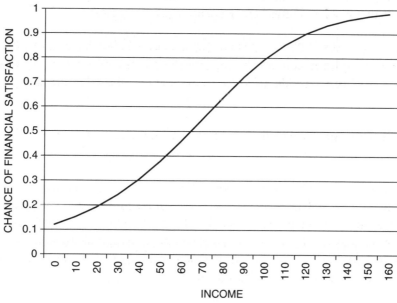

Source: GSS 2012 data.

The results tell a story similar to the non-logistic regression, but in terms of probabilities. For example, increasing income from $50,000 to $60,000 raises the probability of financial satisfaction by 8%, but increasing income from $150,000 to $160,000 raises the probability by only 1%.

GSS EXAMPLE: EDUCATION AND INCOME

I started this chapter with an example using education and income as reference groups to examine this relationship. Let's now use a curvilinear equation. Here are two models for comparison:

■ **Exhibit 15.27:   Linear and Nonlinear Income Models**

Dependent Variable: Respondent's Income in 1000's		
Independent Variable	Model 1	Model 2
Education in years	4.87***	−1.80
Education Squared	—	0.25***
Hours Worked	0.73***	0.73***
Constant	−54.63	−11.85
R^2	0.29	0.30
	$n = 983$	$n = 983$

***$p < .001$ (two-tailed test)
Source: GSS 2012 data.

The R^2 is a bit higher than in the linear model (although not by a whole lot), and the slope for the squared term is highly significant. The graph for Model 2 shows some curve, but just a bit. For comparison's sake, I've included the line from the linear Model 1. I've held hours worked constant at 40 hours per week:

■ **Exhibit 15.28:   Illustrating the Linear and Nonlinear Income Models**

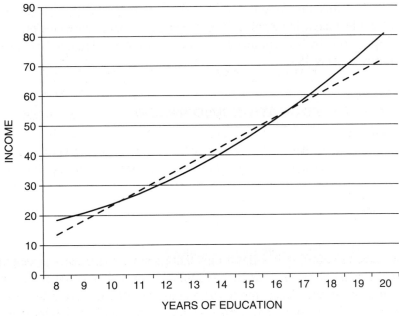

Source: GSS 2012 data.

What the curved line shows us is that education packs a larger effect at the upper end than it does at the lower end. For example, going from 8 years of education to 9 years, income rises $2,420. Going from 18 years of education to 19 years, income rises $7,440. This phenomenon is not captured by the linear equation. In contrast to the previous example, which illustrated diminishing returns, this relationship offers an example of an accelerating relationship: as the values of the independent variable rise, the effect grows larger, not smaller.

GSS EXAMPLE: INCOME AND POLITICAL PARTY

This next GSS example contrasts a linear effect with a nonlinear effect. The stereotypical relationship between income and political party is a simple one: the more money you make, the more Republican you become. We want to know not only if this relationship is supported by data, but whether or not it is a linear relationship, and if it is the same for whites and blacks. I ran two sets of nested models, using income and income-squared as my independent variables and party identification as the dependent variable (measured on a simple scale where strong Democrats are at 0 and strong Republicans are at 6, with people able to choose a 1, 2, 3, 4, or 5). I ran a set for whites and a set for blacks, and here are the resulting models:

■ **Exhibit 15.29: Income and Party Identification for Whites and Blacks**

Dependent Variable: Party ID (0 = Strong Democrat — 6 = Strong Republican)				
Ind. Var.	Whites		Blacks	
	Model 1	Model 2	Model 1	Model 2
Income	0.004*	−0.003	0.001	−0.023*
Income^2	—	0.00005187	—	0.00020696**
Constant	2.792	2.928	0.994	1.396
R^2	0.006	0.009	0.000	0.050
	$n = 821$	$n = 821$	$n = 167$	$n = 167$

*$p < .05$, ***$p < .001$ (two-tailed test)
Source: GSS 2012 data.

For whites, the relationship is a linear one, though not a particularly strong one. The slope for the squared income variable in Model 2 for whites is not statistically significant. In contrast, for blacks, the linear relationship doesn't work: the slope is not statistically significant, and there is no explained variation. The nonlinear model for blacks does substantially better: the non-linear slope is statistically significant and the R^2 is now 0.05. Thus, for one group, the relationship is linear, but for the other group, it is nonlinear. Here is a graph of the relationships:

■ **Exhibit 15.30: Graph of Income and Party ID for Whites and Blacks**

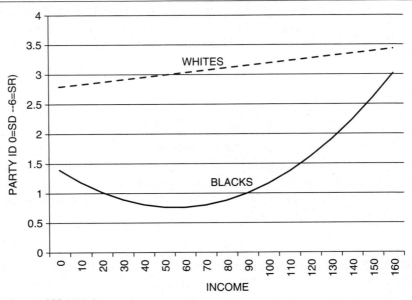

Source: GSS 2012 data.

For whites, the effect of income on party identification is not huge, but it is clearly linear: as income goes up for whites, there is a small but steady move toward Republican. Blacks stay on the Democratic end until around $70,000. In fact, until that point, income and party identification seem to be negatively related: the more income you make, the more Democrat you are. After $70,000, the relationship becomes positive, and at an accelerated rate: a move from $80,000 to $90,000 moves a black person 0.12 toward Republican, whereas a move from $150,000 to $160,000 moves a black person 0.41 toward Republican. Middle-income blacks and whites differ by over two points on this scale, whereas upper-income blacks and whites differ by less than half a point. Had we limited ourselves to linear relationships, we wouldn't have identified these dynamics.

USING LOGARITHMS TO STRAIGHTEN
OUT A RELATIONSHIP

Although most of the time this "independent variable, square of the independent variable" situation is what you will see in the research world, another common transformation involves the use of logarithms. This procedure is a different from the way we used logs with logistic regression. The most frequent situation you will see is this: instead of using income as the dependent variable, a researcher will use the *log* of income as the dependent variable. Let's go over a simple example of this, and you'll see what's going on and why one might choose to do this. Here are the years of education and incomes for ten hypothetical people:

■ **Exhibit 15.31: Ten Hypothetical Educations and Incomes**

Years of Education	Income in 1000s
8	5
8	10
10	15
12	20
16	50
14	100
16	200
16	500
20	750
20	1000

Source: Hypothetical data.

In this situation, some people have very low incomes, and some have very high incomes. If we create a scatterplot and simple regression equation using these data, we get some interesting results. First, the scatterplot:

■ **Exhibit 15.34: Scatterplot with Logged Income**

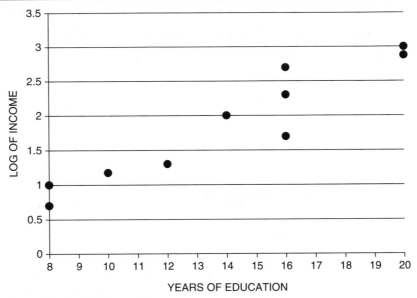

YEARS OF EDUCATION

Source: Hypothetical data.

You can tell from this scatterplot that this changes the relationship between the two variables from an exponential-growth situation to a linear situation. Also, notice that, were we to draw the regression line, the points would be very close to it. Here is the regression equation:

$$\text{LOG OF INCOME} = -0.6027 + 0.177(\text{EDUCATION}) \quad r^2 = 0.90$$

It has a higher r^2. By transforming the dependent variable, we now have a better-fitting model. To use this model to predict incomes, all you need to do is plug in a value for education, take the resulting number, and take 10 to the power of that number. Here are a few examples:

8 years of education:	$-0.6027 + 0.177(8) = 0.8133$	$10^{0.8133} = 6.51$
16 years of education:	$-0.6027 + 0.177(16) = 2.2293$	$10^{2.2293} = 169.55$
20 years of education:	$-0.6027 + 0.177(20) = 2.9373$	$10^{2.9373} = 865.57$

In contrast to the predictions the first model made, these predictions make much more sense. In summary, rather than adding a squared term to capture a nonlinear relationship, we took the dependent variable, logged it, and then used this transformed variable in regular linear regression. Although this is the most frequent transformation you will see, there are others. For example, if your independent variable rises exponentially, and you want to use it in a linear regression, you could log this independent variable. You can even take the log of both the dependent and independent variables. So many possibilities.

LITERATURE EXAMPLE: HOUSEWORK AND GENDER

You might be thinking, "Oh, I already see where this is going: women do more housework than do men." That may be true, but social researchers have greatly increased our understanding of the nuances of this relationship. For example, in his 2012 article in the esteemed *American Journal of Sociology* titled "Gender Deviance and Household Work: The Role of Occupation," Daniel Schneider revealed an intriguing relationship, and it just so happens to be a nonlinear one (how appropriate). Schneider argued that we have preconceptions about the gender-appropriate nature of types of occupations and types of housework. For example, men who are nurses, secretaries, or kindergarten teachers are engaging in "gender deviance": they are not performing their gender correctly because their jobs are within occupations where the vast majority of workers are women. At home, there are also opportunities for gender deviance. For example imagine a heterosexual household in which the husband spends time cooking, shopping, and cleaning but does not spend time doing car repairs and lawn maintenance. Schneider decided to examine the relationship between the type of work a man does at his job and the type of work he does in his home. He used two well-regarded datasets: The National Survey of Families and Households and The American Time Use Survey. Both surveys carefully measure what the man's occupation is and what specific tasks he performs within the home. As with any journal article, Schneider's has far more going on in it than we will go over here. We're just going to look at one of his equations that used the American Time Use Survey. The dependent variable is minutes per day doing male-typed housework (i.e., repairs and lawn care). Although his model controls for lots of other variables (such as age, hours worked, and percent of household earnings husband earns), we'll concentrate on his key independent variable: the proportion of the husband's occupation that is female. For example, if he were a construction worker, that proportion would be very low, but if he were a secretary, that proportion would be very high. Schneider's key move is that he also includes the square of this variable. Here is the model:

■ **Exhibit 15.37: Graph of the Relationship between Seniority and Effectiveness**

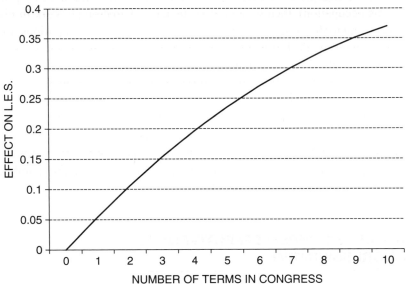

Source: Adapted from Volden et al. (2013).

Although the curve of the line is rather slight, their "tapering off" idea holds. The difference between 1 and 2 terms is 0.05, whereas the difference between 9 and 10 terms is 0.02.

The second set of variables is a vote share variable and its square. If a congressperson received a huge share of the votes, this is a sign her seat is safe and she can spend her time achieving effectiveness rather than campaigning. But perhaps this effect is nonlinear as well. The slope for vote share was 0.030, and for vote share squared the slope was –0.0002. Both were statistically significant. Exhibit 15.38 shows graph of this set of effects. Again, this just shows the shape of the combined effect of these two variables.

■ **Exhibit 15.38: Graph of the Relationship between Vote Share and Effectiveness**

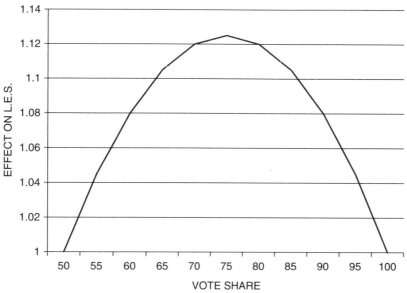

VOTE SHARE

Source: Adapted from Volden et al (2013).

The *x*-axis starts at 50, because in order for a congressperson to win in a two-candidate election, they have to get slightly more than 50% of the vote, and continues up to 100, in which a congressperson wins the election by a landslide margin. Here we see a full parabolic shape. There seems to be a sweet spot in the vote share where a congress-person is most effective. As Volden and his coauthors explained, this effect "indicates that the most effective members on average come from districts that are neither highly contested nor perfectly safe, giving members the leeway and the incentives to advance their legislative priorities" (Volden et al., 2013, p. 337). Winning by a healthy margin gives you clout, but winning by too much might make you complacent.

CONCLUSION

Although we've spent most of our regression time in this book talking about linear relationships, this chapter emphasizes that some of the most interesting relationships are not linear at all. Effects slow down, effects speed up, and effects completely turn around. And now you're prepared to deal with such relationships.

Chapter 16

PROBLEMS AND PROSPECTS: REGRESSION DIAGNOSTICS, ADVANCED TECHNIQUES, AND WHERE TO GO NOW

This chapter covers . . .

. . . potential regression-related problems of which you should be aware

. . . advanced regression techniques of which you should be aware

. . . how to continue your statistical education

INTRODUCTION

Wrapping up a book like this is difficult. We've come a very long way, and you are now well versed in a lot of the statistical techniques that are used in the real world of social research. But social statistics is a huge field, and there is so much more we could cover. So for this last chapter, I've decided on a compromise. There are two more topics I'm going to cover, but I'm going to do so at what I call an "awareness" level. I want you to leave this chapter with an awareness of these two topics, but I will not go into the nitty-gritty details as we have done in previous chapters. The first part of the chapter concerns the field of regression diagnostics, which is basically what it sounds like: diagnosing the health of your regression model and, if your model is "sick," how do you tell what kind of "sickness" it has? This sickness may come from the fact that your regression model violates a regression assumption, such as when you try to use linear regression on a nonlinear relationship. The second part of the chapter briefly introduces you to some of the most popular advanced techniques that are being used in contemporary social research. Again, the goal of this chapter is not to teach you the details of these techniques. Rather, it is designed so that, in your future career when you are using statistics, if someone says "multicollinearity" or "multilevel modeling", you'll at least know what this person is saying and why they are bringing it up.

POTENTIAL PROBLEM ONE: OUTLIERS

We'll start with a problem that I raised briefly early in the book: having one case or a small number of cases that, because of their uniqueness, throws off your regression model, giving you inaccurate results. Recall that an outlier is a case that has a value on a variable of interest that differs dramatically from the rest of the cases. A typical cause of this problem is user error: when inputting the data, someone made a mistake. Then, when someone else was cleaning the data (i.e., looking for such errors), he or she did not catch the mistake. Then, when you started to work with the dataset, you didn't take the initial step to run frequency distributions or descriptive statistics to see if anything looked strange. You just hopped right into running regressions. What I'm trying to point out is that this shouldn't be a problem: reputable datasets have professional data inputters and staff whose job it is to check the dataset, and you should always look carefully at your data before you start any analysis. But sometimes things don't happen as they should, and there is a problem with the data, and there are warning signs in your regression output that tell you that your model is somehow "sick."

Here is an example using a small random sample of thirty cases from the GSS 2012 data. We're interested in the relationship between age and the number of times people say they have sex per month. Below are three versions of these data. The first is the original dataset with the original values. In the second version, I have altered the value of the "times sex" variable for the youngest respondent: this 23-year-old, because of an input error, has gone from having sex an impressive 20 times per month to a ridiculous 200 times per month (that's almost seven times a day). In the third version, I returned the 23-year-old to his original "times sex" value and changed the value for the oldest respondent: the 76-year-old has gone from having sex once a month to 100 times a month:

■ **Exhibit 16.1: Three Versions of a Small Dataset**

ORIGINAL DATA		REVISION 1		REVISION 2	
AGE	#SEX	AGE	#SEX	AGE	#SEX
33	10	33	10	33	10
55	10	55	10	55	10
30	10	30	10	30	10
42	1	42	1	42	1
48	0	48	0	48	0
64	3	64	3	64	3
56	4	56	4	56	4
64	0	64	0	64	0
45	1	45	1	45	1
48	10	48	10	48	10
56	3	56	3	56	3
36	4	36	4	36	4
35	4	35	4	35	4
38	10	38	10	38	10
32	3	32	3	32	3
27	1	27	1	27	1
58	0	58	0	58	0
28	10	28	10	28	10
64	3	64	3	64	3
40	10	40	10	40	10
33	4	33	4	33	4
76	1	76	1	76	100
31	10	31	10	31	10
24	10	24	10	24	10
30	1	30	1	30	1
46	3	46	3	46	3
54	4	54	4	54	4
33	10	33	10	33	10
23	20	23	200	23	20
65	10	65	10	65	10

Note: Shaded cells are "corrupted."
Source: GSS 2012 data, random sample.

Now let's look at the regression results for the three scenarios in order to see how the results differ based on the changes that I made:

■ **Exhibit 16.2: Three Sets of Regression Output**

	ORIGINAL	REVISION 1	REVISION 2
From the Model Summary Output Box:			
R-squared	0.19	0.10	0.09
From the ANOVA Output Box:			
Explained Variation	131.05	3544.93	870.24
Total Variation	678.28	37185.28	9243.43
From the Coefficients Output Box:			
Constant	12.03	45.09	−7.71
Slope	−0.15	−0.77	0.38
Standard Error	0.06	0.45	0.22
T-Value	2.59	1.72	1.71
P-Value	0.015	0.097	0.099

Note: Revisions 1 and 2 use corrupted data.
Source: GSS 2012 data, random sample.

The results change drastically due to a single change in the dataset. Of course we can see this by comparing the original (correct) dataset with the revisions. But what if we didn't have the correct version? What are the clues that there might be a problem in the dataset? A first clue is by looking at the "total variation" values. We'll take both of these from the revised datasets, calculate the variance, and then the standard deviation:

Revision 1: $s^2 = 37,185.28/29 = 1,282.25$ $s = 35.81$
Revision 2: $s^2 = 9,243.43/29 = 318.74$ $s = 17.85$

Think about what these standard deviations tell us: on the times sex variable, the average person deviates from the mean by about 36 sex times per month. This seems like a lot, doesn't it, given that people have sex maybe once or twice a week?

A second clue comes from the fact that the explained variation is 10% even though the slope is not statistically significant. In most other examples we've examined throughout the book, an insignificant slope is accompanied by a very low value for R^2. This tells you that there might be something wrong with the slope.

A third clue comes from the slopes themselves. We'll use them to write out the regression equation and make a prediction for a 25-year-old and a 75-year-old:

Table 16.1: Predictions Using Compromised Data

	25-year-old	75-year-old
Revision 1: sextimes = 45.09 − 0.77(age)	25.84	−12.66
Revision 2: sextimes = −7.71 + 0.38(age)	1.79	20.79

These predictions obviously don't make sense. In other words, they just don't pass the "sniff test": we sniff the results by running a few examples and realize that something just doesn't smell right. Using Revision 1, we have some extremely oversexed young people and some unfortunate old people who are having sex a negative number of times per month. Using Revision 2, we have old people who are having sex much more often than are young people. Not to be ageist, but this just doesn't sound right. As we have done throughout this book, it is important to use your regression model to calculate some predicted values. If these predictions simply don't make any sense, then there may be a problem with the data you used to get to those predictions.

Once you figure out that you do have an outlier (or a set of outliers) that is causing problems, what are your options? If it seems to be a data-entry error, and you are using data that you yourself collected, the solution could be as simple as looking back at your original surveys and making sure the data for the respondent in question are correct and correcting them if they are not. If you are using data from a reputable source, such as the GSS or ANES, the likelihood of a data-entry problem is very low, but you might want to check the dataset's website in order to see if any addenda to the original data about errors have been posted. If you're using secondary data such as these, you should not just change the data yourself.

If the outlier is not caused by a data entry error, then it comes time to decide if you can, for good reason, omit that case (or those cases) from your analysis. Various formulae (which beyond the scope of this chapter) can help you determine if the case in question meets formal guidelines for outliers. In addition, you could make a conceptually driven argument for excluding a case. For example, if you've collected data from Washington State, and somehow Bill Gates has ended up in your sample, you probably have good reason to remove him from your analyses in which net wealth plays a role.

POTENTIAL PROBLEM TWO: MULTICOLLINEARITY

Imagine you and a coworker are working on a project together. Both of you are doing the same tasks as part of the project: you've worked together to collect the data, you worked as a team to input the data, and now you are working on analyzing the data. Your boss calls you both into her office for a progress report. She starts by asking your coworker to explain what's been happening. He describes everything that the two of you have been doing for the last few weeks. He goes on and on and on. Finally, he finishes, and your boss turns to you and asks you to explain what's been happening. You say, "Uhhhh . . ." because, well, you have nothing to add to the explanation. Your coworker stole your thunder when he explained everything that's been going on, leaving you with nothing else to add and making you look bad. How very rude.

The same type of scenario can happen in regression if you have two independent variables that are highly correlated with one another. One variable will explain a lot of the variation in the dependent variable. The second independent variable, since it essentially looks a lot like the first independent variable (because they are highly correlated with one another), is left with nothing else to explain. When two variables are highly correlated, the potential problem is called **multicollinearity**: there are *multi*ple independent variables that *co*vary together in a *lin*ear fashion to a problematic extent.

Let's look at some GSS data, another random sample of 30 cases. We'll use a familiar example: the effect of a mother's and a father's education on the respondent's education. Here are the original data:

■ **Exhibit 16.3: Original Data for Education Example**

YEARS OF EDUCATION FOR...		
...MOTHER	...FATHER	...RESPONDENT
12	12	16
16	16	16
12	12	16
10	10	12
12	12	14
12	12	12
16	16	18
12	12	16
12	12	14
12	12	12
16	16	20
16	16	16
16	15	16
12	12	16
12	9	12
12	11	14
16	20	20
13	12	13
15	20	12
12	12	13
12	9	15
16	12	18
12	13	18
14	14	12
6	0	4
12	8	11
12	8	13
18	12	16
16	16	12
12	3	14

Source: GSS 2012 data, random sample.

Notice that mother's education and father's education are highly correlated. In fact, the correlation coefficient between the two is +0.75: a strong relationship. I then ran a set of nested models using respondent's education as the dependent variable, mother's education as my first independent variable, and father's education as my second independent variable:

■ **Exhibit 16.4: Original Results for Education Example**

Dependent Variable: Respondent's Years of Education		
Independent Variable	Model 1	Model 2
Mother's Years of Education	0.85***	0.62*
Father's Years of Education	—	0.18
Constant	3.21	4.05
R^2	0.43	0.46
n	30	30

Note: Dependent variable: respondent's years of education.
*$p < .05$. ***$p < .001$ (two-tailed test).
Source: GSS 2012 data, random sample.

Father's years of education, though correlated with respondent's years of education, does not perform well in the regression equation. This is because it is highly correlated with mother's education. A clue to the trouble is in the SPSS output you get when you run a nested model (by using the "Next" button just above the Independents box as we went over in Chapter 10). Until now we have not looked at the box of output you get at the very end, after the coefficients. Within this box is a collinearity statistic called **tolerance**. Tolerance is an index that ranges from 0 to 1, with 0 meaning perfect collinearity and 1 meaning no collinearity (I know this seems backward, and on behalf of the field of statistics, I apologize). In a typical regression model, where the independent variables are not correlated with one another, the tolerance will be in the high 0.90s. Generally, we should start to get worried if the Tolerance goes below 0.40 (Allison, 1999). In this situation, the Tolerance for the Father's Education variable is 0.432, so we're right on the edge.

Let's make the situation even worse by making some modifications to our original data:

■ **Exhibit 16.5: Revised Data for Education Example**

YEARS OF EDUCATION FOR...		
...MOTHER	...FATHER	... RESPONDENT
12	12	16
16	16	16
12	12	16
10	10	12
12	12	14
12	12	12
16	16	18
12	12	16
12	12	14
12	12	12
16	16	20
16	16	16
16	15	16
12	12	16
12	12	12
12	11	14
16	16	20
13	12	13
15	15	12
12	12	13
12	12	15
16	12	18
12	13	18
14	14	12
6	6	4
12	12	11
12	12	13
18	12	16
16	16	12
12	12	14

Source: GSS 2012 data, random sample.
Note: Shaded cells are "corrupted."

Note that I changed eight of the fathers' education entries (the shaded ones) to be more similar to the mothers' education entries. This raises the correlation between mother's education and father's education from +0.75 to +0.84. Here are the revised regression results:

■ **Exhibit 16.6: Three Revised Data for Education Example**

Dependent Variable: Respondent's Years of Education		
Independent Variable	Model 1	Model 2
Mother's Years of Education	0.85***	0.56
Father's Years of Education	—	0.38
Constant	3.21	2.14
R^2	0.43	0.45
n	30	30

Note: Data includes "corrupted" data.
***$p < .001$ (two-tailed test).
Source: GSS 2012 data, random sample.

Although the explained variation has gone up, now both independent variables do not have significant effects. Most important, however, is that the tolerance statistic has fallen to an unacceptable 0.29.

What can be done when you have identified collinearity between two independent variables? One option is to make a decision that you won't use one of the independent variables in the regression model. For example, in this scenario, you could decide to use only the mother's education or the father's education. Because they are for many of the cases so close to one another anyway, they're essentially the same. Another option is to combine them into an index. Say we wanted to use two measures of religious activity (religious attendance and prayer) as independent variables, but we find they are too highly correlated. We could create a religious activity index and then use that as a single independent variable.

I don't mean to scare you by bringing up these problems. They are pretty rare, and I doubt you will encounter them. But it's good to know that they exist. And given the awareness approach I took with this section, we've covered only a few details from the field of regression diagnostics. Many other things could go wrong, but outliers and multicollinearity are among the most common.

ADVANCED TECHNIQUES CONCERNING VARIABLES

Now we'll briefly turn our attention to some advanced techniques that are appearing more and more frequently in the social science literature. Again, the goal here is not to learn how the technique works, but to learn why the technique exists and why researchers might turn to the technique instead of other techniques. Researchers are constantly developing new statistical techniques, and eventually, these techniques diffuse throughout the social science disciplines. Take logistic regression as an example. A long time ago, researchers thought nothing of using regular regression with a dichotomous dependent variable. But researchers developed logistic regression, and once it started being taught in graduate programs throughout the country, the technique started to appear more and more in the literature. As this happened, researchers began to expect the use of the technique: if a researcher tried to use regular regression with a dichotomous dependent variable, his colleagues showed him the error of his ways. In an examination of statistical techniques used 20 years ago and today, I found that in the early 1990s, in the top two sociology journals—the *American Journal of Sociology* and the *American Sociological Review*—logistic regression appeared in 20% and 10% of the journals' articles, respectively. By the early 2010s, these had risen to 37% and 21%, respectively.

But now newer techniques have begun to supplant logistic regression. A good number of these techniques concern what the dependent variables look like. For example, let's say you wanted to use GSS data to study factors that affect people's health. The primary GSS variable is called HEALTH, which simply asks the respondent to self-report their overall health. This is what it looks like (with percentages from the 2012 dataset):

Excellent	27%
Good	46%
Fair	21%
Poor	7%

What are our options here? Since this is an ordinal-level variable, we probably shouldn't use regular regression, though some would say that this is not such a bad route to take, and you will even see this done in the social science literature from time to time. We could dichotomize the health variable, but looking at the percentages, there's no great way to do so without losing valuable information. There is, however, an advanced technique called **ordered logistic regression** that is designed for ordinal-level dependent variables with a limited number of categories. It's basically a modified version of logistic regression. For example, in a 2011 article in *American Sociological Review* called "Professional Role Confidence and Gendered Persistence in Engineering," Erin Cech and her coauthors wanted to explain why some students leave an engineering major. One of their dependent variables was "intentional persistence" to become an engineer, and it was measured on a 4-point scale from very unlikely to very likely. Because the dependent variable looks like this, they used ordered logistic regression.

A related technique is called **multinomial logistic regression**. It's pretty much what it sounds like: a version of logistic regression designed to be used with a nominal variable that has multiple categories. This would be the way to go if you wanted to explain, for example, variation in marital status (married, unmarried, divorced) or variation in school choice (public, non-religious private, religious private). In the same article about engineering, Cech and her co-authors want to explain why people stay in an engineering major, switch to another STEM major (science, technology, engineering, math; in this case, I guess they'd switch to a STM major), or leave STEM altogether. Because their dependent variable is measured at the nominal level and has several categories, they use multinominal logistic regression.

If you're going through the social science literature, you might also see other techniques that are closely related to logistic regression: probit and Tobit. **Probit regression** is sometimes used in place of logistic regression. Its primary difference from logistic regression is that with probit it is more difficult to get predicted probabilities close to 0% or close to 100% (a subtle distinction, I realize). Researchers use **Tobit regression** when their dependent variable is a "hybrid" of a dichotomy and a ratio-level variable: a good proportion of the cases have the value of zero on the dependent variable, but the rest of the cases have various values. For example, here is a frequency distribution from a small index I created with GSS data that measures support for allowing people to commit suicide:

Suicide allowed in . . .

. . . 0 situations	40%
. . . 1 situation	41%
. . . 2 situations	7%
. . . 3 situations	2%
. . . 4 situations	10%

Because 40% of the cases have a value of zero, if I wanted to explain variation in support for allowing suicide, I might choose Tobit regression. In an article in the *American Journal of Sociology* in 2010 called "Trouble in Store: Probes, Protests, and Store Openings by Wal-Mart, 1998–2007," Paul Ingram and his coauthors wanted to explain the factors that determined whether a Walmart store was opened or not in various localities. For this, they used probit regression, because the dependent variable was dichotomous. But another one of their dependent variables was the amount that Walmart donated to a community once a store had opened in the community, and this variable could have taken on a value of zero in a good number of the cases, but it could also take on many other values above zero. Therefore, they used Tobit regression for this dependent variable.

Finally, with regard to dependent variables, some researchers get persnickety regarding whether a variable is a **count variable**. We have used "income in $1,000s" time and again as a dependent variable, and you can divide income up almost endlessly: you can have an entire $1,000, but you can have half a thousand, a third, a sixteenth, heck you can even have a nickel to your name (which would be five ten-thousandths of $1,000). But think about other variables that are not so easily divisible. Take the number of cars a family has. I don't know about you, but I wouldn't know what to do with a third of a car. Or how about number of times you have been married. You can't be married 0.37 times (well, perhaps soap operas have figured out how to have their characters do this). Such variables that are ratio-level (0 cars is meaningful, and 4 cars is twice 2) but don't divide up nicely, lead some researchers to two advanced techniques: **negative binomial regression** and **Poisson regression**. These techniques (whose difference is beyond the scope of this book) are designed to deal with such dependent variables. For example, in a fascinating 2012 article in *American Sociological Review* called "The Fringe Effect: Civil Society Organizations and the Evolution of Media Discourse about Islam since the September 11th Attacks," Christopher Bail analyzed how wording from the press releases of anti-Muslim fringe organizations finds its way into mainstream media discourse. In one of Bail's regression models, his dependent variable is the number of words in a press release that are reproduced in national media sources. Number of words is one of these "count" variables: a media source can't really reproduce half of a word. Therefore, Bail uses negative binomial regression instead of regular regression in his analysis.

ADVANCED TECHNIQUES CONCERNING SAMPLES

Some of the most interesting contemporary data collection efforts involve complex forms of sampling. In Chapter 1, I talked about the National Survey of Adolescent Health. This incredible data-collection effort involved studying nearly every student in a carefully selected sample of eighty high schools in the United States. Another complex data-collection effort is the Panel Study of Income Dynamics, which sampled a large number of families, and surveys everyone in those families (and the families that these original families subsequently create). Thus, the data are collected at multiple levels. With Add Health, there are variables that were collected at the school level (i.e., through a survey that the school's principal filled out), at the classroom level (through a survey that a teacher completed about his classroom), at the family level (parents filled out surveys about family characteristics), and at the student level (individual students filled out extensive surveys about their lives and social networks). Say there were two students who were brother and sister and who went to the same school and had some of the same classes. These students would vary on some individual-level variables (i.e., they might study different numbers of hours per week), but some of their information at other levels will be constant: they both share the same parents, same principal, some of the same teachers. In fact, all the students in this one school will share some school-level characteristics. Such complex samples call for advanced statistical techniques.

One such technique that has become very popular in the past generation is called **multilevel modeling**. It also has gone by the name Hierarchical Linear Modeling (HLM), though these days you don't see that term used as much. You may also see the term mixed-linear modeling. Multilevel modeling involves statistical models that take into account the nature of the data, allowing researchers to observe the effects of some of the individual-level variables while controlling for the more macro-level variables. For example, in a 2012 article in *American Sociological Review* called "It's All about Control: Worker Control over Schedule and Hours in Cross-National Context," Karen S. Lyness and her coauthors used schedule control as their dependent variable. Here they describe their statistical model:

We estimate a multilevel model of . . . worker control over working time, defined as control over one's work schedule and hours. Our model includes micro-level worker and job characteristics that research shows are associated with flexibility. Our model also includes effects of several country-level factors . . . these include macroeconomic factors, labor market characteristics, and policy indicators related to social spending and regulation of working time. (Lyness et al., 2012, p. 1028)

They use data from 21 countries that have a variety of worker-related policies, such as length of the standard workweek and family-leave laws. Therefore, in their study they have respondents with different types of jobs and different personal characteristics but living under the same state policies. Their multilevel model allows them to accommodate these complex data.

OTHER ADVANCED TECHNIQUES

Hopefully I convinced you in Chapter 14 that path analysis is an interesting technique useful in examining relationships among variables. While some researchers still use path analysis, others have turned to a more sophisticated technique called **structural equation modeling** (or SEM). Using SEM, a researcher estimates a path model, but instead of using a single variable at each "node" of the model, she uses multiple variables. Then, the researcher uses a special software program that looks at the relationships among all of the variables to develop the betas to place onto the model. For example, in a 2011 article in the journal *Social Forces* titled "Intergenerational Continuity of Taste: Parental and Adolescent Music Preferences," Tom F. M. ter Bogt and his coauthors examined the relationships between mother's musical taste, father's musical taste, and their child's musical taste (ter Bogt et al., 2011). If parents like a particular kind of music, does their child like this kind of music as well? However, they characterize sets of music: pop (includes Top 40, R&B, disco, and hip-hop), rock (rock, alternative, heavy metal, and hardcore punk), and highbrow (classical and jazz). Thus within each genre of music, there are multiple subgenres. This led them to use SEM, and to build models such as this one:

■ **Exhibit 16.7: Model of Parents' Musical Tastes Effects on Adolescent Tastes**

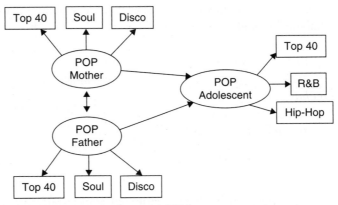

Source: Adapted from ter Bogt et al. (2011).

Each node has three variables attached to it, and the SEM program looks at the relationships among all of these variables (e.g., is Mother's love of Top 40 related to Adolescent's love of R&B?) in order to determine the relationships among all of the nodes.

One final important advanced technique is called **hazard modeling**. Researchers use hazard analyses when their dependent variable is related to time. A criminologist might want to study whether or not a convict, once released from prison, will recidivate (commit crime again). However, this same criminologist could take a different approach: starting at the time released from prison, what factors determine how long it will take the ex-convict to recidivate (if ever)? At one month after release from prison, what is the hazard probability? Then at six months, a year, five years? If one is using a sample of former inmates, the sample will continually be changing, given that some of the sample will have recidivated and the question of "When (if ever) will they recidivate?" becomes moot for them. Hazard modeling allows researchers to account for the special nature of this situation.

A great recent example that uses hazard modeling appeared in the journal *Social Forces* in 2012. In "Delayed Special Education Placement for Learning Disabilities among Children of Immigrants," Jacob Hibel and Andrea D. Jasper examined a sample of immigrant and nonimmigrant children over a period to see when (if ever) they were placed in special education. Because their dependent variable involves time (when will something happen, if ever?), they used hazard modeling. Exhibit 16.8 is one of their graphs that illustrates their results:

■ **Exhibit 16.8: Hazard for Receipt of Special Services, by Parental Nativity**

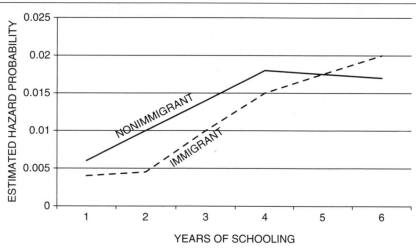

Source: Adapted from Hibel and Jasper (2012).

The hazard, or chance, of receipt of special education services is at first higher for nonimmigrants, but by the fifth year, immigrants have caught up and then surpass nonimmigrants.

NO, REALLY, WE'RE DONE. GO HOME!

When I go to a movie at a theater, I tend to stay for the credits. I love the occasional film that, after the credits have rolled, has a character return to the screen to tell you "Really, that's all there is. It's time for you to go home!" (i.e., *The Muppet Movie*, *Ferris Bueller's Day Off*). And that's where we are. However, even though that's all there is for this book, it's definitely not the case for the field of social statistics. Your instructor and I have taught you a lot, but there's even more for you to learn.

Let's imagine for a moment that my hope at the beginning of the book—that you'll actually start to like statistics—has come to fruition: you now like statistics and you want to continue learning about the techniques in this book, or perhaps some of the advanced techniques I mentioned above. What should you do? Obviously, you could take more courses on any number of topics. Your school may offer them, or you might want to look into short courses that are offered on a number of college campuses in the summer (stats camp!). If you want to self-teach, there are countless books out there. But beware: they may be heavy on mathematical verbiage. There's also the media route, with lots of garage-band-style YouTube videos, but these can be hit or miss.

Another consideration is software. You are perhaps now on a college campus that has a site license for SPSS (and/or other statistical software). But once you enter the cruel real world, one of its cruelties might be a lack of SPSS. Unfortunately, an individual copy of the program is pricy. You might want to look into websites that allow you to analyze data directly on the website. More and more data repositories are making this a reality. One website that has been around for a long time that I like to use is the University of California at Berkeley's Survey Documentation and Analysis. Just type "SDA" into a search engine and it will be one of the first things that pop up (after the Seventh-Day Adventists). This website stores a lot of data (such as the GSS and ANES), but it also allows you to analyze the data right there on the website. It's not as user-friendly as SPSS, but it's not bad. Give it a try.

And now, really, that's all there is. Get out there and spread the word that statistics should not be considered "sadistics" (if I had a dime for every time . . .). Tell people that the field of social statistics is an understandable and useful set of tools to make sense of our increasingly complex, data-driven world. And in whatever you do, be a savvy interpreter of statistical results.

EXERCISES

Exercise 1

Someone claims, "Sure, an outlier in a small dataset can have a huge effect on results. But in a large dataset, it's not a big deal, since once case out of 5,000 is not going to have that big of an effect." Respond to this, explaining why this claim is problematic.

Exercise 2

Using the PewKids dataset, run a frequency distribution (and get descriptive statistics) on the variable for the number of texts the teenager sends per day. Should the kids who replied "500 or more" be considered outliers and removed from analyses involving this variable? Why or why not?

Exercise 3

In an earlier chapter's exercise, you ran a regression model using the ANES knowledge index as your dependent variable and the four media variables as your independent variables. Now after reading this chapter, you're concerned that these four variables might suffer from multicollinearity, given that people who consume one type of news are likely to consume other types of news. Run a set of nested models (entering each independent variable one at a time), and explain why you should or should not be concerned.

Exercise 4 (Answer Available in Appendix D)

For each of these ANES-based scenarios, describe which advanced technique a researcher might want to use and why:

a. a researcher wants to analyze the interaction between income and political views with regard to his or her dependent variable: people's attitudes toward limiting corporations' contributions to campaigns (hint: look at this particular variable).

b. a researcher wants to explain Americans' attitudes toward Affirmative Action (hint: look at the distribution of the Affirmative Action Index).

c. a researcher wants to explain support for environmental legislation, using the Environmental Index as his dependent variable. For his or her independent variables, the researcher wants to use some personal characteristics of the respondent (such as gender and political views) and some legislative data from the respondent's state of residence (such as the stringency of environmental laws in the state).

Appendix A

VARIABLES AND INDEXES FROM THE DATASETS USED IN THE END-OF-CHAPTER EXERCISES

This appendix contains the variables and indexes that are used throughout the end-of-chapter exercises. All of these data are freely available on the Internet, so I could have simply pointed you to them and have you download the original datasets on your own. However, it can be difficult and time-consuming to get these datasets up and running. I have done most of this footwork for you: I have recoded most of the variables and created dozens of indexes. Looking at each dataset in the Variable View in SPSS, you will see the original variables at the top, and all of the recoded variables at the bottom.

The name of any variable that I recoded starts with an "XY." For example, in the ANES dataset, there is an original variable called dem_agegrp: age of the respondent in categories. From this variable, I created two XY variables: XYdem_age (age in years) and XYdem_age4cat (age in four categories). In the PewKids dataset, there is an original variable called psex: sex of the parent, coded Male = 1, Female = 2. Because dichotomies in regression should be coded 0 and 1, I created a variable called XYpsex, where Male = 0, and Female = 1. I also created reference-group sets, interaction terms, and squared variables. These are all explained in the following. The majority of the exercises use these XY variables, though occasionally an exercise will ask you to use a non-recoded variable (i.e., if the original variable "age" was already fine the way it was without recoding). I have included all of the original variables in the dataset in case you want to use the original variables for your own purposes and recodings.

As with any dataset, it is important to recognize that the findings we develop with these datasets are our own, not the responsibility of the creators of the datasets.

AMERICAN NATIONAL ELECTION STUDIES

Variables

<u>Demographics</u>

XYgender_ respondent: gender of respondent
Male: 0
Female: 1

XYdem_marital: marital status of respondent
Married: 0
Partnered: 1
Married, spouse absent: 2
Widowed: 3
Divorced: 4
Separated: 5
Never married: 6

XYdem_maritalmvp: respondent's marital status, married or partnered, with all other answers recoded as missing
Married: 0
Partnered: 1

To see the rest of this appendix, with hundreds of additional variables and indices, please visit the book's website, **www.routledge.com/cw/Linneman**

86 ARTICLES THAT USE STATISTICS IN LESS THAN SCARY WAYS

If I have accomplished with this book what I set out to accomplish, by this point you should be feeling pretty good about this whole statistics thing. My entire goal has been to show you that, if you take all of this step by step, you can understand what's going on in many statistical procedures, even those that use several techniques at once. However, I would be doing you a great disservice if I led you to believe that you were ready for absolutely anything statistical.

Because, if everything you know about statistics is what you learned in this book, you certainly know a whole lot more than most people, but there's a whole lot more going on out there in the real statistical world. It seems like every year researchers develop a new technique that only a few people know how to use. Don't think I'm trying to take the wind out of your sails. This book gets you a good part of the way there. You now have a great foundation, and you can do many analyses on your own with whatever data you happen to be using. But I do want to give you fair warning.

If you open up some scholarly journals, odds are good that you will encounter some of the more esoteric, highfalutin' techniques (I cover some of these techniques briefly in Chapter 16). And, if you try to figure out their statistical models, you will likely feel confused and disheartened. But in these journals are many other great pieces of research that do use the techniques that you now know. And they use statistics to study some very interesting topics. Some of my students and I went through a bunch of journals from a variety of fields (although mostly sociology and political science) and found just such articles. Following is a list of 86 of them. For each article, I briefly describe the authors' overall point, how they use statistics, which parts of the article you might want to study, and aspects of the statistics that might prove confusing (and you can most likely skip). I also give you just a few questions to think about with regard to the results.

Most of these articles are from mainstream journals and are readily available through various online collections. At the end of these descriptions is a list of the journals from which these articles come, and a chart that shows which statistical techniques are used in which articles, in case you want to concentrate on particular techniques.

1

"Identity and Competence: The Use of Culture in the Interpretation of Sexual Images"
Authors: Elizabeth A. Armstrong and Martin S. Weinberg
Journal: *Sociological Perspectives*, Fall 2006, 411–432

Summary: The authors address the age-old question: what is art? This question becomes controversial when the images are sexual in nature. The authors showed 307 undergraduate college students a photograph in which the subject was masturbating (men were shown a photograph of a woman, women were shown a photograph of a man, and both photos were by well-known artistic photographers). The authors had the students fill out surveys asking them to rate the photo as pornography and/or art, and other questions about their identity.

Statistics: On page 421, the authors present two regression models, one with the Pornography Score as the dependent variable, one with the Art Score as the dependent variable. They use regular regression.

Caution: Nothing to worry about.

Questions:

1. Describe the effect of gender.
2. If one has photography experience, how does one tend to rate the photo?
3. If you wanted to contrast the effects of religious identity and conventional identity, does the article have enough information to allow you to do this?

To see the rest of this appendix, with descriptions for the remaining 85 articles, please visit the book's website, **www.routledge.com/cw/Linneman**

Appendix C

STATISTICAL TABLES

APPENDIX C

Abridged from R. A. Fisher and F. Yates. *Statistical Tables for Biological, Agricultural, and Medical Research*, 6th ed. Copyright R.A. Fisher and F. Yates, 1963. Reprinted by permission of Pearson Education Limited.

THE CHI-SQUARE TABLE

	Level of Significance					
	0.20	0.10	0.05	0.02	0.01	0.001
df						
1	1.64	2.71	3.84	5.41	6.64	10.83
2	3.22	4.61	5.99	7.82	9.21	13.82
3	4.64	6.25	7.82	9.84	11.34	16.27
4	5.99	7.78	9.49	11.67	13.28	18.47
5	7.29	9.24	11.07	13.39	15.09	20.52
6	8.56	10.65	12.59	15.03	16.81	22.46
7	9.80	12.02	14.07	16.62	18.48	24.32
8	11.03	13.36	15.51	18.17	20.09	26.13
9	12.24	14.68	16.92	19.68	21.67	27.88
10	13.44	15.99	18.31	21.16	23.21	29.59
11	14.63	17.28	19.68	22.62	24.73	31.26
12	15.81	18.55	21.03	24.05	26.22	32.91
13	16.99	19.81	22.36	25.47	27.69	34.53
14	18.15	21.06	23.69	26.87	29.14	36.12
15	19.31	22.31	25.00	28.26	30.58	37.70
16	20.47	23.54	26.30	29.63	32.00	39.25
17	21.62	24.77	27.59	31.00	33.41	40.79
18	22.76	25.99	28.87	32.35	34.81	42.31
19	23.90	27.20	30.14	33.69	36.19	43.82
20	25.04	28.41	31.41	35.02	37.57	45.32
21	26.17	29.62	32.67	36.34	38.93	46.80
22	27.30	30.81	33.92	37.66	40.29	48.27
23	28.43	32.01	35.17	38.97	41.64	49.73
24	29.55	33.20	36.42	40.27	42.98	51.18
25	30.68	34.38	37.65	41.57	44.31	52.62
26	31.80	35.56	38.89	42.86	45.64	54.05
27	32.91	36.74	40.11	44.14	46.96	55.48
28	34.03	37.92	41.34	45.42	48.28	56.89
29	35.14	39.09	42.56	46.69	49.59	58.30
30	36.25	40.26	43.77	47.96	50.89	59.70

THE *t*-TABLE

	Level of Significance for One-Tailed Test					
	0.10	0.05	0.025	0.01	0.005	0.0005
	Level of Significance for Two-Tailed Test					
	0.20	0.10	0.05	0.02	0.01	0.001
df						
1	3.08	6.31	12.71	31.82	63.66	636.62
2	1.89	2.92	4.30	6.97	9.93	31.60
3	1.64	2.35	3.18	4.54	5.84	12.94
4	1.53	2.13	2.78	3.75	4.60	8.61
5	1.48	2.02	2.57	3.37	4.03	6.86
6	1.44	1.94	2.45	3.14	3.71	5.96
7	1.42	1.90	2.37	3.00	3.50	5.41
8	1.40	1.86	2.31	2.90	3.36	5.04
9	1.38	1.83	2.26	2.82	3.25	4.78
10	1.37	1.81	2.23	2.76	3.17	4.59
11	1.36	1.80	2.20	2.72	3.11	4.44
12	1.36	1.78	2.18	2.68	3.06	4.32
13	1.35	1.77	2.16	2.65	3.01	4.22
14	1.35	1.76	2.15	2.62	2.98	4.14
15	1.34	1.75	2.13	2.60	2.95	4.07
16	1.34	1.75	2.12	2.58	2.92	4.02
17	1.33	1.74	2.11	2.57	2.90	3.97
18	1.33	1.73	2.10	2.55	2.88	3.92
19	1.33	1.73	2.09	2.54	2.86	3.88
20	1.33	1.73	2.09	2.53	2.85	3.85
21	1.32	1.72	2.08	2.52	2.83	3.82
22	1.32	1.72	2.07	2.51	2.82	3.79
23	1.32	1.71	2.07	2.50	2.81	3.77
24	1.32	1.71	2.06	2.49	2.80	3.75
25	1.32	1.71	2.06	2.49	2.79	3.73
26	1.32	1.71	2.06	2.48	2.78	3.71
27	1.31	1.70	2.05	2.47	2.77	3.69
28	1.31	1.70	2.05	2.47	2.76	3.67
29	1.31	1.70	2.05	2.46	2.76	3.66
30	1.31	1.70	2.04	2.46	2.75	3.65
40	1.30	1.68	2.02	2.42	2.70	3.55
60	1.30	1.67	2.00	2.39	2.66	3.46
120	1.29	1.66	1.98	2.36	2.62	3.37
∞	1.28	1.65	1.96	2.33	2.58	3.29

THE *F*-TABLE

P = 0.01

df1 → df2 ↓	1	2	3	4	5	6	8	12	24	∞
1	161.4	199.5	215.7	224.6	230.2	234.0	238.9	243.9	249.0	254.3
2	18.51	19.00	19.16	19.25	19.30	19.33	19.37	19.41	19.45	19.50
3	10.13	9.55	9.28	9.12	9.01	8.94	8.84	8.74	8.64	8.53
4	7.71	6.94	6.59	6.39	6.26	6.16	6.04	5.91	5.77	5.63
5	6.61	5.79	5.41	5.19	5.05	4.95	4.82	4.68	4.53	4.36
6	5.99	5.14	4.76	4.53	4.39	4.28	4.15	4.00	3.84	3.67
7	5.59	4.74	4.35	4.12	3.97	3.87	3.73	3.57	3.41	3.23
8	5.32	4.46	4.07	3.84	3.69	3.58	3.44	3.28	3.12	2.93
9	5.12	4.26	3.86	3.63	3.48	3.37	3.23	3.07	2.90	2.71
10	4.96	4.10	3.71	3.48	3.33	3.22	3.07	2.91	2.74	2.54
11	4.84	3.98	3.59	3.36	3.20	3.09	2.95	2.79	2.61	2.40
12	4.75	3.88	3.49	3.26	3.11	3.00	2.85	2.69	2.50	2.30
13	4.67	3.80	3.41	3.18	3.02	2.92	2.77	2.60	2.42	2.21
14	4.60	3.74	3.34	3.11	2.96	2.85	2.70	2.53	2.35	2.13
15	4.54	3.68	3.29	3.06	2.90	2.79	2.64	2.48	2.29	2.07
16	4.49	3.63	3.24	3.01	2.85	2.74	2.59	2.42	2.24	2.01
17	4.45	3.59	3.20	2.96	2.81	2.70	2.55	2.38	2.19	1.96
18	4.41	3.55	3.16	2.93	2.77	2.66	2.51	2.34	2.15	1.92
19	4.38	3.52	3.13	2.90	2.74	2.63	2.48	2.31	2.11	1.88
20	4.35	3.49	3.10	2.87	2.71	2.60	2.45	2.28	2.08	1.84
21	4.32	3.47	3.07	2.84	2.68	2.57	2.42	2.25	2.05	1.81
22	4.30	3.44	3.05	2.82	2.66	2.55	2.40	2.23	2.03	1.78
23	4.28	3.42	3.03	2.80	2.64	2.53	2.38	2.20	2.00	1.76
24	4.26	3.40	3.01	2.78	2.62	2.51	2.36	2.18	1.98	1.73
25	4.24	3.38	2.99	2.76	2.60	2.49	2.34	2.16	1.96	1.71
26	4.22	3.37	2.98	2.74	2.59	2.47	2.32	2.15	1.95	1.69
27	4.21	3.35	2.96	2.73	2.57	2.46	2.30	2.13	1.93	1.67
28	4.20	3.34	2.95	2.71	2.56	2.44	2.29	2.12	1.91	1.65
29	4.18	3.33	2.93	2.70	2.54	2.43	2.28	2.10	1.90	1.64
30	4.17	3.32	2.92	2.69	2.53	2.42	2.27	2.09	1.89	1.62
40	4.08	3.23	2.84	2.61	2.45	2.34	2.18	2.00	1.79	1.51
60	4.00	3.15	2.76	2.52	2.37	2.25	2.10	1.92	1.70	1.39
120	3.92	3.07	2.68	2.45	2.29	2.17	2.02	1.83	1.61	1.25
∞	3.84	2.99	2.60	2.37	2.21	2.09	1.94	1.75	1.52	1.00

P = 0.01

df1 → df2 ↓	1	2	3	4	5	6	8	12	24	∞
1	4052	4999	5403	5625	5764	5859	5981	6106	6234	6366
2	98.49	99.01	99.17	99.25	99.30	99.33	99.36	99.42	99.46	99.50
3	34.12	30.81	29.46	28.71	28.24	27.91	27.49	27.05	26.60	26.12
4	21.20	18.00	16.69	15.98	15.52	15.21	14.80	14.37	13.93	13.46
5	16.26	13.27	12.06	11.39	10.97	10.67	10.27	9.89	9.47	9.02
6	13.74	10.92	9.78	9.15	8.75	8.47	8.10	7.72	7.31	6.88
7	12.25	9.55	8.45	7.85	7.46	7.19	6.84	6.47	6.07	5.65
8	11.26	8.65	7.59	7.01	6.63	6.37	6.03	5.67	5.28	4.86
9	10.56	8.02	6.99	6.42	6.06	5.80	5.47	5.11	4.73	4.31
10	10.04	7.56	6.55	5.99	5.64	5.39	5.06	4.71	4.33	3.91
11	9.65	7.20	6.22	5.67	5.32	5.07	4.74	4.40	4.02	3.60
12	9.33	6.93	5.95	5.41	5.06	4.82	4.50	4.16	3.78	3.36
13	9.07	6.70	5.74	5.20	4.86	4.62	4.30	3.96	3.59	3.16
14	8.86	6.51	5.56	5.03	4.69	4.46	4.14	3.80	3.43	3.00
15	8.68	3.36	5.42	4.89	4.56	4.32	4.00	3.67	3.29	2.87
16	8.53	6.23	5.29	4.77	4.44	4.20	3.89	3.55	3.18	2.75
17	8.40	6.11	5.18	4.67	4.34	4.10	3.79	3.45	3.08	2.65
18	8.28	6.01	5.09	4.58	4.25	4.01	3.71	3.37	3.00	2.57
19	8.18	5.93	5.01	4.50	4.17	3.94	3.63	3.30	2.92	2.49
20	8.10	5.85	4.94	4.43	4.10	3.87	3.56	3.23	2.86	2.42
21	8.02	5.78	4.87	4.37	4.04	3.81	3.51	3.17	2.80	2.36
22	7.94	5.72	4.82	4.31	3.99	3.76	3.45	3.12	2.75	2.31
23	7.88	5.66	4.76	4.23	3.94	3.71	3.41	3.07	2.70	2.26
24	7.82	5.61	4.72	4.22	3.90	3.67	3.36	3.03	2.66	2.21
25	7.77	5.57	4.68	4.18	3.86	3.63	3.32	2.99	2.62	2.17
26	7.72	5.53	4.64	4.14	3.82	3.59	3.29	2.96	2.58	2.13
27	7.68	5.49	4.60	4.11	3.78	3.56	3.26	2.93	2.55	2.10
28	7.64	5.45	4.57	4.07	3.75	3.53	3.23	2.90	2.52	2.06
29	7.60	5.42	4.54	4.04	3.73	3.50	3.20	2.87	2.49	2.03
30	7.56	5.39	4.51	4.02	3.70	3,47	3.17	2.84	2.47	2.01
40	7.31	5.18	4.31	3.83	3.51	3.29	2.99	2.66	2.29	1.80
60	7.08	4.98	4.13	3.65	3.34	3.12	2.82	2.50	2.12	1.60
120	6.85	4.79	3.95	3.48	3.17	2.96	2.66	2.34	1.95	1.38
∞	6.64	4.60	3.78	3.32	3.02	2.80	2.51	2.18	1.79	1.00

Appendix D

ANSWERS TO SELECTED END-OF-CHAPTER EXERCISES

CHAPTER 1

3. The recoding of the wiretap_toofar variable is straightforward: they're already in the correct order, they just need to be bumped down one (i.e., 1 goes to 0, 2 goes to 1, 3 goes to 2). The recoding of the wiretap warrant variable is trickier: the original variable is 1: favor, 2: oppose, 3: neither favor nor oppose. To favor having to have a warrant is the anti-wiretapping response, so this should get a 0 (so change it from 1 to 0), then those opposed would be recoded from 2 to 2, and the middle response would get recoded from a 3 to a 1.

5. These are merely suggested answers:

a.   level of education:

affects income
is affected by parents' level of education

b.   days per week watch TV news:

affects political knowledge
is affected by hours doing housework

c.   times per month one attends religious services:

affects attitudes toward abortion
is affected by age

d.   number of children:

affects amount of free time
is affected by level of education

e. feeling thermometer toward big business:

affects hours worked per week
is affected by political party

f. political views:

affects attitudes toward government spending
is affected by income

g. having a smartphone:

affects news reading on the Internet
is affected by age

h. hours one works in a week:

affects income
is affected by gender

i. whether one has a dog:

affects stress level
is affected by race

j. support of the environmental movement:

affects likelihood of recycling
is affected by religiosity

9. The critical thing to notice here is that if the respondent's survey was conducted by cell phone, then this respondent was not asked the question: Do you have a cell phone? Only those whose survey was conducted by landline were asked if they had a cell phone. So, to create this overall variable, you would have, in one category, all the respondent whose surveys were conducted by cell phone *plus* the respondents whose survey was conducted by landline but say they have a cell phone. In the other category would be people whose survey was conducted by landline and who said they didn't have a cell phone.

14. Using these three variables, which are measured at the country level of analysis, you could *not* create a variable of the percentage of people who have engaged in all three behaviors. In order to do this, you would need to have a dataset where the variables are measured at the individual level. Then you could figure out which individuals in each country had participated in each. You can't do this with the country-level dataset. For example, we know that 80% of the surveyed Australians had signed a petition, 17% had participated in a boycott, and 22% had participated in a demonstration, but we don't know which respondents did which, so we can't add the percentages together.

CHAPTER 2

2.

Case Summaries

	Case Number	recoded owngun_owngun (1=Y)	recode gun_control (more diff=1)
1	452	No	easier or same ease to get gun
2	1081	Yes	easier or same ease to get gun
3	2001	No	harder to get gun
4	2023	No	harder to get gun
5	2250	No	easier or same ease to get gun
6	2541	No	easier or same ease to get gun
7	2736	No	harder to get gun
8	3060	Yes	easier or same ease to get gun
9	3330	No	harder to get gun
10	3343	Yes	harder to get gun
11	3484	Yes	easier or same ease to get gun
12	3816	Yes	easier or same ease to get gun
13	3948	Yes	harder to get gun
14	3994	No	easier or same ease to get gun
15	4256	No	harder to get gun
16	4266	Yes	easier or same ease to get gun
17	4843	No	harder to get gun
18	4930	No	harder to get gun
19	5367	Yes	easier or same ease to get gun
20	5533	No	harder to get gun
Total N		20	20

Crosstabulation of Support for Gun Control by Gun Ownership

	Owns Gun	No Gun	
For gun control	2	8	10
	25%	67%	
Against gun control	6	4	10
	75%	33%	
	8	12	20
	100%	100%	

Note: only male respondents who are in poor health and very dissatisfied with life.
Source: ANES 2012 data.

6.

Discrimination in the U.S. against Blacks * R race and ethnicity group Crosstabulation

		R race and ethnicity group				
		1. White non-Hispanic	2. Black non-Hispanic	3. Hispanic	4. Other non-Hispanic	Total
Discrimination in the U.S. against Blacks	1. A great deal	179	330	110	54	673
		5.5%	34.9%	12.0%	15.8%	12.3%
	2. A lot	635	327	249	70	1281
		19.5%	34.6%	27.3%	20.5%	23.5%
	3. A moderate amount	1388	215	353	117	2073
		42.7%	22.7%	38.7%	34.2%	38.0%
	4. A little	914	60	169	85	1228
		28.1%	6.3%	18.5%	24.9%	22.5%
	5. None at all	133	14	32	16	195
		4.1%	1.5%	3.5%	4.7%	3.6%
Total		3249	946	913	342	5450
		100.0%	100.0%	100.0%	100.0%	100.0%

Discrimination in the U.S. against Hispanics * R race and ethnicity group Crosstabulation

		R race and ethnicity group				
		1. White non-Hispanic	2. Black non-Hispanic	3. Hispanic	4. Other non-Hispanic	Total
Discrimination in the U.S. against Hispanics	1. A great deal	175	209	132	41	557
		5.4%	22.1%	14.4%	12.0%	10.2%
	2. A lot	726	312	288	81	1407
		22.4%	32.9%	31.4%	23.8%	25.8%
	3. A moderate amount	1404	275	332	125	2136
		43.3%	29.0%	36.2%	36.7%	39.2%
	4. A little	832	121	142	82	1177
		25.6%	12.8%	15.5%	24.0%	21.6%
	5. None at all	108	30	22	12	172
		3.3%	3.2%	2.4%	3.5%	3.2%
Total		3245	947	916	341	5449
		100.0%	100.0%	100.0%	100.0%	100.0%

How much discrimination has R faced personally * R race and ethnicity group Crosstabulation

		R race and ethnicity group				
		1. White non-Hispanic	2. Black non-Hispanic	3. Hispanic	4. Other non-Hispanic	Total
How much discrimination has R faced personally	1. A great deal	37	106	44	30	217
		1.1%	11.2%	4.8%	8.7%	4.0%
	2. A lot	71	136	82	38	327
		2.2%	14.3%	8.9%	11.0%	6.0%
	3. A moderate amount	304	325	245	77	951
		9.3%	34.2%	26.6%	22.3%	17.4%
	4. A little	1094	282	340	131	1847
		33.6%	29.7%	36.9%	37.9%	33.7%
	5. None at all	1750	101	211	70	2132
		53.7%	10.6%	22.9%	20.2%	38.9%
Total		3256	950	922	346	5474
		100.0%	100.0%	100.0%	100.0%	100.0%

Addressing the questions,

a. Yes, blacks do perceive that blacks experience more discrimination than whites do or that Hispanics perceive discrimination toward blacks.

b. No, Hispanics don't perceived that Hispanics experience more discrimination than do whites or that blacks perceive discrimination toward Hispanics.

c. Blacks themselves do experience a higher level of discrimination than do whites or Hispanics.

11.

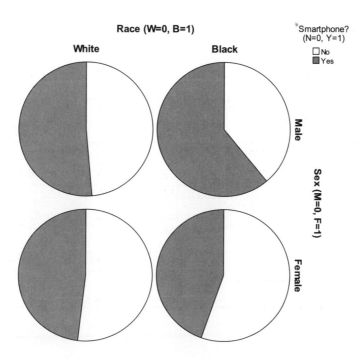

Among whites, there is essentially no difference between men and women. Among blacks, there is a difference: black men are more likely to have a smartphone than are black women.

16.

Child has been bullied in person * Child has been bullied online Crosstabulation

		Child has been bullied online		Total
		No	Yes	
Child has been bullied in person	No	671	28	699
		91.4%	44.4%	87.7%
	Yes	63	35	98
		8.6%	55.6%	12.3%
Total		734	63	797
		100.0%	100.0%	100.0%

Child has been bullied in person * Child has been bullied online * Child's sex (M=0, F=1) Crosstabulation

Child's sex (M=0, F=1)			Child has been bullied online		Total
			No	Yes	
Male	Child has been bullied in person	No	335	12	347
			90.1%	63.2%	88.7%
		Yes	37	7	44
			9.9%	36.8%	11.3%
	Total		372	19	391
			100.0%	100.0%	100.0%
Female	Child has been bullied in person	No	336	16	352
			92.8%	36.4%	86.7%
		Yes	26	28	54
			7.2%	63.6%	13.3%
	Total		362	44	406
			100.0%	100.0%	100.0%

According to the crosstab, being bullied online is clearly related to being bullied in person: only 9% of those who have not been bullied online have been bullied in person, in contrast with 56% of those who have been bullied online. Boys bullied online are almost four times more likely to have been bullied in person (37/10 = 3.7). Girls bullied online are more than nine times more likely to have been bullied in person (64/7 = 9.14).

CHAPTER 3

3.

Case Summaries

Family Income in 1000s

recoded dem_marital	N	Mean	Median	Variance	Std. Deviation
Married	2753	78.90	67.50	3686.033	60.713
Partnered	491	43.21	32.50	2051.973	45.299
Married, spouse absent	334	48.26	32.50	2397.925	48.969
Widowed	577	41.99	32.50	1895.929	43.542
Divorced	339	33.32	26.25	876.897	29.612
Separated	748	43.33	28.75	2565.454	50.650
Never married	469	32.09	21.25	1255.889	35.439
Total	5711	59.10	42.50	3153.243	56.154

z-score for divorced person making \$120,000: $(120 - 33.32)/29.61 = 2.93$

z-score for separated person making \$120,000: $(120 - 43.33)/50.65 = 1.51$

This divorced person is nearly 3 standard deviations away from the mean, making the person highly unique. This separated person is only 1.5 standard deviations away from the mean, making the person not terribly unique.

12.

IQV for bottom bracket:

$61 \times 115 + 61 \times 83 + 61 \times 32 + 115 \times 83 + 115 \times 32 + 83 \times 32 = 29,911$
$29,911/31,755.38 = 0.94$

IQV for top bracket:

$87 \times 84 + 87 \times 9 + 87 \times 3 + 84 \times 9 + 84 \times 3 + 9 \times 3 = 9{,}387$
$9{,}387/12{,}558.38 = 0.75$

15.

Case Summaries

On an average day, about how many text messages do you send
and receive on your cell phone?

Parent's Race	N	Mean	Median	Variance
White	357	108.98	50.00	18394.193
Black	99	135.80	50.00	26227.693
Hispanic	113	146.95	80.00	26530.408
Asian	21	99.29	50.00	15950.714
American Indian	6	108.33	100.00	6176.667
Other	9	205.00	180.00	20675.000
Total	605	121.55	50.00	21239.851

Whites: mean = 108.98, median = 50, variance = 18,394.93
American Indians: mean = 108.33, median = 100, variance = 6,176.67

The white distribution is skewed to the right, implying that there are some whites who
text *a lot*. The American Indian distribution is not very skewed. The white distribution
has around three times the variation as the American Indian distribution. A caution,
however: the American Indian statistics are based on only six kids.

18.

Mean for Western Europe:
$(34.2 + 29.7 + 66.0 + 51.8 + 63.0 + 43.3 + 41.9 + 28.2 + 31.5)/9 = 43.3$

Mean for Eastern Europe:
$(28.4 + 28.5 + 22.8 + 29.7 + 37.9 + 25.0 + 26.6 + 18.6)/8 = 27.2$

Variance for Eastern Europe:

Country	% Confident		
1	34.2	–9.1	82.81
2	29.7	–13.6	184.96
3	66.0	22.7	515.29
4	51.8	8.5	72.25
5	63.0	19.7	388.09
6	43.3	0.0	0.0
7	41.9	–1.4	1.96
8	28.2	15.1	228.01
9	31.5	–11.8	139.24

Variance for Eastern Europe:

Country	% Confident		
1	28.4	1.2	1.44
2	28.5	1.3	1.69
3	22.8	-4.4	19.36
4	29.7	2.5	6.25
5	37.9	10.7	114.49
6	25.0	-2.2	4.84
7	26.6	-0.6	0.36
8	18.6	-8.6	73.96

Variance for Western Europe:
$1612.61/8 = 201.58$

Variance for Eastern Europe:
$222.39/7 = 31.77$

$201.58/31.77 = 6.34$: there is more than six times as much variation among the Western European countries as there is among the Eastern European countries.

CHAPTER 4

2.

recoded dog (Y=1) * recoded orientn_rgay (1=GL) Crosstabulation

			recoded orientn_rgay (1=GL)		
			Heterosexual	Gay or lesbian	Total
recoded dog (Y=1)	No dog		1033	10	1043
			56.0%	35.7%	55.7%
	Yes dog		812	18	830
			44.0%	64.3%	44.3%
Total			1845	28	1873
			100.0%	100.0%	100.0%

Chi-Square Tests

	Value	df	Asymp. Sig. (2-sided)
Pearson Chi-Square	4.595	1	0.032

recoded dog (Y=1) * recoded orientn_rgay (1=GL) * recoded gender (M=0,F=1) Crosstabulation

				recoded orientn_rgay (1=GL)		
recoded gender (M=0,F=1)				Heterosexual	Gay or lesbian	Total
Male	recoded dog (Y=1)	No dog		428	8	436
				53.6%	53.3%	53.6%
		Yes dog		370	7	377
				46.4%	46.7%	46.4%
	Total			798	15	813
				100.0%	100.0%	100.0%
Female	recoded dog (Y=1)	No dog		605	2	607
				57.8%	15.4%	57.3%
		Yes dog		442	11	453
				42.2%	84.6%	42.7%
	Total			1047	13	1060
				100.0%	100.0%	100.0%

Chi-Square Tests

recoded gender (M=0,F=1)		Value	df	Asymp. Sig. (2-sided)
Male	Pearson Chi-Square	0.001	1	0.982
Female	Pearson Chi-Square	9.433	1	0.002

According to the first crosstab, gays and lesbians are more likely have a dog. However, once we elaborate the crosstab, we see that the original relationship exists only for women: lesbians are far more likely to have a dog than heterosexual women are. There is no difference between gay men and heterosexual men.

8.

Purchased online? (N=0, Y=1) * Sex (M=0, F=1) Crosstabulation

		Sex (M=0, F=1)		
		Male	Female	Total
Purchased online? (N=0, Y=1)	Purchased at physical store	49	58	107
		76.6%	87.9%	82.3%
	Purchased online	15	8	23
		23.4%	12.1%	17.7%
Total		64	66	130
		100.0%	100.0%	100.0%

Chi-Square Tests

	Value	df	Asymp. Sig. (2-sided)
Pearson Chi-Square	2.857	1	0.091

Looking at the crosstab, there does seem to be a difference between men and women: men were nearly twice as likely to engage in showrooming as women were. However, the difference is not enough to yield a statistically significant chi-square value. This is likely due to the small sample size: the only people in this crosstab are people who looked up prices on their phone.

10.

Original Crosstab:				Expected Frequencies:			
	Men	Women			Men	Women	
Game	39	24	63	Game	33.6	29.4	63
No Game	9	18	27	No Game	14.4	12.6	27
	48	42	90		48	42	90

fo	fe	fo − fe	(fo− fe)²	(fo− fe)²/fe
39	33.6	5.4	29.16	0.87
24	29.4	−5.4	29.16	0.99
9	14.4	−5.4	29.16	2.03
18	12.6	5.4	29.16	2.31

The chi-square value is 6.2, so with $df = 1$, our p-conclusion is that $p < .02$. Therefore, we can claim with certainty that there is a difference between men and women in the population.

16.

Crosstab

		Child has been bullied online		Total
		No	Yes	
Child's reaction to internet cruelty: defend victim	Frequently	125	17	142
		25.7%	27.9%	25.9%
	Sometimes	164	25	189
		33.7%	41.0%	34.5%
	Once in a while	110	9	119
		22.6%	14.8%	21.7%
	Never	88	10	98
		18.1%	16.4%	17.9%
Total		487	61	548
		100.0%	100.0%	100.0%

Chi-Square Tests

	Value	df	Asymp. Sig. (2-sided)
Pearson Chi-Square	2.558	3	0.465

Chi-Square Tests

	Value	df	Asymp. Sig. (2-sided)
Pearson Chi-Square	2.558	3	0.465

Crosstab

		Child has been bullied online		Total
		No	Yes	
Child's reaction to internet cruelty: ignore	Never	46	7	53
		9.4%	11.5%	9.7%
	Only once in a while	93	11	104
		19.1%	18.0%	18.9%
	Sometimes	171	24	195
		35.0%	39.3%	35.5%
	Frequently	178	19	197
		36.5%	31.1%	35.9%
Total		488	61	549
		100.0%	100.0%	100.0%

Chi-Square Tests

	Value	df	Asymp. Sig. (2-sided)
Pearson Chi-Square	0.978	3	0.807

Crosstab

		Child has been bullied online		Total
		No	Yes	
Child's reaction to internet cruelty: join in	Never	394	39	433
		80.6%	63.9%	78.7%
	Only once in a while	63	17	80
		12.9%	27.9%	14.5%
	Sometimes	25	5	30
		5.1%	8.2%	5.5%
	Frequently	7	0	7
		1.4%	0.0%	1.3%
Total		489	61	550
		100.0%	100.0%	100.0%

Chi-Square Tests

	Value	df	Asymp. Sig. (2-sided)
Pearson Chi-Square	12.099[a]	3	0.007

a. 2 cells (25.0%) have expected count less than 5. The minimum expected count is 0.78.

Crosstab

		Child has been bullied online		Total
		No	Yes	
Child's reaction to internet cruelty: stop it	Frequently	100	21	121
		20.5%	34.4%	22.0%
	Sometimes	189	22	211
		38.7%	36.1%	38.4%
	Once in a while	101	14	115
		20.7%	23.0%	20.9%
	Never	98	4	102
		20.1%	6.6%	18.6%
Total		488	61	549
		100.0%	100.0%	100.0%

Chi-Square Tests

	Value	df	Asymp. Sig. (2-sided)
Pearson Chi-Square	10.347	3	0.016

Two of the independent variables do not have significant relationships with online bullying: defending and ignoring. One of the variables—telling the bully to stop—is significantly related to having been cyberbullied in an expected direction: those who have been cyberbullied are more likely, if someone else is getting cyberbullied, to tell the bully to stop. The last variable—joining in—also has a significant effect, but in an odd direction: those who has experienced cyberbullying are more likely to say they have joined in when someone else is getting cyberbullied.

CHAPTER 5

5.

Descriptives

	Is R's cell phone a smartphone			Statistic	Std. Error
Days in typical week review news on internet	1. Yes, have a smartphone	Mean		3.63	0.084
		95% Confidence Interval for Mean	Lower Bound	3.47	
			Upper Bound	3.80	
		Variance		6.361	
		Std. Deviation		2.522	
	2. No smartphone	Mean		3.08	0.135
		95% Confidence Interval for Mean	Lower Bound	2.81	
			Upper Bound	3.35	
		Variance		6.250	
		Std. Deviation		2.500	

Here are the confidence intervals for the two groups:

For those who have smartphones: $3.47 \leq \mu \leq 3.80$

For those who don't have smartphones: $2.81 \leq \mu \leq 3.35$

The two confidence intervals do not overlap, meaning that we can be sure that these two group's population means are not the same.

10.

Warnings

Index of Health Conditions is constant when Race of respondent = Black. It will be included in any boxplots produced but other output will be omitted.

Case Processing Summary

		Cases					
		Valid		Missing		Total	
	Race of respondent	N	Percent	N	Percent	N	Percent
Index of Health Conditions	White	46	97.9%	1	2.1%	47	100.0%
	Black	1	100.0%	0	0.0%	1	100.0%
	Hispanic	3	75.0%	1	25.0%	4	100.0%
	Other	2	100.0%	0	0.0%	2	100.0%

Colorado may be healthy, but it is also pretty darned white. The sample of Coloradoans (for whom we have data on the Health Conditions Index) has 46 whites, 3 Hispanics, 1 black, and 2 others. With a black sample of 1, SPSS can't calculate many of the statistics. Although it can calculate confidence intervals for the Hispanics and for the people of other races, these intervals are laughably wide given the small number of cases.

13.

Case Processing Summary

	Child has sent sext message	Cases					
		Valid		Missing		Total	
		N	Percent	N	Percent	N	Percent
On an average day, about how many text messages do you send and receive on your cell phone?	No	592	77.0%	177	23.0%	769	100.0%
	Yes	23	92.0%	2	8.0%	25	100.0%

Descriptives

Child has sent sext message				Statistic	Std. Error
On an average day, about how many text messages do you send and receive on your cell phone?	No	Mean		118.48	5.910
		95% Confidence Interval for Mean	Lower Bound	106.87	
			Upper Bound	130.09	
		Variance		20677.908	
		Std. Deviation		143.798	
	Yes	Mean		205.22	37.953
		95% Confidence Interval for Mean	Lower Bound	126.51	
			Upper Bound	283.93	
		Variance		33130.632	
		Std. Deviation		182.018	

The confidence intervals do overlap, so it is possible that the population means are the same. The results are problematic because the sexters' confidence interval is really wide, due to the fact that there are only 23 sexters who went into making the confidence interval. Really, it's a good thing there aren't many more sexters, but in this specific situation, it would be nice to have a few more.

15.

No, we cannot build a confidence interval around this percentage. In order to do this, we would need to know how many American respondents there were, and this information is not in this dataset.

CHAPTER 6

2.

Group Statistics

	Political Views	N	Mean	Std. Deviation	Std. Error Mean
Feeling thermometer: POOR PEOPLE	Extremely liberal	179	76.56	22.563	1.686
	Extremely conservative	194	72.04	23.183	1.664
Feeling thermometer: PEOPLE ON WELFARE	Extremely liberal	178	65.30	23.064	1.729
	Extremely conservative	194	43.05	27.437	1.970

Independent Samples Test

		t-test for Equality of Means			
		t	df	Sig. (2-tailed)	Mean Difference
Feeling thermometer: POOR PEOPLE	Equal variances not assumed	1.909	369.937	0.057	4.523
Feeling thermometer: PEOPLE ON WELFARE	Equal variances not assumed	8.490	367.240	0.000	22.251

With regard to the poor people feeling thermometer, the difference between extreme liberals and extreme conservatives is not statistically significant, so we cannot claim that there is a difference between the populations of these two groups. With regard to the welfare feeling thermometer, the difference is greater than 22 points and is highly statistically significant. Therefore, we can claim with confidence that there is a difference between the populations of extreme liberals and extreme conservatives.

5.

HS or less scores: 21.25, 2.5, 72.5, 2.5, 11.25
HS or less mean: 110/5 = 22
HS or less variance: 3,426.87/4 = 856.72
Some college or more scores: 32.5, 32.5, 47.5, 2.5, 72.5, 37.5
Some college or more mean: 225/6 = 37.5
Some college or more variance: 2,600/5 = 520

With $t = 0.97$, and $df = 9$, our p-conclusion is $p > .20$, so this difference is not statistically significant, and we cannot claim that there is a difference between these two groups in the population of widows with 3 or more kids at home.

13.

Group Statistics

	Sex (M=0, F=1)	N	Mean	Std. Deviation	Std. Error Mean
Internet Health Use Index	Male	1064	2.51	2.665	0.082
	Female	1275	2.92	2.503	0.070

Independent Samples Test

		t-test for Equality of Means			
		t	df	Sig. (2-tailed)	Mean Difference
Internet Health Use Index	Equal variances not assumed	-3.784	2206.337	0.000	-0.407

According to the *t*-test, there is a significant difference: women are more likely to seek out health information on the Internet, and this difference is highly statistically significant, so we can conclude that there is a difference between the populations of men and women.

19.

Descriptives

On an average day, about how many text messages do you send and receive on your cell phone?

	N	Mean	Std. Deviation	Std. Error	95% Confidence Interval for Mean	
					Lower Bound	Upper Bound
Rural	65	107.63	129.202	16.026	75.62	139.65
Suburban	328	122.29	147.139	8.124	106.31	138.28
Urban	219	123.28	147.711	9.981	103.61	142.95
Total	612	121.09	145.402	5.878	109.55	132.63

ANOVA

On an average day, about how many text messages do you send and receive on your cell phone?

	Sum of Squares	df	Mean Square	F	Sig.
Between Groups	13298.185	2	6649.093	0.314	0.731
Within Groups	12904323.05	609	21189.365		
Total	12917621.23	611			

According to the ANOVA, there is far from a significant difference among the three types of communities: the p-value is .731. Although there is a difference in the sample means, the sample standard deviations are huge, which makes it very difficult to achieve statistical significance.

CHAPTER 7

4.

X = Age, Y = Traditionalism Index

	X	Y	X-X̄	Y-Ȳ	(X- X̄)²	(Y-Ȳ)²	(X- X̄)(Y-Ȳ)
	52	13	7.44	4.75	55.32	22.56	35.33
	47	7	2.44	-1.25	5.94	1.56	-3.05
	42	7	-2.56	-1.25	6.57	1.56	3.20
	57	13	12.44	4.75	154.69	22.56	59.08
	67	7	22.44	-1.25	503.44	1.56	-28.05
	42	8	-2.56	-0.25	6.57	0.06	0.64
	27	8	-17.56	-0.25	308.44	0.06	4.39
	22.5	3	-22.06	-5.25	486.75	27.56	115.83
Means	44.56	8.25			1527.72	77.50	187.38

$$b= \frac{187.38}{1527.72} \qquad 0.12265$$

$$r= \frac{\frac{187.38}{344.09}}{} \qquad 0.54$$

$$r^2 \qquad 0.30$$

$$a= 2.7844$$

The regression equation is traditionalism $= 2.78 + 0.12$(age).

The relationship is moderately strong, with an r of 0.54. Age can explain 30% of the variation in scores on the Traditionalism Index.

Health does indeed seem to affect happiness: the healthier a country is, the happier its people are. But in answer to the question in the exercise, health seems to have more of an effect at the lower end of the health spectrum. Notice that at the upper end, even if health goes up, happiness goes up by just a little bit.

CHAPTER 8

3.

Coefficients[a]

Model		Unstandardized Coefficients		Standardized Coefficients	t	Sig.
		B	Std. Error	Beta		
1	(Constant)	1.200	0.049		24.682	0.000
	Age in Years	0.002	0.001	0.028	2.009	0.045

a. Dependent Variable: Wiretapping Index

Here is the regression equation:

WiretapIndex $= 1.20 + 0.002$ (age) $r^2 = 0.001, n = 5,166, p < .05$

The relationship does go in the expected direction: the older you get, the more you are concerned with wiretapping. And the relationship does achieve statistical significance at the $p < .05$ level. Therefore, we can conclude that in the population age does have an effect on concern for wiretapping. However, the effect in the equation is quite small and substantively insignificant. The wiretapping index goes from 0 to 4. To move someone a point up on this index, that person would have to age $1/0.002 = 500$ years!

7. Here is the calculation for the standard error of the slope:

$0.04/0.014 = 2.86, df = 10$, so $p < .05$.

Therefore, this slope is statistically significant and we can claim that this relationship exists in the population of strong Republicans who voted for Obama twice.

12.

Coefficients^a

Model		Unstandardized Coefficients		Standardized Coefficients	t	Sig.
		B	Std. Error	Beta		
1	(Constant)	2.275	0.358		6.362	0.000
	Education in years	-0.067	0.026	-0.183	-2.571	0.011

a. Dependent Variable: Index of Health Conditions

The slope is statistically significant at the $p < .05$ level, so we can conclude that in the population of Americans aged 80+, there is a relationship between education and health conditions.

15.

Here is the correlation matrix using these five variables:

Correlations

		% OF COUNTRY THAT STRONGLY AGREES OR AGREES THAT THEY WOULD GIVE PART OF THEIR INCOME FOR ENVIRONMENT	% OF COUNTRY THAT STRONGLY AGREES OR AGREES THAT THEY WOULD SUPPORT AN INCREASE IN TAXES IF MONEY USED TO PROTEST ENVIRONMENT	% OF COUNTRY THAT SAYS THAT POOR WATER QUALITY IS AN ENVIRONMENTAL PROBLEM IN THEIR COMMUNITY	% OF COUNTRY THAT SAYS THAT POOR AIR QUALITY IS AN ENVIRONMENTAL PROBLEM IN THEIR COMMUNITY	% OF COUNTRY THAT SAYS THAT POOR SEWAGE IS AN ENVIRONMENTAL PROBLEM IN THEIR COMMUNITY
% OF COUNTRY THAT STRONGLY AGREES OR AGREES THAT THEY WOULD GIVE PART OF THEIR INCOME FOR ENVIRONMENT	Pearson Correlation	1	0.859**	−0.006	−0.031	−0.027
	Sig. (2-tailed)		0.000	0.967	0.837	0.859
	N	40	40	46	46	46
% OF COUNTRY THAT STRONGLY AGREES OR AGREES THAT THEY WOULD SUPPORT AN INCREASE IN TAXES IF MONEY USED TO PROTEST ENVIRONMENT	Pearson Correlation	0.859**	1	−0.022	−0.074	−0.049
	Sig. (2-tailed)	0.000		0.885	0.623	0.749
	N	48	48	46	46	46
% OF COUNTRY THAT SAYS THAT POOR WATER QUALITY IS AN ENVIRONMENTAL PROBLEM IN THEIR COMMUNITY	Pearson Correlation	−0.006	−0.022	1	0.960**	0.972**
	Sig. (2-tailed)	0.967	0.885		0.000	0.000
	N	46	46	46	46	46
% OF COUNTRY THAT SAYS THAT POOR AIR QUALITY IS AN ENVIRONMENTAL PROBLEM IN THEIR COMMUNITY	Pearson Correlation	−0.031	−0.074	0.960**	1	0.955**
	Sig. (2-tailed)	0.837	0.623	0.000		0.000
	N	46	46	46	46	46
% OF COUNTRY THAT SAYS THAT POOR SEWAGE IS AN ENVIRONMENTAL PROBLEM IN THEIR COMMUNITY	Pearson Correlation	−0.027	−0.049	0.972**	0.955**	1
	Sig. (2-tailed)	0.859	0.749	0.000	0.000	
	N	46	46	46	46	46

**. Correlation is significant at the 0.01 level (2-tailed).

11.

Coefficients[a,b]

Model		Unstandardized Coefficients		Standardized Coefficients	t	Sig.
		B	Std. Error	Beta		
1	(Constant)	0.403	0.034		11.911	0.000
	Have smartphone (N=0, Y=1)	0.268	0.047	0.156	5.748	0.000

a. Dependent Variable: Review on Internet Index.
b. Selecting only cases for which Race of respondent = White.

Coefficients[a,b]

Model		Unstandardized Coefficients		Standardized Coefficients	t	Sig.
		B	Std. Error	Beta		
1	(Constant)	0.143	0.210		0.680	0.498
	Have smartphone (N=0, Y=1)	0.424	0.233	0.209	1.817	0.073

a. Dependent Variable: Review on Internet Index.
b. Selecting only cases for which Race of respondent = Asian.

The slope for whites is less than the slope for Asians, but only the white slope is statistically significant. This is due to the fact that there are more than 18 times the cases in the white regression compared to the Asian regression.

16.

The slope for South America is not statistically significant (two-tailed test), so we conclude that the South American countries do not differ from Western European countries. The regression equation is

MENEXEC = 18.71 + 39.95(AFRICA) + 23.28(ASIA) + 21.00(E.EUROPE)

The R^2 for this equation is 0.52, meaning that these independent variables together explain slightly more than half the variation in how these countries feel about female executives. According to this equation,

19% of Western Europeans feel that men make better business executives than women do.
59% of Africans feel this way.

42% of Asians feel this way.
40% of Eastern Europeans feel this way.

CHAPTER 10

5.

Dependent Variable: Score on Involvement Index		
(0 = not involved, 5 = very involved)		
Independent Variable	Model 1	Model 2
Household Income in 1000s	0.005***	0.001
Household Education	—	0.24***
Constant	2.02	12.63
R^2	0.03	0.11
n	3,055	3,055

*** $p < .001$ (two-tailed test).
Source: ANES 2012 data.

Income does have the expected effect on involvement in Model 1: for every $1,000 increase in household income, the respondent's involvement rises 0.005. However, once we control for education in Model 2, the effect of income decreases to nonsignificance. It seems that it is really education affecting involvement rather than income. Notice also that income explains only 3%, whereas in Model 2 this rises to 11%.

13.

Dependent Variable: Score on Internet Health Use Index		
Independent Variable	Model 1	Model 2
Score on condition index	0.22***	0.37***
Age in Years	—	-0.022**
Constant	2.60	3.54
R^2	0.007	0.026
n	2,258	2,258

** $p < .01$. *** $p < .001$ (two-tailed test).
Source: PewHealth 2012 data.

In Model 1, we see that for each additional medical condition, score on the Internet Health Use Index goes up by 0.22. Once we control for age, this effect rises from 0.22 to 0.37. Model 1 does not control for the fact that older people have more medical conditions, but they also do not use the Internet as much. So once you control for age, the effect of conditions rises.

16.

Dependent Variable: Child's Score on Bullying Index		
Independent Variable	Model 1	Model 2
Race of Parent (W = 0, B = 1)	−0.17	−0.19*
Family Income in $1,000s	—	0.001
Constant	2.60	3.04
R^2	0.006	0.008
n	513	513

* $p < .05$.
Source: PewKids 2011 data.

First off, neither model explains that much variation: less than 1%, so we should keep that in mind. In Model 1, it seems that blacks get bullied less than whites, but this difference is not statistically significant. Once we control for income (which has an effect in the expected direction, but is not statistically significant), the effect of race goes up just enough to attain statistical significance. So, if we control for income, in essence equalizing incomes between whites and blacks, the income boost gets blacks bullied even less.

19.

Dependent Variable: % of a Country that Says they are Very Happy or Quite Happy		
Independent Variable	Model 1	Model 2
% of country whose health is very good or good	0.50***	0.49**
Income	—	0.21
Constant	48.51	48.02
R^2	0.28	0.28
$n=$	46	46

** $p < .01$. *** $p < .001$ (two-tailed test).
Source: WVS 2005 data.

In Model 1, we see that health affects happiness: for every increased percentage of a country whose health is very good or good, an additional half of a percent of a country is happy. In Model 2, we see that adding the income variable hardly affects things: the effect of health stays almost the same.

CHAPTER 11

4.

Dependent Variable: Hillary Clinton Feeling Thermometer		
Independent Variable	Unstandardized	Standardized
Abortion Index	0.14***	0.08
Gay Rights Index	0.64***	0.16
Health Care Index	2.57***	0.50
Constant	18.20	
R^2	0.39	
n	2,312	

*** $p < .001$ (two-tailed test).
Source: ANES 2012 data.

By far, Hillary, the biggest effect comes from the Health Care Index, so this is the issue that people most associate with you. The effect of this variable is over three times the next closest variable.

7.

Dependent Variable: Technology Index		
Independent Variable	Unstandardized	Standardized
Parent (N = 0, Y = 1)	1.02***	0.33
Family income in $1000s	0.006***	0.20
Education in years	0.06***	0.12
Constant	0.75	
R^2	0.20	
n	869	

*** $p < .001$ (two-tailed test).
Source: ANES 2012 data.

Whether you are a parent for someone younger than 18 has the largest effect on the amount of technology you have, followed by income, then education.

10.

Standard deviations:
Cellphone Use Index: 2.04
Education: 3.00
Family Income: 48.63

Unstandardized slope for education: 0.052
Standardized slope for education = 0.052 × (3.00/2.04) = 0.076

Unstandardize slope for family income: 0.008
Standardized slope for family income: 0.008 × (48.63/2.04) = 0.19

These are just a bit off from the SPSS output due to rounding.

15.

Sports participation has a statistically significant effect on both health and happiness. And looking at the betas, it is almost exactly the same effect: 0.38 for health and 0.39 for happiness. So get out there and be active!

CHAPTER 12

1.

Dependent Variable: Ownership Index (0 = nothing, 3 = home, stocks, & savings)	
Independent Variable	Slope
Race (W = 0, B = 1)	−0.72***
Family Income in $1,000s	0.007***
INT: Race × Income	0.003***
Constant	1.57
R^2	0.27
n	4,063

***$p < .001$ (two-tailed test).
Source: ANES 2012 data.

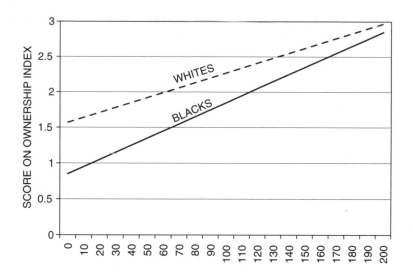

Even poor whites have some ownership (they score above 1.5 on the ownership index), whereas poor blacks are below 1 on the index. However, ever so slowly, as income increases, blacks catch up to whites so that by the time we're talking about people with high incomes, there is little difference between whites and blacks.

7.

Dependent Variable: Shopping Index	
Independent Variable	Slope
Age in years	−0.006*
Smartphone (N = 0, Y = 1)	1.36***
INT: Age × Smartphone	−0.014***
Constant	0.79
R^2	0.26
n	832

*$p < .05$. ***$p < .001$ (two-tailed test).
Source: PewShop 2011 data.

APPENDIX **D**

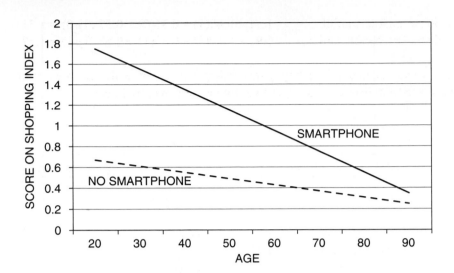

Among young people, whether you have a smartphone plays a big role in how you shop: the difference between young people who do and don't have a smartphone is over a point on the index. Among old people, whether you have a smartphone doesn't play a very large role: old people with smartphones have about the same index score as old people without smartphones.

12.

Dependent Variable: Child's Perception of Parental Check & Blocking Behavior	
Independent Variable	Slope
Parent's Sex (M = 0, F = 1)	−0.40*
Child's Sex (M = 0, F = 1)	−0.31
INT: P's sex × C's sex	0.57*
Constant	1.91
R^2	.012
n	482

*$p < .05$ (two-tailed test).
Source: PewKids2011 data.

Examples:

CPPCBBindex = 1.91 − 0.40 (psex) − 0.31 (csex) + 0.57 (psex)(csex)
male parent, male child: 1.91 − 0.40(0) − 0.31(0) + 0.57 (0)(0) = 1.91
male parent, female child: 1.91 − 0.40(0) − 0.31(1) + 0.57 (0)(1) = 1.60

female parent, male child: $1.91 - 0.40(1) - 0.31(0) + 0.57\ (1)(0) = 1.51$
female parent, female child: $1.91 - 0.40(1) - 0.31(1) + 0.57\ (1)(1) = 1.77$

The most surveiled child is a boy with a male parent. A boy with a female parent is the least surveiled. Girls are more surveiled by mothers than by fathers.

16.

Dependent Variable: Percent of a country saying they are very happy or quite happy	
Independent Variable	Coefficient
% country that saves	.57**
Europe = 0, Africa/Asia = 1	22.39*
INT: %saves and country	−.76*
Constant	65.81
$R^2 = .23$	

Note: n = 38.
* $p < .05.$ ** $p < .001$ (two-tailed test).

Equation:

$\%\text{☺} = 65.81 + 0.57(\%\text{save}) + 22.39(\text{country}) - 0.76(\%\text{save})(\text{country})$

Four examples:

A European country where no one saves:

$\%\text{☺} = 65.81 + 0.57(0) + 22.39(0) - 0.76(0)(0) = 65.81$

A European country where 60% save:

$\%\text{☺} = 65.81 + 0.57(60) + 22.39(0) - 0.76(60)(0) = 100$

An African/Asian country where no one saves:

$\%\text{☺} = 65.81 + 0.57(0) + 22.39(1) - 0.76(0)(1) = 88.20$

An African/Asian country where 60% save:

$\%\text{☺} = 65.81 + 0.57(60) + 22.39(1) - 0.76(60)(1) = 76.80$

In European countries, saving raises happiness, whereas in African/Asian countries the greater the percentage that a country saves, the lower the percentage of the country that is happy. Here is a graph that illustrates this:

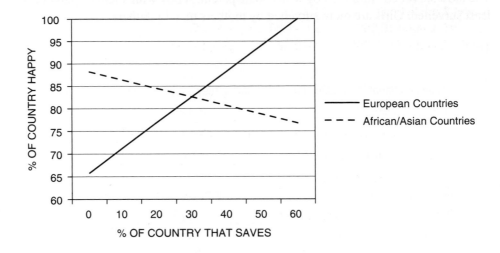

CHAPTER 13

2.

Dependent Variable: Have Passport? (N = 0, Y = 1)		
Independent Variable	Model 1	Model 2
Political party (SD = 0, SR = 6)	0.06***	0.01
Family income in $1,000s	—	0.013***
Constant	−0.47	−1.13
R^2	0.01	0.14
n	5,687	5,687

*** $p < .001$ (two-tailed test).
Source: ANES 2012 data.

In Model 1, it seems that Republicans are more likely than Democrats to have passports. However, in Model 2, once we control for income, the effect of political party goes away. The higher your family income, the more likely you are to have a passport.

Model 1 predictions:

Strong Democrat:	$z = -0.47$	$p = .38$
Strong Republican:	$z = -0.11$	$p = .47$

Model 2 predictions:

Family income \$10,000:	$z = -1.00$	$p = .27$
Family income \$150,000:	$z = 0.82$	$p = .69$

8.

Dependent Variable: Has Gaming Console (Y = 1, N = 0)	
Independent Variable	Slope
Sex (M = 0, F = 1)	-1.44**
Age	-0.072***
Interaction: Sex × Age	0.025*
Constant	2.72
R^2	0.32
n	703

*$p < .05$. ** $p < .01$. ***$p < .001$ (two-tailed test).
Source: PewShop2013 data.

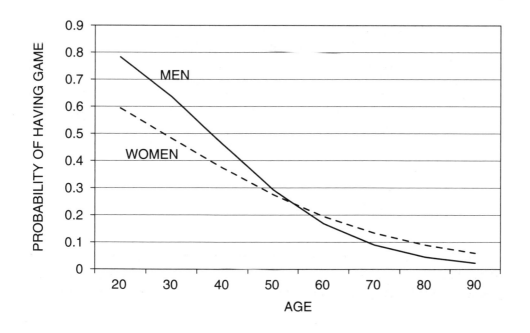

Young men are more likely than young women to have a gaming console. But this difference quickly dissipates as people get older, and men and women around age 50 become equally likely to have a game console.

14.

Dependent Variable: Child Has Smartphone (N = 0, Y = 1)	
Independent Variable	Model 1
Parent's race (W = 0, B = 1)	−0.52
Family income in $1000s	0.002
Interaction: race × income	0.015*
Constant	−0.81
R^2	0.043
n	377

*$p < .05$ (two-tailed test).
Source: PewKids2011 data.

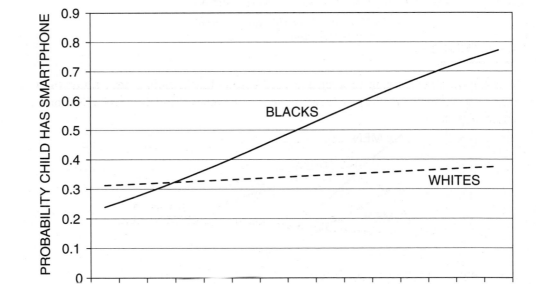

We see from the graph that as family income rises, the probability that white kids have a smartphone goes up slightly. But among black kids, the probability shoots up dramatically.

17.

Regular regression:
PROST = 4.12 – 0.04(%FAVORMEN) $r^2 = 0.34$, $n = 45$

Logistic regression:
PROST2CAT = 2.08 – 0.08(%FAVORMEN) $r^2 = 0.34$, $n = 45$
The slopes in both models are statistically significant.

In a country where 20% favor men over women for jobs:
PROST = 4.12 – 0.04(%FAVORMEN) = 3.32
$z_{PROST2CAT}$ = 2.08 – 0.08(%FAVORMEN) = 0.48 $p = .62$

In a country where 70% favor men over women for jobs:
PROST = 4.12 – 0.04(%FAVORMEN) = 1.32
$z_{PROST2CAT}$ = 2.08 – 0.08(%FAVORMEN) = –3.52 $p = .029$

CHAPTER 14

2. In the simple regression between age and Abortion Index, there is not a statistically significant relationship: the p-value is above .05. However, the path model tells a more interesting story:

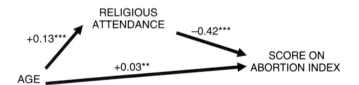

Direct effect of age on Abortion Index	+0.03
Indirect effect of age on Abortion Index: +0.13 × –0.42=	–0.05
Total effect of age on Abortion Index	–0.02

The direct and indirect effects are competing with one another. The direct effect of age is positive. The indirect effect is negative. When you combine the two, you get a very small total effect, which is why in the simple regression there was no significant effect.

7. In the simple regression, the beta for the effect of education on the shopping index is +0.08 and is significant at the $p < .05$ level.

Here is the path model:

The path model tells us that there is no direct effect from education to the shopping index. Rather, its effect is indirect through the technology index.

11.

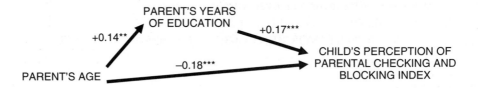

Parent's age has a negative effect on checking/blocking. However, it could have an even more negative effect were it not for the position indirect effect: the older a parent is, the more education the parent has, and this has a positive effect on checking/blocking. So the total effect is:

Direct	−0.18
Indirect: +0.14 × +0.17 =	+0.02
Total:	−0.16

14.

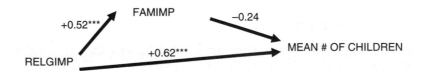

According to the model, there is only a direct effect from RELGIMP to CHILD. Although RELGIMP affects FAMIMP, that's where the indirect effect ends, because the beta from FAMIMP to CHILD was not statistically significant.

CHAPTER 15

4.

Dependent Variable: Economic Peril Index (0 = Not in peril, 24 = In peril)				
Independent Variable	Whites		Blacks	
	Model 1	Model 2	Model 1	Model 2
Age in years	−0.01	0.32***	−0.03**	0.17***
Age squared	—	−0.0036***	—	0.00212**
Income in $1000s	−0.03***	−0.03***	−0.023***	−0.023***
Constant	11.99	4.90	11.32	7.30
R^2	0.09	0.12	0.07	0.08
n	3,057	3,057	874.00	874

*** $p < .001$ (two-tailed test).
Source: ANES 2012 data.

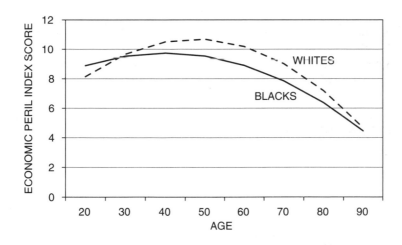

Because the shape of the line is more curved, and because the explained variation increases more from the linear to the nonlinear model, the relationship between age and economic peril is more nonlinear for whites than for blacks. Among young people, whites are slightly less in peril than are blacks. But as age increases, whites rise more quickly on the peril index. By old age, however, whites have dropped precipitously on the index so that they are similarly in peril to blacks.

6.

Dependent Variable: Score on Technology Index		
Independent Variable	Model 1	Model 2
Age in years	−0.033***	0.0012
Age squared	—	0.000346**
Constant	3.94	3.20
R^2	0.198	0.205
n	970	970

**p < .01. ***p < .001 (two-tailed test).
Source: PewShop 2013 data.

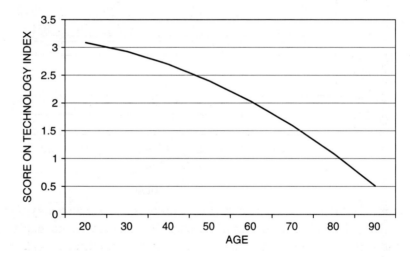

The nonlinear model does just a little better than the linear model: it explains 0.7% more variation. Looking at the line, it has somewhat of a curve. At younger ages, an increase in age causes a small decrease on the technology index. At older ages, an increase in age causes a larger decrease on the technology index.

11.

Dependent Variable: Care for Adult in Past Year (N = 0, Y = 1)		
Independent Variable	Model 1	Model 2
Age	−0.003	0.057***
Age Squared	—	0.0005891***
Constant	−0.41	−1.75
R^2	0.001	0.015
n	2,949	2,949

***$p < .001$ (two-tailed test).
Source: PewHealth2012 data.

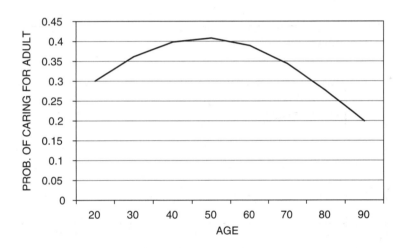

The linear model doesn't reflect the data at all: the slope is not statistically significant and the explained variation is near zero. Although the nonlinear model explains only 1.5% of the variation, both of the slopes are statistically significant. Looking at the graph, the probability of caring for an adult peaks at about age 50 and then starts to decrease.

15.

Dependent Variable: Mean of Country on SCIFAITH		
(1 = pro-science, 10 = pro-faith)		
Independent Variable	Model 1	Model 2
% Country Very Religious	0.002	0.06**
Religiousness Squared	—	−0.0006**
Constant	5.78	4.84
R^2	0.00	0.12
	$n = 45$	$n = 45$

**$p < .01$. ***$p < .001$ (two-tailed test).

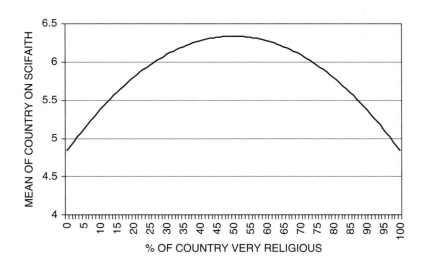

The linear model doesn't work at all: the R^2 value is 0.00. The non-linear model works much better: the R^2 is 0.12. Looking at the graph (which I admit I've made it lie to make the results more clear), we see that a country's responses become more pro-faith until a country is about 50% very religious, and after that the country sways back toward supporting science.

CHAPTER 16

4.

a. The dependent variable is an ordinal-level variable with three categories, so the researcher might want to use ordered logistic regression.
b. The Affirmative Action Index is one of those "hybrid" variables: a huge number of people are at zero, and then there are cases smattered throughout the index above zero, so the researcher might want to use Tobit regression.
c. Because the researcher wants to use data that is at both the individual level and the state level, he or she might want to use multilevel modeling.

BIBLIOGRAPHY

Ainsworth-Darnell, James W., and Douglas B. Downey (1998). "Assessing the Oppositional Culture Explanation for Racial/Ethnic Differences in School Performance." *American Sociological Review* 63:536–553.

Allison, Paul D. (1999). *Multiple Regression: A Primer*. Thousand Oaks, CA: Sage.

American National Election Studies (ANES). (2012). www.electionstudies.org/.

Bail, Christopher A. (2012). "The Fringe Effect: Civil Society Organizations and the Evolution of Media Discourse about Islam since the September 11th Attacks." *American Sociological Review* 77:855–879.

Bohrnstedt, George W., and David Knoke. (1988). *Statistics for Social Data Analysis*. Itasca, IL: Peacock Publishers.

Callanan, Valerie. (2012). "Media Consumption, Perceptions of Crime Risk and Fear of Crime: Examining Race/Ethnic Differences." *Sociological Perspectives* 55:93–115.

Cech, Erin, Brian Rubineau, Susan Silbey, and Caroll Seron. (2011). "Professional Role Confidence and Gendered Persistence in Engineering." *American Sociological Review* 76:641–666.

The College Board. (2013). *Average Debt Levels of Public Section Bachelor's Degree Recipients over Time*. http://trends.collegeboard.org/student-aid/figures-tables/average-debt-levels-public-sector-bachelors-degree-recipients-over-time.

Conley, Dalton. (1999). *Being Black, Living in the Red: Race, Wealth, and Social Policy in America*. Berkeley: University of California Press.

Downey, Douglas B. (1995). "When Bigger Is Not Better: Family Size, Parental Resources, and Children's Educational Performance." *American Sociological Review* 60:746–761.

Fendrich, James Max, and Kenneth L. Lovoy. (1988). "Back to the Future: Adult Political Behavior of Former Student Activists." *American Sociological Review* 53:780–784.

Gartner, Scott Sigmund. (2008). "Ties to the Dead: Connections to Iraq War and 9/11 Casualties and Disapproval of the President." *American Sociological Review* 73:690–695.

General Social Survey (1973–2012). http://publicdata.norc.org:41000/gss/documents//BOOK/GSS_Codebook_AppendixA.pdf.

Glavin, Paul, Scott Schieman, and Sarah Reid. (2011). "Boundary-Spanning Work Demands and Their Consequences for Guilt and Psychological Distress." *Journal of Health and Social Behavior* 52:43–57.

Hetherington, Marc J., and Elizabeth Suhay. (2011). "Authoritarianism, Threat, and Americans' Support for the War on Terror." *American Journal of Political Science* 55:546–560.

Hibel, Jacob and Andrea D. Jasper. (2012). "Delayed Special Education Placement for Learning Disabilities among Children of Immigrants." *Social Forces* 91:503–530.

Hughey, Matthew W. (2009). "Cinethetic Racism: White Redemption and Black Stereotypes in 'Magical Negro' Films." *Social Problems* 56:543–577.

Ingram, Paul, Lori Qingyuan Yue, and Hayagreeva Rao (2010). "Trouble in Store: Probes, Protests, and Store Openings by Wal-Mart, 1998-2007." *American Journal of Sociology* 116:53–92.

Jæger, Mads Meier. (2011). "'A Thing of Beauty is a Joy Forever'?: Returns to Physical Attractiveness over the Life Course." *Social Forces* 89:983–1003.

Konieczny, Piotr. (2009). "Governance, Organization, and Democracy on the Internet: The Iron Law and the Evolution of Wikipedia." *Sociological Forum* 24:162–192.

Loftus, Jeni. (2001). "America's Liberalization in Attitudes toward Homosexuality." *American Sociological Review* 66:762–782.

Lyness, Karen S., Janet C. Gornick, Pamela Stone, and Angela R. Grotto. (2012). "It's All about Control: Worker Control over Schedule and Hours in Cross-National Context." *American Sociological Review* 77:1023–1049.

McAdam, Doug. (1989). "The Biographical Consequences of Activism." *American Sociological Review* 54:744–760.

McAdam, Doug. (1990). *Freedom Summer*. New York: Oxford University Press.

McCright, Aaron M., and Riley E. Dunlap. (2011). "The Politicization of Climate Change and Polarization in the American Public's Views of Global Warming, 2001–2010." *The Sociological Quarterly* 52:155–194.

Pew Internet and American Life Project. (2011). Teens and Online Behavior. www.pewinternet.org/.

Pew Internet and American Life Project. (2012). Health. www.pewinternet.org/.

Pew Internet and American Life Project. (2013). Mobile Shopping. www.pewinternet.org/.

Pugh, S. Douglas. (2001). "Service with a Smile: Emotional Contagion in the Service Encounter." *Academy of Management Journal* 44:1018–1027.

Robnett, Belinda, and James A. Bany. (2011). "Gender, Church Involvement, and African-American Political Participation." *Sociological Perspectives* 54:689–712.

Rosenthal, Jaime A., Xin Lu, and Peter Cram. (2013). "Availability of Consumer Prices from U.S. Hospitals for a Common Surgical Procedure." *JAMA Internal Medicine* 173:427–432.

Rossman, Gabriel. (2012). *Climbing the Charts: What Radio Airplay Tells Us about the Diffusion of Innovation*. Princeton, NJ: Princeton University Press.

Rossman, Gabriel, Nicole Esparza, and Phillip Bonacich (2010). "I'd Like to Thank the Academy, Team Spillovers, and Network Centrality." *American Sociological Review* 75:31–51.

Saguy, Abigail C., Kjerstin Gruys, and Shanna Gong. (2010). "Social Problem Construction and National Context: News Reporting on 'Overweight' and 'Obesity' in the United States and France." *Social Problems* 57:586–610.

Saperstein, Aliya, and Andrew M. Penner. (2012). "Racial Fluidity and Inequality in the United States." *American Journal of Sociology* 118:676–727.

Schneider, Daniel. (2012). "Gender Deviance and Household Work: The Role of Occupation." *American Journal of Sociology* 117:1029–1072.

Schuman, Howard, Edward Walsh, Camille Olson, and Barbara Etheridge (1985). "Effort and Reward: The Assumption that College Grades Are Affected by Quantity of Study." *Social Forces* 63:945–966.

South, Scott J., and Glenna Spitze. (1994). "Housework in Marital and Nonmarital Households." *American Sociological Review* 59:327–347.

Stack, Steven, and Jim Gundlach. (1992). "The Effect of Country Music on Suicide." *Social Forces* 71:211–218.

ter Bogt, Tom F. M., Marc J. M. H. Delsing, Maarten van Zalk, Peter G. Christenson, and Wim H. J. Meeus (2011). "Intergenerational Continuity of Taste: Parental and Adolescent Music Preferences." *Social Forces* 90:297–319.

Tufte, Edward. (2001). *The Visual Display of Quantitative Information*. Cheshire, CT: Graphics Press.

Volden, Craig, Alan E. Wiseman, and Dana E. Wittmer. (2013). "When Are Women More Effective Lawmakers Than Men?" *American Journal of Political Science* 57:326–341.

Weinberg, Martin S., and Colin J. Williams (2005). "Fecal Matters: Habitus, Embodiments, and Deviance." *Social Problems* 52:315–336.

Welch, Kelly, and Allison Ann Payne. (2010). "Racial Threat and Punitive School Discipline." *Social Problems* 57:25–48.

Wheelan, Charles. (2013). *Naked Statistics: Stripping the Dread from Data*. New York: W. W. Norton.

Willer, Robb, Christabel L. Rogalin, Bridget Conlon, and Michael T. Wojnowicz. (2013). "Overdoing Gender: A Test of the Masculine Overcompensation Thesis." *American Journal of Sociology* 118:980–1022.

World Values Survey (WVS). (2012). www.worldvaluessurvey.org/.

GLOSSARY/INDEX

Entries in color include a definition of the term.